ENCYCLOPEDIA

OF

AMERICAN

SOCIAL

MOVEMENTS

VOLUME TWO

EDITED BY

IMMANUEL NESS

SHARPE REFERENCE

an imprint of M.E.Sharpe, Inc.

SHARPE REFERENCE

Sharpe Reference is an imprint of M.E. Sharpe INC.

M.E. Sharpe INC.
80 Business Park Drive
Armonk, NY 10504

Library of Congress Cataloging-in-Publication Data

Encyclopedia of American social movements / Immanuel Ness, editor.
   p. cm.
   Includes bibliographical references and indexes.
   ISBN 0-7656-8045-9 (set: alk. paper)
   1. Social movements—United States—History—Encyclopedias. 2. Social change—
United States—History—Encyclopedias. 3. Social justice—United States—History—
encyclopedias. I. Ness, Immanuel.
HN57 .E594 2004
303.48'4'097303—dc21

                                               2002042613

Publisher: Myron E. Sharpe
Vice President and Editorial Director: Patricia Kolb
Vice President and Production Director: Carmen Chetti
Executive Editor and Manager of Reference: Todd Hallman
Project Manager: Wendy E. Muto
Editorial Assistant: Cathleen Prisco
Cover and Text Design: Jesse Sanchez

CONTENTS

BIRTH CONTROL MOVEMENT

For a movement that spanned a century, the birth control movement retained a remarkably consistent primary objective: to help individuals gain control over reproduction. Underneath this straightforward objective, however, lies a complex history of changing ideologies, strategies, and opinions about who should have access to this control. At the center of much of this change stood Margaret Sanger (1879–1966), the self-proclaimed leader of the movement who dedicated most of her adult life, with varying degrees of success, to the cause. Sanger led the movement through multiple and seemingly discordant permutations ranging from radicalism to medicalization, and it is easy to criticize her functional approach to her cause. It is important, however, to consider Sanger's influence and decision-making process in a historical context because from its radical origins to its linguistic shift to "planned parenthood," the birth control movement ultimately succeeded in convincing the American public and lawmakers that effective and autonomous self-control of reproduction was a desirable goal.

RADICAL ROOTS

Contraceptive devices existed long before there was an organized birth control movement, and many nineteenth-century Americans had relatively easy access to birth control information. The declining birth rate, especially among the white urban middle class, suggests that more and more Americans during this time period used some sort of contraception. This proliferation of contraceptive devices and information, however, troubled Victorian moral reformers, most notably Anthony Comstock (1844–1915), the president of the Society for the Suppression of Vice in New York. According to reformers like Comstock, ready access to contraceptive information threatened the home and drove men towards illicit sexual activity. Comstock launched a crusade to stop this trend. His efforts culminated in the passage of an 1873 anti-obscenity statute that, among other things, made sending contraceptive devices and information through the federal mail illegal. Although many Americans continued to use contraceptives after the passage of what came to be known as the "Comstock Act," fighting for its repeal became a centerpiece in the battle to legalize birth control in the United States.

The earliest birth control advocates, comprised of a small group of suffragists, moral reformers, and free love advocates in the mid-to-late nineteenth century, however, did not support artificial contraception, which they associated with prostitution and immorality. Rather, these women believed in "voluntary motherhood": women, they maintained, should have the political right to choose when they became mothers. Advocates of voluntary motherhood did not hate sex and did not believe that women were asexual—a common Victorian view that gave husbands little motivation to make sexual activity pleasurable for their wives. Advocates of "voluntary motherhood" thought that women could enjoy sexual activity if they had a say in when it took place. Importantly, these activists did not reject the importance of women's role as mothers; rather, they argued that women fulfilled this role more successfully when they had control over when they had babies. Voluntary motherhood, as such, gave women an opportunity to strengthen their positions within their marriages but did not challenge the traditional family structure.

A far more strident challenge to the established sexual and family order occurred during the 1910s. Against a historical backdrop in which scientists and politicians were voicing fears about "race suicide" if the white middle class continued to practice contraception, a group of radicals began to articulate a need to give such information to the working class as well. Believing in birth control's potential to alter both class and sexual relations, these radicals, including anarchist Emma Goldman (1869–1940), distributed sex education materials and talked about birth control as part of their larger revolutionary agenda. They held that the capitalist system benefited from the existence of a large labor force that, in part because of family size, could not afford to challenge the system. They saw that poor women experienced a terrible burden by giving birth many times in often-unsanitary conditions and by having to feed and to clothe their large families. They also felt that it was unjust that white middle-class women had access to birth control information simply because they could afford to pay for medical care. The idea never gained a solid footing on the Socialist political agenda, however, because party leaders deemed birth control too radical for inclusion in its party platform. In their minds, the achievement of women's rights would naturally follow the achievement of workers rights. Nevertheless, these radicals persevered in the promotion of birth control.

Margaret Sanger became part of this intellectual milieu in 1910 when she and her husband moved from the suburbs to New York City, the heart of radicalism and bohemia in the United States. Born Margaret Louise Higgins, the sixth of eleven children in a large Irish Catholic family, Sanger apparently became keenly aware of the hazards of excessive childbearing when her mother died of consumption at age 50. In her youth, Sanger aspired to be a doctor but ultimately decided to study nursing because her family could not afford the expense of further medical training. She married William Sanger, a young architect, in 1902 and briefly settled into domestic life.

A variety of circumstances precipitated the Sangers' decision to move into the city. But once they arrived, the couple quickly became involved in many facets of Socialist politics. Sanger also found part-time work with Lillian Wald's Visiting Nurse Service on the Lower East Side. It was during this work that Sanger claimed to have had an experience that prompted her decision to dedicate her life to birth control. According to the story—which may or may not be true and one that Sanger repeated throughout her career—she had her awakening following the death of Mrs. Sadie Sachs, a young Jewish immigrant who had begged her doctor for contraceptive information to no avail and who died following a botched self-abortion.

Notwithstanding the veracity of the Sachs story, it is true that Sanger began to define herself as a champion of birth control, a term that she adopted as her own in 1915. She became increasingly convinced, especially following a 1914 trip to Europe, that common contraceptive methods such as withdrawal and condoms were undesirable methods because women were dependent on men to use them. Searching for a woman-centered form of birth control, Sanger settled on the diaphragm, which needed to be fitted by a medical specialist. In addition, she began spreading her ideas in *The Woman Rebel*, a magazine she launched in 1914 and was soon a target of the Post Office's enforcement of the Comstock laws. Instead of facing trial, Sanger fled to Europe.

Sanger returned to the United States in 1915 to a changing climate. The Post Office had decided not to press further charges against her. Also during her absence, a group of feminists led by Mary Ware Dennett (1871–1947) formed the National Birth Control League with the goal of repealing the Comstock laws through lobbying on the state and federal level. Sanger, favoring direct action, often criticized the league's lobbying tactics. Sanger also grew increasingly impatient with radicalism and with what she viewed as its divisiveness. She believed that radicals were ignoring her issue as they became more interested in the possible United States entry into World War I in Europe. Sanger began plans to publish *The Birth Control Review* as an alternative to other leftist publications. By October 1916, her vision for the future of the movement became clear when she opened America's first birth control clinic in the Brownsville district of Brooklyn. The clinic operated for ten days before it was raided and closed by the police. Sanger was arrested, convicted for violating anti-obscenity statutes, and spent a month in prison.

MAINSTREAM ALLIES

Sanger lost an appeal on her conviction in 1918 but nevertheless gained an important legal victory for her cause when Judge Frederick Crane ruled that the distribution of physician-prescribed birth control for the prevention of disease was not illegal. Crane's ruling came at a time when many Americans feared that venereal disease was becoming a public health menace. The War Department's decision not to distribute condoms to American armed forces proved to be a disastrous one as more soldiers were infected with venereal disease during World War I than were injured or killed in combat. Crane's framing of the legality of birth control in relation to its disease-fighting capabilities changed the playing field upon which Sanger could base her activism by making birth control a medical, as opposed to a free speech, matter. Sanger turned all of her attention to establishing birth control clinics, which she believed could be legal as

MARGARET LOUISE HIGGINS SANGER (1879–1966)

Margaret Louise Sanger is perhaps the best known figure in the history of the American reproductive rights movement. Sanger was one of eleven children, the daughter of a free-thinker father and a devout Catholic mother. Sanger and her husband William were involved in the intellectual scene of pre–World War I Greenwich Village. She was a member of the New York Socialist Party and participated in Industrial Workers of the World labor actions.

As a nurse working on New York City's Lower East Side, Sanger witnessed the negative consequences of uncontrolled childbearing and botched abortions. The author of several sex education works including *What Every Girl Should Know* (1916) and *Family Limitation* (1914), Sanger became a target of Anthony Comstock's anti-obscenity laws, which banned materials about and devices used for contraception or abortion. She was prosecuted repeatedly for writing and speaking about venereal disease and birth control, and the post office refused to mail her works, including her radical feminist magazine *The Woman Rebel.* Facing imprisonment, Sanger left the county in 1914. After having three children—one of whom died at age five— Margaret and William Sanger separated, and she engaged in affairs with several men, including psychologist Havelock Ellis.

Upon her return to the United States a year later, Sanger embarked upon a national speaking tour to promote family planning, arguing that birth control would help free women from poverty and encourage their sexual autonomy and equality. In October 1916 Sanger, her sister Ethel Byrne, and colleague Fania Mindell opened the first American birth control clinic in the Brownsville neighborhood of Brooklyn. After only a week of operation, the women were arrested for violating state anti-obscenity laws. Sanger's subsequent imprisonment garnered public attention and galvanized support for the issue of birth control. As support for radical and leftist causes waned, Sanger sought support from the medical profession and the eugenics movement. In 1922, she married James Noah Slee, an oil magnate who became a major funder of the family planning movement.

Sanger cofounded the American Birth Control League and the Birth Control Clinical Research Bureau, which merged in 1939 to become the Birth Control Federation of America—later renamed the Planned Parenthood Federation of America. In addition to family planning, the organization also focused on causes such as global population growth and world hunger. In 1926, Sanger helped organize the first World Population Conference in Geneva, Switzerland. She established the National Committee for Federal Legislation on Birth Control but had little success in lobbying politicians to support laws favoring contraception. In 1936, however, a federal judge ruled in *U.S. v. One Package of Japanese Pessaries*—a lawsuit funded by Sanger—that contraceptive devices could not be classified as obscene.

As the U.S. birth control movement became more mainstream in the 1930s, Sanger retired from her active role and relocated to Tucson, Arizona. After World War II, she began to focus on international family planning, cofounding the International Planned Parenthood Foundation in 1952 and serving as its president until 1959. In her later years, Sanger helped secure funding for the research and development of new contraceptive methods—including the first birth control pill, approved in 1960. Sanger died in 1966 at the age of eighty-six, soon after the U.S. Supreme Court's landmark 1965 *Griswold v. Connecticut* ruling that married couples had the right to use contraceptives.

Liz Highleyman

long as they were staffed by medical doctors and served a public health purpose.

Sanger formed the American Birth Control League (ABCL) in 1921 to help gain financial support for birth control and to establish a physician-run birth control clinic. Her first attempt to open a clinic under a doctor's auspices failed later that year. Undaunted by these setbacks, and aided financially by her marriage to millionaire James Noah Henry Slee in 1922, Sanger recruited another physician and opened her Birth Control Clinical Research Bureau in New York City in January 1923 (then called the Clinical Research Bureau). Sanger now voiced a belief that only trained doctors should fit women for diaphragms, despite the fact that she, as a nurse, had successfully performed many such fittings in the past. Given this turn toward medicine, it is no surprise that the ABCL also began attempts to introduce doctors-only legislation in Congress that would have exempted physicians from the Comstock Act and allowed them to prescribe birth control for any reason that they saw fit.

Historians have criticized Sanger for her turn

Margaret Sanger, author of *The Pivot of Civilization*, and Dr. Dorothy Becker, present statistics of patients the New York clinic had served, on December 6, 1923. Both Sanger and Becker were leaders of the Birth Control Movement. *(Brown Brothers)*

away from radicalism and her decision to form a coalition with the medical profession. It is important to remember, however, that radicals came under increasing attack during the 1920s as a Red Scare and general political conservatism took hold in the United States. In addition, feminists refused to support birth control because they viewed the issue as too controversial. Sanger, in fact, had very few allies in radical circles in the 1920s. It is equally important to remember that Sanger alone did not set the terms for the birth control debate. Rulings from judges like Frederick Crane led Sanger to believe that she had little choice but to pursue the support of the medical profession, which was

not, in fact, easily won. Most doctors, in fact, still saw birth control as immoral, and the American Medical Association refused to endorse Sanger's work. Even those doctors who gave limited support for birth control did not necessarily want to ally with Sanger. The Committee on Maternal Health, established by Dr. Robert Dickinson (1861–1950) in 1923, actively tried to wrest control of birth control research out of Sanger's hands. In light of this evidence, it can be argued that Sanger made what is best viewed as a pragmatic choice to pursue the medicalization of birth control.

Another pragmatic, and often-criticized, choice Sanger made was her alliance with the American eu-

THE PIVOT OF CIVILIZATION
APPENDIX: PRINCIPLES AND AIMS OF THE AMERICAN BIRTH CONTROL LEAGUE BY MARGARET SANGER

The Appendix to Margaret Sanger's seminal work, The Pivot of Civilization *(1922), justifies birth control to advance women's rights and health. However, the Appendix also demonstrates the writer's support for eugenics targeting those who are not "the healthy elements of the nation."*

PRINCIPLES:

The complex problems now confronting America as the result of the practice of reckless procreation are fast threatening to grow beyond human control.

Everywhere we see poverty and large families going hand in hand. Those least fit to carry on the race are increasing most rapidly. People who cannot support their own offspring are encouraged by Church and State to produce large families. Many of the children thus begotten are diseased or feeble-minded; many become criminals. The burden of supporting these unwanted types has to be bourne by the healthy elements of the nation. Funds that should be used to raise the standard of our civilization are diverted to the maintenance of those who should never have been born.

In addition to this grave evil we witness the appalling waste of women's health and women's lives by too frequent pregnancies. These unwanted pregnancies often provoke the crime of abortion, or alternatively multiply the number of child-workers and lower the standard of living.

. . . Therefore we hold that every woman must possess the power and freedom to prevent conception except when these conditions can be satisfied.

Every mother must realize her basic position in human society. She must be conscious of her responsibility to the race in bringing children into the world.

. . . These purposes, which are of fundamental importance to the whole of our nation and to the future of mankind, can only be attained if women first receive practical scientific education in the means of Birth Control. That, therefore, is the first object to which the efforts of this League will be directed.

AIMS:

The American Birth Control League aims to enlighten and educate all sections of the American public in the various aspects of the dangers of uncontrolled procreation and the imperative necessity of a world program of Birth Control.

The League aims to correlate the findings of scientists, statisticians, investigators, and social agencies in all fields. To make this possible, it is necessary to organize various departments:

RESEARCH: To collect the findings of scientists, concerning the relation of reckless breeding to the evils of delinquency, defect and dependence;

INVESTIGATION: To derive from these scientifically ascertained facts and figures, conclusions which may aid all public health and social agencies in the study of problems of maternal and infant mortality, child-labor, mental and physical defects and delinquence in relation to the practice of reckless parentage.

HYGIENIC AND PHYSIOLOGICAL instruction by the Medical profession to mothers and potential mothers in harmless and reliable methods of Birth Control in answer to their requests for such knowledge.

STERILIZATION of the insane and feebleminded and the encouragement of this operation upon those afflicted with inherited or transmissible diseases, with the understanding that sterilization does not deprive the individual of his or her sex expression . . .

EDUCATIONAL: The program of education includes: The enlightenment of the public at large, mainly through the education of leaders of thought and opinion—teachers, ministers, editors and writers—to the moral and scientific soundness of the principles of Birth Control and the imperative necessity of its adoption as the basis of national and racial progress.

POLITICAL AND LEGISLATIVE: To enlist the support and cooperation of legal advisers, statesmen and legislators in effecting the removal of state and federal statutes which encourage dysgenic breeding, increase the sum total of disease, misery and poverty and prevent the establishment of a policy of national health and strength.

ORGANIZATION: To send into the various States of the Union field workers to enlist the support and arouse the interest of the masses, to the importance of Birth Control so that laws may be changed and the establishment of clinics made possible in every State.

INTERNATIONAL: This department aims to cooperate with similar organizations in other countries to study Birth Control in its relations to the world population problem, food supplies, national and racial conflicts . . .

Source: Margaret Sanger, *The Pivot of Civilization* (New York: Brentano's, 1922).

genics movement. In the 1920s and 1930s, eugenics was a legitimate field of study taught in most college curriculums and had the potential to lend an air of scientific authority to the birth control movement. Many eugenicists resisted supporting birth control because they feared that the genetically "fit" should be encouraged to have larger families, not to limit their family size. They believed that sterilization, not birth control, was the best method for preventing the "unfit" from having children. But as the focus of eugenics strategy in the 1930s shifted from sterilization to reproduction of the fittest, eugenicists came to believe that giving married couples access to family spacing via birth control served an important purpose.

How much did Sanger believe in the eugenicists' programs for racial betterment? It is difficult to know for sure. She certainly took advantage of the scientific standing that affiliation with eugenics gave to her cause. Less clear, however, is whether she actually believed the movement's racist rhetoric. Sanger established a birth control clinic in Harlem in 1930. Birth control was in fact a divisive issue among African Americans in the 1920s and 1930s. Many black elites believed that family limitation could help support their program of racial uplift, and W.E.B. Du Bois announced his support of birth control as early as 1922. Many African Americans, however, were wary of any sort of medical program forwarded by the white community and questioned the movement's racial motives. This suspicion was not unfounded inasmuch as segregated Southern states actively established birth control clinics for African Americans in an attempt to limit the size of the black population. Although Sanger certainly acted in a patronizing manner toward the African-American clinic board, she never articulated racist goals for her clinic. Pragmatic or not, however, any assessment of Sanger's affiliation with the eugenics movement needs to be balanced carefully with an understanding that she was aware of the class and racial biases of the eugenics movement.

Legal Success

Sanger enjoyed a key legal victory in 1936 when the Supreme Court ruled in *U.S. v. One Package of Japanese Pessaries* that the medical prescription of birth control for disease prevention or well-being was not illegal under the Comstock Act. One year later, the American Medical Association Committee on Contraception issued tentative support for birth control. At this time, Sanger began to lose control of the birth control movement. In 1939, the American Birth Control League and the Birth Control Clinical Research Bureau had

merged to form the Birth Control Federation of America (BCFA). A key indication of the movement's shift away from Sanger's original vision was the 1942 decision to rename the BCFA the Planned Parenthood Federation of America. This linguistic shift eliminated the idea that women should have the right to control their own reproduction from the organization's masthead. Family planning, not birth control, became the movement's main selling point as it moved into the mainstream. Planned Parenthood also became an international leader in the movement for population control, a Neo-Malthusian attempt to eliminate world poverty.

Sanger persisted in her search for an effective, female-controlled contraceptive device. Diaphragms were hard to care for, messy, and eliminated spontaneity in sexual intercourse. Sanger was convinced that scientists could develop an oral contraceptive, and she found a financial ally in Katharine McCormick, whose late husband had been an heir to the International Harvester Company fortune. Their efforts succeeded, and the U.S. Food and Drug Administration approved the first oral contraceptive in 1960.

Even though the *One Package* case had eliminated federal restrictions on the prescription of birth control, many states (especially those states with large Catholic constituencies) still had laws that prevented physicians from prescribing birth control to married women. Following several failed legal challenges, the United States Supreme Court overturned all such laws in a 1965 decision in *Griswold v. Connecticut*. This case was additionally significant because it marked the first time that the Supreme Court articulated the legal doctrine of the right to privacy. The court, under pressure from second-wave feminists, later extended the same rights to unmarried individuals in *Eisenstadt v. Baird* (1972).

The birth control movement, as conceived by leaders like Margaret Sanger, had succeeded in eliminating all legal impediments to distributing birth control information and prescribing contraception. Birth control continued to be a controversial issue, especially internationally, where many native-born activists viewed it as a colonial tool. By the 1970s, however, Planned Parenthood and other activists turned their attention to abortion—a logical outgrowth of the movement's founding idea that women had a right to control their reproduction. In this new manner, therefore, the birth control movement continues to thrive in the United States.

Kristin Celello

BIBLIOGRAPHY

Chesler, Ellen. *Woman of Valor: Margaret Sanger and the Birth Control Movement in America*. New York: Simon and Schuster, 1992.

Gordon, Linda. *Woman's Body, Woman's Right: A Social History of Birth Control in America*. New York: Grossman, 1976.

McCann, Carole R. *Birth Control Politics in the United States, 1916–1945*. Ithaca, NY: Cornell University Press, 1994.

Reed, James. *From Private Vice to Public Virtue: The Birth Control Movement and American Society since 1830*. New York: Basic Books, 1978.

Tone, Andrea. *Devices and Desires: A History of Contraceptives in America*. New York: Hill and Wang, 2001.

WOMEN'S MOVEMENT 1920–1960

The roots of what we now call the first wave of the women's movement can be traced to an event that took place over 150 years ago, when a number of outspoken reformers in Seneca Falls, New York, called "A Convention to Discuss the Social, Civil, and Religious Condition and Rights of Women." For Lucretia C. Mott, Elizabeth Cady Stanton, and other activists already vocal in and committed to the movement to eradicate slavery, the next logical step was to demand rights for women. In July of 1848, the Seneca Falls Conference became the first of its kind to address women's rights and issues. Using the analysis of liberty for all and the Declaration of Independence as a template, the Declaration of Sentiments of the Seneca Falls Convention put forward a formal list of grievances, including: inequity in property rights, education, employment, religion, marriage, and suffrage. In short, Mott, Stanton, and the 100 people who signed the Declaration demanded that women—as citizens—be acknowledged as such.

That meeting fostered a large and diverse movement of reform advocating for the rights of women, one that grew to become one of the most broad-based social movements in America by the turn of the century. Just two years after the Seneca Falls Convention, Lucy Stone and an association of suffragists from the East launched the First National Convention of the Women's Movement in Worcester, Massachusetts. Two years after that, Susan B. Anthony attended her first conference on women's rights in Syracuse, New York, and subsequently joined forces with Stanton, and—in effect—the women's movement. Woman suffrage, as a social and legal concept, was a predictable cause for reformers to adhere to, for many viewed the right of women by law to vote in national and local elections as the pinnacle of equality. Other conventions quickly followed suit, and the struggle for woman suffrage helped the women's movement gain significant strength in numbers.

After the American Civil War (1861–1865), suffragists recognized that attempts to secure the franchise for women at the state level were inadequate at best. The women's movement shifted its strategies accordingly, seeking an amendment to the federal Constitution instead. However, there was contention in the ranks. Disagreement over the issue of suffrage for African-American men caused the burgeoning movement to split into two separate organizations in 1869. One, the American Woman Suffrage Association (AWSA), was founded by Lucy Stone, Henry B. Blackwell, Julia Ward Howe, T.W. Higginson, and other proponents of woman suffrage in Boston, Massachusetts. Considered the more conservative association, the AWSA supported the Republican Party, sought to secure suffrage on the state and local levels, and had abolitionists in its membership. Through grassroots activism and organizing, the AWSA created and disseminated information on the vote for women and encouraged other smaller associations to do the same.

THE NATIONAL AMERICAN WOMAN SUFFRAGE ASSOCIATION

The other, more radical organization founded in 1869 was the National Woman Suffrage Association (NWSA), established in New York by Elizabeth Cady Stanton and Susan B. Anthony. The NWSA held very clear objectives: to create public debate on social issues pertaining to women (including marriage and divorce), and to secure the vote for women through an amendment to the Constitution. The NWSA hosted a national convention on women's rights every year, and its membership increased dramatically. In 1890, the two sister organizations merged after twenty-one years of independent operation, and the National American Woman Suffrage Association (NAWSA) was formed. Led by Stanton, Anthony, and Stone (the former executives of the NWSA and AWSA), the

NAWSA pushed almost exclusively for winning the vote for women through recruitment and lobbying for approval of a federal amendment to the Constitution. Some estimates suggest that almost 95 percent of suffragists in America were organized under the umbrella of the NAWSA.

In 1896, however, a convention held in Washington, D.C., inaugurated the merger of two other active women's organizations: the National Federation of Afro-American Women and the National League of Colored Women. Both had grown from the African American women's club movement, a social movement begun in 1898 largely in reaction to the exclusion of African-American clubs from the General Federation of Women's Clubs (GFWC) founded by Charlotte Emerson Brown and Jane Cunningham Croly in 1890. Initiated and directed by abolitionist Harriet Tubman, author Frances E. W. Harper, journalist Ida B. Wells-Barnett, and educator Mary Church Terrell, the merger produced the National Association of Colored Women (NACW). Terrell became the organization's first president, and set a multifaceted mandate that opposed segregation, set up college scholarships, and also included labor rights, child care, and education. In 1912, the NACW joined the struggle for woman suffrage, two years before its white counterpart, the GFWC.

By 1913, the NAWSA's insistence upon federal enfranchisement on a state-by-state basis led to yet another split within the ranks. The Congressional Union for Woman Suffrage emerged as a result, led by Alice Paul and Lucy Burns. Paul, a Quaker from Philadelphia with vast experience learned from the British suffragette campaigns, advocated a strategy of nonviolence and militancy to the organization, and was a driving force in the changes that were to come. By 1916, the Union reorganized as the National Woman's Party (NWP), focused on direct action and confrontation: participating in hunger strikes, picketing, marches, and acts of civil disobedience. The NWP subsequently became the first group to ever demonstrate in front of the White House. Not surprisingly, the NWP was often at odds with other suffragists, and their tactics made them appear radical and "unreasonable."

The year 1916 also marked the presentation of NAWSA's new president Carrie Chapman Catt's "winning plan." While continuing to mobilize suffragists at the level of the state, the NAWSA refocused on amending the federal Constitution. During the war, their work divided between woman suffrage and support of the war effort, while the NWP focused predominantly on obtaining the vote. Early in 1918, President Woodrow Wilson announced his support for federal enfranchisement for women, but it was not until mid-1919 that the Senate followed suit. On August 26, 1920, the Nineteenth Amendment was finally passed, and approximately twenty-six million women were given the right to vote in the United States.

VICTORY AND AFTERMATH

Achieving the vote was the culmination of decades of organizing and activism by diverse women and different women's associations who unified over the common goal of woman suffrage. After 1920, many thought that the need for a women's rights movement was over. However, women continued organizing and fought for political rights and social reform at the federal, state, and local levels. In other words, the women's movement was very much alive and well after the vote was won, building—slowly at first but then growing in momentum in size—toward what would become known as the women's liberation movement in the 1960s.

Winning the battle for woman suffrage after decades of organized efforts on the part of individual women and organized women's associations was a remarkable victory, but it was a partial one at best. The addition of the Nineteenth Amendment to the Constitution in 1920 was paralleled by the work of Mary McLeod Bethune, an educator from the South who began a voter registration drive for black women—despite the fact that the Ku Klux Klan had launched an unprecedented recruitment campaign for new recruits that same year, and despite death threats from them. In 1917, she became president of the Florida Federation of Colored Women. Bethune would become, in 1923, the president of the National Association of Colored Women, one of the highest national offices a black woman could aspire to at that time.

Although NAWSA disbanded after the suffrage victory, many of the women who were active participants—organizing, petitioning, and lobbying for reform—saw that there was still a need for an organized women's rights movement. Some followed the lead of Carrie Chapman Catt and reorganized as the League of Women Voters at the Chicago convention of the NAWSA in 1919. Catt envisioned an organization that would link women from all states together to work toward progressive legislative reform at all levels of government. By the time their first convention was held in 1920, their nonpartisan, nonsectarian mandate had already expanded to include support for bur-

CARRIE CHAPMAN CATT (1859–1947)

Born Carrie Lane on January 9, 1859, in Ripon, Wisconsin, Carrie Chapman Catt grew up there and from 1866 on, lived in Charles City, Iowa. She worked her way through Iowa State College (now University), graduated in 1880, and after a short time spent reading law became a high school principal in Mason City in 1881. Two years later she was appointed superintendent of schools, one of the first women to hold such a position. In 1885 she married Leo Chapman, a journalist who died in 1886, and then in 1890, George Catt. Her marriage to Catt, an engineer, was unusual in its prenuptial legal contract providing her with four months of free time each year to work exclusively for woman suffrage. Catt encouraged and supported his wife's dedication until his death, in 1905. He left her financially independent to devote the rest of her life to reform activities.

From 1890 to 1892, Catt devoted herself to organizing the Iowa Woman Suffrage Association. She proved a highly effective organizer. She then worked as an organizer for the National American Woman Suffrage Association (NAWSA) from 1892 to 1900 and succeeded Susan B. Anthony as president in 1900. She resigned the presidency in 1904 to care for her ailing husband. Between 1905 and 1915, Catt reorganized the NAWSA along political-district lines and trained women for direct political action and marshaled seasoned campaigners. From 1904 to 1923, she also served as president of the International Woman Suffrage Alliance. She led the campaign to win suffrage through a federal amendment to the U.S. Constitution. Catt's flexible strategy of working at both federal and state levels to build support for woman suffrage and tireless lobbying in Congress directed by Maud Wood Park and then in state legislatures finally produced a ratified Nineteenth Amendment in August 1920. After ratification, she organized the League of Women Voters for the education of women in politics and to work for continuing progressive legislation throughout the nation.

After 1923, Catt devoted her efforts chiefly to the peace movement. She enlisted the cooperation of eleven national women's organizations in the Committee on the Cause and Cure of War (1925) to urge U.S. participation in a world organization for peace. She actively supported the League of Nations, relief for Jewish refugees from Germany, and a child labor amendment. She was also a strong advocate of international disarmament and of Prohibition. Following World War II, she was keenly interested in the United Nations and used her influence to have qualified women placed on certain commissions. With Nettie R. Shuler she wrote *Woman Suffrage and Politics: The Inner Story of the Suffrage Movement* (1923) and co-wrote *Why Wars Must Cease* (1935). Catt died in New Rochelle, New York, on March 9, 1947.

James G. Lewis

geoning international suffrage movements, to provide women voters with political education and information, and to play watchdog over policymaking and legislatures. The League of Women Voters exists to this day, functioning as a broad-based grassroots organization with a focus on political policy and issues, civic engagement, education, and the dissemination of information.

The new post-suffrage era meant that American women could and would face new and perhaps even more challenging struggles. Employment was considered one such issue, and suffragists lobbied for legislation to protect working women. The year 1920 marked the establishment of the Women's Bureau of the Department of Labor. Mary Anderson, a Swedish-born American trade unionist, was appointed as the Bureau's first director. Created by Congress, the Bureau existed—and still functions—as the only federally mandated agency charged with the representation of working women in the processes involved in forming public policy. Initially founded as a database of information on women's status in employment as well as an advocate for women's rights on the job, the Bureau provided legal and political voice to and for all working women, and protection from and recourse to undesirable working conditions, discrimination, and abuse.

Women employed in the public sphere found allies in their colleagues and workplaces, forming associations such as the National Federation of Business and Professional Women's Clubs, Altrusa, and Soroptimist. The National League of American Penwomen was created as an umbrella association for artistic women: composers, painters, poets, and writers. Women in other occupations—particularly in the "caring" professions—also organized, and teachers, nurses, cosmeticians, and mothers found other likeminded women who shared their concerns and wanted to push for equality for the "modern woman."

Other suffragists rejoined the organizations they were active in prior to the push for suffrage, such as the GFWC, the National Consumers League, the

GROWTH OF WOMEN'S ASSOCIATIONS AND ORGANIZATIONS

The membership and influence of women's associations in the immediate post-suffrage years was staggering, and the women who held membership were active participants in their causes. Women's organizations and voluntary associations were not only for adults; young women remained in and returned to a number of clubs begun before the vote was won, including: the Girl Scouts (founded in 1912), the Camp Fire Girls (established in 1910), the Four-H Club (formally organized in 1914), and the Young Women's Christian Association (YWCA, originating in England in 1855 and activated in America in 1858).

The growing number of female university students and graduates of institutions of higher learning also affected the rise of women's organizations in the post-suffrage era. By the time the vote was won, women attending college across the country had already begun to organize on a large scale. Women in Boston began as early as 1882, when a meeting of sixty-five women—all graduates of Wellesley College—led to the creation of the first organization of university women: the Association of Collegiate Alumnae (ACA). By 1883, another organization had emerged. The Western Association of Collegiate Alumnae (WACA) in Chicago (whose mandate highlighted international communication among learned women) eventually merged with the ACA in 1889. By 1903, the Southern Association of College Women (SACW) had emerged, struggling to improve—among other things—academic standards and curricula for women in school.

In 1919, Virginia Gildersleeve, an English professor, dean of Barnard College, and member of the ACA, with Dr. Caroline Spurgeon and Rose Sidgewick, worked together to create the International Federation of University Women (IFUW). At its outset, the IFUW had seven constituencies: the United States, Canada, Great Britain, Italy, the Netherlands, France, and Czechoslovakia. The SACW formally amalgamated with the ACA in the spring of 1921. That merger led to the creation of a single organization of learned women across the country: the American Association of University Women (AAUW). The AAUW remains active and influential to this day, boasting a membership of over 150,000.

WOMEN'S ACTIVISM

The 1920s would prove to be a productive decade for women's social activism and influence, as many is-

Carrying "torches of liberty" along New York's Fifth Avenue during the annual Easter Day Parade, women flaunt their independence by smoking in public. Social barriers restricting women's conduct and behavior relaxed in the 1920s. (© Underwood Photo Archives, Inc.)

Women's Trade Union League, or the women's committees of the various political parties. They and other like-minded women understood that the pursuit of women's rights would be an ongoing and constant struggle that was only accelerated by the vote. Legislative councils were created in virtually every state to keep an eye on the decisions considered and made by legislators. At the federal level, the Women's Joint Congressional Committee represented and lobbied Congress for women's groups. In other words, women sought to put their newly won voting rights to use through a multitude of organizations in an attempt to increase their effectiveness.

sues that were pursued by women's advocacy groups in the years prior would come to the fore. For instance, Congress passed the Sheppard-Towner Act in 1921; this legislation would guarantee the provision of matching federal funds for state-funded health centers created for children in the United States. The concern of women's groups for the health and welfare of women and their children leading up to Sheppard-Towner had begun at the turn of the century, and their lobbying efforts eventually let to the First White House Conference on Children in 1909, which directly influenced the establishment of the Children's Bureau in 1912. The Children's Bureau was a federal agency created to study the status of child welfare across the country, to investigate issues of child mortality, birth rates, orphanages, adoption, accidents, and disease, and to prevent child abuse and neglect on the job and in the home. Housed in the Department of Labor, it was the first federal statutory agency to be headed by a woman, Julia Clifford Lathrop.

Lathrop was a social worker and an activist concerned with child welfare in employment, health, and the law, and she was dedicated to the formal establishment of social services for women and children in need. Prior to her appointment as chief of the Children's Bureau, she was responsible for establishing—among her many other accomplishments—one of the first juvenile courts in the world. As head of the Bureau, and working alongside her successor, Grace Abbott, she was a significant player in passage of the Sheppard-Towner Act of 1921, otherwise known as the Maternity and Infancy Act. She and Abbott, a social worker and educator who had experience working with the Immigrant's Protective League (created in 1909), were fundamentally concerned with the prevention of infant mortality, and traveled to Europe with the American Red Cross to study the effects of World War I on children abroad. Upon their return, Lathrop and Abbott began formulating the Maternity and Infancy Act—a plan that called for a national welfare assistance program that would extend federal aid to state programs to promote maternal and infant healthcare.

Although the American Medical Association, conservative political groups, and others criticized Lathrop and Abbott's plan as "Communist," it received strong support from the Women's Joint Congressional Committee (WJCC). Led by its permanent chairperson, suffragist and reformer Maud Wood Park and boasting membership from a broad range of women's organizations, the WJCC has been described as one of the most powerful lobby groups in American history.

Representing several constituencies, Park and the WJCC directed efforts contributing to the eventual passage of the Sheppard-Towner Maternity and Infancy Protection Act in April of 1921. That moment marked the very first time that federal funding would be allocated to social welfare. Although funding for the Act lapsed in 1929 and was never renewed, the WJCC would go on to secure passage of the Cable Act of 1922; legislation that would provide American women with citizenship rights independent of their husband's status.

Continually attacked and criticized as Socialist and subversive, the WJCC would eventually merge with the newly revamped NWP. In 1921, the NWP had reformed and had begun publishing their own journal entitled *Equal Rights*. Concerned with legal discrimination embedded in legislation, the NWP would join forces with women who had similar views and would lobby for what would become one of the paramount feminist issues of the era: the Equal Rights Amendment (ERA). Proposed that year by former suffragist Alice Paul, the ERA targeted state and common laws that put legal restrictions on women in the realms of jury service, property ownership and control, marriage rights, and guardianship rights over their children. In many ways, people viewed the ERA as the next step—after the vote—in securing full citizenship rights for women in the United States.

The ERA, as envisioned by Paul, would be a constitutional amendment that would apply uniformly across the nation. Designed to nullify the state and federal laws deemed discriminatory to women, the proposed amendment stated that "equality of rights under the law shall not be denied or abridged by the United States or by any State on account of sex," and that "the Congress shall have the power to enforce, by appropriate legislation, the provisions of the article." In other words, the amendment argued that a person's sex should not be the determining factor in the social and legal rights of American people. Formally introduced to Congress in 1923, the ERA did not have full support from all women's organizations. In fact, the amendment caused deep divisions within the women's movement of the era; discord that would last for decades to come.

The proposed amendment received forceful opposition from the National Consumers League, the Women's Trade Union League, the League of Women Voters, and progressive reformer Florence Kelley, who vigorously stated that it would do nothing but compromise the advancements hard won to protect the rights of women in the workforce. In essence, the disagreements among women and between women's organizations over the ERA had its root in what the concept of "equality" did, would, and could mean for women, and illustrated the diversity in opinion that existed within the women's movement even then. The ERA was approved by the Senate in 1972 (forty-nine years after it was introduced to Congress), but was never ratified. What would have become the Twenty-seventh Amendment to the Constitution was never ratified.

THE BIRTH CONTROL MOVEMENT

Margaret Higgins Sanger was the driving force behind another major development in the immediate post-suffrage period: the birth control movement. Sanger, a public health nurse and social reformer, was acutely aware of the connection between poverty, high rates of infant and maternal mortality, and the lethal dangers of abortion. She gave up nursing to devote her attention full time to the struggle to remove the legal obstacles surrounding the publication of information about contraception, believing that all women had the right to control her own reproduction and sexuality, and especially to avoid unwanted pregnancy. To Sanger, the key to women's reproductive and sexual emancipation was to be found in the hands of women themselves. Improving access to information and educating women about the available means of birth control would allow women to choose motherhood for themselves. In addition to having coined the term *birth control* (in 1914), Sanger established the American Birth Control League in 1921 (an early version of what would become the Planned Parenthood Federation of America in 1942) and served as its president for seven years.

As the 1920s roared on, women continued to organize and join forces across groups. In 1927, a joint venture between the National Council of Jewish Women (NCJW), the Young Women's Christian Association (YWCA), and the National Council of Catholic Women (NCCW) exhibited women's influential strength in numbers. Founded by Hannah Greenebaum Solomon in 1893, the NCJW initially focused its efforts on providing assistance and information to new immigrants to the nation. With Jewish values at its core, the NCJW worked as a defender of the rights and freedoms of the public—Jewish and non-Jewish—and stands as the oldest volunteer Jewish women's association in the United States today. The YWCA, a nonsectarian Christian organization founded first in England in 1855 and then in America in 1866, held

aims similar to those of the NCJW and assisted young women with the difficulties in adapting to urban life. The NCCW was established in 1920 at the request of American Catholic bishops who envisioned a national umbrella organization that would assemble the multitude of Catholic women's groups in existence during the war. When the Johnson-Reed Act (legislation instituting rigid and restrictive quotas on immigrant arrivals to America) was passed in 1927, the three organizations united and lobbied against the Department of Immigration and their race-based policies.

WOMEN'S LEADERSHIP IN JUSTICE MOVEMENTS

The business expansion, economic growth and prosperity, mass consumerism, jazz music, increased citizenship rights, increased and improved employment, and changing roles for women that characterized the "Roaring Twenties" (also known as the "new era") came to a grinding halt on October 29, 1929. The stock market crash on "Black Tuesday" was followed by the most devastating economic collapse of the modern industrial world: the Great Depression. Between 1929 and the early 1940s, more than one-quarter of the American workforce (approximately fifteen million people) were unemployed. The real and pervasive threat to Americans' jobs, lives, and livelihoods had dramatic effects on the societal assumptions made about women's place at home and in the public realm. Many reinforced the argument that women should remain where they belonged: as caretakers of the home and hearth, especially in hard times. Others contended that working women were now redundant and that their employment was only taking jobs away from the "breadwinners" of the family: men. Interestingly, and perhaps ironically, the poor economics of the era made women's work outside the home even more necessary for the survival of many families. However, in 1932, the National Economy Act (Section 213) was passed, prohibiting more than one family member from working for the civil service. Many of the jobs lost, until its termination in 1937, were women's.

Although women's social and political organizing in the post-suffrage era peaked in the middle of the 1920s, the onset of the Great Depression witnessed the decline of many of the successful reform activities initiated at the turn of the century. Why participation in associations among women decreased in this era has been debated, but an inability to pay club and association membership dues could be a likely cause. The waning of women's social movement organizing did not last long, however, as the hardships and suffering caused by the Great Depression activated—and reactivated—many women into benevolent work in a variety of areas. In 1930, for example, Jessie Daniel Ames founded the Association of Southern Women for the Prevention of Lynching (ASWPL) in Atlanta, Georgia. Ames, a former suffragist and antiracist reformer, and a multitude of supporters (such as Jewish women's groups, Protestant women's associations, and interracial organizations) believed that white women had to be convinced that they played a role—even through silence—in lynching, and used press releases, brochures, pamphlets, and other resources to educate Southern whites about its causes and prevention. By 1940, there were over 100 associations in the five states where lynching was the most frequent: Georgia, Texas, Louisiana, Florida, and Mississippi.

The life of Jane Addams serves as testament to women's continued dedication to charitable work, organizing, and the struggle for a better society in the post-suffrage era. An active member of numerous local and national associations throughout her life, Addams has become noted particularly for the establishment of Hull-House, a settlement originally begun as a safe space for women and children, which grew into a community service locale and—eventually—into a center of and for social reform. Hull-House boasted residents like Florence Kelley, Dr. Alice Hamilton, Julia Lathrop, Ellen Gates Starr, and Sophonisba Breckinridge, all of whom would continue working for social reform as well and help social work evolve from being considered a benevolent activity to a legitimate profession. A committed suffragist, Addams also played a prominent role in the Campfire Girls, the National Playground Association, the National Child Labor Committee, and the National Association for the Advancement of Colored People (NAACP). An ardent pacifist, she would later become active in the peace movement, joining the Women's Peace Party during World War I. In 1931, Addams was formally—and internationally—recognized for her writing, settlement work, and her efforts in promoting world peace as the first female recipient of the Nobel Peace Prize.

The landslide presidential victory of Franklin D. Roosevelt over Herbert Hoover in 1932 dramatically changed the relationship between the American people and their government and had a significant effect on women's organizing in the United States. Roose-velt's New Deal not only expanded the power of the federal government and reshaped the role of the government in economics, but also drew attention to the vast inequities experienced by women, children, people of color, and laborers. His New Deal solutions also made way for increased political involvement for women and for the appointment of social reformer Frances Perkins to the cabinet (as secretary of labor) in 1933, which marked a significant "first" in American politics. A staunch advocate of fair wages, decent working hours and conditions, child welfare, and Social Security, Perkins was one of the primary executors of Roosevelt's New Deal program.

On June 28, 1934, much to the chagrin of his more conservative critics, Roosevelt announced his intent to implement a social insurance program in the United States. The following day, the Committee on Economic Security was established, responsible for designing a system of social security for America. Appointed chair, Frances Perkins and the committee dealt with (and debated over) a broad array of issues, ranging from old-age assistance, old-age insurance, unemployment, disability, and national health insurance. The latter two were removed from the initial bill, and the remainder went to Congress as the Economic Security Act in early 1935. Despite hostilities from the newspapers and the mass public, the bill was passed, and the Social Security Board was established as an independent agency to deal with the newly renamed Social Security Act within the federal government.

The creation of Social Security established a national system: a federal-state insurance program for the aged and a federal-state unemployment insurance program. However, the persistence of women's organizing led to an expansion of those benefits shortly after their institution. Grace Abbott, Katherine Lenroot, and Martha May Eliot, staff members of the Children's Bureau, worked closely with the Committee on Economic Security right from the Act's beginnings. Together, the three women (supported by a groundswell of voluntary agencies) recommended a program for children with special needs as well as a revised version of the then-defunct Sheppard-Towner Act. In addition, they organized conferences (such as the Conference on Better Care for Mothers and Babies, held in 1938) which highlighted the struggles that prevented *all* women and children from achieving the "democratic ideal." Working for the betterment of the lives of women and children, their efforts were formalized in Title V of the Social Security Act, "Grants to the States for Maternal and Child Welfare." Because of the organized efforts of women—in voluntary associations and in public groups—services for mothers and their children increased and improved exponentially during the 1930s.

ELEANOR ROOSEVELT AND THE NEW DEAL

The First Lady, Anna Eleanor Roosevelt, was also a significant player in the advancement of the New Deal programs, particularly as they pertained to humanitarian issues: child welfare, equal rights, and antidiscrimination. Her vocal and active interest in public welfare, her "hands-on" approach to politics—and her establishment of White House press conferences for female journalists—contributed to her often controversial image as a public personality. As a writer, her syndicated daily column "My Day" (1935–1962) dealt with the issues and activities she encountered while conducting her duties as First Lady. During the twenty-seven years that it ran, she tackled current political events, issues of race and youth, poverty, and women's rights. During World War II, she served as the assistant director of the Office of Civilian Defense, advocated for equal rights for women, and would go on to serve as an American delegate to the United Nations after the death of her husband. As both an activist and a political figure, she came to be one of America's popular leaders of reform and had a significant—and lasting—impact on national policy as it pertained to youth, women, and the disadvantaged.

The mid-1930s marked important gains for black women's organizing in the United States as well. In 1935, Mary McLeod Bethune established the National Council of Negro Women (NCNW) in New York City, and sat as its first president. The NCNW grew from Bethune's belief that African American women's groups needed an umbrella organization that would connect them and their issues on a national and international level. A lobbying coalition founded with fourteen women's organizations, the NCNW expanded to accommodate thirty-five national groups and 250 local associations (comprising more than four million women), and fought job discrimination, racism, and sexism. That same year, Bethune also became the director of Negro Affairs in the National Youth Administration (NYA, an organization created by Eleanor Roosevelt to address the "problem" of unemployment among Depression-era youth.). In 1938, Crystal Bird Fauset, a teacher, YWCA volunteer, public speaker, and race relations activist, ran for state legislature and became the first black woman in history elected to a seat in the Pennsylvania state legislature.

The Democratic National Convention of 1936, held in Philadelphia, was an eventful—albeit uncharacteristically harmonious—one. It marked the renomination of Roosevelt and his vice president John Nance Garner, the dissolution of the "two-thirds" nominating rule, and a continued governmental commitment to the New Deal programs. However, that convention also drew attention to the active leadership and remarkable organizing skills of economist Mary Williams Dewson. Dedicated to public service from an early age, she served as secretary for the Commission on Minimum Wage Legislation in Massachusetts, worked with the Bureau of the Refugees for the American Red Cross in France, was a researcher and secretary for the National Consumers League, and president of the Consumers League in New York before joining forces with the Democratic Party in 1928. Active in his presidential campaign, Dewson soon moved on to women's campaign activities within the party proper: as director of the Women's Division of the Democratic National Committee and the General Advisory Committee of the Women's Division and as a member of the Consumers' Advisory Board of the National Recovery Administration. Culminating with the Convention in 1936, Dewson's successful political mobilizing and organizing secured over 200 female delegates and ensured that women had equal representation in policy-strategizing and agenda-setting. Dewson would go on to work on Roosevelt's third presidential campaign in 1940.

Although achieving the vote in 1920 opened the doors to remarkable avenues for activism and organizing and launched a domino-effect of political, economic, and social gains for many women across the nation, the post-suffrage era was marked by a downturn in women's participation in the military. Although women's activity in the military was comparably less than men's during World War I, advances had been made in terms of women's involvement in all levels of the military. For instance, the 1925 revision of the Naval Act excluded women from enrollment until it was revised again in 1938. In addition, the director of Women's Programs for the Army (a position that fought for the creation of a Women's Service Corps) was eliminated entirely in 1931. By the 1940s, however, an upswing in activism concerned with women's work for and at war occurred once again. In 1939, for example, the American Medical Women's Association (AMWA) began lobbying for the permanent appointment (as opposed to work on a contract-only basis) of women doctors in the Army medical corps. By 1943, Congress permitted temporary commissions (subject to the duration of the war), and permanent hires were allowed by 1953.

WOMEN AND WORLD WAR II

During the first half of 1941, the struggle to secure comparable salaries and benefits for women in the military had already begun. Edith Nourse Rogers, a congresswoman from Massachusetts, introduced a bill that she—and many others—hoped would secure the establishment of a separate unit for women in the Army. Attention to the bill was minimal at best until Japan bombed Pearl Harbor on December 7, 1941, and America formally entered World War II. By May of 1942, the Women's Auxiliary Army Corps (WAAC) accorded official status and salary to female enlistees—without the benefits accorded to their male counterparts—and marked the first time that women (with the exception of nurses) served within the ranks of the U.S. Army. Despite a strong backlash from the public and press who were resistant to women's military service, Commander Oveta Culp Hobby, a public official and publisher, pushed to have the WAAC's "auxiliary" status dropped. By 1943, she was successful, and the WAAC was renamed the Women's Army Corps (WAC).

The WAC recruited women for noncombat duties, and while the majority of those who enlisted performed traditional "woman's work" (mainly clerical tasks, translation, and cooking), others performed more atypical jobs such as technician, photographer, recruiter, electrician, and air traffic controller. The WAC also supplied woman power (Air WACs) to the American Air Force (AAF). Women Accepted for Voluntary Emergency Service (WAVES) was also created for the Navy in 1942, and women who enlisted were automatically granted status equal to that of male recruits. By the end of the war, more than 350,000 women had served in the American armed forces. In 1948, Congress permitted the creation of Women in the Air Force (WAF), passed a bill integrating the WAC in the regular army, and made WAVES a permanent part of the Navy through acceptance of the Women's Armed Services Integration Act. Male and female units of the Army, Navy, and Air Force were amalgamated by 1978.

Enlisting was not the only way women participated in the war efforts. In 1941, a number of women's voluntary associations—the Salvation Army, the YWCA, National Catholic Community Services, and the National Jewish Welfare Board—combined their efforts with the YMCA and the National Travelers Aid Association and created the United Service Organizations (USO). Originally designed to provide on-leave recreation and entertainment for the predominantly male members of the military, the USO's mandate grew rapidly to include social services for women in the armed forces as well as for military families. At war's end, more than 1.5 million volunteers participated in the USO at home and abroad, the bulk of whom were women.

Along with the Red Cross, the USO was the only organization permitted to send staff overseas during the war. However, women were organizing at the national level as well. Alice Throckmorton McLean, a socialite turned social service organizer interested in supporting the war from home, founded the American Women's Voluntary Services (AWVS) in 1940. Working with the Red Cross and the Women's Ambulance and Defense Corps and modeled on a organization already established in Great Britain, the AWVS held a membership of almost 20,000 by 1941, and volunteers trained as drivers, as field medics and attendants, and as mechanics (to name just a few). Despite harsh criticism of its director and its work from the mainstream presses, close to 350,000 women participated in the AWVS, selling millions of dollars in war bonds and stamps, providing food and clothing to those in need, and educating women in do-it-yourself mechanics, agriculture, food preparation and preservation, and the like.

Paralleling the national call for volunteers and recruits was a wartime appeal to women to (temporarily) join the labor force at home for the duration of the war. As men left for war and the need for the production of new goods increased, women were hired in a vast range of occupations. In an abrupt about-face from the Depression era (when women were told to leave jobs for more "deserving" male breadwinners), the media were saturated with calls to women to "do their part" for their families and their country. Appealing to a sense of patriotism and duty, women worked in war industry manufacturing, producing steel as well as heavy machinery, all the while making 35 percent less than their male counterparts and experiencing job segregation and hostility. Although many women who had assumed employment in business, education, and clerical work remained in their positions at war's end, practically all of the women who worked in industry were laid off (estimates have suggested that close to four million women lost their jobs). Although vigorous protests, union grievances, and conferences, committees, and lobbying were launched in objection to discrimination in employment—and reemployment—little support was received from either the labor unions or the War Manpower Commission.

The war opened the doors to women's increased participation in the workforce and changed the profile of these women. Prior to the war, "working women" were overwhelmingly young, single, and without children. However, as the need for wartime production increased, older, married, and maternal women joined the ranks of the employed. Not surprisingly, they faced a challenge perhaps more difficult than even their new working conditions: child care. Although some were lucky enough to have relatives or friends who would care for their children, the remainder had to seek out other options. The Lanham Act, passed by Congress in 1942, was the federal government's attempt to address the pressing need for day care. Established as a temporary measure at a time of national emergency, the Act authorized the use of federal funds for child-care facilities in "war-impacted areas" only. As a result, many mothers continued to go without. When the war ended and many women returned to the home, the funding was terminated and the majority of the child-care facilities were closed. While inherently flawed and ill-defined from the outset, the Lanham Act marked the federal government's widest-ranging foray into child care to date.

WAR VICTORY AND THE STRUGGLE FOR WOMEN'S RIGHTS

America's entry into World War II not only marked the end of the Great Depression and the rise of the United States as a global powerhouse, but it also brought remarkable social and political changes to the shape of the entire country. The movement of women into previously male-only professions was one of the largest. After the war ended, however, those women were either pressed to resign or were laid off to "make room" for America's returning soldiers, and to resume their roles as housewives and mothers. Women's involvement in voluntary associations, public organizations, and charities persisted as part of the wartime relief effort, and certainly did not wane when the conflict ended. Although the Bureau was the only federal organization designed specifically for working women, its work focused on educating women about their rights on the job, promoting legislation that appealed to the needs of women, collecting work-related data, and reporting on their results to Congress and the public at large. The Bureau had managed to have women's work included in the 1938 Fair Labor Standards Act (concerning minimum wage) and fought for policies that addressed employment opportunities, discrimination, and child-raising circumstances. It had become a well-respected and decently funded agency during wartime, and it was backed by organizations such as the YWCA and the League of Women Voters, but, unfortunately, it was unable to provide the immediate support that women seeking recourse for their loss of employment required.

Pay equity rapidly became one of the paramount issues for some members of the women's movement and for the Women's Bureau. During the war, the National Labor Board encouraged the use of wage evaluations based on job descriptions to monitor and maintain fair wage levels. The Women's Equal Pay Act was introduced for the first time in Congress in 1945. If passed immediately, it would have been based on the premise of "equal pay for work of comparable value." Despite an enthusiastic endorsement from the National Association of Manufacturers during the war, resistance to the bill was strong and made its passage slow. It would take eighteen years for the Equal Pay Act to pass.

As late as 1950, Mary Anderson (though technically retired) presented a public statement to a subcommittee of the House Committee on Education and Labor in overwhelming favor of the Equal Pay Act. Speaking on behalf of the National Board of the YWCAs, the League of Women Voters, the National Consumers League, the NCJW, and the Women's Trade Union League (WTUL), Anderson asserted that "equal pay for women is a matter of simple justice," and she urged the Committee to report favorably for the legislation. Congress passed the Equal Pay Act in 1963, thirteen years after Anderson's plea. Equal pay by race would not be mandated until the following year.

By 1948, it was clear that the face of American society was changing. President Harry S Truman, who succeeded Roosevelt after his death in 1945, appointed Eleanor Roosevelt to the United Nations. As chairman of the United Nations Commission on Human Rights (1946–1951), she played a significant role in the creation of the Universal Declaration of Human Rights (adopted in 1948). That same year, Margaret Chase Smith, already a member of the House of Representatives, was elected to the Senate. Smith became the first woman elected to both Houses of Congress in the United States. She would become even more noteworthy two years later, when she publicly condemned the anti-Communist crusade of her colleague, Joseph McCarthy.

INTELLECTUAL DEBATES ADVANCED

Although Congress continued to vote down the ERA (in 1946, 1950, and again in 1953), things were changing on the ground. In 1949, Harvard Law School publicly announced that it would begin admitting women to its prestigious program. In addition, the early activism of the suffragists, centered on obtaining formal citizenship rights for women in the form of the vote, was reinforced on an international level. The 1952 United Nations Convention on the Political Rights of Women, the first of its kind, formally announced that "women shall be entitled to vote in all elections on equal terms with men, without any discrimination." The following year marked the English translation and American publication of Simone de Beauvoir's *The Second Sex*. De Beauvoir, a French existentialist, novelist, and social essayist, analyzed the history of women's oppression in what would become her most noted work. Her thesis, that "one is not born, but rather becomes, a woman," has been credited for inspiring the women's liberation movement that would emerge a little more than a decade later.

The postwar period has come to be characterized by economic gains, an improved standard of living, and the Baby Boom. A revival of the importance placed on women's role as caregiver of the home—as well as on the nuclear family—also followed the war. Postwar sentiments were strong, and the family was deemed supreme: marriage was praised, divorce frowned upon, and childbearing exalted. Despite, or perhaps because of, the preoccupation with the continuation of the nuclear family, information on sexuality flourished in the postwar years. The publication of the Kinsey reports, *Sexual Behavior in the Human Male* in 1948 and *Sexual Behavior in the Human Female* in 1953, marked the first of many challenges to mainstream assumptions about sexuality and brought sexuality into public discussion. Kinsey concluded that his research failed to find any significant anatomic or physiological evidence to support the assumed sexual difference between men and women. Public reaction to the volume on female sexuality was overwhelmingly negative: critics questioned the potential moral implications of the project's findings and doubted the ethical foundation of the research. In less than one year, the clamor over the female volume led to a public denouncement of Kinsey by the American

Medical Association. The Rockefeller Foundation withdrew its funding for the Institute of Sex Research shortly thereafter.

Despite the controversy, the Kinsey reports served as reference guides for policymaking throughout the later postwar years and helped to legitimize the discussion of sex in the mainstream media. Radio, television, and the print media all provided outlets for a variety of commentaries on sexuality. Attitudes toward sexuality were changing, albeit slowly. The year 1953 also marked the release of the premiere issue of *Playboy*, a glossy publication featuring images of "photographic fantasy" for the "modern man." Seventy-thousand copies of the first issue (featuring Marilyn Monroe on the cover and in centerfold) hit North American newsstands in December, and 54,175 issues of the 44-page magazine were promptly sold.

In 1955, American states prohibited female homosexual activities, even though the Constitution allotted all of its citizens, in writing, the right to the pursuit of pleasure and happiness. That year, Phyllis Lyon and Del Martin founded the Daughters of Bilitis (DOB) (an intentionally inconspicuous name borrowed from a poem by Pierre Louys called "Songs of Bilitis"), the first lesbian organization in America. Established in San Francisco, Lyon and Martin envisioned a space where lesbians could meet free from fear of the law and as a location for community and political action. The following year, the DOB published its first issue of *The Ladder*, a national newsletter for lesbians. It wasn't long before their membership grew, and independent versions of the group emerged across the country. By January 1957, the DOB officially became a nonprofit in the state of California. Although the DOB received significant support from members of the gay rights movement in its early years, the burgeoning women's liberation movement would significantly affect that collaboration, as "women's rights" became an issue separate from "gay rights."

CONCLUSION

Clearly, the United States emerged from World War II a changed nation. While promoting and defending democracy abroad and maintaining Cold War attitudes at home, however, internal challenges remained. In 1955, for instance, women still earned an average of only 63 cents for every dollar earned by men. Moreover, and significantly more striking, the federal government had not yet addressed the denial of civil liberties and civil rights of racial minorities.

The year 1955 marked the arrest of Rosa Parks, a seamstress and member of the Alabama chapter of the NAACP who refused to relinquish her seat on a public bus to a white man—a breach of the city's racial segregation ordinances. The Montgomery Bus Boycott, led by Ralph Abernathy and Martin Luther King Jr. and backed by the Women's Political Council and the NAACP, was an overwhelming success, and the regular users of the municipal bus company held out for more than a year. Park's defiance and strength, together with the boycott that followed, captured the imagination of the entire country, launched the public recognition of King, and set the tone for the political struggles that would ensue. Rosa Parks has since become known as the mother of the civil rights movement.

Although the suffrage movement succeeded in introducing partial citizenship rights to some women in America, few women occupied "official" positions within the legislature in the post-suffrage era. They were, however, actively participating in other, less visible, political arenas. Between 1920 and the late 1950s, women maintained membership in women's voluntary associations, created national women's coalitions, lobbied on issues pertinent to women and children, and were involved in women's auxiliaries and in trade and labor unions. Contrary to popular opinion, women did not withdraw from political life after the ratification of the suffrage amendment, but instead continued to struggle for the complementary goals of full citizenship for women and the development of policies made with women in mind. Surprisingly, only recently has it become clear in historical documents that women were indeed political creatures—and were actively engaged in effective political participation and affecting political change—after the vote was won.

Suffrage marked a pivotal moment in political history and the women's movement, as it was a tangible mechanism with potential for major societal transformation. In a very real way, securing the vote for women was a prerequisite for challenging assumptions about women's "place" (be it public, in the workforce or in politics; or private, in the home), for women's political socialization and mobilization, as well as for emerging ideas about social change. Significant gains were made for women in virtually every sector of American society in the post-suffrage era, but a great deal remained to be accomplished. Securing rights for women in education, employment, politics, and the law were still battles to be fought, and the ERA remained a pressing concern.

The period between 1920 and 1960 was once considered to be a politically dormant era for women's activism, feminism, and the women's movement, and it was largely assumed that once women won the vote their political activity "paused" until the second wave "revival" in the 1960s. A glimpse into some of the challenges faced by revolutionary women and men during the period—ranging from the birth control movement to the New Deal to civil rights—as well as their remarkable successes, illustrate that the women's movement was alive and well and still very much kicking after the vote was won. Some activists of the era pushed for public policy changes that would augment women's formal equality (including, for instance, the promotion of a federal healthcare program that acknowledged the needs of women and children), while others worked diligently in smaller women's associations, affecting change at the local level on a one-on-one (or case-by-case) basis. Regardless of their strategies or political persuasion, women in the United States were actively and deftly engaged in advancing women's political and social rights during this period. In many ways, the work of women during the post-suffrage era paved the way for the next stage in the contemporary women's movement's history; one that promised to be as turbulent, as troubling, and as fulfilling as the wave that came before.

Candis Steenbergen

BIBLIOGRAPHY

Backhouse, Constance, and David Flaherty. *Challenging Times: The Women's Movement in Canada and the United States.* Montreal: McGill-Queens University Press, 1992.

Buechler, Steven. *Women's Movements in the United States: Woman Suffrage, Equal Rights, and Beyond.* New Brunswick, NJ: Rutgers University Press, 1990.

Cott, Nancy. *The Grounding of Modern Feminism.* New Haven, CT: Yale University Press, 1989.

DeHart, Jane Sherron., and Donald Matthews. *Sex, Gender and the Politics of the ERA.* New York: Oxford University Press, 1990.

Evans, Sara. *Personal Politics: The Roots of Women's Liberation in the Civil Rights Movement and the New Left.* New York: Vintage Books, 1979.

Gluck, Sherna Berger, ed. *Rosie the Riveter Revisited: Women, the War and Social Change.* Boston: Twayne, 1987.

Gordon, Linda. *Pitied But Not Entitled: Single Mothers and the History of Welfare.* Boston: Harvard University Press, 1995.

Higonnet, Margaret, Jane Jenson, and Margaret Weitz. *Behind the Lines: Gender and the Two World Wars.* New Haven, CT: Yale University Press, 1987.

Hine, Darlene Clark, and Kathleen Thompson. *A Shining Thread of Hope: The History of Black Women in America.* New York: Broadway Books, 1998.

Kerber, Linda, and Jane Sherron De Hart, eds. *Women's America: Refocusing the Past.* 5th ed. New York: Oxford University Press, 2000.

Kish Sklar, Kathryn, and Thomas Dublin, eds. *Women and Social Movements in the United States, 1830–1930.* Binghamton: State University of New York, 1999.

Koven, Seth, and Sonya Michel, eds. *Mothers of a New World. Maternalist Politics and the Origins of Welfare States.* New York: Routledge, 1993.

Scott, Anne Firor. *Natural Allies: Women's Associations in American History.* Urbana: University of Illinois Press, 1992.

Skocpol, Theda. *Protecting Soldiers and Mothers: The Political Origins of Social Policy in the United States.* Boston: Harvard University Press, 1992.

EQUAL RIGHTS AMENDMENT

In 1848, over 300 women and men gathered in Seneca Falls, New York, to hold the nation's first women's rights convention. Seventy-two years later, when the passage of the Nineteenth Amendment to the U.S. Constitution in 1920 granted women the right to vote, many political activists felt that the vision of the Seneca Falls convention had been realized. Others believed that securing suffrage was just one marker in a broader struggle for women's equality and immediately began working for the passage of another constitutional amendment, the Equal Rights Amendment (ERA). The story of the ERA is an ongoing and dynamic one. Throughout the amendment's more than eighty-year history, public interest has ranged from intensity to indifference; coalitions for and against it have been formed, disassembled, and reconstructed; opponents have become allies; and the playing field has moved between the federal government and the states.

ROOTS OF THE ERA: THE STRUGGLE FOR SUFFRAGE

The originator of the Equal Rights Amendment was lawyer and social reformer Alice Paul (1885–1977). As a young woman she spent time in England, where she studied law and social work and became acquainted with Emmeline and Sylvia Pankhurst, militant leaders of the British women's suffrage movement. As part of the Pankhursts' Women's Social and Political Union, Paul was arrested and imprisoned several times and was forcibly fed after going on a hunger strike.

After returning to the United States in 1912, Paul earned a Ph.D. at the University of Pennsylvania and directed her commitment to women's rights toward passage of the Nineteenth Amendment. Paul soon joined the National American Woman Suffrage Association (NAWSA), the principal women's rights organization. Her intelligence and enthusiasm quickly propelled her into a leadership role, leading to her being named head of the Congressional Committee, the organization's lobbying arm. From the beginning of her work with NAWSA, Paul clashed with the group's president, Carrie Chapman Catt (1859–1947), over the direction of the suffrage campaign and the strategies it employed. The younger Paul advocated applying pressure on the federal level, while Catt advocated a state-by-state grassroots push. Paul was successful at bringing young, radical women into the organization, while Catt owed her leadership position to older members. Most important, Paul advocated using the confrontational methods that she learned from the Pankhursts, while Catt insisted on more conservative strategies, such as public speaking and lobbying elected officials. With the support of her followers, Paul sponsored a suffrage parade on March 3, 1913, in Washington that ended in a riot, which infuriated Catt. In further defiance of Catt, Paul organized the Congressional Union as a fund-raising arm of the Congressional Committee in order to have more resources to fund her activities. Tensions between Paul and Catt and their respective followers continued to escalate until Paul left the NAWSA to form her own organization, the National Woman's Party (NWP), in 1917.

The two groups continued working for passage of the Nineteenth Amendment, utilizing strategies and tactics that reflected the differences between their two leaders. Not surprisingly, when the amendment was ratified in 1920, members of both the NWP and the NAWSA took credit for the victory.

EARLY BATTLE LINES

After ratification of the Nineteenth Amendment, the NWP immediately turned to what they considered the unfinished business of women's equality by advocating for an Equal Rights Amendment to the U.S. Constitution. They believed that there was still a lot of work to do in terms of making women's economic, educational, political, legal, and social realities equal to those of men. The NWP had several reasons for not wanting to settle for anything less than an amendment to the Constitution. First, they argued that only a constitutional amendment would protect women's rights from future legislative bodies whose members might not support gender equality. Second, they believed that a campaign to change the Constitution was the quickest and least costly strategy. Third, they believed that women would be perceived as equal to men only if the Constitution said they were.

In 1923, the NWP celebrated the seventy-fifth anniversary of the first women's rights convention by holding their own convention in Seneca Falls, New York. It was at this meeting that Alice Paul first introduced the Equal Rights Amendment, which read, "men and women shall have equal rights throughout the U.S. and every place subject to its jurisdiction." Later that year, the amendment, dubbed the Lucretia Mott Amendment, in honor of the early women's rights activist, was introduced in the U.S. House of Representatives by Kansas Representative Daniel Read Anthony, a distant relative of women's rights leader the late Susan B. Anthony.

Throughout the first five decades of the movement to pass the ERA, the most vocal and powerful opponent of the ERA was the League of Women Voters (LWV), founded by Carrie Chapman Catt to succeed the NAWSA. Members argued that the amendment was unnecessary inasmuch as the right to vote was all that was needed to guarantee women's equality. In keeping with this perspective, local LWV branches across the country launched programs to educate newly enfranchised women about political issues of the day and to teach them how to influence the political process by becoming active in local, regional, and national party politics. In addition, the LWV rejected the universalizing effect of the ERA as dangerous to women. Although they advocated for women's increased participation in the public world of work and politics, they believed women needed special protections against the types of abuses that such public activities might elicit. Thus, a major component of their reform agenda was protective workplace legislation, such as laws guaranteeing that women's pay would be equal to men's, limits on the total number of hours a woman could be employed, minimum pay scales for women, and restrictions on women's employment in occupations considered morally or physically dangerous. They argued that the sweeping equality advocated by the pro-ERA forces would not take into consideration the special circumstances of women as would their "specific-bills-for-specific-ills" legislative approach.

The early battle lines over the ERA had been drawn. Although the NWP failed to win grassroots support for the ERA, owing to their radical reputation during the suffrage campaign, hundreds of state and local LWV chapters moved forward with voter education programs and their specific-bills-for-specific-ills legislative agenda. Initially, Catt's legislative agenda triumphed over Paul's amendment proposal. However, after a rash of Progressive reform measures were passed throughout the 1920s, the political climate began to change in the 1930s. With threats of global economic depression and war in Europe looming, political support for social reform on the domestic front began to erode. Even more important to the fate of the ERA, workplace protective legislation came under attack as women's rights advocates identified instances of protective measures being used to discriminate against women in the workplace. For example, reports circulated that minimum wage and maximum hour standards made women less attractive to employers.

LEGISLATIVE CHESS

As workplace legislation fell out of favor because of abuses, the ERA was increasingly seen as a remedy for workplace discrimination. By the late 1930s, a variety of national women's groups, concerned that the discriminatory consequences of protective labor laws outweighed their equalizing benefits, added their endorsements to the ERA effort. In addition, business and industry interests began to weigh in on the side of the ERA as a way of overturning protective legislation laws that they viewed as promoting government interference in free enterprise. In pursuit of the business vote, both the Republican and Democratic national parties included support for the ERA in their party platforms by 1940. Throughout this time period, the lobbying efforts of ERA advocates kept the amendment on the congressional agenda by getting it introduced in every session of Congress. They succeeded in advancing it to Judiciary Committee subcommittee hearings several times in the 1930s. However, anti-ERA forces remained powerful enough to block movement beyond the subcommittee. A turning point in the national debate occurred in 1938, when Congress passed the Fair Labor Standards Act of 1938 (FLSA) as part of President Franklin D. Roosevelt's New Deal programming for economic and social welfare. This bill guaranteed minimum wage and maximum hour standards for all workers, and, therefore, strengthened the idea of blanket protection advanced by the ERA.

With their economic arguments validated by the FLSA, pro-ERA forces next took advantage of the nation's wartime climate of patriotism to strengthen their position. They argued that American women who had entered the workplace, joined the women's divisions of the armed forces, and endured sacrifices at home deserved the justice and equality that was at the heart of American values. These arguments were successful. After two decades of persistence, advocates were rewarded in 1942, when the Judiciary Committees of both houses of Congress passed the amendment. In 1946, the ERA was brought up for a vote in the Senate for the first time in its twenty-three year history. However, through the political maneuvering of anti-ERA forces, who continued to question the value of the ERA, the vote was called without prior notice, taking ERA supporters by surprise. With little time for proponents to rally speakers in support of the amendment, it failed. In 1950, 1953, and 1956, ERA forces withdrew their support for the proposed amendment when protective legislation provisions were added to it. Following this flurry of activity, there was no congressional action on the ERA for the next fourteen years. During this period, amendment supporters were largely unsuccessful in their attempts to keep the issue on the public agenda, as Cold War politics and the booming postwar economy consumed the nation's attention. But the ERA was not dead; it was just hibernating.

REVITALIZED SUPPORT

After the fierce battles over the ERA of earlier decades, all but a small core of devoted NWP members abandoned the ERA. In 1960, under pressure from women's groups, President John F. Kennedy created a presidential committee charged with identifying the status of women in terms of education, employment, violence, child care, and other issues. Kennedy appointed labor leader Esther Peterson, who had worked against the ERA as head of the Labor Department's Women's Bureau, as the chair of his newly formed President's Commission on the Status of Women. Motivated by a desire to represent multiple perspectives on the committee, Peterson made a decision that inadvertently reintroduced the ERA as a viable solution to the obstacles to women's equality. Underestimating the dormant power of the ERA, Peterson invited representatives of a number of pro-ERA groups to serve on the commission. They used the committee as a platform for reestablishing a base of support for the amendment, and the ERA secured a new political foothold.

THE RATIFICATION BATTLE

During the 1970s, the ERA became a symbolic rallying point for a host of feminist groups with broadly diverse agendas, including sexual and reproductive rights and services, gay rights, child-care services, child-welfare reform, and economic and education opportunity reforms. Support for the ERA transcended the political and organizational differences of these groups, and the ERA enjoyed the most widespread support in its forty-five-year history. In July 1970 and October 1971, under renewed pressure from a united feminist front that now included the ERA's traditional foe, the League of Women Voters, the U.S. House of Representatives passed the amendment. Only Senate approval stood between the ERA and its first chance for ratification by the states. On March 22, 1972, after forty-nine years of public and congressional debate, the Senate approved the amendment, which would add the following words to the U.S. Constitution in the form of the Twenty-Seventh Amendment to the Constitution:

Section 1: Equality of rights under the law shall not be denied or abridged by the United States or by any state on account of sex.

Section 2: The Congress shall have the power to enforce, by appropriate legislation, the provision of the article.

Section 3: This amendment shall take effect two years after the date of ratification.

In order for the ERA to become part of the U.S. Constitution, it had to be ratified by three-fourths of the state legislatures prior to a seven-year deadline. In the first year of the ratification process, twenty-two states ratified it. During the second twelve months, eight more signed on, and advocates believed they were on their way to an easy victory. However, in 1973 the ERA suffered its first defeat in Utah. Then, in 1974 only three new states voted to ratify, and several ratifying states considered rescinding their yes vote. Between 1975 and 1978, only two more states voted for ratification, leaving the amendment three states short of the thirty-eight necessary for ratification.

At the center of the ERA's falling fortunes was a coalition composed of political and religious conser-

Supporters of the Equal Rights Amendment cheer First Lady Betty Ford's endorsement. *(The Schlesinger Library, Radcliffe Institute, Harvard University)*

vatives. Their arguments against the amendment focused on perceived threats to the traditional family posed by abortion, gay rights, and working mothers, as well as concerns about the power of the federal government to dictate social policy to states. Under the leadership of ultraconservative lawyer, author, and anti-Communist political crusader Phyllis Schlafly and her STOP ERA organization, thousands of grassroots volunteers organized phone banks, managed direct mail campaigns, sent speakers out to churches, distributed leaflets door-to-door, called in to radio talk shows, and even baked cookies for state legislators in their quest to stop what had seemed to be the ERA's inevitable ratification.

As ERA supporters began to envision a defeat that had been unthinkable only a few years earlier, they adopted two new strategies. First, they began to work for the extension of the amendment's original seven-year ratification deadline. A three-year exten-

sion was granted, moving the ratification deadline to June 30, 1982. However, no states ratified the amendment during the extension period, and the second ratification deadline passed without the required state approval. On the federal level, the ERA continues to be introduced to every session of Congress, as it has been since 1923. However, it has failed to generate any action.

A second strategy implemented by pro-ERA forces was to add ERA language to individual state constitutions. In 1971, before the ratification process, when the ERA debate was still raging in Congress, Pennsylvania, Illinois, and Virginia passed state ERAs. Before the federal ERA reached its first ratification deadline in 1979, eleven additional states added sexual equality provisions to their constitutions. By 1980, however, like the federal ERA, state ERAs were losing support, and several attempts failed. After 1986, only one state, Iowa, attempted to pass a state ERA. In 1992, a public referendum on a state ERA failed; in 1998, Iowans approved the addition of an Equal Rights Amendment to their state constitution.

Despite the victory in Iowa and the continued reintroduction of the ERA in Congress, the question of a federal ERA appears to be in a dormant stage, not unlike the 1950s when, except for a small core of devoted ERA activists, the ERA appeared to have vanished from the public agenda. Many people claim that an ERA is no longer necessary because the protections it called for have already been achieved through a variety of legislative actions. Others claim the ERA is still important for no other reason than the symbolic value of adding a constitutional guarantee of gender equality. Still others continue to oppose the ERA as antifamily. These divergent opinions suggest that, given the right social and political context, the ERA controversy may reappear in the future.

Linda Czuba Brigance

BIBLIOGRAPHY

Becker, Susan D. *The Origins of the Equal Rights Amendment: American Feminism Between the Wars.* Westport, CT: Greenwood Press, 1981.

Berry, Mary Francis. *Why ERA Failed: Politics, Women's Rights, and the Amending Process of the Constitution.* Bloomington: Indiana University Press, 1998.

Mathews, Donald G., and Jane Sherron De Hart. *Sex, Gender, and the Politics of ERA: A State and the Nation.* New York: Oxford University Press, 1990.

Rupp, Leila J., and Verta Taylor. *Survival in the Doldrums: The American Women's Rights Movement, 1945 to the 1960s.* New York: Oxford University Press, 1987.

ABORTION RIGHTS MOVEMENT

Perhaps the most significant decision women face in their lifetimes is whether or not to have children, and, if so, at what point during their lives and under what conditions. The ability to freely make these decisions and have significant control over reproduction has been the driving force behind what has come to be known as the abortion rights movement. Although *Roe v. Wade* (1973) is often thought of as the catalyst to the abortion debate, the current struggle over abortion rights has its roots in the nineteenth century, and the use of abortion dates back even further.

Yet, what distinguishes the modern abortion movement and the counter, pro-life movement from their predecessors is the expansive and salient nature of the debate. For example, between 1989 and 1999 the *New York Times* covered, on average, 730 abortion-related stories a year. Moreover, the abortion conflict has permeated every level of government, from the Supreme Court to state legislatures to local bureaucracies.

The historical roots of the abortion rights movement can be traced to the nineteenth century. During this time period, abortion went from being a fairly common practice to one increasingly dominated and stigmatized by the emerging medical community. By the mid-twentieth century, the topic of abortion reappeared in both elite and public discourse. The Court's ruling in *Roe v. Wade* ushered in a new era in the abortion debate—leading to the rise in the pro-life movement and a flurry of national and state policymaking. Later, the abortion rights movement revived itself, partly as a response to growing abortion clinic violence and increasing governmental restrictions on abortion services.

ABORTION IN THE NINETEENTH CENTURY

The early American colonists inherited Puritan beliefs that opposed both birth control and abortion. The Puritans feared that married people would use birth control and reduce their population, which had economic consequences for an agrarian society dependent on free or relatively cheap labor. However, the nineteenth century ushered in major demographic changes. America began a transition from an agricultural society into a more urban and industrialized society. The need for many children was disappearing—birth rates dove from an average of 7.04 children per woman in 1800 to an average of 3.56 per woman in 1900. But nineteenth-century America's conceptions about the family and motherhood were also changing. These changes all contributed to an increasing demand for abortion and to the subsequent rise of abortion as a public issue.

By the 1800s, abortion was a common practice, but it was also largely unregulated. Guidelines pertaining to abortion were inherited from the English common law tradition, which generally held that an abortion prior to quickening (the point in pregnancy when a woman can feel the fetus move) was at most a misdemeanor. Furthermore, violations of the law were difficult to prosecute because a woman was the only reliable person who could testify as to when quickening occurred. Indeed, the first statutory abortion regulation did not surface until 1821 in the state of Connecticut, and the statute only prohibited the use of dangerous poisons to induce abortion, rather than actually restricting the practice of abortion.

Society was fairly tolerant of abortion services during the 1830s; "disguised" advertisements for abortion services regularly appeared in newspapers. Throughout the 1850s and 1860s, abortion services were readily available in most urban areas. Given the relative availability of abortion services, no impetus existed for the development of a pro-choice or abortion rights movement.

Yet, by the late 1800s, the permissibility and availability of abortion services began to wane. The impetus for this change began in the medical community. Although there was a genuine and legit-

Ever since the Supreme Court legalized abortion during the first trimester in 1973, reproductive rights have proved a controversial issue among Americans. Here, pro-choice and pro-life activists demonstrate in front of the Supreme Court on July 3, 1989, after the justices had upheld a Missouri law limiting abortion in *Webster v. Reproductive Health Services. (AP Wide World Photos)*

imate health concern related to abortion services, many scholars argue that the medical community's crusade against abortion was based primarily on economic concerns. At the time, the medical profession was largely unregulated. Medical professionals who received some formal training found themselves in direct competition with midwives, herbalists, alternative healers, and quacks. Importantly, "real" doctors wanted to regulate and license the profession. Medical doctors were generally from the upper classes of society and had more expensive training compared to their sectarian competitors. As such, they wanted to restrict access to medical service delivery.

In 1847, the American Medical Association (AMA) was formed to improve the standards of medicine and to professionalize the field. Through the AMA, doctors began to attack the legitimacy of abortion providers who were not trained medical doctors. The AMA formally launched its crusade against abor-

tion in 1859 by passing an anti-abortion resolution and encouraging government action. Next, the AMA lobbied to restrict abortion advertising and to prosecute illegal abortion providers, while also beginning a public crusade against abortion.

Doctors published books and wrote editorials pointing out both the medical and moral reasons abortion should be illegal. They argued that women, by virtue of their ignorance about pregnancy, were inadvertently committing a sin. Medical doctors, on the other hand, possessed expert knowledge on the subject. Framing abortion as an education and ethical issue provided physicians with leverage over their competitors.

The medical doctors' framing efforts began to pay off in 1873 when Congress passed the Act for the Suppression of Trade in and Circulation of Obscene Literature and Articles of Immoral Use, commonly called the Comstock Act. The Comstock Act included a provision banning any advertisements for abortions; this law represented the first federal involvement in abortion-related policies.

Over the next fifteen years, forty anti-abortion statutes were passed in the states, and by 1910 every state had anti-abortion laws. Most of the laws contained a clause authorizing physicians to perform therapeutic abortions at their discretion, thereby providing doctors with a monopoly over the services. Abortion soon faded from the political agenda, but upper-class women continued to have abortions at approximately the same rate as they did before abortion was criminalized. Thus, the impetus for a broad-based abortion rights movement had not yet been created.

ABORTION IN THE 1950s TO
ROE v. WADE

Reliance on doctors' medical judgment and interpretation of the need for therapeutic abortions created inequalities. In the 1950s, stories began to surface in the media focusing on the plight of poor women in need of abortion services. These stories typically detailed the thousands of maternal deaths resulting from abortions, unsafe conditions, and unnecessary risks women had to take because abortion services were illegal. Complications resulting from illegal abortion were so prevalent that many hospitals had wards specifically set aside for (mostly poor) women injured from illegal abortions. The unfairness of this system led some doctors, lawyers, and theologians to reevaluate their stance on abortion laws.

Initially, the medical community took a leading role in the call for reform but was joined by women's rights activists following two highly publicized events, which catapulted abortion into the public spotlight. In 1962, Sherri Finkbine, a mother of four, discovered early in her fifth month of pregnancy that she had taken the drug thalidomide. The horrific side effects of thalidomide on a fetus were well documented. Sherri and her doctor agreed that an immediate abortion was necessary. Wanting to warn other pregnant women about the dangers of the drug, Sherri called a friend who worked at a local television station. The story received considerable media attention, and the hospital where Sherri was scheduled to have an abortion denied her one. Unable to abort in the United States, Sherri flew to Sweden to obtain a legal abortion.

Around the same time (1962–1965), there was an outbreak of the German measles, which caused serious birth defects in approximately 15,000 babies. Physicians were moved to evaluate the restrictive abortion laws that allowed this tragedy to occur, and by 1967 the AMA issued a statement favoring liberalization of abortion laws. Moreover, public outrage followed both the Finkbine and measles cases, mobilizing many women to form ad hoc groups to legalize abortion. However, the general absence of women from the abortion access debate reflected the societal taboos on female sexuality and abortion—it was believed that abortion would lead to promiscuity and a breakdown of traditional sex roles.

THE SEEDS OF A PROTO-MOVEMENT

By the 1960s, the status of women was visibly improving. Breaking with tradition, women were delaying marriage, attending college, and entering the labor force at unprecedented rates. Coinciding with these demographic changes, society was also beginning to emphasize the importance of individual rights and freedom over traditional religious values and morals. As the abortion issue gained visibility, women began to get involved in the debate. And as more women became involved, they began to frame abortion rights as an individual rights issue. The Society for Humane Abortions (SHA) was one of the first organizations to frame abortion in this light, but it was also one of the first abortion rights movement organizations (see Table 1).

The SHA set out to change public opinion, declaring that "the right to elective abortion, whether you dream of doing it or not, is the cornerstone of the women's movement." Following the civil rights and student movements' tactics, SHA activists declared civil disobedience against abortion laws—setting up networks that provided women with information on how to perform abortions or where to go to obtain them. Another women's organization, Jane, trained members to perform abortions for women in need of service, regardless of their financial circumstances. The proto-movement engaged in a public education campaign that included lectures, speak-outs, and television and radio talk show appearances—all of which were intended to raise peoples' consciousness and demonstrate how reproductive rights were crucial for women's equality.

Reframing abortion as a rights issue and reducing the criminal and immoral representations of abortion mobilized more women. As more individuals came forward during speak-outs, women increasingly recognized that abortion was not a personal problem, it was an issue that collectively affected women, which prompted other women's organizations to champion abortion rights. By 1967, a year after its inception, the

TABLE 1. Selected Abortion Rights Movement Groups and Formation Dates

Group	Formation Year
Planned Parenthood Federation	c. 1916
Association of Reproductive Health Professionals	1963
Society for Humane Abortions	1963
National Organization for Women	1966
Alan Guttmacher Institute	1968
Zero Population Growth	1968
National Abortion and Reproductive Rights Action League	1969
Religion Coalition for Abortion Rights	1972
National Women's Health Network	1975
National Abortion Federation	1977
Reproductive Rights National Network	1978
CARAL Pro-Choice Education Fund	1987
Feminist Majority Foundation	1987

National Organization for Women (NOW) added reproductive rights to their bill of rights.

The women's movement crystallized the definition of abortion rights as a fundamental aspect of equality and individual autonomy. By de-stigmatizing the issue, activists transformed abortion from a taboo subject to a public policy issue. Abortion rights advocates emerged from the medical community, women's groups, elected officials, and even members of the clergy. New abortion rights groups formed, including the National Association for the Repeal of Abortion Laws (which changed names before settling with the current National Abortion and Reproductive Rights Action League). Furthermore, chapters of many national abortion rights groups were established throughout the country, making coordinated action across states more feasible.

The coalition of abortion rights supporters continued to grow throughout the 1960s. Initially, the reform movement was designed to liberalize abortion laws; however, the results of reform were mixed, sometimes resulting in greater access and other times not. Reform was typically limited to those states that had public support for abortion law liberalization, interest group support, and little electoral competition within districts.

Many of the state-initiated reforms still contained stipulations that prevented women from making their reproductive decisions without medical or legal involvement. Unhappy with the haphazard legislative reform effort in the states, activists started to campaign for outright repeal of existing abortion laws. Their efforts led Hawaii to become the first state to legalize abortion in 1970. Following Hawaii's lead, other states began to liberalize their policies. New York was the next state to reform in July 1970, and California, Alaska, and Washington soon followed. In sum, by 1971, fourteen states allowed abortions under certain conditions. The efforts of the abortion rights movement had provided significant, but limited, dividends. Two years later, states' resistance to abortion reform came to a halt with the U.S. Supreme Court's 1973 intervention in the abortion debate.

THE IMPACT OF *ROE V. WADE*

Sarah Weddington and Linda Coffee were two recently graduated and inexperienced lawyers who wanted to challenge the constitutionality of an 1857 Texas statute outlawing abortion. But Weddington and Coffee needed to prove that someone was injured as a consequence of the law (called "standing") and to find a legal argument for overturning the law. In the U.S. Supreme Court's ruling in *Griswald v. Connecticut* (1965), which struck down Connecticut's law prohibiting the dissemination of contraception information, Weddington and Coffee found both a rationale for standing and an argument for a constitutional "right to privacy" on reproductive decisions. Armed with a legal position, Weddington and Coffee filed a class action suit, brought forth on behalf of all women who faced obstacles when making reproduction decisions.

After much deliberation in the spring of 1972, the U.S. Supreme Court ruled in a seven to two majority that a woman's right to an abortion was a fundamental right and therefore the government lacked the authority to interfere with her private decision to abort in the first trimester of pregnancy. The Supreme Court's decision in *Roe* legalized abortion in all states.

Roe v. Wade dramatically changed the abortion debate. Within a month following the Supreme Court's decision, the Catholic Church hierarchy called for civil disobedience against the ruling. The Church provided immediate leadership, organizational capacity, community organization, and resources needed to launch an anti-abortion movement. Essentially overnight the pro-life movement emerged as a widespread, predominantly single-issue grassroots movement. As the 1980s approached, new actors joined, including evangelical, fundamentalist, and Pentecostal churches.

In contrast, following *Roe*, abortion rights groups moved away from grassroots mobilization. Abortion rights groups generally believed that *Roe* settled the abortion question, and so they moved on to address other issues. In fact, Staggenborg (1999) argues that during the immediate years following *Roe*, abortion rights groups that survived became increasingly formalized and professionalized by creating formal bureaucratic structures, hiring professional staff, and increasingly moving away from direct action tactics, preferring instead to work within governmental institutions. Thus, *Roe* helped to institutionalize the abortion rights movement. This institutionalization helped to ensure that group leaders were able to recruit members with professional campaigns and to increase their budgets by soliciting foundation money even as public interest in protecting or expanding legalized abortion declined. These efforts helped to sustain existing abortion rights groups through the "lean" period of most of the 1970s.

PRO-LIFE MOBILIZATION AND THE RESURGENCE OF THE ABORTION RIGHTS MOVEMENT

Throughout the 1980s and 1990s, the anti-abortion movement gained momentum—it attracted members, launched aggressive campaigns against clinics, and achieved several policy victories at the national and state level. Over time, the frequency and prevalence of the movement's confrontational tactics did not wane. In 1985, 85 percent of abortion providers were experiencing some form of harassment (including activities such as picketing, clinic blockades, and invasion of the facility). By the 1990s, 86 percent of abortion providers continued to be the recipients of harassment. Extreme violence also plagued providers. Between 1984 and 1998 there were 311 death threats, 71 attempted bombings, 31 actual bombings, 16 attempted murders, 7 murders, and 760 acts of vandalism.

The pro-life movement's aggressive protest campaign at clinics was matched by their efforts at policy changes. Following *Roe*, the anti-abortion movement attempted to overturn the Court's decision by introducing the 1974 Right to Life Amendment in Congress. Ultimately, this legislation was unsuccessful, but the movement was able to pass the 1976 Hyde Amendment, which eliminated federal funding for abortions. Building on the Hyde Amendment victory, the pro-life movement looked for other means of restricting access to abortion, thus turning to state legislatures, where they focused on supporting pro-life candidates, public funding of abortions, and curbing access to abortion services.

Within state legislatures, the pro-life movement helped introduce bills intended to restrict access to

services. And although abortion rights groups, such as the National Abortion and Reproductive Rights Action League (NARAL), lobbied heavily, anti-abortion measures such as spousal notification, informed consent, and parental notification laws were passed in several states. By 1989, the constitutionality of states' abortion restrictions was challenged in *Webster v. Reproductive Health Services* (1988). Marking a sharp departure from its ruling in *Roe*, the Supreme Court upheld many of the anti-abortion restrictions and, in turn, opened the door for future restrictions. Two other cases (*Ohio v. Akron Center for Reproductive Health, 1990,* and *Planned Parenthood of Southeastern Pennsylvania v. Casey, 1882*) reaffirmed the Supreme Court's willingness to allow restrictions against abortion services. The Court's decisions fueled the pro-life movement—for example, in 1990, 465 abortion-related bills were introduced in state legislatures, and the vast majority were anti-abortion bills. In 1992, the number of abortion-related bills introduced in state legislatures dropped to 100 but jumped to 220 in 1996, 245 in 1998, 395 in 2000, and 620 in 2001.

Even though abortion rights groups were mobilized in the states, in each year from 1990 to 2001, state anti-abortion legislation outnumbered pro-choice legislation, and more anti-abortion measures were enacted. For example, in 2000, 138 bills were pro-choice and 257 were anti-abortion. In 2001, 222 bills were pro-choice and 398 were anti-abortion. Similarly, in 2001, 39 anti-abortion measures were enacted, while 27 pro-choice measures were adopted. Indeed, between 1995 and 2001, 301 anti-abortion measures were adopted in the states, with the peak occurring in 1999 at 70 measures adopted.

Furthermore, in the 1980s and 1990s, the abortion rights movement increasingly became involved in direct democracy (initiative and referenda) campaigns in which abortion questions were being decided at the ballot box. Both sides in the abortion debate made use of this venue, with Washington State first repealing some abortion restrictions in 1970, maintaining public funding of abortion in 1984, and reaffirming access to abortion in 1991. Colorado faced four similar measures between 1984 and 1998, with a parental notification measure passing as a partial birth abortion ban failed in 1998. Oregon, Arkansas, Massachusetts, Michigan, Nevada, and Maryland all considered abortion questions at the ballot box, and more often than not, abortion rights forces won these contests by mobilizing considerable financial resources and grassroots activity. However, in one major 1984 defeat, a

Figure 1. Spending by Two Main Pro- and Anti-Abortion PACS, 1979–2000 Election Cycles

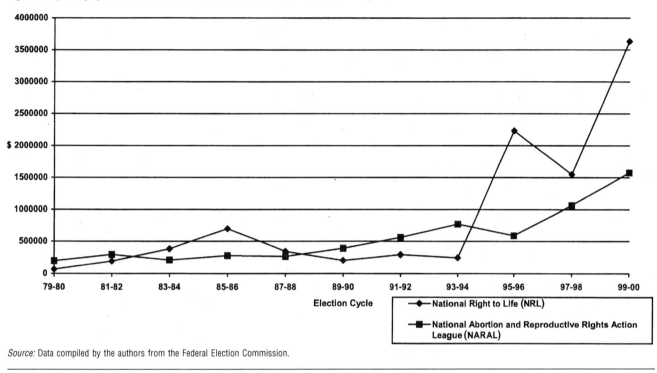

Source: Data compiled by the authors from the Federal Election Commission.

coalition of abortion rights groups that included the local chapters of Planned Parenthood, NARAL, the Religious Coalition for Abortion Rights, and NOW were unable to block a proposal to repeal public funding of abortions in Colorado. In this contest, the pro-life movement was well organized in the state, primarily through Catholic and fundamentalist churches. Furthermore, abortion rights groups were not able to effectively deliver their message that it was unfair to deny poor women and teenagers access to abortion, especially if they had become pregnant through rape or incest. Polls suggested that most voters thought the abortion funding ban did not discriminate against indigent women, and proponents of the ban were able to convince voters that not only was abortion morally wrong, but also that public funding of abortions increased taxes. This same message helped to defeat a 1988 Colorado measure that would have restored public funding.

The *Webster* decision signaled the Supreme Court's ability to restructure the foundation of abortion rights and, in turn, galvanized the abortion rights movement. Recognizing the changing composition of the Court, which was being stacked with conservative judges, coupled with the indefatigable clinic protesting, the abortion rights movement became reenergi-

zed. Membership in the most visible abortion rights interest group, NARAL, soared between 1989 and 1990, and NARAL worked with NOW, Planned Parenthood, and the American Civil Liberties Union (ACLU) to coordinate their efforts in combating the pro-life movement's policy progress at the state and national level, as well as counter the activities occurring at clinics.

Consequently, the pro-choice movement resurfaced as a major political player in the abortion debate; 1989 marked the first year that the pro-choice movement raised significantly more money than the pro-life movement, a pattern that is still prevalent today. However, as Figure 1 demonstrates, the main pro-choice political action committee (PAC) at the national level, NARAL, began to be outspent by the main pro-life PAC, National Right to Life (NRL), during the 1996 election cycle. Interestingly, some research suggests that as NARAL spending was outpaced, the pro-choice movement actually gained more lobbying influence in Congress in the 1990s.

The abortion rights movement developed a multi-tiered strategy: supporting pro-choice candidates, monitoring abortion-related policy proposals at the state and national level, and lobbying politicians and engaging in coalition building with like-minded interest groups. With the rise of the pro-life group Operation Rescue in 1988, and its tactic of abortion clinic blockades and harassment, abortion rights groups began counter-demonstrations to protect the clinics and women seeking abortions. Pro-choice groups such as Planned Parenthood, NOW, and NARAL set up escort services to physically walk with women into clinics, coordinated with clinic operators, and tried to work with police in identifying and arresting pro-life protesters who violated the law. These activities at the local level helped the abortion rights movement to re-energize grassroots activists by giving them concrete activities that directly engaged the pro-life movement.

The activities of the more traditional abortion rights groups at the local level helped to mobilize radical abortion rights activists as well. In an effort to divert media attention from the pro-life groups blocking clinics, radical activists formed new groups, such as Refuse & Resist, the Coalition Opposing Operation Rescue (COOR), and the Bay Area Coalition Against Operation Rescue (BACAOR), and even drew on the memberships of existing radical groups, such as AIDS Coalition to Unleash Power (ACT UP). These radical activists physically and verbally confronted pro-life protesters, which sometimes led to pushing, shoving, and other forms of fighting. Such violent confrontations sometimes led to the arrests of both pro-life and pro-choice protesters. Although some mainstream groups, such as NOW, had hesitated to encourage confrontational counter-protests during clinic blockades, eventually they did notice the effectiveness of radical groups in decreasing the number and intensity of pro-life blockades. The abortion rights counter-protesters also helped dispel a growing media image of pro-life activists as victims during the blockades by encouraging the media to capture images of pro-life protesters shouting in the faces of women seeking abortions as well as abortion rights counter-protesters. As the media image of those blocking the clinics shifted, mainstream leaders of the pro-life movement began distancing themselves from the protesters. Cutting the ties between radical grassroots pro-life activists and more mainstream pro-life leaders helped discourage the continuation of large-scale clinic blockades.

The radical tactics of local abortion rights activists were complemented nationally, as the mainstream abortion rights groups were eventually successful in passing the Freedom of Access to Clinic Entrances Act (FACE) in May 1994. The FACE Act made obstructing the entrance of a clinic or damaging the clinic a punishable offense under federal law, with fines of up to $10,000 and six months in jail.

The abortion rights movement maintained its presence in politics throughout the 1990s and into the twenty-first century. Abortion rights advocates constantly find themselves on the defensive as the pro-life movement continues to pursue new abortion-related issues intended to curb—and eventually eliminate—access to abortion services. Based on the lessons of the 1980s and early 1990s, the pro-choice movement has emerged as a stronger, more coordinated, and dedicated movement in the American political landscape.

CONCLUSION

Although access to abortion in the United States was fairly easy in the country's early history, the professionalization of medical doctors and American cultural ambiguity about female sexuality led to severe restrictions on access to abortion in the nineteenth and twentieth centuries. But even during this restrictive period, many upper- and middle-class women could still obtain legal abortions under the discretion allowed to medical doctors. As this inequity became more apparent and as cultural norms about the traditional family and gender roles began to change in the 1950s and 1960s, the seeds of a proto-abortion rights movement began in the United States.

By the 1960s, the notion of abortion rights was firmly tied to the movement for women's rights and rode on a wave of social movement activism focused on achieving equality for all groups in all aspects of life. The fledgling abortion rights movement was able to effectively frame access to abortion not only as an individual right, but also as an equity and health issue for women. These framing efforts helped the movement enlist the help of professionals, including doctors and lawyers, and to successfully reform abortion laws in several states. However, many members of the movement believed that simple reform was not enough—only full legalization would solve the problems associated with illegal abortions.

As a relative surprise to many, the U.S. Supreme Court provided the movement with its biggest victory in the 1972 decision in Roe v. Wade, legalizing abortions in the first trimester of pregnancy. However, this same decision made the abortion rights movement complacent, while also giving rise to the first significant grassroots movement against abortion. For the next ten years the pro-life movement attacked abortion in popular culture, public policy, and finally, at the source—abortion providers. Ironically, these successes of the pro-life movement, and at times, its violent tactics, served to reenergize the abortion rights movement in the 1980s. By the 1990s, the abortion rights movement could claim new policy successes, but it had achieved a relative stalemate with the pro-life movement—neither side could claim a 100 percent victory. With public opinion relatively divided on the issue, the two main political parties polarized, and two broad-based social movements continuously active on the issue, abortion is likely to remain on the political agenda for years to come, with no policy solution forthcoming.

It is precisely this unending battle that has dragged fairly new issues into the abortion debate, some of which, such as so-called partial birth abortion, have hurt the efforts of the abortion rights movement. Indeed, pro-life groups successfully lobbied Congress to pass a federal Partial Birth Abortion Ban in 1996 and 1997 (even though both were vetoed by President Clinton), and thirty-one states passed some version of a partial birth abortion ban by 2003. The U.S. Senate passed a revised version in March 2003, which President Bush has promised he would sign. However, opinion polls consistently suggest that the pro-life movement has won the debate over late-term abortions.

The pro-life movement will likely continue to try to establish the personhood of the fetus and from there try to whittle down the number of weeks that abortion is socially acceptable. This will assist the movement not only in passing bans on late-term abortions, but also in establishing "fetal rights," (i.e., the Unborn Victims of Violence Act of 1999), which, according to the National Abortion and Reproductive Rights Action League, are designed to create a separate criminal offense if a person causes death or injury to "a member of the species homo sapiens at all stages of development who is carried in the womb from conception to birth." To date, the act hasn't been successful at the national level, but abortion rights activists seem to be at a disadvantage in this debate.

Other issues, such as fetal tissue and human cloning research may have helped the cause of the abortion rights movement by demonstrating the health benefits of medical research. Indeed, as these issues have been debated in the United States, many stalwart pro-life elected officials have taken positions in support of medical research efforts.

With advances in medical technology, technologies such as the "abortion pill" (RU-486) may make much of the debate over abortion a moot point. Other advances, such as frozen sperm, eggs, and embryos,

that could eventually be used to begin and complete a pregnancy, pose dilemmas for the rights of those who produced them, as well as for pro-life activists who see all potential human life as sacred. How will the abortion rights movement address these issues, especially when they cannot be so readily attached to the notion of women's rights?

The abortion debate can be expected to continue to grow more complex rather than become more black and white. Thus, the movement will continue to face many challenges and will need to reestablish its definition of the issue—shifting the focus back to women's rights rather than allowing the fetus to be treated as a separate entity from women in policy and public discourse. Indeed, the original success of the abortion rights movement did come from effectively framing the issue in terms of a woman's autonomy over her body and her ability to control her own reproduction.

Alesha E. Doan and Donald P. Haider-Markel

BIBLIOGRAPHY

Adams, Greg D. "Abortion: Evidence of an Issue Evolution," *American Journal of Political Science* 4:3 (1997): 718–737.

American Civil Liberties Union. "ACLU Calls Ban on Safe Abortion Procedures Dangerous Political Power Play, Promises to Sue." Press release, March 26, 2003. Washington, DC: ACLU.

Berkman, Michael B., and Robert E. O'Connor. "Do Women Legislators Matter?: Female Legislators and State Abortion Policy." *American Politics Quarterly* 21:1 (1993): 102–124.

Blanchard, Dallas. *The Anti-Abortion Movement and the Rise of the Religious Right: From Polite to Fiery Protest.* New York: Twayne, 1994.

Cohen, Jeffery E., and Charles Barrilleaux. "Public Opinion, Interest Groups and Public Policy Making: Abortion Policy in the American States." In *Understanding the New Politics of Abortion*, ed. Malcolm L. Goggin. Newbury Park, CA: Sage, 1994.

Conover, Pamela Hohnston, and Virginia Gray. *Feminism and the New Right: Conflict over the American Family.* New York: Praeger, 1983.

Cook, Elizabeth Adell, Ted G. Jelen, and Clyde Wilcox. *Between Two Absolutes: Public Opinion and the Politics of Abortion.* Boulder, CO: Westview Press, 1992.

Cozzarelli, Catherine, and Brenda Major. "The Impact of Antiabortion Activities on Women." In *The New Civil War: The Psychology, and Politics of Abortion*, eds. Linda J. Beckman and S. Marie Harvey. Washington, DC: American Psychological Association, 1998.

Craig, Barbara Hinkson, and David M. O'Brien. *Abortion and American Politics.* Chatham, NJ: Chatham House, 1993.

Donovan, Patricia. "The 1988 Abortion Referenda: Lessons for the Future." *Family Planning Perspectives* 21:5 (1989): 218–223.

———. "The People Vote on Abortion Funding: Colorado and Washington." *Family Planning Perspectives* 17:4 (1985): 155–159.

Epstein, Lee, and Joseph F. Kobylka. *The Supreme Court and Legal Change: Abortion and the Death Penalty.* Chapel Hill: University of North Carolina Press, 1992.

Falik, Marilyn. *Ideology and Abortion Policy Politics.* New York: Praeger, 1983.

Forrest, Jacqueline D., and Stanley K. Henshaw. "The Harassment of U.S. Abortion Providers." *Family Planning Perspectives* 19 (January/February 1987): 9–13.

Garrow, David J. *Liberty and Sexuality.* New York: Macmillan, 1994.

Graber, Mark A. *Rethinking Abortion: Equal Choice, the Constitution, and Reproductive Politics.* Princeton, NJ: Princeton University Press, 1996.

Haider-Markel, Donald P., and Alesha Doan. "Money and Morality: Abortion Groups in the U.S. Congress." Paper presented at the annual meeting of the American Political Science Association, September 1998.

Henshaw, Stanley K. "Factors Hindering Access to Abortion Services." *Family Planning Perspectives* 2 (March/April 1995): 54–59, 87.

Jacoby, Kerry N. *Souls, Bodies, Spirits: The Drive to Abolish Abortion Since 1973.* Westport, CT: Praeger, 1998.

Johnson, Victoria. "The Strategic Determinants of a Countermovement: The Emergence and Impact of Operation Rescue Blockades." In *Waves of Protest: Social Movements Since the Sixties*, eds. Jo Freeman and Victoria Johnson, 241–266. Lanham, MD: Rowman and Littlefield, 1999.

Kaplan, Laura. "Beyond Safe and Legal: The Lessons of Jane." In *Abortion Wars: A Half Century of Struggle, 1950–2000*, ed. Rickie Solinger. Los Angeles: University of California Press, 1998.

Luke, Kristin. *Abortion and the Politics of Motherhood.* Los Angeles: University of California Press, 1984.

McCarthy, John D. "Pro-Life and Pro-Choice Mobilization: Infrastructure Deficits and New Technologies." In *Social Movements in an Organizational Society*, eds. John McCarthy and Mayer N. Zald, 49–66. New Brunswick, NJ: Transaction Books, 1992.

Merton, Andrew H. *Enemies of Choice: The Right-to-Life Movement and Its Threat to Abortion.* Boston: Beacon, 1981.

Mooney, Christopher Z., and Mei-Hsien Lee. "Legislative Morality in the American States: The Case of Pre-Roe Abortion Regulation Reform." *American Journal of Political Science* 39:3 (1995): 599–627.

National Abortion and Reproductive Rights Action League. *Who Decides: A State-by-State Review of Abortion and Reproductive Rights.* Washington, DC: National Abortion and Reproductive Rights Action League, 2002.

Olasky, Marvin. *The Press and Abortion, 1838–1988.* Hillsdale, NJ: Lawrence Erlbaum, 1988.

Petchesky, Rosalind Pollack. "Reproductive Freedom: Beyond a 'Woman's Right to Choose.'" *Signs* 5 (1980): 661–685.

Reagan, Leslie J. "'About to Meet Her Maker:' Women, Doctors, Dying Declarations, and the State's Investigation of Abortion, Chicago, 1867–1940." *Journal of American History* 78 (1997): 1240–1264.

Reed, James. *From Public Vice to Private Virtue.* New York: Basic Books, 1978.

Risen, James, and Judy L. Thomas. *Wrath of Angels: The American Abortion War.* New York: Basic Books, 1998.

Rubin, Eva. *The Abortion Controversy: A Documentary History.* Westport, CT: Greenwood Press, 1994.

Schnucker, Robert V. "Elizabethan Birth Control and Puritan Attitudes." *Journal of Interdisciplinary History* 4 (Spring 1975): 655–667.

Smith, Daniel Scott. "Family Limitation, Sexual Control, and Domestic Feminism in Victorian America." In *Controlling Reproduction: An American History*, ed. Andrea Tone. Wilmington, DE: Scholarly Resources, 1997.

Solinger, Rickie. "Pregnancy and Power before *Roe v. Wade*, 1950–1970." In *Abortion Wars: A Half a Century of Struggle, 1950–2000*, ed. Rickie Solinger. Los Angeles: University of California Press, 1998.

Staggenborg, Suzanne. "The Consequences of Professionalization and Formalization in the Pro-Choice Movement." In *Waves of Protest: Social Movements Since the Sixties*, eds. Jo Freeman and Victoria Johnson, 99–134. Lanham, MD: Rowman and Littlefield, 1999.

Tone, Andrea. *Controlling Reproduction: An American History.* Wilmington, DE: Scholarly Resources, 1997.

Tribe, Lawrence H. *Abortion: The Clash of Absolutes.* New York: W.W. Norton, 1992.

Woodward, Bob, and Scott Armstrong. *The Brethren: Inside the Supreme Court.* New York: Simon and Schuster, 1979.

African-American Women's Movement

1930s–1940s

The African-American women's movement of the 1930s and 1940s focused almost exclusively on black female employment and economic opportunities. With the very survival of the black family threatened by the Great Depression, the self-help programs that had dominated the thoughts of organized women in the previous decades became an unaffordable luxury. Black men could rarely find work, and the responsibility for maintaining the family fell almost entirely upon black women. World War II brought little change to the women's movement as it continued to focus on economic concerns. Throughout these decades, the major women's organizations steered black spending toward black businesses, pushed for the inclusion of black women in government programs and positions, advocated protective labor legislation, and protested restrictions on the enlistment of black women in the armed forces.

UPLIFTING THE RACE

When the 1930s began, many black women were deeply involved in the activities of such mixed-gender African-American organizations as the Urban League and the National Association for the Advancement of Colored People (NAACP). While the interracial efforts promoted by the largest black women's organization of the day, the National Association of Colored Women (NACW), enjoyed renewed support, the group itself often seemed behind the times. The NACW had a distinguished history as a network of hundreds of women's organizations, but the faults that would bring about its demise were already evident.

Formed in 1896 to protest slurs against black women, the NACW employed "Lifting as We Climb" as its motto, while it called on a united black womanhood to better the race. As the motto indicates, the black women's movement differed in significant ways from the movement led by white women. Club women in the 1930s and 1940s focused on matters related to race rather than gender. Although white men had obvious advantages over white women, African-American men were not significantly better off than the women of the race. The sense of real equality that developed between the sexes meant that organized black women firmly believed that they could and would solve the problems of all African Americans. The black women's movement never focused solely on the problems of women.

Through its various member organizations, NACW promoted intensive social service at the local level to boost the quality of African-American home life and educate the mothers of the race. Its members believed that character development was dependent on intellectual growth and that black people had been denied such growth.

During the 1920s, the organization had lost much influence, and this trend would continue through the 1930s. The NACW's local focus on uplift activities seemed to many black women activists to be an inadequate response to the disastrous position of African-American families during the Great Depression and a tepid response to the uncertainty of the New Deal.

UPLIFTING ECONOMIC STATUS

In 1930, most African Americans were disenfranchised and economically challenged. The majority of blacks belonged to the working class because a combined lack of access to income-generating property and well-paying jobs had prevented them from socioeconomic advancement. While about 60 percent of all black women worked as domestics during the 1930s, racism prevented many black men from finding any kind of employment. Relief efforts commonly failed to reach many black families, often because racist government officials simply refused to assist African Americans. The survival of the black family came to

387

rest on the labor of wives and mothers, as many organized women recognized, and economics became the chief concern of women.

The leaders of the NACW proved slow to acknowledge changing currents of black thought, but they did attempt to address economic concerns. The association continued to promote social justice in the 1930s by pushing for integration, and it exposed the unequal wage rates provided in the National Industrial Recovery Act through a joint publicity effort with the Urban League and NAACP. The NACW named economic inequality as a major oppressor of African Americans, and it officially supported higher wages and shorter working hours for women. Despite these efforts, the NACW continued to lose influence in the black community.

The Depression forced the abandonment of many NACW self-help projects as money woes forced the association to modify its agenda and narrow its function, but class divisions did not abate and they continued to be a source of racial disunity. Mary Church Terrell, a long-time Republican Party activist and a founder of the NACW, and Mary Waring, head of the NACW in the 1930s, largely presumed that all black women faced the same issues. They advocated dedication to racial uplift, but many other women disagreed with this strategy. In practice, NACW programs often meant that conservative, light-skinned, socially prominent African-American women preached moral purity and socially correct behavior to their darker-skinned, poorer, and increasingly liberal sisters. To many African Americans, it seemed that the club women were more concerned about respectable behavior than about the exploitation of the working class.

NEW STRATEGIES

The Great Depression and the uncertain outlook of the New Deal had a profound effect on the women's movement by prompting many black leaders, particularly among the younger generation, to develop new racial ideologies and strategies. This led to an ideological division between race leaders, as a younger generation of women activists began to debate with the older ones as to whether the problems of African Americans related more to race or to class. Terrell could not accept any program that de-emphasized racial integration, while new-style leaders like educator Mary McLeod Bethune suggested that the black working class align itself with white workers to better the economic position of both.

Bethune, the daughter of former slaves and the founder of Bethune-Cookman College, proved more attuned to the new attitudes of black women and the practical concerns that they faced than the NACW leadership. Unlike most of the other women leaders, Bethune had once been poor, and she possessed strongly African features in which she took great pride. She had no interest in maintaining a color/class hierarchy, a charge frequently leveled at NACW activists by other black women. Bethune, who had headed NACW in the 1920s, would emerge as one of the greatest African-American leaders of the era by abandoning NACW's local approach to racial problems.

THE NATIONAL COUNCIL OF NEGRO WOMEN

The dominant women's organization of the 1930s and 1940s, the National Council of Negro Women (NCNW), began when Bethune decided that there was a need for a black women's organization to project itself at the national level. On December 5, 1935, she created the NCNW by bringing together representatives of fourteen organizations, including the sororities Alpha Kappa Alpha, Delta Sigma Theta, and Sigma Gamma Rho; black occupational societies such as the National Business and Professional Women's Clubs and the National Association of Colored Graduate Nurses; various auxiliaries, including the Women's Auxiliary of the National Medical Association and the Ladies Auxiliary of the Brotherhood of Sleeping Car Porters; and the women's associations of the African Methodist Episcopal and African Methodist Episcopal Zion churches. The NCNW had the multiple objectives of creating a national movement; educating, encouraging, and effecting the participation of blacks in civic, political, economic, and educational activities and institutions; serving as a clearinghouse for the dissemination of information concerning women; and planning, initiating, and carrying out projects to develop, benefit, and integrate African Americans within the nation. Bethune situated the headquarters of NCNW in Washington, D.C., in order to be in a better position to lobby national leaders.

Much of Bethune's success in the women's movement came because she found a best friend in the White House. Eleanor Roosevelt began to recognize racial discrimination only after her husband, Franklin, assumed the presidency in 1933. While promoting an agenda that accepted segregation and championed equal opportunity, Roosevelt lobbied government officials to include African Americans more fully in the

New Deal. As a result of her efforts, Bethune received an unpaid position in 1935 with the national advisory committee of the National Youth Administration (NYA), the New Deal agency created to help young adults secure education and job training. Bethune accepted a paid position with the NYA in 1936 to oversee activities involving African Americans and three years later became the chief of the NYA's Division of Negro Affairs.

Bethune took advantage of her position as the most influential black woman in the United States to extend the reach of the New Deal into black communities. In 1936, she presented the concerns of the NCNW to Roosevelt. Bethune sought appointments of professional black women to the Children's Bureau, the Women's Bureau, and each department of the Bureau of Education that dealt with the welfare of women and children. The NCNW lobbied for positions that black women had never held. It also sought the appointment of black women to administrative positions in the Federal Housing Administration and the Social Security Board. In 1938, Bethune organized a conference of the NCNW called "The Participation of Negro Women and Children in Federal Programs" in Washington, D.C., which attracted sixty-five black women leaders including Terrell. Resolutions at the conference decried black women's limited access to federal relief programs and challenged the exclusion of agricultural and domestic workers, over half of all black workers, from Social Security benefits.

Bethune had only limited success in lobbying the Roosevelt administration, but all the same she persuaded many blacks to switch allegiance from the Republican "Party of Lincoln" to the Democratic Party of FDR. The subsequent link of African-American women activists with the Democrats, a tie that has lasted to the present era, is one of Bethune's legacies.

During World War II, the NCNW worked to establish a Fair Employment Practice Commission, intervened in the notorious court-martial of four black Women's Army Corps members who were disciplined without an opportunity to defend themselves, and worked successfully to secure the admission of black women to the WAVES, a naval branch. With the cessation of hostilities, the association continued to focus on fighting for jobs and civil rights. It began to pay more attention to housing discrimination and to the provision of equal facilities. In 1949, Bethune stepped down as head of the NCNW to be succeeded by Dr. Dorothy Ferebee. The organization had laid a foundation for civil rights work by helping to raise wage standards, broaden Social Security benefits, and in-

crease government salaries for African Americans. It had established a foothold that women could use to guide the nation to full democracy.

BLACK ACTIVISM OUTSIDE OF THE NCNW

Although the NCNW focused on the national government, some of its member associations continued the local work traditionally associated with black women activists. Alpha Kappa Alpha sorority (AKA), a founding member of the NCNW, improved the health of African-American agricultural workers in Mississippi by creating the first mobile healthcare clinic in U.S. history. The members of the sorority had learned that an appalling number of blacks in the Magnolia State suffered from nutritional ailments and a complete absence of any professional medical care. For several weeks every summer between 1935 and 1942, AKA Mississippi Health Project activists led by Ferebee drove to the Deep South to provide nutritional advice and basic medical treatment. Suspicious white planters often refused to allow the AKA members to treat "their" blacks, but persistence and diplomacy usually gained the sorority members access to plantation workers.

Black health activists in the era of segregation had to cultivate diplomatic skills to secure their personal safety and circumvent white resistance to social change. AKA never explicitly described the Mississippi Health Project as a civil rights activity because doing so would antagonize the white power structure and prevent the sorority from aiding sharecroppers. AKA did use the health project to focus federal attention on the destitute conditions of African Americans in the rural South, but it carefully sought support through NCNW lobbying efforts. Black health reform straddled the line between social service work and political activity. In order to improve health conditions for sharecroppers, AKA leaders had to do more than establish summertime clinics. They had to secure the cooperation of the predominantly white federal, state, and local health officials.

To extend its reach, AKA established the Non-Partisan Council on Public Affairs, which produced the first full-time congressional lobby for minority group rights. The council, the brainchild of AKA president Norma Boyd, campaigned to promote integration, decent living conditions, and permanent jobs, and to ensure that the federal government responded to the social welfare needs of all Americans. In 1948, the council disbanded when AKA joined with six other sororities and fraternities to form the American

Council on Human Rights, which engaged in similar lobbying.

While the NCNW and its member clubs pushed for a New Deal for blacks, an unaffiliated grassroots movement of women activists sprang up to promote black financial power. Established in 1930, the Housewives' League of Detroit aimed to stabilize the economic status of African Americans through directed spending. Members intended to retain higher proportions of material resources within the African-American communities by pledging to patronize only those stores that employed blacks in various capacities; by buying black products and utilizing black professionals; by supporting institutions that trained black youth for trades and commercial activities; and by conducting educational campaigns to teach African Americans the value of their spending.

Although organized black women focused on the economic situation of African Americans, other issues were not entirely neglected. Lynching had long been a concern of organized women, and, throughout the 1930s and 1940s, black women continued to press for federal legislation against this outrage through various organizations, including NCNW and AKA. Much more than a murder, a lynching was an organized attack by a mob of whites, often with the complicity of local and state law enforcement agencies, that was designed to intimidate an entire African-American community. Although a federal antilynching bill never passed Congress, public opinion gradually changed because of lobbying by black groups. By 1950, most whites had come to recognize lynching as a barbarous and criminal act. Recorded incidents of lynching ceased by that year.

BLACK SUCCESS

The organized black women's movement of the 1930s and 1940s endeavored first and foremost to guarantee the well-being of the race. Debate over the methods of giving every individual a fair chance to achieve health and enjoy a family life resulted in the collapse of the NACW and the rise of the NCNW. The guard passed to NCNW when the goal of organized black women became racial progress through economic power. Filled with hope by New Deal promises, African-American women anticipated a second Reconstruction, but many of the gains that they sought would only be achieved by a later generation.

Caryn E. Neumann

BIBLIOGRAPHY

Cash, Floris Barnett. *African American Women and Social Action: The Clubwomen and Volunteerism from Jim Crow to the New Deal, 1896–1936*. Westport, CT: Greenwood Press, 2001.

Giddings, Paula. *When and Where I Enter: The Impact of Black Women on Race and Sex in America*. New York: William Morrow, 1984.

Hine, Darlene Clark. "The Housewives' League of Detroit: Black Women and Economic Nationalism." In *Visible Women: New Essays on American Activism*, ed. Nancy A. Hewitt and Suzanne Lebsock, 223–241. Urbana: University of Illinois Press, 1993.

McCluskey, Audrey Thomas, and Elaine M. Smith, eds. *Mary McLeod Bethune: Building a Better World*. Bloomington: Indiana University Press, 2001.

White, Deborah Gray. *Too Heavy a Load: Black Women in Defense of Themselves, 1894–1994*. New York: W.W. Norton, 1999.

African-American Women's Movement

Black feminism is a social movement in that it performs the task of uniting identity, grievances, culture, and a desire for social transformation. With influences culled from literature, the arts, popular culture, and the social sciences, black feminism is not merely an offshoot of "regular" feminism or the women's movement, but rather an integral part to the evolution of the women's movement. The basic tenet of black feminism is primarily the analysis of black women's position at the intersection of race, class, and gender identities and oppressions. This definition, like the definition of feminism itself, is under constant debate and challenge from those who would also add sexual orientation and physical ability to the web of socially constructed identities that impact black women and black communities. With its historical antecedents in the nineteenth-century abolition movement and the black women's club movement of the early twentieth century, black women's activism on behalf of their gender *and* race concerns manifests itself in the civil rights movement in the 1950s–1960s on into present struggles around welfare reform, antiprison work, healthcare, reproductive rights, and representations of black women in the media.

Black Feminism in the 1950s

Black women continued the legacy of activism begun by pioneers such as Ida B. Wells, Anna Julia Cooper, Mary Church Terrell, Claudia Jones, and Amy Jacques Garvey, who made linkages early on between black women's oppression as women and as blacks. In the 1950s, artists, academics, and grassroots organizers questioned the dominant mentality of home and hearth for women and how that played out for black women. After all, black women adeptly cared for their families under the involuntary servitude of slavery and were present in the workplace long before white American women.

Florynce Kennedy, for example, explored how black women could be better served by the women's rights movement and a specifically black feminist approach in her essay, "A Comparative Study: Accentuating the Similarities of the Societal Position of Women and Negroes." Though written while she was an undergraduate at Columbia University, the essay portends Kennedy's later activism in predominantly white feminist organizations, such as the National Organization for Women (NOW), and her role in founding the National Black Feminist Organization (NBFO) in New York City in 1973. Kennedy bridged different segments of the feminist movement with an outspoken, take-no-prisoners attitude.

Artists were, and continue to be, central to the formulation and dissemination of black feminist thought and practice. Born May 19, 1930, playwright Lorraine Hansberry is most often noted for being the first black woman with a play produced on Broadway. The play, *A Raisin in the Sun,* debuted in March 1959 and garnered Hansberry the New York Drama Critics' Circle Award. Hansberry's play served as a dramatization of black feminist thought, drawing on the themes of race, class, and gender for a working-class family facing the dilemmas black self-determination and the personal aspirations of family members in the face of racism and societal resistance to change. Hansberry tackled these dilemmas through the play, as well as in the 1964 production *The Sign in Sidney Brustein's Window.* In addition, Hansberry began an essay in 1957 after reading Simone de Beauvoir's classic feminist text, *The Second Sex* (1953). Published posthumously in her essay "Simone de Beauvoir and *The Second Sex:* An American Commentary," Hansberry wondered why more women had not grappled with this text, as it illuminated for her the social construction of gender.

Another active black feminist thinker during this time was Pauli Murray, the first black woman to be ordained an Episcopalian priest. Like many black women involved in the black feminist movement, Murray held multiple allegiances that influenced her view of institutionalized sexism and racism. As a lawyer, professor, long-time civil rights activist, and an active member of President John F. Kennedy's Commission on the Status of Women, Murray infused her black feminist activism with insights from each of her areas of expertise. Like Florynce Kennedy, Murray made crucial connections between white feminists and black feminists, particularly in her role as a founding member of NOW in 1966. Notably, Murray also took on masculinist posturing within the black liberation movement, questioning how there could ever be liberation for half the black race.

BLACK FEMINISM IN THE 1960S

The roots of the contemporary black feminist movement, though nurtured by the club women's movement and individual black feminist activists in the 1930s–1950s, are firmly entrenched in the activism and ideology of the civil rights movement. Organizations such as the National Association for the Advancement of Colored People (NAACP), the Congress on Racial Equality (CORE), and the Student Nonviolent Coordinating Committee (SNCC) served as the training ground for young black women who would later become leaders in black feminist theorizing and organizing. Barbara Smith, for example, participated in Cleveland's CORE chapter as a high school student. She would later help form the Combahee River Collective, using her organizing experience with CORE, which included black women in leadership positions. The same can be said for countless other young black women activists, including Francis Beal, Margaret Sloan, and Linda Burnham.

The most direct connection between the civil rights and black feminist movements is the case of the Third World Women's Alliance (TWWA). The TWWA began in 1968 as a black women's caucus in SNCC. Initially called the Black Women's Liberation Committee (BWLC), the group convened to discuss the impact of racism and sexism on their lives as black women. For example, in the days before the *Roe v. Wade* (1973) decision, nonconsensual sterilization and back alley abortions had a disproportionate impact on poor and working-class women of color. BWLC members met to discuss how the civil rights movement might better address issues affecting black women on the basis of race and gender. Like the incipient contemporary white feminist movement, BWLC also touched on some fundamental feminist issues, such

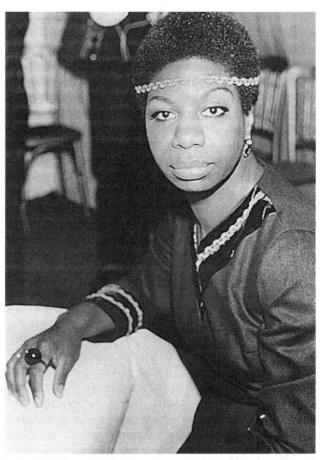

In the 1960s, buoyed by the dramatic events of the civil rights movement and the violent responses to efforts to achieve racial equality, Nina Simone wrote and performed protest songs about racism in America. *(AP Wide World Photos)*

as women's body awareness, educational barriers, parenting, and strategies for combating daily sexism.

The civil rights movement was also, of course, the training ground for white women activists. Two of those women, Mary King and Casey Hayden, belonged to SNCC and, although they gained valuable organizing experience that they would later use in the predominantly white feminist and antiwar movements, they issued a personnel memo addressing the sexism they experienced in SNCC (e.g., secretarial duties). This memo, combined with the legend of SNCC leader Stokely Carmichael's infamous response to a query about the position of women in the student movement (Carmichael allegedly quipped, "Prone."), led scholars to stereotype the civil rights movement as a hostile environment for women without regard to the experiences of *black* women. Black women gained significant organizing experience, as well as a

NINA SIMONE (1933–2003)

Born Eunice Kathleen Waymon on February 21, 1933, in Tyron, North Carolina, Nina Simone became the personification of African-American protest music in the 1960s. A gifted singer and pianist as a child, Simone attended the Juilliard School of Music, leaving after one year. Later, Simone began to hone her skills as a jazz, pop, and soul pianist and singer, appearing in bars and clubs throughout the United States. By the 1950s, she was a nationally known musician, dubbed the "High Priestess of Soul" by her followers.

In the 1960s, buoyed by the dramatic events of the civil rights movement and the violent responses to efforts to achieve racial equality, Simone wrote and performed protest songs about racism in America. In particular, Simone was shocked and angered by the Ku Klux Klan's bombing of the 16th Street Baptist Church in Birmingham, Alabama, that killed four young girls. Her songs became representations of the rage and discrimination many African Americans throughout the United States felt. Simone channeled the anger of a generation through songs that captured the imagination of blacks and educated whites. Her most well known songs include "Mississippi Goddam," "To Be Young, Gifted and Black," and "Four Women." In the 1970s, disillusioned with what she believed to be the failure of the civil rights movement, as well as with the persistence of racism in the United States, Simone fled the country to live in the south of France, where she died on April 21, 2003.

Immanuel Ness

theoretical basis for actively resisting racism, sexism, and classism through the civil rights movement and organizations. Gloria Richardson, Ruby Doris Smith Robinson, Cynthia Washington, and Gwen Patton all found their activist identities and cultivated their leadership abilities, regardless of their gender and the behind-the-scenes roles to which they were relegated by the social constructions of civil rights leaders as male, middle-class, and clergy. Instead, they became bridge leaders, women who—according to civil rights historian Belinda Robnett—had the unique ability to serve as a vital link between civil rights organizations and their grassroots constituencies. On the cultural front, in the 1960s, Nina Simone, the black singer known as "The Priestess of Soul," embraced the civil rights movement and black power movement through

her music. Although Simone became disillusioned that the problems of racism would be solved in the United States, her consummate musical prodigy still pushed the movement forward, evoked most prominently in her "Mississippi Goddam," written after the white racial violence against African Americans in Alabama and Mississippi. That black women's social, historical, and lived experiences of racist discrimination paralleled their experiences of sexist discrimination was undeniable, but black women began to realize that neither the civil rights movement nor the women's liberation movement could fully articulate the black woman's position in U.S. society.

BLACK FEMINISM IN THE 1970S

The 1970s saw the most obvious and productive phase of black feminists' formal organizations. From coast to coast, black women, in an effort to expand the women's liberation movement agenda, met to discuss what it meant to be black and female. A few of the organizations that did this work included the NBFO, the TWWA, the National Alliance of Black Feminists (NABF), the Combahee River Collective, and Black Women Organized for Action (BWOA). Predominantly active in major U.S. cities—New York, Boston, Chicago, and San Francisco—these organizations had structures that were influenced by black women's civil rights and student activism. The TWWA and Combahee, for example, both operated as collectives and, at least theoretically, modeled participatory democracy as espoused in SNCC. The NBFO and the NABF, having members with backgrounds in civil rights, students, and government organizations, organized hierarchically. The outlier, BWOA, demonstrated a unique way of organizing that combined the collective and the hierarchical, with the leadership of the organization rotating every three months among three different members.

Each of these organizations espoused different political approaches to black feminism and, as such, reflected those varied beliefs in their organizational structures. The range of organizational structures served to emphasize the many voices of black feminist organizing. The NBFO, NABF, and BWOA can all be characterized as reform-minded organizations that sought the full inclusion of black women into the existing capitalist system. They offered a critique of patriarchy that challenged the racism, sexism, and classism that excluded black women from certain occupations, equal pay, and adequate child care, and they actively supported the Equal Rights Amendment through coalition work with predominantly white feminist organizations.

The TWWA and the Combahee, on the other hand, offered a critique of capitalism *and* patriarchy. Positing that black women were on the bottom of race, gender, and class hierarchies, Combahee and the TWWA advocated a Socialist overthrow of capitalism in which black women would be recognized as workers and black community leaders. In their classic "A Black Feminist Statement" (1977), Combahee noted that the synthesis of racial and sexual oppression as critical factors undermining the quality of women and people of color's work lives and class positions required the destruction of capitalist exploitation.

With feminist organizing gaining mainstream notoriety, black women faced an increasing number of community pressures to abandon the women's movement and feminism. Pressure from some black men and women not to get involved with a "white women's thing" faced black feminists each time they participated in a speaking engagement, such as lectures for community groups, college courses, or even as guests on *The Phil Donahue Show*. Many blacks considered black feminism and its adherents "divisive" to the civil rights and black liberation movements. Some of these views were based on the idea that black women had a finite amount of time and energy, and daily survival issues should be at the forefront of any truly black struggle as opposed to consciousness-raising around housework. Popular culture was rife with examples of the potentially negative consequences for black women engaging feminism as a liberating ideology. In the 1970s, black exploitation, or "blaxploitation," films were a prime example of conflating feminism and lesbianism. If a black woman were truly a "Strong Black Woman," she would resist feminism's pull and maintain racial loyalty as a protector of the black community, as depicted in the film *Cleopatra Jones* (1973).

Such a view trivialized the real issues feminists faced, such as battering and sexual assault, and it also ignored the very dire consequences of patriarchy affecting black families. Black feminist organizations actively resisted this marginalization and insisted that gender issues assume a more prominent place in the black liberation struggle. The range of activities of these organizations included rallies and contributions to funds to free political prisoners, such as Angela Davis; hosting community health fairs that focused on issues severely impacting the black community, such as high infant mortality rates; cosponsoring anti-rape events such as Take Back the Night marches; speaking

out in favor of abortion rights and advocating for new regulations against nonconsensual sterilization; protesting racist and sexist employment discrimination against black women in blue-collar and professional positions; and coalition work with predominantly white feminist organizations on projects such as feminist credit unions.

Black feminist organizations lasted a collective total of twelve years. All were defunct by the 1980s with the rise of conservatism, or more specifically, Ronald Reagan's election to the presidency, and the Christian Right's conservative agenda. Although there is no direct causality between the change in political climate and the decline of black feminist organizations, BWOA, for instance, noted in their final newsletter, *What It Is*, that after the flurry of feminist activity in the 1970s, the group was taking an indefinite hiatus to recoup for the anticipated backlash against women's and civil rights gains. Other causes for the decline of black feminist organizations included a lack of adequate funding on the same large scale as predominantly white feminist organizations, leadership disputes over the definition of black feminism, and the continued pull between struggling for black rights and struggling for women's rights. Most significantly, some activists were simply burned out after two decades of struggle.

In addition to formal organizing, black women writers continued the legacy of black feminist literacy and activism into the 1970s. Writers such as Alice Walker, Audre Lorde, Margaret Okazawa-Rey, Michele Wallace, and Pat Parker participated in black feminist organizations, but also made enormous contributions to the literature and philosophical thought of the black feminist movement. Walker's fictional account, *The Color Purple* (1982), and Wallace's *Black Macho and the Myth of the Superwoman* (1979) both took black male sexism to task and decried its impact on black women. Both works were the subject of controversy and derided as instigating a "battle between the sexes" and being divisive. However, these authors, as well as many others published during the 1970s, sparked much-needed debates about the role of black women in the black community and in society at large. This was a particularly important contribution as black women began to make inroads into the echelons of higher education, secured elected positions at the local and national levels, and assumed greater roles of power in the entertainment industry—all in an effort to redefine how black women were portrayed in the media and perceived by the American public. Dispelling myths about black female sexuality that depicted black women as voracious "Jezebels" or, contradictorily, as asexual, subservient Mammy-figures defined the mission of black feminist activists well into the 1980s.

BLACK FEMINISM 1980s–1990s

A persistent tension within the black feminist movement continues to surround the use of the word "feminist" itself. In 1983, novelist and essayist Alice Walker coined the term "womanist" in her collection of essays *In Search of Our Mothers' Gardens.* Although the first definition she gives states that a womanist is a black feminist, many black women, in the United States and abroad, have taken on the term as a distinct form of activism on behalf of black women and the black community that is outside traditional definitions of feminism. Notably, although Walker also defined womanism as a way of relating to black women and black men sexually and/or nonsexually, this aspect of the definition is often ignored in a heterosexist cooptation of Walker's original meaning. Thus, Africana womanism purports to be more closely aligned with the black liberation struggle, espousing an essentialist view of black women as uniquely morally equipped to wage this struggle. Despite the contention, black feminism and black womanism share certain perspectives on race, gender, and class and act as two separate streams feeding into the central aims of the black feminist movement.

Interestingly, black women academics in theology, religion, and ethics have taken on the mantle of black womanism and elucidated its contours, effectively bringing the black feminist movement into the black church. Black womanists, such as Renita Weems, Cheryl Sanders, and Katie G. Cannon, challenge patriarchal readings of biblical Scriptures through womanist reinterpretations, and they call for reevaluating black women's roles in the church as an untapped leadership resource.

Because of the lasting controversy surrounding the label "feminist," beginning in the 1980s some black women chose to avoid the feminist label in an effort to be more successful in advocating on behalf of black women. This black woman–centered activism was most prominent in the area of health. The National Black Women's Health Project (NBWHP) formed in 1984 with the stated mission of self-help. NBWHP's guiding principle led to the organization of small, autonomous groups focused on prevention through Afrocentric principles of holistic health, as well as attention to the particular ramifications of ra-

cism on black women's physical, spiritual, emotional, and mental health. Similar work was done by a group of women, several of whom were also members of the NBWHP, in a statement entitled "African American Women Are for Reproductive Freedom." This late 1980s statement extended the mainstream feminist agenda on abortion to reproductive rights, noting the historical impact of slavery on black women's present-day reproductive choices. They include not only the maintenance of legal abortions, but also *accessible* abortions, as well as the right to parent without interference from the state.

In the 1990s, the black feminist movement also challenged the state for its treatment of former University of Oklahoma law professor Anita Hill during the confirmation of Clarence Thomas to the U.S. Supreme Court. When Hill came forward to reveal allegations of sexual harassment while working for the Equal Employment Opportunity Commission under Thomas's directorship, her mistreatment by the Federal Bureau of Investigation and the Senate Judiciary Committee sparked an exemplary dilemma for the black feminist movement. The black community alleged a racist plot to derail Thomas's nomination and questioned Professor Hill's racial loyalty in coming forward. Predominantly white feminist organizations championed Professor Hill as a brave pioneer in women's rights for speaking out against gender discrimination.

No national black women's organization stepped forward to defend Hill or to explain the race and sex implications of Thomas's confirmation. Instead, a group of black women academics started a grassroots campaign called African American Women in Defense of Ourselves (AAWDO) to respond. Within one month, Barbara Ransby, Elsa Barkley Brown, Susie King, and Deborah Gray gathered over 1,600 signatures and donations to take out a full-page advertisement in the *New York Times* Sunday edition. The statement served the dual purpose of challenging the racist *and* sexist treatment of Professor Hill, as well as protesting the threat that the politically conservative Thomas nomination posed for the black community's economic and political well-being. The statement ultimately affirmed that black women would continue to speak out on behalf of one another, the black community, and those antagonistic to social justice regardless of race. Much like their nineteenth-century foremothers, AAWDO reasserted that only the black woman could adequately speak to the vagaries of life lived at the intersection of gender and race identities.

THE PRESENT

Today, the momentum of the black feminist movement proceeds unabated as racism, sexism, classism, and heterosexism transmutate in a postindustrial, capitalist society. Specifically, the black feminist movement faces the dilemma of accounting for the social and political advances of black women while at the same time dealing with persisting racial and gender discrimination. The lack of a national black feminist organizational presence remains a sticking point among black women searching for an organized response to discrimination against black women and black communities. However, as evidenced by the AAWDO mobilization, the many voices raised in protest against the exclusion of black women from the Million Man March, and the growth of black feminist caucuses at academic and activist conferences (e.g., the Black Feminist Caucus of the 1998 Chicago Black Radical Congress), black feminism remains an active theoretical basis for struggle for black women nationally. Black women active in the black feminist movement of the late 1960s and early 1970s are carrying on their activism, as well as inspiring younger generations to explore their black feminist history and apply those lessons to combat welfare reform, attacks on affirmative action, and the increasing mass incarceration of black women, men, and children in the United States.

Kimberly Springer

BIBLIOGRAPHY

African American Women Are for Reproductive Freedom. "We Remember." In *Still Lifting, Still Climbing: African American Women's Contemporary Activism,* ed. Kimberly Springer, 38–41. New York: New York University Press, 1999.

"African American Women in Defense of Ourselves." In *Still Lifting, Still Climbing: African American Women's Contemporary Activism,* ed. Kimberly Springer, 42–43. New York: New York University Press, 1999.

Cannon, Katie Geneva. *Katie's Canon: Womanism and the Soul of the Black Community.* New York: Continuum, 1996.

Combahee River Collective. "A Black Feminist Statement." In *Still Lifting, Still Climbing: African American Women's Contemporary Activism,* ed. Kimberly Springer, 232–240. New York: New York University Press, 1999.

Hansberry, Lorraine. "Simone de Beauvior and *The Second Sex:* An American Commentary." In *Words of Fire: An Anthology of African American Feminist Thought,* ed. Beverly Guy-Sheftall, 128–142. New York: New Press, 1995.

Kennedy, Florynce. "A Comparative Study: Accentuating the Similarities of the Societal Position of Women and Negroes." In *Words of Fire: An Anthology of African American Feminist Thought,* ed. Beverly Guy-Sheftall, 102–106. New York: New Press, 1995.

National Black Women's Health Project. "Vision Statement." In *Still Lifting, Still Climbing: African American Women's Contemporary Activism,* ed. Kimberly Springer, 37. New York: New York University Press, 1999.

Robnett, Belinda. *How Long? How Long?: African American Women in the Struggle for Civil Rights.* New York: Oxford University Press, 1997.

Sanders, Cheryl, ed. *Living at the Intersection: Womanism and Afrocentrism in Theology.* Minneapolis, MN: Fortress, 1995.

Springer, Kimberly. "Politics in the Cracks: The Interstitial Politics of Black Feminist Organizations." *Meridians: Feminism, Race, and Transnationalism* 1:2 (March 2001): 155–191.

Walker, Alice. *The Color Purple.* New York: Pocket Books, 1982.

———. *In Search of Our Mothers' Gardens: Womanist Prose.* San Diego: Harcourt Brace Jovanovich, 1983.

Wallace, Michelle. *Black Macho and the Myth of the Superwoman.* New York: Warner Books, 1978.

Weems, Renita. *Just a Sister Away: A Womanist Vision of Women's Relationships in the Bible.* Philadelphia: Innisfree, 1991.

WOMEN'S MOVEMENT 1960–1990

The 1960s—these two words conjure up images of civil rights marches, war protesters, and hippies. This decade retains its grip on the American imagination some forty years later and for good reason: the 1960s initiated a series of profound changes in U.S. society. In 1960, John F. Kennedy was elected to the presidency, signaling an unparalleled confidence in the young. The contraceptive pill appeared, paving the way for the sexual revolution. But by 1960, the optimism and prosperity that swept through the United States following World War II faced increasing challenges. The Beatniks offered young people a critique of American materialism and the hypocrisy of their parents' generation. The civil rights movement took a more confrontational approach as sit-ins in Greenville, North Carolina's Woolworth's brought public protests to the national eye. The Student Nonviolent Coordinating Committee (SNCC) was founded, leading ultimately to the Black Power movement. In the West, migrant farm workers were organizing. And although few people knew it then, over 10,000 American soldiers were in a small country in Southeast Asia called Vietnam.

After a decade of declining age at marriage and increasing birth rates, in 1960 the media discovered that all was not well behind the white picket fences that divided suburbia. Newspapers, magazines, and television all ran stories about women's dissatisfaction. And women had much to be unhappy about. The U.S. Senate contained only one woman. Working women earned, on average, just 60 cents for every dollar men made. Most working women occupied low-status clerical and service jobs. Of the 58 percent of African-American women who worked outside the home, most were employed as domestic servants.

Three major social movements shaped the decade we now call the 1960s: civil rights, the movement against the war in Vietnam, and the women's movement. What will be referred to here as the women's movement was also called women's liberation, the feminist movement, radical feminism, and women's rights. In the early analysis of the women's movement, groups were sometimes differentiated as the women's rights groups and the women's liberation groups, or, respectively, the older and the younger women's movement branches. Women's rights advocates sought to create a role for women in the present society. This earlier date of origin and the overall older median age of women involved in this branch, estimated at the late twenties and early thirties, led to the designation of it as the "older" branch of the feminist movement. The women's liberationist can be generalized as one wanting radical changes to "liberate" or free women from constraining social roles. This impetus was usually combined with another social reform ideology such as socialism or anarchism. These "radical feminists" wanted to change the structure of society as a whole, with women's role being only one of many altered. Most of the women in this branch of the movement were generally in their middle and late twenties. This led to the nomenclature of the "younger" or more "radical" branch. All these women shared a commitment to feminism, an ideology maintaining that women in the United States were oppressed and that change needed to occur. Feminists varied widely in their beliefs as to the cause of that oppression and as to the best way to overcome it.

The origins of the women's movement are as varied as the terms used to refer to it. Some scholars find the origins of the women's movement in World War II. This view, which is most closely associated with the historian William Chafe, holds that changes in the labor force participation rates of married women—that is, the percentage of married women employed outside the home—led to changes in women's role in U.S. society. This interpretation is not without challenge. Some historians have argued that, while the

BETTY FRIEDAN (1921–)

Bettye Naomi Goldstein was born in Peoria, Illinois, on February 4, 1921, to Miriam (Horwitz) and Harry Goldstein. A psychology student at Smith College, Betty (who dropped the *e* from her name during school) was a star student and a solid writer: she sat as editor in chief of the college's newspaper and graduated summa cum laude in 1942. In 1943, Friedan continued her studies as a doctoral student in psychology at the University of California at Berkeley. However, after receiving (and then declining) a prestigious scholarship from the institution, she dropped out of the program and moved to New York City to pursue a career in journalism. She married Carl Friedan in 1947 and settled into the role of suburban housewife and mother to three children while also working as a freelance journalist for the Federated Press, the labor press, and a variety of popular women's magazines including *Good Housekeeping*.

In 1957, prior to her fifteenth class reunion, Friedan designed and sent a questionnaire to her Smith College contemporaries, asking whether or not they felt content with their lives since college. She received in-depth responses from over 200 women, and the results were extraordinary: the majority felt unfulfilled, and many outlined the details of the dissatisfaction with their lives. The common thread among them all was an effort to conform to their supposedly "natural" gender roles while simultaneously harboring a frustration and a desire for something *more*. Finding commonality among her former classmates not only legitimized her own discontent in her marriage and her life, but also led to an extension of research into the topic. She expanded her study dramatically, formulating more questionnaires and surveys, conducting interviews, and consulting with psychologists and behaviorists. The results of her investigations would provide the data for what would become a landmark work: *The Feminine Mystique*.

Published in 1963, *The Feminine Mystique* was a combination of the results of her qualitative research and her own stifling experience in the domestic realm. Friedan defined and described "the problem that had no name," that women were the victims of deception, expected to glean happiness and fulfillment from their sole role as caregiver of their husbands and children. According to Friedan, the glorification of "wife" and "mother" not only led to frustration and a loss of self-esteem, but also prevented women from pursuing other work and/or creative self-expression. Translated into multiple languages, Betty Friedan's *The Feminine Mystique* was an almost instant best seller and has since been credited with inspiring the second wave of the women's movement in North America.

The Feminine Mystique sparked controversy over women's "place" in American society, and the groundbreaking work launched Friedan into the public spotlight. Appearing on the radio, on television, and at academic conferences, she rapidly established herself as a women's movement leader. By the mid-1960s, Friedan had become a household name, and she had joined forces with other women interested in the advancement of women's rights. In October of 1966, at the Third National Conference of the Commission on the Status of Women in Washington, D.C., she and twenty-eight other women cofounded the National Organization for Women (NOW). As its first president (until 1970), Friedan fought for civil rights and directed campaigns to challenge stereotypes of women in the media, to improve women's political participation, and to develop accessible child care. NOW was also at the forefront of the fight to legalize abortion, and in 1969 Friedan helped found the National Conference for the Repeal of Abortion Laws. Soon after abortion was legalized, the group changed its name to the National Abortion Rights Action League (NARAL). During her last year as NOW's leader, she led the Women's Strike for Equality, a public and vocal commemoration of the fiftieth anniversary of women's suffrage in America.

Friedan continued working for women's rights by assisting in the establishment of the National Women's Political Caucus in 1971, as well as helping with the organization of the International Feminist Congress and the creation of the first Women's Bank in New York in 1973. Soon after, she turned her attention to writing (she was a regular columnist for *McCall's* magazine) and teaching. Her teaching posts included the New School for Social Research and Temple University in 1972, Yale in 1974, and Queen's College in 1975. A winner of multiple awards and honors (including the Eleanor Roosevelt Leadership Award in 1989, an induction in the National Women's Hall of Fame in 1993, and a Lifetime Achievement Award for Literary Arts in 1998), Betty Friedan has, through years of activism and writing, been established as one of the most effective leaders of the second-wave women's movement. Her memoir, *Life So Far*, was published in 2000.

Candis Steenbergen

NATIONAL ORGANIZATION FOR WOMEN
STATEMENT OF PURPOSE 1966

The National Organization for Women (NOW), founded in October 1966 at an organizing conference in Washington, D.C., became the leading women's rights organization in the 1960s.

We, men and women, who hereby constitute ourselves as the National Organization for Women, believe that the time has come for a new movement toward true equality for all women in America, and toward a fully equal partnership of the sexes, as part of the worldwide revolution of human rights. . . .

The purpose of NOW is to take action to bring women into full participation in the mainstream of American society . . . exercising all the privileges and responsibilities . . . in truly equal partnership with men.

We believe the time has come to move beyond the abstract argument, discussion and symposia over the status and special nature of women which has raged in America . . . ; the time has come to confront, with concrete action, the conditions that now prevent women from enjoying the equality of opportunity and freedom of which is their right, as individual Americans, and as human beings. . . .

Despite all the talk about the status of American women in recent years, the actual position of women in the United States has declined . . . to an alarming degree. . . . Although 46.4 percent of all American women between the ages of 18 and 65 now work outside the home, the overwhelming majority—75 percent—are in routine clerical, sales, or factory jobs, or they are household workers, cleaning women, hospital attendants.

. . . Discrimination in employment on the basis of sex is now prohibited by federal law, in the Civil Rights Act of 1964. But although nearly one-third of the cases brought before the Equal Employment Opportunity Commission during the first year dealt with sex discrimination and the proportion is increasing dramatically, the Commission has not made clear its intention to enforce the law with the same seriousness on behalf of women as of other victims of discrimination. . . .

WE BELIEVE that the power of American law, and the protection guaranteed by the U.S. Constitution to the civil rights of all individuals, must be effectively applied and enforced to isolate and remove patterns of sex discrimination, to ensure equality of opportunity in employment and education, and equality of civil and political rights and responsibilities on behalf of women, as well as for Negroes and other deprived groups. . . .

WE DO NOT ACCEPT the token appointment of a few women to high-level positions in government and industry as a substitute for a serious continuing effort to recruit and advance women. . . .

WE BELIEVE that this nation has a capacity . . . to innovate new social institutions which will enable women to enjoy true equality of opportunity and responsibility in society, without conflict with their responsibilities as mothers and homemakers. . . .

WE BELIEVE that it is as essential for every girl to be educated to her full potential of human ability as it is for every boy—with the knowledge that such education is the key to effective participation in today's economy and that . . . education can only be serious where there is expectation that it be used in society. . . .

WE REJECT the current assumptions that a man must carry the sole burden of supporting himself, his wife, and family, and that a woman is automatically entitled to lifelong support by a man upon her marriage, or that marriage, home and family are primarily woman's world and responsibility. . . . We believe that proper recognition should be given to the economic and social value of homemaking and child-care. To these ends we will seek to open a reexamination of laws and mores governing marriage and divorce, for we believe that the current state of "half-equality" between the sexes discriminates against both men and women . . .

WE BELIEVE that women must now exercise their political rights and responsibilities as American citizens. . . .

IN THE INTERESTS OF THE HUMAN DIGNITY OF WOMEN, we will protest, and endeavor to change, the false image of women now prevalent in the mass media, and in the texts, ceremonies, laws, and practices of our major social institutions. Such images perpetuate contempt for women by society and by women for themselves. . . .

NOW WILL HOLD ITSELF INDEPENDENT OF ANY POLITICAL PARTY in order to mobilize the political power of all women and men intent on our goals. We will strive to ensure that no party, candidate, president, senator, governor, congressman, or any public official who betrays or ignores the principle of full equality between the sexes is elected or appointed to office. . . .

WE BELIEVE THAT women will do most to create a new image of women by acting now, and by speaking out in behalf of their own equality, freedom, and human dignity . . . in an active, self-respecting partnership with men. By so doing, women will develop confidence in their own ability to determine actively, in partnership with men, the conditions of their life, their choices, their future and their society.

Source: National Organization for Women. Washington, DC, October 29, 1966. Available at www.now.org/history/purpos66.html.

change noted by Chafe accurately describes the circumstances of white, middle-class women, women of color and poor white women had worked outside the home prior to World War II.

Changes in the political landscape may have also contributed to the resurgence in women's activism. In 1961, President Kennedy created a Presidential Commission on the Status of Women. This group of twenty members, appointed by the president, issued a report on women's economic, legal, and political status in 1963. *American Women* detailed in depth the inequities in women's status. As a result, thirty-three states established Commissions on the Status of Women, and at the federal level, an Interdepartmental Committee on the Status of Women and a Citizen's Advisory Council were established by Executive Order to follow up on the report of the president's commission. The commission's findings were amplified by Betty Friedan's study *The Feminine Mystique* (1963) which documented the dissatisfaction of many middle-class housewives with their position in U.S. society.

In 1964, a Civil Rights Act was introduced that included a prohibition of employment discrimination based on sex. The bill also called for the establishment of an Equal Employment Opportunity Commission (EEOC) to enforce the law. However, following passage of the 1964 Civil Rights Act, the EEOC refused to enforce Title VII, the part of the bill specifically pertaining to sex discrimination. This refusal provided a cause for feminists to rally around. At the Third National Conference of Commissions on the Status of Women on June 30, 1966, delegates attempted to pass a resolution urging the EEOC to enforce Title VII. When the resolution did not pass, the women who proposed it decided to form a lobbying organization for women's rights to pressure the EEOC on behalf of women. They sketched out, on a napkin, what became the National Organization for Women (NOW). Twenty-eight women joined the first day. By the following October, there were more than 300 members. NOW's Bill of Rights for women outlined seven goals: an equal rights constitutional amendment; enforcement of the law banning sexual discrimination in employment (Title VII of the 1964 Civil Rights Act); maternity leave rights in employment and in Social Security benefits; tax deductions for home and childcare expenses for working parents; child day-care centers; equal job training and allowance opportunities for women in poverty; and the right of women to control their reproductive lives. This last demand, for legalized abortion, would prove so controversial within NOW that within two years a group of women left to

form Women's Equity Action League (WEAL), which excluded abortion rights from its focus.

THE WOMEN'S MOVEMENT AND OTHER SOCIAL MOVEMENTS

While the changing political climate inspired some women to become involved in the women's movement, other historians have cited participation in two important social movements as key to explaining the reemergence of feminism during the 1960s. This interpretation holds that white women who participated in civil rights organizations began to see similarities between themselves and the blacks they sought to help, much as the suffrage movement grew out of women's involvement with abolition a century before. Other women were involved in the New Left, a term that refers to a loosely affiliated movement of young people critical of U.S. society and politics, particularly foreign policy and the war in Vietnam. Women involved in both movements became dissatisfied with the limited role allotted to them.

Between 1964 and 1967, many papers circulated concerning the unequal position of women in the civil movements. In 1964, at a Student Nonviolent Coordinating Committee staff meeting, Ruby Doris Smith presented a paper on "The Position of Women in SNCC" in which she criticized the limited role afforded to women within the group. SNCC leader Stokely Carmichael's infamous remark, "The only position for women in SNCC is prone," has been seen as indicative of the disregard for women within some parts of the civil rights movement. Similarly, in 1965 Casey Hayden and Mary King wrote a paper called "A Kind of Memo" in which they criticized the subordinate position of women within the civil rights movement. Essays like "The Grand Coolie Damn" (1969) by Marge Piercy and "Goodbye to All That" (1970) by Robin Morgan offered similar analyses of men in the New Left. Although these authors may not have intended to launch a movement for women, they can be seen as an impetus behind some groups within the women's movement.

Just as women's suffrage has its roots in the exclusion of Lucretia Mott and Elizabeth Cady Stanton at the World Anti-Slavery Conference in 1840, women's mistreatment at the New Left National Conference for a New Politics (NCNP) over Labor Day weekend in 1967 resulted in a pivotal women's movement group forming in Chicago. During the spring of 1967, two women, Heather Booth and Naomi Weinstein, conducted a seminar on women's issues at the free university of the University of Chicago. Out of this seminar some women formed a group to discuss the possibility of presenting a list of demands at the NCNP. The members of this group who attended the conference were so angered by the committee's refusal to discuss their platform plank concerning women's inequality that they continued as a group after the convention. This original group eventually split into two: the Women's Radical Action Project and the Westside Group. The Westside group in March 1968 began the first feminist newsletter, *Voice of the Women's Liberation Movement*, coining the term *women's liberation*.

In 1967, women's liberation groups formed across the United States. Some groups, like those in Seattle, Gainesville, Detroit, and Toronto, seem to have arisen spontaneously. At other times, new groups started when a member from one of the few existing groups relocated and started another group. For example, in October 1967 Shulamith Firestone, a member of the original Chicago women's liberation group, moved to New York, where she and Pam Allen attempted to form a New York women's group. They received an unfavorable response from the women contacted through New Left political organizations, but a breakthrough finally occurred in the late fall of 1967 at a convention at Princeton of another New Left group, the Students for a Democratic Society (SDS). A workshop held there on women's issues inspired the formation of the New York Radical Women. The group's first demonstration occurred on January 15, 1968, when about 500 radical women split off from 4,500 women marching to protest the war in Vietnam to participate in a counterdemonstration staged by the New York Radical Feminists. The counterdemonstration involved symbolically burying the coffin of traditional womanhood, complete with a funeral orientation that explained the relationship between feminism and the women's peace movement.

In a similar action, on September 7, 1968, the New York Radical Feminists demonstrated in Atlantic City at the Miss America Pageant. That night television beamed radical feminism into America's living rooms, garnering in thirty seconds more attention for the cause than any number of community meetings or mimeographed newsletters ever could. Organizers created a Freedom Trash Can, in which the demonstrators threw objects representing women's imprisonment to beauty standards, including makeup, high heels, and women's undergarments. In an effort to gain more news media coverage, someone had leaked the plan. Proving that any publicity was not necessarily good publicity, the news media seized on the image of women burning their bras, which became the seed of the false epithet "bra burner"—a term used to trivialize the feminist issue and to deflect from the issue of women's objectification. Although the Miss America Pageant protest failed to end beauty pageants, the resulting publicity helped spread the feminist message. Women's groups began organizing throughout the United States to address women's oppressed status.

Just a little over a year after women were prevented from presenting their resolution on women's rights at the National Conference for a New Politics, more than 200 women from thirty-seven different states attended a women's liberation conference over Thanksgiving weekend, 1968, in Chicago. Among the important papers presented at this conference was "A Program for Feminist Consciousness-Raising." For both branches of the movement, consciousness raising (C-R) provided a means of unifying women through an understanding of common experiences with sexism. Consciousness raising provided women with a forum to discuss their dissatisfaction with the societal role allotted to women and helped to foster an understanding of sexism by exploring the common experiences in each woman's life. Because this movement was founded on personal experiences, consciousness raising helped to liberate women's minds. For some C-R was their introduction to feminism. Through C-R, women from different situations and backgrounds discovered the similarities in their lives and realized that the problem lay with society and not themselves. The knowledge that women were victims of societal oppression was very empowering, and angry women channeled their energy into feminist activities. C-R groups, as they were called, began forming throughout the United States as word of this technique spread through women's movement periodicals. A C-R group often provided women with their introduction to the women's movement and to the many issues that feminists addressed in the ensuing decade.

Within a few years, women's movement organizations sprang up across the United States. In Los Angeles, in the fall of 1969 a conference was held at Immaculate Heart College to decide what direction the Los Angeles women's movement should take. Someone had heard about a women's center in New York, and the conference participants all thought that was the perfect project for them. The first women's center in Los Angeles opened as a joint effort of the University of California at Los Angeles (UCLA) and community women. Two years later, the Westside Women's Center was founded to reach more women through another center located in another part of town.

THE 1970S

By the year 1970, the women's movement was major media news, and it made good copy. In March 1970, 200 women journalists occupied the editorial offices of *Ladies' Home Journal* to demand child care for *Journal* employees, better pay for women journalists, and the installation of a female editor for the magazine. On August 26, 1970, 50,000 women marched down the middle of Fifth Avenue in New York to commemorate the fiftieth anniversary of women's suffrage. That same year, three books about feminism appeared: *The Female Eunuch* by Germaine Greer, *Sexual Politics* by Kate Millett, and *The Dialectic of Sex* by Shulamith Firestone. Women of color also began feminist organizing, as the North American Indian Women's Association and the Comisión Femenil Mexicana Nacional were founded. The women's movement began to make inroads into major institutions of American life. In 1970, the first women's studies program was created at San Diego State College, the Lutheran Church in American authorized the ordination of women, and the Equal Rights Amendment was reintroduced into Congress.

THE WOMEN'S MOVEMENT FINDS POLITICS

Throughout the early 1970s, women made major gains in the political arena. Although the Equal Rights Amendment was first introduced in Congress in 1923, it was not until the 1970s that a widespread movement for passage reemerged. The National Organization for Women (NOW) spearheaded this resurgence. In 1970, twenty NOW leaders disrupted hearings of the U.S. Senate Subcommittee on Constitutional Amendments to demand that the ERA be heard by the full Congress. In 1972, Congress finally passed the ERA, and the drive for ratification began. Despite a strong national movement and the granting of an extension to the usual seven years to acquire ratification by the required thirty-eight states, by the 1982 deadline, only thirty-five states had ratified the amendment.

Although the ERA brought together a large number of women interested in greater political power for women, some participants felt that male-dominated legislatures would never pass the ERA. The National Women's Political Caucus was founded by Washington, D.C., women in July 1971. NWPC saw increased numbers of women in all aspects of political life as a way to combat sexism, racism, and institutional discrimination against women. NWPC focused its efforts on gaining political appointments for women, working with political parties to elect more women candidates and to increase the visibility of women's issues in electoral politics.

Similar efforts occurred on the state level. For example, in Texas a women's caucus formed within the Raza Unida Party. Although women served in many positions of party leadership, they faced discrimination from some men. In 1973, women decided to form the Mujeres Por La Raza caucus to obtain leadership positions for women in the Raza Unida Party and to elect Chicanas to office in Texas. They held conferences throughout Texas in 1973 to increase women's involvement with politics. In addition to organizing conferences for community women, the Mujeres worked to combat racism and classism among white women.

These efforts bore fruition as politicians began paying greater attention to women's issues. In 1972, Congress passed Title IX of the Education Amendment. This law requires that "No person in the United States shall, on the basis of sex, be excluded from participation in, be denied the benefits of, or be subjected to discrimination under any education program or activity receiving federal financial assistance." The amendment took effect in 1976 and opened the way for women's increased participation in athletics programs and professional schools. Despite legal challenges, Title IX remains in effect today.

THE MOVEMENT TO LEGALIZE ABORTION

The women's movement's largest foray into politics occurred in the area of abortion rights. The U.S. Supreme Court ruling of January 1973 that legalized abortion might be called the greatest success of the women's movement. Abortion served as a unifying focus for many groups involved in the women's movement as liberal feminists and radicals, young and old women alike, all worked to secure women's access to safe and legal abortions. The movement to re-legalize abortion predates the women's movement, as physicians and clergy members, mostly men, had been working throughout the 1960s to liberalize abortion laws. However, with the advent of the women's movement, women became active in demanding the repeal of all abortion laws. In January 1969, members of New York NOW's Abortion Committee formed New Yorkers for Abortion Law Repeal (NYALR). That same month the National Association for the Repeal

GERMAINE GREER (1939–   )

Germaine Greer was born in Melbourne, Australia, on January 29, 1939, the daughter of Eric Reginal (a newspaper advertising manager) and Margaret May Mary (Lanfrancan) Greer. After attending the Star of the Sea Convent, an all-girl Catholic Academy in Victoria, she pursued an undergraduate degree in English and French literature at the University of Melbourne at the age of eighteen. Greer graduated with her B.A. in 1959, and moved to Sydney to complete her master's degree in 1961. In 1964, she moved again—this time to the United Kingdom on scholarship to study English literature at Cambridge University. Her dissertation, entitled *The Ethic of Love and Marriage in Shakespeare's Early Comedies*, earned Greer her doctoral degree in 1967. Ph.D. in hand, Greer accepted a lecturer position in Warwick University's English department, and taught there until 1973. After the completion of her degree, she wrote for a variety of journals and magazines, appeared on television, and married—and divorced—Paul de Feu; their union lasted three weeks.

Her first book was both highly controversial and overwhelmingly successful. Published in Britain in 1970, *The Female Eunuch* was considered—and is still believed to be—a landmark feminist text, one that launched Greer in the public eye and made her a noteworthy—but problematic—figure in both the sexual liberation and women's movements. In *The Female Eunuch*, Greer challenged society's misrepresentations of women's sexuality, argued that marriage was a modern and legal form of slavery, and maintained that the stereotype of females as passive sexual creatures was nothing more than the psychological castration of women by society. The book was published in the United States in 1971, and, following a highly publicized book tour (and a public debate with Norman Mailer at New York's Town Hall), Greer had become one of the new faces of 1970s feminism.

An international celebrity by the 1970s, Greer continued to give public talks and to publish, constantly stirring up controversy, rejecting narrow views of femininity and womanhood, and urging women to struggle against such characterizations through their own investigations into sexuality and creativity. The success garnered from *The Female Eunuch* not only transformed Greer into a media sensation; she also wrote vigorously for publications like *Spare Rib*, *Esquire*, and *The Sunday Times*, and continued teaching: she sat as director of the Tulsa Centre for the Study of Women's Literature in Oklahoma (where she founded a center for the study of women's literature), and has, since 1989, been a special lecturer and unofficial fellow at Cambridge. She currently splits a part-time appointment between the Department of English and Comparative Literary Studies, the Centre for British and Comparative Cultural Studies, and the Centre for the Study of Women and Gender at the University of Warwick.

In many ways, Greer has led a double life: one as distinguished scholar, lecturer, and writer of women's achievements in the literary arts (see *The Obstacle Race: The Fortunes of Female Painters and Their Work* [1979], *Shakespeare* [1986], and *Slip-Shod Sibyls: Recognition, Rejection and The Woman Poet* [1995]), and another as the outspoken and contentious feminist spokeswoman of the late twentieth century. In 1999, she wrote the book she had said she would never write: the sequel to *The Female Eunuch*. *The Whole Woman* examined the status of the women's movement as it neared the millennium and attacked what she saw as current and dangerous trends in feminist theory and practice. Receiving mixed reviews from feminists and the popular presses, Greer has proven—at the age of sixty—that she has still *got it*: her writing is stirring, her questions are pertinent, and her style is provocative, entertaining, and sexy.

Candis Steenbergen

---

of Abortion Laws, which included both members of NOW as well as male abortion advocates, was founded.

To members of the women's movement, it was important for women's voices to be heard in the debate over legalized abortion. Thus, on February 13, 1969, members of the radical feminist group the Redstockings interrupted hearings on abortion law reform being held by the New York State legislature to protest that witnesses before the committee consisted of fourteen men and one nun. The following month, on March 21, 1969, the Redstockings organized their own "hearings" on abortion, which included a speakout, at which hundreds of women went public with their own experiences with mostly illegal abortions. In a similar move in 1972, fifty-three prominent American women publicly stated in the inaugural issue of *Ms.*, the pioneering feminist magazine founded by Gloria Steinem, that they had had abortions.

Although some groups focused on legalizing abortion, others worked to circumvent the law. In 1969, members of the Chicago Women's Liberation

GLORIA STEINEM (1934–)

Steinem gained prominence as an articulate spokeswoman for women's rights both in lectures and in television appearances. She helped found the National Women's Political Caucus (1971), the Women's Action Alliance (1971), and the Coalition of Labor Union Women (1974). She was also the founding editor (1972–1987) of *Ms.*, a feminist magazine.

Gloria Steinem was born in Toledo, Ohio, on March 25, 1934, and spent her early years traveling in a house trailer with her parents. After her parents divorced in 1946, Steinem moved with her mother to Toledo and began attending school on a regular basis for the first time. During her senior year of high school, Steinem moved to Washington, D.C., to live with her older sister.

Steinem graduated from Smith College in 1956 and traveled to India on a scholarship. While in India, she participated in nonviolent protests against government policy. By 1960, she had moved to New York City and found work as a writer and journalist. Her article "I Was a Playboy Bunny," which recounted her brief experience as a waitress at Hugh Hefner's Playboy Club in 1963, garnered Steinem her first national attention. Steinem's work became more overtly political over the next few years, and she began writing a column, "The City Politic," for *New York* magazine in 1968. She also moved into politics more directly, working for Democratic candidates such as Norman Mailer, Eugene McCarthy, Robert Kennedy, and later George McGovern.

She also worked with Cesar Chavez in his efforts on behalf of the United Farm Workers.

Her politics took on a feminist bent after 1968 when she attended a meeting of a radical feminist group, the Redstockings. Three years later, along with Betty Friedan, Bella Abzug, and Shirley Chisholm, Steinem founded the National Women's Political Caucus. She also began investigating the viability of a new magazine for women, one that approached contemporary issues from a feminist perspective. The preview issue sold out, and within five years *Ms.* had a circulation of 500,000. As the magazine's editor, Steinem attracted national attention as a feminist leader and became an influential spokesperson for women's rights issues.

Throughout the late 1970s and 1980s, Steinem devoted much of her time to political organizations and became a noted spokesperson for the women's liberation movement. She was a founding member of the Coalition of Labor Union Women, Voters for Choice, and Women Against Pornography. Around 1987, *Ms.* magazine was sold to owners who, Steinem realized later, did not share Steinem's vision for the magazine. The magazine changed hands two more times before Steinem and a group of backers bought the magazine back in 1999. In December 2001, the Feminist Majority Foundation, a feminist research and action organization, purchased the magazine and provided it with much-needed financial stability.

James G. Lewis

Group formed the Abortion Counseling Service, widely known by its code name, Jane, after the name women seeking abortions used when calling the service. Jane provided women with safe, low-cost abortions while they were still illegal. Although the members of Jane initially provided referrals to medical personnel to provide illegal abortions, dissatisfaction with the treatment women received at the hands of these men eventually led the women themselves to learn to perform abortions. Between 1969 and 1973, when the U.S. Supreme Court detained women's legal access to abortion, Jane provided over 11,000 women with abortions that were safer and cheaper than those provided by the male-dominated illegal abortion industry.

THE WOMEN'S HEALTH MOVEMENT

Women's activism in abortion led to greater involvement in women's healthcare. The Boston Women's Health Collective emerged from a group of women who began meeting in the late 1960s after involvement in Students for a Democratic Society and the civil rights and antiwar movements. In the spring of 1969 at a women's liberation conference held in Boston, one of these women, Nancy Hawley, gave a workshop called "Control of Our Bodies." This workshop provided the women with the focus of their discussions for the next months. After sharing personal experiences with the medical establishment, the women turned to researching women's health issues. This research provided the foundation for *Our Bodies, Our Selves*, first published in 1969 by the New England Free Press. The first commercially published edition appeared in 1972; it is now in its seventh edition as *Our Bodies, Ourselves for the New Century* (1998).

Although members of the Boston Women's Health Collective sought to raise consciousness about women's health through their book, feminists in Los Angeles took a more hands-on approach. In late 1970, a group of women in Los Angeles began meeting at the Everywoman Bookstore to discuss health and abortion issues. Searching for a means for women to regain control of their bodies, one of the members, Carol Downer, inserted a speculum into her vagina and invited the other women present to observe her cervix. Thus, on April 7, 1971, the concept of "self-help" gynecology was developed. The original self-help group continued meeting at the Everywoman Bookstore while forming new groups for several more months to teach women this radical technique. Members of the self-help gynecology group also ran self-help clinics. Self-help gynecology gained such notoriety that in September 1971 national NOW invited the self-help group to present a demonstration at the national convention held in Los Angeles. Between 200 and 250 women participated in the demonstrations during the conference. In addition, members of the original Los Angeles group traveled to publicize self-help gynecology, which spread their innovative methods across the United States.

In October 1971, the self-help gynecology clinic began holding an open clinic for women every Saturday staffed by women who had gone through self-help training. In 1972, the group acquired its own building and officially initiated the Feminist Women's Health Center (FWHC). On September 20, 1972, members of the FWHC were charged with practicing medicine without a license. During the trial, the women were acquitted, which served to provide legal legitimization of self-help gynecology as an alternative form of healthcare. In January 1973, after the Supreme Court's legalization of abortion, the FWHC opened the first women-controlled legal abortion clinic.

Although many women of color were involved in efforts to legalize abortion and in the alternative women's health movement, women of color faced an additional challenge to their reproductive rights. Whereas some women struggled for the right to prevent and end pregnancy, women of color also were more likely to be denied their reproductive capabilities through involuntary sterilization. In 1973, two black sisters, aged 12 and 14, were declared mentally incompetent by their Alabama physician, who sterilized them using federal funds to pay for the procedures after their mother, who could not read or write, had "signed" her X on the consent forms. In *Madrigal vs. Quilligan* (1975), a group of ten Spanish-speaking Chicanas sued Los Angeles County Hospital for involuntary sterilization after they were given consent forms in English. Although the case was initially thrown out of court, the women eventually won their suit. As these cases gained notoriety, many other women of color came forward to share similar experiences.

As news of involuntary sterilization spread throughout the United States, organizations sprang up to address this issue. Committees to End Sterilization Abuse formed in New York and in Chicago, where membership drew on the Chicago Women's Liberation Union, Puerto Rico Solidarity Committee, and Mujeres Latinas. A similar group, the Committee for Abortion Rights and Against Sterilization Abuse, formed in Los Angeles and New York. These efforts resulted in changes to laws governing sterilization. New York was the first state, in 1975, to create sterilization consent guidelines. In 1979, the federal government standardized consent forms, required that they be made available in the patient's first language, and mandated that they include information about alternative contraceptives and statements regarding the irreversibility of sterilization. The federal government also instituted a thirty-day waiting period and prohibited hysterectomy for the purpose of sterilization.

The women's health movement gave rise to national organizations that now exist to address the health concerns of almost every community of women. For example, in the early 1970s, the Women's Union of the Young Lords Party organized health centers for women in Harlem. This work continues today as the Peoples Alternative Health Center and the First World Women of Color Healing Circle. The Older Women's League (OWL), founded in 1980, works to bring universal high-quality, affordable healthcare to women from birth to death. In addition, OWL has focused on women's role as informal healthcare providers and has advocated for acknowledgment and financial support for this role. In 1983, the Black Women's Health Project was founded by women in Washington, D.C. In 1985, a group of Native Americans living in South Dakota formed the Native American Community Board, which organized the Native American Women's Health Education Resource Center. This group has advocated for reproductive rights in addition to launching educational campaigns about AIDS, domestic violence, and prenatal nutrition. The Lesbian Health Fund, founded in 1992 as part of the Gay and Lesbian Medical Association, is the only organization dedicated to research on lesbian health. The National Asian Women's Health Organization, founded in 1993, works to end racial and ethnic health disparities, to educate Asian Americans about healthcare, and to ensure awareness and research about specific issues that Asian Americans face.

VIOLENCE AGAINST WOMEN

In addition to abortion and women's healthcare, feminists put the issue of rape on the national agenda. Prior to the women's movement, rape was a taboo subject. Newspapers routinely withheld the names of women who had been raped in order to "protect" them. A woman's past sexual history was admissible as evidence during rape trials. Husbands could not be charged with raping their wives because the law provided a marital exemption to most rape laws. The women's movement changed all of this. In 1976, Nebraska became the first state to outlaw marital rape. Today forty-nine states, all except Arizona, provide rape shield laws, which preclude the use of a rape victim's prior sexual history to undermine her credibility.

Because the police, hospitals, and society in general tended to blame women at least partially for rape, feminists sought to redefine ideas about rape as well as alter the treatment of victims. The first feminist action against rape occurred on January 24, 1971, when the New York Radical Feminists held the first "Speak Out on Rape," at which women who had been raped publicly recounted the experience. Personal testimony served to destigmatize rape and to help women see rape as a crime committed against women, and not as a crime caused by women dressing too provocatively, leading a man on, or being where they shouldn't have been. As a follow-up, in April 1971, the New York Radical Feminists sponsored a day-long conference about rape. Based on the experiences that women shared during that conference, women began to understand that boyfriends and husbands perpetrate rapes. This central revelation would have a profound influence on American society where women had been taught to fear the stranger lurking in dark shadows but not the boy next door. The most concrete outgrowth of increased awareness about rape were the hundreds of rape crisis intervention centers and hotlines created by women. In 1972, the first emergency rape crisis hotline opened in Washington, D.C., and by 1976 more than 400 independent rape crisis centers existed throughout the United States. In 1978, the National Coalition Against Sexual Assault was formed.

As the rape crisis movement evolved, women began targeting the institutions that legitimized rape. They focused on images of violence against women, particularly the media and pornography. In 1976, Julia

London founded the group Women against Violence against Women in Los Angeles. The group's first demonstration occurred as part of a media boycott organized by NOW against sexually violent images in the music industry. In 1978, the first national feminist conference on pornography was held in San Francisco. As part of this conference, women took to the streets organizing a large demonstration in the red-light district. This "Take Back the Night" march became the impetus for similar events that occur throughout the country to this day.

Like rape, domestic violence was considered a dirty little secret until the women's movement brought national attention to the issue. The first shelter for women victims of physical abuse is generally thought to be Chiswick Women's Aid in England, which opened in 1971. In 1972, women in St. Paul, Minnesota, formed the first battered women's hotline, and Haven House in Pasadena, California, became the first such shelter in the United States. The movement to establish hotlines and shelters for women victims of male violence spread quickly throughout the United States. In 1978, the National Coalition Against Domestic Violence formed, bringing shelters and other groups together to publicize the issue and to seek legal change in the treatment of battered women.

THE PROLIFERATION OF THE WOMEN'S MOVEMENT

In addition to revolutionizing institutions of American life such as government, education, and the family, throughout the 1970s, the women's movement politicized existing groups of women. Lesbians, women of color, and working women all formed feminist organizations during the 1970s, in the process both broadening and amplifying earlier women's movement activities.

Lesbian Feminism

Along with many other communities within the United States during the 1960s, gays and lesbians were inspired to organize for their own liberation. Although several groups, most notably Daughters of Bilitis and the Mattachine Society, existed in the 1950s, the 1970s saw the rise of a widespread, public gay liberation movement. Lesbian feminists became early, active participants in the women's movement. However, lesbians were not always welcome in women's movement organizations. The term *lavender menace* was first used in 1969 by members of NOW to refer to lesbians, whom they feared were discrediting the women's movement. In May 1970, a group of lesbian feminists, the Radicalesbians, disrupted the second Congress to Unite Women in New York. Wearing T-shirts that proclaimed themselves the "lavender menace," the women took over the conference to protest the discrimination against lesbians within the women's movement. The Radicalesbians did not continue for long as a group but made an important contribution to lesbian feminism by articulating the connections between lesbianism and feminism. In their essay "The Woman-Identified Woman" (1970), they redefined lesbianism from a sexual practice to a political position in which women give their allegiance primarily to women. This position of "political lesbian" was seen as a choice that feminists made in solidarity with other women. On December 17, 1970, Kate Millett, a noted feminist author who had been "outed" as a lesbian by *Time* magazine (May 1970), and a number of high-profile members of the women's movement held a press conference to address the issue of lesbianism.

The first lesbian feminist organization in the United States was founded in Seattle, Washington, in 1971. Like many similar groups across the country, women involved in the Seattle Gay Liberation Front broke away to form an independent group, initially called the Gay Women's Alliance. The alliance created a resource center that housed a library and an information hotline, offered support groups, and provided speakers on lesbian issues. The organization, which eventually changed its name to the Lesbian Resource Center, expanded over the years to include political activism, particularly in fighting antigay laws, offering job training through federally funded programs, and eventually occupying an independent building.

As lesbian feminists became more vocal within the women's movement, "gay/straight," as the two groups were called at the time, dialogues were one strategy used to address homophobia. These dialogues were based on the technique of C-R. On February 20, 1971, the Women's Center in Los Angeles held its first Sexual Dialogue, as it was then called. Approximately 135 to 150 women attended that first dialogue, which was so successful that another one was scheduled for April. Unlike chapters in some areas of the United States, the Los Angeles NOW chapter led the charge against homophobia within the organization. The Los Angeles chapter held a gay/straight dialogue after a local group, the Lesbian Feminists, accused them of persecuting lesbians. On May 16, 1971, the NOW Center for Women's Studies

hosted a gay/straight dialogue, the first such ever meeting held by a NOW chapter. Women responded so strongly that an additional third dialogue at the Women's Center was scheduled for May 22. At the National NOW conference held in Los Angeles over Labor Day weekend 1971, the Los Angeles NOW chapter resolution accepting lesbian rights as part of the feminist movement was adopted to the National NOW constitution. The resolution stated that lesbians suffered from a double oppression, that NOW recognized the validity of their lifestyle, and that therefore the oppression of lesbian women was a feminist concern.

In April 1973, the West Coast Lesbian Conference, the largest lesbian conference in the United States to that date, was held in Los Angeles. A total of 1,500 women attended to hear keynote speakers Robin Morgan and Kate Millet. As was to be expected at any gathering this large, many different factions were in attendance. Problems stemming from political differences and lesbian/straight relations disrupted the conferences from the beginning. Conflict arose when some Socialist Worker's Party (SWP) material was included in the registration packet. In addition, many of the more radical women reacted negatively to the idea of keynote speakers Kate Millet and Robin Morgan for two reasons. First, they disliked the use of the "star" system, which placed more value on certain women's ideas than others. Both Morgan and Millet had very successful books at the time, and the press labeled them "leaders" of the feminist movement. Second, they felt that since both Morgan and Millet claimed to be lesbians, although both were married to men, they should not be addressing a conference of lesbians. This conflict between political lesbians and "sexual" lesbians mirrored the conflict that occurred throughout women's movements groups. Conflict over definitions of sexual identity resulted in a schism as well. When a transsexual who had caused a major rift in the San Francisco chapter of the Daughters of Bilitis got on stage to perform a song, the conference went wild. Half the women said she should be able to perform, while the other half stated that because he was preoperative and had enjoyed male privilege his entire life, he should be kicked out. Therefore, the many differences in political and sexual views caused tension and splits at an event designed to unify lesbian women.

Some lesbian feminists, weary of fighting homophobia within the women's movement, began organizing separately from straight feminists. In 1970, The Furies Collective formed in Washington, D.C. Members of The Furies included some of the most influential lesbian feminist separatists, such as Joan Biren, Charlotte Bunch, Rita Mae Brown, and Helaine Harris. During their brief history, the Furies attempted to create a model of lesbian separatism. Although the conflict that plagued the group is well documented, the Furies was nonetheless an extremely influential group, in part because of its newspaper, which published virtually all of the "classic" articles about lesbian feminist separatism.

Homophobia within the women's movement and schisms within lesbian feminist communities threatened to divide the women's movement. Adrienne Rich's important article "Lesbianism and Compulsory Heterosexuality" (1986) voiced the sentiments that had helped to heal the various divides in the late 1970s. By positing the existence of a lesbian continuum, a spectrum of woman-identified behaviors that ranged from emotional relationships to sexual relationships, Rich opened up common ground for all women in the movement. In addition, by making an explicit connection between homophobia and the limitations that heterosexuality placed on women, Rich highlighted the ways that lesbians and straight women both suffered under this ideology.

Although lesbian feminist separatism became a less pressing issue as the 1970s progressed, the increased visibility of lesbians of color during the late 1970s and 1980s raised more issues for the women's movement as a whole. Writers such as Audre Lorde, Barbara Smith, and Cherríe Moraga, among others, challenged the racism of the women's movement, including lesbian feminist groups.

Women of Color

The history of women of color and the women's movement is extremely complex. Women's movement organizations founded by women of color do not look like primarily white women's organizations, as a result of which they have frequently been excluded from the historical record. Some historians, such as Rosalyn Baxandall and Sherna Gluck, have suggested that, in fact, groups of women of color that "predate" the "beginning" of the women's movement should be credited as the first women's movement organizations. However, many women of color did not claim the word "feminism," which they saw as belonging to white feminists. Many of the "rights" that white feminists wanted, such as access to abortion and work outside the home, were not the rights women of color wanted, in the case of abortion, or needed, in the case of working outside of the home. Indeed, the ideology

of the women's movement often conflicted with the cultural values of some women of color. Some women of color saw the women's movement as too separatist, and because they experienced both racial and sexual discrimination, in addition to other oppressions, they chose to continue to work with men of color. Many women of color found that the women's movement was dominated by white women who were unwilling to confront their own racism or the racism that pervades U.S. society. It is considered all-embracing—to include African Americans, Latinos, and other minority populations—but the term minority is considered pejorative. These same women often felt that organizations for people of color ignored their needs as women. It seemed that all too often "women" were seen as "white" and men were seen as "people of color," leaving women of color nowhere to call home. This fact was poignantly reflected in the title of an early essay collection by black women called *All the Women Are White, All the Men Are Black, But Some of Us Are Brave*.

Feminism among African-American women grew out of the involvement of both the black liberation movement and the women's movement itself. For example, women members of SNCC formed the Black Women's Liberation Committee in December 1968 to discuss the intersections of racism and sexism. These women soon formed an independent group, the Black Women's Alliance, and by 1970 they had expanded to include all women of color, calling themselves the Third World Women's Alliance. Although the women of SNCC found the answer in a women-only group, the issue of separatism from men proved difficult for women of color. For black women, organizing as women was sometimes difficult. Women who had been active in civil rights or Black Power groups sometimes faced harsh criticism from their male counterparts when they formed women's groups. Various arguments were used to dissuade black women from organizing as women, including: "black women are already liberated," "the problem is racism, not sexism, so organizing as women is apolitical," and "feminists hate men and are lesbians."

The National Black Feminist Organization (NBFO) was founded in 1973, bringing together many prominent black women who had been involved in various social movements. Approximately thirty women attended the first meeting in May 1973, held in the offices of New York NOW. The NBFO organized a press conference in New York in the following summer and received over 400 phone calls the next day and 200 attendees for a meeting a week later. The

AUDRE LORDE (1934–1992)

Audre Geraldine Lorde was born to Linda Gertrude Belmar and Frederic Byron Lorde, immigrants from Grenada, on February 18, 1934, in Harlem, New York, the youngest of three sisters. She began writing poetry at a very early age, and published her first love poem in *Seventeen* magazine while attending Hunter High School in New York City. She studied for a short while at the University of New Mexico (1954), and completed her undergraduate degree in Literature and Philosophy at Hunter College (now Hunter College of the City University of New York) in 1959. In 1961, she graduated from Columbia University with a master's degree in library science, worked as a librarian, and married Edwin Rollins, a lawyer, in 1962. They had two children and divorced in 1970.

The 1960s were a busy decade for the poet. Lorde had already published in black literary magazines and in a number of anthologies, and she had become active in the civil rights movement, the burgeoning second-wave women's movement, and antiwar efforts. In 1968, upon receiving a National Endowment for the Arts grant, she left her job at a New York library and accepted a post as poet-in-residence at Tougaloo College in Jackson, Mississippi. For six weeks, she taught and wrote in a locale rife with civil rights movement activity. It was here that she met Frances Clayton (who would become her life partner for many years), and published her first volume of poetry, *The First Cities*. Released by the Poets Press, a small publishing house, it received rave reviews, and critics described it as "innovative" and quietly "introspective."

Her second collection of poems, *Cables to Rage*, was written during her stay at Tougaloo and was published in 1970. That work touched on issues that would reemerge in poems and prose to come later: violence, voice, love, hope, relationships, and family. It also contained Lorde's first explicitly lesbian poem published, "Martha." The volume that quickly followed, *From a Land Where Other People Live* (1973), was nominated for a National Book Award for poetry in 1974. *The New York Head Shot and Museum* was published in 1974 and was characterized as her most radical and political work to date. *Coal* (1976) was a compilation of poetry from her first two collections along with new additions. It was a significant volume in that it was her first to be released by a major publisher, W.W. Norton, making Lorde's writing available to a broader audience.

Lorde was diagnosed with breast cancer in the late 1970s, and her writing both incorporated and reflected her changed reality. Her first nonfiction work, *The Cancer Journals* (1980), chronicled her battle with both the disease and the medical establishment. A three-part book gleaned from journal entries and essays, it detailed the discovery and removal of her first tumor, the progression of the disease, her decision to not wear a prosthesis, and—most important—the fundamental tenets of "survival": the need for positive role models and the importance of friendship and love. *The Cancer Journals* was awarded the Gay Caucus Book of the Year award from the American Library Association in 1981. Six years after her initial brush with cancer and a mastectomy, Lord was diagnosed with liver cancer. Her work again reflected that fact, and *A Burst of Light* was published in 1988.

Lorde was a self-described "black-lesbian feminist mother lover poet," and her work reflected the multiplicity of her identity as well as divergent—and often contradictory—perspectives. As a teacher, she educated students in English literature, writing, and poetry at John Jay College of Criminal Justice and her alma mater, Hunter College, where she later sat as the Thomas Hunter Chair of Literature. She was also New York's poet laureate from 1991 to 1992. As a noted feminist, she expressed the necessity of assembling different groups to work against domination in all of its forms, and articulated it in writing in *Sister Outsider: Essays and Speeches* (1984). That text would soon become part of the canon of Women's Studies, and the title of an essay in the collection, "The Master's Tools Will Never Dismantle the Master's House," rapidly came to be one of the most often quoted lines in the women's movement. As an activist, she co-founded (with Barbara Smith) Kitchen Table: Women of Color Press, sat on the editorial boards of *Chrysalis*, *Black Box*, and *Black Scholar*, and was an active supporter of writers' organizations and arts councils. She wove the intricacies of oppression and marginalization into all of her work, and challenged women to find common ground through their differences.

Lorde died on November 17, 1992, in St. Croix at the age of fifty-eight.

Candis Steenbergen

most significant outcome was the organization of a national conference for black feminists held the following November, attended by 400 to 500 women. Chapters opened in city after city. However, the membership had difficulty reaching consensus about the purpose of the organization, and so it closed in 1977.

In 1975, the Boston chapter of the NBFO split off to form the Combahee River Collective. Its statement of purpose signaled its more radical orientation as it keyed in to the interlocking systems of oppression, racism, sexism, and classism that black women faced. Its members included Barbara Smith, who in addition to producing some of the most influential writing by feminists of color, became involved in local politics: support for a black doctor who was arrested for performing a legal abortion, the defense of a black woman accused of murder, and labor issues within the black community. In addition to local political work, the Combahee River Collective worked to connect women of color. Between 1977 and 1979, they sponsored retreats to discuss the status of black women in the women's movement, to learn about participants' political projects, and to explore ways to politically organize black women.

For some African-American women, the term *feminism* was so closely allied with white women that they rejected the label entirely. Efforts to redefine feminism for black women occurred throughout the movement, although the best known is probably Alice Walker's. Walker offered the term *womanist* as an alternative to feminist. Womanist meant the opposite of "girlish," which is to say frivolous, irresponsible, and not serious. Walker further refined the definition by stating that womanist included women who loved other women, sexually and/or nonsexually, and women who appreciated women's culture, women's emotionality, and strength. Walker explicitly addressed the issue of separatism by claiming that womanist meant a commitment to the survival and wholeness of all people.

Many black feminists have made major theoretical contributions to the women's movement. Among the earliest and most influential was Angela Davis, who in 1971 offered an interpretation of slavery that put women at the center of black people's survival. The poet, essayist, and activist Audre Lorde advocated a feminism that acknowledged the importance of culture, the political uses of the erotic, and the necessity of addressing women's differences. Prior to her untimely death at the age of fifty-eight, Lorde had published fifteen books. Her life's work continues in the nonprofit organization the Audre Lorde Project. bell

hooks began writing her first book, *Ain't I a Woman: Black Women and Feminism* (1981), at the age of nineteen and has published nineteen subsequent works. Her lyrical, yet unwavering, insistence on the viability of a feminism that embraces all people has made her a central figure in feminist theory for over twenty years. Finally, the sociologist Patricia Hill Collins has explored black feminisms and their relationship to other feminist theories.

Latina Feminism

With a long history in community service organizations and labor movements, Latinas in the United States began organizing for their own liberation in the wake of student movements among Puerto Ricans, Cubans, and Chicanos. Like African-American women, these women often faced criticism from their male peers and found the issue of separatism from men a difficult one to resolve. Chicanas who became involved with women's groups often found themselves facing the epithet *malinchista*—a reference to the historical, now near mythical, figure La Malinche, the native woman who was given to Cortes during his conquest of Mexico and is viewed as a traitor to her people.

Just as Alice Walker offered an alternative feminism for black women, Ana Castillo coined the term *Xicanisma* to replace the phrase *Latina feminism*. Like Walker's recasting of feminism for black women, Castillo's alternative recognizes the importance of Latinas working with men to end discrimination. She, too, points to the interdependency of people as opposed to the individualism that often pervaded calls for women's rights.

In October 1970, approximately forty women involved in the women's workshop at the Mexican American National Issues Conference in Sacramento discussed the need for an organization specifically for Mexican-American women. The four specific resolutions made concerned the right of women to self-determination and control of their own bodies, the establishment of links with other women's groups, proportional representation of Mexican-American women on the State and Federal Commissions on the Status of Women, and finally, formation of the Comisión Femenil Mexicana (CFM) to organize Mexican-American women. CFM's statement of purpose includes four specific goals: to develop female leadership skills; to disseminate information regarding the work and achievements of Mexican/Chicana women; to plan programs that help, assist, and promote solutions to Mexican-American women and their families' problems; and to assure their inclusion in the larger women's movement by establishing relationships with other women's organizations and movements. The CFM's concerns did not revolve around improving solely the material position of Chicanas, but also their position within society as equal participants with men in expanding the roles available for Mexican Americans.

In 1972, CFM founded the Chicana Service Action Center, an employment and training program. In 1973, at a CFM conference of 800 women, a national organization was founded by adding Nacional to the name Comisión Femenil Mexicana. By 1985, the Comisión had organized twenty-three chapters across the nation. Members of CFM focused on education, child care, sex education, and family planning. They created two bilingual and bicultural child development centers called Centro de Niños for women in school or in job-training programs. Casa Victoria provided girls who had been involved in the juvenile justice system with counseling, family therapy, and educational and vocational training. CFM became involved in the movement to ratify the ERA and to end sterilization abuse.

Although the majority of Latinas lived on the West Coast, organizations did form in the East as well. In 1974, the Mexican-American Women's National Association (MANA) was founded in Washington, D.C., and soon had members in sixteen states. MANA's original intent was to provide a voice for Mexican-American women at the national, state, and local levels. In January 1994, members voted to remove the emphasis on Mexican-American women by changing the organization's official name to ANA, a national Latina organization, a move that reflected the growing diversity of its membership.

Latina feminists have produced some of the most important works on feminism and women of color. Gloria Anzaldua and Cherrie Moraga edited the influential *This Bridge Called My Back: Writings by Radical Women of Color* (1983). These essays, written by women from many different backgrounds, explored the connections among sexism, racism, homophobia, and class exploitation. While offering a profound critique of the women's movement as it currently existed, the volume spoke to the need for a feminism that women of color could embrace. Both Moraga and Anzaldua have published additional works individually that have explored Latina lesbian feminism and the role of culture in political liberation. Latina femi-

nist authors have proved so numerous that in 1982 they formed the group Mujeres Activas en Letras y Cambio Social (Women Active in Letters and Social Change) to support writers and scholars who address Latina and Native American women's issues.

Women in the United States of Asian descent have been involved in many social movements, particularly those that address the status of immigrants, labor, and housing. In addition, existing ethnic cultural, political, and economic organizations have provided Asian-American women with opportunities for involvement in women's issues. In the 1960s, Asian-American feminist groups started organizing. The Organization of Chinese American Women and the Organization of Pan Asian American Women were both located in Washington, D.C., but local groups also formed such as Asian American Women United, Vietnamese Women's Association, Filipino American Women Network, and Cambodian Women for Progress. Gradually, as immigration from South Asia increased, these women began organizing feminist groups as well. Manavi, founded in New Jersey in 1985, educates South Asian women about their rights and works to end violence against women. In Texas, the Committee on South Asian Women, founded in 1983, publishes a nationally circulated newsletter and organizes and participates in conferences.

Working Women and the Women's Movement

Women's efforts to improve working conditions are as old as the labor movement itself. During the 1970s, several prominent women, such as Dolores Huerta in the United Farm Workers, rose to national prominence. Strikes by women drew support from the women's movement as well as labor communities. For example, from 1972 to 1974, women workers at the Farrah Manufacturing Company fought for the right to unionize and gained better working conditions. Many women union leaders were also active in forming women's movement organizations like NOW and WEAL, and some women members of the New Left worked in labor organizing. However, because many of the central concerns of women's movement organizations seemed driven by middle-class women's agenda, during the mid-1970s working women formed their own women's organizations. In 1974, the Coalition for Labor Union Women (CLUW) was founded to organize women workers, make unions more responsive to women workers' needs, promote Affirmative Action in the workplace, put more women into union leadership positions, and create links between the women's movement and organized labor. CLUW's most significant achievement was its persistent focus on the needs of working women to balance the demands of family and work. After decades of research and lobbying, CLUW was instrumental in passage of the Family and Medical Leave Act (1993).

Although CLUW tried to make labor unions work for women, Nine to Five concentrated on helping women workers to see themselves as important members of society. In 1973, a group of clerical workers in Boston formed the organization to change workplace conditions for women. Through consciousness raising, public demonstrations, and other tactics drawn from the women's movement, Nine to Five sought greater recognition for the contributions made by working women, most of whom labored in clerical positions. In 1976, the National Association for Office Workers was formed, and in just four years it had over 10,000 members.

THE WOMEN'S MOVEMENT AND U.S. CULTURE

By the mid-1970s, no aspect of American society remained untouched by the women's movement. Music, literature and poetry, and art began to reflect feminism as women gave voice to their experience. Building on the alternative media that grew in the 1960s, women's movement periodicals brought news of feminism to every corner of America. The year 1968 saw the publication of the first women's movement periodicals—*Voice of the Women's Liberation Movement* (Chicago), *Notes from the First Year* (New York), *No More Fun and Games, A Journal of Female Liberation* (Boston), and *Lilith* (Seattle). Within a year, the women's movement periodicals would become too numerous to count. As feminist periodicals developed, new titles appeared that appealed to specific communities within the women's movement. The year 1971 alone saw the Third World Women's Alliance in New York publishing *Triple Jeopardy; Hijas de Cuantemoc* appearing out of Long Beach, California; Asian Women of University of California offering *Asian Women*; and the advent *of The Lesbian Tide* in Los Angeles. *off our backs,* founded in 1970, is the longest-surviving feminist newspaper in the United States. *Ms.,* a feminist magazine designed to compete with mainstream women's magazines, appeared in the winter of 1972. Gradually, the more informal women's movement periodicals were supplemented by feminist journals such as *Sojourner* (Boston, 1975), *Signs*

(Chicago, 1975), *Chrysalis* (Los Angeles, 1977), and *Heresies* (New York, 1977).

Feminist authors began exploring various women's experiences in their writings. Early women's movement activists also wrote fiction and poetry that often incorporated aspects of the women's movement. For example, Rita Mae Brown's *Rubyfruit Jungle* offered a lesbian coming of age story (1973), while Marge Piercy's *Woman on the Edge of Time* (1976) imagined a nonsexist, communitarian future. Maya Angelou's *I Know Why the Caged Bird Sings* (1970) became a *New York Times* best-selling paperback, while Toni Morrison's *The Bluest Eye* (1970) and many other subsequent novels that explored black women's lives resulted in a Nobel Prize for Literature for Morrison in 1993. Ntozake Shange's play *For Colored Girls Who Have Considered Suicide When the Rainbow Is Enuf* (1974) and Alice Walker's Pulitzer Prize–winning novel and, later, film *The Color Purple* (1982) brought black feminism to the cultural forefront of American society, often sparking national debates about the status of black women. In 1976, two works by Asian American feminists appeared: *The Woman Warrior* by Maxine Hong Kingston and Mitsuye Yamada's *Camp Notes and Other Poems. The Woman Warrior* provoked controversy among Asian Americans, who questioned Kingston's "authenticity" in portraying Chinese culture as patriarchal. Many readers were introduced to Native American women's writing through Leslie Marmon Silko's *Ceremony* (1977). The early 1980s saw Latina authors Cherrie Moraga's *Loving in the War Years* (1983) and Sandra Cisneros's *The House on Mango Street* (1983); Cisneros's work won the Before Columbus American Book Award; both works offered female coming-of-age stories.

The explosion of feminist literature, poetry, and nonfiction reflected in women's movement periodicals soon led to a need for feminist publishers. Although a few titles appeared under mainstream imprints, the vast majority of presses were unwilling to gamble on feminist texts. The Women's Press Collective and the Feminist Press were both founded in 1970. In the ensuing years, many new presses, including Diana Press (1972), Daughters, Inc. (1972), All of Us Press (1973), and Persephone Press (1976), appeared.

Music festivals for women were held across the country, including the Sacramento Women's Music Festival (1973), the First National Women's Music Festival in Champaign-Urbana, Illinois (1974), and the Boston Women's Music Festival (1974). The largest women's music festival, the Michigan Womyn's Music

Festival, started in 1976 and continues today. Olivia Records, a recording label that produced only women's works, was founded in 1973.

Goddess worship became another important aspect of women's culture in the 1970s. Many members of the women's movement found goddess worship appealing because it offered a relationship with nature and greater respect for women, as well as a female deity. Works such as Zsuzsanna Budapest's *The Holy Book of Women's Mysteries* (1975), Merlin Stone's *When God Was a Woman* (1976), and Starhawk's *The Spiral Dance* (1979) introduced women to Wiccan teachings and rituals, and covens formed across the United States. Some feminist wiccan practitioners, such as Budapest, do not include men or God in their worship practices.

One of the most visible symbols of the feminist transformation of culture was the Woman's Building, which opened in 1973 in Los Angeles, California. Conceived as a public center for women's culture, the Woman's Building housed a feminist art school, *Chrysalis, a journal of women's culture,* and women's art galleries, in addition to hosting women's cultural events and speakers until its closing in 1991.

"DEATH" OF THE WOMEN'S MOVEMENT

Assessing the women's movement is difficult because there is no yardstick to measure the success of a social movement that sought to transform society. Some achievements of the movement are easy to quantify. Women now earn, on average, seventy-six cents for every dollar a man makes. In the early twenty-first century, thirteen women were serving in the Senate and sixty women were in the House of Representatives. More women work outside the home than ever before. Men have started participating in household work and child care in ways that would have seemed unfathomable in the 1950s. However, changes in attitudes, beliefs, and behaviors are more difficult to "count," and it is in these areas that the women's movement exerted the greatest influence on U.S. society. Although most Americans today do not identify themselves as feminists, many people support the issues addressed by the women's movement, such as equal pay for equal work, reproductive rights, and more equal gender roles.

It is equally difficult to explain the decline in the women's movement. The election of Ronald Reagan to the presidency in 1980 signaled the "end" of the 1960s for many people and led to the fragmentation and decline of social movements in general. Some historians have speculated that the women's movement may have been a victim of its own success. Women's status in society seemed to change so quickly that a women's movement may have appeared unnecessary. Other historians have pointed to increasing conflict within the movement itself as responsible for its decline. All of these theories may in part explain "what happened to the women's movement." Although the women's movement of the 1990s certainly looked different from that of the 1970s and 1980s, feminist activism continued. Women struggled to defend the gains made during the previous decades and to answer the many issues raised as a result of their activism in the 1970s and 1980s. Fortunately, the 1990s saw the inception of the "third wave," which brought new perspectives and new women to feminism. Today a variety of organizations and a range of publications are bringing feminism to a new generation.

Michelle Moravec

BIBLIOGRAPHY

"American Women. The Report of the President's Commission on the Status of Women." In *Feminism in Our Time: The Essential Writings, World War II to the Present,* ed. Miriam Schneir, pp. 38–47. New York: Vintage Books, 1994.

Angelou, Maya. *I Know Why the Caged Bird Sings.* New York: Bantam, 1983.

Anzaldua, Gloria. *La Frontera/Borderlands.* San Francisco: Aunt Lute Books, 1987.

———, ed. *Making Face, Making Soul.* San Francisco: Aunt Lute Books, 1990.

Anzaldua, Gloria, and Cherrie Moraga, eds. *This Bridge Called My Back: Writings by Radical Women of Color.* 2d ed. New York: Kitchen Table, 1983.

Atkinson, Ti-Grace. *Amazon Odyssey.* New York: Link Books, 1974.

Baxandall, Rosalyn, and Linda Gordon, eds. *Dear Sisters: Dispatches from the Women's Liberation Movement.* New York: Basic Books, 2000.

Bevacqua, Maria. *Rape on the Public Agenda: Feminism and the Politics of Sexual Assault.* Chicago: Northeastern University Press, 2000.

Boston Women's Health Collective. *Our Bodies, Ourselves.* New York: Simon and Schuster, 1973.

Brown, Rita Mae. *A Plain Brown Rapper.* Oakland, CA: Diana, 1976.

———. *Rubyfruit Jungle.* 1973. Reprint, New York: Bantam Books, 1983.

Budapest, Zsuzsanna. *The Holy Book of Women's Mysteries.* Berkeley, CA: Wingbow, 1989.

Bulkin, Elly, Minnie Bruce Pratt, and Barbara Smith. *Yours in Struggle: Three Feminist Perspectives on Anti-Semitism and Racism.* Ithaca, NY: Firebrand Books, 1984.

Castillo, Ana. *Massacre of the Dreamers: Essays on Xicanisma.* New York: Plume Books, 1995.

Chafe, William. *The American Woman: Her Changing Social, Economic, and Political Roles, 1920–1970.* New York: Oxford University Press, 1974.

Cisneros, Sandra. *The House on Mango Street.* New York: Vintage Books, 1991.

Collins, Patricia Hill. *Black Feminist Thought: Knowledge, Consciousness, and the Politics of Empowerment.* 2d ed. New York: Routledge, 2000.

"Combahee River Collective Statement." In *Feminism in Our Time: The Essential Writings, World War II to the Present,* ed. Miriam Schneir, pp. 175–198. New York: Vintage Books, 1994.

Crow, Barbara. *Radical Feminism: A Documentary Reader.* New York: New York University Press, 2000.

Duplessis, Rachel Blau, and Ann Snitow, eds. *The Feminist Memoir Project: Voices from Women's Liberation.* New York: Three Rivers, 1998.

Echols, Alice. *Daring to Be Bad: Radical Feminism in America 1967–1975.* Minneapolis: University of Minnesota Press, 1989.

Evans, Sara. *Personal Politics: The Roots of Women's Liberation in the Civil Rights Movement and the New Left.* New York: Vintage Books, 1979.

Faderman, Lillian. *Odd Girls and Twilight Lovers: A History of Lesbian Life in Twentieth-Century America.* New York: Columbia University Press, 1991.

Firestone, Shulamith. *The Dialectic of Sex: The Case for Feminist Revolution.* New York: Morrow, 1970.

Friedan, Betty. *The Feminine Mystique.* New York: W.W. Norton, 1963.

Hayden, Casey, and Mary King "A Kind of Memo . . . to a Number of the Women in the Peace and Freedom Movements." In *Feminism in Our Time: The Essential Writings, World War II to the Present,* ed. Miriam Schneir, pp. 89–94. New York: Vintage Books, 1994.

hooks, bell. *Ain't I a Woman: Black Women and Feminism.* Cambridge, MA: South End, 1981.

Hull, Gloria T., et al., eds. *But Some of Us Are Brave: Black Women's Studies.* New York: Feminist, 1986.

Kaplan, Laura. *The Story of Jane: The Legendary Underground Feminist Abortion Service.* Chicago: University of Chicago Press, 1997.

Kingston, Maxine Hong. *The Woman Warrior: Memoir of a Girlhood Among Ghosts.* New York: Vintage Books, 1989.

Lorde, Audre. *Sister Outsider.* Trumansburg, NY: Crossing, 1984.

Mankiller, Wilma, et al., eds. *The Reader's Companion to U.S. Women's History.* Boston: Houghton Mifflin, 1998.

Millett, Kate. *Sexual Politics.* Garden City, NY: Doubleday, 1970.

Moraga, Cherrie. *Loving in the War Years.* 2d ed. Cambridge, MA: South End, 2000.

Morgan, Robin. *Going Too Far: The Personal Chronicle of a Feminist.* New York: Random House, 1977.

———. *Goodbye to all That.* 1970. Reprint, Pittsburgh, PA: Know, Inc., 1971.

———, ed. *Sisterhood Is Powerful: An Anthology of Writings from the Women's Liberation Movement.* New York: Vintage Books, 1970.

Morrison, Toni. *The Bluest Eye.* 1970. Reprint, New York: Penguin, 2000.

"National Black Feminist Organization Statement of Purpose." In *Feminism in Our Time: The Essential Writings, World War II to the Present,* ed. Miriam Schneir, pp. 171–174. New York: Vintage Books, 1994.

Piercy, Marge. "The Grand Coolie Damn." In *Sisterhood Is Powerful: An Anthology of Writings from the Women's Liberation Movement,* ed. Robin Morgan, pp. 473–492. New York: Vintage Books, 1970.

———. *Woman on the Edge of Time.* New York: Knopf, 1997.

Radicalesbians. "The Woman-Identified Woman," (1970). http://scriptorium.lib.duke.edu/wlm.

Rich, Adrienne. "Compulsory Heterosexuality and Lesbianism." In *Feminism in Our Time: The Essential Writings, World War II to the Present,* ed. Miriam Schneir, pp. 310–328. New York: Vintage Books, 1994.

Rosen, Ruth. *The World Split Open: How the Modern Women's Movement Changed America.* New York: Viking, 2000.

Schneir, Miriam, ed. *Feminism in Our Time: The Essential Writings, World War II to the Present.* New York: Vintage Books, 1994.

Shange, Ntozake. *For Colored Girls Who Have Considered Suicide When the Rainbow Is Enuf.* New York: Scribner Poetry, 1997.

Silko, Leslie Marmon. *Ceremony.* New York: Penguin, 1988.

Stone, Merlin. *When God Was a Woman.* 1976. Reprint, New York: Harcourt, 1978.

Spretnak, Charlene, ed. *The Politics of Women's Spirituality.* Garden City, NY: Anchor Books, 1982.

Starhawk. *The Spiral Dance.* 20th anniversary ed. San Francisco: Harpers, 1999.

Walker, Alice. *The Color Purple.* Pocket Books, 1996.

Whittier, Nancy. *Feminist Generations: The Persistence of the Radical Women's Movement.* Philadelphia: Temple University Press, 1995.

Yamada, Mitsuye. *Camp Notes and Other Poems.* New Brunswick, NJ: Rutgers University Press, 1998.

WOMEN'S STUDIES MOVEMENT

Women's Studies emerged in American higher education in the late 1960s as a result of the organized efforts of scholars who promoted teaching and research on women that challenged both the existing curriculum and traditional pedagogy. It is simultaneously a grassroots movement, led by specific people, particular campuses, and selected communities, *and* a national phenomenon, with organizations and events that fostered and helped link the local initiatives.

The story of the movement to create an academic space for the study of women and gender has at least three separate trajectories. The first involves the growth of educational opportunities for women and the increasing numbers of women holding positions of authority within American society. The second trajectory acknowledges events on hundreds of individual campuses as newly minted female scholars, many influenced by the women's liberation movement, began to research and teach. And the third trajectory concerns the national organizations and developments that enabled faculty and their students to build the discipline of women's studies. The relationships among these three trajectories are, and have been, dynamic. Read together, they tell the story of how ideas and people interacted to change American colleges and universities in the twentieth century.

THE INCREASING PRESENCE OF WOMEN ON CAMPUS

The number of women graduating from American colleges and universities steadily increased from the 1950s until the 1990s, when women became the majority of recipients of associate and bachelor's degrees as well as nearly half of those who earned master's and doctorate degrees. As the numbers of women earning advanced degrees grew, cultural norms about women's roles in society shifted, and larger numbers of women remained in the salaried workforce over the

course of their lives. Socioeconomic factors helped to fuel these changes. One of these factors was the demand in the post-Sputnik era of the late 1950s to increase the number of college students generally and the number of scientists in particular. National foundations, primarily the Woodrow Wilson National Fellowship Foundation, the Carnegie Foundation, and the Ford Foundation, promoted study by women and helped to fund their advanced degrees.

A second factor was the presence of women who were reentering the academy. In the 1960s, a group of women educators founded the National Coalition for Research on Women's Education and Development to encourage adult women to return to school to complete undergraduate degrees and to pursue higher ones. Led by figures such as Mary Bunting, then president of Radcliffe College, and Helen Astin, the author of *Some Action of Her Own: The Adult Woman and Higher Education* (1976), the coalition advocated collegiate policies that were more responsive to the empirical realities of women's lives.

A third factor leading to the growth of women's studies involved the legal system. Beginning with Title VII of the Civil Rights Act of 1964, which dealt with equal employment opportunities, federal legislation was passed and executive orders were issued to promote equal rights and opportunities for racial minorities and for women. The inclusion of women in this landmark piece of civil rights legislation was primarily the result of the work of U.S. congressional Representative Martha Griffiths (D-MI). Parallel policies were often enacted at the state and municipal levels as well. The Equal Opportunity Employment Commission, set up to handle the complaints that arose from the act, became a central source of redress for women to combat discrimination. Another piece of federal legislation, Title IX of the Education Act Amendments of 1972, addressed discrimination specifically in educational settings. Finally, Executive Order 11375, 1967, reinforced Affirmative Action by requiring contractors working for the federal government to make good faith efforts to meet the objectives of the law. These policies worked together on multiple levels to help women gain access to colleges and universities and to give them the legal tools with which to pursue broader rights and opportunities.

Bernice Sandler's career illustrates how all of these factors operated together. A graduate student at the University of Maryland, Sandler was instrumental in filing the complaint that led to the passage of Title IX. In the forty years since then, she has been writing and speaking on how to improve campus culture for women. The impact that her actions have had was highlighted in 1997 when she keynoted a conference held at The Citadel. This previously all-male military institution had been forced to admit women to its campus because of the legislation she had helped instigate. When the doors finally opened, the college's staff said, Sandler's work on campus culture had guided them in dealing with the changes. An early product of those changes was evident in another conference event: In addition to being the keynote speaker, Sandler was part of a panel that included The Citadel's first graduating female cadet. The importance of individuals, their ideas, and their actions in producing systemwide effects is dramatically shown in public events like this.

But legal remedies were not the only avenue of change that led to the growth of women's studies. Women's advocacy organizations emerged on campuses to help formulate policies, to provide support, and to give advice for and about women's issues. Some of these Women's Centers grew out of student organizations or campus commissions on women. Others were outgrowths of faculty and staff caucuses to promote women's affairs. Still others formed in cooperation with community groups.

The formation of these organizations on the local level was paralleled by the growth of national advocacy groups geared toward increasing the number of women on college campuses as well as the number of women in positions of authority there. The American Council on Education (ACE), for instance, created an Office of Women's Affairs in 1973, after an almost fifty-year hiatus in attention to women's issues. Headed by Emily Taylor, a well-known dean of women from the University of Kansas, the ACE office was dedicated to promoting women as college presidents—and was stunningly successful; their numbers increased fourfold in thirty years. Other national ed-

ucational associations also played a part: The American Association of University Women and the Association of American Colleges and Universities, along with many ad hoc groups, cooperated to articulate and advocate for women students, staff, and faculty through lobbying, conferences, scholarships, and publications.

The women who arrived on campus—whether as students, as staff, or as faculty—were quick to demand that the education they were receiving, the policies they were enforcing, and the research and teaching they were conducting be relevant to women. These demands led to the development of courses, essays, and books. Two early collections provided material to teach in these classes and documented the need for the kind of scholarly research that would become the discipline of women's studies over the next three decades. The first of these books, *Sisterhood Is Powerful: An Anthology of Writings from the Women's Liberation Movement* (1970), edited by Robin Morgan, was the first comprehensive collection of writings from the women's liberation movement that helped fuel political activities on campus. The second, *Woman in Sexist Society: Studies in Power and Powerlessness* (1971), edited by Vivian Gornik and Barbara Moran, was the first collection of interdisciplinary scholarly essays to investigate the cultural construction of women's lives.

BUILDING THE SCHOLARLY FOUNDATIONS OF AN INTERDISCIPLINARY FIELD

Marilyn Boxer begins her comprehensive history of the women's studies movement, *When Women Ask the Questions: Creating Women's Studies in America* (1998), with the observation that "Women's Studies in higher education grew out of advocacy for and inquiry about women, and the experiences of the women who collectively built a new academic field."

The women's liberation movement energized and directed many of the women who entered higher education in the late 1960s and early 1970s. Their political arena was the college campus. As the number of women increased, their relative lack of power and authority underscored their outsider status, whether as newcomers to previously all-male institutions or as minorities in historically coeducational institutions. The central insight of the women's liberation movement—that women were marginal, without substantial or sustained influence in the majority of America's institutions—was readily apparent in academic settings.

The changes these early feminist scholars sought were vast, morally grounded, and achieved largely through persuasion. From campus to campus, women went about organizing to achieve their goals. The story of the first women's studies program, at San Diego State University, offers one example. As Boxer relates the story, a group of twenty women—faculty, students, staff, and community—had formed a committee and lobbied the administration (successfully) for new courses on women for the fall term in 1969. *Newsweek*'s issue of October 26, 1969, called these new courses "one of the hottest new wrinkles in higher education," citing the large enrollment in Lois Kessler's class at San Diego State. That same year, her colleague Sheila Tobias collected syllabi for women's studies classes and published them as *Female Studies I*, the first of a series that became a founding women's studies classic. In the 1970–1971 academic year, Cornell University launched what appears to have been the second women's studies program in the nation.

Over the next three decades, the numbers of courses and programs grew exponentially. In public research universities, pressure often came from the graduate students who were pursuing research on women. In smaller private colleges, women's studies frequently began when faculty sought to teach a most comprehensive liberal arts curriculum. Foundation grants to further the transition to coeducation became the vehicle by which women's studies was introduced in many formerly all-male colleges. Private research universities were sometimes slower to launch full-scale women's studies programs, relying instead on the courses on women taught by junior women faculty within already-existing disciplines. Whatever the setting, students brought the women's liberation movement to campuses and advocated for the new scholarship.

The response of administrations to these pressures varied. In some cases, deans, provosts, and presidents responded readily to the call for inclusion of this new scholarship, prodded as they were by the growth of the research literature (see below). In most cases, a small and dedicated group of campus women had to lobby year after year for the resources to teach a course, for cooperation from other departments to offer courses that would build toward a women's studies certificate, a minor, or a major, and for the administrative infrastructure to organize collateral activities such as lectures and discussion groups. The setup and funding of women's studies units was thus a politically fraught activity. The subject matter was new, the advocates usually held marginal positions,

and what was being taught and researched directly challenged the status quo. Nonetheless, from some 200 programs of women's studies in the 1970s, the number has risen to over 700 in the last thirty years.

Although the origins and strategies of the women's studies movement were campus based, nationally the feminist scholars who led the women's studies movement clustered around common goals. *Feminist Scholarship: Kindling in the Groves of Academe*, edited by Ellen Dubois et. al. (1985), illustrates an early stage of goal articulation. Five authors, each an expert in her field, collaborated on this book project. First, they described how the scholars who were creating feminist scholarship and teaching in women's studies programs straddled a complex divide. Trained in and rewarded by departmental structures that reflected historic disciplinary mores, these scholars were reaching beyond their training in terms of subject matter, methodology, and pedagogy in order to investigate women's experiences, past and present. A thorough investigation required that they leave traditional disciplinary boundaries and become interdisciplinary; but to become thoroughly interdisciplinary carried risks for their professional development. Women's studies leaders adopted the strategy of naming the politics of this situation and demanding responsiveness from institutions.

Second, the authors described the emergent research in women's studies. They characterized it as documenting the existence and origins of women's oppression, ideologically and psychologically, and investigating the instances of women's agency. All feminist scholarship, whether historical or contemporary, whether in the social sciences or the humanities, whether highly theoretical or grounded in empirical observations, has revolved around these two poles of discrimination and liberation. Placing the study of women and gender systems into a matrix of other identity variables such as race, nationality, class, sexuality, age, and ability has brought more adherents—and complexities—to the field. Because this women's studies subject matter has such direct relevance to students' lives, teaching methods in the field had to evolve in order to accommodate sometimes intense personal reactions to the topics under discussion.

Positive student response increased the legitimacy and popularity of women's studies. Florence Howe, one of the early pioneers in women's studies, claimed in "Toward Women's Studies in the Eighties: Part l" (Fall 1979) that the field was the quintessential liberal arts subject because (1) it was interdisciplinary and unifying; (2) it taught skills in critical analysis; (3) it

CONSTITUTION OF THE NATIONAL WOMEN'S STUDIES ASSOCIATION
FOUNDING PREAMBLE (1977 [1982])

The National Women's Studies Association (NWSA) is an organization that supports and promotes feminist teaching, learning, research, and professional and community service at the pre-K through post-secondary levels and serves as a locus of information about the interdisciplinary field of Women's Studies for those outside the profession.

The National Women's Studies Association was formed in 1977 to further the social, political, and professional development of Women's Studies throughout the country and the world, at every educational level and in every educational setting. To this end, this organization is committed to being a forum conducive to dialogue and collective action among women dedicated to feminist education and change.

Women's Studies owes its existence to the movement for the liberation of women; the feminist movement exists because women are oppressed. Women's Studies, diverse as its components are, has at its best shared a vision of a world free from sexism and racism. Freedom from sexism by necessity must include a commitment to freedom from national chauvinism, class and ethnic bias, anti-Semitism, as directed against both Arabs and Jews; ageism; heterosexual bias—from all the ideologies and institutions that have consciously or unconsciously oppressed and exploited some for the advantage of others. The development of Women's Studies in the past decade, the remarkable proliferation of programs that necessitated this Association, is a history of creative struggle to evolve knowledge, theory, pedagogy, and organizational models appropriate to that vision.

Women's Studies is the educational strategy of a breakthrough in consciousness and knowledge. The uniqueness of Women's Studies has been and remains its refusal to accept sterile divisions between academy and community, between the growth of the mind and the health of the body, between intellect and passion, between the individual and society.

Women's Studies, then, is equipping women not only to enter society as whole, as productive human beings, but to transform the world to one that will be free of all oppression. This Constitution reaffirms that commitment. Ratified 1982.

The 1977 founding Preamble, with some changes in 1982, has introduced every NWSA Constitution. Although the constitution and the way it articulates NWSA's Mission have undergone revision, most recently in 1988, the historical Preamble marks the point of origin.

Source: National Women's Studies Association. http://www.nwsa.org/constitution.htm.

---

assumed a problem-solving stance; (4) it clarified the issues of value judgment in education; and (5) it promoted socially useful ends. Arguments like Howe's grounded the women's studies endeavor in established values and simultaneously claimed that women's studies took those values further than other fields. This strategy often proved persuasive to faculty colleagues, administrators, and parents, who were impressed with student enthusiasm despite their caution about the novelty of this field of study.

Women's studies scholars continue to do battle for their subject matter, their means of researching it, and their practices of conveying it to the next generation of scholars. This is not to say that the process of change has been negligible. It has been, for both supporters and detractors, enormous. Rather, it is to acknowledge the essentially conservative nature of American higher education and its practitioners.

Ellen Messer-Davidow's analysis in *Disciplining Feminism: From Social Activism to Academic Discourse* (2002) follows the women's studies movement further. She demonstrates how women's studies, begun in the women's liberation movement, initially defied institutional structures in making its claims for change. She goes on to show that its very success in being institutionalized into departments with tenure lines has altered its goals and reshaped its claims for change in the wider, conservative political climate of the early twenty-first century.

CREATING THE INSTITUTIONAL FRAMEWORK FOR THE PROFESSION

National networks consisting of organizations, scholarly journals and books, and faculty exchanges for speaking engagements and administrative reviews encouraged the women's studies movement on campuses throughout the United States. One of these networks, the National Women's Studies Association (NWSA), was formed in 1977. Its history highlights both the innovation to be found in women's studies and the controversies that surrounded it. Prior to its beginning, women's studies faculty had created re-

In 1975, scholar Catherine Stimpson helped found the pioneering feminist publication *Signs: Journal of Women in Culture and Society.* (Photo provided by Catherine Stimpson)

gional associations such as the Southeastern Women's Studies Association and the Great Lakes College Association's subgroup on women's studies. But unlike these and other professional associations, the NWSA has always included both scholars and activists. The agendas of these two groups of people often diverged, with scholars seeking to institutionalize women's studies on campuses and activists pushing for political agendas that addressed a wider range of women's needs. The organizational structure of NWSA reflects this dual focus of its constituency: membership (for individuals and organizations) and voting rights are channeled through both identity groups and professional positions. The organization's national meetings, which attract some 2,000 participants, have been sites for both networking across the academic-community divide and contesting control of the association. With

the development of the Ph.D. in Women's Studies on campuses in the late 1990s and early 2000s, the absence of a strictly professional academic association to set standards, provide scholarly conference venues, and advocate for the field remains a contentious issue.

A second scholarly association was founded in 1981, the National Council for Research on Women (NCRW). Originally, this association consisted only of research institutes, either campus based (like the Wellesley Center for Research on Women) or free-standing (such as the National Organization for Women's Legal Defense Fund), and it worked primarily in the policy arena. Over its twenty-year history, however, NCRW has expanded its mission in at least three ways. It has come to include a wider range of organizations devoted to development and application of research on women and girls (Girls, INC.). It has increased its membership to over 100, including women's studies programs that have research components. And it has issued publications (for instance, reports on women and science), developed policy circles of corporate women, and held annual conferences with a global focus. There is some overlap in membership between NWSA and NCRW, and occasionally the leaders have held discussions about the possibilities of closer coalition activity. However, given their differences in membership, goals, and strategies, these two primary organizations in the field of women's studies have remained distinct.

The women's studies movement created and was nurtured by scholarly journals, both interdisciplinary and discipline-based. The primary interdisciplinary journals have distinct origins. Conceptualized in 1969 and first published in 1973, *Feminist Studies* emerged from the work of scholars involved in the women's liberation movement. Some thirty years later, under the editorship of Claire Moses of the University of Maryland, it continues to follow a tradition of collective editorship for the publication of scholarly articles. *Frontiers* and *Signs: Journal of Women in Culture and Society* both began publishing in 1975. *Frontiers*, run independently by a collective of scholars and initially based at the University of Colorado, attempted to bridge the gap between academic and community women. *Signs* developed at the University of Chicago Press, where managing editor, Jean Sacks, sensing the evolution of the field of feminist scholarship, asked Catharine Stimpson of Barnard College to assemble an editorial board to launch the journal. African-American women scholars Patricia Bell-Scott, Beverly Guy-Sheftall, and Ruby Sales began publishing *Sage:*

bell hooks (1952–)

Born Gloria Jean Watkins in Hopkinsville, Kentucky, on September 25, 1952, bell hooks adopted the pseudonym both in honor of her great-grandmother and in an effort to re-create and reclaim her identity. As a poet and writer, the decision to shirk capitalization was meant to remove attention from herself as author and to shift it, instead, to the ideas within the text itself. To hooks, her ideas override her personal identity. She engaged in undergraduate work in English at Stanford University in the mid-1970s, where she earned her B.A. in 1973; received her master's degree from the University of Wisconsin in 1976, and continued her doctoral research at the University of California at Santa Cruz, where she earned her Ph.D. in 1983. Her dissertation examined the work of American author Toni Morrison. Since that time, she has held academic positions at Yale University (as Professor of English), Oberlin College (1988–1993, as Professor of English and Women's Studies), the City University of New York (1994–2001, as Distinguished Professor of English), and is currently a Brown Visiting Scholar in Feminist Studies at Southwestern University.

hooks began work on her first book, *Ain't I a Woman: Black Women and Feminism* (1981), during her undergraduate years, and it was named one of the "twenty most influential women's books of the last twenty years" by *Publishers Weekly* in 1992. Her second book, *Feminist Theory: From Margin to Center* (1984), followed shortly thereafter. These early works set the stage for what would become the overarching paradigms of her imminent work: a focus on black feminist theory, the "white supremacist capitalist patriarchy," and accessibility to readers of all walks of life. The speed with which her ideas reached print foreshadowed hooks's future as a prolific writer, poet, feminist, theorist, and cultural critic.

The numerous books and articles that followed, including, but not limited to, *Yearning: Race, Gender, and Cultural Politics* (1990), which won an American Book Award in 1991, *Teaching to Transgress: Education as the Practice of Freedom* (1994), and her most recent *Communion: The Female Search for Love* (2002), examined topics ranging from cultural criticism, pedagogy, and healing, as well as issues of sexuality, families, and communities—all with a feminist perspective and with particular emphasis paid to black politics and culture. Common to all of hooks's works has been a challenge to her readers to consider the linkages between race, class, gender, education, and popular media as fundamentally connected to the ways in which society has been and continues to be structured. In so doing, she asks her readers to address their own roles in perpetuating existing societal forms of oppression, privilege, and power. She particularly emphasizes the need to read all texts with a "critical eye."

Today, hooks continues to actively write; in addition to her multiple books, she has written children's stories, innumerable poems, memoirs, essays, and articles for publications such as *Essence, Z magazine, Artforum, Postmodern Culture,* and the *Black American Literature Forum.* Challenging and disrupting prevailing notions of feminism, the women's movement, antiracist movements, educational institutions, and popular culture, bell hooks will undoubtedly continue the push for dialogue on oppression and domination, and for real social change.

Candis Steenbergen

A Scholarly Journal on Black Women at the Women's Research and Resource Center at Spelman College in 1984. The NWSA launched its own scholarly publication, *The NWSA Journal,* in 1988. These journals inspired the work of many scholars, including bell hooks, whose myriad books, articles, and poems have explored the intersection of gender, race, sexuality, and culture.

By the 1980s, every professional field had begun to publish a journal devoted to research on women, gender, and feminism. Examples number nearly 100 and include *Differences: A Journal of Feminist Cultural Studies, Journal of Women's History, Psychology of Women Quarterly,* and *Sex Roles: A Journal of Research.* Simultaneously, community-based journals on women like *Conditions: A Magazine of Writing with an Emphasis on Writing by Lesbians* as well as popular magazines like *Ms.* produced additional material that fed the women's studies movement.

University presses as well as trade publishers like Beacon quickly recognized the developing market for women's studies and developed lists for feminist scholarship. Press catalogs, sections in bookstores, and online ordering houses all attest to the thousands of titles published annually. One monthly newspaper, *The Women's Review of Books,* is dedicated to the review of books on or of special interest to women, and the substantial book review sections of most academic journals also indicate the importance of these kinds of titles in contemporary scholarship.

Feminist activists and scholars have come together in classes, in publications, and in organizations for more than thirty years to promote the study of women, gender, and feminism—all in the face of countervailing pressures to remain within the established canon of texts and interpretations and inside the dominant organizational frameworks. That the movement has succeeded is due primarily to the persuasion (and persuasiveness) of its advocates, the merit of its arguments, and the success of its human and scholarly products.

Jean Fox O'Barr

BIBLIOGRAPHY

Astin, Helen. *Some Action of Her Own: Adult Women and Higher Education.* Lexington, MA: Lexington Books, 1976.

Boxer, Marilyn. *When Women Ask the Questions: Creating Women's Studies in America.* Baltimore, MD: Johns Hopkins University Press, 1998.

Dubois, Ellen, et al., eds. *Feminist Scholarship: Kindling in the Groves of Academe.* Urbana: University of Illinois Press, 1985.

Gornik, Vivian, and Barbara Moran, eds. *Woman in Sexist Society: Studies in Power and Powerlessness.* New York: Basic Books, 1971.

Howe, Florence, ed. *The Politics of Women's Studies: Testimony from 30 Founding Mothers.* New York: Feminist, 2000.

Howe, Florence. "Toward Women's Studies in the Eighties: Part 1," *Women's Studies Newsletter* 8:4 (Fall 1979): 2.

Messer-Davidow, Ellen. *Disciplining Feminism: From Social Activism to Academic Discourse.* Durham, NC: Duke University Press, 2002.

Morgan, Robin, ed. *Sisterhood Is Powerful: An Anthology of Writings from the Women's Liberation Movement.* New York: Random House, 1970.

Tobias, Sheila. *Female Studies I.* 1969. Mimeographed.

WOMEN'S LIBERATION MOVEMENT
1965–1975

The women's liberation movement refers to the development of a political self-consciousness among women beginning in the late 1960s. The movement was characterized by its critique of sexual discrimination as well as by its challenge to traditional gender roles and social attitudes that denied women opportunities in both the wider society and personal relationships with men. Arguing that sex was the primary source of their oppression, women's liberationists challenged the inequalities that prevailed in the family, as well as the sexism that existed in legal, economic, and social institutions, which were causes championed by "women's rights" activists.

HISTORICAL CONTEXT

Like all social movements, women's liberation did not emerge in a vacuum but was shaped by political, social, and economic developments. The modern civil rights movement that was propelled to the nation's center stage in the 1954 U.S. Supreme Court *Brown v. Board of Education* decision and in the 1955 Montgomery bus boycott signaled that previously marginalized groups were challenging their peripheral status. For women, the signs were less dramatic but no less significant.

Although the women's liberation movement highlighted the inequities in women's personal lives, the political and ideological groundwork that created a receptive environment for such challenges to society's views of women was laid by women who focused on women's institutional oppression. In 1963, John F. Kennedy's Presidential Commission on the Status of Women, made up of women from various organizational backgrounds, reported that women were discriminated against in almost every area of life, from career mobility to divorce laws. Indeed, the very existence of the commission symbolized how women in the postwar period were increasingly mobilizing around a whole host of issues, including gaining a greater voice in unions, religious groups, and political organization.

As the commission laid part of the foundation for the emergence of the women's liberation movement, the ideological base was prepared partially by Betty Friedan in her groundbreaking book, *The Feminine Mystique* (1963). She argued that women were oppressed by a pervasive ideology that glorified domesticity as women's ultimate fulfillment; this idea was promoted heavily in women's magazines and in popularized psychological literature. Contending that housewifery and motherhood stunted women, Friedan challenged women to find additional aspirations such as outside employment and higher education. Although Friedan's book provided an analysis of the circumstances many white middle-class women faced, the conditions she described had already begun to change. In fact, married women's employment had been steadily rising in the postwar era, suggesting that the feminine mystique was not embraced universally. Friedan's descriptions notwithstanding, women received mixed signals about their proper place in American society, which prepared the way for accepting an all-out assault on traditional views of women.

The passage of the 1964 Civil Rights Act further contributed to a political climate in which women could contest their exclusion and their oppression. This legislation included Title VII, which prohibited discrimination on the basis of race, religion, creed, national origin, and, significantly, sex. The Johnson administration's priority was eliminating racial discrimination and not sex discrimination, but the law established the Equal Employment Opportunity Commission (EEOC) to enforce the provisions of the act; the failure of the EEOC to address sexual discrimination seriously prompted predominantly professional women to form the National Organization for Women (NOW) in 1966.

Pioneering feminist Betty Friedan sits on a couch beside two of her influential works, *The Feminist Mystique* and *It Changed My Life: Writings on the Women's Movement.* (*The Schlesinger Library, Radcliffe Institute, Harvard University*)

Together, these developments set the stage for the emergence of the women's liberation movement toward the end of the 1960s.

ORIGINS

The most important influences in the creation of the women's liberation movement were the social movements that preceded and later coexisted alongside it, namely, the civil rights movement, the New Left, and the Vietnam antiwar movement. All of these movements put forth a critique of and demanded fundamental change for American society. Female and male activists condemned American society for failing to live up to its rhetoric of freedom and democracy. Although some activists hoped to reform the system through existing channels, others were more disillu-

sioned with a country they viewed as greedy, empty, and corrupt.

The civil rights movement served multiple functions for subsequent social movements—it was a training ground for future activists and a source of ideologies, tactics, and strategies. For future women's liberationists, the black movement was both a model for change and a microcosm of the problems that needed their attention. Motivated by a sense of justice, self-determination, and, for some, a calling to transform their country into a genuine democracy, black and white women participated in the struggle as sitters-in, freedom riders, picketers, and boycotters among a host of other roles. They soon realized, however, that their movement's rhetoric in support of democracy, freedom, and self-determination often fell short of the reality where women activists were concerned. The Student Nonviolent Coordinating Committee (SNCC), the organization at the forefront of introducing new tactics and ideologies in the movement, was particularly insensitive to its female members.

In response, several SNCC women wrote position papers in 1964 and 1965, drawing parallels between the treatment of blacks in society and the treatment of women in the civil rights movement. They charged that women often performed clerical jobs and were excluded from leadership positions—this in an organization that not only struggled for black equality, but promised equality to its own activists. Male SNCC activists replied that sexual discrimination was a minor issue and an unnecessary diversion from the more important issue of racial oppression. SNCC was vulnerable to attack precisely because it held itself up as the model for real democracy.

The New Left was similarly guilty of failing to live up to its promises of inclusion. Modeled after SNCC, Students for a Democratic Society (SDS) experimented with prefigurative politics, which is the principle that your organization and your processes should be models for the type of society you are trying to create. For SDS, that meant an egalitarian, democratic, and meaningful experience, dedicated to improving their own lives and the lives of others, including southern blacks and the inner-city poor. As some women of SNCC discovered, some SDS women felt marginalized by a group that imitated the broader society's gender stereotypes. This was manifested in women often being relegated to the most menial office tasks while the men of SDS were the spokespeople, the ideologues, and the leaders.

Initially, most women members of SNCC and SDS

believed that there was room in their groups to address the concerns they raised—it was now time to broaden the agendas to include women's oppression alongside that of African Americans, draft-age men, and the Vietnamese. When women tried to transform the movements in which they were initially active, they were usually met with resistance, prompting some women to form an independent women's movement.

Several events solidified this decision. One such event was the trend that was developing in the black and white movements in which only members of the oppressed group could participate in their own liberation. Hence, by 1966, the radical branch of the black movement rejected integrationism and embraced black nationalism. Similarly, beginning in 1967, the white male Left concentrated on undermining, through draft resistance, the source of their oppression, the Selective Service System. Women in the black movement, the male Left, and the Vietnam antiwar movement realized that they had been struggling for the liberation of others while being denied the legitimacy of their own oppression.

When women raised the issue of their secondary status in the movement, they were derided and humiliated. A case in point: when SDS women demanded that a statement on women's liberation be included in the organization's official paper, *New Left Notes*, SDS men finally relented. The statement, however, appeared next to a cartoon of a girl in a polka dot dress with visible matching underwear, holding a sign demanding women's rights. SDS men tolerated women's liberation at best, but at worst, they demeaned women, trivializing and infantilizing them and diminishing the importance of their demands. Further evidence of women's marginalization occurred at the 1967 National Conference for New Politics (NCNP). Activists from various struggles met to develop a more cohesive strategy on black rights, the Vietnam War, and other issues. After black delegates had petitioned successfully for greater representation on committees, white female activists attempted the same tactic. White male conference leaders, however, dismissed women's demands.

ORGANIZATIONS

Nineteen sixty-seven was a watershed year for women's liberation. The movement took several forms: Either women formed women's groups within larger organizations, the preferred method for politicos, who remained connected to, but independent from, the male-dominated movement; or women either broke from the male Left altogether or were never a part of it, characteristics of radical feminists. While radical feminists created a separate movement and did not cooperate with male activists, politicos pursued both women's liberation and other causes such as civil rights, and anticapitalist and antiwar work.

Small-scale women's liberation groups began proliferating through 1967. Involving many veterans of other social movements, groups such as New York Radical Women (NYRW) and Westside Group in Chicago were the first to form. Many of the earliest collectives lasted only a short time, only to dissolve and re-form with new members and new names. New York Radical Women, for example, dissolved in 1969, but New York Radical Feminists, which functioned until 1972, replaced it. These groups were primarily radical feminist in orientation while groups such as Bread and Roses in Boston, operating from 1969 until 1973, and D.C. Women's Liberation, operating from 1968 until 1971, were political.

The first formal and large-scale conference of women's liberationists occurred in Sandy Springs, Maryland, in 1968. The meeting included twenty-two women from women's liberation groups active across the country. Although the conference exposed much contention, particularly over the issues of race, class, and ideology, it also provided an opportunity for women radicals to meet independently from men at a more national level.

IDEOLOGIES AND TACTICS

An outstanding feature of the women's liberation movement was how its ideologies were tightly connected to its tactics; that is, the process of doing something was as important as what was being done. While some ideologies were inherited, others were created using small intimate groups, or consciousness-raising, which became a defining aspect of the movement.

Women's liberationists who were veterans of other causes inherited the commitment to radical change, to self-determination, and to other tenets of the movements in which they had participated. Indeed, they created their own independent movement because of the inability of men in the other struggles to apply those ideologies to women. Women's liberation, then, represented an ideological hybrid by combining the "old" ideas of previous social movements with "new" ideas stemming from the shortcomings of the old approaches and those that developed from methods pioneered by women's liberationists themselves.

INTELLECTUAL FOUNDATIONS

Despite women's liberationists' frustration with the male Left, many of them shared its anticapitalist, antiracist, and anti-imperialist position. Women's liberationists, however, saw the primary source of oppression as gender-based, while acknowledging that women were affected by other forms of oppression.

One of the early influential articles was "Toward a Female Liberation Movement" also known as the "Florida Paper," written by two Gainesville activists, Beverly Jones and Judith Brown, and published in 1971. The Florida Paper put women's oppression front and center and advocated for a separatist strategy in which women would be completely independent from men.

Shulamith Firestone became one of the movement's most visible intellectuals with the publication of her 1970 book, *The Dialectic of Sex: The Case for Feminist Revolution*. Warning against any cooperation with the Left, she urged women to put themselves first in an independent movement that sought to liberate women from patriarchy. She also considered the role that biology, sexuality, psychology, and cultural influences played in women's oppression. A member of the NYRW and other groups, Firestone honed her analyses in discussions with other women.

Women's liberation began as a diffuse movement of radical women connected by previously established contacts and by mail. The movement snowballed once women such as Jones and Brown wrote about their experiences in other movements and in society. Sue Munaker, for instance, a veteran of the draft resistance movement in Berkeley, wrote "A Call for Women's Liberation" in 1968, in which she articulated the marginalization women felt in a male-dominated movement. Her article was then distributed among women in other cities, prompting the creation of women's liberation groups there.

Such pieces literally spread the word, giving radical women the sense that their experiences were not isolated, but that they represented a general pattern of mistreatment and discontent. These early writers served as the foundation of communication for the emerging movement, linking thousands of women together. Lacking national organizations and leaders, this movement relied on such informal contacts and networks. This fact not only revealed that women were excluded from more formal avenues of communication, but also demonstrated the extent to which this movement was a decentralized grassroots movement.

The anthologies that resulted from the exchanges and communication were testament to women's growing politicization. While books such as Robin Morgan's 1970 *Sisterhood Is Powerful*, Kate Millet's 1970 *Sexual Politics*, and Anne Koedt, Ellen Levine, and Anita Rapone's 1973 *Radical Feminism* represented a broad spectrum of political views on women and by women, their very existence was in itself a political act. The publication of such anthologies challenged assumptions about women's ability to organize themselves and to develop skills and ideologies.

Once word spread via these books and articles, women around the country began talking to other women about their experiences at work, in their families, and in society. They soon began organizing informal meetings, or consciousness-raising groups, usually of about ten to twelve women. Women wanted to create an environment where women's oppression and liberation were accorded the same, if not more, seriousness than those of other groups. To do so, they pioneered in the development of new tactics that allowed women to voice their concerns openly, free from male derision. Consciousness-raising allowed women to speak on issues that they once believed were unimportant or too personal, such as housework, sexuality, marriage, family, and children. Discussions also covered workforce issues, gender stereotypes, and depictions of women in popular culture, among innumerable other topics. Women gained confidence as they spoke, many for the first time in any type of public way. As they did so, they realized that many other women shared their interests, fears, and concerns. This enabled some women to understand that what had previously been thought to be personal, or an isolated experience, was actually more widespread and had political dimensions. Women's oppression was found to have broader systematic causes and ramifications, requiring a grassroots search for solutions.

One such solution was to contest media images of women as sexual objects. In 1968, the media were beginning to cover the women's liberation movement. Americans outside the movement were first exposed to it with the 1968 Miss America pageant. Protesting the sexual objectification and commercial exploitation of women, a group of 100 women's liberationists organized a counter-pageant in Atlantic City, outside the official pageant venue. They crowned a live sheep Miss America, drawing parallels between how women and animals were judged. Participants also tossed objects representative of women's oppression such as *Playboy* magazine, *Ladies Home Journal,* and high-heeled shoes into a "Freedom Trash Can." For the first time, Americans saw one side, albeit a skewed view presented by the media, of a multifaceted movement that challenged society's fundamental assumptions about women.

INSTITUTIONS

Although some women's liberationists criticized the excessive use of consciousness-raising as overly individualistic, the issues raised in these sessions and in creative protests became the social, political, and economic goals of the movement. Because the movement was so decentralized and organized, quite literally, out of participants' living rooms, it encompassed a broad range of issues. Once women became politicized in consciousness-raising sessions, they often turned to more outward activism.

Because the women's liberation movement challenged society's sexism and its institutional manifestations, one of its goals became the establishment of alternative institutions. Women formed their own health collectives to counter the treatment they had received by male physicians; they created female-centered bookstores, theater groups, and radio programs.

Women inside the movement realized the benefits of female institutions. However, they wanted to reach women who would never read newsletters that were circulated in small groups. To address this issue, women established a more formal media outlet that women controlled to spread feminist writings. In 1972, *Ms.* magazine was born. The brainchild of Gloria Steinem, *Ms.* sought to introduce the ideas of the new feminist movement to a broader constituency. With a circulation in the hundreds of thousands, the magazine pioneered in covering contentious issues such as rape, domestic violence, child abuse, and abortion.

GOALS

From these female-focused institutions arose a feminist political challenge to women's social, legal, and political oppression. Abortion, in particular, became a feminist issue once women learned about how their own bodies functioned, prompting them to reassess their position regarding how decisions were made about medical treatment and how women were treated by the medical establishment. The 1970 publication of *Women and Their Bodies* (later *Our Bodies, Ourselves*) by a Boston feminist group contributed to

a growing awareness about women's health issues and to the politicization of these issues. Feminists began demanding more information about pregnancy, medication, and the birthing procedures, raising issues related to birth control, fertility, sexuality, and, finally, abortion. Although abortion laws had been liberalized in the 1960s, women wanted unrestricted access to abortion and wanted to remove the decision-making aspects of it from the medical establishment. Although falling short of feminist demands, the breakthrough on abortion came in the 1973 Supreme Court decision, *Roe v. Wade*, which declared that women's right to privacy included the right to terminate a pregnancy.

While both radical and liberal feminists made abortion a public issue, other issues related to women's bodies were raised. Previously private issues such as rape and domestic violence were now catapulted onto the national political agenda. Feminists succeeded in changing how rapes were investigated and prosecuted; for example, eliminating the required third-party corroboration for a rape victim's story inasmuch as most rapes were not witnessed by a third party. Women's groups also pressured various levels of governments to establish shelters for victims of domestic violence and to fund family violence prevention programs.

Feminists from both the liberal and radical branches were responsible for successfully raising public awareness about women's issues. As the radical branch became mired in factionalism, especially over the issues of race, class, and sexual orientation, many radicals found common cause with the liberals and cooperated on many issues, including abortion rights.

DIVISIONS

Once the euphoria of the early women's movement began to wane, differences among women that had been obscured resurfaced. By 1970, lesbians, black women, and working-class women began challenging the contention that women could speak in a single voice of "sisterhood." While some veteran women's liberationists reacted defensively, charging that such critiques were the actions of outside saboteurs who wished to derail the women's movement, it eventually became obvious that differences needed to be addressed.

Early women's liberationists had prided themselves on not re-creating the hierarchies of society and male-dominated movements, thereby allowing for all women in the movement to participate. Activists soon realized, however, that their unwillingness to appoint spokespeople and leaders meant that others would do that for them. The media often singled out individuals like Gloria Steinem, a pro-feminist journalist, as a leader, even though she had not been known in movement circles. The devotion to anti-elitism became a divisive force when almost anybody who could contribute something as an individual was demonized for trying to attract attention to herself at the expense of the movement. This was particularly true for feminist writers such as Shulamith Firestone, who was accused of trying to profit from the movement, despite her theoretical and intellectual contributions to feminism.

Anti-elitism coupled with lesbianism created insurmountable divisions in the radical feminist movement. At the movement's inception, lesbianism was not a pressing issue. As women built alternative institutions and arrangements, however, they came into closer contact with one another, and many became involved intimately with one another. Sexuality and the power dynamic in personal relations were central to women's liberationists' critique of gender roles. Contradictorily, many straight women's liberationists viewed lesbianism as a sexual issue and not a political one. While heterosexual feminists feared that "lesbian-baiting" might discredit the movement, lesbians took them to task for failing to recognize the political dimensions of sexuality and for failing to see their unique form of oppression. In fact, lesbian feminists argued that lesbianism was the natural progression of women's liberation as it freed women completely from patriarchy in personal relationships. As the "gay–straight split" continued, lesbianism emerged as the vanguard of radical feminism, whereby how one lived one's life became as important as one's political philosophy. By 1975, lesbians dominated the movement.

The focus on lesbianism set the stage for the emergence of cultural feminism. The movement's earlier experimentation on alternative women's institutions foreshadowed cultural feminism's separatism. Cultural feminists maintained that women were essentially different from men; they were more peaceful, democratic, and superior to men. This brand of feminism encouraged women to construct female institutions based on women's values and culture. These concepts appeared escapist to many radical feminists, who believed that cultural feminism encouraged women to withdraw from society rather than fight to change it. The contention over sexual orientation and the rise of cultural feminism prompted many radical feminists to merge into the more mainstream liberal branch of feminism. In so doing, liberal feminism adopted radical positions on many feminist issues such as abortion.

OUTCOMES

By 1975, the radical branch of the women's movement, originally self-labeled women's liberation, had realized many of its goals. Its dedication to political self-consciousness among women was infectious. As millions of women were politicized, they raised awareness of issues that were previously deemed private or unimportant but that had profound consequences for women. Women's health issues, abortion, rape, and domestic violence became national political issues, as did those associated with liberal feminism, including equal opportunity in education and employment. Furthermore, the movement challenged society's traditionally held views about the proper place of women. Its emphasis on eliminating gender stereotypes and the objectification of women forced many Americans to rethink their views about what it meant to be male and female.

As many women and men incorporated the ideas of the women's movement into their daily lives, other Americans rejected such concepts in favor of traditional views about the family and about women and men. Just as feminists were celebrating their victories on a whole host of fronts, opponents of those victories mobilized. As part of the New Right, antifeminists promoted an agenda that sought to reverse many of the gains made by feminists of all stripes. Rejecting the Equal Rights Amendment, abortion rights, and Affirmative Action, among other issues trumpeted by the women's movement, the New Right envisioned a return to conservative American values, rooted in traditional gender roles. This movement gained momentum through the 1970s, culminating in the election of Ronald Reagan in 1980.

Natalie Atkin

BIBLIOGRAPHY

Berkeley, Kathleen. *The Women's Liberation Movement in America.* Westport, CT: Greenwood Press, 1999.

Boston Women's Health Collective. *Our Bodies, Ourselves.* New York: Simon and Schuster, 1973.

DuPlessis, Rachel Blau, and Ann Snitow, eds. *The Feminist Memoir Project: Voices from Women's Liberation.* New York: Three Rivers, 1998.

Echols, Alice. *Daring to Be Bad: Radical Feminism in America.* Minneapolis: University of Minnesota Press, 1989.

Evans, Sara. *Personal Politics: The Roots of Women's Liberation in the Civil Rights Movement and the New Left*. New York: Vintage, 1980.

Friedan, Betty. *The Feminine Mystique*. New York: W.W. Norton & Company, 1963.

Jones, Beverly, and Judith Brown. "Toward a Female Liberation Movement." In *Voices from Women's Liberation*, ed. Leslie Tammer, 362–415. New York: Signet, 1971.

Koedt, Anne, Ellen Levine, and Anita Rapone. *Radical Feminism*. New York: Crown Publishing Group, 1973.

Millet, Kate. *Sexual Politics*. Garden City, NY: Doubleday, 1970.

Morgan, Robin, ed. *Sisterhood Is Powerful: An Anthology of Writings From the Women's Liberation Movement*. New York: Random House, 1970.

Munaker, Sue. "A Call for Women's Liberation." *The Resistance*, January 1968.

Rosen, Ruth. *The World Split Open: How the Women's Movement Changed America*. New York: Penguin, 2000.

WOMEN'S MOVEMENT 1990–PRESENT

Third Wave feminism has been carried forward by young women across America in the late twentieth and early twenty-first centuries. The women's movement, like all social movements, has mutated and transformed to meet contemporary concerns—not the least of which is to combat stereotypes about youths and feminism.

Third Wave is the current embodiment of the women's movement in the United States. Referring to waves, in the sense that there are substantial disconnects between generations of feminists, is somewhat misleading. However, the term *Third Wave* acknowledges that feminism has changed over the course of the past 150 years but still references this larger movement in American history.

Prior waves focused on specific political and legal agendas. The First Wave came at the turn of the twentieth century between the Seneca Falls Convention in 1848 and 1920 when suffragists gained the right for women to vote, and the Second Wave in the 1960s and 1970s when women were uniting to gain legal and political equality to men and to reform traditional sex roles. Both waves were marked by large, distinct activist movements. No large, distinctive activist mobilization of the Third Wave is occurring, even though a strong identity is emerging. Third Wave sets out new cultural territory for young women and critiques the work left to do from the Second Wave. Sharing an emphasis on the single status as young women and the occasional young man (those born around 1970), Third Wave constitutes a new generation of feminist politics.

The new generation of American feminists possesses a unique culture, political agenda, and set of challenges. Some of the issues include monitoring the increasing power that corporations have to set public policy agendas, sexual and reproductive freedom, the continued threat of harassment and violence against women, hate crimes based on sexual orientation and gender identity, and women's experience of multiple oppressions.

Third Wave fights misrepresentation of women in the media, works with and talks back to older generations of feminist activists, and recognizes that not much has changed in men's roles in the nearly three decades since the earlier women's movement. With a focus on sex and pleasure, popular culture, and the media, activism is more local, specific, and private. Third Wave challenges the common assumption that there are adhered-to doctrines of feminism that designate one to be a "card-carrying" member. Overall, Third Wave demonstrates that there are many ways to "do feminism" and be a feminist.

DIVERSITY

If one word were to sum up the goals of the Third Wave, it would be diversity. A central tenet of Third Wave feminism is to include women who have previously been excluded from social movements due to race, class, and sexual orientation prejudice. Because of their advantaged status in society, white middle-class (and typically married) women often dominated the activist efforts of First Wave and Second Wave; and, accordingly, race, class, and sexuality issues often fell to the side. Earlier feminists were criticized by women of color, lesbians, and working poor women for excluding issues that were specific to their needs.

Third Wave can be seen as a push against all forms of discrimination simultaneously—sexism, racism, classism, ageism, and homophobia. As a result, the diversity of feminists in the twenty-first century is being addressed and embraced. Third Wave feminists promote a vision of liberation in which there is a wide-ranging plurality rather than any single ideal or notion of a liberated woman. Liberation is seen as diversity in the options available for gender identity and sexual relations. As Third Wavers ac-

Ms. Magazine **founder Gloria Steinem (left) and National Asian Women's Health Organization leader Mary Chung (right) march in San Francisco on April 14, 1996, during a "Fight the Right" march sponsored by the National Organization for Women.** *(AP Wide World Photos)*

knowledge how they are different from each other, they join together with men to fight various systems of oppression.

MEN AND FEMINISM

One of the differences between Third Wave and Second Wave feminists is the role of men in their movements. This new wave of feminism does not fight men—but rather combats injustices based on gender. Men are not seen as the enemy or cause of all women's oppression. Still, Third Wavers demand that men's roles and attitudes change to meet women's gains.

Third Wavers also take a different approach to understanding what "women's issues" are today. Third Wavers acknowledge that feminism is about men and masculinity, too, for stereotypes about masculinity are seen as just as limiting and harmful as those about femininity.

And to be female is seen as a misnomer in terms

of being a feminist requirement since more and more Third Wavers are sympathetic men. Third Wave sees that the feminist movement needs men to participate in activist causes and to assist in social change. Sex segregation and opting out of society are no longer seen as part of a utopian vision or a valid (let alone practical) solution, such as the earlier attempts at all-women artist and community collectives of the 1970s. Thus, by including men and reaching out to many different types of women, Third Wave is much broader and larger than prior women's movements.

ORGANIZATIONS AND ACTIVISM

Third Wave feminists are the ideological descendants—and literally often the daughters—of the leaders of the 1960s and 1970s Second Wave. One of the most popular and widely recognized Third Wave organizations, the Third Wave Foundation, was founded in 1996 by Rebecca Walker, daughter of acclaimed writer Alice Walker. The New York–based Third Wave Foundation, a national not-for-profit organization, is devoted to cultivating young women's leadership and activism for women between the ages of fifteen and thirty. One of a handful of national activist organizations for young women, this philanthropic association contests inequalities that result from differences in age, race, sexual orientation, economic status, and level of education. Through grant making, Third Wave Foundation gives direct financial support to young women activists and the projects and groups they lead.

Third Wave activism takes a variety of forms. One increasingly popular event, typically held on college campuses, is the National Young Women's Day of Action (NYWDA). October 2002 marked the tenth annual National Young Women's Day of Action, a grassroots campaign organized by and for young women to raise awareness of reproductive rights that places reproductive and sexual freedom in the context of larger goals, such as racial and economic justice, accessible healthcare, an end to punitive immigration and welfare policies, freedom from violence for lesbian, gay, bisexual, and transgendered people, and greater sex education in public schools.

Third Wave organized the first National Young Women's Day of Action in 1992 to commemorate the death of Rosie Jiménez, a young college student who died because she could not afford a safe and legal abortion. She was the first woman known to have died as a result of the Hyde Amendment, a federal law that denies women federal Medicaid funding for

On January 30, 1998, Lisa Santer and Jack Ashcraft serve as abortion clinic escorts—volunteers who protect women seeking to end their pregnancies—in Birmingham, Alabama. A day earlier, anti-abortion protesters had bombed a clinic two blocks away, killing a nurse and police officer. *(AP Wide World Photos)*

abortions. Now, NYWDA provides student and community activists with the tools to raise awareness, develop coalitions, and educate and activate local communities. By teaching young activists how to write a press release, how to contact local media outlets, how to talk to reporters about feminist concerns, and how to create banners, stickers, and leaflets that generate public awareness, these activist days on college campuses every October are helping Third Wavers use savvy media techniques to get their messages across.

Third Wave Foundation and National Young Women's Day of Action are two examples of Third Wave activism, yet Third Wave lacks a unified political platform. Many young women's organizations have been established, yet there is no central membership group or activist planning committee. Third Wave, in fact, refuses a tight and tidy definition of feminist activism, claiming that the most important feminist issues are those most important to each feminist. Ironically, Third Wave feminists are resistant to being identified as a social movement.

HISTORY—GROWING UP FEMINIST, TALKING BACK

Third Wave women grew up in a world shaped by the Second Wave; feminism is a given, and the idea of gender equality is taken for granted. Typically coming of age in 1983, when Sally Ride became the first American woman to travel in space, many Third Wavers have taken Women's Studies or Gender Studies courses at college and have jobs in feminist not-for-profit organizations. Feminism is now old enough that those who were raised from within look back and talk back to those who blazed the trails before them.

Young women writers and activists who came of age in the 1980s, typically college-educated and racially and sexually diverse with an increasingly global focus on issues of concern to women, called for a Third Wave of feminism in the early 1990s. This meant making a conscious break from the attitudes and ideas of the Second Wave of the 1960s and 1970s. While carrying on the unfinished business of Second Wave leaders like Gloria Steinem and Betty Friedan, Third Wave addresses problems internal to the women's movement.

Third Wave questions the Second Wave assumption that patriarchal oppression was a universal experience for all women. Different types of women have historically experienced oppression in different ways. And Third Wavers disagree with each other, and all recognize that is okay. In agreeing to disagree, Third Wave recognizes that feminism was never monolithic and that it never will be. Projects and goals that are still in progress from thirty years ago have been burdened by the difficult task of coalition building with different types of women and the historical—and often legendary—disputes between feminists. Disagreements, say Third Wavers, are productive.

Young women have begun to speak up about feeling ignored, slighted, or patronized by older feminists. Third Wavers criticize Second Wavers for implicit ageism and a condescending "We know better than you" attitude. A paternalistic assumption to know what the "real" feminism is and what "real" women's issues are only furthers stereotypes and slows political gains, claim Third Wavers like Jennifer Baumgardner and Amy Richards. Their collection of Third Wave writings, *Manifesta: Young Women, Feminism, and the Future* (2000), argues for the continued relevance of feminism in young women's lives.

Baumgardner and Richards write about the complexities of coming of age with political ideals molded by Second Wave gains, but where differences and compromises have replaced what they see as the absolutes of the Second Wave. The Second Wave slogans such as "I am woman, hear me roar!" and "Sisterhood is powerful"—slogans put forward primarily by middle-class, white, and heterosexual women—have been reformulated to a notion of "girl power." Third Wave feminists have even changed the definition of "feminist" to be more inclusive since the emergence of gay and lesbian, transgender, and transsexual civil rights movements.

Third Wavers have incorporated the gains and lessons of the 1960s and 1970s into their own lives. Third Wavers grapple with how to combine some version of feminist politics with what Leslie Heywood and Jennifer Drake, the editors of *Third Wave Agenda: Being Feminist, Doing Feminism* (1997), call the "lived messiness" of real life: such as celebrating women's freedom to buy lingerie at high-end lingerie boutiques and devices at sex toy shops, and enjoy makeup and pornography, while also confronting eating disorders, antifeminist media images, and the stereotypical portrayals of women's sexuality by the fashion and cosmetic industries.

BODY IMAGE, FEMININITY, AND SEXUALITY

Fighting unrealistic standards of beauty set by the mass media is central to Third Wave. Third Wavers are fed up with the pressure to look perfect and wear a size six. The first two waves of feminism focused on clearly defined political and economic gains in relation to men's status, such as to vote, own property, divorce, and inherit money, at the turn of the twentieth century, and then, for reproductive rights, equal pay for equal work, and freedom from sexual harassment and rape—struggles that still continue since Second Wave. Now, Third Wave has extended the fights in the political and economic arenas to the cultural one.

Second Wave faced the difficult task of arguing that women are not naturally feminine or born feminine but are socialized to be "ladylike." Now, Third Wave recuperates and values feminine traits while also contending with new forms of oppressive and objectifying femininity. Third Wave is very concerned about the increase in cosmetic surgery among women—about breast implants, facial reconstruction, and liposuction in particular—that is perpetuating racist, classist, weight-obsessed, sexually objectifying standards of femininity. So, while Third Wave monitors the icons of femininity in popular culture like su-

permodels and the ascendancy of trendy quick-fixes to women's aging like Botox treatments—those that may have drastic effects on girls' body image and self-esteem—at the same time Third Wave celebrates each woman's choice to apply makeup, bare her belly in midriffs, or select plastic surgery.

And because Third Wavers are just as likely to be both pro-sex and pro-porn, they may carry trendy coin purses that contain the latest lipsticks. Often, this question of "to wear make-up" or "not to wear make-up" is trivialized as if compacts and skin care were Third Wave cause celebres. While lipstick, according to Third Wave, is not seen as a feminist issue, the ability to freely choose to wear it for one's own pleasure is. Ultimately, Third Wave advocates the need to be comfortable and happy with one's appearance and to affirm that every woman has the right to wear what she wants without an assumption of behavior or personality.

GROWN-UPS AND GIRLIE CULTURE

At the same time Third Wave says "bye-bye" to the beauty standards set by Mattel's Barbie doll, they are embracing once outrageous epithets. Even though Second Wavers fought against calling women "girls," Third Wavers willingly use this once-nasty word to name themselves for fun.

Grrrl. It is a word that describes a no-nonsense young woman who, with a smirk and sense of pride, can tackle all that comes her way. Kathleen Hanna, lead singer of the punk band Bikini Kill, coined the term in the mid-1990s. It is a Third Wave reclamation of the world "girl," which is intended to recall the confident and curious, and possibly precocious, preteens that women once were before they understood the message that "proper" ladies don't break rules, investigate to go it alone, or get into trouble. Third Wave websites such as cybergrrl.com relish the term and encourage all to use it. Now, "Girl Power" refers to an expression of brazen individuality. Hype about "girl power"—that strength employed by such cultural icons as the Spice Girls, Buffy the Vampire Slayer, and the Power Puff Girls—continues to make girlie culture trendy.

Similarly, some women have reclaimed the word "bitch" to describe themselves defiantly. For example, Elizabeth Wurtzel published *Bitch: In Praise of Difficult Women* in 1998 to talk about her riot-grrrl rage, and *Bitch: Feminist Response to Popular Culture*, a magazine based out of San Francisco by Lisa Miya-Jervis and Andi Zeisler, continues to grow in national circulation.

Third Wavers take pleasure in evoking playful, flirtatious, enthusiastic femininity for personal expression and political purposes. In addition to recuperating terms typically used to put women down, Third Wave sees "girlie culture" as a style of femininity that connotes maturity and rebellion while calling to mind all-pink bedrooms with frilly curtains. Flavored lip gloss and sparkling bracelets are girlie. In other words, girliness mimics the traditional markers of American female adolescence. This style became increasingly popular in the 1990s among Third Wavers who felt alienated by the media image of feminism.

Over the years, the term *feminist* has developed a very negative meaning; it has become a dirty word. Indeed, Third Wave refers to it as the new "f-word." Some assumptions that are synonymous (even though many are erroneous) with being a feminist include man hating, lesbianism, bra burning, and not being very feminine. As a result, young women may fear being labeled feminist because of these negative implications. One Third Wave goal is to eliminate the swear-word stigma associated with being a feminist. And they are making feminism all the rage with their own savvy backtalk and media messages by using the childlike sweetness of girlie culture to combat the stereotype that feminists are hairy militants who can't put an outfit together.

FIGHTING BACKLASH

Despite three decades of feminist social movement, American mainstream popular culture is still very misinformed about what feminism is and who feminists are. And Third Wavers monitor mainstream media constantly for erroneous portrayals.

In 1991, Susan Faludi's *Backlash: The Undeclared War Against American Women* documented the ridicule and opposition women faced in the media in the 1980s at the height of conservative national politics. Faludi showed how TV, newspapers, advertisements, movies, and fashion trends perpetuate stereotypes about women that ultimately diminish the advances made toward gender equality. Faludi argued that the same media messages also convince women that they had already won all the rights they needed and feminism was stodgy, passé, and terminally unhip.

Backlash furthers many feminist misnomers, according to Third Wave. "Is Feminism Dead?" was the query of a *Time* magazine cover story in June 1998. The cover counterpoised a photo of the TV character Ally McBeal against pictures of Susan B. Anthony, Betty Friedan, and Gloria Steinem. As if a fictional character could somehow represent all young American women, Third Wave began a large-scale critique of many more similar images: a TV sitcom vision of apathetic and selfish thirtysomethings that only want to be sexy, sassy, and successful.

Third Wavers disparage these sitcoms and paperbacks-turned-movies such as *Bridget Jones's Diary* (which hit bookstores in 1998 and theaters in 2001) because they rely on seemingly strong young women professionals as main characters, but these characters are ultimately self-absorbed and obsessed with the eternal hunt for a man and a sex life. These media stereotypes, Third Wavers argue, also pretend that work and love—or career and family—are still mutually exclusive for modern women.

Another contentious example of backlash against young women's efforts, argues Third Wave, is simply naming the current era "post-feminist," which implies that women are in a utopia of equality where feminism isn't necessary. Defining the millennium as post-feminist encourages young women to remain unconcerned with feminism if they haven't felt personally disadvantaged or discounted, warns Third Wave. As a result, many young women will agree with feminist issues—and expect equality in employment, healthcare, and access to public institutions, and feel free to run for political office or to express themselves sexually and artistically—but do not identify with the feminist label. This is referred to as the "I'm not a feminist, but" problem: or the refusal of many young women to identify with feminism.

Third Wave feminism proclaims that the movement is not dead, Americans are not in a post-feminist utopia, and women are not satisfied. Ultimately, Third Wavers lament the general taken-for-grantedness of young women who are apathetic about securing greater rights and freedoms for women. Third Wavers constantly work to attack this lack of feminist self-identification while reaching out to more young women who agree with their issues without identifying these issues as "feminist."

Groups such as The Guerrilla Girls, women artists anonymously attempting since 1985 to improve the general outlook on feminism through parodies, humor, printed projects, and sometimes defacing mainstream media, fight backlash and expose sexism and racism in the art world and the culture at large. In order to draw attention away from their individual personalities so that onlookers cannot define them only as women or as "feminists," they wear gorilla masks during their performances and appearances.

Media backlash has galvanized Third Wave to attack misrepresentations of feminists and young women in the mainstream media. Since the social and political climate is different from three decades ago, Third Wave uses different strategies. They are taking the media into their own hands and are creating their own.

A Media of One's Own

New York– and San Francisco–based and popular culture–oriented, the largest membership base of Third Wave is media-wielding thirtysomethings—many who work in the media as magazine writers and online journalists. Typically attending college during the televised Clarence Thomas–Anita Hill sexual harassment hearings in 1991 and later contributing strong opinions to the media hype around Monica Lewinsky and President Bill Clinton in the late 1990s, Third Wavers have set out to make media of their own.

Third Wave has focused attacks on popular culture to effect social change. Confronting mass media as very visible, big business, and patriarchal, Third Wavers are reformulating political protest. Political expression often takes the form of a "zine," a website, punk music, or all-women music festivals, independently produced documentary videos, or a performance art piece. Third Wavers create and distribute subversive feminist messages in order to counteract images deemed insulting or derogatory.

In homespun popular culture, Third Wavers work to ensure that the complexity of women's experiences is represented and that young women everywhere are aware of their rights. The Guerrilla Girls use witty and sarcastic graphics to mock inequalities in the professional art and media industries. Musician activists like Tori Amos and Ani Difranco combine reproductive rights and antiviolence campaigns with their song lyrics. Magazines like *Bitch* and *BUST* (billed by New York City's Lower East Side creators Debbie Stoller and Marcelle Karp as "a magazine for women with something to get off their chests") are widely distributed outlets for young women's anger and promote a healthier self-image for women. On a smaller scale, zines are edgy, grassroots magazines. Distributed in print or online versions, zines share conversations between women and girls of all different races, ethnicities, nationalities, sexualities, and lifestyles, hash out disagreements between feminists, and discuss current controversies in women's and girls' lives.

While broadening the issues and definitions of feminism, Third Wave makes feminist issues and ideas more accessible to the public and to more women. Crafting popular cultural messages and disseminating them over listservs extends the political activism from the 1960s into today's era of high-speed global telecommunications and the Internet. Although feminism could not continue to be popularized without addressing whatever popular culture controversies emerge around women and gender, that is not to say that Third Wave is successful as a social movement.

A Movement?

Third Wave has accomplished a collective character based on different individual attitudes and styles. The movement is diffuse. It cannot be criticized as disorganized (a common criticism of social movements) because Third Wave hasn't necessarily attempted to organize or represent those who agree with them on feminist issues. Still, Third Wave may be too diverse for its own good. Third Wave insists that it exists, yet it seems to be lots of young women and no one. Third Wave incorporates all young women's concerns as feminist issues while refusing a singular definition of feminism itself.

Despite the difficulty of overcoming mainstream media stereotypes about youths and feminism, young women who might otherwise get behind Third Wave issues have no large activist body to join. Without membership drives to large national organizations, Third Wave is not recognizable as collective action. Third Wave does not look like the Second or First Waves because it does not have a unifying political agenda. There is no unilateral rally around changes in legislation, public policy, or social customs. And Third Wave has shunned suggesting how to specifically bring about social and political change. Their comprehensive approach to gender equality looks fragmented, impossibly broad, and sometimes contradictory.

Feminism for Third Wavers seems to be more about image than social movement. Third Wave seems to be more of an academic rather than an activist construct, a cultural rather than a political identity. Certainly, there should be more to a social movement than simply watching TV or reading magazines from a particular perspective. It remains to be evidenced that Third Wave actually initiates changes that make society a better place for women to live and grow up in.

Sarah L. Rasmusson

BIBLIOGRAPHY

Baumgardner, Jennifer, and Amy Richards. *Manifesta: Young Women, Feminism, and the Future.* New York: Farrar, Straus & Giroux, 2000.

Faludi, Susan. *Backlash: The Undeclared War Against American Women.* New York: Anchor Books, 1991.

Findlen, Barbara, ed. *Listen Up: Voices from the Next Generation.* 2d ed. Seattle, WA: Seal Pr Feminist, 2001.

Heywood, Leslie, and Jennifer Drake, eds. *Third Wave Agenda: Being Feminist, Doing Feminism.* Minneapolis: University of Minnesota Press, 1997.

Karp, Marcelle, and Debbie Stoller. *The Bust Guide to the New Girl Order.* New York: Penguin USA, 1999.

Walker, Rebecca. "Becoming the Third Wave." In *WOMEN: Images and Realities, A Multicultural Anthology,* 2d ed., ed. Amy Kesselman, Lily D. McNair, and Nancy Schniedewind, 532–533. Mountain View, CA: Mayfield, 1999.

Walker, Rebecca, ed. *To Be Real: Telling the Truth and Changing the Face of Feminism.* New York: Anchor Books, 1995.

FEMINIST/LESBIAN SEPARATISM MOVEMENT

The use of the term *separatism* within the second-wave radical feminist movement is today widely misunderstood. Even many scholars believe that it referred only to lesbian separatism, which was actually a rather late development in an ongoing process of self-definition that began in the earliest days of the movement's deliberate separation from the New Left. Within radical feminism, separatism was understood in at least three senses: to refer to (1) the creation and maintenance of an autonomous women's liberation movement "outside" the New Left; (2) "feminist separatism," created by women who defined themselves mostly (at least at first) as heterosexual, as what was sometimes seen as a "strike against men"; and (3) lesbian separatism, in which lesbian feminists sought to build a movement separate from both men and heterosexual women.

CREATION OF AN AUTONOMOUS WOMEN'S MOVEMENT

Second-wave radical feminism was born in the women's caucuses and discussion groups that radical women formed, starting in the mid-1960s within the "projects" and organizations of the anti-Vietnam War and the civil rights movements, often referred to collectively as "the movement." Some of the dissatisfaction that led up to the formation of these groups was evident as early as 1964, when Ruby Doris Smith Robinson, one of the black women founders of the Student Nonviolent Coordinating Committee (SNCC), wrote a paper analyzing the position of women in the organization. Mary King, a white woman who joined the Atlanta staff of SNCC in 1963, along with Casey Hayden, another white SNCC staffer, wrote a similar position paper for SNCC's 1964 meeting in Waveland, Mississippi, on the future of the organization, in which King sought to raise the question of how her growing awareness of herself "as a woman might af-fect the structure and program of SNCC," given the utter absence of any attention to women's rights within the civil rights movement. King and Hayden's indictment of SNCC's unexamined male supremacy, which they argued was as pervasive and damaging as white supremacy, was met at Waveland with withering criticism. Nevertheless, a year later, King and Hayden coauthored a second version of their statement on women in SNCC, which they mailed to forty fellow women activists and which was subsequently published in the pacifist periodical, *Liberation* magazine. In 1966, after years of escalating tension over women's roles in the organization, Students for a Democratic Society (SDS) women who demanded a plank on women's liberation in the SDS platform for the year were answered with a hail of rotten tomatoes and ejection from the group's convention.

In November 1967, a radical faction of the thousands of women who marched on Washington as the Jeanette Rankin Brigade to protest the Vietnam War, alienated by what they saw as the "Establishment" nature of the march, split off to talk about creating an autonomous women's movement. New York's first Women's Liberation meeting was held the same November. In January 1968, New York Radical Women—whose members included Shulamith Firestone, Kathie Amatniek, Anne Koedt, and Carol Hanisch—was accused of trying to divide the antiwar movement by marching with their own float, a papier-mâché coffin bedecked with banners reading, "The Death of Traditional Womanhood" and "Don't Cry! Resist!" in an anti-Vietnam War rally called by Women Strike for Peace. Throughout the turmoil that was 1968, small Women's Liberation groups proliferated around the country, sparked by women's dissatisfaction with their second-class status in the movement. The participants in these groups—as cogently analyzed by Marge Piercy in "The Grand Coolie Damn" (1969)—came to see that the movement, in which women did so much of the actual work itself oppressed and exploited them *as women*. Although many of them had built lives and identities around their work in the antiwar and civil rights movement, giving to it significant labor, years of time, and huge quantities of emotional energy, they were thoroughly fed up with the hostile reception that the idea of focusing any part of movement action and organizing on the liberation of women was receiving from both men and "politico" women. The term *politico*, as Alice Echols explains in *Daring to Be Bad: Radical Feminism in America 1967–1975* (1989), was used to refer to those movement women "who attributed women's oppression to capitalism, whose primary loyalty was to the left, and who longed for the imprimatur of the 'invisible audience' of male leftists."

The new radical feminists found themselves no longer able to support the dominant leftist position: that male supremacy is a manifestation of capitalism, sure to whither away once the liberation of the proletariat is won. This position required the subordination of the struggle for women's liberation "after the revolution" against capitalism was victorious. Instead, many of these feminists began to develop an analysis of patriarchy as a system of male dominance, existing in forms always historically specific and inflected by reigning in the economic system, but in important ways separate from—and far older than—capitalism.

It was in the early radical feminists' split from the antiwar and civil rights movement to form an autonomous Women's Liberation Movement (WLM), and its immediate aftermath, that separatism received its first meaning, referring to the actual split through which the WLM was formed. For many radical women, this separatism was a strategy aimed specifically at the movement to make a point "within the people." Radical feminists wanted to remain "on the left" while creating structures and institutions designed to allow women to focus on women's concerns without the continual imposition of male-defined theories and perspectives. They were tired of being told that their concerns were not important; tired of working on oppressions other than their own; tired of fighting over issues such as whether or not women like themselves could be seen as "oppressed"; and tired of being blatantly disrespected and treated as second-class citizens, low-status workers, and sex objects by the almost totally male leadership of movement organizations. Yet they were also not insensitive to charges that in engineering this split, they were "dividing the left" and eviscerating the antiwar and civil rights movement, impairing its ability to do

work that they themselves believed was vital. Nevertheless, after suffering much abuse and hostility within the movement as a result of their attempts to advance women's issues, they ultimately concluded that the split—and a continuing separation between feminist and movement organizing—was necessary in order to allow them effectively to work directly on women's oppression. They were through having to justify their theories or their actions in terms of the male-centered goals and priorities of the larger movement. They also wanted to demonstrate to the movement leaders how much it had depended on women's work and how little it could afford to do without this work. At least in calmer moments, the hope was that as a result, the antiwar and civil rights movement would change, confronting its own sexism and complicity in perpetuating the oppression of women.

However much these early radical feminists opposed some of the views then dominant on the left, most of them were not about to align themselves with the earlier first-wave feminism of suffrage and women's equal rights, any more than with the equal-opportunity liberal feminism of the National Organization for Women (NOW), both of which they saw as irredeemably "bourgeois." As Susan Brownmiller reports in *In Our Time: Memoir of a Revolution* (1999), even women who were to become feminist stalwarts of the second wave, such as Robin Morgan, were initially disdainful of the term *feminist*, which they saw as allying them with liberalism. These antipathies are clearly illustrated in an early feminist action staged by New York Radical Women (NYRW) at the National Mobilization Committee to End the War in Vietnam's (MOBE) Counter-Inaugural of January 1969. On the one hand, NYRW, intent on burning their voter registration cards, tried to convince suffragist Alice Paul to join them in "giving back the vote." (Paul angrily declined.) On the other, NYRW's intent to raise the slogan "Feminism Lives" drew an enraged response from Women's International Terrorist Conspiracy from Hell (WITCH), whose members included Morgan, and a threat to counter with sashes reading, "Feminism Sucks"—a threat never carried out, to Morgan's later relief: "Thank God, or Goddess, we did not do that. . . . But we came *this* close. I still thought of 'feminism' as a dirty word." The radical women who split off from the antiwar and civil rights movement to form an autonomous women's movement saw themselves as revolutionaries, whose goal was not to reform the liberal-capitalist system, but to eliminate it, root and branch, along with patriarchy.

The movement they formed called itself the Women's Liberation Movement (WLM), to make clear its distinction from earlier and contemporary liberal feminisms.

FEMINIST SEPARATISM

As separatism in its first sense was directed at the male-centered movement, separatism in its second sense was directed at first at movement men, though it later changed form to include men in general. Called "feminist separatism," this separatism began with the notion that women should "go on strike," not only against the movement, but also against the individual men with whom they had previously been affiliated. Most of the women who founded the WLM were (at least at this time in their lives) heterosexually identified. Indeed, some of the organizations they founded, such as Redstockings, did not even permit lesbian membership, defining lesbianism as a "deviance"; an impediment to working with the mass of women, who could not be expected to have progressive attitudes toward lesbians; and a liability to feminism, which would then be discredited as representing only a narrow and "deviant" dissatisfaction with the status quo.

Women who were self-identified lesbians and who wanted to work in the WLM were at this time generally expected to keep their lesbianism hidden, lest it become a "distraction" from the "important" issues, divisive within movement projects, and an "embarrassment" to the movement as a whole. They were generally more than willing to do so, for the costs of being publicly identified as a lesbian at the time were extraordinarily high. Nevertheless, many of the early feminists of the WLM were sure that, like the larger movement, men would not confront their sexism unless they were forced to. Women's oppression was "real," in that men derived material benefits from it. Men would not give up their real privileges without a fight. That fight must be pursued collectively, not individually, because the problem was structural and universal, rather than one of any individual woman's relationship with any individual man. To go to the root of the problem, women must join together in solidarity as a class to do battle with the class of men, because for all women, at least at some level and at least at the time in history to which they had come, "men are the enemy." As both the "Florida Paper," authored by Beverly Jones and Judith Brown, and the "Redstockings Manifesto" argued, to go to the root of the problem, women must join together in solidarity as a class to do battle with the class of men, because for all women, at least at some level and at least at the time in history to which they had come, men themselves were the enemy.

CONSCIOUSNESS RAISING

Critical to forming solidarity among women was establishing a collective consciousness of women's common oppression and their common interest in ending that oppression. Although women might objectively be a class—in Marxist terminology, a "class in itself"—they could not move purposefully to combat their oppression until they became a "class for itself," that is, a class conscious of itself *as* a class and of its common interests. To forge this transition in consciousness, radical feminists invented consciousness raising (CR), probably taking their inspiration from the "Speak Pains to Recall Pains" practice of Maoist groups seeking to understand the strategic needs of revolution in specific contexts of decadent capitalism. CR became the WLM's central means of understanding women's oppression. Through collective examination in the woman-only sharing of consciousness-raising groups, participants worked to uncover the hidden patterns and meaning of their experiences of daily lives as embodied women living in patriarchy. As trust was established, and as ever more intimate and even embarrassing stories about women's lives in male-dominated society poured out, common patterns of experience continued to show up in what they had previously assumed—and been told all their lives by the culture and almost everyone in it—were private and individual discouragements, slights, and assaults. By this method, they began to reveal the structure of women's oppression as a group. Through CR, feminists came to see—and to communicate by writing theory and by organizing mass actions—that "the personal is political," that is, that most of women's oppression in capitalist-patriarchy (or patriarchal-capitalism) is constructed and maintained outside the official liberal realm of "the political": in the family, in religion, in traditional arrangements of gender and male supremacy, all areas allegedly outside the purview of the state. Catharine A. MacKinnon has argued that through the "feminist method [of] consciousness raising: the meaning of women's social experience" created a new way of looking at what "counts" as knowledge, building a politics that starts from women's lived experience. In creating this politics, men were viewed as an impediment: there was nothing useful they could possibly add to a process of analysis that starts from the standpoint of life experienced by a woman in a culture of male supremacy.

REDSTOCKINGS MANIFESTO

July 7, 1969

Redstockings, one of many grassroots women's organizations, was founded in 1969 by radical feminists dedicated to defending the women's liberation movement from male supremacy. The following is their manifesto.

1. After centuries of individual and preliminary political struggle, women are uniting to achieve their final liberation from male supremacy. Redstockings is dedicated to building this unity and winning our freedom.

2. Women are an oppressed class. Our oppression is total, affecting every facet of our lives. We are exploited as sex objects, breeders, domestic servants, and cheap labor. We are considered inferior beings, whose only purpose is to enhance men's lives. Our humanity is denied. Our prescribed behavior is enforced by the threat of physical violence.

Because we have lived so intimately with our oppressors, in isolation from each other, we have been kept from seeing our personal suffering as a political condition. This creates the illusion that a woman's relationship with her man is a matter of interplay between two unique personalities, and can be worked out individually. In reality, every such relationship is a class relationship, and the conflicts between individual men and women are political conflicts that can only be solved collectively.

3. We identify the agents of our oppression as men. Male supremacy is the oldest, most basic form of domination. All other forms of exploitation and oppression (racism, capitalism, imperialism, etc.) are extensions of male supremacy: men dominate women, a few men dominate the rest. All power structures throughout history have been male-dominated and male-oriented. Men have controlled all political, economic and cultural institutions and backed up this control with physical force. They have used their power to keep women in an inferior position. *All men* receive economic, sexual, and psychological benefits from male supremacy. *All men* have oppressed women.

4. Attempts have been made to shift the burden of responsibility from men to institutions or to women themselves. We condemn these arguments as evasions. Institutions alone do not oppress; they are merely tools of the oppressor. To blame institutions implies that men and women are equally victimized, obscures the fact that men benefit from the subordination of women, and gives men the excuse that they are forced to be oppressors. On the contrary, any man is free to renounce his superior position provided that he is willing to be treated like a woman by other men.

We also reject the idea that women consent to or are to blame for their own oppression. Women's submission is not the result of brainwashing, stupidity, or mental illness but of continual, daily pressure from men. We do not need to change ourselves, but to change men.

The most slanderous evasion of all is that women can oppress men. The basis for this illusion is the isolation of individual relationships from their political context and the tendency of men to see any legitimate challenge to their privileges as persecution.

5. We regard our personal experience, and our feelings about that experience, as the basis for an analysis of our common situation. We cannot rely on existing ideologies as they are all products of male supremacist culture. We question every generalization and accept none that are not confirmed by our experience.

Our chief task at present is to develop female class consciousness through sharing experience and publicly exposing the sexist foundation of all our institutions. Consciousness-raising is not "therapy," which implies the existence of individual solutions and falsely assumes that the male-female relationship is purely personal, but the only method by which we can ensure that our program for liberation is based on the concrete realities of our lives.

The first requirement for raising class consciousness is honesty, in private and in public, with ourselves and other women.

6. We identify with all women. We define our best interest as that of the poorest, most brutally exploited woman.

We repudiate all economic, racial, educational or status priveleges that divide us from other women. We are determined to recognize and eliminate any prejudices we may hold against other women. . . .

7. We call on all our sisters to unite with us in struggle.

We call on all men to give up their male privileges and support women's liberation in the interest of our humanity and their own.

In fighting for our liberation we will always take the side of the women against their oppressors. We will not ask what is "revolutionary" or "reformist," only what is good for women.

The time for individual skirmishes has passed. This time we are going all the way.

Source: Sisterhood Is Powerful: An Anthology of Writings from the Women's Liberation Movement (New York: Vintage Books, 1970), 598–601.

Furthermore, because of their male privilege and their male-dominant standpoint in the world, their contributions would actually be damaging to the process, skewing it by their ascribed male authority.

A MOVEMENT OF WOMEN ONLY

The early radical feminists had come of age in a world in which—even more so than today—expertise and authority were gendered male. Just as the men of the movement had felt little compunction about telling them what women "needed," so they had been told all their lives by male experts, teachers, doctors, and scholars what was wrong with them and how they should go about fixing it. In addition, they had lived all their lives with the assumption that they would submit to male authority, defer to male egos, live under male protection, and provide service and comfort to males in ways that men would prescribe. In splitting off from the antiwar and civil rights movement, feminists had separated themselves from some of this male control, claiming space in which to create their own analyses and theories of their situation, sometimes explaining that they needed "to get away from the male voices, in order to be able to hear ourselves." This phrase was often used by radical feminists to explain their separatism to outsiders. But male voices were everywhere. How far was it possible to separate oneself from incessant masculinist pronouncements and proscriptions? And how far was that even a good thing? These questions remained for radical feminism throughout its history, and they were answered in many different ways in many different places.

It might seem that the establishment of an autonomous WLM did not require that this new radical feminist movement be populated only by women. As a body of knowledge or an ideology, there appears to be no reason feminism could not be embraced by men as well as women. Yet although liberal-feminist NOW explicitly defined itself as an organization of "men and women," the WLM was not NOW. It recognized no liberal requirement to be inclusive. and it was committed to the belief that men and women have fundamentally opposed real interests in terms of the continuation of patriarchy. Furthermore, as in CR, men had nothing to contribute, and because of their social status and privilege, they must inevitably exert patriarchal power over the women for whom the movement existed. As Robin Morgan wrote in the introduction to *Sisterhood Is Powerful* (1970), "women's liberation is . . . the genuine radical movement. . . . I haven't the faintest notion what possible revolutionary roles white heterosexual men could fulfill, since they are the very embodiment of reactionary-vested-interest-power[–except] possibly not exist? No, I really don't mean that. Yes, I really do." In her influential farewell to the left, "Goodbye to All That," printed in the inaugural issue that followed radical women's takeover of the underground New York journal *Rat* (February 9–23, 1970), Morgan asked why "white men [who] are the most responsible for the destruction of human life on the planet . . . [are] controlling the supposed revolution to change all that? . . . A legitimate revolution must be led by, *made* by those who have been most oppressed: black, brown, and white *women*—with men relating to that the best they can." She concluded, "[Women] are rising with a fury older and potentially greater than any force in history, and this time we will be free or no one will survive. *Power to all the people or to none. All the way down, this time.*"

The anger that experiences in the New Left and with men's social power in general had engendered in many early radical feminists is apparent in Morgan's statements. This anger was for most feminists only exacerbated by the consciousness-raising process, where "click" experience piled up upon "click" experience to reveal to them what a bad situation the patriarchy had put them in. (A "click" experience was a sudden moment of enlightenment when the hidden sexist meaning of a social convention previously thought to be benign suddenly became apparent.) It was said at the time that "every good feminist goes through her really *angry* period, when she really *hates* all men." Whether or not that was universally true, it was clear that a significant number of early radical feminists were nakedly angry at the lot in life that patriarchy had assigned to them and directed that anger—at least for a time—at men in general. The WLM was uniformly assumed by the women in it to be "women only" in its day-to-day operations, though exceptions might be made in some rare circumstances. Flyers for meetings, rallies, and marches commonly bore the tag line "all women welcome," telling men explicitly to stay away. In some feminist projects, such as bookstores, which were necessarily open to the general public, it was a common practice to establish "womanspace" or "women's space," as a realm into which men were not to go.

PERSONAL SEPARATISM

Although separatism was controversial within the WLM, many individual radical feminists sought to live feminist-separatist personal lives. Some groups, such as NYRW, sought to keep separatism a short-term strategy confined to the political realm; others, such as Judith Brown, a founder of Gainesville Women's Liberation and Boston's Cell 16, and Beverly Jones of the influential "Florida Paper" of June 1968, advocated at least temporary personal separation from men. Women who maintained personal separatism sought to keep all their interactions with men—and the institutions of patriarchy—to a minimum. Besides deliberately separating themselves from male lovers—and perhaps remaining celibate—many radical feminists also rejected male friends and sought to avoid patriarchal culture, living without televisions and staying away from mainstream ("male-stream") media, relying on alternative WLM and movement news sources, and reading only feminist books and publications. Many also refused to vote or otherwise participate in "in-system" politics and would not become involved with the police under almost any circumstance, even should they themselves become the victims of crime. For many of these women, paid employment was one context in which they were regularly required to interact with men, though some managed even to avoid that by securing employment in WLM projects or through self-employment.

Family relationships were a source of some consternation for many of these women, and all manner of personal strategies were pursued, from maintaining relatively unaffected relationships with male relatives to cutting them off completely along with the rest of the male world. A particular source of controversy within the WLM in this regard was the case of women who were the mothers of male children. Although the WLM was happy to welcome these mothers themselves, groups and projects took very different positions on when and where their male children were also welcome. For example, in defining who might come into womanspace, policies varied. Sometimes a blanket "no men or male children" prohibition existed; other times policies might be age-specific, allowing male infants or children up to a certain age. These policies and their determination were always very contentious, owing to the recognition that barring the male children was, in most instances, tantamount to shunning their mothers as well.

THE WOMAN-IDENTIFIED WOMAN

These tendencies were extended by the development within the WLM of the idea of the "woman-identified woman" and of an analysis of "compulsory heterosexuality." Early radical feminists did not particularly celebrate the feminine. Like Emma Goldman, who was a huge influence on many of them—as reflected by the popularity within the movement of the reader, *Red Emma Speaks*, edited by Alix Kates Shulman (1972)—they often disdained what they saw as the weakness, passivity, silliness, and vanity of "ordinary" women. Styling themselves as serious revolutionaries embodying the toughness that role implies, early radical feminists (though they might espouse a model of androgyny as their personal ideal) tended to adopt the style of argument and relating in their interpersonal interactions that they had learned in the movement. This style was decidedly "male": aggressive, intellectual, uncompromising, and deadly serious.

In time, however, a critique began to develop within the WLM of "male-identification." A "male-identified" woman was one who longed for male approval, who privileged masculine values and ways of being, and who internalized patriarchy's definition of women. Because patriarchy elevated masculine traits and values as the ideal for both men and human beings, and rejected and devalued women, in a patriarchal society "androgyny" must privilege the masculine, unless active attention were paid to resisting misogyny and revaluing the feminine. In this revaluing, as Radicalesbians wrote in "The Woman-Identified Woman" (1970), what passed for "femininity" in patriarchal culture was revealed to be a "slave status . . . [conferred by] the man whose name we bear . . . [as] what we have to be in order to be acceptable by him." Feminists instead needed to realize that "irrespective of where our love and sexual energies flow, if we are male-identified in our heads, we cannot realize our autonomy as human beings."

Radicalesbians was an ephemeral group formed around the "Lavender Menace" action organized by Rita Mae Brown, Artemis March, Ellen Shumsky, and several others to raise the issue of lesbianism at the second Congress to Unite Women of May 1970. Fortified by a group of Vassar students, they decided to bring forth the issue of the movement's fear of lesbians and of being labeled as a lesbian movement. This fear was prevalent, with women who were lesbians encouraged to "keep it to themselves." Lesbians were generally looked upon as something of an embarrassment or, as Rita Mae decided, a "menace." The women who called themselves "Radicalesbians" wrote a statement entitled "The Woman-Identified Woman," and stenciled two dozen T-shirts with the words "Lavender Menace." At the Second Congress to Unite Women, they seized the stage and poet Martha Shelley took the microphone. For the next two hours, numerous women joined them in revealing their own lesbianism and standing in solidarity with the group. The group had coined the term *woman-identified* in an effort to find a term that was less threatening to heterosexual women than "lesbian." The power of their redefinition of lesbianism as a choice that was primarily political and their explanation of lesbianism in terms of the logic of feminist separatism worked in the WLM to fuel what was called the "gay-straight split" that roiled the WLM between 1970 and 1972. By 1972, however, the model of the "woman-identified woman," who refused to participate in cultural misogyny, loved and valued women, and recognized the true social value of women's ways of being, had become ascendant As understood within the WLM, this woman need not be lesbian in terms of sexual practice, but should be a "political lesbian" in her solidarity with and direction toward women. It was also important that she understand that heterosexuality was not a choice for women, but an institution in which women were forced to participate under threat of severe punishment. As Adrienne Rich later explained it in "Compulsory Heterosexuality and Lesbian Existence," even in patriarchy all women, in their emotional and relational lives, exist somewhere on a "lesbian continuum." Yet female solidarity is frustrated by the coercive institution of compulsory heterosexuality, which seeks to destroy woman-identification, to set women against one another, and to mold them to male ends.

LESBIAN SEPARATISM

The women who participated in the WLM were struggling to liberate themselves from male dominance. They were also, in the main, feminist separatists and angry at patriarchy and men, countercultural and generally iconoclastic and rebellious. It should therefore not be surprising that, at least in part activated by these ideas, it wasn't long before large numbers of them were purposely choosing lesbianism and "coming out in the women's movement." As a member of the *Big Mama Rag* collective in Denver put it in their founding edition late in 1971, "How can you conquer an oppressor when you sleep with him every night?" It was a later aftermath of this "chosen" lesbianism that resulted in the third expression of separatism in the WLM, lesbian separatism.

From the elevation of the ideal of the woman-identification within the WLM to the status of the proper model for a radical-feminist woman, to the no-

tion that that woman is also lesbian in her life-orientation and sexuality, required only a very small step. Traditional ideals of sexual morality, revealed by the analysis of compulsory heterosexuality to be nothing more than operations of patriarchal power, were irrelevant. Why, therefore, would any woman-identified woman and political lesbian not also choose to be an actual lesbian? Was it because she was unable to free her mind and herself from compulsory heterosexuality? Or was she "still" sleeping with men because she was actually male-identified?

Eventually, a tension arose around this issue and ultimately split the WLM. Some—though far from all—of the women who had embraced lesbianism within the WLM as a political choice and an act of personal liberation, began to argue that a "true" radical feminist was also a lesbian. Expressions of disdain for heterosexual women began to be heard in many radical feminist projects and organizations, along with assertions that all "the real work" of the movement was being done by lesbians. Heterosexual women were criticized for continuing to participate in an institution well known to be oppressive and unhealthy for women, rather than directing all their energies toward women and the WLM. Furthermore, some lesbians began to argue that not only did heterosexual women improperly give their own energy to men, but also served as transmitters of the energy of other feminist women to men, depriving the WLM of that energy as well. This argument held that because heterosexuality is so negative for women, those women in the WLM who continued to participate in it were constantly complaining to other women, many of them lesbians, about their relationships and demanding continual support from those other women in order to be able to sustain the relationships, thereby transferring lesbian energy to men.

These critiques and assertions of lesbian superiority eventually found expression in the creation within the WLM of groups and projects that identified themselves as lesbian separatists. Lesbian separatists demanded that lesbian feminists construct a movement separate not only from men but from heterosexual women as well. However, they were from the outset vigorously opposed by many other radical feminists who also identified as lesbian, but who refused to sanction any move that would split the WLM and eject women from it because of their sexuality. A great deal of debate and controversy within WLM journals and projects resulted from this development. The conflict was further exacerbated by the fact that some lesbian separatists began to invoke a body of essentialist feminist theory, exemplified by Elizabeth Gould Davis's *The First Sex* (1971), which argued that women were inherently superior to men, who were the "deformed" products of a mutation in one of the female x-chromosomes that had resulted in the stunted and misshapen male y-chromosome. As might be anticipated, to the politically astute women steeped in progressive theory who had built the WLM from its outset, and who refused to participate in lesbian separatism, such arguments appeared nothing short of fascism.

WOMEN OF COLOR REJECT SEPARATISM

By the mid-1970s, women of color had begun to organize themselves into separate black feminist groups and to advance powerful critiques of the WLM's separatism as rooted in both racism and classism. The best known of these critiques is contained in "The Combahee River Collective Statement," produced in 1977 by a collective of women of color who had been meeting together in Boston since 1974. Taking their name from a guerrilla campaign organized and led by Harriet Tubman which freed more than 750 slaves, the Collective was animated over the years by numerous women veterans of the New Left and WLM, as well as civil rights, black nationalism, and the Black Panthers. These women came to Combahee because their disillusionment with their earlier movement experiences had led them "to the need to develop a politics that was anti-racist, unlike those of white women, and anti-sexist, unlike those of Black and white men." The "Statement" argues that separatism is a luxury predicated on the privilege of white women, in which women of color—though they may be feminists and lesbians, as were the members of Combahee—could not participate. Their first loyalty must be to their communities, under siege by the policies and practices of institutionalized racism; to split them by separatism would leave everyone in them even more vulnerable to racist attacks: "Our situation as Black people necessitates that we have solidarity around the fact of race, which white women of course do not need to have with white men, unless it is their negative solidarity as racial oppressors. We struggle together with Black men against racism, while we also struggle with Black men about sexism."

Throughout the 1970s, the Combahee River Collective extended their influence by sponsoring a series of seven black feminist retreats which created connections among large numbers of women of color activists. In the early 1980s, Collective member Barbara Smith, along with Audre Lorde, cofounded Kitchen Table: Women of Color Press. In her introduction to *Home Girls: A Black Feminist Anthology* (1983), Smith emphasizes the need that a comprehension of the "simultaneity of oppressions" creates for coalition building, which seeks to bring about "racial change in a way that unites oppressions instead of isolating them."

In summary, we can see in the radical-feminist WLM a progressive development over a number of years of variants of separatism. Beginning with the creation of the autonomous women's movement separate from the New Left, this separatism found expression in a "feminist" form of separation from men and a "lesbian" form of separation from men and heterosexual women. As each of these separatisms developed, some women stayed behind. Among them were many women of color, who saw separatism as predicated on white privilege and dangerous to their communities in a racist society.

Eileen Bresnahan

BIBLIOGRAPHY

Brownmiller, Susan. *In Our Time: Memoir of a Revolution*. New York: Dial Press, 1999.

Combahee River Collective. "The Combahee River Collective Statement." 1977. In *Home Girls: A Black Feminist Anthology*, ed. Barbara Smith, 272–282. New York: Kitchen Table: Women of Color, 1983.

Davis, Elizabeth Gould. *The First Sex*. New York: Penguin Books, 1971.

Echols, Alice. *Daring to Be Bad: Radical Feminism in America 1967–1975*. Minneapolis: University of Minnesota Press, 1989.

Evans, Sarah. *Personal Politics: The Roots of Women's Liberation in the Civil Rights Movement and the New Left*. New York: Vintage Books, 1979.

Firestone, Shulamith. *The Dialectic of Sex: The Case for Feminist Revolution*. New York: Bantam Books, 1970.

Gitlin, Todd. *The Sixties: Years of Hope, Days of Rage*. New York: Bantam Books, 1987.

Hartsock, Nancy C.M. "The Feminist Standpoint: Developing the Ground for a Specifically Feminist Historical Materialism." In *The Second Wave: A Reader in Feminist Theory*, ed. Linda Nicholson, 216–240. New York: Routledge, 1997.

Hayden, Casey, and Mary King. "A Kind of Memo for Casey Hayden and Mary King to a Number of Other Women in the Peace and Freedom Movements." In *Feminism in Our Time: The Essential Writings, World War II to the Present*, ed. Miriam Schneir, 89–94. New York: Vintage Books, 1965.

Jones, Beverly, and Judith Brown. "Toward a Female Liberation Movement," also known as the "Florida Paper." In *Voices from Women's Liberation*, ed. Leslie B. Tanner, 362–415. New York: New American Library, 1970.

King, Mary. *Freedom Song: A Personal Story of the 1960s Civil Rights Movement*. New York: Morrow, 1987.

MacKinnon, Catharine A. "Consciousness Raising." In *Toward a Feminist Theory of the State*, 83–105. Cambridge, MA: Harvard University Press, 1989.

Morgan, Robin. "Introduction: The Women's Revolution." In *Sisterhood Is Powerful: An Anthology of Writings from the Women's Liberation Movement*, xv–xvi. New York: Vintage Books, 1970.

———, ed. *Sisterhood Is Powerful: An Anthology of Writings from the Women's Liberation Movement*. New York: Vintage Books, 1970.

Nicholson, Linda, ed. *The Second Wave: A Reader in Feminist Theory*. New York: Routledge, 1997.

Piercy, Marge. "The Grand Coolie Damn." In *Sisterhood Is Powerful: An Anthology of Writings from the Women's Liberation Movement*, 473–492. New York: Vintage Books, 1969.

Radicalesbians. "The Woman Identified Woman." In *Radical Feminism*, ed. Anne Koedt, Anita Rapone, and Ellen Levine, 240–246. New York: St. Martin's Press, 1987.

Redstockings. "Redstockings Manifesto." In *Sisterhood Is Powerful: An Anthology of Writings from the Women's Liberation Movement*, ed. Robin Morgan, 598–601. New York: Vintage Books, 1970.

Rich, Adrienne. "Compulsory Heterosexuality and Lesbian Existence." In *Blood, Bread, and Poetry: Selected Prose 1979–1985*, 23–60. New York: W.W. Norton, 1986.

Rosen, Ruth. *The World Split Open: How the Modern Women's Movement Changed America*. New York: Viking, 2000.

Ryan, Barbara. *Feminism and the Women's Movement: Dynamics of Change in Social Movement, Ideology and Activism*. New York: Routledge, 1992.

Ryan, Barbara, ed. *Identity Politics in the Women's Movement*. New York: New York University Press, 2001.

Schneir, Miriam, ed. *Feminism in Our Time: The Essential Writings, World War II to the Present*. New York: Vintage Books, 1994.

Shulman, Alix Kates. *Red Emma Speaks: An Emma Goldman Reader*. New York: Schocken Books, 1983. Originally published as *Red Emma Speaks: Selected Writings and Speeches*. New York: Random House, 1972.

Smith, Barbara. "Introduction." In *Home Girls: A Black Feminist Anthology*, ed. Barbara Smith. New York: Kitchen Table: Women of Color, 1983.

Smith, Barbara, ed. *Home Girls: A Black Feminist Anthology*. New York: Kitchen Table: Women of Color, 1983.

Tobias, Sheila. *Faces of Feminism: An Activist's Reflections on the Women's Movement*. Boulder, CO: Westview Press, 1997.

Tong, Rosemarie Putnam. *Feminist Thought: A More Comprehensive Introduction*. 2d ed. Boulder, CO: Westview Press, 1998.

Anti-Rape Movement

Any list of the accomplishments of the contemporary American women's movement, or the second wave of feminism, is likely to include the feminist movement against rape as a major highlight. It is because of the anti-rape movement that we, as a society, benefit from the availability of rape crisis centers and hotlines, more victim-friendly laws, and a better understanding of the impact of this crime. This movement also helped give rise to campaigns against domestic abuse, sexual harassment, and child sexual abuse. Today, every rape victim is likely to have access to services and receive sympathetic treatment from law enforcement and prosecutors, thanks to the activism of the feminists who first dared to say *rape* in public. In spite of these activists' years of work to elevate societal consciousness, however, their ultimate goal of ending rape has yet to be achieved.

The term *anti-rape movement* might suggest the existence of some explicitly *pro-rape* force, but very few people would express favorable attitudes toward rape. In fact, American society has long treated rape as criminal behavior. The movement against rape has instead sought to uproot deeply held societal attitudes that make rape persist as a social problem. These include the beliefs that women secretly crave rape, women say no to sex when they really mean yes, black men are especially prone to raping (white women in particular), and rapists are deranged psychopaths or sex-crazed villains. Anti-rape campaigners sought to dismantle such myths in both public institutions and personal attitudes. They were successful in removing the taboo of rape and raising public awareness of this issue.

EMERGENCE OF THE ANTI-RAPE MOVEMENT

The anti-rape movement originated and took shape within the larger context of the U.S. women's movement. As a result, the anti-rape movement can be considered a submovement or a spinoff of the larger second wave. Although it took a unique form and had its own leaders and organizations, it was never divorced from the larger movement. Activist Susan Griffin wrote, "The issue of rape was in no way ever separate from the question of the whole liberation of women as we have been defined by patriarchy, and we did not see it as separate." Feminist politics and analysis were crucial to the budding anti-rape campaign.

Women's Liberation and the Anti-Rape Movement

Rape arrived on the feminist agenda in the context of the women's liberation movement, or radical feminism. This branch of second-wave feminism took the form of decentralized grassroots groups, loosely organized mainly in cities and college towns around the United States. Radical feminists believed that women could achieve freedom only through the eradication of male supremacy and the societal institutions (marriage, the family, and the state, for example) that support it. The members of this branch of the women's movement were unafraid of engaging in flamboyant actions that challenged widely held taboos, and they had no interest in maintaining respectability in the public eye. They were thus well-suited to call attention to controversial sexual matters. The women's liberation movement provided the organizational context that set the stage for the anti-rape movement.

In fall 1970, the New York Radical Feminists (NYRF) first raised the rape issue in their consciousness-raising groups and made it their centerpiece issue. Consciousness raising was the process by which women connected the intimate features of their personal lives with the larger picture of male dominance. Well-known anti-rape activist, Susan

445

Brownmiller explains that a NYRF member brought up the issue in a meeting. Three women present spoke up to tell about their own experiences of rape or attempted rape. Women were shocked to realize how common rape was. Through this process, feminists realized that rape was not an isolated incident based on bad luck or victim behavior. It was not a racist frame-up of a black man by a white woman. It was not something the victims secretly enjoyed. Instead, it was a symbolic and real demonstration of male dominance over women. Feminists defined rape as a crime of violence, not of sexual passion. Radical feminists challenged the sexual entitlement of men and demanded sexual autonomy for women.

In early 1971, NYRF, soon joined by New York Women Against Rape, began coordinating "speak-outs" in which women told about their rape experiences in public settings. Susan Brownmiller was one crucial player in organizing these events. The speak-outs served as mobilizing events that drew public attention, including media coverage, to the new movement. In addition, the radical feminist media began publishing information and theory about rape, helping to spread the word about this "new" issue. Between 1970 and 1973, consciousness of rape was being raised among women's liberation groups in all parts of the country—New York, Santa Monica, Los Angeles, Berkeley, Washington, D.C., Chicago, Seattle, Denver—and with this consciousness, the anti-rape movement was born.

Liberal Feminism and the Anti-Rape Movement

The other main branch of the second wave—women's rights or liberal feminism—was less crucial to the formation of the anti-rape movement. But its activists did become aware of the radical feminist activism on rape and helped to advance the movement beginning around 1973. The liberal feminists were centrally organized, with national groups and local chapters. Their most visible organization was the National Organization for Women (NOW), which today remains one of the largest feminists groups. Women's rights advocates believed that feminists must work to secure the rights and responsibilities of full and equal citizenship for women. They pressed for legal reform and economic equality between women and men within the existing sociopolitical structure. These activists were much more concerned about maintaining a respectable public image than radical feminists were. Thus, liberal feminists did not address the sexual subject of rape until after the women's liberationists started removing the taboo.

The most active liberal feminist anti-rape campaigner was Mary Ann Largen of Virginia, elected to be the first coordinator of the NOW Rape Task Force (NOWRTF) in 1973. NOWRTF encouraged local and state NOW chapters to investigate the rape laws and policies in their areas in order to develop action plans for legal and institutional reform. The liberal feminist anti-rape activism in NOW inspired the development of grassroots law reform efforts in numerous states and cities around the country. Because NOW poured the vast majority of its resources into pressing for the Equal Rights Amendment, an important liberal feminist goal, NOWRTF was short-lived.

Women of Color and the Anti-Rape Movement

The participation of women of color—that is, female members of minority ethnic or racial groups in the United States—in the anti-rape movement was influenced by larger trends. Feminists have noted that mainly white, middle-class women have made up the women's movement and that its agenda has largely reflected the priorities of this group of women. Feminists encouraged each other to ignore differences based on race, class, ethnicity, and sexual orientation, and to focus on the common bond of womanhood in designing feminist goals and strategies. The mostly white groups attempted to include women of color in their membership, and some of them did assume leadership positions, but the groups failed to attract large numbers of nonwhite women. By focusing on gender oppression at the expense of racial and economic oppression, white feminists often overlooked the ways that gender, race, and class work together to maintain oppression. Women of color did form independent feminist organizations to bring to the fore those issues affecting themselves and poor women, such as the National Black Feminist Organization and the Combahee River Collective.

Black women, among them the noted activist and writer Angela Davis, sometimes expressed distrust of the anti-rape movement. They stressed that white anti-rape activists ignored the special circumstances of women of color, who experience rape and other forms of gender oppression differently from white women. African-American women also feared that greater regulation of rape by the criminal justice system would disproportionately target men of color. The history of lynching in the United States, which was built on fraudulent rape charges against black men, is a powerful reminder that racism and rape frequently connect.

Nevertheless, women of color did participate in

the anti-rape movement. For example, in 1976 in Los Angeles, Latina women created a bilingual rape hotline for Spanish-speaking women, although real diversity in the anti-rape movement of that city did not come about until the mid-1980s. Furthermore, the rape crisis center in Washington, D.C., served as a hub of organizing for black women in the 1970s. White women who founded the center realized that it would be undesirable for a majority-white center to serve a majority-black city. Women of color affiliated with the center did not wait for white women to invite them to join the movement; instead, they developed analyses of rape that fit the experiences of women in their communities. They took their awareness of rape into their neighborhoods and educated others about the seriousness of this crime, and they took information about their communities to their work at the center. Loretta Ross and Nkenge Toure, Washington, D.C., Rape Crisis Center activists from the 1970s and 1980s, together with other women of color, shaped a center that could meet the needs of their communities.

ORGANIZING AND STRATEGIES

Since the emergence of the anti-rape movement, activists have built social movement organizations to address the problem in many ways. These groups reflected a range of feminist ideologies. Some organizations, identified with liberal feminist goals, focused on legal and institutional reform. Others, identified with the radical feminist branch, viewed rape as one piece in a larger system of white male dominance. The distinctions between liberal and radical dissolved somewhat only a few years into the anti-rape movement, as activists sought to do whatever was necessary to serve victims and challenge the persistence of rape. In the early 1970s, and even today, organizing has focused on several different but related strategies: self-defense, Take Back the Night rallies, crisis center development, and law reform.

Self-defense

Efforts focusing on fighting off attackers were among the first activities by women's groups to organize around the rape issue. In 1969, members of Cell 16 in Cambridge, Massachusetts, advanced an agenda of martial arts training and self-sufficiency for women. When the anti-rape movement emerged in 1970, the advantages of self-defense became clear: through self-defense, women might become empowered to overcome their socialized passivity and resist rape. Organizing focused on martial arts, assertiveness training, and providing women with fighting skills.

In the 1960s and 1970s, men dominated the martial arts, and instructors often viewed women's fear as a source of profit. To provide a feminist alternative, in 1971 martial artist Py Bateman founded the Feminist Karate Union (FKU) in Seattle. The FKU united martial arts instruction with consciousness raising, giving women the opportunity to discuss their fears and experiences of self-defense. On the East Coast, feminists founded the Women's Martial Arts Union to bring together women practitioners in Philadelphia, New York, and Baltimore. The periodicals *Black Belt Woman* (Medford, MA) and *Fighting Woman News* (New York) emerged in the mid-1970s to keep interested women connected. Furthermore, feminists combined self-defense projects with other strategies, such as rape crisis centers and Take Back the Night. Today, rape crisis centers, universities, and community centers routinely offer women's self-defense classes. Anti-rape writers and activists have argued eloquently in favor of self-defense as a way to empower women to feel less vulnerable and to fight an attacker.

Take Back the Night

One of the most enduring and recognizable anti-rape collective actions is the Take Back the Night (TBN) march and rally. In this action, women gather to reclaim—at least symbolically—the night and the streets as women's rightful place. Activists designed the action as a one-time or annual event, not typically as an ongoing project. One of the first actions bearing the TBN name took place in Pittsburgh in 1977, featuring speaker Anne Pride delivering a violence against women memorial by the same name.

The idea of "taking back the night" goes back further, however. For example, the 1971 pamphlet "Stop Rape" by Detroit Women Against Rape suggested that feminists patrol the streets to resist women's unwritten exclusion from the public sphere after dark. In 1975, in celebration of Women's Equality Day (August 26), NOW called for members of its chapters across the country to engage in protests and actions in the streets at night and resist women's victimization. These examples of women symbolically reclaiming the streets and the night bear striking resemblance to what has come to be called Take Back the Night. TBN marches and rallies continue to take place on college campuses and in communities throughout the country.

Rape Crisis Centers

Rape crisis centers (RCCs) have been the primary organizations of the anti-rape movement. Centers vary in the resources they provide, but all offer some direct services to victims, have some process to reach out to victims, and contain some form of internal rape education and training. Today, RCCs exist as independently operated agencies in some locales; elsewhere, they act as departments within hospitals or district attorneys' offices or in conjunction with battered women's shelters. The relationship between individual centers and the feminist movement also varies.

Radical feminist activists founded the first RCC in Washington, D.C., in 1972. Among the founders were Elizabethann O'Sullivan, Karen Kollias, and about ten other women. All of the founders were themselves survivors of rape. In deciding what services the center should offer, they were determined to provide the kinds of support they would have wanted when they were raped. When the center opened its doors, it offered emergency telephone counseling, escorts to police stations and hospitals, support groups, and public education. The D.C. Rape Crisis Center (DCRCC) embraced a philosophy of self-help: they hoped to empower rape victims to make their own choices about how to proceed after a rape. The center recognized that police and hospital staff often mistreated victims, so some women might prefer to avoid these institutions. This meant that the staff did not take a position on whether victims should report to law enforcement; they believed that only the victim herself knows what course is best. They put the victim's needs first and sought mainly to support her in whatever choices she made.

Rape crisis centers soon became the focal point of much anti-rape organizing around the country. Within less than two years of the founding of DCRCC, centers opened in Florida, New York, North Carolina, Michigan, Wisconsin, Arizona, Illinois, California, and Pennsylvania. In 1974, Washington, D.C., activists formed the Feminist Alliance Against Rape, a national coalition of anti-rape projects that made an explicit connection with antiracist feminist politics, which remained active through the mid-1980s. The more professionally oriented National Coalition Against Sexual Assault was founded in 1978. Presently, RCCs are in place in nearly every locale in the United States. A pro-victim, self-help philosophy remains the guiding force behind all rape crisis centers.

Rape Law Reform

Social movement activists have a long tradition of using legal strategies to create social change. Early in the anti-rape campaign, activists began examining the law of rape and learned that rape itself had always been treated as criminal, punishable behavior. They came to understand, however, that existing laws made prosecution and conviction very difficult and only rarely succeeded in punishing rapists. In most states' rape laws, prosecutors had to prove that victims did not consent to sexual intercourse. Usually, the only evidence of nonconsent were signs that the victims vigorously fought their attackers (bruises on the victim, marks on the body of the accused, and so on). Thus, a victim who was afraid for her life and did not put up a struggle could be seen as consenting to sex. It did not matter whether she resisted verbally or was too afraid to fight. This requirement made rape cases very difficult to prosecute. The law permitted the defense to introduce evidence of a victim's sexual history, and most people assumed that a woman with sexual experience could not or would not say *no* to sexual activity or deserved to be raped. In addition, rape laws did not apply to marital relationships, shielding men from charges of raping their spouses. These laws, known together as the common law of rape, were held in place by a distrust of women's claims.

Anti-rape activists teamed up with feminist lawyers and law students—a group that grew very quickly in the early 1970s—to analyze existing law and propose reforms. Applying the new feminist understanding of rape, these activists formulated strategies to pass more pro-victim statutes. Activities in Michigan provide an early example of feminist success. The Michigan Women's Task force on Rape (MWTFR) began as a division of the Women's Crisis Center of Ann Arbor. MWTFR members decided to pursue rape law reform and enlisted the help of law instructor Virginia Nordby, who worked with the task force and law students to research the existing law and formulate reforms. The task force wrote a sweeping reform statute, one that revised all aspects of the existing laws (in most other states, reform took place in a more piecemeal fashion). The new law, known as the Criminal Sexual Conduct statute, redefined rape to include a wider range of sexual violations. Furthermore, the law introduced gender-neutrality and a degree structure for the crime. The proposed law removed the requirement that a victim resist her attacker. It also contained a rape shield provision, which restricts the amount of evidence of a victim's sexual history admitted at trial. The Michigan legislature passed the law, with few changes to the MWTFR version, and it went into effect in 1974. Significantly, the legislature refused to accept the removal of the spousal exemption, though that reform took place several years later. This statute is widely considered a feminist reform.

Law reform activities took place all around the nation. By 1980, all fifty states and the District of Columbia had considered or passed small and large reforms. All of the elements of the Michigan law were pursued by law reform activists in the other states: redefinition of the crime, staircasing of offenses, evidentiary reform, rape shield, and removal of the marital exemption. Because of the incremental nature of changes in public policy, the reform effort continues in many states even today. In Georgia, for example, law students, rape crisis center activists, and lawyers began working together to propose a comprehensive reform of the rape law as recently as 1999.

RAPE ON THE PUBLIC AGENDA

A major achievement of the anti-rape movement has been to move this issue from the strictly feminist agenda to the national public policy agenda. For more than three decades, the activists of this campaign have been able to persuade some of the major institutions of our society—government, the media, law enforcement, medicine, and education—to think about the problem of rape in ways they never had before.

The 1970s saw an unprecedented amount of policymaking on the rape issue at every level of the federal government. In the states, legislators were rewriting rape laws at the prompting of anti-rape activists, as we have seen. States and counties also wrote or rewrote policies governing the way institutions—including hospitals, police departments, and prosecutors' offices—managed rape cases and rape victims. At the federal legislative level, Senator Charles Mathias (R-MD) proposed the first anti-rape bill to create a National Center for the Prevention and Control of Rape (NCPCR) in 1973. The bill became law in 1975. NCPCR was a funding organization designed to support research and anti-rape projects. It succumbed to President Ronald Reagan's budget cuts in the early 1980s. Another federal legislative initiative was the Rape Victims Privacy Act, sponsored by Representative Elizabeth Holtzman (D-NY), which amended the federal rules of evidence to include a rape shield provision. It became law in 1978. Even the U.S. Supreme Court decided two rape-related cases (*Cox Broadcast-*

ing Corporation v. Cohn, 1975; and *Coker v. Georgia*, 1977). These are just a few examples of the flurry of public policy attention to the rape issue in the 1970s.

There are two explanations for the policy successes. First, the 1970s witnessed a deluge of rhetoric prompting politicians to get tough on crime. Lawmakers carefully avoided casting votes that would make them appear "soft" on crime. Anti-rape activists were effectively handing these politicians a crime issue to support. Unfortunately, this law and order agenda was based largely on white fears of minority criminality. This tough-on-crime agenda has only intensified in recent years.

Another reason for the policy successes of the anti-rape movement was the growing media attention to rape. Media coverage can be crucial if a social movement intends to effect social change. Through the mainstream media, rape came to be defined as a major social problem. The press attention to rape increased dramatically over the course of the 1970s. Stories ranged from routine reporting of crimes committed to case studies using a specific victim's story, to general stories about rape as a social problem. The change in reporting, however, was not only quantitative but also qualitative; the press was now willing to discuss rape in victim-sympathetic ways. In addition, high-profile rape cases, such as those of Inez Garcia in California and singer Connie Francis in New Jersey, called heightened attention to the issue. The media even paid attention to the anti-rape movement itself, highlighting turning points in activism. Because the issue was so prevalent in the media and public consciousness, policymakers had little choice but to take rape seriously.

Although feminists usually saw the policy developments of the 1970s as positive, they did understand that their own definition of rape did not match the public's or policymakers' definition. For example, anti-rape activists viewed rape as one part of a larger picture of female subordination, as the symbolic and real expression of male dominance. They theorized rape as a problem grounded in women's socialized passivity and men's socialized aggression. Activists understood that most victims were raped by men they knew, often men with whom they had been intimate. And they knew that law enforcement typically targeted poor men and men of color when investigating and prosecuting sexual assault. Very little of this feminist rape consciousness was translated onto the public anti-rape agenda. To policymakers, rape was the act of a few criminally minded individuals, was committed only by strangers, took place primarily on urban streets, and defied explanation. In the policy setting, then, anti-rape ideology existed only in a diluted form.

RECENT DEVELOPMENTS

The anti-rape movement continues today in spite of a political and social movement context that differs dramatically from that of the early 1970s when it emerged. The media have continued to pay attention to the issue. For example, high-profile rape cases involving charges against William Kennedy Smith and Mike Tyson sparked debates on the problem of acquaintance rape. Celebrities have also gotten involved in the fight against rape: with the support of recording artist Tori Amos, herself a rape survivor, the Rape, Abuse & Incest National Network was founded in 1994. It provides a national sexual assault hotline (800–656-HOPE) that refers callers to local rape and abuse services. These issues help to keep rape on the public agenda. In at least two additional settings—college campuses and legislative bodies—the struggle to end rape ebbs and flows.

Campus Activism

Beginning in the 1980s, the public discourse and feminist analysis of rape paid new attention to the date rape phenomenon, highlighting research findings that most victims are raped by men they know. Of course, this fact was well known in feminist circles for some time; but the media picked up the discussion relatively late. Much of the new awareness of the problem originated in university settings and focused on young women's experiences. Beginning in the 1980s and reaching into the 1990s, student anti-rape groups started springing up around the country. Among them were Students United for Rape Elimination (SURE) at Stanford, Students Concerned About Rape (SCARE) at Syracuse, and a host of other such groups. At some schools, women's groups expanded their focus to include rape, such as Sisters in Solidarity to Eradicate Sexism (SISTERS) at Spelman and Students for Women's Concerns at Vanderbilt. Campus men's groups, for example Tulane Men Against Rape (T-MAR) and Rape Education and Active Leadership (REAL-Men) at North Carolina State, have concluded that men must be active in the fight to prevent rape.

The focus of each group varies. They might organize educational programs, staff helplines and escort programs, or sponsor Take Back the Night marches. One recent national effort has been organized by the V-Day Campaign. This is an effort, spearheaded by playwright Eve Ensler, to perform the Obie-award winning *The Vagina Monologues* on campuses and in other community settings. The campaign focuses on raising awareness of violence against women worldwide, and all funds raised go to anti-violence causes. Since 1998, V-Day has energized the anti-rape movement on college campuses and beyond. No matter what their focus, all campus anti-rape groups have a commitment to upholding sexual autonomy and preventing acquaintance rape. University administrators have generally welcomed these forms of student organizing, but whether they are motivated by fear of liability or a real commitment to rape prevention may never be known.

Legislative Efforts—The Violence Against Women Act

Rape remained on the public policy agenda throughout the 1980s and 1990s in the states and nationally. The capstone federal policy initiative was the passage in 1994 of the Violence Against Women Act (VAWA), the most visible legislative success of the anti-rape movement (in conjunction with the battered women's movement). The NOW Legal Defense and Education Fund, together with the coalition group National Task Force to End Sexual Assault and Domestic Violence, were the main activists behind VAWA. This legislation created a federal civil rights provision for rape and domestic violence. This provision created a federal right to be free of violent crimes motivated by gender—rape, sexual assault, and domestic violence—and allowed victims to sue perpetrators for damages in federal court. In addition, VAWA allocated millions of federal dollars to promote violence-prevention efforts in the states. This landmark legislation was widely celebrated as an unprecedented success by activists in the movement. The celebration was short-lived, however: in *United States v. Morrison* (2000), in a five to four decision, the U.S. Supreme Court struck down the civil rights provision, stating that Congress had no constitutional authority to pass the provision. Antiviolence activists are now left wondering whether any federal recourse for gender-motivated violence is possible.

CONCLUSION

The multifaceted anti-rape movement has made its mark on the American political and social landscape. Beginning with the 1970s' radical feminist analysis of rape—which challenged not only rape myths but also male dominance in all its forms—the movement has effected an ideological shift in society. No longer must rape survivors live with the pain of silence and shame. They now may seek help from agencies and counselors who are likely to tell them simply, "It is not your fault." Police departments and hospitals have made improvements in their treatment of rape victims, and legal reforms have removed many of the obstacles to pressing charges. Rape crisis centers offer educational programs in the hopes of preventing rape from happening in the first place. Colleges and universities routinely offer rape prevention programming and sometimes make attendance mandatory. This is a far cry from the hostility most rape victims experienced, if they told anyone at all, over three decades ago. But problems from within and without persist. Fear of minority criminality continues to inform the rape issue and the movement, and women of color continue to feel marginalized. Moreover, a backlash of sorts has called into question many of the basic tenets of anti-rape feminism. Thus, the work of the movement remains unfinished. The revolution in popular attitudes, begun in the consciousness-raising sessions of the 1970s, will continue well into the twenty-first century.

Maria Bevacqua

BIBLIOGRAPHY

Bevacqua, Maria. *Rape on the Public Agenda: Feminism and the Politics of Sexual Assault.* Boston: Northeastern University Press, 2000.

Brownmiller, Susan. *Against Our Will: Men, Women and Rape.* New York: Simon and Schuster, 1975.

Davis, Angela Y. *Women, Culture, and Politics.* New York: Random House, Vintage, 1990.

Estrich, Susan. *Real Rape.* Cambridge, MA: Harvard University Press, 1987.

Gold, Jodi, and Susan Villari, eds. *Just Sex: Students Rewrite the Rules on Sex, Violence, Activism, and Equality.* Lanham, MD: Rowman and Littlefield, 2000.

Gornick, Vivian, Martha Burt, and Karen J. Pittman. "Structure and Activities of Rape Crisis Centers in the Early 1980s." *Crime and Delinquency* 31 (1985): 247–268.

Griffin, Susan. *Rape: The Politics of Consciousness.* Rev. ed. San Francisco: Harper & Row, 1986.

Koss, Mary P. "Hidden Rape: Sexual Aggression and Victimization in a National Sample of Students in Higher Education." In *Rape and Sexual Assault II,* ed. Ann Wolbert Burgess, pp. 3–25. New York: Garland, 1988.

MacKinnon, Catharine A. *Toward a Feminist Theory of the State.* Cambridge, MA: Harvard University Press, 1989.

Matthews, Nancy A. *Confronting Rape: The Feminist Anti-Rape Movement and the State.* New York: Routledge, 1994.

McCaughey, Martha. *Real Knockouts: The Physical Feminism of Women's Self-Defense.* New York: New York University Press, 1997.

Roiphe, Katie. *The Morning After: Sex, Fear, and Feminism.* Boston: Little, Brown, 1994.

Warshaw, Robin. *I Never Called It Rape: The Ms. Report on Recognizing, Fighting and Surviving Date and Acquaintance Rape.* New York: Harper & Row, 1988.

4

LABOR MOVEMENT

INTRODUCTION

In most of the world, labor movements are conventionally considered to be the most critical force in civilizing society. From a comparative and historical standpoint, labor is intimately related to the creation of social democracy on a global basis. From the dawn of industrial capitalism, labor movements have advocated greater levels of political and economic equality, giving rise to the creation of liberal-democratic states in the West that have conferred systems of universal electoral participation which have in turn engendered social programs that promote the provision and more equitable distribution of basic human needs: healthcare, education, housing, food, and dignity at the workplace.

A comparative examination of the historical trajectory of social democracy demonstrates that social democracy emerged in the nineteenth and twentieth centuries in an uneven fashion: some countries developed comprehensive systems of social welfare, while others developed programs in a more piecemeal manner. In view of the general global trend toward social democracy, pushed through by workers movements, the U.S. labor movement has had a uniquely divergent historical trajectory that accounts for its relative weakness in demarcating the system of social protection for working-class people.

Today, although labor is in a defensive position throughout the world, organized labor in the United States has more limited power and effectiveness than labor movements in comparable developed countries in Western Europe and North America. Thus, in nearly every category of economic security, American workers lag far behind those in other advanced industrial countries. On average, American workers continue to earn less and work harder than workers in countries with stronger labor movements.

Thus, is the U.S. working class and concomitant labor movement more conservative than labor in comparable countries? To the contrary, although the United States has a limited social safety net, ironically, American workers have demonstrated a solid record of militancy that in many ways eclipsed that of their counterparts in Western Europe. This militancy, however, is expressed not through the ballot box or the political arena, but through collective action at the workplace. The tradition of worker syndicalism in the United States can be explained by the fact that American democracy emerged in the late eighteenth century, well before the apogee of the American labor movement. Electoral participation in the United States was truncated at its inception.

At the time of America's founding, only white upper-class males could vote. Unlike comparable European democracies, voting participation did not occur in one fell swoop but was granted gradually for women and African Americans, in the wake of the abolition, women's, and civil rights movements. Although much of labor has been excluded periodically from participation, the working class was divided on the basis of identity, and the means of recourse were severely circumscribed by bitter opposition to political rights to be obtained through the state. Thus, the history of the labor movement is viewed more prominently through the lens of class struggle at the point of production. Since workers could not gain power through the state, voluntary action by associations of workers through the workplace was the most prominent form of resistance.

Unlike European social democracies that developed labor-based parties, the U.S. constitutional framework of divided and fragmented government restricted working-class activity through party formation. However, it would be a great mistake to conclude that the absence of a working-class party is a sign of moderation and complacency. Contrary to prevailing wisdom, American workers were and are interested in militant action, but the delimited political means of dissent through the formation of an authentic party pushed labor to seek economic and legal rights directly at the workplace. Thus, since the workplace was the major point of contention, workers in the United States have engaged in strike action to a significantly greater degree than their European counterparts. Working-class militancy sweeps through American labor history. Moreover, American labor history is marked by the independence of the working class from institutions. Although a smaller percentage of U.S. workers are in unions, many have engaged in autonomous wildcat and unauthorized strike activity that challenged the hegemony of U.S. business.

The stillborn efforts to create a labor-based party in the nineteenth and twentieth centuries did not stop working people from rebelling against oppressive conditions. In the nineteenth century, workers and their unions made demands against employers for better pay, improved working conditions, and respect on the job. The movement to reduce the workday and to ameliorate dangerous workplace conditions in the nineteenth century forced public officials to respond. Without the right to form recognized labor organizations, working people engaged in militant strike activity in the face of violent repression by state armed squads and almost universal court rulings equating unions with criminal conspiracies. That working people continued to resist, risking not just their jobs but their lives, provides evidence of the remarkable human spirit for equality and justice.

Once again, in the early twentieth century, employers and the state resisted worker movements to establish unions of their own. Although craft unions represented a small fraction of the working class, the rise of mass production created uncontrollable pressure by workers to create unions in manufacturing industries.

The advent of the New Deal and the National Labor Relations Act in the 1930s produced labor-management accords that have demobilized worker militancy and the ferment of industrial workers. The accords produced gains for members and nonmembers of unions by setting industrial standards and demanding improved healthcare, education, and government social programs that resulted in the rise of the public sector labor movement in the 1960s. Still, the labor-management accords demobilized much of the working class, who relied on union leaders to do the bidding for them. Moreover, many unions abandoned organizing drives and became relatively lethargic in representing the broader working class. However, by the late 1960s, as a result of declining profitability, business waged a new offensive against organized labor as a means to increase productivity. As a consequence, unions are not as adept at protecting worker interests as they once were. Organized labor's density in the workforce declined from some 35 percent in 1955 to less than 13 percent in 2001.

The decline in organized labor does not mean that workers have no way of resisting unfair employers. Indeed, workers continue to oppose abusive employer practices by independent nonunion action, holding unauthorized strikes, calling in sick, and slowing down the work process.

Still, in order to build a strong labor movement, unions will have to organize new members. However, labor now recognizes that many of the laws and agreements crafted in the 1930s and watered down since do not correspond to the contemporary workplace, since a growing number of workers are now employed in the service sector. Since the 1970s, the service sector that has tended not to be unionized has superseded manufacturing. The new challenge for the labor movement will be to organize service sector workers—the vast majority of whom are low-wage support workers. In addition, many of the workers ripe for organizing are women, people of color, and immigrants that do not form part of the leadership of the mainstream labor movement.

The labor movement also must confront the reality of globalization of work. Not only is the United States losing manufacturing jobs to low-wage countries, but service jobs in the communications industry are now increasingly being exported to low-wage regions. Globalization of work necessitates the U.S. labor movement to form strategic alliances with labor throughout the world in defending the dignity of work and the human rights of workers. In the United States, globalization has also increased the number of workers employed under sweatshop conditions—jobs that are essentially unregulated by the state. Workers employed by sweatshops of all kinds are paid below minimum wages, work longer hours, and do not have health and safety protection.

The labor movement will not regain its strength without a new commitment to organizing workers and challenging the dominant political structure to change labor law to facilitate joining unions and improving conditions of work. U.S. labor history demonstrates that working conditions and wages were improved only when a strong labor movement emerged to challenge unfair employers and state and federal laws that impeded their ability to band together to form unions of their own. Success always emerged in the wake of rank-and-file pressure for more responsible and democratic unions. In times of quiescence, employers and the state watered down laws that protected workers. Throughout U.S. history a strong social democracy is dependent on a vibrant labor movement that demands the expansion of state protection for workers, a larger public sphere that guarantees greater access to public education, healthcare, social welfare, and other protections that create a modicum of equality. In every era corporations, unchecked by a strong labor movement, will not be deterred in reducing social protection through privatizing essential social services, advocating for the reduction of the tax base, and eliminating programs that keep the population educated and healthy.

As the entries in this section demonstrate, workers in the past have always defied management power that is wielded abusively. Implicit in many of the essays that follow is the fact that workers will need to find new repertoires of solidarity to sustain their wages and working conditions and improve and help build a stronger social democracy.

Immanuel Ness

LABOR MOVEMENT

The groundwork for the U.S. labor movement that spiraled in the nineteenth century was set in the seventeenth and eighteenth centuries, spanning the colonial period and the American Revolutionary era. Although there was little in the way of a formalized labor movement during the colonial period—where workers organized with the express purpose of furthering their collective interest—this early period would lead to the factory system, which gave rise to the modern labor movement.

Samuel McKee Jr. distinguishes labor in early America into four categories: free (skilled or unskilled), apprentices, indentured servants, and slaves. These classifications were all imported from Europe. Labor in colonial America was shifted across time and region. So, while slavery for all intents and purposes ended in New York at the end of the eighteenth century, it would be nearly another century before America would see its demise in the South. Each category provides a glimpse of the opportunities and constraints placed upon labor activism, no less the formation of a movement.

FREE LABOR

To be free in the colonies meant that one was an artisan or mechanic and paid one's way from England and Europe or one was an indentured servant who had served his contract period and was released from further obligation. American society was mostly agrarian—more than 90 percent of the first settlers relied on agriculture to survive. Land was plentiful and could be obtained cheaply. Family members performed much of the farm labor. The remainder of the population settled in the towns and cities that would become America's economic hubs, New York, Philadelphia, and Charleston. These towns, which were the sites of local and international trading, required a more diverse workforce. Millers, carpenters, coopers, printers, and handicraftsmen of various skills were in

steady shortage and, thus, were in high demand. Though general, unskilled labor was also needed, the pervasive shortage of skilled workers was a demand Europe found difficult to fill.

Numerous enticements were offered to skilled workers to leave their homes and settle in the unknown and often difficult American terrain. Free land, high wages, and the opportunity for self-proprietorship were proffered to those willing to make the harsh voyage. England abandoned these offers, however, when legislators there feared that too many of their skilled workers were leaving to build up a colony that could eventually sever its economic dependency on England. The English parliament began restricting emigration of skilled workers to the colony as early as 1718. England forbade emigration of both workers and machinery plans in the textile industry and then gradually extended the prohibition to include iron, steel, and coal industry workers.

Despite the hardships of the long and often harrowing Atlantic voyage, those Europeans who settled in America often enjoyed a better life than their brethren in the Old World. Foster Rhea Dulles and Melvin Dubofsky writing in *Labor in America* (1984) note that life in the New World generally meant more material comforts, improved health, and longer life expectancies, despite class differences. There was a high level of literacy and learning, even among ordinary colonists, that was unprecedented. Furthermore, the ownership of land and the independence of business that many free laborers experienced did not allow for the transference of traditional, feudal English rule and greatly shaped the character of the American mythology of individualism and equality.

Itinerant work was common. Workers would ply their trades and skills from home to home, bringing their tools with them. Skilled workers did not begin setting up shops to serve customers on a widespread basis until the eighteenth century. Often, craftsmen would take on an apprentice or purchase a servant to assist in the business.

As towns grew, demand for artisanal work increased. Master craftsmen who owned their own ships hired journeymen workers to assist with them. The journeymen workers were artisans and mechanics who worked for wages. Master craftsmen also received labor from apprentices.

APPRENTICESHIPS

To gain entry into a trade, workers would apprentice themselves to master craftsmen who were willing and able to pass on knowledge of the craft in exchange for cheap labor. Apprenticeship was regulated by both the state and English guilds. Contracts bound the apprentice to serve his or her master or mistress. In turn, the master or mistress agreed to teach the apprentice a trade and house, feed, and clothe him or her. As with indentured servants, the agreement varied and would generally last four to seven years. In New York, masters were obliged to pay any registration fees to ensure the freedom of the apprentice upon completion of training. Many masters and mistresses educated their apprentices beyond the craft, teaching them reading and writing skills.

It was not uncommon for apprentices to be children given by their parents to a master or mistress to secure a trade. In some instances, children were given at a very young age, constituting more of an adoption than an apprenticeship. Despite the trappings of security and education, some apprentices subjected to abuse and cruelty ran away from their masters. Parents would sometimes instigate their child's fleeing from the master if they suspected that their child was not being cared for properly or was not imparted sufficient training and knowledge. If a judge determined that apprentices were abused or untrained, contracts could be rendered void.

Apprentices worked in any number of trades such as glaziers (glassblowers), smiths, or printers, to name a few examples. Female apprentices often did domestic work and learned spinning or sewing. Upon completion of their contracts, apprentices received a set of clothes, tools, and sometimes a small sum of cash.

INDENTURED SERVANTS

Many skilled and unskilled settlers to America came from Europe as indentured servants. Indentured servitude meant that emigrants would have their passage paid. In return, they promised to work for an agreed term of service. This enabled emigrants to come to America without the initial outlay, which

some did not want to spend and most did not have. Family groups that came as indentured servants were known as "redemptioners" because they paid a portion of their passage at the time of their departure and promised to redeem the balance by working in the colony.

Masters of indentured servants did not have the same responsibility as masters of apprentices, obligated to impart skills or a trade to the apprentice. The master was obligated to provide indentured servants adequate food, shelter, clothing, and protection. Although property ownership was generally allowed, voting, marriage, or engaging in a trade for personal gain was forbidden without the consent of the master. Upon completion of the term, servants were given clothing, tools, and other goods to make their way in the world. Male servants performed a wide variety of tasks while female servants generally performed domestic duties.

Although skilled workers from England were eventually prevented from leaving England to settle in the colony, unskilled workers, especially the "unwanted elements" of society, were encouraged to leave. It was erroneously believed at the time that England was overpopulated. Also called "transports," vagrants, the unemployed, criminals, widows, and orphans were shipped wholesale from England, often involuntarily, with the dual purpose of reducing England's underclass while developing a larger consumer society in the colonies. A quarter of all British immigrants were convicts. Colonists were disgusted and upset at the export of England's "undesirables" and eventually succeeded in halting the migration of criminals. Transports also included political prisoners who were frequently exiled for their religious beliefs. The tide of sending transports to America changed near the beginning of the Revolution, when England curbed all emigration. American governors were prohibited from issuing land titles and naturalization bills to immigrants from Great Britain and Ireland. This issue was taken up in the Declaration of Independence.

Some impoverished Americans willingly accepted servitude, most likely because no alternative remunerative jobs were available or because they owed a debt. Christians were legally prevented from going into servitude. Indentured servants and slaves were advertised for sale in the newspapers in much the same way that other property was. Following English law, masters were not allowed to dismiss servants before the end of their agreed upon term without sufficient reason and approval of town council members and its chief officer. In the event of incurable illness, dismissal of servants was forbidden. When a servant became injured while employed, the master provided for all costs incurred. Unwarranted and unnecessary dismissals, it was reasoned, would place an undue amount of burden on poor relief agencies. Conversely, workers were not permitted to leave their positions at will. This was done primarily to prevent masters from luring potential employees away from their present master.

Servants also conspired with each other and slaves to help each other run away. In the early days of the colonies, blacks were sold as indentured servants as well as slaves. Servants escaped from ships before they could be sold or ran away during their bondage. Servants departed from their masters for a variety reasons—cruel masters, change of heart, and the realization that they could earn higher wages selling their services in the free market.

For white servants, especially early in the colonial period, running away successfully required, at best, a change of appearance, because their parting was usually advertised in local newspapers with only a description of their physical features. Being white, they could slip into general society fairly easily. For blacks, it was much more difficult to integrate into society because of the color of their skin, even in areas with free blacks, because their numbers were so small. If a black runaway was detained and unclaimed, the finder would retain him or her, the same way any other property might be retained.

Slave Labor

In *Race and Nationality in American Life* (1957), historian Oscar Handlin writes that prior to the eighteenth century, only two categories of persons existed: free and unfree. With the institutionalization of slavery, the new categories distinguishing Americans became free and slave. The development of slavery in America has a unique history. White unfree workers as well as black workers were referred to as slaves in equal measure, with the trafficking of Irish servants also known as slave trade. In fact, the terms "slave" and "servant" were used somewhat interchangeably, slave being an epithet whose usage did not necessarily imply increased subservience, at least in terms of race or personage. There were also little differences in bondage times between blacks and whites. Although some blacks were kept in bondage permanently, others were held in servitude for a limited number of years or were able to purchase their freedom perhaps through the tending of small plots of land when not working

for their master. Blacks who served out their service periods became artisans and farmers on their own land and enjoyed a similar status to free whites. In fact, in 1668, in a county in eastern Virginia, 29 percent of blacks were free.

Christianity was also taken into account in determining slave and servant status, and those who converted were often released. After labor's value increased, however, legislators rethought this religious loophole and between 1667 and 1671 enacted laws that negated conversion as a determinant for manumission.

Furthermore, many parts of the colonies, especially in the North, had smaller and more seasonal agricultural economies that did not require investment in a perpetual and relatively expensive labor force. It was simply more economical to hire workers for the short term than to have to feed, clothe, and house them year round.

Shifting economic conditions and the increasing desire to institutionalize racism as a means of social control hastened the entrenchment of slavery in the American way of life. August 1619 opened the chapter of black slavery in America when twenty Africans were brought to Virginia. Although many white transports were brought to the colony under duress, as Handlin notes, *all* blacks were brought to America involuntarily. Slavery began gradually, with a significant number of blacks being sold as indentured servants as well as slaves. In 1664, England took over New Amsterdam from the Dutch and declared in law that service terms for black servants were to be "perpetual." By the last half of the seventeenth century, slavery became legal in all thirteen colonies.

After 1690, South Carolina began to move its economy away from the naval and fur trade industries toward large-scale agriculture, including rice, cotton, and indigo plantations. Plantation owners immediately recognized that having a permanent labor supply, which could be exploited, was the most profitable way to farm. The enormous profits in trafficking and ownership of slaves "steadily sucked slaves" to the plantation. Those who owned slaves already realized they were sitting on goldmines and encouraged the breeding of future slaves. The opening of Africa in 1698 to free trade brought large numbers of slaves to the Chesapeake and South Carolina areas, and by the eighteenth century there were heavy and rapid increases in the slave population due in part to importation but also in great measure to births.

Although the early colonial period was comparatively less racialized, at least in legal terms, white masters still preferred white workers to black ones. Recently imported Africans were seen as strange and unruly, lacking English-language skills and an understanding of European customs and mores. In the hierarchy of desirable black workers, preference was given to skilled native-born black males, while unskilled recent arrivals were the least preferred.

Workers from Europe became increasingly reluctant to come to the colonies because of the harsh life they would experience as recounted by other emigrants. To encourage more white workers to come to America, contract periods were shortened and land was offered as part of the freedom dues for many Europeans, including the Irish, who were not regarded in the same social category as those with English ancestry. This period initiated the Irish into a higher social category, separating them from blacks and Native Americans, who were increasingly thought of as the lowest elements in American society. The shortage of white workers and the inability or unwillingness to grant land to servants completing their contract also precipitated the buildup of black slave labor.

Slaves did mostly agricultural work. Women as well as men toiled in the fields; women also did domestic work: cooking, cleaning, spinning, and child rearing, including working as wet nurses. On larger plantations, slaves were divided into house servants and field hands, who were the majority on any plantation. Slave compensation was, of course, nil, and the basic necessities slaves received were mostly abominable. Housing was poor, usually without windows or flooring. The food was meager, consisting of starch and low-quality meat. Clothing—or cloth for the women to sew—was distributed once or twice year, with each adult receiving a pair of shoes that were usually the same for men and women and with children receiving no shoes until they could work in the field.

The American economy began to diversify more after 1720. In addition, artisanal indentured servants often left their respective trade to become independent farmers upon completing their contracts. The influence of these shifts trickled down to black slaves, enabling them to acquire more mechanical skills. Slave owners diversified the skills of their slaves to make up for seasonal slowdowns and inflationary periods. It was also not unusual for slave owners to rent out their slaves; this alternative was often very profitable for the owners.

The training of slaves as artisans was problematic for free white artisans. Most notably in the South where there were more blacks than in the North,

skilled white workers complained that skilled black workers were competing for their jobs. By and large, this was true, especially in the towns. Legislation was enacted to restrict the hiring out of slaves and to prevent blacks from sharing in the income from their labor.

Despite the fact that businessmen working in tandem with the state developed a divisive strategy aimed at weakening attempts to formulate any sort of working class, black, white, and Native American workers still managed to form bonds. In the early colonial period, it was not uncommon for servants and slaves to work together to escape their lot. Punishment for those captured was harsh, usually hanging or immolation. But even for minor infractions, servants and slaves alike received lashings and beatings. Because of their impoverished nature, it was impossible to levy fines for most infractions.

The rapidly growing numbers of blacks in the South encouraged whites to enact strict legislation against slaves. In South Carolina, nearly two-thirds of their population was black, and in Virginia it was 50 percent. Whites lived in constant fear of slave uprisings. The gathering of blacks, even on Sundays, was severely limited, and when runaways were caught, slaves not involved in fleeing were also punished.

WOMEN

Women have been generally overlooked in research studies, even though women in the colonial and Revolutionary periods performed work both inside and outside the home. Barbara Mayer Wertheimer begins her chronicle of women workers by noting that Native American women were the first women to work in America. They were the first people known to grow corn and to produce maple sugar. Generally, in most tribes, they were responsible for agriculture and domestic work including child rearing. If it was not for these women, who shared their knowledge of the land, the earliest colonial settlers would not have survived.

The first settlers to America came from England in 1607, settling in what they called Jamestown. Shortly thereafter, large numbers of women were brought from England to keep the male settlers content and to populate the new colony. Originally, women were allotted land in similar fashion to male settlers, but this policy was halted because it impeded women's need, and perhaps even desire, to marry quickly.

The harsh colonial life was especially taxing to women. Women married young and bore many children. They often died young, and their husbands usually sought to remarry quickly. Women who did not have their own family, land, or business were often supported by relatives. Referred to as "spinsters," they labored in the home, were given no privacy, and had no spending money. Widows in New York, however, organized themselves to protest their treatment by society, stating that they supported the government by paying taxes and carrying businesses.

Women maintained the household and reared the children. Husbands and sons usually ran the small businesses that sustained the early colonists, and wives and daughters often provided additional labor. The women, therefore, learned to shoe animals, work with metals, keep the books, and operate tools. Girls did not learn trades the way apprenticed boys did; their instruction was done in the home by helping family members.

Some women earned their living through the few professions that were allowed women. Keeping a tavern or inn was mostly a woman's business. Midwifery and doctoring were other professions in which women dominated, at least until the Revolutionary period. However, because women were not seen as equal in the eyes of the law, they had their own unique difficulties. A Maryland doctor named Katherine Hebden was unable to collect her payment for services rendered. Her husband had to take the case to court on the grounds that he was entitled to money owed him for work his wife had performed.

LABOR ORGANIZING

Unions, in the modern sense of the term, developed in the nineteenth century. In the colonial and early independence era, some workers formed mutual aid societies to provide death benefits to workers and other rudimentary services, but the organizations typically did not protest harsh conditions. Nor did they advocate politically or socially the improvement of worker rights.

The guild system that protected worker rights in Europe did not readily transfer to American society. Still, workers organized protests against government regulations that impinged on their survival and dignity on the job. Attempts were made in the colonial era to regulate the maximum level of wages and to fix prices for goods and services to prevent workers from earning more than necessary for subsistence.

Although there were certainly instances of labor disputes in colonial America, scholars continue to debate whether these disputes can be conflated to be equivalent to strikes. Undoubtedly, a number of individual work stoppages and demands for changes in the workplace, whether in compensation, hours, or treatment, flared up from time to time. However, strikes—the collective stoppage of work and services to obtain improvement in wages and working conditions—began at the end of the eighteenth century, as the unbridling of workers from their masters or slaveholders through the development of capitalism became pervasive, particularly in urban industrial areas. Thus, the strike is indelibly associated with capitalist social relations.

Various examples of early strikes are recorded by numerous sources. Thomas R. Brooks writes that America's first labor strike occurred in Philadelphia in 1786 by printers who "turned-out" to obtain a minimum wage of six dollars per week. Dulles and Dubofsky claim that the first recorded strike in U.S. labor history did not occur until 1799 by a group of organized cordwainers—shoemakers who work with Cordovan leather—in Philadelphia. After staying off the job for ten weeks, the cordwainers won a new contract from the master shoemakers.

In John R. Commons' comprehensive series, *History of Labour in the United States* (1918), David J. Saposs writes on the problem of distinguishing between strikes by master workmen and those by journeymen. The master workmen generally revolted against price regulation by public authorities, whereas the journeymen struck against employers to maintain wages. In the instance of the strike in 1786 by printers in Philadelphia, the printers were both merchants and laborers, so the "purity" of their strike, as a true workers' protest, becomes somewhat suspect. Brooks notes that black sweepers' refusal to work in Charlestown, South Carolina (present day Charleston), in 1761 might well constitute the first worker-led work stoppage.

Other labor disturbances in the colonial period include a mutiny of indentured servants and fishermen in 1636 off the coast of Maine, protesting the withholding of wages. In 1661, indentured servants in Virginia planned a rebellion. Officials in Maryland faced a public disturbance attended by workers in 1663. Protesting against their conditions, ship carpenters in 1675 issued a formal protest against their conditions. New York City recorded a work stoppage by licensed carters in 1677. Ordered to clean the streets of New York for 3 pence per cartload, they protested the pay and their treatment by the city as well. The carters protested their conditions again in 1684. Also in New

York, bakers stopped baking bread in 1741 and tailors stopped sewing in 1768. In 1768, indentured servants revolted in what is now Florida. That same year also saw a turnout by journeymen tailors in New York protesting their low wages and offering to perform their services for private employers.

During the Revolutionary period there were instances of strikes and disturbances, which were spurred by inflationary prices and declining purchasing power and, undoubtedly, encouraged by the rebellious nature of the times. In November 1778, journeymen printers in New York demanded and received pay increases. Similar protests were waged in 1779 by seamen in Philadelphia, shoemakers in New York in 1785, and journeymen printers in Philadelphia the following year.

The independence era also saw public debate about the inhumanity of the system of slavery. Prior to this time, abolitionist groups and individuals demanded cessation of slavery on moral grounds. The eighteenth century witnessed the development and questioning of the rights of citizens in general, and the question of slavery became part of that discussion. The hypocrisy of demanding full rights from the British while enslaving a significant number of their own was not lost to many colonialists. Indentured servitude had already begun waning, and after the war, slave importation ceased.

Malini Cadambi

BIBLIOGRAPHY

Brooks, Thomas R. *Toil and Trouble: A History of American Labor.* New York: Delacorte, 1971.

Cahn, William. *A Pictorial History of American Labor: The Contributions of the Working Man and Woman to America's Growth, from Colonial Times to the Present.* New York: Crown, 1972.

Commons, John R., et al. *History of Labour in the United States.* 1918. Reprint, New York: A.M. Kelley, 1966.

Dulles, Foster Rhea, and Melvin Dubofsky. *Labor in America: A History.* Arlington Heights, IL: Harlan Davidson, 1984.

Handlin, Oscar. *Race and Nationality in American Life.* Garden City, NY: Doubleday Anchor Books, 1957.

Jernegan, Marcus Wilson. *Laboring and Dependent Classes in Colonial America: 1607–1783.* New York: Frederick Ungar, 1931.

McKee, Samuel, Jr. *Labor in Colonial New York: 1664–1776.* New York: Columbia University Press; London: P.S. King & Son, 1935.

Morris, Richard B. *Government and Labor in Early America.* New York: Harper & Row, 1965.

Saposs, David J. *History of Labour in the United States.* Edited by John R. Commons. New York: Augustus M. Kelley, 1966.

Wertheimer, Barbara Mayer. *We Were There: The Story of Working Women in America.* New York: Pantheon Books, 1977.

LABOR MOVEMENT 1790–1860

If there is a single development that marked the beginning of the antebellum labor movement, it occurred in 1827 when skilled artisans from across more than a dozen unions in Philadelphia organized that city's Mechanics' Union of Trade Associations (MUTA). As the preamble to its constitution announced, the organization aimed "to raise the mechanical and productive classes to that condition of true independence and equality which their practical skill and ingenuity, their immense utility to the nation, and their growing intelligence are beginning imperiously to demand." To be sure, collective action by skilled workers in the new American republic well predated the MUTA. In the quarter-century following the American Revolution, mechanics' institutes emerged to celebrate the productive role and promote the economic interests of their members, and to uphold such hallmarks of artisanship as the traditional apprenticeship system. Early craft unions such as the Federal Society of Journeymen Cordwainers (shoemakers) in Philadelphia (1794), appeared, and these in turn became vehicles for strikes.

Still, the MUTA represented a critical new departure and the next phase in the history of organized American labor—the nation's first citywide confederation of trade unions. This innovation, together with Working Men's parties, local trade unions, cooperative workshops, and (in the 1850s) national unions, comprised the basic institutional landscape of the antebellum labor movement and, at least in terms of trade unionism, of the American labor movement ever since.

SOCIOECONOMIC ORIGINS OF THE MOVEMENT

Not quite forty years before the founding of the Philadelphia confederation, artisans in Boston, New York, Philadelphia, and elsewhere had paraded in commemoration of the ratification by their respective states of the new Federal Constitution (1788), which they believed would enhance their economic prospects by creating a central government able to stimulate American industry and thus national prosperity. Their elaborate floats celebrated not only the new federal edifice but also their deep-felt pride of place in it—their essential role as the nation's "bone and sinew" and, related intimately to that, their claim, if as yet not fully realized, to independence and equality. By the age of Jackson, however, growing numbers of skilled white workingmen, like the members of Philadelphia's central labor union, were building not floats but a labor movement, were declaring not the ascendancy but the degradation and decline of workingmen and labor in republican America. These tightly intertwined institutional and ideological developments would, however unevenly and sporadically, persist, broaden, and deepen between the late 1820s and the Civil War.

Behind these developments lay a profound and ongoing transformation of work wrought by the market revolution of the late eighteenth and early nineteenth centuries (c. 1780–1830). With the growth of markets, itself the product of revolutionary changes in transportation (first roads and turnpikes, then canals, then railroads), more and more Americans were drawn more deeply and regularly into commercial exchanges and contractual relationships. For craftsmen, as for all free adult white Americans, this brought liberating choice and opportunity, but also increasing social inequality. Thus, ambitious master craftsmen with adequate capital could, and did, join the growing ranks of entrepreneurial merchant capitalist employers who sought financial gain and upward mobility by manufacturing a particular good for an extensive market. In most cases (printing and textiles were the notable exceptions), this involved for most of the period not mechanization but rather the "sweated" sub-

FACTORY RULES FROM THE HANDBOOK TO LOWELL   1848

The "Lowell System," imposed on young women working in a textile mill for Frances Cabot Lowell, a manufacturer, became a prototype for many workers employed in the embryonic manufacturing industries of mid-nineteenth-century America. Under the harsh system, "mill girls" worked long hours under unsafe conditions for low pay.

REGULATIONS TO BE OBSERVED by all persons employed in the factories of the Hamilton Manufacturing Company. The overseers are to be always in their rooms at the starting of the mill, and not absent unnecessarily during working hours. They are to see that all those employed in their rooms, are in their places in due season, and keep a correct account of their time and work. They may grant leave of absence to those employed under them, when they have spare hands to supply their places, and not otherwise, except in cases of absolute necessity.

All persons in the employ of the Hamilton Manufacturing Company, are to observe the regulations of the room where they are employed. They are not to be absent from their work without the consent of the overseer, except in cases of sickness, and then they are to send him word of the cause of their absence. They are to board in one of the houses of the company and give information at the counting room, where they board, when they begin, or, whenever they change their boarding place; and are to observe the regulations of their boarding-house.

Those intending to leave the employment of the company, are to give at least two weeks' notice thereof to their overseer.

All persons entering into the employment of the company, are considered as engaged for twelve months, and those who leave sooner, or do not comply with all these regulations, will not be entitled to a regular discharge.

The company will not employ any one who is habitually absent from public worship on the Sabbath, or known to be guilty of immorality.

A physician will attend once in every month at the counting-room, to vaccinate all who may need it, free of expense.

Any one who shall take from the mills or the yard, any yarn, cloth or other article belonging to the company, will be considered guilty of stealing and be liable to prosecution.

Payment will be made monthly, including board and wages. The accounts will be made up to the last Saturday but one in every month, and paid in the course of the following week.

These regulations are considered part of the contract, with which all persons entering into the employment of the Hamilton Manufacturing Company, engage to comply.

JOHN AVERY, Agent.

Source: Factory Rules from the Handbook to Lowell, 1848. (Chicago, IL: Illinois Labor History Society, 1848).

division of skilled manual work among dependent journeymen (now the "employed") concentrated in central workshops and paid low wages.

Under these exploitative conditions, journeymen found it increasingly difficult, if not impossible, to follow the traditional artisanal path to master status and the "competency," or modest independent means, that status conferred. Nor could the traditional apprentice system survive cost-cutting masters–employers who turned it into a source of cheap child labor. In short, even as the market revolution enabled some craftsmen (well-situated masters in particular) to prosper, the handicrafts—both as a system of production and as a social relationship that bound journeymen and masters together around historically mutual interests— were undergoing "bastardization," and artisans were in turn bifurcating into bosses and wageworkers. By the late antebellum period, a large and permanent

wage-earning working class had emerged in the United States.

Journeymen in the reorganized handicrafts were neither the only wageworkers in the industrial sector nor the only workers to engage in collective labor protest. The emerging factory system—symbolized most famously to contemporaries by the water-powered textile mills of Lowell, Massachusetts—provided a second, if less common, path to wagework and a setting for employer–employee conflict. By mid-century, unskilled laborers like dockworkers and those who built the canals and railroads essential to the market revolution formed another permanent segment of the new wage-earning working class and engaged in strikes against employers.

Still, in composition and ideology, the antebellum labor movement was dominated by skilled and semiskilled workingmen experiencing and resisting their own proletarianization. If not all labor protest was their protest, it was through their organized collective actions, as well as their ideas, that the labor movement largely arose and developed.

IDEOLOGY AND AIMS

Antebellum labor activists articulated a mobilizing ideology focused on both the exploitation of artisanal labor and, more broadly, the growing social inequality attendant on the market revolution and industrialization. Refashioning the republicanism of the American Revolution, they linked the progress (and thus the fate) of the republic to the labor, the virtue, and the welfare of its workingmen, and they mounted a moral critique of free-labor capitalism that located the root cause of degraded labor and social inequality in a pervasive and selfish "spirit of avarice." That rapacious spirit, they believed, warped government and society, creating the conditions under which parasitical "nonproducers" (or "the aristocracy"), themselves possessed and morally deranged by avarice, unjustly deprived workingmen of the fruits of their labor. As a result, the discourse of the movement warned, workingmen were on the verge of enslavement through loss of their personal independence, and the republic itself was on the verge of that fatal corruption that (history and republican theory taught) was the inevitable consequence when love of liberty succumbed to love of gain. It was thus their urgent, momentous, and heroic duty to rescue, through organized collective action, labor and the republic from tyrannical wealth and the grotesque inequality it fostered.

Important as these themes were, there was significantly more to the movement's ideology than the "artisan [or labor] republicanism" stressed by a generation of labor historians. For one thing, as those historians themselves have noted, republicanism combined labor rhetoric with an emphasis on equal rights and the labor theory of value. Thus, workingmen proclaimed their right to organize for their own protection and sang countless paeans to the generative and civilizing powers of their useful (skilled) labor. Moreover, they juxtaposed such paeans with laments of labor's degradation, thereby highlighting and protesting what they saw as a jarring, telling, and dangerous contradiction between the dignity and respect labor deserved and the contempt and exploitation it suffered.

From the complementary currents of evangelical Protestantism, with its promise of salvation through free will and free-labor capitalism, with its promise of economic gain through individual exertion, came the theme of collective self-agency that saturated workingmen's ideology and lent it effectiveness in rallying workers to the cause. If workingmen awoke to their imminent slavery and united to resist those who would enslave them, this theme promised, victory—and with it the gratitude of "posterity"—would be theirs. Its logical counterpoint was that workingmen ultimately had only themselves to blame for their oppression. Indeed, the notion of workingmen's ironic and perverse complicity in their own degradation figured prominently in the movement's ideology, complementing and reinforcing republicanism's emphasis on vigilant citizenship.

The parallels with antebellum revivalist Protestantism's treatment of individual sin and salvation are revealing. Labor ideology in this period (and beyond) was, on the whole, saturated with evangelical language and themes, a fact too often obscured by the almost single-minded stress placed by most labor historians on artisan republicanism. Scripture, for example, provided rich material for pointed condemnations of unjust (that is, ungodly) accumulations of wealth, especially on the backs of those who labored. As prominent labor leader Seth Luther declared, quoting Jesus, in his *Address on the Origins and Progress of Avarice* (1834): "YE CANNOT SERVE GOD AND MAMMON." (It is worth noting here that "avarice" was at once a republican and religious trope, and like similar multivalent keywords in labor discourse it at once facilitated and reflected labor activists' blending of the two traditions.) Protestant millennialism not only supplied assurances that, as already noted, workingmen aroused and united in defense of their rights would prevail, but simultaneously elevated their cause to the plane of cosmic Christian conflict between light and darkness. On their cause, on their redemptive mission, rested the fate not simply of workingmen but of humanity itself.

Religion, then, lent labor protest legitimacy, hope, momentousness, and a clarifying moral critique that blasted the exploitation of labor and social inequality. Simultaneously, like republicanism's fear of class privilege and in conjunction with it, Christianity's emphasis on forgiveness muddied class ways of thinking and blunted the movement's radical edge.

Antebellum labor ideology was also highly racialized and gendered in tightly intertwined ways. In a republic where the vast majority of freemen were white men, whiteness was virtually synonymous with republican independence and citizenship, and blackness with dependence and servility (both external and internal). Such a context ensured that jeremiads about workingmen's (imminent) descent into "white slavery" (a term far more common than "wage slavery") bespoke racialized anxieties about the security of workingmen's whiteness. Blacks loomed as the Other whose fate workingmen feared, abhorred, and seemed in danger of sharing. In such a context, as historian David Roediger (drawing on W.E.B. Du Bois) has argued in *The Wages of Whiteness* (1999), workingmen sought refuge in their whiteness, and whiteness (or more precisely, its privileges) in turn provided them with a psychological "wage" that could compensate for their economic exploitation.

The racialized anxieties workingmen's rhetoric bespoke were intimately bound up with dread of emasculation. The attributes of a slave—most notably, dependence and physical and mental servility—were precisely those of an unmanly man. Hence, antebellum labor ideology represented the labor movement as at once the expression and redemption of (white) worker manhood. Manly workingmen, it instructed time and again, were organized and united in defense of their rights; responsive to the heroic duty to which they were called as deliverers of labor, the republic, humanity, and posterity from the thralldom of oppressive wealth; and ultimately invincible. Manliness was also invoked, explicitly and implicitly, to contrast fair (i.e., manly) workingmen with their unjust (i.e., unmanly) oppressors.

In manliness, in short, race, class, and gender converged. As a trope, moreover, it served to condense and make even more compelling the major discursive elements of the labor ideology it pervaded. At the same time, in its accent on character and respectability, shared with and strengthened by the discourse of whiteness, manliness rhetoric muted even as it amplified the movement's class timbre.

The manliness trope occasionally inflected even the rhetoric of protesting women workers and their female allies in interesting ways. In 1844, New England activist Sarah Bagley combined feminist overtones with deference to workingmen's manly agency when, on one hand, she firmly protested the economic and political circumstances of New England's female factory operatives, while on the other she looked to workingmen "to protect your daughters and sisters."

In contrast, a contemporary of Bagley mocked men's pretensions to manliness ("Prate no more of your manliness") and asserted that not men but "the strong and resolute of their own sex" would protect women. Other female labor leaders conceived of mo-

bilized and united workingwomen in ways that paralleled the concept of manliness among their male counterparts.

Nor were the twinned tropes of slavery and whiteness confined to male workers' rhetoric. Urging the women shoebinders of Lynn, Massachusetts, to strike for a higher wage in 1860, Clara Brown was quoted in the *New York Times* in language that brought a sharp rebuke followed by a revealing clarification on her part: "Don't let them make niggers of you; (Shame, there are colored persons here.) I meant Southern niggers."

The ideology of the antebellum labor movement was thus multidimensional and complex. It was also elastic. For these reasons it lent itself to no single, specific program, but rather to a variety of movement objectives, some more pronounced in one phase than in another, all of them intended to redress labor's degradation and the social inequality it so glaringly reflected. For the same reasons, it lent itself equally well to excoriations of "nonproducers" and "purse-proud aristocrats," "grinding employers," and "capital" (a term invoked with increasing regularity in the period's second half).

Among the principal demands that defined the movement as it first emerged in its early years were public funding of public schools; restrictions on (or even the abolition of) state-chartered corporations (paper-money-issuing banks were judged to be particularly dangerous); abolition of imprisonment for debt; restrictions on convict labor; mechanics' lien laws to ensure payment for work done; reform of militia service so as not to burden workingmen financially; and the dispersal of public land in the West to small homesteaders rather than speculators (an aim that, with varying intensity, persisted throughout the period). As this list suggests, privileges and monopolies obtained through "class" legislation favoring "the few" at the expense of "the many" were perceived as the primary problem.

This early antimonopoly stance and related concern with government-sponsored "artificial" privileges would to varying degrees remain a general feature of the movement. At the same time, from the early-1830s on, labor activists as a whole repeatedly focused on developing trade unionism at the craft, city, and national levels; staging strikes over wages and hours; securing the ten-hour day; and, as an alternative to the wage system, establishing worker-owned cooperative workshops (in addition to land reform).

The ideology (and related objectives) of antebellum labor protest at once cast doubt on, critiqued, and suggested alternatives to the period's dominant free-labor ideology. Free laborism stressed the imperative and possibility of virtually unlimited (white male) self-making in a world where wagework was (supposedly) but a temporary condition, a waystation on the road to becoming one's own boss, who in turn hired other men on their way up. It took as givens and represented as natural the values and workings of the marketplace, above all competitive individualism and the law of supply and demand.

Organized workingmen did not reject upward mobility; indeed, their rhetoric occasionally pointed with pride to mechanics who, through their own skill (or genius) and hard work, had risen out of the ranks of labor. But neither did they embrace the unbridled, exploitative, selfish race for wealth they perceived all around them and to which they attributed their own, and the republic's, alarming situation. Their ideology represented the scramble for gain as immoral and corrupting of republican simplicity and virtue, as rewarding only a few, and as exposing the hypocrisy in free-labor rhetoric about the dignity of labor ("If labor of the hands is thus honored and rewarded," a leading labor paper of the 1840s pointedly asked, "why such a universal scramble . . . to forego its honors and rewards, by entering into speculation and trade?"). And it rejected the arguments of free-labor proponents that the price of workmen's labor—their property, some labor advocates called it—should be determined by supply and demand, and that unions were both unjust and unnecessary. Labor ideology was not revolutionary—it did not envision the violent overthrow of one class by another; but, as the foregoing suggests, it was radically oppositional in its challenge to the basic thrust and dominance of free-labor values.

PHASES AND LEADERSHIP

The early years of the movement were dominated not by trade unionism but by labor politics in the form of Working Men's parties, the most important of which were centered in the metropolitan Northeast. Philadelphia led the way when the MUTA resolved in early 1829 to organize a party in that city. New York and Boston soon followed suit. Party platforms shared a thoroughgoing antimonopolism focused on the evils of legislatively created corporations in the financial and manufacturing sectors. Despite the impressive showing of some at the polls—Philadelphia Working Men, for example, won more than 30 percent of the vote in 1829, while that same year the New York party

elected a journeyman carpenter to the state assembly (and came close to sending six others to Albany with him). The parties proved short-lived. Inexperience, factionalism, and the lure of Andrew Jackson's Democratic Party, which attracted workingmen's votes with its antimonopoly agenda and its celebration of producers over nonproducers, all took their toll.

Wary of labor politics, workingmen's advocates in the early 1830s concentrated instead on trade unionism. A flurry of union building and strikes ensued, fueled in no small part by the ten-hour day demand. (That demand, it should be noted, entailed political pressure brought to bear at the state and federal levels, and thus the labor movement never eschewed politics altogether in this period of surging unionism and beyond.) Led by the General Trades' Union (GTU) of New York (1833), citywide federations of local unions soon emerged in more than a dozen cities in the East and trans-Allegheny West. The GTUs not only lent financial support to strikes by member unions but also sponsored lectures and labor newspapers. Their conventions and committees, moreover, schooled journeymen in participatory union democracy. Trade union membership probably hovered between one-fifth and one-third of urban journeymen, a proportion never again attained before the Civil War.

Beyond the citywide federations, two innovative organizations of this period were the New England Association of Farmers, Mechanics, and Other Working Men (1832) and the National Trades' Union (1834). The association dedicated itself to the ten-hour day and set March 20, 1832, as the date on which, absent overtime pay, all members of the organization "except practical farmers" were "to labor no more than ten hours for one day." As its title suggests, it was the first attempt at industrial unionism in the United States, seeking to unite in a single organization factory operatives, unskilled laborers, and skilled tradesmen. The Trades' Union, whose founding convention attracted delegates representing more than 25,000 workers in six Eastern city centrals, marked the first national organization of American workers, though during its two-year existence it remained geographically narrower than its name promised.

The upsurge in unionism was accompanied by a veritable wave of strikes, with some of the most important action occurring in Boston, Philadelphia, and New York. In 1835, Boston carpenters, masons, and stonecutters, joined eventually by the city's housewrights, struck for the ten-hour day. Though ultimately unsuccessful, the strike produced a stirring and influential document in the antebellum struggle for shorter hours, the "Ten-Hour Circular." Depicting the struggle as one between workingmen and "Capital," the circular declared in language redolent with republicanism, evangelical Protestantism, whiteness, and manliness: "We cannot, we will not, longer be mere slaves to inhuman, insatiable and unpitying avarice." Sentiments like these helped that same year to inspire a general strike in Philadelphia (the nation's first) for the ten-hour day. The strike was notable for including skilled and unskilled, Irish and native-born workers. Aided by a petition campaign, it succeeded in pressuring the city council to limit the hours of workingmen employed by the city to ten. Other employers quickly followed the council's example.

In New York the next year, striking journeymen tailors became the object of an employer offensive against unions and strikes that left twenty tailors convicted of conspiracy. Both the conviction and the presiding judge became instantly notorious among the workingmen of New York and beyond. Some 27,000 of the city's residents rallied in protest, burning Judge Ogden Edwards in effigy and blasting the prosecution of the tailors as "a concerted plan of the aristocracy to take from them that Liberty which was bequeathed to them as a sacred inheritance by their revolutionary sires." In Philadelphia, protests led to an unprecedented formal alliance between skilled and unskilled workers when the Trades' Union voted to include dockworkers.

Some women workers were also caught up in the strike wave of the 1830s. The New York Tailoresses' Society, organized in 1831 and 1,600 strong, struck that same year. In mid-decade Philadelphia, women shoe and clothing workers struck with the support of unionized male shoemakers and tailors. Among female textile operatives, the most notable strikes occurred in Lowell, Massachusetts, where mill owners' vaunted paternalism was both challenged and exposed as selfish when women stopped working in 1834 to resist wage cuts (unsuccessfully) and again in 1836 to oppose higher boardinghouse rents (resulting in compromise).

It was against this backdrop of surging and, for unions, resource-draining strike activity that the labor movement after mid-1836 began to embrace cooperative production as the "more permanent" answer to workingmen's oppression called for by the National Trades' Union. Cooperation, that organization maintained, would enable workingmen to sell "their labor directly to the consumer," thereby ending speculation and ensuring "they would receive the full product." As historian Bruce Laurie more pointedly summed up

this program in *Artisans into Workers* (1989), it was "a collective project to achieve social equality and worker control." Though many cooperative workshops were indeed soon established, they, like the labor movement itself, succumbed to economic depression in 1837.

In its first decade, the movement was led by an array of talented activists, some of whom would continue as leaders when the movement revived in the 1840s. William Heighton, a cordwainer born in England, founded Philadelphia's MUTA; edited the Union's newspaper, the *Mechanics' Free Press;* and authored three speeches, the first of which ("An Address to the Members of Trade Societies, and to the Working Classes Generally. [1827]) profoundly influenced the rising of workingmen in his city and perhaps beyond.

The career of another Philadelphia cordwainer, William English, illustrates how thoroughly involved activists could be in the full range of existing labor institutions. English served as a leader of the Philadelphia Working Men's party, as a founding delegate to the National Trades' Union, and as president of the Philadelphia Trades' Union. He orated in favor of the ten-hour day and helped to found the National Association of Cordwainers before being elected state representative in 1836.

Among the New York leadership, machinist Thomas Skidmore created a considerable stir with his *The Rights of Men to Property!* (1829), a proposal for eliminating social inequality through an agrarian program of redistribution and expropriation. His approach was too extreme even for the Working Men's party to which he belonged before being expelled. Breaking with Skidmore, labor editor George Henry Evans developed a moderate land reform proposal that would figure prominently in the labor movement in the 1840s. Other leaders benefited the city's GTU, especially printer Ely Moore, its first president, and chairmaker John Commerford, who succeeded Moore in 1835. Moore had been elected the previous year to the chairmanship of the National Trades' Union and to the U.S. House of Representatives. New York also produced Sarah Monroe, leader of the Tailoresses' Society, about whom little is known.

In Boston and New England, the carpenter Seth Luther emerged as probably the region's most influential and best known labor activist. A brilliant orator and agitator, several of whose addresses were published as pamphlets, Luther helped to organize the Boston Trades' Union and also championed factory hands. He was likely principal author of the "Ten-Hour Circular" and was still agitating the cause eleven years later in 1846, the year he died. No antebellum labor leader produced more scorching jeremiads on the evils of avarice and factory work.

Luther's agitation in the 1840s was part of the labor movement's post-Depression revival around especially the ten-hour day demand. The struggle galvanized New England journeymen and female mill workers who cooperated across lines of skill and gender. Women played a critical role by engaging in petition campaigns to pressure state legislatures to enact ten-hour statutes. Male–female cooperation was institutionalized when the New England Workingmen's Association (1844) agreed in 1845 to admit the Lowell Female Labor Reform Association (1844). Both groups led the way organizationally.

Sarah Bagley rose to prominence as leader of the Lowell Female Labor Reform Association. A Lowell operative herself, Bagley spearheaded a petition drive aimed at the Massachusetts legislature, organized factory women in New Hampshire, and published critiques of factory conditions and owners. She collaborated with harness maker William F. Young, editor of the influential *Voice of Industry*, organ of the Workingmen's Association, and a key figure himself in the decade's labor agitation. For a brief period, Bagley edited the *Voice* after her association acquired it.

The ten-hour struggle of the 1840s had mixed results. New Hampshire passed the nation's first state ten-hour law in 1847 ("ALL HAIL NEW HAMPSHIRE," exulted the *Voice*), and Pennsylvania followed suit a year later after strikes and political pressure dating from 1845. Both laws, however, had loopholes. The Massachusetts legislature, notwithstanding the testimony of Sarah Bagley and six other women before a House committee, and a subsequent intensified petition campaign, refused to act.

Even as the ten-hour contest unfolded, workers and their leaders sought alternatives to the wage-labor system in cooperative workshops and land reform. From shoemakers in Lynn to German tailoresses in Cleveland, they established cooperatives throughout the North and West. Under the leadership of George Henry Evans, the National Reform Association (1844) promoted land reform as the solution to workers' ills. With its slogan "Vote Yourself a Farm," the organization sought to make public lands available for free to homesteading families. Both cooperationists and land reformers were represented in the Industrial Congresses that nourished labor activism across the urban North from the mid-1840s to the mid-1850s.

The 1850s witnessed a major development in the

THE FACTORY BELL
BY AN UNKNOWN FACTORY GIRL 1844

Most nineteenth-century Americans did not own a clock or a watch of their own to keep time. The tolling of the factory bell signified the beginning and end of the harsh workday for young women employed in the New England textile mills.

Loud the morning bell is ringing,
Up, up sleepers, haste away;
Yonder sits the redbreast singing,
but to list we must not stay.

Not for us is morning breaking,
Though we with Aurora rise;
Nor for us is Nature waking,
All her smiles through earth and skies.

Sisters, haste, the bell is tolling,
Soon will close the dreadful gate;
Then, alas! we must go strolling,
Through the counting-room, too late.

Now the sun is upward climbing,
And the breakfast hour has come;
Ding, dong, ding, the bell is chiming,
Hasten, sisters, hasten home.

Quickly now we take our ration,
For the bell will babble soon;
Each must hurry to her station,
There to toil till weary noon.

Mid-day sun in heaven is shining,
Merrily now the clear bell rings,
And the grateful hour of dining,
To us weary sisters brings.

Now we give a welcome greeting,
To these viands cooked so well;
Horrors! Oh! not half done eating—
Rattle, rattle goes the bell!

Sol behind the hills descended,
Upward throws his ruby light;
Ding dong ding,—our toil is ended,
Joyous bell, good night, good night.

Source: Factory Girl's Garland, Exeter, New Hampshire, May 25, 1844.

history of organized labor in the United States with the rise of national unions in various trades (among them the hatfinishers, cigar makers, typesetters, shoemakers, machinists and blacksmiths, and iron molders). Some were short-lived; all were important as a next stage in labor's organization-building. With the national unions came new leaders like molder William Sylvis, principal founder of the Iron Molders' International Union (1859), who grasped the need for strong national organizations in the context of nationwide markets and employers' associations. Sylvis himself would emerge as the nation's single most important Civil War–era labor leader.

The decade also saw continued agitation for the ten-hour day and episodes of intense strike activity culminating in what was then the largest strike in U.S. history, the Lynn shoemakers' strike of 1860. More than 20,000 men and women participated, bolstered by their numbers and placards like the one proclaiming, "American ladies will not be slaves: Give us a fair compensation and we labor cheerfully." Leadership came from men like Alonzo B. Draper, editor of the *New England Mechanic*, president of the Lynn Mechanics' Association, and an advocate of women's participation in support of higher wages for journeymen, and from women like Clara Brown, a young factory stitcher who sought to raise women's wages along with men's. After two months the strike ended in defeat. Its size, its mass mobilization of factory workers, and the presence of the militia were all harbingers of labor–capital conflict in the future.

Assessment

The antebellum labor movement, like all social movements, was characterized by strengths and weaknesses, some more easily seen with the advantages of hindsight and historical study. Certainly, the movement succeeded in bequeathing to American workers in the Gilded Age and beyond a core set of institutions—trade unions, city centrals, and at least fledgling nationals—as well as attendant institutional practices that would empower and sustain them in their conflicts with capital and would form the basis of the modern American labor movement. It succeeded, too, in developing and passing on the weapon of the strike, along with a program for radical change—cooperative production—that promised to make both strikes and wage labor obsolete. It ameliorated the exploitation of some, though by no means all, workers, prepared the way for the eight-hour day struggles, and engendered working-class pride and self-respect. More generally, the movement established organized labor protest as a permanent, if contested, part of the American political and social landscape.

And yet the divisive lines of ethnicity, race, gender, and skill seriously hobbled the movement. Nativism, together with the massive influx of German and especially Irish immigrants in the decade 1845–1854, created a fragmented working class, though there were hopeful instances of solidarity across ethnic lines. The movement also excluded blacks and marginalized white women. Even when male unionists supported, or sought the support of, women workers, they did so typically out of a sense of chivalry or a desire to lend legitimacy to their own cause.

The very language of labor, with its densely intertwined tropes of whiteness and manliness, iterated and reiterated racial and gender lines. And since lack of skill was readily associated with blacks, women, and Irish immigrants—who in turn were easily associated with dependence and lack of self-control—skilled workingmen most often shunned the unskilled. A different kind of line, between North and South, also limited the movement as Southern white male artisans actively cast their lot not with one another but with the slaveholding elite.

The movement's language and ideology were also problematic. There was a melodramatic and romantic cast to both that tended toward oversimplification—for example, the notion that aroused and united workingmen were invincible, which ultimately left only workingmen themselves to blame for their oppression. And for all that republicanism, evangelical Protestantism, whiteness, and manliness fed the movement's class-inflected oppositional critique of free-labor capitalism, they simultaneously muted classist ways of thinking and blunted labor radicalism.

Nonetheless, the antebellum labor movement stands as a significant and inspiring, if flawed, movement for social justice that first confronted more than 175 years ago issues of economic fairness that are with us still.

Gregory L. Kaster

Bibliography

Blewett, Mary H. *We Will Rise in Our Might*. Ithaca, NY: Cornell University Press, 1991.

Bronstein, Jamie L. *Land Reform and Working-Class Experience in Britain and the United States, 1800–1862*. Stanford, CA: Stanford University Press, 1999.

Commons, John R. *History of Labour in the United States*. Vol. 1. New York: Macmillan, 1918.

Fink, Gary M., ed. *Biographical Dictionary of American Labor*. Westport, CT: Greenwood Press, 1984.

Gillespie, Michele. *Free Labor in an Unfree World*. Athens: University of Georgia Press, 2000.

Kaster, Gregory L. "Labour's True Man: Organised Workingmen and the Language of Manliness in the USA, 1827–1877." *Gender & History* 13:1 (April 2001): 24–64.

Laurie, Bruce. *Artisans into Workers*. New York: Noonday, 1989.

Lazerow, Jama. *Religion and the Working Class in Antebellum America*. Washington, DC: Smithsonian Institution, 1995.

Levine, Bruce, Stephen Brier, et al. *Who Built America*. Vol. 1. New York: Pantheon Books, 1989.

Murphy, Teresa Anne. *Ten Hours' Labor*. Ithaca, NY: Cornell University Press, 1992.

Pessen, Edward. *Most Uncommon Jacksonians*. Albany: State University of New York Press, 1967.

Roediger, David R. *The Wages of Whiteness*. Rev. ed. London: Verso, 1999.

Roediger, David R., and Philip S. Foner. *Our Own Time*. London: Verso, 1989.

Ross, Steve J. *Workers on the Edge*. New York: Columbia University Press, 1985.

Sutton, William R. *Journeymen for Jesus*. University Park: Pennsylvania State University Press, 1998.

Wilentz, Sean. *Chants Democratic*. New York: Oxford University Press, 1984.

LABOR MOVEMENT

The years 1860 to 1877 were a pivotal era in the history of American labor. The Civil War was the catalyst that transformed both the economy and society, hastening the pace of industrialization and concentration of wealth in America. Monopolies and trusts were consolidating control of the nation's most important industries, making it more difficult for smaller firms to compete. Two interrelated trends posed a serious threat to workers' welfare: declining wages and the loss of jobs due to mechanization of the work process. The war brought prosperity to many businessmen and financiers, but most workers saw prices increase and their earning power decline. Male workers' earnings dropped, but women earned less than half of what men did, and children could be exploited for even less. Employers regularly pitted each against the other to keep wages down. Despite full employment conditions during the Civil War, the effects of labor-eliminating mechanization and unskilled workers had caused real wages in 1865 to drop by one-third from their 1860 level. Mechanization of many industries also meant that work could be simplified to the point where employers did not have to pay a premium for skilled workers.

This upheaval in the workplace challenged labor, which was primarily organized on local levels, or along craft lines, to organize unskilled and semi-skilled workers along industry lines on a national scale. The question for organized labor was whether it would remain as a narrow-based pressure group of craft workers, or transform itself into a broad-based working-class social movement open to all workers. The Civil War, which gave America, as President Abraham Lincoln put it, "a new birth of freedom," unleashed social forces of egalitarian reform in the labor movement. As a result, unions had to grapple with how they would respond to questions of race, gender, and immigration.

THE IRON WORKERS

During the mid-nineteenth century, the Iron Molders' International Union played an important leadership role in the effort to unite labor and mobilize it as a social movement. The Iron Molders was one of the most militant unions of the day, seeking social reforms through political action. Its president, William H. Sylvis, was one of the era's most dynamic labor leaders. Under his leadership, the Iron Molders established small-scale, worker-owned cooperatives, so that they could keep the fruits of their labor. But their cooperative efforts were overwhelmed by the growing industrial capitalist system. Workers cooperatives could not raise the capital necessary to update their relatively small factories with the latest equipment and technology, and therefore could not compete with the larger, corporate-owned factories. Sylvis also supported women's rights and labor solidarity, both domestic and international. Having witnessed firsthand how strikes had almost wiped out the strike fund, Sylvis was persuaded that strikes were not the best instrument for advancing labor's cause. Instead, he argued for political action and was instrumental in the formation of the National Labor Union and the National Labor and Reform Party, both of which strove to organize mutual aid associations and to challenge employers directly at the workplace.

THE EIGHT-HOUR MOVEMENT

Since there were no regulations governing the length of the working day, it was not uncommon during this period for workers to labor ten to eighteen hours a day, six days a week. The issue of shorter hours was a top priority for the labor movement, and the fight for the eight-hour day was the historical continuation of labor's pre–Civil War struggle for the ten-hour day. A machinist named Ira Steward, who worked twelve-hour days, became one of its chief proponents. As a delegate to the International Union of Machinists and Blacksmiths' convention in 1863, he was instrumental in the passage of a resolution calling for the enactment of a law to guarantee workers the eight-hour day. The union donated $400 and put Steward in charge of organizing the movement. He was president of the Boston Eight Hour League and the National Ten Hour League. In 1864, he formed the Labor Reform Association to push the fight for the eight-hour day. The next year, he teamed up with the abolitionist Wendell Phillips to found the Grand Eight Hour League. With the end of slavery, Phillips and many other abolitionists turned their attention to the problems associated with wage slavery. However, this potentially powerful coalition broke up when union members wanted to bar the importation of Chinese workers from America.

Borrowing a political tactic from the land reform movement, the Grand Eight Hour League of Massachusetts lobbied politicians in 1865 to secure their pledge of support for the cause. This political strategy secured only twenty-three supporters in the Massachusetts legislature, but the depression of 1866 spurred worker interest in political reform, especially the eight-hour day. Steward argued that cutting working hours without cutting pay would not only give workers more leisure time, but it would also increase employment and workers' purchasing power. In *Toil and Trouble: A History of American Labor* (1971), Thomas R. Brooks cites a popular rhyme that summed up Steward's idea: "Whether you work by piece or by day; decreasing the hours increases the pay."

The momentum for the eight-hour movement increased as Connecticut, Illinois, Missouri, New York, and Wisconsin passed laws during the late 1860s. However, these state laws contained glaring loopholes; they permitted employers to require that their employees sign ten-hour contracts. The eight-hour provision applied only if employers failed to mandate longer hours, and Wisconsin's law applied only to women and children. These laws were short-lived since the desperate search for work during the depression years of the 1870s effectively nullified this modest advance. The movement had better success on the federal level when Congress passed an eight-hour law in 1868. However, it applied only to laborers and mechanics working for the federal government. The eight-hour day was a plank in the Republican Party's platform in 1872, but most workers would have to wait until 1886 for the labor movement to take up the issue again. Shorter working hours remains a goal of many in the labor movement today.

THE NATIONAL LABOR UNION

Rapid industrialization and technological developments such as the railroads and telegraph during the Civil War hastened the process of the nationalization of the economy that had begun prior to 1860. It became apparent to a handful of labor leaders that the traditional system of isolated local trades' assemblies was no longer sufficient to cope with the threat posed by large corporations and trusts whose reach spanned the nation, and beyond. Two unsuccessful attempts were made to form a national federation of unions in 1864. First, Robert Gilchrist, president of the Louisville Trades' Assembly, called for a national convention, but his call went unheeded. But a second call in September resulted in a meeting of twelve delegates from eight local trades' assemblies under the rubric of the International Industrial Assembly of North America. The assembly never met again, but its constitution called for the establishment of a strike fund based on per capita union membership, a concept later used by unions such as the Knights of Labor and the Cigar Makers. Moreover, its organizational structure, which rested on local trades' assemblies, became the model for the National Labor Union.

Although the eight-hour movement did not achieve its goal, it did give birth to the first national federation of labor, the National Labor Union. The process began when the Grand Eight Hour League of Indiana called for state conventions across the land to elect worker representatives to attend a national convention. In March 1866, representatives of all but two national unions met in New York and called for a national convention to be held in Baltimore in August. The local orientation of most unions of the day is illustrated by the fact that local trade unionists in New York City quickly accused the national leaders of exceeding their authority by calling for the national convention. A compromise was reached allowing the Baltimore convention to be held on August 20 and the National Labor Union to be founded.

William Sylvis was a moving force in the formation and leadership of the National Labor Union and became its first president. The political center of gravity was the local trades assemblies as the distribution of delegates to the 1866 convention shows: seventy-seven delegates representing 60,000 workers answered the call, including fifty delegates from fifty local trade unions, seventeen delegates from thirteen trades' assemblies, seven delegates from five eight-hour leagues; and three delegates from two national unions. The National Labor Union was not a union per se; rather, it was a loose federation of unions, and it also included political reformers from the suffrage, abolitionist, and other movements. It was too unwieldy to hold together for long, but it represented an important effort to bring unity and a semblance of national cohesion to the decentralized American labor movement.

The National Labor Union's leadership was dominated by political reformers and intellectuals, more so than labor leaders. Its political reform agenda was expressed through committees established to address a wide variety of concerns: the eight-hour day and other labor concerns, land reform, currency reform, women's rights, cooperation, inflation, the abolition of contract prison labor, and the establishment of a public works program. However, the National Labor Union's political reform goals were often in conflict with the racist outlook, and "pure and simple" unionism, of many of its local union members. The goals of political reform were beautifully expressed by one National Labor Union leader quoted in Brooks's *Toil and Trouble:* "What is wanted is for every union to help inculcate the grand ennobling idea that the interests of labor are one; that there should be no distinction of race or nationality; no classification of Jew or gentile; Christian or infidel; that there is one dividing line, that which separates mankind into two great classes, the class that labors and the class that lives by others' labor." Although the 1869 convention admitted Isaac Myers, president of the Colored National Labor Union, as a delegate, it sidestepped the issue of race, effectively killing any action to effect racial unity in labor's ranks. The importation of Chinese laborers was another issue that divided the National Labor Union. Many in the labor movement urged the repeal of the Burlingame Treaty (1868), which recognized the right of the peoples of the United States and China to emigrate to each other's country.

National leaders, some of whom were not workers, pursued broader political goals, but local trades' assemblies, which made up the National Labor Union's backbone, wanted concrete benefits for their members. Political conflict between its constituent parts was a major cause of the union's demise. Moreover, the lack of adequate revenue, due to poor recordkeeping and assessment of dues, meant that the National Labor Union had trouble funding its operations from the start. Sylvis died in 1869, and the National Labor Union began to decline in 1870. Political bickering between the political reform and pure and simple unionism factions led to the ultimate demise of the National Labor Union. The Industrial Congresses held between 1873 and 1875 represented a futile attempt to resurrect the mission of the National Labor Union without its focus on political reform. This was a seeming impossibility, and the congresses, like the National Labor Union before it, represented a national leadership body in search of a membership base.

THE NATIONAL LABOR AND REFORM PARTY

Sylvis recognized that labor was in a weak position; even when workers won a strike, employers often regained their advantage through firing, blacklisting, wage cuts, increasing production requirements, and breaking unions. Instead, he argued for political action. The National Labor and Reform Party was the result of his vision that labor should have its own political voice. Like the National Labor Union, the National Labor and Reform Party reflected the ideas of political reformers and intellectuals more than those of labor leaders. On February 21, 1872, the National Labor Union held a political convention in Columbus, Ohio, and adopted its political reform goals as the National Labor and Reform Party's platform. Its platform called on the federal government to bypass the banks and directly issue a national currency ("Greenbacks"); establish the eight-hour day; provide public land for landless homesteaders, not corporations or real estate speculators; regulate the railroads and telegraph companies; enact civil service reform; and abolish prison contract labor.

The convention nominated Judge David Davis of Illinois to be its candidate for president, but he declined the offer and the party was left without a presidential candidate. Although this fiasco effectively killed the National Labor and Reform Party, it met again in Cleveland in September to nominate a second candidate, Charles O'Connor, a New York lawyer. O'Connor was the first Roman Catholic to run for president, but he received only 18,602 votes.

THE ORDER OF THE KNIGHTS OF ST. CRISPIN

Named for the patron saint of their trade, the Order of the Knights of St. Crispin was founded in 1867 by Newell Daniels. Although it was founded in Milwaukee, the order's roots lie in Massachusetts. Daniels was a refugee of the Massachusetts shoemaker strike of 1860 where the order was well received. The order was formed in response to pay decreases brought on by the introduction of shoemaking machinery prior to the Civil War that could be operated by unskilled workers. Shoemaking was once a proud craft that commanded decent wages, but even low-paid children could now make shoes. With increased competition in a labor market where sixteen-hour days were not uncommon, the prevailing wage was only $3 a week for men and as little as $1 for women. These adverse social conditions set the stage for the order's founding.

The Knights of St. Crispin were greeted by shoemakers who realized that collective action was needed to stem the loss of jobs and falling wages. Nationwide, its growth was so rapid and widespread that 600 local lodges were represented at the first Grand Lodge, the nationwide gathering of the order, in 1868. For the next five years, it was the most powerful labor union in the United States. At its peak, the Crispins had an estimated 50,000 members, and their reach was international. The Crispins sought legislation and collective bargaining agreements to protect their jobs from unskilled workers, "green hands" as they called them. The order's political influence was such that the politicians sought its endorsement. They established producer's cooperative stores to help insulate workers from the vicissitudes of the labor market. They also favored the idea of consumer cooperatives that were pioneered in England by the Rochdale plan (one of the earliest worker cooperatives) in the 1840s. But, as with other worker cooperatives, they could not compete with larger, better-financed corporate enterprises.

During 1868–1869, the Knights of St. Crispin successfully conducted many strikes, which took employers by surprise. It also successfully fought against pay cuts for its members. Female shoemakers also united, forming the Daughters of St. Crispin in 1870 to maintain wages and improve working conditions. Although many male-dominated unions of the era discriminated against female members in their trade, the Knights were supportive of the Daughters. The Daughters of St. Crispin, in turn, worked closely with their male brethren, gaining the Knights support in several strikes. When female shoemakers were fired in Baltimore for their union membership, the local Knights conducted a sympathy strike to show support for their sisters' right to belong to a union.

Employers countered the Knights of St. Crispin's success by organizing into trade associations, blacklisting union agitators, and hiring strikebreakers. In 1870, a North Adams, Massachusetts, employer could not find any local strikebreakers to hire. He transported seventy-five Chinese workers from San Fran-cisco by transcontinental railroad, paid them less than half the wages earned by the order, and broke the strike. In Philip Foner's *History of the Labor Movement in the United States: From Colonial Times to the Founding of the American Federation of Labor* (1947), the employer is quoted as declaring that he would continue to break strikes in order "to free himself from the cramping tyranny of the worst of American trades-unions—the Knights of St. Crispin"—illustrating the extent to which employers feared the collective power of the Crispins. However, the Crispins could not compete with this tactic and so turned their ire against the Chinese strikebreakers as much, if not more than, the employers. From 1872 onward, employers were consistently able to break strikes. The Knights of St. Crispin failed to adapt to the changing times by not reaching out to organize the unorganized, such as the Chinese immigrants. By 1875, the Crispins had all but dissolved as a labor union. Labor circles at the time widely believed that strikes were a weak tool, so the Crispins eschewed strikes in favor of arbitration, that is, collective bargaining and negotiation, with employers. However, it was too late for the Crispins to change strategy, and they completely disappeared by 1878.

Although the Knights of St. Crispin disbanded in 1878, so many of its leaders and members joined the more successful Knights of Labor that they became its backbone. As a result, the Knights of Labor adopted many of the innovations pioneered by the Knights of St. Crispin.

THE CIGAR MAKERS INTERNATIONAL UNION

Originally founded on June 21, 1864, as the National Cigar Makers Union, it changed its name to the Cigar Makers Union International in 1867. The union was a skilled trade union whose membership was predominantly made up of male cigar rollers. Female cigar rollers tried to join the union in 1864 but were rejected by their male counterparts, who did not see a compelling need to admit women. Men were suspicious that women, who were paid less by employers, were competing for their jobs. Subsequently, the women formed their own union and built it to the point that the men accepted them for membership three years later. But in 1872, the men took the self-defeating step of excluding women from membership when skilled female Bohemian cigar makers entered the market. Employers were quick to hire the women as strikebreakers. Adolph Strasser ruled the union with an

When railroad workers walked out in Martinsburg, West Virginia, then blocked a train from passing through town until the company rescinded a wage cut, President Rutherford B. Hayes sent in federal troops to disperse them. This action ignited the first nationwide strike in July 1877. *(Brown Brothers)*

iron hand, establishing top-down control over the locals. A young cigar roller named Samuel Gompers came to prominence in the Cigar Makers Union as a result of his political skill at reorganizing and stabilizing the New York local during this time period. The union, like others during this time period, faced increasing threats to their jobs posed by the introduction of labor-eliminating machinery.

THE PANIC OF 1873

In 1873, the overproduction of industrial and agricultural goods, combined with a decline in demand, created conditions of economic instability. Excessive stock speculation on railroad construction projects further weakened the economy to the point where, on September 18, the prominent banking firm Jay Cooke and Company collapsed. The resulting bank panic sparked a stock market crash that resulted in more than 5,000 business failures by year's end, a sharp

drop in national income, and widespread unemployment, especially for working-class Americans.

The panic of 1873 had a devastating effect on organized labor, especially the national unions that had gained a foothold during the 1860s and early 1870s. In 1873, there were thirty national unions in existence, but only eight were left by 1877. From the end of the Civil War to 1873, organized workers' wages rose due largely to their success at building national unions, winning strikes, and engaging in collective bargaining. But the panic of 1873 triggered a long depression that lasted until 1878 and caused a serious decline in union membership, employment, and wage rates. Employers had the upper hand, and tactics such as blacklists, lockouts, "yellow dog" contracts (signed between employers and union leaders, without the participation of workers), and lawsuits were effective tools for disciplining a workforce that was living in desperate circumstances.

THE NATIONAL STRIKE OF 1877

By 1877, workers had suffered through four years of depression, unemployment, and wage cuts. When the Baltimore and Ohio Railroad cut wages by 10 percent on July 16, the second pay cut in eight months, railroad workers went out on a wildcat strike. The strike rapidly spread to other railroads across the nation. Enraged workers demonstrated and rioted in protest in Baltimore, Chicago, Pittsburgh, and St. Louis, as well as in many smaller cities and towns across the nation. Militia had to be called in from as far away as Philadelphia to restore order after the Pittsburgh militia failed to restore order; in some cases, they refused to shoot civilians, but they failed to subdue the strikers who destroyed railroad tracks and burned down machine shops and the Union Depot. Workers in other industries also went on strike, transforming a railroad strike into a general strike that spread to all regions of the country. For a few days the workers were in control of, and operated, railroads, bakeries, and other businesses.

President Rutherford B. Hayes called out federal troops to quell the uprisings at Martinsburg, West Virginia, and Pittsburgh to subdue the striking workers and their sympathizers. Nine people were killed in Martinsburg, eighteen in Chicago, and twenty-six died in Pittsburgh. Hayes's use of federal troops broke the strike. Property damage was estimated in the range of $5 to $10 million. Perhaps the closest the United States has come to a sustained nationwide general strike, the National Strike of 1877 was a great social upheaval that sent shock waves through the upper echelons of society. Frightened state legislators around the nation responded by passing repressive conspiracy laws aimed at hamstringing organized labor and authorizing funds to build massive National Guard armories to house troops and munitions to guard against future worker uprisings.

CONCLUSION

America's break with its prewar past was so dramatic that historian Charles Beard labeled the Civil War the Second American Revolution. But revolutions are usually followed by periods of reaction and retrenchment by elites and conservative social forces, and this period was no exception. Labor's story during this era was one of trying, and failing, to form national unions to counter the growing power of capital. Labor's failure to meet this challenge was largely due to the fact that power in most unions of the time was lodged in the locals. Efforts to establish a national labor feder-

ation, such as the National Labor Union, foundered because of its top-down organizational structure. The National Labor Union's leaders had few followers, and its power base was in the local trades' assemblies. The Knights of St. Crispin was more successful in this regard largely because its national organization grew out of its grassroots base. This period was also noteworthy for the clash between labor's political reformist and its pure and simple unionism wings. Conflict arose on issues dealing with race, gender, and immigration between those in the National Labor Union who wanted to go into the political arena to reform society along more egalitarian lines and those, such as the Knights of St. Crispin and the Cigar Makers, who preferred to accept the status quo and concentrate on gaining immediate material benefits for their members. There was also conflict between the former group, which wanted to organize all workers, and the latter, which wanted to limit the focus to craft workers. Ultimately, these issues overwhelmed attempts to unite the two factions and build a national federation of labor of skilled and less skilled labor. Progress on these fronts would come in slow, incremental steps with future generations of workers, but the seeds of reform were planted during this era.

Vernon Mogensen

BIBLIOGRAPHY

Beard, Charles, and Mary Beard. *The Rise of American Civilization.* New York: Macmillan, 1927.

Brecher, Jeremy. *Strike!* Boston: South End, 1972.

Brooks, Thomas R. *Toil and Trouble: A History of American Labor.* 2d ed. New York: Dell, 1971.

Bruce, Robert V. *1877: Year of Violence.* Indianapolis, IN: Bobbs-Merrill, 1959.

Commons, John R., et al. *History of Labour in the United States.* 4 vols. New York: A.M. Kelley, 1966.

Ely, Richard T. *The Labor Movement in America.* New York: Thomas Y. Crowell, 1886.

Foner, Eric. *Reconstruction: America's Unfinished Revolution, 1863–1877.* New York: Harper & Row, 1988.

Foner, Philip S. *History of the Labor Movement in the United States: From Colonial Times to the Founding of the American Federation of Labor.* New York: International, 1947.

Gompers, Samuel. *Seventy Years of Life and Labor.* 2 vols. New York: E.P. Dutton, 1934.

Groat, George Gorham. *An Introduction to the Study of Organized Labor in America.* New York: Macmillan, 1926.

Grob, Gerald N. *Workers and Utopia: A Study of Ideological Conflict in the American Labor Movement, 1865–1900.* Chicago: Quadrangle Books, 1969.

Grossman, Jonathan P. *William Sylvis, Pioneer of American Labor.* New York: Columbia University Press, 1945.

Gutman, Herbert G. *Work, Culture and Society in Industrializing America: Essays in American Working-Class and Social History.* New York: Vintage Books, 1977.

Kessler-Harris, Alice. *Out to Work: A History of Wage-Earning Women in the United States.* New York: Oxford University Press, 1982.

Lescohier, Dan D. *The Knights of St. Crispin, 1867–74.* New York: Arno Books, 1969.

Ware, Norman J. *The Labor Movement in the United States, 1860–1890: A Study in Democracy.* New York: Vintage Books, 1964.

KNIGHTS OF LABOR

It is instructive to begin a discussion of the Knights of Labor as a social movement with two observations and two metaphors. First, the Knights of Labor was the largest labor organization in the United States in the nineteenth century. During its heyday in the 1885–1887 period, when it grew almost sixfold, it dwarfed its rival, the American Federation of Labor. The second observation is that the amazing growth of the Knights appeared to thoughtful onlookers to be a knitting together of America's highly diverse workers into a modern class, willing and able to act on its own interests. Karl Marx's associate, Friedrich Engels, opined in *The Labor Movement in America* (1887) that the Knights "are the first national organization created by the American working class as a whole."

But we must beware of imputing too much motive power to the organization known as the Knights of Labor. For the most part, the Knights did not organize and direct the social movement of workers in the mid-1880s as much as it served as a vehicle for that movement. In this regard two metaphors for the Knights are relevant: that of an umbrella and that of a parade. The Knights by its organizational openness, its grand ambitions, and its devotion to humanitarian reform was able to link together a wide variety of reformers—Single Taxers (followers of Henry George), Irish Land Leaguers, Greenbackers, Anarchists, Socialists—and diverse ethnic groups—Germans, Irish, Scandinavians, African Americans, and Central Europeans—workers of all skill levels, and women as well as men. Put together in almost a decade of growth, this heterogeneous mixture never quite congealed and ultimately proved quite combustible.

The second metaphor, that of a parade, should be understood in nineteenth-century terms. Political candidates and agitators often used parades led by impressive brass bands on the platforms of wagons to "drum up" support for speeches and rallies. The idea was to create a stir so that bystanders joined from the enthusiasm of the moment or "the bandwagon effect." The parade went on, but its membership was usually different from moment to moment. Such, in many respects, was the Knights of Labor, an organization characterized by enormous membership turnover at the local level and a succession of groups at its leadership helm. With only tenuous membership loyalty, the Knights' prospects were precariously dependent on the successes and failures of the strikes (there was little compromise bargaining in this era) into which it entered and the resulting fluctuations in public opinion (the bandwagon effect). That very dependence makes a strong argument for considering the Knights as a social movement rather than merely a labor organization.

FORMATION OF AN INDUSTRIAL WORKING CLASS

One of the most important and influential insights of social movement theory into the process of movement formation is that the existence of deep-seated and valid grievances is not sufficient of itself to mobilize a social movement. In order to convert political opportunities into a social movement, the aggrieved group must have access to organizational resources. Rather than being recruited into a movement one by one out of an amorphous mass, aggrieved individuals usually join social movements as part of preestablished networks, organizations, or communities that are coopted by emergent social movements. Such associational networks provide social movements with the necessary legitimacy and incentives to participate, communication networks, and leadership resources. Thus, grievances may exist for many years until the resources become available that allow potential participants to take advantage of new political opportunities.

Such was the case with America's new industrial

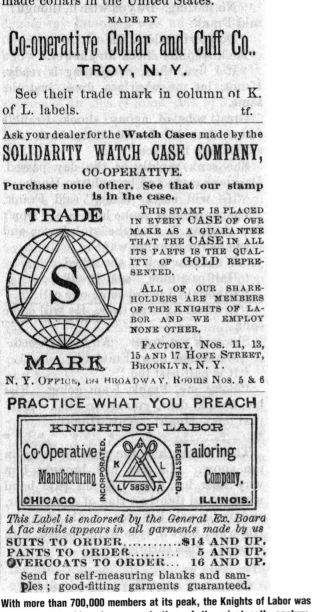

With more than 700,000 members at its peak, the Knights of Labor was the largest working-class organization of the nineteenth century. Knights established cooperative factories and—as this advertisement shows—urged consumers to purchase only union-made goods. *(Wisconsin Historical Society/WHi 5068)*

working class, which in the mid-century was composed largely of recent immigrants from Ireland and Germany, the bulk of them Catholics. By the 1870s, the core industrial region was expanding from New England and the Mid-Atlantic region into the Great Lakes states. Pittsburgh, Detroit, Cleveland, Buffalo, Chicago, and Milwaukee became fast-growing industrial centers. The population of these cities was approximately 30 percent immigrant, with the percentage rising to over 67 if children were included. The immigrant percentage was far higher—sometimes double—in industrial employment. Perhaps as many as half of these new industrial workers were Catholics.

Unskilled immigrant industrial workers labored upwards of sixty-hour work weeks at poverty wages. Employment was highly uncertain, with busy periods alternating with slack ones and factory shutdowns. Families lived in overcrowded tenements or dilapidated shacks without paved streets or indoor plumbing; hence, in the summer typhoid and other epidemic diseases were common. In the winter, these urban districts were covered with a thick dust from the coal used to heat their homes.

Yet, with the exception of the skilled craftsmen among them, immigrant industrial workers rarely formed or joined protest movements until the 1880s. In large part, this was because they were marginalized by the nation's dominant reform discourse, which was Evangelical Protestant. Though it had figured heavily in the struggle against slavery, Protestant discourse had little to say about the wrongs done to immigrant workers. Indeed, the 1850s antislavery reformers were often tinged with anti-Catholic Know-Nothingism. In the two decades after the Civil War, the native reform tradition began to adapt to new industrial realities. The Knights of Labor would lead in that transition.

At first, the Knights were squarely within the dominant reform tradition. Uriah Stephens, the founder in 1869 of the Knights of Labor, was trained to be a Baptist minister and had been a proponent of John Fremont, the radical antislavery alternative in 1864 to Abraham Lincoln. When Stephens spoke, as he often did, about the need for "solidarity" of skilled with unskilled workers, this had as much to do with the Protestant reform tradition of benevolence and Christian brotherhood as it did with class consciousness. Likewise, his opposition to wage slavery drew as much from an abhorrence of the sin of idolatry of wealth as it did from the secular movements of labor and socialism. In addition to this element of Protestant reform, Stephens emphasized—as did other Protestant trade union leaders of this era—character formation and personal uplift, manifested in a commitment to temperance and abstinence and opposition to saloons.

Stephens had also been a Mason, and he made the Knights a secret, oath-bound organization. During the initiation ceremony, which seemed to take up most of the local meetings, members in disguises read the elaborate initiation ritual, while new members wore blindfolds. Meeting times and places, even the very name Knights of Labor, were kept from the public.

At first, the secrecy, ritual, and reform language of the Knights were well suited to its existence as a small craft organization of garment cutters in Philadelphia. Secrecy served as a protective coloration to conceal it from its enemies among the employer class. And the crusading rhetoric of Christian brotherhood gave to its organizing a transcendent mission. But by 1876 a few organizers had begun to admit "sojourners"—new members not of the same craft—from the coal mines and unskilled trades in the Pittsburgh area.

The contradiction grew even greater after the Great Upheaval of 1877, a railroad strike against intolerable wage cuts that mushroomed into a pitched battle between industrial workers in the new Western (now Midwestern) industrial region of the country and the forces of order, including the U.S. Army. For the tens of thousands of workers who had participated in the collective actions of 1877, the Knights' grand idea of the organizational solidarity of all toilers promised to harness the newly displayed power of workers to bring the country's industry leaders to its knees. The number of district assemblies (which governed the local assemblies) jumped from three to fourteen immediately after the strike. Knights' assemblies also appeared in cities like Chicago and Detroit where the Knights offered a viable alternative to trade unions, which had been destroyed by the depression and unemployment.

Almost immediately, in the tradition of the older reform associations, these assemblies went into politics usually in conjunction with Greenback reformers. Yet, despite its growth, the extension of the order into the Great West, and its electoral success, the Knights was constrained in its develoment by its fundamental makeup. The secrecy and ritual antagonized the Catholic Church, which had historically been opposed to secret societies as dangerous competitors. The turn to politics in keeping with its reform tradition also had its drawbacks, for when the depression ended in 1879, the party movement collapsed and with it so did

many Knights assemblies. Meanwhile, the revival of prosperity restored the fortunes of the trade unions, and labor activists left the temporary umbrella of the Knights. By 1879, with membership dwindling and dues income in freefall, the order was in crisis.

It was at this juncture that Terence Powderly, the Knights' Grand Master Workman who had succeeded Stephens in 1878, engineered a fundamental shift in the organization. An Irish Catholic machinist with roots in the trade unions and Catholic workers, Powderly understood the importance of mollifying church authorities. Under his leadership, the 1881 convention of the Knights abandoned secrecy and the oath. It also shifted the organizing and fund-raising efforts of the order from Philadelphia to Pittsburgh. The shift was almost revolutionary in its impact. The order shed its reputation that it excluded Catholics, and it opened itself to new and radical currents that were sweeping the Irish Catholic working class.

Virtually at the same moment that the Knights made their shift, Irish American working people began joining clubs by the thousands to support the Irish National Land League (INLL). The INLL was a "new departure" in Irish nationalist politics, uniting the movement for home rule in Ireland led by Charles Parnell, the revolutionary movement for Irish independence led by the Clan na Gael, and the agrarian movement of Irish peasants to regain title to the land. In America the INLL's drive to raise funds for the Irish movement was met with a great outpouring of enthusiasm and generosity among all segments of the Irish American community from the lace curtain Irish and the church to Democratic Party politicians and ordinary working people. Most significantly, the issue of land reform became an opening wedge for radicals like Patrick Ford, editor of the *Irish World and American Industrial Liberator,* to preach their doctrines of social reform to Irish Catholic workers. Ford's "Spread the Light" clubs enrolled hundreds of industrial workers, Knights of Labor activists, trade unionists of all backgrounds, and Socialists. The potentially explosive movement to override the prerogatives of property in (Irish) land became a broad movement transcending ethnic and religious backgrounds.

Just as important, members of the INLL popularized the Irish practice of shunning those who collaborated with the British enemy. The INLL's support for the "boycott," which originated in the struggle against a British land agent, Captain Boycott, was quickly exploited by trade unionists and Knights leaders for working-class purposes. In Chicago, for example, the Knights led two major boycotts during strikes in

1881–1882. During that period, Myles McPadden, an Irish nationalist Knights organizer, whom Powderly had dispatched to Chicago, brilliantly capitalized on the popularity of land reform and the boycott to organize dozens of new Knights of Labor local assemblies, most of them in industrial areas of Chicago. By the end of 1882, the Knights organization in Chicago and elsewhere had been transformed from a body of political reformers in mixed local assemblies devoted to Greenback politics to a labor organization of industrial workers, with a plurality of Irish Catholics. Fully 40 percent of the names of all delegates and officers of Chicago's two district assemblies were Irish. Nationally, the order began to grow rapidly in 1882, with a majority of new local assemblies being trade in character.

The reorientation of the Knights under Powderly's leadership and its use of the Land League and Irish nationalist movements to draw in Irish Catholic workers exemplified how social movements must co-opt existing organizational, communication, and leadership networks to be successful. It also exemplified another critical element in social movement formation—"framing"—that is, the social process by which grievances are generalized and shaped into political claims that resonate with public opinion. Framing often involves a "dressing up" of collective actors in symbolic clothing. The new popularity of the boycott exemplified that symbolic process. Boycotting was not something new. The American revolutionary movement had used it in the 1760s–1770s, and trade unions had boycotted sporadically well before the 1880s. Clothing that tactic in the rhetoric of Irish nationalism served to ease the way of Irish workers into the labor movement and to spur the spread of boycotting in the movement at large. As McPadden put it, the power of the Knights lay not in strikes but in the ability to "boycott" scabs.

By the same token, framing could also involve a change in meaning of old symbols. Thus, what was once Christian brotherhood and universal humanitarianism—expressed in the Knights motto, "an injury to one is the concern of all"—became a synonym for a labor principle, amalgamation across craft lines, and a working-class identity. Only the Knights of Labor, an organization with one foot in the reform tradition and the other in the labor movement, could have effected this symbolic transformation.

EXPANSION AND TURBULENCE

By 1882–1883, the Knights were poised to make another transition—to leadership of a broad national movement of industrial workers for the eight-hour day. Labor's Great Upheaval from approximately spring 1885 to fall 1887 illustrates an important development in social movement theory, the notion of "cycles of contention." Under the right circumstances, social movements can rapidly diffuse, wavelike, across the social system, overwhelming existing institutions, and then just as quickly recede and demobilize after succumbing to repression and dissension. A cycle of contention usually begins when "political opportunities" appear for well-placed "contenders." When they find their demands frustrated by authorities, they reframe their claims to draw in additional claimants. The "mobilization phase" is normally marked by the following: the rapid diffusion and intensification of conflict; the development of new routine forms of collective action (what theorists call repertoires); the appearance of new organizations and the expansion of existing ones; and the creation of new "master frames." The ensuing demobilization phase involves a mixture of participant exhaustion and organizational factionalism between radicals and moderates, followed by selective state repression and selective acceptance of movement demands.

Political opportunities converged in the mid-1880s from several sources. With the start of the 1883–1885 depression, a series of wage reductions spread across the Wabash rail system, in the hands of Wall Street tycoon Jay Gould. With Gould's railway running full bore to cover high fixed costs amidst falling prices, it could ill afford a strike. Just as critically, public opinion supported the railway workers, organized in a Knights' District Assembly. With the governors of three states arbitrating, the Knights beat back the wage reduction; the men won an additional strike in September 1885 using a boycott of the Wabash Railroad's rolling stock. Altogether in the 1884–1885 period, the order engaged in five railway strikes and won four of them.

All rail strikes in this era had national repercussions, but because this one involved a national organization with the grand pretension to organize the entire working class, its effect was nothing short of electric. The defeat of a large national corporation using the new weapon of the boycott greatly heartened workers. Once-fearful railroad workers flooded into the Knights assemblies, especially in the Midwest. Isolated local trade unions—the American Federation of Labor had not yet been born, and its predecessor, the Federation of Organized Trades and Labor Unions (FOTLU), was moribund—sought national-level solidarity by affiliating with the Knights. Accession of the unions brought thousands of new members to the Knights.

Unorganized, unskilled workers also rushed into the order en masse. The list of entrants was nothing short of a cross section of the American working class: thousands of working women, many of them sweated garment workers from New York and Chicago; hundreds of African-American waiters, barbers, and printers, including thirty-five local assemblies in the Richmond area alone; Socialist German furniture craftsmen together with machine hands from the Midwest; and Polish rolling mill workers from Milwaukee all marched under the banner of the order. Nothing like it had ever been seen before, and the press, by exaggerating the organizational cohesion and effectiveness of the Knights, contributed mightily to its meteoric growth. Within a period of not more than six months, the Knights of Labor grew from a national organization of approximately 104,000 in 1885 to 725,000 in 1886.

A similar mix of opportunities helped the Knights win prestige and grow in mushroom style on the local level. In Chicago, the heart of the movement, local trades unions had benefited from the support of the Democratic Party regime of Mayor Carter Harrison. By refusing to use police to intervene during strikes in the early 1880s, Harrison enabled unions to defeat employers and establish footholds in the city's industrial economy. With the advent of falling prices during the 1883–1885 depression, unionized employers counterattacked, and these same unions struck again. This time the opportunity structure proved unfavorable.

Facing possible defection of anticorruption Democrats and criticism from the local Citizens Association and press for buying votes with his police policy, Harrison turned to a little known police captain. John Bonfield, to mollify employers. In protecting strikebreakers crossing picket lines in February 1886, the police forced local unions to turn to the Knights of Labor and the boycott as an alternative. When striking boxmakers, who had been stymied by Bonfield, won their struggle with the help of the Knights, and another Knights' boycott against prison-made shoes proved successful as well, the mood in the city shifted dramatically. In what one student of social movements has called a "moment of madness"—a time in which all things seem possible and social learning is intensified and telescoped in time—the Knights reaped a bountiful harvest of recruits. By late March, the *Chicago Tribune* reported that the local order was growing at the rate of a thousand per week. From 1885 to 1886, Chicago Knights had increased mem-

In 1886, the Knights of Labor boasted a membership of more than 700,000, making it the largest working-class organization of the nineteenth century. The Knights quickly declined, however, racked by internal dissension and—as this 1887 cartoon shows—the unpopular leadership of Grand Master Workman Terence V. Powderley. *(Brown Brothers)*

bership tenfold, and the number of workers on strike in the city had increased from 6,618 to 87,849. Similar moments of madness occurred in New York, Cincinnati, Milwaukee, Kansas City, and other cities following Knights' boycott or strike victories, though on a smaller scale than in Chicago.

Once within the fold of the order, workers gravitated toward the shorter hours movement, a demand that had long been a staple of the American labor movement. In 1884, the FOTLU had called for a strike on May 1, 1886, to institute an eight-hour day for American workers. In advance of the date, local Eight-Hour Associations formed in many cities to spread the word. The eight-hour demand was framed in a new way. Hitherto, it had been viewed as a means of uplifting workers as virtuous citizens of the republic; some Socialists supported the fight for eight hours as a way of accelerating the evolution away from wage labor and toward a new order of producers cooperation. The argument of the Eight Hour Leagues, however, was economic and social in nature. Shorter hours would decrease unemployment, unite the interests of all workers, and increase consumer demand, thus counteracting overproduction. From 1886 to the turn of the century, the eight-hour day demand and its portrayal as labor's solution to depressions and unemployment would become the movement's new master frame.

For the short span of time between the success of the boycott and the May 1886 strike, the movement for the eight-hour day seemed to possess the force of a tidal wave. Almost 50,000 Chicago workers had won the demand by the end of April, and on May 1 another 60,000 struck. Nationally, New York had 45,000 strikers, Cincinnati 32,000, Baltimore 9,000, Milwaukee 7,000, and Boston, Pittsburgh, and Detroit each boasted between 3,000 and 4,700 strikers. Altogether, about 200,000 struck on May 1. Chicago's 35,000 packinghouse workers were the largest single group to win shorter hours. More lasting victories were won by building trades and cigarmaker unionists.

Just as the boycotting "mania" and shorter hours rage reached their peaks, a counterforce was gathering steam that would deal a crushing blow to the Great Upheaval. Internally, a brewing conflict between militants and moderates split the Knights asunder, leaving the entire movement vulnerable to attack. On March 13, 1886, Powderly issued a secret circular that disavowed Knights of Labor support for the May 1 strike. Nationally, the Knights were facing demands for strike funds and boycotts from tens of thousands of raw, undisciplined recruits, in addition to requests for support from viable bodies of trades unions. If the order had possessed a centralized strike fund, it might have been able to exert some control over the mania that had gripped the nation's workers. But, in contrast to the most advanced national unions, the order's strike fund was collected and controlled by local and state district assemblies. Powderly's circular was a desperate attempt to regain control over the distended order.

Exacerbating the difficulty of focusing the energies of the mushrooming shorter hours movement was the large-scale involvement of the Anarchists in Chicago. Although they had at first scorned the eight-hour day demand as a mere palliative, by fall 1885 they began to view it as an occasion for a mass strike that might be turned into a revolution. In furtherance of that goal, the Anarchists championed the demand of eight hours of work for ten hours of pay because it had less chance of being accepted by employers than the trade union demand of eight hours of work for eight hours of pay. When German furniture work-

ers endorsed the more radical demand on April 10, the eight-hour movement in Chicago lost its unity, and the press began identifying the entire movement with anarchism.

By the end of the month, the formation of anti-union employers associations in the furniture, metal trades, and boot and shoe industries made it evident that employer resistance was stiffening. But the events of May 4, 1886, at Haymarket Square utterly demoralized the movement. Police under Bonfield confronted an Anarchist-convened meeting in Haymarket Square protesting the shooting of strikers the day before and ordered it to disperse. In almost the same instant, some unknown person threw a dynamite bomb into the ranks of the police. The exploding bomb killed at least four policemen, while the indiscriminate shooting by the remaining police killed at least another sixty people, including three fellow officers.

Called a "riot" by the press, the Haymarket Affair set off a widespread panic, kindling the nation's first major Red Scare. The press fed the public fear that a revolutionary conspiracy existed among foreign-born radicals to overthrow the Republic and called for the sternest actions to vindicate law and order. Under pressure from leading businessmen, Mayor Harrison banned public meetings and processions, and the police ruthlessly suppressed existing strike activities and arrested over two hundred Anarchist leaders and suspects. Eventually, eight leaders stood trial for murder and conspiracy, and four were hanged, even though the identity of the bomb thrower was never ascertained.

The Haymarket Affair gravely split the movement. Powderly condemned the Anarchists in terms indistinguishable from that of mainstream public opinion, while Samuel Gompers, newly elected president of the American Federation of Labor, condemned the violation of workers' civil liberties by the police and supported clemency for the Anarchists. Within the Knights of Labor, many criticized Powderly's one-sided attempt to disassociate the order from anarchism. All at once, it seemed, a major opposition movement had coalesced against Powderly, which would have important public repercussions on the order's ability to maintain the confidence of its members.

Even under the best of circumstances, however, it would have been difficult to prosecute strikes in the face of a public hysteria that conflated labor organizations with dangerous foreign radicalism. The Chicago garment leader Abraham Bisno wrote in his

KNIGHTS OF LABOR REPUDIATE AND DENOUNCE HIM
DAVID B. HILL   1888

The Knights of Labor, founded in 1869, became the leading national workers organization in the late nineteenth century. In the following document, the Elmira Local Assembly 1965 unanimously denounces the governor for his opposition to laws that would permit "a poor man" to compete for political office.

The following resolutions were unanimously adopted by Elmira Local Assembly 1965, K. of L., Oct. 2, 1888:

Whereas, On December 10, 1887, at a regular meeting of 1965 K. of L., a committee was appointed to draft resolutions for the purpose of petitioning the Legislature to amend the election laws by making it a criminal offense for any person to use money at any National, State, or Municipal election, in buying votes, knowing full well that in the purity of the ballot, free from the influence of money, depends the future welfare of our free institutions and the safety of our country; and

Whereas, On March 19, 1888, such a bill was introduced in the Senate by Senator J. Sloat Fassett, known as the "Anti-Bribery Bill," which passed the Senate and Assembly; this same bill having been earnestly supported by D.A. 15, K. of L.; therefore be it

Resolved, That we censure Governor D.B. Hill for not signing this bill, and for treating with such contempt the well known wishes of the K. of L., and a vast majority of law-abiding citizens.

Resolved, We, the K. of L., do also denounce and condemn Governor Hill for his action on the "Electoral Bill," known as the "Saxton Bill," a bill framed solely in the interests of the poor man; a bill which would enable a poor man to compete for an office with a man of wealth.

Resolved, That in withholding his assent to those two great measures, Governor Hill proves himself an enemy to the deserving poor man, and an ally of corruptionists.

Resolved, That we, the K. of L., will do our utmost to defeat Governor Hill for re-election to the office of Governor, and call on all labor organizations and law-abiding citizens to aid us in our endeavors to preserve a pure ballot.

Resolved, That we send a copy to each D.A. in the State, under the seal of the order, and that they be given to the press for publication.

Unanimously adopted.

Source: Library of Congress, *An American Time Capsule: Three Centuries of Broadsides and Other Printed Ephemera.* Printed Ephemera Collection, portfolio 129, Folder 40b.

---

autobiography (1967): "[P]icketing became absolutely impossible. The police arrested all pickets, even two or three. The attitude on the part of the police was practically the same as though the city was under martial law." Samuel Gompers observed, "[T]hat bomb not only killed the policemen, but it killed our eight-hour movement."

On the national level, the employer reaction occurred virtually at the same point in time. The Knights called a strike against Jay Gould's southwest system of railways on March 6, 1886, after a Knights member was discharged. Heretofore, public opinion and the support of public officials had aided the Knights. But in this affair the public was little interested, and the railroad refused arbitration. After a violent confrontation killed nine in East St. Louis, National Guard troops entered the fray. The order's public reputation suffered, and an unhappy Powderly gave the back-to-work order on May 4, the same day as the Haymarket bombing. In retrospect that date emerges as "the tipping point" of the Great Upheaval, the time at which mobilization turned into demobilization.

From that point onward, the Knights were beset with employer intransigence and state repression, compounding the difficulties created by internal dissension aired in public. The most notable case was the loss of the packinghouse workers strike in Chicago in fall 1886. The order, which had earlier been viewed as the savior of poor workingmen, suddenly appeared impotent. Meanwhile, well-placed trade unionists were able to win disputes with the aid of their national unions' strike funds. Local unions demanding "trade autonomy" left the order in droves for national unions of their trade. When the Knights responded by chartering more Trade District Assemblies (the equivalent of national unions), they triggered jurisdictional disputes with the national unions affiliated with the AFL. By 1888, the once mighty Chicago Knights of Labor had declined from 18,000 members in 1886 to about 3,000. Nationally during the same period, the Knights lost over two-thirds from their membership peak of 702,000.

The united front of the courts, public officials, and employers against the boycotts and strikes of labor organizations beginning in March led activists to turn to independent labor parties. A comprehensive study of labor parties in 1886–1887 detected their existence in at least 189 American cities—including every large industrial center—in thirty-four out of thirty-eight states. In New York City a coalition of trade union and Knights leaders, Socialists, and Single Taxers nominated Henry George for mayor. In 1886, George finished second in a three-man race, winning 31 percent of the vote. In Chicago, a less distinguished candidate representing the same coalition won a like percentage of the mayoral vote in April 1887. In these and other cities a host of state legislators, city councilmen, and judges won office on the labor ticket.

Nonetheless, the impressive vote totals concealed two salient facts. The parties represented political protests against the use of the courts and the repressive apparatus of the state against the Great Upheaval. When the Great Upheaval dissipated and the repression let up, so did the protests. The new parties, moreover, were quite ambivalent about the long-term uses of the state to right the injustices in society.

Second, the major parties were willing to selectively endorse—thus coopting—many of the goals championed by the labor parties and thereby stealing their thunder. For example, in Chicago, the Republican mayor suspended Bonfield from the police force in 1889. Later that year, the newly elected Democratic mayor outdid the old Harrison regime by adopting important elements of the labor party's program, granting expanded patronage to union leaders, and reviving and extending the hands-off police policy during strikes. In short, the willingness of the democratic polity to partially meet the demands and concerns of the Great Upheaval and the moderating of the state's severe repression of 1886 kept workers from embracing either Anarchist insurrection or an independent labor party strategy.

LEGACY OF THE KNIGHTS OF LABOR

Social movements are usually driven by grand ambitions. Not just the Anarchists, but the Knights of Labor, demanded an end to the wage system and the inclusion of all working people, whatever their skill level, nationality, race, or sex in the ranks of organized labor. Because circumstances frustrated these ambitions, and the Knights were succeeded by a more enduring but less inclusive and more pragmatic organization—the AFL and its affiliated national unions—historians have tended to paint the post–Great Upheaval period in broad-brush terms as one of defeat, disillusionment, and decline.

Recent social movement theory, however, provides us with a broader array of concepts and terms to assess outcomes. In between the extremes of outright defeat and victory, one popular typology offers the policy alternatives of preemption and cooptation. Another theorist stresses as an outcome the diffusion of new values and the politics of agenda setting; still others point to the creation of enduring networks of activists—a kind of "social capital" movement. In this latter category of enduring developments internal to the movement, we have the possibility of innovations in frames, repertoires (routine forms of collective action), and organizations. It is here that we note most obviously the long-term impact of the Knights of Labor and the Great Upheaval of which it was a vehicle.

Historians of the Gilded Age and Progressive Era often speak of that era as being characterized by an "organizational revolution." Large-scale, centralized organizations in the hands of professional managers using technical knowledge afforded Americans the capacity to bring order and purpose to chaotic and dysfunctional markets. Although the corporation most often comes to mind in this regard, workers too sought order, purpose, and control of markets through their own functional organizations. In this context, the Knights of Labor stands out as a series of related organizational hypotheses tested in the experience of the Great Upheaval. Notably, certain elements were found wanting. Activists found that geographically organized associations like the district assembly were relatively ineffective in focusing the energies of organized workers. In place of these community-based associations, labor activists, even within the Knights of Labor, turned to functionally organized and centrally controlled national unions. Other aspects of the Knights organization, however, survived and prospered, though within the confines of the national unions and the AFL.

The new master frame of the eight-hour day, which originated during the Great Upheaval, has already been mentioned as an innovation that dated to this period. The Knights also initiated industrial councils of related crafts—for example, in the metal, printing, building, and railway trades—which proliferated in the 1890s and the first decade of the twentieth century. Moreover, in the tradition of the solidarity manifested in the Knights, the AFL allowed the paramount craft in various industries to organize the entire industry under its wing. By 1890, the Knights' national district assembly of miners became the AFL's most influential industrial union, the United Mine Workers. The mixed local assembly combining workers of different trades also survived the Knights in the form of the "federal labor unions" directly affiliated with the AFL (rather than national unions).

Even more significant for the future of the labor movement was the spread of new repertoires in the form of the boycott and the secondary boycott or sympathy strike. One form it took was the union label boycott. By the end of the 1880s, nine national unions had adopted the union label; eight of these nine unions began using it during the Great Upheaval. By the turn of the century, thirty-one different unions used the boycott. The sympathy strike also survived the Knights and reached its peak in the early 1890s, notably the Pullman strike and boycott. So effective and so widely used had the boycott become by the turn of the century that it sparked an Open Shop counterattack and the widespread use of the labor injunction. Notably, the 1880s Knights leaders had originated and popularized this new repertoire as an alternative to striking.

In sum, by taking the focus off the Knights of Labor as an organization with a discrete emergence, decline, and fall, and instead viewing the order from the perspective of a social movement, we find that the experience of the Knights in the era of the mid-1880s Great Upheaval had an enduring impact on the American labor movement's direction, methods, and organizational culture.

Richard Schneirov

BIBLIOGRAPHY

Bisno, Abraham. *Abraham Bisno: Union Pioneer*. Madison: University of Wisconsin, 1967.

Browne, Henry J. *The Catholic Church and the Knights of Labor*. Washington, DC: Catholic University Press, 1949.

Engels, Friedrich. *The Labor Movement in America*. New York: Louis Weiss, 1887.

Fink, Leon. *Workingmen's Democracy: The Knights of Labor and American Politics*. Urbana: University of Illinois Press, 1983.

Foner, Eric. "Class, Ethnicity, and Radicalism in the Gilded Age: The Irish Land League and Irish-America." In *Politics and Ideology in the Age of the Civil War*, 150–200. New York: Oxford University Press, 1980.

Friedman, Gerald. *Statemaking and Labor Movements, France and the United States, 1876–1901*. Ithaca, NY: Cornell University Press, 1998.

Kealey, Gregory, and Bryan D. Palmer. *Dreaming of What Might Be: The Knights of Labor in Ontario, 1880–1900*. New York: Cambridge University Press, 1982.

Levine, Susan. "Labor's True Women: Domesticity and Equal Rights in the Knights of Labor." *Journal of American History* 70 (1983): 323–339.

Oestreicher, Richard Jules. *Solidarity and Fragmentation: Working People and Class Consciousness in Detroit, 1875–1900*. Urbana: University of Illinois Press, 1989.

Perlman, Selig. "Upheaval and Reorganization (since 1876)." In *History of Labour in the United States*. Vol. 2., ed. John R. Commons, et al. New York: Macmillan, 1918.

Phelan, Craig. *Grand Master Workman: Terence Powderly and the Knights of Labor*. Westport, CT: Greenwood Press, 2000.

Rachleff, Peter J. *Black Labor in the South, 1865–1890*. Philadelphia: Temple University Press, 1984.

Ross, Steven J. "The Politicization of the Working Class: Production, Ideology, Culture, and Politics in Late Nineteenth-Century Cincinnati." *Social History* II:8 (May 1986): 171–195.

Schneirov, Richard. *Labor and Urban Politics: Class Conflict and the Origins of Modern Liberalism in Chicago, 1864–97*. Urbana: University of Illinois Press, 1998.

Scobey, David. "Boycotting the Politics Factory: Labor Radicalism and the New York City Mayoral Election of 1886." *Radical History Review* 28–30 (1984): 280–325.

Tarrow, Sidney. *Power in Movement: Social Movements and Contentious Politics*. 2d ed. Cambridge, MA: Cambridge University Press, 1998.

Voss, Kim. *The Making of American Exceptionalism: The Knights of Labor and Class Formation in the Nineteenth Century*. Ithaca, NY: Cornell University Press, 1993.

Ware, Norman J. *The Labor Movement in the United States 1860–1895: A Study in Democracy*. New York: Vintage Books, 1929.

Weir, Robert E. *Knights Unhorsed: Internal Conflict in a Gilded Age Social Movement*. Detroit: Wayne State University Press, 2000.

Zolberg, Aristide R. "Moment of Madness." *Politics and Society* 2 (1978): 183–207.

MINERS' MOVEMENT IN THE WEST

West of the Mississippi River, class war between militant miners and corporations produced an early and genuine working-class culture attended by an indigenous radical unionism. Corporate intrusion into "people's" mining ground is a well-documented historical process in the United States—readily apparent not only in Western hard-rock mining but earlier, in the upper Mississippi Valley lead mines of the early 1800s and in the coal-mining communities of Pennsylvania beginning in the 1840s. In the lead mines, independent miners profitably worked publicly owned mines until driven out by a fledgling capitalist class that claimed the ground as private property—abetted by the relentlessly expansionist senator, Thomas Hart Benton. Physical violence against working miners and coercive legal practices figured prominently in this deliberate ouster of one class by another. More familiar are narratives of coal-mining wars in Pennsylvania that pitted encroaching coal and railroad companies against independent contract miners who set their own conditions of work and perceived contracts with companies as agreements between equals. In the heat of the Civil War, coal bosses disabused contract miners of these leveling ideas by meeting strikes with federal troops supplied by a government firmly committed to economic growth on the capitalist plan. Juxtaposed with class war in the lead and coal mines are the fundamentally egalitarian "southern mines" of Georgia during the gold rush of 1829. Although the violent displacement of native peoples to make way for mining cannot be ignored or downplayed here, thousands of miners, in the absence of a strong central government and powerful corporations, constructed in the Georgia mines their version of a "moral economy." Moral economies aim for an equitable division of resources intended to promote genuine participatory democracy. Workers in this period tended to perceive embryonic capitalist practices as amoral for granting privileged individuals com-plete freedom in their quest for profit—a freedom that undermined both community welfare and principles of democracy.

WORKING-CLASS CULTURE AND THE CALIFORNIA EXPERIENCE

Thousands of "Argonauts," or Forty-niners, streamed into the Sierra Nevada range of California with the discovery of gold in 1848. They clearly articulated the idea of the gold fields as the "people's mines," meaning they envisioned a vast economic region where workers themselves maintained control of production. Among the Argonauts we find Mississippi Valley lead miners, Pennsylvania coal miners, and veterans of the rush to the Georgia mines, many imbued with a strong sense of class consciousness and a strong distrust of concentrated power in any form. Immigrant miners with experience of industrial warfare abroad often shared this thinking and contributed their own home-grown class strategies. Many novice miners quickly assimilated this sense of worker militancy and upheld ideas of the dignity of independent manual labor within an egalitarian social structure.

Argonauts' journals and diaries reveal perceptions of California as an escape from the contradictions and inequities of the new capitalist order. Throughout the gold fields, ordinary miners organized regular mandatory meetings where they hammered out democratic codes of law that worked to both ensure participatory democracy and to obstruct capitalist practices. Mining laws both reflected the California experience and drew heavily from earlier Spanish and European practices dictating small claims intended to spread wealth and requiring claimants to work the ground regularly or give it up. In California, such laws discouraged holding claims for speculation and forbade the amassing of claims by individuals and small groups, thus upholding the dignity of manual work. Argonauts policed themselves effectively through miners' courts. California's well-attended public hangings are most often construed as barbarism in action. Yet when compared with increasingly "hidden" executions in the East (behind prison walls), a case can be made that California represents a survival of older "republican crowd" actions with their affirmation of a people's right to fully participate in and draw moral instruction from all aspects of public life. As Argonauts followed subsequent gold and silver rushes into the interior, they put into service a repertoire of crowd actions as a means of asserting labor power. Vigilante actions in the West are often linked, especially in the popular media, to unruly mobs of miners, quick to implement summary justice. In truth, during later industrial wars, mining bosses and some elements of the middle classes far more often inflicted extralegal violence and terror on miners.

Producer (working-class) ideology and practices nurtured in California and imported to gold and silver rushes farther inland therefore embrace a moral economy, a propensity for radical participatory democracy, the use of various crowd actions, a discourse favoring independent "producerism," and the elevation of manual labor. Additional elements of an emerging working-class culture in California include a studied generosity in times of trouble, a thriving saloon and gambling culture, a grudging acceptance of women in the public sphere, and an assessment of wage work as fundamentally demeaning and degrading. Producerism certainly filtered into the constitutions of miners' unions later in the century, including documents taking a decidedly Socialist/Syndicalist turn. Striking miners also engaged in time-honored crowd tactics such as food riots, public humiliation of owners and managers, and protest marches carrying the tools of their trade—the pick and shovel. Union members gave generously to support striking miners and their families elsewhere. And in the absence of union halls, early organizing and union meetings often took place in saloons, which also served as hiring halls and temporary boarding houses. Miners' unions also established women's auxiliaries and women's unions, which played an important role in the economic and social life of many camps. Indeed, women sometimes took the places of their husbands, sons, and brothers during strikes, knowing that troops would be more reluctant to brutalize them. First nurtured in California, these beliefs and practices served miners and their families well as they built the most radical union movement in the nation, culminating in the Syndicalist Industrial Workers of the World.

THE 1872 MINING LAW: PRIVATIZATION AND PROLETARIANIZATION

As a successful economic system, capitalism requires not only the commodification of goods and services, but more important, the commodification of human labor, so that work is transformed from the pursuit of subsistence and individual fulfillment into a product to be traded for profit in the marketplace. This process played out quickly in the mining camps of the West. The Mining Law of 1872, still essentially in effect today, helped ensure that corporations, not working miners, would control the nation's most valuable mining properties. The 1872 law overturned the federal government's original vision for public mineral lands as demonstrated in the Mississippi lead mines—a project of leasing mines to independent producers who would turn over a portion of their income to the government in the form of royalties.

The 1872 law was a direct attack on local common-law mining codes grounded in the California experience, which prevented rich ground from falling into the hands of speculators and capitalists. California laws that strictly limited claim size also required that mining ground be regularly worked or forfeited. That is, miners owned their ground only as long as they worked it. The 1872 law nullified all local mining common law, giving hegemony over mineral law to the legislatures of individual states and territories—government entities that, from the beginning, used the law and the court system to sanction, encourage, and smooth the path of capitalist state formation. In this vein, the 1872 law included the claim-patent system, which grants secure or free title (unrestricted permanent ownership) to claim holders. Secure ownership also gives possessors, whether individuals or corporations, the right to bring suit. When small claim holders refused to sell out, corporations simply engaged them in crippling lawsuits over a variety of issues. Expensive, lengthy litigation nearly always forced a sale, since judges suspended independents from active mining during these prolonged show trials.

The mines on Nevada's Comstock lode were notorious for generating costly litigation between mining barons, who in turn were famous for using shady legal tactics against the independent miners who first located the silver. The example of Immanuel Penrod, one of the original locators of the district, demonstrates capitalist state formation in action. California capitalists descended on the district following the discovery of high-grade silver in 1859 and made a practice of taking into partnership independent claim owners, such as Penrod, who refused to sell and insisted on a partnership. Penrod's new partners made use of the "freeze-out" strategy, assessing his personal funds to build an expensive new mill, at a cost well beyond his means. Penrod sold his interest for $5,500, a trifle considering the millions his claim yielded later. In 1863, Comstock capitalists used their influence with lawmakers to pass a measure legitimizing the freeze-out.

The claim-patent system also worked to effectively privatize the nation's Western mines, in converting them from public to private ownership. Until the 1872 law went into effect, the federal government understood mining on public lands in the West as legal trespass, though it seldom acted to evict—mainly because local police and militia tended also to be local miners who fought back. Working miners in turn regarded mining ground as a sort of mineral commons, open to those who intended to work the ground (with the notable exclusion from the commons of native peoples and other excluded groups, especially Hispanics and Chinese in the West). The claim-patent system, in allowing permanent ownership to those who spent $500 on claim "improvements," thus privatized the ground—the people's mines—for $500 and a nominal fee. Royalties are also basically dispensed with, so that the 1872 law stands as a massive giveaway of public lands to a privileged class. After 1872, with secure title guaranteed, capitalists, domestic and foreign, poured money into Western mines.

THE COMSTOCK UNIONS

Not surprisingly, as corporations consolidated in Nevada, some of the most militant and long-lived miners' unions emerged on the Comstock, the nerve center of early industrial mining in the West. For independent miners forced from their claims and for most newcomers to the district, despised wagework presented the only option. Most historians assign the later stimulus and style of unionism in the West to the Comstock model. From the beginning, miners fought mine owners, an understandable development, considering the aversion of the miners to take on highly dangerous and unhealthy underground work for the substandard wages offered by the mine owners. An initial labor shortage obliged big companies to offer $4 a day, barely adequate pay in light of the astronomical cost of living in Virginia City. In 1863, rumors of a pay cut led the miners to organize a protective association intended to preserve the $4 day, aid mem-

bers in need, and end wildcat speculation in mining stocks, which often led to the closing of mines. Frequent shutdowns in mines throughout the West cut sharply into wages that some historians construe as unusually generous.

Although the protective association did not comprise a formal union, it represented a fundamental and venerable component of working-class formation under capitalism. In a town less than five years old, the materialization of such an organization signals both rapid capitalist state formation and a perceived need of workers to protect themselves as a class. The following year, in response to losses incurred by expensive lawsuits, runaway speculation, and mismanagement, Comstock companies attempted to economize by dropping wages to $3.50 a day. Absentee owners of the Uncle Sam mine acted first, with orders to foreman John Trembath to announce the cut. On March 19, 1864, an assembly of miners answered the challenge by affixing Trembath to the main hoist with ropes, attaching the label "dump this pile of waste from Cornwall," and requesting the hoist engineer to raise and lower the foreman a few times along the length of the main shaft. Trembath, greatly subdued, insisted that he acted on company orders. The company, lacking strong military or police backing, rescinded the order but bided its time. Lack of police and military power reflected the miners' policy of appointing and electing their own as enforcers of the law, militia members, and firefighters. Early on, unions recognized the power of such arrangements and used the vote and volunteerism to obtain them. As long as power struggles remained local, this tactic succeeded admirably.

In response to worker mobilization, Virginia City mining companies met secretly to propose and carry out antilabor policies, such as the blacklisting of leaders and the drafting of secret agreements with a number of anti-union miners to work below the living wage. The outcome was a disappointment, however. When owners announced an across-the-board wage cut to $3.50 in July 1864, the miners engaged in a two-day disciplined crowd action to show their collective strength. On the first day, they marched behind the Gold Hill Brass Band in a parade of solidarity and listened to a speech by Frank Tilford, a friendly judge, who announced that reducing wages meant driving the miners to "despair and death." The charge was not unfounded, considering how coal companies in the East utilized wage cuts, expanded hours of work, juridical attacks, and seasonal work—cumulatively, owners intended these measures to drive miners and their families to the edge of starvation and into sub-mission. On the second day, the miners spoke for themselves. Carrying the picks, sledges, and shovels of their trade, they marched on each Comstock mine and mill, giving notice to managers that the $4 wage would stand. Every foreman promised compliance, perhaps mindful of both Trembath's experience and Judge Tilford's speech the day before, likening mining companies to ancient Roman traitors who were punished by tossing them from the Tarpeian rock adorned with girdles of burning faggots.

Most significantly, on August 6, the miners proclaimed the birth of a new union, the Miners' League of Storey County, dedicated to the preservation of the $4 day for all underground workers—signifying a bona fide industrial union. The league encompassed unions in Virginia City, Gold Hill, and Silver City, towns built around the mines. New members pledged to work for no less than $4, to discover men who worked for less and expose them to public humiliation, and to accept wages paid only in silver or gold (rather than scrip). Predictably, members swore to march on offending companies and convince them, by force of numbers, to rethink inequitable policies. A sustained class struggle followed, with the unions, supportive townspeople, and newspapers on one side, arrayed against the big companies and some elements of the small middle class. Owners could not profitably fire united union men en masse and so resorted to the weak expedient of dismissing leaders by concocting dubious charges unrelated to unionism. Companies also continued secret hirings below the standard wage.

In September, to counter continuing corporate tactics, the Miners' League debated the establishment of a union camp on the Comstock. Termed a "closed shop" by anti-union propagandists, a union camp or union "shop" requires all prospective workers to join a union before applying for work. In using the expression "closed shop" to denote an arbitrary and coercive forcing of workers into unions, mine owners ignored the function of unions to protect and further the interests and rights of all workers. Within a few decades, some mining towns, such as Butte, Montana, stood as genuine union camps, with virtually every occupation unionized, including those dominated by women. The possibility of a union camp led Governor James Nye, a mine owner, to summon two companies of calvary, armed to the teeth, to Virginia City in a bid to dissuade the league from its purpose. To avert a bloodbath, the Miners' League wisely postponed the union camp decision but temporarily weakened the

organizing impulse, allowing owners to hire increasing numbers of miners for $3.50. Mine owners got up their own "league," the Citizens' Protective Association, to disseminate a public discourse representing capitalists as guardians of democracy, intent on upholding the rights of individual miners to "choose" union membership. Companies avoided carrying this discourse to its logical conclusion—that miners would freely elect to descend underground and risk their lives and health for less than $4 a day.

A second mining boom on the Comstock in 1866 worked to the miners' advantage by producing a new labor shortage. This time the miners, beaten down once by management, restructured the union and committed themselves to a union camp. The original preamble to their constitution described the "tyrannical oppressive power of Capital" (a response, perhaps, to Nye's troops) and the enormous capability of workers to redress the imbalance. A contingent of conciliatory union men persuaded their more radical brothers to moderate the militant tone for public consumption, but members continued to use the original preamble at meetings and induction ceremonies. This time the union prevailed, safeguarding the $4 day and establishing an eight-hour shift until the bonanza ore played out in the 1880s. Mine bosses had no choice but to comply; attacks on these rights meant a general strike and the shutdown of production. In the deep mines of the Comstock, a strike of all workers also posed the danger of pump operators walking off the job and the consequent flooding of the mines. The miners' victory rested on solidarity—a general consensus for both a union camp and an industrial brand of unionism that extended the living wage and reduced hours to all miners regardless of skill or job status. Comstock unions also built up social weight by using dues to provide critical social services for miners and their families, including sick benefits and money for funeral expenses. Other union contributions to Virginia City and its suburbs included the camp's only public library and an excellent private hospital.

Collective action on the Comstock marked the emergence of a genuine working-class culture in the mines of the West and the appearance of class consciousness among workers in the context of capitalist state formation. Thousands of Comstock miners carried a discourse of self-help and mutualism to industrializing camps throughout the West and inspired armies of Western miners to press for industrial unionism and the union shop. Toward the turn of the century, many miners would go a step further and

Striking miners stand at the site of their tent colony, destroyed by the state militia in Forbes, Colorado. Capital–labor violence—with the government often intervening on behalf of management—was endemic in the West in the late nineteenth and early twentieth centuries. *(Denver Public Library)*

adopt clear Socialist ideals and objectives. Through it all, miners' militancy and the determination of mining companies to dictate all conditions of work guaranteed endemic class war. As new camps took shape, miners articulated and put into practice a mission to preserve the dignity of labor, to ensure workplace democracy, and to force adequate compensation for dangerous and difficult work. Not all miners, of course, shared this sense of militancy; nor should we minimize policies of racism and exclusion directed against targeted groups. Still, as miners' unions grew more radical, they tended to grow more inclusive of marginalized groups.

CAPITAL–LABOR WARS IN THE COEUR D'ALENES

In the rich silver mines of Idaho, workers' struggles against absentee corporations played an important

role in founding the radical Western Federation of Miners (WFM), which in turn influenced the organizing of the Syndicalist Industrial Workers of the World. Idaho miners responded to the ongoing corporate deskilling and degrading of labor by forging a district federation of local unions. Local Idaho unions adopted the Virginia City model and federated almost as quickly as corporate interests took over the mines. In 1887, Simon Reed, owner of the newly incorporated Bunker Hill and Sullivan Mining Company (BH&S), based at Wardner, announced a cut in the customary wage for all underground workers from the Butte scale of $3.50 a day (won by Butte miners in 1878) to $3.00 for skilled miners and $2.50 for unskilled men. Reed, in using wages to distinguish skill levels, intended the cut to erode worker solidarity. To compound the insult, he introduced deadly Burleigh machine drills in place of skilled hand-drilling methods. Although Burleigh drills, called "widow makers" by the miners, sped up production and increased profits, they also spewed fatal clouds of silica dust into the still underground air. Razor-sharp particles of dust, still a health hazard in mines today, lodge in the lungs and trace a network of scars that eventually asphyxiate the victim. Silicosis, also called "miners' con" (consumption) or "black lung" by coal miners, is responsible historically for the deaths of thousands of American miners. This danger, coupled with the possibility of death or permanent injury underground, makes militancy in response to owners' pronouncements no surprise.

Historian Richard Lingenfelter's graphic description of underground dangers in *The Hardrock Miners* (1974) aids greatly in understanding the brand of radicalism that characterized the Idaho miners:

> He could be blown to bits in an explosion, drowned in a sump, suffocated and incinerated in a fire, scalded by hot water, crushed by falling rocks or cave-ins, wound up in the machinery, ground under the wheels of an ore car, have his head split open with an ax or pick, his neck broken by being run up into the hoist frame, or his whole body smashed out of shape and reduced to a pulp, or ripped apart and scattered in shreds by falling down a shaft. Moreover [with the introduction of new technologies] new accidents were constantly happening, the likes of which were never before heard of.

In the year of its incorporation, Bunker Hill and Sullivan policies led to the secret organization of unions in the scattered silver camps. These unions soon announced their presence by winning minor concessions from smaller companies in the district, then by coming together and federating early in 1891, as the Miners' Union of the Coeur d'Alenes. By summer, the federation employed a series of strikes to restore the $3.50 day at all but the BH&S mines. The empowered union then resolved to go after BH&S, now controlled by powerful San Francisco and Eastern capitalists, including the Guggenheim family and Cyrus McCormick. Besides the wage issue, BH&S miners strongly resented the "check-off" in which the company deducted $1 a month from each man's paycheck to subsidize a substandard health care system and retained the balance as profit. Union members determined to recover the check-off money and build a first-class hospital with a competent staff.

To enforce their demands for an end to the check-off and an across-the-board living wage of $3.50, min-

ers walked off the job late in the summer of 1891. Company president John Jays Hammond telegraphed superintendent Victor Clement to avoid at all costs giving into these demands. Clement floundered at first. Sheriff Cunningham of Wardner owed his election to the miners and refused to send deputies to the mine to break up the strike. Nonminers in the camps repudiated offers from the company to scab. In the absence of district support and in the face of plummeting profits, the company agreed to both demands in late summer, determined to renege in due time.

A newly organized Mine Owners' Protective Association (MOPA) appeared in the district in October, bent on beating down the $3.50 day and crushing the union. On the advice of lawyers, the MOPA hired industrial spies (Pinkertons and Thiel detectives) to infiltrate local unions. As the livelihood of spies rested on detecting "sedition" among the miners, they predictably found "anarchists" lurking in every underground tunnel. Then, without warning, in January 1892, the MOPA shut down nearly every mine in the district, except the smallest, throwing 2,000 men, many with families, out of work in the dead of winter. Yet the ploy backfired. Local farmers supplied the strikers with wagon-loads of food, and the federation made use of its own well-stocked commissary. In desperation, again on the advice of company lawyers, the MOPA turned to the importation of scab labor. Obliging railroad companies rushed trainloads of scabs into the district, and high court judges barred miners from interfering in any way with the process. By June, the mines resumed full production with scab labor. Still the miners persevered, recruiting perhaps one-half of the scab workers to their side. Thousands of dollars continued to pour in regularly from outside unions in support of the workers. The membership of the large Butte Miners' Union, for example, assessed each man $5 per month for their Idaho comrades until the strike ended.

As the summer wore on, tension heightened among miners, mine guards, and scabs as BH&S anticipated the outbreak of violence. On July 10, the company rejoiced when a gun battle broke out between Gem and Frisco mine guards and striking miners. Three miners and three guards died in a rain of bullets. Miners proceeded to capture both mines and take 150 scab prisoners, whom they loaded in boxcars and dispatched from the district. Throughout the district, miners engaged in similar actions, clearing the Coeur d'Alenes of scab labor and occupying the mines. These events not only gratified mine owners, who could now call in troops, but alarmed the camps' prosperous middle classes to the extent that some withdrew support from the workers. Military and vigilante action became the order of the day as Governor Wiley declared martial law and called on President Benjamin Harrison for aid. State and federal troops converged on the district on July 14, and despite meeting no resistance, rounded up hundreds of miners (sources report up to 1,000 men), and confined them for two months in filthy stockades called "bull pens," in which three men eventually died. Local residents who supported the companies used the opportunity not only to aid in the roundup, but to engage in a witch hunt against personal enemies and business competitors by accusing them of supporting the miners. Enforcers of martial law ordered union commissaries closed, officials elected by union vote removed from office, and the closing of mines whose owners bargained with the unions. Until March 1893, when a U.S. Supreme Court decision cleared every miner of criminal charges, the charged men experienced grave violations of their civil rights that tended to further radicalize them rather than render them docile. Indeed, veterans of the Coeur d'Alenes bull pens figure prominently as original members of the Westchester Federation of Miners (WFM).

The frustrating experiences of Idaho miners and similar occurrences in industrializing camps elsewhere in the West led to the organization in 1893, in Butte, of the WFM, which successfully brought together smaller district federations throughout the mining West. The Butte Miners' Union ranked as the nation's largest local industrial union in this "Gibraltar of Unionism," while Butte itself stood as the second-fastest-growing city in the country. Extraordinarily rich in copper and other metals, Butte boasted a crazy-quilt of bustling ethnic neighborhoods, a rich cultural life, and a remarkable degree of worker solidarity. In the spring of 1893, the recent specter of the Idaho bull pens produced a sense of crisis that led representatives of seventeen local unions throughout the West to converge on the city to organize a miners' federation that would match the national power of corporations. The 1893 WFM constitution welcomed all workers involved in mining and processing ore, including coal miners. This founding document is a mixture of bread-and-butter issues and incipient socialism; the latter appeared in full force in subsequent constitutions. The 1893 founders called for economic justice, major improvements in mine safety and independent inspectors to enforce them, payment of wages in lawful money rather than company scrip, the abolition of company stores and

housing, a ban on employment of boys under sixteen in the mines, and the interdiction of industrial spies, private mine guards, contract labor, and all conspiracy laws that trampled the rights of miners as citizens.

As the turn of the century approached and then passed, industrial warfare in the mines of the West intensified. WFM leaders along with many rank-and-file members veered decidedly left. Hasty industrialization of the mines by a capitalist class determined to maximize profit in the shortest time played a crucial role in the process. Corporate mining requires heavy capitalization, and investors are disinclined to wait long for dividends; paying a living wage, providing basic benefits, and attending to mine safety cut into anticipated profits. By 1901, we find delegates to WFM conventions demanding the "emancipation of the toiler" and "a complete revolution of present social and economic conditions . . . that justice be meted out to all people of the earth."

Sentiments such as these attracted the attention of labor leader Eugene Debs. He perceived the bare-knuckles nature of capital–labor wars in the West as proof of his conviction that workplace struggles involving direct action produced the most meaningful and lasting social and economic change. More conservative Socialists of the period (better termed "progressives") favored the ballot box and working through established political parties over shop-floor agitation as the means to a more egalitarian order. In June 1905, as mine bosses showed no sign of negotiating fairly with workers and every inclination of persevering in their crusade to destroy WFM locals, the federation dispatched leaders and delegates to a meeting in Chicago. There, 186 delegates representing 40,000 workers organized the Syndicalist Industrial Workers of the World, commonly called the "Wobblies." WFM delegates represented some 27,000 miners, comprising by far the largest occupational group. Labor luminaries included Debs; president Charles Moyer of the WFM; labor activist Mary Harris "Mother" Jones; Lucy Parsons, wife of Haymarket martyr Albert Parsons; Socialist Labor Party president Daniel DeLeon; and "Big Bill" Haywood, veteran of the Idaho bull pens and WFM leader. Haywood and Moyer sat on the executive board at the pleasure of the rank and file, which held the right of recall. The IWW recruited workers in all occupations, regardless of skill, gender, or race, standing in sharp contrast to the larger AFL, which recruited skilled, white, male workers. The Wobblies also promoted a Socialist agenda of the most radical tone. According to the original preamble:

The working class and the employing class have nothing in common. There can be no peace so long as hunger and want are found among millions of working people and the few, who make up the employing class, have all the good things of life. Between these two classes a struggle must go on until all the toilers come together on the political, as well as on the industrial field, and take and hold that which they produce by their labor through an economic organization of the working class, without affiliation with any political party.

A later version of the preamble pulled no punches and called for outright abolition of the wage system.

WFM president Moyer abruptly withdrew the federation from the IWW in 1907, perhaps in reaction to his narrow escape with Big Bill Haywood from a 1905 murder frame-up. Clarence Darrow would defend the pair in a trial that absorbed the nation's attention for months. Moyer's disassociation of the federation from the IWW did little to dampen the enthusiasm of ordinary miners for the Wobbly project. Many retained membership in both the WFM and (often secretly) in the IWW until relentless persecution by an alliance of big business, the state, and the middle classes during World War I stopped Wobbly Syndicalism dead in its tracks. In 1916, WFM leaders, growing ever more conservative, rechristened the organization the International Union of Mine, Mill, and Smelter Workers and focused increasingly on bread-and-butter issues. Debs, too, broke with the IWW in 1908 over the Wobblies' espousal of implementing workplace sabotage when necessary in waging class war. Haywood, however, remained with the Wobblies until the patriotic hysteria of World War I opened the way for his conviction under the Espionage Act for opposition to the war. He escaped to Russia, where he died in 1928.

Precisely defined, "radical" denotes going to the root of a thing, as in radical change or reform. Just as American revolutionaries sought radical reform in declaring war on England in 1776, Western miners perceived themselves as very much in the mainstream of this American tradition of righteous resistance. In the West, miners took the democracy project seriously and fought to vest social, political, and economic control in the hands of the people, rather than giving it over to a self-interested few. Miners and their families also constructed a genuine working-class culture in the camps. They not only resisted capitalist culture, but contested it with a coherent alternative vision of America that appealed to many. Finally, the failure of miners and their supporters to shape a more egalitarian society in the decades around the turn of the twentieth century can be traced more to the implementation of various forms of physical and legal coercion by corporations and the state than to any disunity among miners or to a weak or flawed producers' rationale.

Jeanette Rodda

BIBLIOGRAPHY

Aiken, Katherine G. " 'It May Be Too Soon to Crow': Bunker Hill and Sullivan Company Efforts to Defeat the Miners' Union, 1890–1900." *Western Historical Quarterly* 24:3 (August 1993): 308–331.

———. " 'Not So Long Ago a Smoking Chimney Was a Sign of Prosperity': Corporate and Community Response to Pollution at the Bunker Hill Smelter in Kellogg, Idaho." *Environmental History Review* 18:2 (Summer 1994): 67–85.

Allcorn, D.H., and C.M. Marsh. "Occupational Communities—Communities of What?" In *Working-Class Images of Society*, ed. Martin Bulmer. London: Routledge, 1975.

Aronowitz, Stanley. *The Politics of Identity: Class, Culture, Social Movements*. New York: Routledge, 1992.

Barger, Harold, and Sam H. Schurr. *The Mining Industries, 1899–1939: A Study of Output, Employment, and Productivity*. New York: National Bureau of Economic Research, 1994.

Boswell, Terry, and Diane Mitsch Bush. "Labor Force Composition and Union Organizing in the Arizona Copper Industry: A Comment on Jimenez." *Review* (Fernand Braudel Center) 8:1 (Summer 1984).

Boyer, Richard O., and Herbert M. Morais. *Labor's Untold Story*. New York: United Electrical, Radio, and Machine Workers of America, 1955.

Brinley, John Ervin. "The Western Federation of Miners." Ph.D. diss., University of Utah, 1972.

Calvert, Jerry. *The Gibraltar: Socialism and Labor in Butte, Montana, 1895–1920*. Helena: Montana Historical Society, 1988.

Conlin, Joseph R. *Bacon, Beans, and Galantines: Food and Foodways on the Western Mining Frontier*. Reno: University of Nevada Press, 1986.

Dawley, Alan. "Workers, Capital, and the State in the Twentieth Century." In *Perspectives on American Labor History: The Problems of Synthesis*, ed. J. Carroll Moody and Alice Kessler-Harris. DeKalb: Northern Illinois University Press, 1989.

Derrickson, Alan. *Workers' Health, Workers' Democracy: The Western Miners' Struggle, 1891–1925*. Ithaca, NY: Cornell University Press, 1988.

Emmons, David. *The Butte Irish*. Champaign: University of Illinois Press, 1990.

Esposito, Anthony. *Ideology of the Socialist Party of America, 1901–1917*. New York: Garland, 1997.

Francaviglia, Richard V. *Hard Places: Reading the Landscape of America's Historic Mining Districts*. Iowa City: University of Iowa Press, 1991.

Frisch, Paul Andrew. "The Gibraltar of Unionism: The Working Class at Butte, Montana, 1878–1906." Ph.D. diss., UCLA, 1992.

Gordon, David, et al. *Segmented Work, Divided Workers: The Historical Transformation of Labor in the United States*. New York: Cambridge University Press, 1982.

Graham, Hugh David, and Ted Robert Gurr. *Violence in America: Historical and Comparative Perspectives: A Staff Report to the National Commission on the Causes and Prevention of Violence*. Vol. 1. Washington, DC: U.S. Government Printing Office, 1969.

Greever, William S. *The Bonanza West: The Story of the Western Mining Rushes*. Norman: University of Oklahoma Press, 1963.

Hardesty, Donald. *The Archaeology of Mining and Miner: A View from the Silver State*. Special Publications Series #6: Society for Historical Archaeology, 1988.

Haywood, William D. *Bill Haywood's Book: The Autobiography of William D. Haywood*. New York: International, 1929.

Huginnie, Andrea Yvette. " 'Strikitos': Race, Class, and Work in the Arizona Copper Industry, 1870–1920." Ph.D. diss., Yale University, 1991.

James, Ronald M. "Drunks, Fools, and Lunatics: History and Folklore of the Early Comstock." *Nevada Historical Society Quarterly* 35 (Winter 1992): 215–238.

Jameson, Elizabeth Ann. *All That Glitters: Class, Conflict, and Community in Cripple Creek*. Chicago and Champaign: University of Illinois Press, 1998.

Jensen, Vernon H. *Heritage of Conflict: Labor Relations in the Nonferrous Metals Industry up to 1930*. Westport, CT: Greenwood Press, 1968.

Laslett, John H.M. *Labor and the Left: A Study of Socialist and Radical Influences in the American Labor Movement 1881–1924*. New York: Basic Books, 1970.

Leach, Eugene E. "Chaining the Tiger: The Mob Stigma and the Working Class, 1863–1894." *Labor History* 35:2 (Spring 1994): 187–215.

Limerick, Patricia Nelson, et al. *Trails: Toward a New Western History*. Lawrence: University of Kansas, 1991.

Lingenfelter, Richard E. *The Hardrock Miners: A History of the Mining Labor Movement in the American West, 1863–1893*. Berkeley: University of California Press, 1974.

Lord, Eliot. *Comstock Mining and Miners*. 1883. Reprint, Berkeley: Howell-North, 1959.

Malone, Michael P. *The Battle for Butte: Mining and Politics on the Northern Frontier, 1864–1906*. Seattle and London: University of Washington Press, 1981.

Marks, Gary. *Unions in Politics: Britain, Germany, and the United States in the Nineteenth and Early Twentieth Centuries*. Princeton, NJ: Princeton University Press, 1989.

Maynard, Steven. "Rough Work and Rugged Men: The Social Construction of Masculinity in Working-Class History." *Labor/Le Travail* (Canada) 23 (1989).

Mellinger, Philip J. *Race and Labor in Western Copper: The Fight for Equality, 1896–1918*. Tucson and London: University of Arizona Press, 1995.

Mercier, Laurie. *Anaconda: Labor, Community, and Culture in Montana's Smelter City*. Champaign: University of Illinois Press, 2001.

Milner, Clyde A., II, et al. *The Oxford History of the American West*. New York and Oxford: Oxford University Press, 1994.

Montgomery, David. *Citizen Worker: The Experience of Workers in the United States with Democracy and the Free Market During the Nineteenth Century*. New York: Cambridge University Press, 1993.

Nash, Gerald D. *Creating the West: Historical Interpretations, 1890–1990*. Albuquerque: University of New Mexico Press, 1991.

Neuschatz, Michael. *The Golden Sword: The Coming of Capitalism to the Colorado Mining Frontier*. Westport, CT: Greenwood Press, 1986.

Paul, Rodman. *Mining Frontiers of the Far West, 1848–1880*. New York: Holt, Rinehart and Winston, 1963.

Peterson, Richard H. *Bonanza Rich: Lifestyles of the Western Mining Entrepreneurs*. Moscow: University of Idaho Press, 1991.

Phipps, Stanley S. *From Bull Pen to Bargaining Table: The Tumultuous Struggle of the Coeur D'Alene Miners for the Right to Organize, 1887–1942*. New York: Garland, 1988.

Prichard, Nancy Lee. "Paradise Found: Opportunity for Mexican, Irish, Italian and Chinese-born Individuals in the Jerome Copper Mining District, 1890–1910." Ph.D. diss., University of Colorado, 1992.

Robbins, William G. *Colony and Empire: The Capitalist Transformation of the American West*. Lawrence: University Press of Kansas, 1994.

Rosner, David, and Gerald Markowitz. *Deadly Dust: Silicosis and the Politics of Occupational Disease in Twentieth-Century America*. Princeton, NJ: Princeton University Press, 1991.

Rueschemeyer, Dietrich. *Power and the Division of Labor*. Oxford: Polity, 1986.

Schwantes, Carlos A. "Images of the Wageworkers' Frontier." *Montana: The Magazine of Western History* 38:4 (Autumn 1988).

Scott, James. *Domination and the Arts of Resistance: Hidden Transcripts*. New Haven, CT: Yale University Press, 1990.

Shovers, Brian. "The Perils of Working in the Butte Underground: Industrial Fatalities in the Copper Mines, 1880–1920." *Montana: The Magazine of Western History* 37:2 (Spring 1987).

Slotkin, Richard. *The Fatal Environment: The Myth of the Frontier in the Age of Industrialization*. New York: Atheneum, 1985.

———. *Gunfighter Nation: The Myth of the Frontier in Twentieth-Century America*. New York: Atheneum, 1992.

Smith, Grant H. *The History of the Comstock Lode, 1850–1920*. Reno: Nevada State Bureau of Mines and the Mackay School of Mines, 1943.

Smith, Norma. "The Rise and Fall of the Butte Miners' Union, 1878–1914." Master's thesis, Montana State College, 1961.

Thompson, E.P. *The Making of the English Working Class*. New York: Pantheon, 1964.

Todd, Arthur Cecil. *The Cornish Miner in America.* Truro, Cornwall: D. Bradford Barton, 1967.

Townsend, John Clendenin. *Running the Gauntlet: Cultural Sources of Violence Against the IWW.* New York: Garland, 1986.

Trimble, William J. *The Mining Advance into the Inland Empire.* New York: Johnson Reprint, 1972.

Watts, Sarah Lyons. *Order Against Chaos: Business Culture and Labor Ideology in America, 1880–1915.* Westport, CT: Greenwood Press, 1991.

White, Richard. *"It's Your Misfortune and None of My Own": A New History of the American West.* Norman: University of Oklahoma Press, 1992.

Wilentz, Sean. "The Rise of the American Working Class, 1776–1877." In *Perspectives on American Labor History: The Problem of Synthesis,* ed. J. Carroll Moody and Alice Kessler-Harris. Dekalb: Northern Illinois University Press, 1989.

WPA Writers' Program. *Copper Camp: Stories of the World's Greatest Mining Town—Butte, Montana.* New York: Hastings House, 1943.

Wyman, Mark. *Hard Rock Epic: Western Miners and the Industrial Revolution, 1860–1910.* Berkeley: University of California Press, 1979.

Zanjani, Sally. *Goldfield: The Last Gold Rush on the Western Frontier.* Athens: Ohio University Press, 1992.

ANARCHISM AND THE LABOR MOVEMENT

The historian Paul Avrich notes in *Anarchist Portraits* (1988), "Of all the major movements of social reform, anarchism has been subject to the grossest distortions of its nature and objectives." Indeed, no political philosophy has been as demonized and misrepresented as Anarchism. Anarchism in its most basic formulation simply means the absence of government, not the absence of organizational structures. Specifically, Anarchism is the political belief that society should have no government, laws, police, or other authority, but should be a free association of all its members. Portrayed as the refuge of scoundrels and deviants, Anarchism actually played an influential role in the development and growth of the labor movement in Europe and the Americas.

Anarchism was present in the United States prior to the arrival of European activists. However, North American Anarchism lacked the activist orientation of European Anarchism because it tended to be more individualistic and disdained attempts to organize cohesive federations. At this time, it was essentially a philosophical and pacifist movement. In the United States, the most significant figure in the Anarchist movement was Benjamin Tucker. In his journal *Liberty*, he published the work of European Anarchists, including Peter Kropotkin, Mikhail Bakunin, and Leo Tolstoy.

Avrich notes in *The Haymarket Tragedy* (1984): "Representatives from twenty-six cities met in Pittsburgh to form the revolutionary socialist and anarchist groups into one body, the International Working Peoples Association. The formative period of its history was marked by three important events: the London Social Revolutionary Congress of July 1881, the Chicago Social Revolutionary Congress of October 1881, and the arrival of Johann Most in America in 1882."

THE INFLUENCE OF EUROPEAN ÉMIGRÉS

Radical Anarchism arrived in the United States through European émigrés fleeing political repression (e.g., the anti-Socialist laws passed in Germany in 1878–1879, the pogroms in the Russian Pale, etc.) or seeking economic opportunity. Despite its international pretensions, Anarchism developed in European ethnic communities—Russian, Italian, Jewish, and so on. An exemplar of this is Johann Most, a committed Socialist and early member of the International Working Men's Association (the First International). In 1874, he was elected to the German Reichstag, but after passage of anti-Socialist laws he was forced to flee the country.

When Most was released from prison in 1882 (he had called for the assassination of Tsar Alexander II), he immigrated to the United States and settled in Chicago. Most published the newspaper *Die Freiheit* and soon became the best-known Anarchist in America. His views were incredibly influential among German and Yiddish-speaking Anarchists in the United States. He argued that the state should be ruled by a collective group of citizens. He believed that before this could happen people would have to use violence to overthrow the government. He even compiled a text explicating the construction and use of explosive devices, *The Science of Revolutionary Warfare* (1885).

In addition to the outspoken Most, many other German Anarchists were active in the movement. Perhaps the most well known are the Haymarket defendants Albert Parsons, August Spies, Adolph Fischer, George Engel, Michael Schwar, Samuel Fielden, Oscar Neebe, and Louis Lingg. Although they had their share of differences, Parsons, Spies, Schwab, and the other Haymarket defendants were exemplars of the Chicago Idea, named after the convention of social revolutionary groups assembled in Chicago in October 1881. They were advocates of union organization, direct action, and avoidance of electoral politics. All were active in the struggle for the eight-hour day and were also committed to armed self-defense.

THE HAYMARKET AFFAIR

In 1886, a series of strikes swept in and around Chicago. At the McCormick Reaper Works, August Spies was addressing a crowd of workers when the scabs left the factory. An intense battle erupted. The police were called in, and when pelted with stones they opened fire on the crowd, shooting indiscriminately at the men, women, and children. The police killed six and wounded more.

The following evening, May 4, a mass meeting was called at the Haymarket. About 2,000 workers attended the meeting, far short of the 20,000 Spies originally expected. The mayor observed the activities, and when he was satisfied that they posed no danger, left the scene. However, Chicago police captain Bonfield sent over 170 policemen to the scene to break up the small crowd that remained. Captain Ward, the officer in charge at the scene, demanded that the meeting disperse. As Samuel Fielden began to explain to the officers that the meeting was peaceful, a bomb was thrown into the group of policemen. The police reacted by emptying their pistols into the crowd, once again shooting men, women, and children. Although the bomb killed one to two policemen at most, more were killed due to friendly fire. The numbers of injured workers remain unknown because many were afraid to go to the hospital in the belief that they would be turned in to the authorities and persecuted.

The press was quick to blame the Anarchists in headlines such as "Chicago Anarchists Throw Bomb in Midst of Police" and "Anarchy's Red Hand," and called for severe reprisals. Anarchism was linked to immigrants and was said to be an "alien doctrine" of the "scum and offal" of the Old World. Even labor joined the hue and cry. Typographical Union No. 16, notwithstanding Parsons's membership, adopted a resolution denouncing "the heinous acts of the mob at the Haymarket" and offered a reward of $100 for the capture of the bomb thrower. The Knights of Labor also ignored Parsons's longtime association with the organization, while the Grand Master Workman of the order, Terrence W. Powderly, made frantic efforts to dissociate his organization from the Anarchists. Although the authorities were unable to identify the bomb thrower, Parsons, Spies, Fischer, Lingg, and Engel—organizers of the Haymarket meet-

ing—were sentenced to death for "conspiracy to murder."

JEWISH INFLUENCE IN THE ANARCHIST MOVEMENT

The Haymarket trial precipitated the formation of the first Jewish Anarchist group in the United States, the Pioneers of Liberty (*Pionire der Frayhayt*), who affiliated themselves with the International Working People's Association. They were also greatly influenced by Most. Their inauguration occurred on October 9, 1886, the day that the sentences were handed down. Their initial task was to prevent the execution of the Haymarket defendants. To this end, they held meetings, sponsored rallies, and gathered funds for judicial appeals. Their first paper, *Varhayt* (Truth) (1889), was short-lived (five months, twenty issues). However their subsequent effort, *Freie Arbeiter Stimme* (Free Voice of Labor) (1890) lasted eighty-seven years.

The *Freie Arbeiter Stimme* claimed to represent

Anarchist, feminist, and passionate advocate of personal liberation, "Red Emma" Goldman spoke widely on behalf of workers and the poor.
(Brown Brothers)

EMMA GOLDMAN (1869–1940)

Emma Goldman was born to Abraham and Taube Goldman in a middle-class Jewish family in Kovno, Russia (now part of Lithuania) on June 27, 1869. Influenced by radical politics as a young teenager, she began working in garment factories in St. Petersburg. She later went to America to join an older sister in Rochester, New York, where she worked as a seamstress and was briefly married. Outraged by the execution of the Haymarket Square Anarchists, Goldman moved to New York City at age twenty to become a radical activist.

Goldman became a popular speaker, making several cross-country lecture tours and numerous visits to Europe. A fervent Anarchist, she advocated for free speech, labor rights, birth control, and women's equality. A proponent of free love, she critiqued traditional marriage and supported the rights of prostitutes. She combined class, gender, and sexual politics, declining to join groups focused exclusively on women's issues. Goldman wrote widely and published the radical magazine *Mother Earth;* among her most well-known works are *The Traffic in Women and Other Essays on Feminism* (1971) and her autobiography *Living My Life* (1931).

Goldman was committed to personal freedom, believing that anarchism "stands for the liberation of the human mind from the dominion of religion; the liberation of the human body from the dominion of property . . . an order that will guarantee to every human being free access to the earth and full enjoyment of the necessities of life, according to individual desires, tastes, and inclinations." Her belief in personal liberty is exemplified by a story in her autobiography in which a fellow activist told her that her dancing did not behoove a political agitator. She wrote, "I did not believe that a cause which stood for a beautiful ideal, for anarchism, for release and freedom from conventions and prejudice, should demand the denial of life and joy. . . . If it meant that, I did not want it." From this was derived the most famous quote attributed to Goldman—"If I can't dance, I don't want to be part of your revolution"—which she never actually said.

In her early years, Goldman supported "propaganda by deed," although her later experiences led her to reject terrorism. In 1892, she and Alexander Berkman planned to assassinate Henry Clay Frick, who suppressed the Homestead strike in Pittsburgh; Berkman injured but did not kill Frick and was sentenced to prison. Goldman's lectures were routinely disrupted by authorities, and she was imprisoned on various occasions for incitement to riot, distributing birth control information, and organizing against World War I and the draft. Some of her works were suppressed under the Comstock anti-obscenity laws. As the country's most well-known proponent of anarchism, Goldman was hounded after Anarchist Leon Czolgosz assassinated President William McKinley in 1901. In 1919, she and Berkman were deported to Russia.

Although she had supported the Russian Revolution while in America, "Red Emma" became increasingly disillusioned with the Bolsheviks after witnessing increased bureaucratization, political persecution, and Leon Trotsky's violent suppression of the Kronstadt rebellion. In 1921, she left Russia for England. In 1936, she went to Spain to support the Anarchists fighting Generalissimo Franco's fascists in the Spanish Civil War. Goldman died in Toronto in 1940 and is buried in Chicago near the Haymarket Anarchists.

Liz Highleyman

thirty-two Jewish workers' associations and in Avrich's words, "combined the functions of a labor paper, a journal of radical opinion, a literary magazine, and a people's university." Its most well-known editors were David Edelstadt, the Yiddish labor poet, and Saul Yanovsky, who steered the paper away from "propaganda of the deed" as advocated by Most and toward more mainstream and reformist efforts like union organizing.

During the four years from 1886 to 1890, Anarchism emerged as probably the largest and certainly the most dynamic movement among Jewish radicals in the United States. The Jewish Anarchists, predominantly workers, took part in the first strikes against sweatshop labor and helped organize some of the first Jewish trade unions, such as those of the New York cloakmakers and kneepants workers.

Another key event of the period was the attempt by Alexander Berkman (a Pioneers of Liberty member) on the life of Henry Clay Frick, manager of the Carnegie steelworks near Pittsburgh. Berkman's act was in retaliation for the violence meted against workers during the Homestead Steel Strike of 1892. Touring the country raising money for Berkman's defense catapulted Emma Goldman into the political limelight. A fiery orator and talented editor of *Mother Earth*, she was active in a number of labor causes, including decrying the Triangle Shirtwaist Fire and publishing articles defending Tom Mooney and Warren Billings.

In the early 1900s, emphasis in the Jewish Anarchist community began to shift away from individual acts of violence toward the organization of unions in all trades in which Jewish workers were employed—from bookbinding and cigarmaking to tailoring and housepainting. They were especially active in the International Ladies' Garment Workers' Union (ILGWU) and in the Amalgamated Clothing Workers of America (ACWA), participating in strikes, rooting out corruption, and fighting against bureaucracy and indifference.

They were also active in the *Arbeiter Ring*, or Workmen's Circle, a Socialist fraternal order in North America that provided life insurance, sickness and accident benefits, burial plots, and educational and cul-

tural programs. Between 1910 and 1918, at least ten Jewish Anarchist groups existed in New York alone. By the 1920s, Anarchist branches were established in New York, Philadelphia, Baltimore, and Los Angeles. The Jewish Anarchists were also engaged in a variety of cooperative endeavors in New York and developed by the ILGWU and ACWA.

Besides the Jewish Anarchists, Russian workers also organized themselves. At the peak of its membership, the Union of Russian Workers in the United States and Canada numbered nearly 10,000 members. Italian Anarchists also played a role in the unions but disdained leadership positions owing to the anti-organization influence of their leader Luigi Galleani. Nonetheless, they were active in demonstrations and

Emma Goldman addresses a meeting of the National Federation of Labor in London, England, on January 20, 1937. Goldman had spoken out against imperialism, fascism, and oppression. *(AP Wide World Photos)*

strikes in Lawrence, Massachusetts (1912), Paterson, New Jersey (1913), and Plymouth, Massachusetts (1916).

INTERNATIONAL FORCES

Anarcho-syndicalism, the amalgamation of Anarchist ideology with the structure of a trade union, never caught on in the United States. This does not discount the fact that anarcho-syndicalists were active in the United States. However, they never formed anarcho-syndicalist unions. Nonetheless, the revolutionary Syndicalist Industrial Workers of the World (or Wobblies) placed an emphasis on direct action and self-organization of the working-class. In contrast to the slogan of Samuel Gompers's American Federation of Labor, "Honest pay for an honest day's work," the Wobblies called for "Abolition of the wage system," which they termed wage slavery. As a result, the press and government derided them as Communists, Anarchists, and criminals. When the Wobblies and Anarchists took an antimilitarist position during World War I, they were thrown in jail and in some cases deported.

During the Red Scare in 1919, a large number of Anarchists, including Emma Goldman and Alexander Berkman, were deported from the United States. Some historians have argued that Nicola Sacco and Bartolomeo Vanzetti, two Italian immigrants found guilty of murder, were both executed in 1927 for their Anarchist beliefs. Unlike its stance in the Haymarket affair, labor rallied to the case of Sacco and Vanzetti but to no avail.

In the early part of the twentieth century, the lure of the Bolshevik Revolution, the Red Scare, the Palmer Raids, and deportations had a disastrous impact on the Anarchist movement in the United States—one from which it would never recover. With its leadership in prison or deported and crippled by infighting, the movement continued to atrophy, experiencing a brief revival during the Spanish Revolution and Civil War (1936–1937) when the anarcho-syndicalist Confederacion Nacional del Trabajo (CNT) collectivized industries in Catalonia and agriculture in Andalusia.

Evan Daniel

BIBLIOGRAPHY

Avrich, Paul. *Anarchist Portraits*. Princeton, NJ: Princeton University Press, 1988.

———. *The Haymarket Tragedy*. Princeton, NJ: Princeton University Press, 1984.

Berkman, Alexander. *Prison Memoirs of an Anarchist*. New York: New York Review of Books, 1999.

———. *What Is Communist Anarchism?* New York: Dover Publications, 1972.

Dubofsky, Melvyn. *We Shall Be All*. New York: Quadrangle/New York Times Books, 1969.

Foner, Philip S. *Autobiographies of the Haymarket Martyrs*. New York: Pathfinder, 1969.

Glassgold, Peter, ed. *Anarchy!: An Anthology of Emma Goldman's Mother Earth*. New York: Counterpoint, 2001.

Goldman, Emma. *Living My Life*. New York: Dover, 1930.

Goldman, Emma, and Alix Kates, eds. *Red Emma Speaks: An Emma Goldman Reader*. New York: Schocken Books, 1983.

Guérin, Daniel, and Mary Klopper, trans. *Anarchism: From Theory to Practice*. New York: Monthly Review Press, 1970.

Hunter, Robert. *Violence and the Labor Movement*. New York: Arno and New York Times, 1969.

Most, Johann. *Revolutionare Kriegswissenschaft (The Science of Revolutionary Warfare)*. New York: Internationalen Zeitungs-Vereins, 1885.

Woodcock, George. *What Is Anarchism?* London: Freedom, 1945.

LABOR MOVEMENT

1877–1919

The history of the American working people's collective attempts to resist dependence and inequality remains largely unknown and misunderstood in popular culture, perhaps, as one historian speculated, because it does not accord well with the nation's dominant narrative of individual struggle and success. Because of state intervention and employers' use of technology and new production processes to increase labor competition, working-class movements between 1877 and 1920 were, on the whole, unsuccessful in realizing both their broader visions of a just industrial society and many of their less ambitious demands in regard to wages and working conditions for the majority of working people. Those failures had the effect of narrowing and tempering the aspirations of the dominant sector of the labor movement. Historians who favored this development interpreted what *was*—that is, the conservative approach of the country's most powerful unions—as what had always been, and the labor movement's more complex, radical past receded from popular memory.

AMERICAN WORKERS IN THE INDUSTRIAL ERA 1877–1920

The period 1877 to 1920 saw rapid, wrenching changes in American society and culture. An agrarian country in 1877, by the end of World War I the United States was an urban nation in which most adult inhabitants labored under employers and 40 percent of the workforce was involved in manufacturing. Modern cities, such as New York City, San Francisco, Philadelphia, Chicago, and Brooklyn (until it was incorporated into New York City), attracted most of the nation's industries, and their neighborhoods reflected the great divides in wealth, between the rich, the new urban middle class, and the poor, that emerged with the growth of industrial capitalism. These same developments, though on a smaller scale and at a slower rate, occurred in Southern cities, such as New Or-

leans, Louisiana, Birmingham, Alabama, and Chattanooga, Tennessee, where blacks and whites entered the tobacco, iron, steel, and shipping industries as waged laborers. Outside the South, city populations swelled with immigrants, over 26 million of whom arrived in the United States between 1871 and 1920. For much of the nineteenth century, immigrants typically hailed from northern and western Europe. Between 1890 and 1920, this pattern shifted. "New immigrants" from central, eastern, and southern Europe and from Mexico flooded into the nation, and, in contrast to the mainly Protestant "old immigrants," they included large numbers of Catholics, Jews, and Greek and Russian Orthodox.

The impact of these changes was tremendous. The wave of immigrants to the United States remade the American working class, which by the end of this period was more ethnically diverse than the workforces of Canada, Australia, and Great Britain. It was also racially and ethnically stratified. White, Protestant, native-born men, and the sons of northwestern European immigrants dominated skilled work, while "new immigrants" filled the ranks of the unskilled and semiskilled. African Americans, Mexican and Chinese immigrants, and, in the Northeast and Midwest, the Irish typically worked in the most irregular and poorly paid menial jobs.

Employers were tempted to play upon racial and ethnic divisions when labor competition was high, and they met with some success in doing so. This was especially the case in the South, where blacks, owing to disenfranchisement campaigns and debt peonage, lacked both political and economic power by 1900. However, an employer who experimented with black labor in the South risked a boycott by white customers or a race strike by white employees. North and South, "white" jobs were almost always cleaner, safer, and better paid than "black" ones. Few whites challenged a system that benefited them.

The rise of the factory further segmented the American workforce, as the proportion of women engaged in factory work more than quadrupled, from 4 percent in 1870 to 17 percent in 1900. In the Northeast, female industrial workers were typically foreign-born or the daughters of foreign-born parents. They worked mainly in the garment industry but also labored in canneries, box-making factories, book binderies, and commercial laundries. Women almost always held "women's jobs." As with men, racial hierarchies shaped in crucial ways the division of work among women. In Southern tobacco-processing plants, for example, white women operated the machines, while black women were relegated to the harder and dirtier job of stripping the tobacco leaves by hand. All female workers, white and black, shared an exclusion from skilled work, which was reserved for men. "Women's work" was invariably poorly paid, unskilled, and competitive. Obstacles to skilled labor positions included not only the hostility of male craft workers but also the hesitancy of employers to train women workers whom, they believed, sought only temporary employment.

Industrialization demanded a discipline and rhythm of work that was new to many workers who had arrived at the factory gates from either rural areas of America and Europe or from employment in small factories and shops in which custom rather than the clock governed the speed, quality, and nature of work. These workers carried with them into the factories notions of a flexible relationship between work and living. Thus, immigrant Jews and Slavs, for example, mystified native-born employers by missing work in order to honor religious holidays or to participate in festivals. Skilled coopers, also to the amazement of manufacturers, worked steadily Tuesday through Friday but then insisted upon their traditional long weekend. Even the job-hungry unskilled risked taking periodic breaks or attempted to set their own speed of work according to customary understandings of a "fair day's work" rather than conform to the industrialists' dictum that "Time is money."

Skilled workers were more able to resist the harsh industrial discipline sought by business owners and managers. In his book, the *Fall of the House of Labor: The Workplace, the State, and American Labor Activism, 1865–1925* (1987), historian David Montgomery described the control exerted by Ohio iron workers during the 1870s and 1880s as a result of their highly sought skills: "The workers . . . decided collectively, among themselves, what portion of [the] rate should go to each of them . . . how work should be allocated among them; how many rounds on the rolls should be undertaken each day. . . . To put it another way, all the boss did was to buy the equipment and raw materials and sell the finished product."

Yet, during this period, mechanization took a huge toll on many skilled workers, including brass workers, puddlers, dressmakers, coopers, and shoemakers. Men who had enjoyed some leverage at work because of their skill confronted new processes in which each worker repeated a small, separate task that required little skill or training. One unionist fumed, "The men are looked upon as nothing more than parts of the machinery that they work."

Manufacturers' introduction of machinery proved an effective tool in reducing many skilled workers to the level of the semiskilled or unskilled. Still, the tension between pre-industrial and industrial work habits remained frequent between 1877 and 1920, because, as historian Herbert Gutman pointed out in his classic study, *Work, Culture, and Society in Industrializing America: Essays in American Working-Class and Social History* (1976), "The American working class was continually altered in its composition by infusions, from within and without the nation, of peasants, farmers, skilled artisans, and casual day laborers who brought into industrial society ways of work and other habits and values not associated with industrial necessities and the industrial ethos."

Industrialization entailed other hardships for workers. Although highly skilled workers received a large share of the era's prosperity, and wages in the United States were far higher than in industrializing Europe, testimonies before investigative committees and the reports of state and federal agencies suggest that the average American worker had to struggle in order to subsist under industrialism. Immigrant families and families supported by women workers in particular fell below the minimum required earnings for a healthy, decent life. The main reason for this is that although working men and women benefited from economic booms, the busts that followed booms brought unemployment or underemployment to thousands, even millions, without regard to talent or productivity. Five serious economic depressions cut into working people's earnings and opportunities between 1877 and 1914. For most working people, poverty was an inevitable condition that they faced at some point in their lives. Government at this time did not provide any sort of safety net for the unemployed, and during economic crises the needs of the poor far outstripped the resources of private charities. The poor were left to ride out bad times as best they could on their own.

One way in which working people supplemented family income was to send their children to work in factories, mines, and mills. By 1900, about 1.7 million children were engaged in industry. Child labor was especially common in the mines and in the silk mills of the anthracite region because miners so often lost their lives or were disabled at work, leaving their families destitute. In addition, miners' low wages necessitated that children supplement the family income.

In addition to these problems, long hours and intensive rates of work resulted in a larger number of industrial accidents in the United States relative to other industrializing nations. The mines, railroads, and steel mills were particularly dangerous. Two thousand fatalities occurred each year between 1905 and 1920 in the coal mines, and in 1901 one in eleven operating trainmen suffered injury, often the loss or mangling of a limb or limbs. Every year between 1907 and 1920, one in four immigrant workers at the Carnegie South Works was injured or killed.

Unhealthy, demoralizing working conditions also plagued workers. Immigrant women labored in the hot, noisy, steam-filled rooms of commercial laundries and breweries, and in attics and basements they were "packed like sardines in a box." In mining camps and towns, "breaker" boys, mostly ten to fourteen years old, breathed in thick clouds of coal dust as they separated debris from loads of coal. Italian immigrant track workers in the North American West made makeshift homes out of railway boxcars that provided little relief from the elements. Their company-supplied food was, in the words of one laborer, "not even fit for dogs."

THE 1877 RAILWAY STRIKE

Although strikes were frequent in the decade following the Civil War, labor activists during that time drew largely upon free-labor ideology to emphasize cooperation between capital and labor. This ideology originated in antebellum days, when most "workingmen" labored under an employer who was onsite and reliant upon his employees' skills in producing a product. Looking back to this era of relative autonomy, postbellum labor leaders tended to avoid the image of class conflict in their analysis of "the labor question" and sought instead to restore the independence that skill had brought antebellum industrial workers. Some hoped that projects such as worker-owned cooperatives would help laborers to amass capital and thus escape wage labor. Others agitated

for legislation to limit the working day so that workers might reclaim the time usurped by manufacturers and spend it instead participating in the nation's political and social life. On the railroads, skilled trainmen stuck to a conservative course, paying dues to brotherhoods that sought to focus their energies on protecting members and their families from financial loss in case of injury or death.

The Panic of 1873 caused many labor activists to reconsider the relationship between laborers and their employers. The 1873 crisis stemmed from the overexpansion of the railroad industry, much of which speculative credit had financed. This produced a rash of defaults on bonds by railroad companies and their takeover by receivers. Railroads, in turn, attempted to minimize costs by cutting train crews to dangerously low numbers, neglecting equipment and track, and repeatedly slashing railroaders' wages. These measures increased the frustrations of railroad men, who throughout the 1870s had endured numerous exploitative work rules and conditions, including inhumanly long hours at jobs that required dexterity and alertness to ensure the safety of passengers and coworkers. Railroaders also worked "double-headers" in which they operated trains twice the usual length without the help of extra hands. Furthermore, these wage cuts came in a context in which as many as three million people were without work and more than four-fifths of those with a job were underemployed.

On July 16, 1877, railroad workers struck en masse. By July 22, nearly one million had walked off their job. Within a week, the strike had spread from Martinsburg, West Virginia, to Pittsburgh, Reading, Columbus, Chicago, Terre Haute, Kansas City, and San Francisco. In Baltimore, St. Louis, Philadelphia, and other cities and towns, discontented nonrailroaders joined strikers and in some areas destroyed railroad property and attacked militia units sent to crush the strike. According to contemporary estimates, more than 80,000 railroad workers, perhaps one-third of them Irish, and about a half million sympathetic nonrailroaders were involved in the unrest at its height. In St. Louis, a relatively peaceful general strike closed about sixty factories, while in Philadelphia, Pittsburgh, Chicago, and elsewhere riots and bloody confrontations broke out between strikers and militia.

The 1877 strike produced an important shift in the mainstream press's understanding of labor issues. Prior to the conflict, leading editorialists and commentators had mainly associated mob action with immigrant groups and Communists, not native-born, skilled workingmen. In his 1994 article "Chaining the

Soldiers of the Sixth Maryland Regiment fire on workers of the Baltimore and Ohio Railroad in July 1877. A turning point in the nation's history, the national railroad strike ushered in a long era of bloody conflict between labor and capital. *(Brown Brothers)*

Tiger: The Mob Stigma and the Working Class, 1863–1984," historian Eugene Leach argued that the strike "confounded the crucial distinction between riotous workers and law-abiding ones" that had dominated previous views of crowd action. "The riots seemed to spill across divisions of occupation, ethnicity, geography, and even gender, expressing resentments widely shared in the working class," Leach observed. It was therefore difficult for mainstream critics to explain away labor unrest and violence as the work of immigrants, agitators, and lawless elements.

The discipline that characterized the parades of thousands of strikers and their sympathizers through the streets of St. Louis and Philadelphia in 1877 caused elite and middle-class onlookers to fear the coming of a class-based revolution. Influential analysts laid responsibility for the unrest at the feet of strikers themselves. The press urged railroads to refuse to make concessions of any kind and bitterly attacked those companies that capitulated to workers' demands. As a result of the 1877 strike, then, dominant opinion solidified against independent working-class organization and against strikes in particular.

GILDED AGE LABOR MOVEMENTS

In the years following the 1877 railway strike, various labor leaders debated the causes of labor violence. In 1883, John Swinton, the publisher of a popular working-class newspaper, warned Americans that the unbearable conditions that had precipitated labor violence in 1877 must radically improve: "Don't let us have a tiger among us that needs to be chained; let us have neither tiger nor chains; away with the Wrongs by which he is generated." In contrast to Swinton's solution to the "labor question," which entailed a radical restructuring of society, trade unionist Samuel Gompers emphasized the need for organization among skilled workers. The future leader of the American Federation of Labor (AFL) viewed workers' lack of organization as the chief cause of strike and of labor unrest in general. Without the discipline of a trade union, he argued, workers tended to act "upon ill-considered plans, hastily adopted," and "upon passion." Trade unions would act as "conservators of the public peace" and "check the more radical elements in society."

Trade unions did gain new life in the decade following the 1877 strike. Although blacklists and dismissals in the immediate aftermath of the riots almost destroyed the railroad brotherhoods, these craft associations and others, particularly the cigar makers and construction unions, steadily rebuilt their membership. By 1886, about 350,000 craft workers belonged to a national body, the Federation of Organized Trades and Labor Unions of the United States, and in Cincinnati, Boston, Chicago, Denver, New Orleans, and San Francisco, craft unions had formed powerful citywide organizations.

The labor organization that made the greatest strides during the late 1870s and early 1880s was not limited to craft workers but was instead industrial in character. Called the Knights of Labor, the organization had its start in a number of secret societies formed among Philadelphia artisans following the Civil War. Despite the hostile climate toward unions, a growing number joined the Knights after 1878, when the order rejected secrecy and began to organize openly on a national scale. Rather than limit membership to skilled white male workers, as labor unions had done in the past, the Knights admitted and actively recruited a far broader range of people: blacks and whites, native-born and immigrant, Catholic and Protestant, the skilled and unskilled, sympathetic shopkeepers and business-owners, and beginning in 1881, women. Although it excluded the Chinese and played a leading role in anti-Chinese violence in California, Wyoming, and Oregon, by the mid-1880s the order was in other respects the first mass organization of its kind.

Led by machinist Terence Vincent Powderly, the Knights gave voice to the widespread concern that industrialists' power posed a danger to the Republic. If, as the founders contended, the liberty of citizens turned on their independence, then, the Knights reasoned, the nation's industrial path had undermined liberty by introducing machines and processes that degraded skilled labor and vastly enlarged the nation's permanent underclass of the dispossessed. In sum, industrialism had created the widespread economic dependence of working people on employers. It left workers little time or energy to exercise the rights of citizenship, and it threatened social anarchy. These developments, the Knights charged, represented the harbingers of tyranny.

Trade unionists and industrial unionists cooperated on a number of fronts. In 1885, New York City's massive citywide labor organization, the Central Labor Union, represented over 200 unions of both skilled and unskilled workers, in San Francisco skilled cigar makers found widespread support for their boycott of Chinese-made cigars among the city's white working poor, and unskilled and semiskilled Poles joined German American craft workers in Milwaukee's Knights of Labor union halls. Across the country, working-class communities proved enthusiastic supporters of the eight-hour-day campaign. In 1886, the year that labor historians term "The Great Upheaval," about 400,000 workers struck in support of this demand, with the Knights often in the lead.

On the western railways, the industrial credo of the Knights brought impressive gains. As railroad companies slashed wages and implemented other cost-saving measures in order to remain competitive, the railroad brotherhoods, which since the debacle of 1877 had eschewed labor conflict and emphasized the shared interests of capital and labor, came under increasing pressure from members to combine with shop workers, brakemen, switchmen, and track laborers in an effort to gain a more powerful voice for labor on the railroads. Engineers and firemen respected shop worker-led strikes on the Union Pacific in 1884 and on Jay Gould's sprawling Southwest system of roads in 1885, both of which won promises from management to rescind wage cuts. These victories, along with a much-celebrated agreement negotiated be-

tween Terence Powderly and Jay Gould in September 1885, swelled the Knights' membership rolls to between 700,000 and one million.

The Knights' language of antimonopoly appealed to residents of towns and cities across the United States that in many ways remained "island communities" during the nineteenth century. In *The Search for Order, 1877–1920* (1967) historian Robert H. Wiebe wrote, "The heart of American democracy was local autonomy. . . . American institutions were still oriented toward a community life where family and church, education and press, professions and government, all largely found their meaning by the way they fit one with another inside a town or a detached portion of a city." Local citizens saw their communities thrown into chaos by economic forces that were national in scope and often indifferent or hostile to their interests as well as the interests of their working-class neighbors.

The relationship between local communities and railroads is a case in point. Striking railroaders in the Southwest found widespread sympathy for their plight among farmers and small merchants who resented the discriminatory rates charged by railroad companies. City officials angered by the Missouri Pacific's negligence in paying local taxes also identified with strikers. In *A Generation of Boomers: The Pattern of Railroad Labor Conflict in Nineteenth-Century America* (1987), Shelton Stromquist pointed out that local support for railroad labor struggles was not by any means universal. In market cities such as Burlington, Illinois, the reduced railroad rates that manufacturers enjoyed often led them to side with railroads, and "social solidarity" among large and diverse working-class populations was "more fragile and fragmented." Still, in numerous smaller railroad towns, where railroaders' economic well-being was tied to that of retailers and where dependence on railroads "bred a fierce independence," citizens of varied backgrounds and means cast the railroaders' fight against impoverishing wage cuts as a struggle for local rights and concerns against the impositions of an alien power.

By the turn of the century, however, the industrial unionists such as the Knights numbered in the thousands rather than the hundreds of thousands. Many labor activists had rejected or put aside the order's radical republican vision. In the Knights' place stood the AFL. In contrast to the Knights, its leadership accepted industrial capitalism and aimed to secure gains in wages and working conditions for its members, craft workers, in return for labor peace. Rather than seek government's help in restoring the

SAMUEL GOMPERS (1850–1924)

Born to Jewish working-class parents in London on January 27, 1850, Gompers migrated to the United States with his parents in 1863 and became a naturalized citizen in 1872. He followed his father into the trade of cigar making and in 1864 joined the local union, serving as its president from 1874 to 1881. Influenced by British trade union principles and by the Marxist emphasis on the primacy of the economic organization of workers, Gompers worked to create strong, centralized trade union institutions that would help grow and direct local unions. He and Adolph Strasser founded the Federation of Organized Trades and Labor Unions in 1881 along these principles, as well as its successor as the American Federation of Labor (AFL) in 1886. Gompers was the AFL's first president and remained president, except for the year 1895, until his death.

Like many Marxists, Gompers believed that trade unions would develop awareness of a broad class interest among workers, and that political activity and reform did little for the workers unless organized workers in the factories and craft shops enforced change. Yet, despite his Marxist beliefs, as a labor leader, Gompers gained a reputation for conservatism. Even in the lowest paying jobs, the influx of immigrants to the American workforce was deeply resented because their presence kept wages low. Gompers, a self-described champion of the working man, shared this resentment. He directed the successful battle with the all-inclusive Knights of Labor for supremacy over organized labor. But even after the downfall of the Knights of Labor by the end of the 1800s, by 1904, the AFL accounted for around 10 percent of all nonagricultural workers. Its emphasis on recruiting skilled craft workers excluded the less skilled at a time when these

workers were growing in numbers and contributed to the drop in membership over the next decade. Gompers distrusted the influence of intellectual reformers, fearing any activity that would divert labor's energy from economic goals. To that end, he kept the union out of politics in the early days and refused cooperative business plans, socialistic ideas, and radical programs, maintaining that more wages, shorter hours, and greater freedom were the just aims of labor. To differentiate the AFL from more radical elements in the labor movement and to make the organization appear more respectable, he encouraged binding, written trade agreements.

Gompers came to be recognized as the leading spokesman for the labor movement, and his pronouncements carried much weight. As government regulation of industrial relations increased, Gompers led the AFL into political alliances and even actively supported Woodrow Wilson's presidential candidacy in 1912. During Wilson's two terms, Gompers helped push the Clayton Anti-Trust Act of 1914 and the Seamen's Act of 1915 through Congress. With the outbreak of World War I, Gompers organized and headed the War Committee on Labor. As a member of the Advisory Commission to the Council of National Defense, he helped to hold organized labor loyal to the government program. As a result, during the war, union membership more than doubled to nearly 4 million from its earlier peak of 1.7 million members in 1904. After the war, however, several failed strikes left the union weakened. It slumped further in the pro-business atmosphere of the 1920s. Gompers died in San Antonio, Texas on December 13, 1924. His autobiography, *Seventy Years of Life and Labor* (1925), was published after his death.

James G. Lewis

Republic to industrial America, the AFL embraced "volunteerism"—an antistatist outlook that opposed the extension of government's role in industrial relations, specifically, the hostile intervention of the courts in labor conflicts.

A number of factors led to the Knights' demise. First, Knights on the Southwest system lost an 1886 strike that involved almost 9,000 workers. Many participants had to move elsewhere in search of work; others landed in jail for allegedly violating court injunctions against interference with railroad property or for assault or intimidation of strikebreakers. At about the same time, on May 4, 1886, a bomb killed

a policeman at Haymarket Square in Chicago, where Socialists and Anarchists led a meeting of about 300 workers to protest the deaths of two unarmed workers involved in a strike at the McCormick Reaper Works. An antiradical, anti-immigrant hysteria followed in which the meetings' Anarchist leaders were convicted and hanged for their politics rather than any involvement in the bombing. Although Powderly distanced the order from the accused, the Knights' fortunes suffered in the wake of the Haymarket Affair. The frenzy encouraged employers to vigorously fight and defeat a number of major Knights of Labor strikes in 1886, and further widened the divide that had

MARY HARRIS "MOTHER JONES" JONES (1830–1930)

Born in Cork, Ireland, on May 1, 1830, Mary Harris was brought to America some time after 1835 by her father, who had preceded the rest of the family in emigrating. In 1867, Jones lost her husband and four children to yellow fever, and then all of her personal belongings in the great Chicago fire four years later. Attracted by the Knights of Labor campaign for improved working conditions, she turned to them for assistance, and became involved in the American labor movement. She won fame as an effective speaker and by 1880 was a prominent figure in the movement.

An active proponent of legislation to prohibit child labor, Jones also organized miners, garment workers, and streetcar workers. One of the founders of the Social Democratic Party (1898) and the Industrial Workers of the World (1905), she was a lecturer for the Socialist Party of America. She traveled across the country, both organizing for the United Mine Workers and speaking on her own, supporting strikes, and galvanizing public support for labor with her slogan, "Join the union, boys."

In 1913, her organizing activities were blamed for violence in the West Virginia coal mines, and she was convicted of conspiracy to commit murder. Her ordeal ended when the governor released her. The U.S. Senate ordered a committee to investigate conditions in the West Virginia coalfields. In 1914, her graphic description of the massacre of twenty people by machine-gun fire during a Ludlow, Colorado, miners' strike convinced President Woodrow Wilson to try to mediate the dispute. A long-time champion of laws to end child labor, she continued as a union organizer and agitator into her nineties. She wrote *Autobiography of Mother Jones* in 1925, which contains some factual inaccuracies. She died in Silver Spring, Maryland, on November 30, 1930, and is buried in the Union Miners Cemetery at Mount Olive, Illinois.

James G. Lewis

emerged between trade unionists and industrial unionists, as trade unionists sought to disassociate their organizations from radicalism.

Differences in philosophy and strategy between trade unionists and industrial unionists rose to the surface in the mid-1880s. In order to protect the fa-

vorable contract gained in the 1885 strike, most engineers and firemen obeyed their brotherhoods' order to continue work during the 1886 Southwest railway strike, vastly complicating Gould system Knights' efforts to win company recognition of employees' executive committee. In May 1886, Samuel Gompers, then head of the Cigar Makers International Union, called a meeting of national unions to discuss the relationship of trade unionists and the Knights after Socialist cigar makers, supported by the Knights, threatened his conservative leadership. The meeting rejected the tradition of dual unionism, which had allowed skilled workers to belong both to their craft unions and the Knights, and formed the AFL. The efforts of Gompers and other AFL leaders to avert a general strike in Chicago in support of the 1894 Pullman boycott illustrates the union's continued commitment to an independent, more conservative path.

Nonetheless, although the AFL's approach differed considerably from that of the Knights, the line between trade unionists and reformers was a porous one in the Gilded Age. Historian William Forbath, in his book *Law and the Shaping of the American Labor Movement* (1991), contended that the typical AFL activist "shared the Knights' radical ambitions and their faith in lawmaking and the ballot as ways of ending the 'tyranny of capital.'" AFL leaders joined the Knights in lobbying state governments and Washington on behalf of legislation that mandated an eight-hour day and a ban on tenement manufacturing and payment in scrip, and members of the AFL and Knights alike exhibited strong support for independent and third-party candidates. These political efforts faced huge obstacles, including ethnic and racial divisions, single-member constituencies, the cost of running candidates at the federal level, and party loyalties shaped by the Civil War and Reconstruction. Despite such serious impediments, during the 1870s and 1880s many labor activists tried and some succeeded in winning office on the state and local level. Labor-supported candidate Henry George lost the New York mayoral race but succeeded in polling one-third of votes cast, and labor parties won in municipal races across the nation.

Forbath argued that it was only after labor activists suffered a series of defeats in the courts during the 1880s and 1890s that "trade unionists' views of what was possible and desirable in politics and industry" changed, from an emphasis on "broad, positive reforms" to a focus on winning "bread and butter" gains for its members through collective bargaining. Judicial hostility to the boycott, the sympathy strike, reformist legislation, and even the right to strike itself "shaped labor's strategic calculus" so that by the turn of the century radicals in the AFL were a distinct minority.

Although strikes remained legal throughout the nineteenth century, boycotts and sympathy strikes came increasingly under judicial attack. These attacks began in response to railway labor disputes, as judges tended to see railway strikes, especially nationwide actions, as a threat to the public interest, and unionists' attempts to control shop-floor rules as a threat to the rule of property and contract. The courts laid the basis for state intervention when they ordered federal troops to intervene in the 1877 strike in order to restore commerce and social order when state and local officials sympathetic to the railroaders refused to deputize volunteers or call in state militia. In 1886, injunctions issued against those engaged in work stoppages on roads under receivership (bankrupt roads under public management) doomed the Knights' strike on the Southwest system. The courts expanded the scope of the labor injunction to workers who boycotted handling of struck company cars in the 1888 Burlington strike, even though the railroad brotherhoods had long used the secondary strike to win collective bargaining agreements for its members. By the time the industrial American Railway Union (ARU) waged a strike in 1894 to restore the wages of employees of the Pullman Palace Car Company, the legal groundwork for the injunctions that ultimately doomed the Pullman strike were in place. Federal and state troops enforced a court decree against the ARU boycott of Pullman cars, crushing a strike that had involved at its height almost 260,000 railroad workers from Chicago to the Pacific.

The federal courts were reluctant to intervene in nonrailroad labor disputes for much of the nineteenth century, but the rise of the citywide boycott, which enlisted the sympathy of broad segments of working-class populations with boycotts of "unfair" goods and shops, changed this. Beginning in the late 1880s, courts redefined property to include the ownership not only of objects but also anything that had "exchangeable value." The redefinition later allowed courts to cast the boycott as a "combination" under the Sherman Anti-Trust Act and the picket line as intimidation and thus a violation of workers' property right to pursue their vocations. Judicial hostility to strikes for work-rule changes and closed shops pushed state and local authorities to intervene on their own. In 1892, the governor of Pennsylvania dealt the strike against Andrew Carnegie's Homestead steel

The indefatigable Mary Harris "Mother" Jones traveled widely to organize workers, mobilize strikers, and fight for better labor conditions. She remained active well into her nineties. (Brown Brothers)

works a severe blow when he ordered the state militia to restore law and order after strikers drove back company-hired and armed Pinkerton agents brought in to protect strikebreakers. The loss decimated the unions of skilled iron and steelworkers.

Gilded Age labor activists, including AFL leaders, sought redress in the political arena with little success. Federal judges were mostly from the ranks of elite Republicans unsympathetic to labor, and professional associations governed the process of selecting candidates for state judgeships, diminishing labor's influence from the outset. The courts determined the fate of reformist legislation, usually in the employers' favor. In 1885, a federal court overturned an AFL-supported New York statute outlawing the manufacture of cigars in tenements on the grounds that sweatshop workers were free laborers entitled to make their own decisions about employment. On similar grounds, the Illinois Supreme Court struck down a hard-fought Illinois law restricting the hours worked by women and children. When AFL members debated whether to pursue state involvement in labor disputes in the 1890s, "volunteerists" cited invalidated labor laws as evidence that the federation should reject state intervention in favor of the economic power of craft unions.

Although the Knights' numbers had diminished significantly by the 1890s, the order's producer ideology remained a potent force among a number of industrial workers, as the extensive support among railroad workers for the Pullman boycott illustrates. The United Mine Workers of America preserved the Knights' inclusive organizing strategy, organizing white and black, skilled and unskilled alike. The alliance formed between industrial workers, farmers, and sharecroppers in the mid-1890s in support of Populist Party candidates revived for a brief time working-class support for independent parties. Many of the Southern black tenants, miners, day laborers, and domestic workers who had joined the Knights in the late 1880s and early 1890s likely lent their support to the Colored Farmers' Alliance and to Populist candidates in 1894 and 1896, as a sizable number of industrial workers did in their search for relief from the economic depression that began in 1893.

The Populist coalition collapsed, however, owing in part to regional differences but mostly to key material conflicts between agricultural and industrial populations. Farmers wanted cheap money, inflation, an end to the protective tariff, and free silver, while industrial workers favored cheap food, hard money, high wages, and protection from foreign competition. The Republican victory in the 1896 presidential election was largely a result of these divisions. The producer ideology that had moved thousands to cross lines of race, skill, gender, ethnicity, and religion to challenge industrialists' values in the 1880s had by the end of the century entered a period of decline from which it never fully recovered. In its wake, the exclusive, antistatist strategy of the AFL dominated. Although the broader vision of an industrial Republic remained unfulfilled in 1900, over the succeeding two decades middle-class Progressives and their working-class allies drew upon elements of this vision to launch a series of reforms that reshaped and reinvigorated American labor movements.

PROGRESSIVISM AND LABOR

Following five years of depression, the American economy expanded after 1897, and with it the AFL grew. Shortages of skilled workers in numerous industries, including railroading, construction, and coal mining, inspired union-organizing drives that brought AFL membership to 1.7 million by 1904. The AFL's growth was in large part due to the success of its strategy of "business unionism," which won for many AFL members improved wages and working conditions. "Business unionism" refers to the approach best summed up by Gompers, who viewed unions as "business organizations of wage-earners." Accordingly, the AFL made material objectives its central concern and pursued these objectives by resorting to the strike as an economic weapon only after a careful calculation of risk, securing labor contracts that codified rules and procedures negotiated by a professional class of labor bureaucrats, and, in order to reduce labor competition, seeking immigration restrictions and resisting the inclusion of immigrants, women, and nonwhites. There were costs associated with this strategy. Bureaucracy, and the alliance of some member unions with corrupt urban political machines, eroded the organization's democratic traditions and its idealism. Still, AFL unions, especially the United Mine Workers and the International Typographical Union, railroad brotherhoods, and building trades, won significant victories during this period.

The vast majority of working people stood outside of trade unions and thus received few of the rewards brought by "business unionism." The AFL leadership and many of its members saw black labor as a threat to white labor; the organization issued only about 82,000, or 3 percent, of its union cards to black workers, and most of its member unions excluded blacks entirely. In these policies, the AFL mirrored larger developments in American race relations: Northern acquiescence to the solidification of segregation in the South, the dramatic increase in lynching, and, in the wake of the Populists' defeat, the passage of numerous laws that effectively disenfranchised Southern black men.

In spite of these obstacles, some African Americans found a place in the AFL. In Alabama, for example, black industrial workers joined all-black and integrated unions and occupied leadership positions in the state federation. In Birmingham-area mines, blacks comprised 60 percent of the miners' biracial union by 1915. Biracial unions did not necessarily provide a haven of racial equality and brotherhood. The Knights of Labor's biracial approach, after all, had involved the acceptance of segregated locals in the South and a racial hierarchy in employment, the relegation of blacks to secondary leadership positions, and white paternalism toward black members. The same traditions of white supremacy shaped relationships between Alabama's black and white miners. Nonetheless, their commitment to an integrated, industrial union represented a sharp departure from the approach taken to race relations by other social organizations in the South and the nation's most powerful labor organization.

Women did not find a place in the AFL, mostly because employers banned their entrance into the skilled trades but also because of the AFL's view of female industrial workers as intruders in the labor market and, more to the point, as saboteurs of male privilege. The proper role of the father and the husband was, in most AFL members' eyes, the family breadwinner, while women and children were properly the dependents of men. The AFL therefore sought special protections for women in industry and a family wage, by which the AFL meant higher male wages, in order to render female paid labor unnecessary and restore male power in the household. In viewing female workers as unnatural, the AFL did not differ much from most Knights of Labor, but Gilded Age labor activists, male and female, tended to support the family wage as a means to benefit the whole family.

By 1920, women were working for wages in record numbers. In 1910, virtually all of the two million Americans engaged in domestic service were women, many of them Irish-born or African American, and women dominated unskilled and semiskilled work in the garment industry. Some worked to supplement a male family member's wages, others to support their own household, and still others to gain some independence and security for themselves. Although most female workers stood outside of organized labor, like male workers they sought, in various ways, to exert control over their working conditions. In New York City, for example, native-born women joined working girls' clubs that offered opportunities for recreation but also a forum for expressing workplace grievances, sympathy for labor organizations, and a desire for co-operation. Black domestic workers in the South challenged employers who demanded long hours and low wages by quitting and seeking employment elsewhere and sharing information about employers with other domestics in mutual aid societies and neighborhood associations.

The growth of the AFL at first drew a cautious but accommodative response from a number of major industrialists who joined the National Civic Federation (NCF), an organization which, in the hope of promoting labor peace, endorsed employer cooperation with conservative unionists. However, many small business owners, who could less afford the welfare capitalism proposed by industrialists of the NCF, waged a full frontal assault upon the closed shop. Appealing to the ideals of individualism and liberty, and meeting with much success, organizations such as the National Association of Manufacturers defended employees' right to refuse to join unions, disseminated anti-union pamphlets, and used private armed guards, strikebreakers, and the blacklist to defeat workers who struck in protest. Moreover, employers turned to mechanization and scientific management techniques that reduced the power and prestige of skilled workers in numerous industries.

At the same time that AFL unions went on the defensive, garment workers unions underwent a period of explosive growth. About 400,000 mostly unskilled and semiskilled Italian and east European immigrant women joined unions in the space of four years (1909–1913). Their success was probably partly due to the highly competitive and unstable nature of the industry, which encouraged large employers to see unionization as one way to rationalize their trade. Progressive reformers also proved helpful, as their support for industrial harmony through arbitration played a role in convincing employers to negotiate with the garment workers when they struck the industry. But the main impetus for reform came from below, in 1909 and 1910—first among shirtwaist workers, whose general strike drew 20,000 participants, and then among 100,000 male and female clothing industry workers.

The upheaval in the garment industry coincided with, and was in part influenced by, the rise of the Socialist Party and the International Workers of the World (IWW). Led by Eugene V. Debs, who had embraced socialism while serving jail time for his role in leading the Pullman strike as president of the ARU, the Socialist Party found supporters among many unskilled workers, such as those in the garment, textile, and shoe industries, some skilled workers and middle-class women, farmers threatened by tenancy in the Southwest, and "new" immigrants. At the national level, the party garnered a substantial number of votes in 1904 and 1908, and numerous Socialists won elections at the state and city level. In contrast to the Socialist Party cohorts, who were by and large

After destroying a strikers' tent camp in Ludlow, Colorado, on the night of Easter Sunday in 1914, members of the Colorado National Guard pose with their rifles. Soldiers killed fourteen people—including eleven children—making the "Ludlow Massacre" one of the bloodiest state-sanctioned attacks on workers during the Progressive Era. *(Denver Public Library)*

gradualists willing to pursue an electoral strategy, IWW members, or "Wobblies," renounced politics and sought the immediate emancipation of workers through spontaneous, direct action. An estimated two to three million Americans were "Wobblies" between 1909 and 1919.

Although no stable union emerged from the Wobblies' efforts, and the Socialist Party's electoral strength was eventually sapped by the Democratic Party's concessions to labor under President Wilson, both were important because they offered organization to unskilled workers, particularly immigrants, when the AFL did not. IWW influence can be seen especially in the textile strikes in Lawrence, Massachusetts, in 1912 and in Paterson, New Jersey, the following year. These strikes involved mostly immigrant men, women, and children, working people spurned by the AFL.

In Paterson, strikers met defeat after English-speaking skilled workers, who had joined with Italian and Jewish workers, returned to work. Garment workers did not obtain recognition for their union, the International Ladies' Garment Workers' Union, and

the spread of industrial unrest to other immigrant laborers faltered after Paterson. But in Lawrence, where police attacks on women and children raised public ire against mill owners, and in the garment industry, strikers were able to wring concessions from owners, including reduced hours, pay raises, improved conditions, and overtime pay. Moreover, their well-publicized struggles, along with the violent repression of miners at Ludlow, Colorado, in 1914, convinced a significant segment of the middle class that only progressive, rational reform efforts could reestablish order and democracy in industrial America.

Middle-class and working-class Progressive-Era reformers pushed for and won a slew of labor legislation aimed at correcting industrialism's ills. As president, Theodore Roosevelt brought the federal government for the first time into an industrial dispute on the side of labor when he pressured mine operators to negotiate a strike by United Mine Workers in Pennsylvania in 1902. The AFL, female unionists, and social feminists allied to win protective legislation for women workers, measures that the Supreme Court upheld in principle in 1908. Encouraged,

"Breaker boys" as young as nine years old worked up to fourteen hours a day separating coal from waste products. More than 300,000 children worked in the nation's mines, factories, and mills in the early 1900s. *(Brown Brothers)*

thirty-eight states put child labor laws on the books in 1912, and twenty-eight states limited women's hours of labor. States also passed workers' compensation laws and codes regarding safety and sanitation. To reward the AFL for its support of his election in 1912, Woodrow Wilson appointed labor leaders to federal office, established the Department of Labor, and helped to push through Congress the Clayton Act, which laid out a "bill of rights" for labor unions and sought to end the courts' use of the Sherman Anti-Trust Act against labor "combinations." The Ad-

amson Act and the Seamen's Act, respectively, limited railroad workers' hours and mitigated the abusive authority of ship captains over sailors.

Progressive reforms signaled a dramatic transformation in many Americans' ideas about the relationship between people and the government. The acceptance of government intervention on behalf of workers to protect them from the excesses of industrialism was widespread, whereas in the 1870s middle-class and elite thinkers routinely denounced as Communism the idea that a worker should, for in-

NO REST FOR THE WEARY: CHILDREN IN THE COAL MINES
BY JOHN SPARGO

John Spargo, labor advocate and organizer, was a leading critic of the early twentieth-century labor system that relied on child labor working under dangerous conditions. In this excerpt from his book, Spargo exposes the dangerous conditions in the American coal mining industry that depended so much on children for its labor needs.

Work in the coal breakers is exceedingly hard and dangerous. Crouched over the chutes, the boys sit hour after hour, picking out the pieces of slate and other refuse from the coal as it rushes past to the washers. From the cramped position they have to assume, most of them become more or less deformed and bent-backed like old men. When a boy has been working for some time and begins to get round-shouldered, his fellows say that "He's got his boy to carry round wherever he goes."

The coal is hard, and accidents to the hands, such as cut, broken, or crushed fingers, are common among the boys. Sometimes there is a worse accident: a terrified shriek is heard, and a boy is mangled and torn in the machinery, or disappears in the chute to be picked out later smothered and dead. Clouds of dust fill the breakers and are inhaled by the boys, laying the foundations for asthma and miners' consumption.

I once stood in a breaker for half an hour and tried to do the work a twelve-year-old boy was doing day after day, for ten hours at a stretch, for sixty cents a day. The gloom of the breaker appalled me. Outside the sun shone brightly, the air was pellucid [clear], and the birds sang in chorus with the trees and the rivers. Within the breaker there was blackness, clouds of deadly dust enfolded everything, the harsh, grinding roar of the machinery and the ceaseless rushing of coal through the chutes filled the ears. I tried to pick out the pieces of slate from the hurrying stream of coal, often missing them; my hands were bruised and cut in a few minutes; I was covered from head to foot with coal dust, and for many hours afterwards I was expectorating some of the small particles of anthracite I had swallowed.

I could not do that work and live, but there were boys of ten and twelve years of age doing it for fifty and sixty cents a day. Some of them had never been inside of a school; few of them could read a child's primer. True, some of them attended the night schools, but after working ten hours in the breaker the educational results from attending school were practically nil.

. . . From the breakers the boys graduate to the mine depths, where they become door tenders, switch boys, or mule drivers. Here, far below the surface, work is still more dangerous. At fourteen or fifteen the boys assume the same risks as the men, and are surrounded by the same perils. Nor is it in Pennsylvania only that these conditions exist. In the bituminous mines of West Virginia, boys of nine or ten are frequently employed. I met one little fellow ten years old in Mt. Carbon, W. Va., last year, who was employed as a "trap boy." Think of what it means to be a trap boy at ten years of age. It means to sit alone in a dark mine passage hour after hour, with no human soul near; to see no living creature except the mules as they pass with their loads, or a rat or two seeking to share one's meal; to stand in water or mud that covers the ankles, chilled to the marrow by the cold draughts that rush in when you open the trap door for the mules to pass through; to work for fourteen hours—waiting—opening and shutting a door—then waiting again for sixty cents; to reach the surface when all is wrapped in the mantle of night, and to fall to the earth exhausted and have to be carried away to the nearest "shack" to be revived before it is possible to walk to the farther shack called "home."

Boys twelve years of age may be *legally* employed in the mines of West Virginia, by day or by night, and for as many hours as the employers care to make them toil or their bodies will stand the strain. Where the disregard of child life is such that this may be done openly and with legal sanction, it is easy to believe what miners have again and again told me—that there are hundreds of little boys of nine and ten years of age employed in the coal mines of this state.

Source: John Spargo, *The Bitter Cry of Children* (New York: Macmillan, 1906).

stance, have the right to be paid a living wage. Later, in the 1930s, working Americans built upon that transformation to promote both labor peace and labor justice.

This accomplishment was a long-term one. In the short term, the results were much more mixed. Progressive reforms, the end products of compromise between groups with very different interests and belief systems, tended to favor skilled workers and those engaged in factory work in which inspectors were an effective presence. These reforms did not touch the working lives of many other workers—unskilled laborers, domestic servants, and the rural poor. Key pieces of legislation, namely, the Clayton Act and the 1916 federal law banning child labor, were rendered meaningless by the courts, which narrowly interpreted the Clayton Act and rejected the 1916 law as unconstitutional. Indeed, the Progressive impulse to provide labor with a voice in industry did not find much appeal among judges. The courts either struck down or read out of existence virtually all of the fifty anti-injunction laws won by labor between 1900 and 1920.

WORLD WAR I AND BEYOND 1914–1919

Labor activists confronted a new set of circumstances in the years before the United States entered World War I. Employers faced labor shortages because the war in Europe stemmed the tide of immigrants arriving on American shores. At the same time, American industry and agriculture strained to fulfill the Allied Powers' demands for food, raw materials, and manufactured goods. Working people used their power in the tightened labor market to secure improved wages and working conditions. Strikes that annually involved more than a million workers, representing a wide spectrum of employees, rocked U.S. industry between 1916 and 1920. Increased pay was a particularly important issue for most, since wartime inflation doubled consumer prices by 1920, eroding much of the gains that workers had made in wages. As the demand for goods expanded, employers attempted to increase production by introducing scientific management techniques and pushing employees to speed up their work.

Six months after the United States officially joined the Allied Powers' war effort, a colossal series of strikes in shipbuilding, coal mining, and metal industries led the federal government to institute labor commissions to adjudicate labor disputes during the war. Although some labor agency officials believed that unionization would calm labor relations, and certainly the AFL's pro-war stance helped to persuade them of this position, rather than union rights the government more consistently supported shop councils elected by employees to deal with worker grievances. When employers proved intractable, Washington pressured them to concede to their workers' demands, inducing millions to join the ranks of organized labor, which grew to five million by 1920.

The wartime demand for labor also brought hundreds of thousands of Southern rural working people into Northern and Midwestern cities—about a half million white Southerners and an equal number of black Southerners, and, into the Southwest, 185,000 Mexicans. For black migrants, the war represented a turning point. Previously barred from most skilled jobs, blacks eagerly left the Jim Crow order of the South (and the boll weevil and floods that decimated cotton crops in 1916) for the North's higher wages, voting booths, integrated busses, and superior schools. The jobs offered blacks were largely those that white people did not want, and racial tensions often simmered below the surface as blacks and whites competed for work and housing. Such tensions turned to violent conflict in East St. Louis in 1917, where white mobs murdered forty blacks in a bloody riot. Despite these obstacles and terrors, the relative freedom enjoyed by African-American migrants to the North encouraged many to commit to a fight for equal rights.

Women, too, experienced a new sense of self-purpose during the war, as industry recruited them to fill the places of men fighting in Europe and to keep up with the demand for goods. Women worked as streetcar conductors, as metalworkers and munitions workers, and an increasing number as clerical workers, among other jobs. The entrance of women into nontraditional occupations, and the hostility they often encountered from male coworkers and unionists, led many women to support women's suffrage. Without the vote, these women argued, how could they hope to change or ameliorate their working and living conditions? Women's suffrage gained force in the states and, after a hard-fought battle, became law under the Nineteenth Amendment to the Constitution in 1920.

The wartime gains in industry made by women, African Americans, and labor were quickly reversed when soldiers returned home in 1919. The prewar economy in which blacks were fired to make room for whites—both foreign and native born—was back. Women left nontraditional jobs or were driven out. Labor leaders had possessed no small amount of faith in the unions' ability to maintain and even expand their membership base and the apparatus set up during the war to resolve labor disputes, but business leaders had viewed labor's wartime role as purely temporary. Unionists responded to attempted rollbacks with large-scale protests in 1919: a general strike in Seattle, strikes of 50,000 male clothing workers in New York, 120,000 textile workers in New England

and New Jersey, 400,000 soft coal miners, and 300,000 steelworkers. White workers also expressed their anxieties over labor competition and race in the riots that swept the nation during the summer of 1919. In Washington, D.C., Chicago, Omaha, rural Arkansas, and other towns and cities, white mobs attacked black neighborhoods, but in contrast to past riots, blacks in Chicago fought back.

In combating strikes, employers built upon the antiradical politics that had developed during the war. Steel companies painted its mainly immigrant striking workforce as revolutionary, exploiting divisions between foreign-born and native-born. Fearful of the spread of radicalism in Germany, Russia, and Hungary, state militias, city police, and the federal courts backed business leaders' equation of radicalism with labor activism. The "Red Scare" primarily targeted the foreign-born, Communists, and Anarchists, but it also shaped the public's view of labor and legitimated federal or state intervention in strikes. The confidence and optimism of wartime labor quickly turned to disillusionment. Not until the 1930s would American labor movements experience rebirth and renewal.

CONCLUSION

John R. Commons was a Progressive-Era historian and reformer whose multivolume *History of Labour in the United States* (1946) contested the reigning assumption of Gilded Age economists that labor's collective action jeopardized the free market and thus liberty itself. Commons saw trade unions as central to the cause of industrial peace and democracy. He viewed the AFL's narrow, exclusive strategy and focus on economic gains as not only practical but desirable, as a reflection of Americans' acceptance of the basic values of industrial capitalism.

In his historical work, Commons took an institutional approach that limited the study of labor history to trade unions and collective bargaining. Since the 1960s, however, historians have uncovered a far richer story involving a clash between the values of industrialism and those of large segments of the working population. During the Gilded Age, this clash spawned labor movements that shared a republican vision of industrial relations. The differences in their approaches to this vision became more pronounced and significant in the 1880s and 1890s as the courts and employers gradually imposed an expanded definition of property that effectively outlawed many of the weapons that were key to a broad-based, reformist labor movement, namely, strikes and mutual aid

aimed at changing the terms and nature of work. On this constricted ground, the Knights declined, and the AFL abandoned radicalism and moved to an exclusive, accommodative strategy for winning a respected place within the capitalist order.

The AFL met with considerable success in improving material standards for many of its members during the Progressive and World War I eras. The majority of working Americans did not enjoy these gains, however, and the inclusive, radical visions of Gilded Age labor movements found new life. Among craft workers confronting mechanization and open shop campaigns, and among immigrant workers in the garment industry especially, deteriorating conditions pushed many to engage in massive strikes that fundamentally altered government's role in industrial disputes but did little to effect immediate and tangible change in the working lives of most Americans. The courts undermined much of the labor legislation passed during the Gilded Age and the much-celebrated Age of Reform, the Progressive Era. Although labor experienced resurgence during World War I, its achievements were largely temporary. Antiradicalism, labor competition, and racial warfare left U.S, labor movements in disarray after the war. Although women and African Americans exhibited new resolve concerning civil and political rights after the war, the hope of many working-class Americans, whatever their skill, background, or philosophy, that they might gain a voice in the workplace would not again be revived until the 1930s.

Theresa Ann Case

BIBLIOGRAPHY

American Social History Productions. *Who Built America: Working People and the Nation's Economy, Politics, Culture, and Society.* New York: Pantheon Books, 1992.

Case, Theresa A. "Free Labor on the Southwestern Railways: The 1885–1886 Gould System Strikes." Ph.D. diss., University of Texas at Austin, 2002.

Commons, John R. *History of Labour in the United States.* New York: Macmillan, 1946.

Dubofsky, Melvin. *Industrialism and the American Worker, 1865–1920.* 2d ed. Arlington Heights, IL: Harlan Davidson, 1985.

Fink, Leon. *Workingmen's Democracy: The Knights of Labor and American Politics.* Urbana: University of Illinois Press, 1983.

Foner, Eric. *Reconstruction: America's First Unfinished Revolution, 1863–1877.* New York: Harper & Row, 1988.

Foner, Philip S. *The Great Labor Uprising of 1877.* New York: Monad, 1977.

Forbath, William. *Law and the Shaping of the American Labor Movement*. Cambridge, MA: Harvard University Press, 1991.

Gutman, Herbert G. *Work, Culture, and Society in Industrializing America*. New York: Vintage Books, 1977.

Hunter, Tera W. " 'Work That Body': African-American Women, Work, and Leisure in Atlanta and the New South." In *Labor Histories: Class, Politics, and the Working-Class Experience*, ed. Eric Arnesen, Julie Greene, and Bruce Laurie. Urbana: University of Illinois Press, 1998.

Jones, Jacqueline. *American Work: Four Centuries of Black and White Labor*. New York: W.W. Norton, 1998.

Kenny, Kevin. *The American Irish: A History*. Essex, UK: Pearson Education Limited, 2000.

Leach, Eugene E. "Chaining the Tiger: The Mob Stigma and the Working Class, 1863–1984." *Labor History* 35 (Spring 1994): 187–215.

Letwin, Daniel. *The Challenge of Interracial Unionism: Alabama Coal Miners, 1878–1921*. Chapel Hill: University of North Carolina Press, 1998.

Milkman, Ruth, ed. *Women, Work, and Protest: A Century of US Women's Labor History*. Boston: Routledge & Kegan Paul, 1985.

Montgomery, David. *The Fall of the House of Labor: The Workplace, The State, and American Labor Activism, 1865–1925*. New York: Cambridge University Press, 1987.

Painter, Nell Irvin. *Standing at Armageddon: The United States, 1877–1919*. New York: W.W. Norton, 1987.

Peck, Gunther. *Reinventing Free Labor: Padrones and Immigrant Workers in the North American West, 1880–1930*. Cambridge, MA: Cambridge University Press, 2000.

Schneirov, Richard, Shelton Stromquist, and Nick Salvatore, eds. *The Pullman Strike and the Crisis of the 1890s: Essays on Labor and Politics*. Urbana: University of Illinois Press, 1999.

Stromquist, Shelton. *Generation of Boomers: The Pattern of Railroad Labor Conflict in Nineteenth-Century America*. Urbana: University of Illinois Press, 1987.

Wiebe, Robert H. *The Search for Order, 1877–1920*. New York: Hill & Wang, 1967.

Woloch, Nancy. *Women and the American Experience*, Concise Edition. New York: McGraw-Hill, 2002.

EIGHT-HOUR DAY MOVEMENT

The American labor movement has fought a long struggle to establish eight hours as a standard workday. As industrialization overtook the nation and skilled crafts became unskilled due to the increased use of machinery, the amount of time workers spent on the job went as high as fourteen hours a day for little pay. The fight to establish eight hours as the standard workday would go through legislatures, courts, the streets, and cost much in time and lives.

With the growth of industrialism in America also came a dramatic change of life. From what was once an economic system based on agriculture was rapidly overcome by early machinery and its forms of power sources. From textiles to shoemaking and beyond, the ability to produce more goods at a faster and cheaper cost spread rapidly. Those who once were skilled in cherished valued crafts, like shoemaking and carpentry, rapidly saw their art reduced to simply pulling a lever or cutting a predetermined pattern. Although competition within the marketplace was always present, increased industrialization meant producing even more goods at an accelerated pace. With competition between producers growing even fiercer, new ways would have to be found to minimize cost and maximize profit. The first place to cut expenses was the workforce. Having employees work longer hours at even lower pay rates would help achieve the goal of producing more goods faster and cheaper.

The comparable growth in international trade especially influenced this increased competition. As Western countries began to open up markets, whether by negotiation or force, in places such as Asia and Africa, a scramble to establish economic superiority emerged and expanded. Furthermore, these areas also provided a rich supply of natural resources that was needed by these growing industries.

Long before industrialism took the country completely by storm, there was concern over how hard to work employees. Even the earliest American guilds and unions argued for shorter working hours, first pressing for ten hours as the standard day. But the increased use of machines, the opening of international trade routes, and finding new ways to exploit natural resources would take precedence over the number of hours someone would have to stand behind a machine.

With the Civil War came a need for increased production. When the war ended, and industry resumed on a peacetime basis, the labor movement, in comparison to industrialism, also grew at an accelerated rate. Workers began to organize more into trade unions, and one of their chief concerns was the number of hours in which employees were required to work. Hours expanded while wages shrank. Increased European immigration did not help at all, for while American workers might refuse a job with low wages and long hours, those from foreign countries, looking for a better life, had nothing to lose. Regardless of workers' feelings, employers set the number of hours, and workers either agreed or did not have a job.

In 1866, the move to establish the eight-hour day gained momentum. This movement stretched across racial, ethnic, and even gender lines. The National Labor Union was organized in Baltimore in 1866. At the forefront was Ira Steward, a machinist from Boston. Steward saw the eight-hour day movement as not just a labor but an economic concern. To Steward, working people at incredibly long hours and paying them low wages were harmful practices for both worker and employer. If people worked a shorter day for better pay, they would have time on their hands and more money in their pockets. Thus, people could purchase and enjoy more, and industry would have a steady market. Although some did not share Steward's idea of consumption, by this time the use of machines was irrefutable, even by those whose crafts were threatened, if not overtaken, by industrialism.

Several states made attempts to establish eight

hours as the legal workday. Illinois, Wisconsin, Missouri, and New York were the forerunners by passing eight-hour laws in 1886. Passing such legislation always met with fierce opposition from employers who wished to maintain a ten-hour day, with no additional pay for overtime. To many employers, the current economic situation reflected the abilities of those who could rise above. Monetary success was proof that one was capable in rising above the crowd. If one did not wish to work the shift, there would be plenty of others right behind willing to take the job.

Those states that did pass eight-hour laws found problems in enforcement. For example, Illinois law did not provide penalties for noncompliance, a point at which employers took note. Despite strikes and demonstrations, no help in enforcement came forth, only animosity toward the movement. Relief did seem to come in 1868 when Congress created an eight-hour day for laborers and mechanics working for the federal government, but this law would not have much influence on the state level.

In 1884, the movement for an eight-hour day truly took flight, although the initial declaration originally went unnoticed. The Federation of Organized Trade and Labor Unions called for the eight-hour day to start as of May 1, 1886. Although this might have been somewhat ignored at first, in 1886 demonstrations did in fact break out in many major cities. Thousands of workers in places such as Pittsburgh, Baltimore, and St. Louis went on strike or demonstrated in an effort to advance this cause.

The eight-hour issue culminated in Chicago in May of 1886. Chicago was considered to be the center of the eight-hour day movement, and with relations between workers and employers already at a feverish pitch, violence became virtually inevitable. Demonstrations at the McCormick Reaper Works in early May ended in violence between striking workers and police, resulting in several deaths. A group of Anarchists, led by August Spies and Albert Parsons, called for a demonstration on May 4 to protest the police brutality. Although Chicago mayor Carter Harrison found the assembly to be peaceful, and having warned the police not to interfere, the police did in fact raid the meeting just after Harrison left. An unknown person threw a dynamite bomb, killing several policemen. Remaining police opened fire on the crowd, killing other members of the crowd. Spies and Parsons were among the four men who would eventually be convicted and executed for the bombing and conspiracy, although there was no evidence linking them to the act.

As the labor movement became more organized in associations such as the Knights of Labor and the American Federation of Labor (AFL), so did the call for eight-hour day legislation, even though many labor leaders such as the AFL's Samuel Gompers did not always believe legislation would help much. Laws could be easily repealed by a future legislature or declared unconstitutional by the courts. Local labor organizations especially led the drive for legislation. But, again, enforcement was difficult. In the states where laws were passed and upheld by the courts, compliance was easily evaded. One reason was a loophole in many of these laws. Employers could contract with their workers for a longer day. Of course, the employee would either comply in the "request" for longer hours or not have a job. Furthermore, state enforcement might fall under any number of departments, or, just be ignored altogether. What also added to the situation was that farmers had little, if any, sympathy for the eight-hour day. Many farmers considered the urban factory workers to be whiners, especially since agricultural production could run as long as sixteen hours a day.

A landmark case involving the limitation of work hours came in 1908 with the U.S. Supreme Court case of *Muller v. Oregon*. In 1903, the state of Oregon passed a law limiting the number of hours females could work to ten. The law was, of course, challenged. The case reached the Supreme Court, which upheld the act. Arguing in favor of the law was the future Supreme Court justice Louis Brandeis, who did not rely upon legal precedent but instead presented a variety of arguments based on sociological, medical, and historical evidence. Opponents to the law argued that the act violated the freedom of contract as protected by both the Constitution and the Fourteenth Amendment. The Supreme Court, however, saw that the law protected the health and well-being of women.

Regardless of any shortcomings, the eight-hour day movement continued to gain momentum in the early twentieth century. At the AFL convention in 1913, there was a push to institute the eight-hour day along with stringent enforcement provisions. One issue surrounding this drive was who should be included, such as specific trades, women, and minority groups. Many argued that any laws should cover all workers, regardless of trade, race, or gender. The AFL would often back away from the eight-hour issue, and the issues of enforcement and inclusion would continue to divide the labor movement for years.

The federal government passed eight-hour laws on an irregular basis. During the presidential admin-

EIGHT HOURS
MUSIC BY JESSE HENRY JONES

ca. 1866

"Eight Hours," written sometime around 1866, was a popular song among trade unionists and labor activists in the nineteenth-century struggle to improve working conditions in the workplace through reducing the workday.

We mean to make things over, we are tired of toil for naught,
With but bare enough to live upon, and never an hour for thought;
We want to feel the sunshine, and we want to smell the flowers,
We are sure that God has will'd it, and we mean to have eight hours.
We're summoning our forces from the shipyard, shop, and mill:
Eight hours for work, eight hours for rest, eight hours for what we will!
Eight hours for work, eight hours for rest, eight hours for what we will!

The beasts that graze the hillside, and the birds that wander free,
In the life that God has meted have a better lot than we.
Oh! hands and hearts are weary, and homes are heavy with dole;
If our life's to be filled with drudgery, what need of a human soul!
Shout, shout the lusty rally from shipyard, shop, and mill:
Eight hours for work, eight hours for rest, eight hours for what we will!
Eight hours for work, eight hours for rest, eight hours for what we will!

The voice of God within us is calling us to stand
Erect, as is becoming to the work of his right hand.
Should he, to whom the maker his glorious image gave,
The meanest of his creatures crouch, a bread and butter slave?
Let the shout ring down the valleys and echo from ev'ry hill:

Eight hours for work, eight hours for rest, eight hours for what we will!
Eight hours for work, eight hours for rest, eight hours for what we will!

Ye deem they're feeble voices that are raised in labor's cause?
But bethink ye of the torrent, and the wild tornado's laws!
We say not toil's uprising in terror's shape will come,
Yet the world were wise to listen to the monitory hum,
Soon, soon the deep-toned rally shall all the nations thrill:
Eight hours for work, eight hours for rest, eight hours for what we will!
Eight hours for work, eight hours for rest, eight hours for what we will!

From factories and workshops, in long and weary lines,
From all the sweltering forges, and from out the sunless mines,
Wherever toil is wasting the force of life to live,
There the bent and battered armies come to claim what God doth give,
And the blazon on their banner doth with hope the nations fill:
Eight hours for work, eight hours for rest, eight hours for what we will!
Eight hours for work, eight hours for rest, eight hours for what we will!

Hurrah, hurrah for labor! for it shall arise in might;
It has filled the world with plenty, it shall fill the world with light;
Hurrah, hurrah for labor! it is mustering all its powers,
And shall march along to victory with the banner of Eight Hours!
Shout, shout the echoing rally till all the welkin thrill:
Eight hours for work, eight hours for rest, eight hours for what we will!
Eight hours for work, eight hours for rest, eight hours for what we will!

Source: Philip S. Foner, *American Labor Songs of the Nineteenth Century* (Urbana: University of Illinois Press, 1975).

istration of Woodrow Wilson, Congress passed an eight-hour law for railroad workers, which was met with fierce opposition by railroad employers. The law was set to take effect on January 1, 1917. With America's growing involvement in World War I, a compromise was needed and was ultimately reached.

Upon the conclusion of World War I, strikes for the eight-hour day swept through many segments of the labor movement, beginning with textiles and moving on from there. However, with the Great Depression and subsequent New Deal, the eight-hour day took a back seat to more pressing matters at first. Franklin D. Roosevelt's New Deal was more inter-

ested in jump-starting the economy and putting people back to work than worrying about hours. Although people were certainly interested in not having to work incredibly long hours, having a job at all was more important. Then, in 1936, came the Walsh-Healey Public Contracts Act. This law concerned government contractors, with one of the provisions limiting the number of work hours a day to eight, with time-and-a-half pay for overtime worked within a twenty-four-hour period.

Later in the New Deal came the Fair Labor Standards Act (FLSA) of 1938. Although this Act included exemptions for people engaged in fields such as agriculture and domestic service, businesses involved in or affecting interstate commerce were required to have a forty-hour work week. Other provisions were made regarding wages and overtime pay.

The eight-hour workday is still considered to be ideal. Although there might be legislation, local or national, establishing the number of hours in which one might work, contracting the number of hours in a work week is still between the employer and employee. Many companies today utilize "flex time," whereby employees can select their daily starting and finishing times, as long as they work the minimum required weekly hours. In many positions overtime is not paid but is merely considered to be part of the job. For those working under union contracts, the standard work week is laid out, along with provisions for overtime compensation. Although the eight-hour day, with forty hours per week, is thought to be the standard, the actual work week varies from profession to profession. Some companies do not even require forty hours, with work weeks from thirty-five to thirty-seven and a half hours.

The fight for the eight-hour day was long and hard-fought. Many people died for the cause, and the issue even divided the labor movement at times. Regardless, the drive to establish eight hours as a standard workday would leave long-lasting marks on those who must work for a living.

Mitchell Newton-Matza

BIBLIOGRAPHY

Brecher, Jeremy. *Strike!* Boston: South End, 1972.

Foner, Philip S. *History of the Labor Movement in the United States.* Vol. 3, *The Policies and Practices of the American Federation of Labor, 1900–1909.* New York: International, 1964.

Foner, Philip S., and David R. Roediger. *Our Own Time: A History of American Labor and the Working Day.* Westport, CT: Greenwood Press, 1989.

Friedman, Lawrence. *A History of American Law.* New York: Simon and Schuster, 1985.

Lichtenstein, Nelson, ed. *Who Built America?* Vols. 1 and 2. New York: Worth, 2000.

Mandel, Bernard. *Samuel Gompers.* Yellow Springs, OH: Antioch Press, 1963.

Rosenzweig, Roy. *Eight Hours for What We Will: Workers and Leisure in an Industrial City, 1870–1920.* New York: Cambridge University Press, 1985.

Tomlins, Christopher. *The State and the Unions.* Cambridge: Cambridge University Press, 1985.

SYNDICALISM AND THE INDUSTRIAL WORKERS OF THE WORLD

Many scholars consider Syndicalism as one of the influential "left" ideologies of the twentieth century, within the increasingly problematic definition of a left-right political spectrum. However, consensus seems to end there, and the history of Syndicalism and its role in the United States has proven to be one of the oldest scholarly battlegrounds, perhaps rightly reflecting the colorful and often violent memories associated with this term. Controversies emerge as soon as the term is used, along with a plethora of meanings and experiences associated with Syndicalism. Is Syndicalism the same thing as "revolutionary syndicalism," or perhaps "anarcho-syndicalism"? Are they significantly different versions of the same basic concepts, diverging in their paths through time? Or is it the same idea everywhere, but with different experiences? Is the United States "exceptional"? The list of questions can certainly get exhaustive.

Perhaps a good place to start would be to describe what Syndicalism *is not*. A common thread observable through all Syndicalist movements has been their sometimes incoherent efforts to distinguish themselves from Socialist (and later Communist) movements. Drawing exact lines between movements and people associated with labels such as "Syndicalist" or "Socialist" is often not a very meaningful task, for there is significant overlap and confusion in ideas and actions. However, distinctions and differences exist, and Syndicalist movements' insistence on rejecting most legal-political forms of action and deep skepticism of Socialist parliamentary tactics can be considered as major division lines among "left" labor movements. By far the most spectacular and observable Syndicalist tactics to achieve social change as well as short-term gains include direct action, sabotage, and the general strike. Political participation and change through the formal political system are considered a waste of effort; the real power to change society goes through direct action, where workplace problems are solved without intermediaries, augmented by carefully aimed acts of industrial sabotage, all leading to the ultimate Syndicalist weapon, the general strike. The general strike, conceived as the point where workers' control and initiative of production is depicted and ultimately realized, brings about the end of capitalism by paralyzing its vital productive and commercial elements, while at the same time opening the way for a new society based on the control of all production through *syndicats*, or (in a historically specific context) "industrial unions."

Historically, Syndicalism can be traced back to nineteenth-century "left" political and workers' movements defining themselves as Socialist or Anarchist. Late-nineteenth-century continental Europe, especially France, is considered to have witnessed the creation of what would be called "anarcho-syndicalism," "Syndicalism," or an early version of "industrial unionism" around the world. Various elements of Socialist labor organization, such as the perception of the working class as the key agent of social change, as well as elements of Anarchism, observable in the lack of trust toward centralization and state authority, form the ideological foundation on which Syndicalism stands. The French experience is usually associated with the *Confédération Générale du Travail* (CGT), with an ongoing debate concerning its exact influence on the American experience. Syndicalism seems to be alive in the twenty-first century, with all the characteristic, eclectic togetherness of ideologies and images. One can see the black cat of sabotage on the walls, along with environmentalist slogans, black-and-red flags, and pro-labor pamphlets in the so-called antiglobalization" rallies. Tracing the story of Syndicalism in the United States requires an almost exclusive attention to the Industrial Workers of the World (IWW), whose fate and influence very closely reflect the fortunes of the ideology and movement in its context.

THE INDUSTRIAL WORKERS OF THE WORLD

The Industrial Workers of the World (IWW) was founded at a 1905 convention in Chicago after a series of conferences and was immediately welcomed by the first speaker, "Big Bill" Haywood, as "the Continental Congress of the working class." It appears that the phrasing was somewhat exaggerated, for although the convention had brought together numerous unions and political organizations, the number of workers represented with voting rights was a mere 50,000 (overall, indirect representation was around 140,000)—a very small portion of organized labor at the time and a fraction of all workers in the United States. Although numbers would never prove to be a significant strength of the IWW through its history, its historical influence, either as exercised by the IWW as an active organization or as a myth, had little to do with numerical strength.

If the first convention in Chicago did not represent a numerical strength, it certainly succeeded in assembling an impressive variety of groups and ideas. From the populous Western Federation of Miners (WFM) represented by the influential Haywood to a variety of small American Federation of Labor (AFL) locals, the IWW represented a chaotic and eclectic amalgam of purposes, ideologies, and characters. Branding the organization at its creation as Syndicalist or Socialist would be an unsupported speculation, because what would later become the Syndicalist elements coexisted with Daniel De Leon's doctrinaire Socialist Labor Party (SLP; it was represented through the party's union wing, the Socialist Trade and Labor Alliance), Eugene V. Debs's Socialist Party of America

Founded in 1905, the Industrial Workers of the World sought to organize unskilled, factory, and migrant workers—groups often ignored by other unions. *(Brown Brothers)*

WILLIAM D. "Big Bill" HAYWOOD (1869–1928)

Born in Salt Lake City, Utah, on February 9, 1869, William Dudley Haywood began work as a miner at a young age to help support his family. In 1896, he joined the newly organized Western Federation of Miners (WFM), and in 1900 he became a member of the executive board and national secretary-treasurer of the organization. He traveled throughout the West as a union organizer. Because of increasing conflicts between miners and mine owners, Haywood often traveled secretly through embattled mining camps to avoid arrest. Haywood and the Western Federation of Miners campaigned for eight-hour working days for underground miners. Most mining camps required underground workers to labor ten hours on the job each day, not counting transportation time up and down the mine shafts, and to work thirteen out of fourteen days. Because of the WFM efforts, Utah became the first state in the nation to enact an eight-hour workday for miners.

A militant leader, Haywood was often accused of inciting violence, especially in the Colorado troubles culminating in the Cripple Creek strike of 1904. He was also accused of instigating the assassination of former governor Frank Steunenberg of Idaho in 1905, but was acquitted in a trial in which the high-profile trial attorney Clarence S. Darrow defended him. The trial attracted nationwide attention. Though eventually found not guilty, the ordeal led to fighting between Haywood and Charles Moyer, one of the other leaders of the WFM, about the direction of the organization. Haywood left it in 1908.

In 1905, Haywood helped organize the Industrial Workers of the World (IWW). He joined the Socialist Party and became a member of its national executive board, but because of his advocacy of violence was forced out of the party. He led the famous Lawrence and Paterson textile workers' strikes in 1912 and 1913, respectively. Repudiating the crafts union ideal and the cooperation policy of the American Federation of Labor, he preached the IWW doctrines of class struggle, no compromise, and mass action. He became head of it in 1915 and forged an image of the IWW as a group that would use any means at its disposal to change a system it despised. At its peak, the group had more than three million members.

When the United States entered World War I, Haywood was arrested on a charge of sedition, and was tried, convicted, and sentenced to twenty years' imprisonment. While awaiting a new trial in 1921, he forfeited bail and escaped to the Soviet Union, where he lived for the rest of his life. He became a trusted adviser to the new Bolshevik government. He died on May 18, 1928. Half of his ashes were ceremoniously buried in a wall of honor at the Kremlin, next to the remains of American journalist and Communist sympathizer John Reed. The remainder were quietly returned to the United States and buried in Chicago, near a monument to American workers.

James G. Lewis

(SP), numerous labor organizers who for various reasons had been unable to achieve career ambitions with the AFL, and colorful individuals like "father" Thomas J. Hagerty—the author of the famous preamble to the IWW constitution, the 1905 manifesto, and the creator of an organizational chart of industrial unions, also known as "Father Hagerty's Wheel of Fortune," forming the "One Big Union."

Haywood's opening speech was supported and well received by the audience; his emphases on themes of solidarity, class struggle, and disdain for the "pure and simple" craft unionism of the AFL had reached a crowd very much in agreement with these sentiments. Controversial issues remained in place, however, and would prove to be dangerous fault lines that would endure throughout the history of the IWW.

The WFM, forming the core membership and financial source of the newly created IWW, had brought its experience of bitter struggles and a fiery, independent "Western" streak, as well as the conviction that a peaceful coexistence of employers (or "capitalists") and workers was unattainable. Experiences gained through hard-fought—and lost—strikes and struggles in Colorado had shown the WFM the futility of favorable court decisions when governors would refuse to enforce them. Losing strikes while locals were dismantled only served to enhance the idea that dependence on legal institutions for protection against employers was a recipe for disaster. This line, along with a distrust of political affiliations and the political processes in general, had a lot in common with what would be called American Syndicalism in a few years.

Among the purely political groups, both the SLP and the SP intended to steer the newly formed organization as a branch of the party apparatus. Homogeneity had never been one of the defining elements of socialist movements, however, and this situation was no different. To summarize, certain elements within the SLP as well as the SP advocated a position against the dominant "boring from within" attitude. As a tactic, "boring from within" meant that socialists would organize within existing trade unions, radicalize, or "educate" the workers who had "false consciousness" in these unions, and place them in line with party functions and ideals. The opposing groups saw in the IWW a potential to become a genuine class-conscious organization of industrial unions, making the trade unions and AFL craft unionism obsolescent by its very existence. Most Socialists still had high hopes for converting the AFL, but the IWW was at the center of many arguments nevertheless. What made many Socialists most uncomfortable with the IWW was the strong position of ideas that advocated success primarily at the workshop, not the ballot box.

The IWW and its Opponents

Problems within the IWW were to play a decisive role throughout its history, but the IWW fully expected opposition from a variety of outside sources as well and had no trouble finding it. The AFL, under Samuel Gompers, had grown from its small beginnings when the Knights of Labor dominated the scene briefly in the second half of the nineteenth century, into the largest federation of unions in the United States. Gompers had created an organization that thrived not on conflict but on agreements that brought small, immediate, incremental gains. Gompers's insistence on craft unionism and the significant number of skilled workers organized within the AFL meant that it mostly aimed to represent the interests of the skilled minority while a large majority of the working class in the United States was left out. Although the IWW represented a small number of workers, its radical rhetoric and aims led Gompers to believe that the IWW posed a threat, aiming to replace the AFL, although his agents within the IWW had informed him otherwise after observing the chaos and conflict of interests already evident in the infant organization. Consequently, Gompers told all members not to support IWW strikes and reminded them that strikebreaking was acceptable in such situations. WFM locals were purged from AFL-affiliated organizations, and aid to the WFM was halted.

As the AFL attack continued, suspicious SP members also voiced their opinions about the IWW. Although Debs and other prominent names of the SP endorsed the organization, there was widespread suspicion among Socialists concerning De Leon and the SLP. The IWW seemed to have united the SP and the SLP at least on a small common ground, but suspicion of another split led by De Leon never wavered. The "boring from within" attitude also continued to dominate the SP, and supporters of the tactic became increasingly aggressive as they perceived the IWW as not only a hopeless attempt, but also a weakening influence on their work within the AFL, since it attracted socialists and other radicals.

As the newly created IWW struggled with problems inside and outside, government authorities, backed by negative public sentiment, were about to start a long and torturous period of harassment at all levels. The first event exemplifying this attitude was triggered by the murder of a former governor of Idaho in Caldwell. As soon as the local authorities had a suspect, they started working on establishing connections to prominent figures of the WFM.

The fact that a connection had not been established and that the suspected conspirators were in Colorado did not deter the authorities. After an interstate abduction spree, Haywood, Charles Moyer (president of the WFM), and George A. Pettibone were brought to Idaho and imprisoned. Appeals by union attorneys ended in failure, and although the juries eventually found them to be not guilty, they did spend a critical time in prison. A critical time indeed, since the IWW was experiencing severe crises and the absence of experienced, charismatic leadership at such a time seriously hampered its survival efforts, let alone attempts to grow. During the absence of Haywood and Moyer, the IWW experienced an ossification of existing differences among its groups, as socialists struggled against De Leon's SLP, and the WFM was torn between factions favoring a "revolutionary" IWW and a "respectable" IWW. In the meantime, the first (and only) IWW president, Charles O. Sherman, and secretary-treasurer William E. Trautmann became involved in these factional struggles and were positioned against each other. It certainly appeared that a serious conflict was going to take place at the second convention, and there would be no surprises. The long-term result of the second convention became clearer as the years 1907–1908 would witness the first big schism in the history of the IWW, with major consequences.

DECLINE OF THE IWW AND ITS HISTORICAL LEGACY

Meanwhile, the factional struggles within the WFM gathered momentum, as Vincent St. John and his supporters who favored a revolutionary IWW slowly lost ground. After bitter struggling, efforts to keep the WFM in the IWW failed, and this most populous and resourceful element of the IWW withdrew, leaving what appeared to be a union on the brink of collapse. By the time Haywood and St. John were trying to save the IWW, De Leon's aims and tactics had attracted much suspicion and hostility. Through his attempts to stop SP influence in the IWW, De Leon had succeeded in implementing what was called a "political clause," where a party affiliation was not allowed, but political action was acceptable. However, the alliances he had established with direct action supporters two years before had crumbled, while his image as an intellectual alienated from the workers grew in strength. The year 1908 witnessed the second split, this time during the convention. De Leon and his followers, banished by the IWW, left and established a paper IWW in New Jersey, and then moved to Detroit. The paper IWW never had much influence, and after the death of its founder in 1914, it eventually died out.

By the time the damaging internal struggles in 1908 came to a climax, the IWW had lost a significant portion of its membership and resources with the loss of the WFM (in 1907), alienated remaining SP figures such as Debs, and thrown out De Leon and the SLP affiliates. Even during such a time of troubles, however, the IWW had organized and engaged in conflicts in a wide geographic area. From the textile workers in the East (Paterson, New Jersey, Providence, Rhode Island, Lawrence, Massachusetts, et al.) to Goldfield, Nevada, and timber workers of the Northwest, the IWW worked actively in organizing and striking, even if the strikes were not necessarily successes.

Although the IWW had organized some skilled and permanent workers, it also proved to be the only

Leaders of the Industrial Workers of the World pose in front of a dye factory. Among those featured are William "Big Bill" Haywood (seated, far right) and, beside him, Elizabeth Gurley Flynn. *(Brown Brothers)*

union that actively attempted to organize unskilled immigrants (including Japanese workers, who were excluded by all other unions) and itinerant workers. The internal success of the "Syndicalist faction," combined with what critics labeled as "hobo unionism," created an image of the IWW as an alienated, weak union of anarchists and unemployed workers. Although badly shaken by lack of funds and organizational chaos, the IWW nevertheless survived and possessed the basis of what was to constitute the "Wobbly" myth for decades.

The ideological product of developments in the IWW during this period was a mixture of elements: they borrowed a significant amount from Marx, in terms of the understanding of history as class struggle and "laws" of social change, from Anarchists' and Syndicalists' notions such as direct action, sabotage, and the general strike, and mixed these with already-existing elements such as the spirit of frontier activism and initiative, among others. The result was hardly a coherent body forming a unique ideological framework; but it was certainly not a repetition of other movements and ideas, within or without the United States. A good example of the particular mixture of ideas the IWW created is the antipathy concerning political action. Although Anarchists and many Syndicalists had looked upon political action unfavorably, if not with hostility, the attitude of the IWW was as much a result of such external influences and previous experience of some of its members as it was the result of direct, new experience gained during the bitter battles involving Socialists and the SLP. Although the IWW never let go of its vision of revolution, socially ultimate ends were not necessarily of foremost importance on the agenda in the struggles that it pursued, trying to improve the immediate conditions of the workers it tried to organize.

In the aftermath of the 1907–1908 emigration, the IWW began a period of intensive struggles in both the West and the East. In the West, what would be known as "free speech fights" erupted, with significant results in locations such as Spokane, Washington (1909–1910) and Fresno, California (1910–1911). In Spokane, the IWW organized a number of migratory workers who had to work in primitive, brutal conditions. Their success did not go unnoticed, as the city council soon banned IWW soapboxers from the streets, employing an argument of nationalism and religion. The IWW refused to stop, and in less than a month, the Spokane jail was overfilled with Wobblies who had continued to give speeches. As workers started to leave Spokane for jobs, the IWW orators were released. As soon as

the workers returned, a similar procession of events commenced; IWW orators started making speeches, and they were promptly put in jail. By the time the struggle ended, hundreds of Wobblies would be imprisoned. The conditions in the prisons were not only primitive, but also designed to weaken and break the spirits of the prisoners. Climatic extremes, lack of sanitary measures, and brutality in general left a majority of prisoners with permanent health problems.

As the fight became ever more costly for the authorities in Spokane, they wavered. The jails were full, but the IWW was still there, in numbers. The numerous tales of brutality and injustice against the IWW influenced even public opinion, resulting in more pressure on city authorities. Finally, in 1910, nonviolent resistance and determination prevailed, and the IWW achieved its goals. They could publish the *Industrial Worker* and freely organize indoor or outdoor meetings. Similar "free speech fights" with similar results took place in a variety of Western cities for a few more years, with exceptions such as San Diego, California, where success proved to be elusive in the face of determined opposition by local authorities and lack of intervention by higher authorities.

The IWW had gained a number of skilled organizers and a larger number of determined followers by the end of the "free speech fights," and it would need them all in the immediate future. Joseph Ettor, one of the highly skilled and experienced organizers of the IWW, arrived in Lawrence, Massachusetts, in early 1912, invited by a local Italian IWW.

Low wages and long hours in the textile mills of Lawrence had culminated in widespread anger and dissatisfaction among the workers who were mostly immigrants. However, not all ethnicities supported the idea of a strike; from the start, the most enthusiastic support for a strike came from the less well-established groups, mostly from Southern and Eastern Europe. Haywood also marked his return to active organizing when he showed up in Lawrence and was warmly greeted by a great number of workers. Accompanying Ettor was Arturo Giovannitti, soon to become a well-known character in the history of the IWW. Strike committees and relief committees were immediately formed with the combined work of the local strikers and national IWW organizers. Limited demands were drawn up, and they were put forth again and again in regular parades, picket lines, and music. In a short time, the number of workers who stopped work grew so that the mills were crippled and the strike was well under way.

Although the IWW in Lawrence never supported

violence, perhaps inevitably, clashes among militia, the police, and the strikers occurred. By the time strikebreakers were introduced, the atmosphere was already full of tension. When a police officer was stabbed and a striker was shot and killed, a group of people including, unsurprisingly, Ettor and Giovannitti were identified as the conspirators by the police. As the leaders of the strike were put in jail, however, reinforcements from the IWW had come; Elizabeth Gurley Flynn (the "rebel girl") and William E. Trautmann had joined Haywood to replace them. The IWW proved to be extremely resourceful in organizing the strike, creating committees to alleviate the problems strikers faced, and even imported the tactic of sending strikers' children outside the strike zone so they could be taken care of by willing families. Every act contributed to greater publicity, and the local businesses and authorities contributed to the publicity by acts of brutality and stubbornness. In about two months, the mill owners capitulated, accepting the demands of the strike committee. Haywood and other Wobblies were ecstatic over the victory; things appeared to be changing for the IWW indeed. Ettor and Giovannitti were acquitted a few months following the strike.

Through the success of the Lawrence strike, the IWW had succeeded in signing up new members and had gained a lot of publicity. The successes did not follow, however, even in Lawrence, as mill owners (the American Woolen Company) playing one ethnicity against the other and using spies to infiltrate the union and the media influenced public opinion negatively toward the IWW. The following year would put all the strength and morale of the organization to the test, at Paterson, New Jersey.

Similar in some ways to Lawrence, Paterson was also an old industrial town, and labor was similarly divided into ethnic groups. The IWW did not really "lead" the strike here but served as organizing and advisory assistance. In addition to figures like Flynn and Haywood, Carlo Tresca, an anarchist with close ties to syndicalism—and to Flynn—made an appearance. Although similar tactics to those used in Lawrence were employed, Paterson proved to be a different testing ground. When material support for the strikers wavered and new drives for funding (John Reed's famous Pageant of the strike included) were unsuccessful, cracks along ethnic and ideological lines appeared fast. Things fell apart quickly, and the strike ended in defeat, with Socialists, the AFL, and the media all critiquing the IWW.

ELIZABETH GURLEY FLYNN
(1890–1964)

Born on August 7, 1890, in Concord, New Hampshire, Elizabeth Gurley Flynn was the daughter of working-class Socialists. She showed an early talent for public speaking on social issues. Thrown out of school in 1907 for her political activities, she became an organizer for the Industrial Workers of the World (IWW). She took part in the IWW's "free speech" campaigns in western mining towns and was arrested dozens of times; she also helped organize strikes or raise relief and legal defense funds. In 1918, she helped establish the Workers' Liberty Defense Union, which was founded to protect immigrants from being deported and to give them financial and legal help. She served as secretary of the Workers' Liberty Defense Union until 1922. She also worked for women's suffrage, peace, birth control, and other progressive causes, and was one of the founders of the American Civil Liberties Union in 1920.

In the 1920s, Flynn was a key fundraiser in the Nicola Sacco and Bartolomeo Vanzetti case. After that case ended in 1927, a heart ailment forced her out of action for several years. In 1936, she joined the Communist Party and became one of its outspoken leaders in the United States. Three years later she was removed from the national committee of the American Civil Liberties Union for her Communist Party membership. She was arrested along with twelve other Communist leaders in 1951, at the height of the McCarthy period, and was incarcerated in January 1951. She published *I Speak My Own Piece: Autobiography of "The Rebel Girl"* in 1955.

Flynn served as chair of the Communist Party of America from 1961 to 1964, the first woman to hold that post. In a suit that went to the U.S. Supreme Court, *Aptheker v. Secretary of State* (1964), she and Herbert Aptheker, the editor of the Party's journal *Political Affairs*, challenged the constitutionality of a provision of the Subversive Activities Control Act of 1950 that denied the issuance of passports to Communists. When they won the suit in 1964, she promptly secured a passport in order to visit the Soviet Union. She died in Moscow on September 5, 1964, and was given a state funeral in Red Square.

James G. Lewis

LEGACY OF THE IWW

If the IWW won limited gains and lost most of the time in actual industrial warfare, it certainly did not lack in mythology and influential discourse. IWW songs, slogans, caricatures, and language would prove to be enduring aspects of the IWW legacy. Martyrs also added to the charisma and culture of the Wobbly phenomenon. Joe Hill, a "Wobbly bard," was tried and sentenced to death for a murder charge in 1914; the resulting effort to defend him had international dimensions, but the uproar did not help him. In 1915, he was executed in Utah and after an elaborate funeral, buried near the Haymarket martyrs. Two years later, Frank Little, a well-known IWW organizer, would be added to the martyr mythology after being lynched by a Butte, Montana, vigilante mob for his "unpatriotic" antiwar speeches and agitation.

On the organizing front, the IWW experienced significant successes through most of World War I (when it was particularly under attack after 1917 for being "subversive and unpatriotic," with allegations that it received "Kaiser's gold"), especially during 1916 when it successfully organized the agricultural migratory workers of the Midwest under the Agricultural Workers Organization (AWO). Several short-lived successes followed in the Mesabi range (Minnesota) mining region, but once again, the IWW was unable to build a lasting organization after the gains it had helped achieve. Meanwhile, the IWW had returned to organize the lumber workers of the Northwest, and trouble was not far behind.

Trying to support the soapboxers who were jailed and then taken out in the middle of a forest and made to run back naked as they were beaten by the vigilantes (dubbed the "Everett Massacre"), the IWW planned to invade Everett, Washington, with hundreds of workers from Seattle. As the boats from Seattle arrived at Everett's docks, they were met by a group of vigilantes, led by local authorities. It is still not clear who fired the first shot, but the scene immediately degenerated into a bloody confrontation, and by the time the boats left the docks, several people on both sides were dead, with many wounded. The massacre increased publicity and sympathy for the IWW, however, and the brutality it did not fear to face made an impression on many workers.

The 1916 convention of the IWW came at a time when, for the first time in its history, the organization had some funds thanks to the successes of the AWO, lots of publicity, and morale boosting from recent events; Haywood tried to transform the IWW from an organization of agitators and soapboxers into one of more permanent labor organizers. The entry of the United States into World War I in 1917, however, along with the renewed hostility the IWW was about to face, changed the course of events in a way Haywood probably never wanted to witness. The immediate result of the United States' entry into the war was an increase in demand for labor, which seemed to be an opportunity for IWW organizers. They also recognized the danger in producing antiwar propaganda without addressing the patriotism of the workers. The turn toward patriotism by the working classes of Europe when the war started stood as a dark example before the IWW. One of the poems produced at the time reflects the IWW's position rather brightly:

> I love my flag, I do, I do,
> Which floats upon the breeze,
> I also love my arms and legs,
> And neck, and nose, and knees.
> One little shell might spoil them all
> Or give them such a twist,
> They would be of no use to me;
> I guess I won't enlist.

The indirect approach to the issue of conscription, however, proved to be insufficient to protect the IWW from aggression. Employers, realizing the opportunity to use the rhetoric of patriotism and treason, responded to the recent gains of the IWW with public opinion at their back. The industries IWW had organized most successfully—agriculture, lumber, mining, and transport—were also among the most critical for the ongoing U.S. war effort, a situation that certainly did not help the IWW in strikes. Opposed by the government at all levels, as well as the judicial system, employers, and vigilante mobs, the Wobblies faced perhaps the greatest crisis of survival in their history, which ultimately ended in disaster. Authorized or supported by every possible agency and authority, federal agents conducted massive raids at all locations where the IWW was organized. They took away documents, publishing material, office supplies, and publications, apparently in order to prove the IWW had indeed accepted German gold and that it was involved in treason. The actual aim was more general, however: the destruction of the IWW. A massive wave of arrests followed soon after, with all the leadership and many members placed under arrest, facing a variety of charges. During 1918–1919, as the massive IWW trials continued, the aftershocks of the Revolution in Russia were being felt. The hysteria that would aid the infamous "Red Scare" (or "Palmer Raids") of 1919–1921 was in the making. The trials, where the IWW still had some hope since it had won courtroom battles before, have been defined by many scholars as a circus, and the leadership was found guilty on all charges.

By 1919, the IWW was certainly in disarray, though not yet destroyed. A series of decisions taken at the 1919 convention of the IWW, however, resulted in the exclusion of all experienced leadership in the organization. At a time when massive waves of arrests followed by speedy trials (or no trials) and prompt deportations or imprisonment was about to begin, getting rid of the seasoned leadership did not help. The first instances of the Palmer Raids also coincided with an armed conflict and lynching where the IWW was involved, this time in Centralia, Washington. What followed, with the arrests, deportations, and laws in supporting these acts (the Criminal Syndicalism Law), was the dismantling of not only the IWW, but also most radical organizations housing immigrants in the United States.

The flight to Russia of Haywood, who had symbolized the IWW for such a long time, was a particularly traumatic event, and it probably signifies the end of the IWW's truly influential and significant years. He died in 1928 in Moscow, a lonely and disillusioned man. Some of his ashes were buried under the Kremlin wall, and the rest were placed in Chicago, near the burial place of the Haymarket Anarchists.

As the issue of Communism took a greater part of the debates within the dissolving IWW, the lack of experienced leadership, internal factional divisions, and chronic lack of funds pushed the organization into complete collapse by 1924. Unlike the 1906–1908 splits, however, there was no new energy, and the context had changed. Communism was going to be the central paradigm and topic of debate in the "left" for decades to come, and the battered remnants of the IWW could not hope to challenge a triumphant alliance of employers, courts, and governments as it had done so many times before.

Although the IWW did not cease to exist, after 1924 it was a mere shadow of what it had been, and as an organization it never regained the strength and momentum it had during the first two decades of the twentieth century. However, the influence the Wob-

blies exerted on labor and the "left" in general is certainly disproportionate to their organizational successes. Many Wobblies joined the Congress of Industrial Organizations in the 1930s, which successfully championed the cause of industrial unionism (although not really associated with Syndicalism anymore), used direct action tactics, and drew on the movement culture and mythology of the IWW. The influence was not limited to the United States either: the IWW existed in a large variety of contexts and geographical space, ranging from Australia to Norway, from South America to Canada. The lasting legacy of the Wobblies has been observed more in their songs, culture, language, and relentless determination and courage against impossible odds, and not the details of internal, organizational, or structural struggles. Characters such as Haywood, St. John, Ralph Chaplin, Joe Hill, Flynn, Ettor, and many others occupy a quasi-mythological space with the struggles, slogans, pamphlets, and caricatures of the IWW. The risk of romanticizing or underemphasizing the IWW has always existed, and the scholarship is full of examples of both, as well as examples of greater ambition, scope, and controlled historical perspective. The existing mythology might be the greatest injustice to the significance of the IWW today. One thing is certain: the legacy of the IWW, with all its different perceptions, interpretations, and analyses, is still very much with us.

Alex B. Corlu

BIBLIOGRAPHY

Dubofsky, Melvyn. *"Big Bill" Haywood.* New York: St. Martin's Press, 1987.

———. *We Shall Be All: A History of the Industrial Workers of the World,* ed. J.A. McCartin. Rev. ed. Urbana: University of Illinois Press, 2000.

Kornbluh, Joyce L. *Rebel Voices: An IWW Anthology.* Ann Arbor: University of Michigan Press, 1964.

Miles, Dione. *Something in Common: An IWW Bibliography.* Detroit: Wayne State University Press, 1986.

Renshaw, Patrick. *The Wobblies: The Story of Syndicalism in the United States.* Garden City, NY: Doubleday, 1967.

Salerno, Salvatore. *Red November/Black November: Culture and Community in the IWW.* Albany: State University of New York Press, 1989.

Thompson, Fred, and Patrick Murfin. *The I.W.W.: Its First 70 Years.* Chicago: IWW, 1976.

RAILROAD WORKERS MOVEMENT

Railroad unions in the United States generally are not regarded as social movements, nor typically are they considered "movement" unions. Indeed, the railroad industry's almost bewildering number of unions—organized primarily along craft lines—have earned reputations as looking primarily after their own "bread-and-butter" interests. Yet, while craft unionism ultimately triumphed, the railroad industry also gave rise to some of the most celebrated industrially organized unions possessing genuine visions of larger social change. The diverse, or bipolar, nature of railroad unionism resulted from the railroads' complex occupational and racial hierarchy as well as the industry's close relationship with the national state.

Over the nineteenth and twentieth centuries, as historian Gerald Friedman has written of the broader labor movement, railroad unions organized and evolved to take advantage of economic and political opportunities, becoming more radical when the railroad corporations and the state were friendly and retreating into conservative postures under employer counterattack and hostile governmental policies. Although these "cycles of contention" help explain the rise of the "Big Four" brotherhoods of engineers, conductors, firemen, and brakemen, as well as the rest of the "standard" railway unions representing shopcraft, clerical, and maintenance-of-way workers, railwaymen nevertheless persisted in the idea of a broad organization encompassing the various railroad trades. However, craft jealousies, racial attitudes, job segmentation, and employer and state hostility prevented the emergence of "one big union."

Still, railroad unions were involved in some of the most dramatic and important instances of labor conflict, and their persistence contributed to the development of some of the most important industrial relations and social welfare legislation in U.S. history. Moreover, those railroaders who faced the greatest struggle—African Americans—played an important role in the modern civil rights movement.

The earliest known railroad union developed among skilled workers in the running trades (or "operating crafts") following the first major wave of nineteenth-century railroad construction and consolidation in the 1850s. The Brotherhood of Locomotive Engineers (BLE), founded in 1863, had its origins in a union of engineers that existed briefly in the mid-1850s. Vigorously led by William D. Robinson, who had served as secretary of the earlier union, the BLE distinguished itself by its aggressive defense of wages on a national level, conducting a series of strikes in 1864. However, the force of the railroad corporations' response precipitated a debate within the BLE, resulting in the ousting of Robinson and his replacement by the careful Charles Wilson as Grand Chief Engineer later that year. With Wilson, the BLE backed away from direct confrontation with capital, choosing instead to emphasize benevolent work. In the process, it took on the conservative character that it and the brotherhoods of conductors, firemen, and brakemen would be known for.

The Order of Railway Conductors (ORC), the Brotherhood of Locomotive Firemen (BLF), and the Brotherhood of Railroad Brakemen (later renamed Brotherhood of Railroad Trainmen, BRT) followed the Locomotive Engineers' example, organizing themselves in 1868, 1873, and 1883, respectively. Together, these unions became known as the Big Four railroad brotherhoods. Sometimes the Switchmen's Mutual Aid Association (SMAA), which came into being in the late 1870s and was succeeded by the Switchmen's Union of North America (SUNA) after 1900, is included in this group.

The distinctive features of the Big Four railroad brotherhoods were their craft conservatism and fraternal character. Drawing upon Masonic fraternalism, early brotherhood leaders emphasized the principles of mutual aid, ranging from the visiting of sick or injured members to the provision of death and disability insurance, and moral uplift, ranging from technical instruction to the inculcation of sober and industrious habits through speeches and prescriptive literature. The efforts at mutual aid met a very real material need among men who labored in a hazardous industry, while the attention to moral uplift emphasized the individual self-improvement and upward mobility of laboring men. Brotherhood leaders believed that the magic and drama of fraternal ritual, the promise of moral uplift, and the tangible benefits of fraternal insurance would make them attractive to skilled railwaymen. At the same time, they hoped the mainstream legitimacy of fraternalism, together with their own benefit work, moral uplift practice, stated reluctance to strike, and scrupulous observance of contracts, would make them acceptable to railway managers as trustworthy representatives of skilled railway labor. And, indeed, during the 1880s, the brotherhoods experienced something of a golden age as railroad expansion and a tight labor market enabled them to negotiate favorable agreements on a number of roads. Together with their craft orientation, this success encouraged the brotherhoods to chart a separate course from that of the larger labor movement, refusing protective alliances with other segments of organized railroad labor and declining affiliation with the American Federation of Labor (AFL).

The railroad brotherhoods were not the only unions to organize railwaymen in the United States, a fact demonstrated by the rise and fall of a number of more broadly based unions from the mid-1870s through the mid-1890s. During the depression and labor conflict of the 1870s, a number of railroad workers organized episodic proto-industrial unions, the most significant of which was the Brakemen's Brotherhood and Trainmen's Union, organized in 1873 and 1877, respectively. These unions either included multiple grades of railroad workers or acted to provide organizational support for broader industrial action, and in the case of the nationwide railroad strikes that played the central role in the "Great Uprising of 1877," they served to mobilize railwaymen against wage cuts. However, these unions did not survive the Great Uprising, with its massive employer and state response. Nevertheless, their members carried their experiences with them into the Knights of Labor (KoL).

The Knights of Labor not only stood as the most important, inclusively organized railway labor organization of the 1880s but the most important labor organization of the Gilded Age. Founded in Philadel-phia in 1869, the Knights, like the brotherhoods, partook of the fraternal form, practicing secrecy and ritual, but distinguished themselves from other trade unionists by their belief in the creation of an organization that would bring together all workers, regardless of race, nationality, or occupation.

Guided by this broad moral vision, the KoL developed a genuine movement culture that at its broadest envisioned the abolition of the "wages system" and the wholesale transformation of American society. The organization grew explosively in the mid-1880s, propelled in part by the dramatic strike victory of KoL railwaymen, based mainly in the roundhouses and repair shops, against Jay Gould's Southwestern railroad system in 1885. However, a second strike in 1886 against the Gould system met with defeat and, together with the Haymarket Affair of 1886, contributed to the rapid decline of the organization. Nevertheless, the Knights remained a presence on a number of railroads and continued to provide an organizational framework linking men across trade lines and serving as "strikers' unions" when conditions on those roads became unfavorable. However, the railroad assemblies of the KoL suffered serious defeat in their strikes and by the early 1890s had all but been swept away.

The migratory streams generated by the breaking up of the Knights, as historian Shelton Stromquist has shown, led to the formation of the most important industrial railroad union of the nineteenth century, the American Railway Union (ARU), but not before the brotherhoods had encountered a series of reversals and had themselves experimented with a broader form of organization. By the late 1880s, the favorable conditions that had fostered the brotherhoods' "go it alone" attitude had changed as new railroad construction tapered off and railroad corporations adopted policies aimed at increasing the supply of skilled labor. In the Chicago, Burlington & Quincy Railroad strike of 1888, the "brotherhood" style of organization proved a bust as management easily replaced striking engineers and firemen.

For many of the men involved, the experience pointed to the need for some sort of federation among the brotherhoods; the result was the Supreme Council of the United Orders of Railway Employees. Formed in 1889, the outcome of negotiations among the firemen, brakemen, and switchmen, the Supreme Council was successful in its first year. (Conspicuously, the Engineers declined to participate, and remaining Knights assemblies were ignored.) However, jurisdictional conflict between the BRT and the SMAA, together with the reluctance of the brotherhood leaders to endorse sym-

EUGENE VICTOR DEBS (1855–1926)

Eugene Debs was a significant labor leader and the most important spokesman for the Socialist Party of America. He was born in his lifelong home of Terre Haute, Indiana. The son of French immigrants, he lived a comfortable childhood and completed a ninth-grade education. He left school to become a paint scraper on the Vandalia Railroad.

Shortly thereafter, Debs became a locomotive fireman and was an organizing member of the Terre Haute lodge of the Brotherhood of Locomotive Firemen. In his early days, Debs's approach to industrial capitalism was based on old-fashioned republican values. He believed deeply in industrial citizenship and thought that unions should build a positive and cooperative relationship with industrial capital.

In 1879, Debs tested the local political waters by serving two terms as city clerk and then a term in the Indiana state legislature. He remained an active member of the local union and saw himself as an independent citizen living in relative equality. In 1885, he married Katherine Metzel. The marriage was largely loveless, and they had no children.

Debs's concepts of harmony and cooperation were shattered by a difficult strike in 1888 against the Burlington Railroad. Burlington's unyielding position and the failure of the different railroad brotherhoods to work in unity convinced Debs that a radical departure from the present structure in terms of industrial capitalism and union structure was needed. He, therefore, turned to militant industrial unionism and a broader concept of class struggle.

Debs's first response was to develop an industrial union for all railroad workers. The American Railway Union (ARU) was established in 1893 and quickly won a strike against the Great Northern Railway. Fresh from victory, the ARU faced a much greater challenge when it took over a strike launched by workers against the Pullman Palace Car Company in 1894. When negotiations failed, Debs called for a national boycott against Pullman cars, which was resoundingly successful. But

United States Attorney General Richard Olney convinced President Grover Cleveland to send federal troops to break the strike. The strike was in fact broken, and Debs was arrested and sentenced to prison for six months.

While in prison, Debs began to read Marxist literature and met with leading Socialist politicians like Victor Berger. Upon his release, Debs announced his conversion to socialism. In 1900, he became a Socialist candidate for president and then helped to organize the Socialist Party of America (SPA), formally launched in 1901. He wanted to develop a specially American-based Socialist movement that would appeal to rank-and-file workers. He avoided inner-party discussions and warfare. Instead, he traveled widely and spoke constantly to workers, always carrying the message of class struggle and empowerment. He used the four presidential campaigns from 1900 to 1912 to urge workers to support socialism, to educate, to support strikes and to help organize unions. Debs always saw the SPA as an organ to build solidarity. Though Socialist votes for president never reached more than 900,000, his speeches were enormously popular with Socialists and attracted workers, scores of local officials, and even congressmen. In 1905, he was also a founding member of the Industrial Workers of the World (known as the "Wobblies").

By 1916, the constant travels and massive physical effort left Debs tired and ill. Although he did not run for president in 1916, he spoke out against the war in Europe. And when the United States entered the war in 1918, Debs launched a tour of protest speeches. In Canton, Ohio, he was arrested for sedition, convicted, and sentenced to federal prison. While in prison, the SPA ran him for president in 1920 and attracted a large protest vote. Pardoned in 1921 by President Warren Harding, Debs was released from prison. Over the next five years, his health continued to deteriorate, though he never lost his dedication to working-class issues. On October 20, 1926, he died in an Illinois sanitarium.

R. David Myers

pathy strikes, led to its disillusion in its second year, rendering it dead by the summer of 1891.

THE PULLMAN STRIKE AND BOYCOTT

Even as the Supreme Council came off the rails, figures within the federation movement, most notably BLF secretary Eugene V. Debs, and the Knights, particularly District Assembly 82 representing men on

the Union Pacific Railroad, began discussing the possibility of a general union of railwaymen. In early 1893, these men met to form the American Railway Union. As the first truly industrial railroad union, the ARU declared itself in favor of organizing all classes of railway employees (excepting black workers) and committed itself to thoroughgoing sympathetic action. With its vision of a strikeless era to come, the ARU

At the behest of railroad owners, President Grover Cleveland sent federal troops to break the Pullman Strike in 1894. In this violent scene, soldiers fire on a crowd of workers at the corner of Loomis and 49th streets in Chicago. *(Brown Brothers)*

caught on among railwaymen as no industrial union had before, especially among the less skilled and previously unorganized. It was this excitement and commitment to complete organization that led the young union in June 1894 to declare a boycott of Pullman cars in support of striking workers at the Pullman Palace Car Company in Chicago.

The action resulted in a near nationwide tie-up of the railroads and one of the most momentous episodes of labor conflict in U.S. history. However, railroad managers acting in concert discharged and blacklisted employees who refused to handle Pullman cars and persuaded the federal government to intervene with federal troops and a sweeping injunction effectively outlawing the boycott. By mid-July, the strike and boycott were over. In the bitter aftermath,

Debs and other ARU leaders were convicted of civil contempt and sentenced to prison; many blacklisted strikers were unable to find railroad employment again.

The events surrounding the Pullman strike and boycott of 1894 spelled a crushing defeat for industrial unionism on North American railroads while ensuring that the brotherhoods' style of craft unionism would triumph. The Big Four not only studiously avoided the conflict, but they also expelled members who supported the boycott and assisted the railroad corporations in identifying and blacklisting strikers. In the aftermath of the conflagration, the federal government and the railroad corporations took favorable note of the brotherhoods' actions and set about including them in a state-sanctioned system of mediation and arbitration designed to prevent conflicts of the Pullman boycott variety and to ensure that the railroads remained free of "radical," industrial-style unionism. The Erdman Act of 1898 provided the framework for the nation's first real system of collective bargaining as well as the first, if de facto, recognition of the right of unions like the brotherhoods to exist.

WAR, WORSENING WAGES AND CONDITIONS

The Erdman Act provided the brotherhoods with a level of security and stability that enabled them to become quite powerful by the eve of the United States' entry into World War I. In the years after 1897, with the return of prosperity following the 1890s depression, running-trades workers found themselves working longer, more intensive hours as the railroads strained to meet the increased demand placed upon them by the rapidly expanding national economy. Combined with a steadily rising cost of living, deteriorating working conditions produced rank-and-file cries for higher wages and shorter hours. With pressure from below and an "opportunity structure" provided by the state from above, some brotherhood leaders recalled the lessons of their brief experiment with federation and the need for cooperation among themselves at some level.

Leading the way in 1902, the Order of Railway Conductors and Brotherhood of Railroad Trainmen formed an association to present coordinated wage demands to the railroad corporations. Followed by the Brotherhood of Locomotive Engineers and Brotherhood of Locomotive Firemen and Enginemen (which amended its name in 1907, a reflection of the long-standing jurisdictional friction between the two unions), the brotherhoods engaged in a pattern of ever-widening, and increasingly synchronized, industrial action, including successive rounds of "concerted movements," as the presenting of uniform demands was termed, and mediation and arbitration under federal auspices. Although the brotherhoods became adept at the courtlike proceedings, marshalling and presenting mountains of detailed evidence, and although they won important gains, they became increasingly disappointed with the arbitrators' awards, which tended to favor the railroads, and frustrated with the arbitration system itself.

The showdown between the brotherhoods and the railroads began in March 1916 when the Big Four jointly presented demands for an eight-hour day in the train service without a corresponding reduction in wages. The brotherhoods made clear that under no circumstances would they submit the matter to arbitration. A series of negotiations with management, union meetings, and strike ballots concluded with a national-strike deadline set for Labor Day, September 4, 1916.

By the end of the summer, after a publications relations campaign on the part of both labor and capital, the two sides were hunkering down for the deadline when President Woodrow Wilson, with the nation on the verge of entry into World War I and facing the most serious tie-up of the national transportation system since the 1890s, intervened. Going before Congress, he asked for and received legislation granting the eight-hour workday. Narrowly upheld by the U.S. Supreme Court in early 1917, the Adamson Act provided the first nationally legislated eight-hour day for nongovernment workers and marked a historic shift in the federal government's ability to intervene in and regulate labor relations. It also marked the power and aggressiveness the brotherhoods had commanded and set the stage for the role these unions would play in labor politics during World War I and the 1920s.

As the United States mobilized for war during 1917, the railroads buckled under the strain of national transportation demands. The situation, which reached crisis proportions by the end of the year, had been in the making for at least a decade as the railroads, hampered by Interstate Commerce Commission caps on shipping rates and burdened by an increasing wage bill, failed to expand sufficiently. In December, the Wilson administration moved to nationalize the railroads, and for the duration of the war the federal government operated the national rail system through the United States Railroad Administration (USRA). The government's takeover, together with the wartime rhetoric of industrial democracy, had an enormous impact on railroad labor of all grades. Although the grievance and collective bargaining machinery utilized by the USRA enabled the Big Four to gain formal recognition and extend their membership, its impact on nonoperating employees was even greater.

Dating back to the late nineteenth century, a variety of unions had attempted to organize the wide range of nonoperating railroad workers. Skilled shopmen, particularly machinists, but also boilermakers, blacksmiths, and the other metal workers who built and maintained the locomotives, had organized, primarily through the Knights of Labor as early as the 1870s. With the disillusion of the KoL and the shat-

Labor leader and Socialist Eugene V. Debs ran for president five times. In 1920, he won more than 900,000 votes despite being imprisoned for violating the Espionage Act by publicly opposing World War I. *(Brown Brothers)*

tering of the ARU, however, the union that came to represent railroad machinists and that stood at the forefront of the shopcraft unions, was the International Association of Machinists (IAM). Other unions such as the International Brotherhood of Blacksmiths and International Brotherhood of Boiler Makers represented the rest of the railroad metals trades.

The militancy and tendency of the shopcraft unions to engage in joint action and to form systemwide federations, a legacy of the Knights, prompted the American Federation of Labor to inaugurate a Railway Employees' Department (RED) in 1908. After the turn of the century, unions like the Brotherhood of Railway Carmen, Brotherhood of Railway and Steam-

ship Clerks, Brotherhood of Railway Telegraphers, and Brotherhood of Maintenance of Way Workers came into being to represent nonoperating workers in the yards, stations, communications, and track maintenance. By the World War I period, reflecting the segmented nature of the railroad labor force, some sixteen different unions represented railroad workers. All but the Big Four would affiliate with the AFL. Diverse as their membership was, one thing the nonoperating unions had in common was the fact that the industrial relations machinery put in place by the Erdman Act did not extend to them. Consequently, in the years before World War I, these unions faced an uphill battle to organize and gain recognition from the railroad corporations. During the war, the USRA permitted these unions to significantly extend their membership, which had consistently lagged behind that of the Big Four, win important wage gains, and sign national agreements standardizing wages and working conditions.

RACIAL INEQUALITY

The workers who arguably expected the most of, and were most bitterly disappointed by, the Railroad Administration were African Americans. Since the period of slavery, Southern railways had engaged the labor of black men in the construction, maintenance, and operation of their roads. After the Civil War and emancipation, many of these workers remained in railway service, establishing a tradition of black labor, notably, in the brakemen's and firemen's positions in the South. But when it came to unionization, these men faced dual obstacles: the obstruction of railroad management and the antipathy of the railroad brotherhoods, not to mention the racial climate of the New South. Management profited from black labor, which it paid at a lower rate than white and easily ignored or beat back black attempts at organization.

White unionists, particularly the Firemen and Brakemen, for their part, not only excluded black workers from their unions but did everything they could to drive them from railroad employment entirely. From the first decade of the twentieth century well into the 1920s and 1930s, the BLFE and BRT conducted a series of often violent "race strikes," political lobbying, and outright terrorism to eliminate black brakemen and firemen from the railways. Black workers, however, refused to voluntarily give up their jobs and persisted at unionization.

Over the course of the 1910s and 1920s, black firemen, brakemen, switchmen, and Pullman porters established numerous local and regional associations, including the Colored Trainmen of America (CTA), the Colored Association of Railroad Employees, and the well-known Brotherhood of Sleeping Car Porters (BSCP), headed by Socialist journalist A. Philip Randolph. One group, the Railway Men's International Benevolent Industrial Association, led by Robert L. Mays, sought to transcend craft divisions and build a single federation of all black railroaders. During the war, these men leapt at the chance offered by the USRA to claim for themselves the rights enjoyed by their white counterparts. Because the USRA directly oversaw the nation's rail system, it provided blacks with a set of bureaucratic procedures they could follow in pursuit of their rights. But the Administration often moved slowly to make good on promised improvements and, in fact, acted against black workers when their frustration spilled over into strike action. Moreover, USRA labor relations machinery favored the established white unions, and the white unions themselves continued in their hostility to their black counterparts. Nevertheless, the World War I period and equity principles established by the USRA raised black aspirations and resulted in the persistence of black labor unions through the 1920s and 1930s, despite continued white hostility.

If the war experience was transformative for black railroaders, it also reoriented the white railroad unions toward social reform and taught them the virtues of government administration, developments that fed directly into their most ambitious political campaign: the Plumb Plan for government ownership of the national rail system. Proposed and elaborated by the brotherhoods' general counsel, Glenn E. Plumb, and progressives within the railroad unions—the Engineers' Warren S. Stone, the Machinists' William H. Johnston, and Bert Jewell of the AFL Railway Employees' Department—the Plumb Plan envisioned a tripartite rail administration drawn equally from labor, shippers, and bondholders. Coordinated by the Plumb Plan League, the campaign for the Plumb Plan reflected the rail unions' new social consciousness as well as the effect of wartime industrial democracy rhetoric, especially in the campaign's emphasis on the unions as defenders of the public interest and the Plan as a democratic way to administer the railroads.

THE RAILROAD LABOR BOARD AND POLITICAL ACTION

In the context of postwar labor militancy, however, the Republican-controlled Congress was not only determined to return the railroads to private ownership, but it almost included in the bill returning the railroads to their owners a provision outlawing strikes. In the end, the Transportation Act of 1920 established the Railroad Labor Board (RLB), a quasi-judicial body itself empowered to decide labor disputes. Smacking of compulsory arbitration and inconsistent in its efforts to obtain compliance with its decisions, the RLB permitted the railroad corporations to roll back trade unionism among the nonoperating employees and introduce company unionism. The Board, then, became the target of labor antagonism. So deeply did labor's grievances run that on July 1, 1922, roughly 400,000 shopcraft and other nonoperating employees walked off the job. The first nationwide railroad strike since

1894, the Shopmen's Strike of 1922 met with employers determined to oust trade unions from their shops and a federal government with little compunction about using extraordinarily sweeping injunctions and the military to break the walkout.

Railway labor's defeats during these years spurred the railroad unions into political action. Although these organizations, especially the Big Four, had been politically active as early as the 1890s and encouraged members to vote for candidates friendly to labor, they had focused their efforts on monitoring and influencing legislation affecting railway labor. Early on, the brotherhoods had recognized that the terrain on which they operated was defined by government. Certainly, the injunctions issued against boycotts and strikes made this clear. But railwaymen also understood that in many instances it was only government that could meaningfully address crucial workplace issues. Accordingly, the brotherhoods maintained lobbyists in the state and national legislatures and, working with reform-minded activists outside the labor movement, won important safety, workmen's compensation, and hours legislation in the years before World War I. With the events of 1919–1922, the railroad unions decisively shifted into electoral politics.

Following passage of the Transportation Act in 1920, the railroad unions organized a nonpartisan campaign that defeated one of the Act's co-authors and other labor-unfriendly congressmen. In the fall of 1922, the unions founded the Conference for Progressive Political Action, an organization that quickly became the focal point for a wide range of reformers, farm leaders, and intellectuals and succeeded in electing to Congress a number of labor-friendly candidates in the off-year election. This Progressive bloc briefly flirted with the idea of a formal labor party, but the Big Four steered the movement toward independent action and in 1924 backed Wisconsin Senator Robert M. La Follette (R-WI) in his unsuccessful insurgent campaign for the presidency.

Although the rail unions failed in their goal of electing a Progressive labor-friendly candidate to the White House, their 1920s political activity set in motion events that would shape railroad labor relations in the 1930s and after. The Republicans who controlled the federal government during the decade remained in power, but they nevertheless took notice of labor's political power and dissatisfaction with the RLB. The result was the Railway Labor Act of 1926, which introduced a Board of Mediation and marked

the first time Congress recognized the right of workers to join unions without employer interference.

The Act established the basic framework that would govern railroad industrial relations into the post–World War II era, with expanded provisions provided by the Amended Railway Labor Act of 1934. As the Depression of the 1930s deepened, the railroad unions used their political power to address the problem of unemployment in the industry. Thus, the unions supported full-crew, train-limit, and six-hour-day legislation. But the measure with the greatest significance was the Railroad Retirement Act of 1937, which established a separate system of social security for railroad employees. Together, these railway laws represented important New Deal industrial relations and social welfare legislation that paralleled the better-known Wagner and Social Security Acts. For the railroad unions themselves, this legislation enabled them to secure national agreements covering almost all operating and most nonoperating employees by the end of the decade.

THE NEW DEAL AND WORLD WAR II

The New Deal policies of the 1930s that proved favorable to organized labor on the railroads and elsewhere had a mixed effect on black railroad unions. The 1934 Railway Act rescued the Brotherhood of Sleeping Car Porters from oblivion, but the same machinery that worked to BSCP's advantage provided the standard (white) unions with a virtual monopoly over their respective job categories, effectively depriving black workers in the operating crafts of their workplace and bargaining rights. (The Congress of Industrial Organizations encountered the same obstacle when it attempted to organize nonoperating workers during the 1930s and 1940s.)

Nevertheless, unions like the Association of Colored Railway Trainmen and Locomotive Firemen persisted. Following the path blazed by their World War I-era predecessors, they translated their exclusion from the larger labor movement into a tradition of independent unionism that fostered a fierce racial solidarity and pride among black craft workers. The World War II period and the return of prosperity prompted the railroad unions to recover the ground they had lost in terms of wages during the Depression. Despite a no-strike pledge, labor militancy actually increased during the war as a number of small, wildcat strikes, usually as a result of disputes over the application of national agreements or wartime wage stabilization policies, resulted in a number of temporary government seizures of railroads. But the real labor conflict of the era emerged in the years immediately following the war as both the operating and nonoperating unions presented demands for increased wages, shorter hours, and work rules revisions. All but the Engineers and Trainmen, who had grown frustrated with the tedious process of working through the Railway Labor Act machinery, settled their issues. In early 1946, the two holdouts conducted strike votes and after a series of emergency conferences walked out on May 23, initiating the first major strike of operating employees since the Burlington Strike of 1888.

Under threat by President Harry Truman, who had seized the railroads, to draft striking employees into the military, the union chiefs called off the strike after only forty-eight hours. Successive rounds of demands and presidential seizures in 1948 and 1950 completed railroad labor's part in the broader strike wave of the post–World War II era.

Black railwaymen took advantage of the war's moral climate, as a war for democracy, to fight the pervasive discrimination they faced. The March on Washington Movement of 1941, conceived by A. Philip Randolph to force the Roosevelt administration to take action against racial discrimination in defense-related industries, resulted in the creation of the Fair Employment Practices Committee (FEPC). The FEPC conducted hearings and investigations into the railroads and a number of other industries and ordered the elimination of discriminatory practices. However, it was another matter to enforce such calls. Thus, in addition to the FEPC, black railroaders turned to the courts and with civil rights lawyer Charles H. Houston won important decisions in the 1944 U.S. Supreme Court cases of *Steele v. Louisville & Nashville R.R. Co.* and *Tunstall v. Brotherhood of Locomotive Firemen and Enginemen* requiring white unions to represent fairly black workers over whom they had jurisdiction. The *Steele* and *Tunstall* decisions stood alongside the other World War II-era Supreme Court decisions that laid the groundwork for the eventual ending of legal discrimination against African Americans. In this way, writes historian Eric Arnesen, the "civil rights unionism" of black railwaymen flowed into the larger African-American civil rights movement. Nevertheless, it would not be until the 1960s and its landmark civil rights legislation that black operating employees would be able to break down the rigid color bars that blocked their advancement.

Sadly, black railwaymen achieved their greatest victories just as the railroad industry entered a period of terminal decline, continuing a trend dating from the 1920s. Competition from interstate trucking, intercity bussing, the airlines, and the automobile severely cut into the railroads' passenger and freight traffic and revenues. By 1965, only a little over a third of the U.S. rail network provided passenger service, and it was only the creation of the quasi-public Amtrak by the Rail Passenger Service Act of 1970 that kept any service available. Railroad employment dropped correspondingly, declining 32 percent between 1950 and 1960 and total jobs decreasing from 909,000 to 683,000 between 1960 and 1968. Moreover, locomotive firemen faced technological extinction as the diesel locomotive replaced steam power. From the 1950s onward, the railroad unions fought largely defensive battles, attempting to preserve jobs and maintain wages and working conditions, and, by the 1980s and 1990s, resisting White House efforts to undo social welfare legislation such as the Federal Employers Liability Act.

For the railroad unions, white and black, these difficult times manifested themselves organizationally. The operating brotherhoods, with the exception of the BLE (which followed suit in 1988), reflected the strain when they petitioned and were admitted to the American Federation of Labor-Congress of Industrial Organizations (AFL-CIO) in the 1960s. The pressure of civil rights laws and AFL-CIO admission requirements forced the brotherhoods to drop their color bars, but this contributed to the decline of the independent black railway unions. After the BRT successfully challenged the Colored Trainmen of America (CTA) as the bargaining agent of brakemen and yardmen on the Missouri Pacific Railroad, the CTA met for the final time in 1969. Similarly, the Brotherhood of Sleeping Car Porters ceased to exist when financial and organizational difficulties forced it to merge with the Brotherhood of Railway and Airline Clerks in 1978, thus ending a history of independent black unionism. But, to a large extent, independent brotherhood unionism also ended when in 1969, the BRT, BLFE, ORC, and SUNA came together to form the United Transportation Union (UTU), bringing closer than ever before Eugene V. Debs's dream of "one big union" of railroad workers, but not exactly under the circumstances he had envisioned. In 1989, the UTU attempted an expensive, but unsuccessful, bid to take over the BLE in a representation election on the Norfolk Southern Railroad.

Railroad unionism continues in the twenty-first century but in rather attenuated form compared with its earlier history. Although the railroads continue to haul much of the nation's freight, with Amtrak repeatedly on the brink of bankruptcy and the challenges facing the larger labor movement, railroad unions face an uncertain future. Nevertheless, the industry's complex nature and its relationship to government will continue to influence the character of railroad unionism.

Paul Michel Taillon

BIBLIOGRAPHY

Arnesen, Eric. *Brotherhoods of Color: Black Railroad Workers and the Struggle for Equality.* Cambridge, MA: Harvard University Press, 2001.

Friedman, Gerald. *State-Making and Labor Movements: France and the United States, 1876–1914.* Ithaca, NY: Cornell University Press, 1998.

Kaufman, Jacob. *Collective Bargaining in the Railroad Industry.* New York: King's Crown, 1954.

Lecht, Leonard A. *Experience under Railway Labor Legislation.* New York: Columbia University Press, 1955.

Olssen, Erik. "The Making of a Political Machine: The Railroad Unions Enter Politics." *Labor History* 19 (Summer 1978): 273–296.

Perlman, Mark. *The Machinists: A New Study in American Trade Unionism.* Cambridge, MA: Harvard University Press, 1961.

Richardson, Reed C. *The Locomotive Engineer, 1863–1963: A Century of Railway Labor Relations and Work Rules.* Ann Arbor: University of Michigan Press, 1963.

Robbins, Edwin C. *Railway Conductors: A Study in Organized Labor.* New York: Columbia University Studies in Social Sciences, 1914.

Seidman, Joel. *The Brotherhood of Railroad Trainmen: The Internal Political Life of a National Union.* New York: John Wiley & Sons, 1962.

Stromquist, Shelton. *A Generation of Boomers: The Pattern of Railroad Labor Conflict in Nineteenth Century America.* Urbana: University of Illinois Press, 1987.

Taillon, Paul. " 'To Make Men out of Crude Material': Work Culture, Manhood, and Unionism in the Railroad Running Trades, c. 1870–1900." In *Boys and Their Toys: Masculinity, Technology, and Class,* ed. Roger Horowitz, pp. 33–54. New York: Routledge, 2001.

Tarrow, Sidney. *Power in Movement: Social Movements, Collective Action, and Politics.* New York: Cambridge University Press, 1994.

Troy, Leo. "Labor Representation on American Railways." *Labor History* 2 (Fall 1961): 295–322.

Zieger, Robert. "From Hostility to Moderation: Railroad Labor Policy in the 1920s." *Labor History* 9 (Winter 1968): 23–38.

STEELWORKERS MOVEMENT

In the approximately 125-year history of the American steel industry, steelworkers have had little success organizing lasting social movements. The most important reasons for this failure do not rest on the steelworkers themselves. External factors such as changing production technology, resistance from their employers, the nature of American labor law, and foreign competition for the firms they work in have thwarted repeated efforts by workers to bring lasting changes to this industry.

EARLY STEELWORKER MOVEMENTS

Andrew Carnegie pioneered the mass production of steel in the United States during the mid-1870s. Before that time, iron fulfilled the requirements of most metal consumers. Because it took years to develop the skills needed to puddle iron (stir it in such a way as to remove impurities), iron workers exercised enormous control over the production process. This changed when Carnegie introduced the Bessemer process to America. Bessemer converters blew air through molten slag, thereby eliminating the need for hand puddling and making the mass production of steel possible. Faced with the emerging threat of technological obsolescence and the immediate threat of the Panic of 1873, local organizations of skilled puddlers organized the Amalgamated Association of Iron, Steel and Tin Workers in 1876. The Amalgamated Association believed strongly in craft unionism, meaning it had little interest in the fate of less-skilled workers.

Despite having the word "steel" in its name, the Amalgamated Association was always strongest in the ironmaking sector of the iron and steel industry. But unfortunately for iron workers, steelmaking was the wave of the future. Since Bessemer steelmaking did not require highly skilled workers, steelmakers had lower wage bills than ironmakers. Moreover, the amount of output produced at a Bessemer steel plant dwarfed that of a typical iron mill. Steel and iron were almost interchangeable, and since steel was more useful in key markets like rail manufacture, many ironmaking firms shifted to steelmaking in the 1880s and early-1890s, eliminating their union in the process. At the same time, many new steelmakers began production union-free. In this way, the steel industry pulled the rug out from under the Amalgamated Association.

ANDREW CARNEGIE AND THE HOMESTEAD STRIKE

This does not mean that the transition from iron to steel produced no labor difficulties. There were many local disputes in America's steelmaking region during this transition. However, management invariably won these battles. The most famous of these conflicts occurred at Andrew Carnegie's Homestead Works (located just outside of Pittsburgh) in 1892. In two famous essays written in 1886, Carnegie had endorsed the idea of labor unions. He did this because his superior production technology had allowed him to pay union wages and still undersell his competitors who had to face periodic strikes. By 1892, that advantage had disappeared because of a glut in the steel market and an increase in technologically sophisticated non-union rival firms. Therefore, Carnegie and his on-site partner, Henry Clay Frick, were determined to eliminate the Amalgamated Association from their mill once and for all.

Homestead's Amalgamated local expected negotiations for their new contract to go smoothly in 1892. Instead, Frick made demands he knew the union could not accept. Then, when the contract expired, he erected a fence around the Homestead Works to facilitate locking the union workers out. On July 6, 1892, the company brought a boatload of Pinkerton guards up the Monongahela River. Tipped off that the Pinkertons were coming to protect permanent replacement workers, the strikers and other citizens of Homestead,

Pennsylvania, met them at the dock in order to prevent them from landing. Twelve people died in the ensuing firefight, and many more were wounded. After the Pinkertons surrendered, the strikers marched them around town to be kicked and beaten by the local population. This uprising convinced the governor of Pennsylvania to send in the National Guard, which protected the permanent replacement workers who restarted operations at the mill. The Amalgamated gave up later that year since many of their members had already returned to work on a non-union basis.

Many historians credit the Homestead Lockout with destroying trade unionism in the steel industry for the next forty-five years. In fact, technological change had already made the survival of a strong union in this industry impossible. The Amalgamated Association temporarily maintained strength in a few small sectors in this industry, such as tin plate manufacture, because the production process for these types of steel still required skill. In order to prevent the Amalgamated Association from mounting a comeback, Carnegie Steel employed a series of questionable tactics such as maintaining a blacklist of union members that it would not hire and spying on their workmen in order to weed out organizers. The rest of the industry would come to use similar tactics in order to stay union-free.

FIGHTING THE UNION—STRIKES AND UNION BUSTING

The Amalgamated had some hope of revival when most of the industry consolidated as the United States Steel Corporation in 1901. The union struck U.S. Steel almost immediately, hoping that the firm would be willing to negotiate so it could concentrate on establishing itself on a firm financial footing. In doing so, the Amalgamated Association underestimated the firm's tolerance for labor organization. U.S. Steel chairman Elbert Gary, like many other steel magnates, hated trade unions. To him, they not only cost employers money in higher wages, but they violated the spirit of individual achievement that American capitalism depended upon. Therefore, rather than negotiate, U.S. Steel took advantage of the 1901 strike to eliminate the Amalgamated Association from more mills than ever before. For the next eight years, the company waged war on the few unions that remained, all of which represented workers in the few sectors of the industry that still required a skilled

workforce. Other firms in the industry followed suit. By the end of 1909, the Amalgamated Association was as good as dead, party only to a few contracts with independent specialty steelmakers in the Midwest.

Although management eliminated the union from the industry, labor conditions steadily deteriorated. Wages for the few skilled workers in the industry decreased dramatically. The twelve-hour day and the long turn (a twenty-four-hour shift every two weeks) became commonplace. Steel companies came to depend upon new Eastern and Southern European immigrants to fill their ranks because few native-born Americans would accept these circumstances. These new employees tended to live in crowded slums located near the steel mills where they worked because they did not make enough money to live in better neighborhoods. Steel companies dominated the governments of many steel towns and used that power to keep union organizers away from their workers. At the same time, U.S. Steel created elaborate welfare programs to win loyalty from their most skilled employees. It offered workers subsidies to buy company stock and gave them a pension plan if they served the company long enough. The vast majority of workers, however, got very little from their employer.

Despite the absence of an effective union, steelworkers continued to attempt to organize in order to improve their labor conditions. There were major local strikes at McKees Rocks, Pennsylvania, in 1909 and at Bethlehem Steel in eastern Pennsylvania in 1910. After economic mobilization for World War I began, steelworkers tried to take advantage of the demand for labor and the need for continued production by beginning a nationwide organizing campaign. John Fitzpatrick of the Chicago Federation of Labor and ex-Industrial Workers of the World (IWW) organizer William Z. Foster, fresh from organizing Chicago packinghouse workers, started the National Committee for Organizing Iron and Steel Workers in 1918. During wartime, the Committee had great success signing up steelworkers, particularly less skilled immigrant workers, because employers did not want to risk disruptions in production when business was booming.

When the war ended, Committee leaders called on U.S. Steel Chairman Elbert Gary to open negotiations for a formal contract. Gary refused to recognize or even meet with them. Once again, other steelmakers followed U.S. Steel's lead. The National Committee wanted more time to organize, but rank-and-file

COMING OUT OF THE SMOKE.

This antilabor cartoon aimed to taint the nationwide steel strike of 1919 with the specter of communism. *(Brown Brothers)*

pressure forced it to call a nationwide steel strike on September 22, 1919. The Committee's primary goals were to win union recognition and bring about the end of the twelve-hour day. Approximately 250,000 employees, about half the workforce in the industry, answered the strike call.

Because of their ideological resistance to trade unionism, steel producers were determined to fight the strike by using any means necessary. When the strike began, many firms hired replacements for as many striking workers as possible. Since the Committee tended to attract unskilled workers, it proved relatively easy to replace them. Steelmakers also inflamed racial and ethnic tensions among their workers in order to combat the strike. For example, U.S. Steel distributed handbills in Chicago that charged Italians and Eastern Europeans with trying to take jobs away from Americans. Media revelations about William Z. Foster's IWW past did not help the Committee's cause. This allowed employers to paint all the leaders of the strike as dangerous radicals.

As the weeks dragged on, more and more steelworkers went back to work without union contracts. The single worst blow to the strike came from within

labor's own ranks when the Amalgamated Association told its few skilled members to return to work in December. The National Committee formally ended the strike on January 8, 1920, although production had returned to normal levels weeks before. It disbanded shortly thereafter.

NATIONAL LABOR LEGISLATION AND UNIONIZATION EFFORTS

Steelworkers remained docile throughout the 1920s and even into the Great Depression as wage cuts and layoffs shook the industry. It took the passage of the National Industrial Recovery Act (NIRA) in 1933 to bring about another union drive. The moribund Amalgamated Association remained the only union in the iron and steel industry at this time. Still wedded to craft unionism, its deeply conservative leadership felt no need to mount a new organizing campaign, even though Section 7(a) of the NIRA formally recognized the right of labor to organize for the first time. Unlike the United Mine Workers (UMW), which made much of the NIRA, the Amalgamated Association sent only a few organizers into the field after its passage.

Yet steelworkers did not require help from the Amalgamated Association in order to organize. In the months following passage of the NIRA, independent employee organizations sprang up on their own throughout the industry. The names of these locals (one was called the Franklin D. Roosevelt lodge; another the ARIN lodge—ARIN is NIRA spelled backwards) underscore the reason for their existence. As they had done before, steelmakers fought these organizations bitterly. Some firms created company unions (worker organizations started and dominated by management) in order to steal the thunder of reform from outside organizations; others simply refused to bargain with any union. Therefore, the majority of these new worker organizations proved short-lived.

THE STEELWORKERS ORGANIZING COMMITTEE

It took new legislation, the National Labor Relations Act of 1935, and a new organizing philosophy, to bring real change to the industry's labor relations. John L. Lewis of the UMW started the Committee for Industrial Organization (later the Congress of Industrial Organizations or CIO) in 1935. Although interested in organizing less-skilled workers in many mass production industries, the CIO was particularly interested in organizing steelworkers because many steel companies controlled mines that supplied their mills. The CIO started the Steel Workers Organizing Committee (SWOC) in 1936. It began by concentrating its efforts on winning over workers involved in the company unions at U.S. Steel. By encouraging these organizations to defy management, SWOC hoped to convince the rank-and-file that only outside unions could truly represent their interests. The success of these efforts led to secret talks between John L. Lewis and U.S. Steel chairman Myron Taylor. These talks culminated in U.S. Steel's March 1937 decision to sign a contract with SWOC so as to avoid a costly strike and possible involvement by the federal government. Many other steel firms followed suit.

U.S. Steel's main competitors, such as Bethlehem Steel and Republic Steel, did not, however. These leading firms in the industry were known collectively as "Little Steel" because they were smaller than U.S. Steel Corporation, but they were all very large enterprises. Unlike U.S. Steel, which had new blood in its management ranks by the 1930s, the leaders of Little Steel continued to oppose the presence of any outside union in their plants. Therefore, when SWOC began to organize their workers in the spring of 1937, Little Steel chose to fight.

The most famous incident of the Little Steel Strike is known as the "Memorial Day Massacre." It occurred on May 30, Memorial Day, outside a Republic Steel plant in Chicago. Chicago policemen shot into a crowd of strikers, killing ten, seven of whom were shot in the back. SWOC did not get a single union contract from the Little Steel strike. However, pressure from the Roosevelt administration to keep production going during World War II led each Little Steel firm to recognize the union. By the end of the war, SWOC's successor organization, the United Steelworkers of America (USWA), represented the vast majority of workers in the industry.

Nevertheless, many steel firms only bargained with the USWA under duress. The government's National War Labor Board had forced them to do so to guarantee steel for the war effort. Because of this and other assistance from the Roosevelt administration, USWA membership grew rapidly during the war. After the war ended, the USWA had grown too large to destroy. Management attempts to roll back union power led to industrywide strikes in 1946, 1949, 1952, 1956, and 1959. The last of these strikes lasted 116 days and was the largest single strike in American history. In these disputes, the USWA invariably sought higher wages and more control over the production process. The union usually won the first issue and lost the second. By 1960, steelworkers were among the best-paid workers in all of American industry, but they were also vulnerable to technological unemployment and changing economic fortunes.

GLOBAL AND REGIONAL COMPETITION AND STEEL MILL CLOSURES

The downturn that has destroyed the potential for lasting social movements in the American steel industry began in the mid-1960s. Continuous labor tension, high wage bills, and the failure of American steelmakers to modernize their production methods led steel consumers to increasingly buy cheaper product from overseas. The USWA responded to the industry's economic crisis by promoting conciliation. For ten years, starting in 1973, it even forfeited the right to strike (in favor of mandatory arbitration) under a novel arrangement called the Experimental Negotiating Agreement.

As old mills stopped operations around Pittsburgh, Youngstown, Chicago, and elsewhere, some employees organized protests, but this did not change their fate. By the mid-1980s, the union broke pattern bargaining and fought austerity measures at surviving firms like U.S. Steel (by then known as USX Corporation because it had bought two oil companies and did not want to be primarily identified with a failing industry). Like its forerunner Carnegie Steel did in 1892, USX locked out the union in 1986. Although the USWA has survived in some mills (including those of USX), unionization rates in American steelmaking continue to decline with the industry's fortunes.

Since 1980, the only new steel mills built in the United States have been mini-mills, small-scale operations that recycle scrap steel rather than create new product from scratch. Since mini-mills require few skilled workers, they tend to operate on a nonunion basis. Furthermore, because of recent technological innovations, mini-mills have increasingly started competing with traditional unionized steel producers.

Foreign competition, nonunion mini-mills, and an unfavorable political climate for organized labor in general have all hurt the prospects for further unionization in the steel industry in recent years. After mergers with other unions, most notably the United Rubber Workers in 1995, the United Steelworkers of

America has increasingly devoted more of its attention to organizing and serving different kinds of workers. The acceleration of the American steel industry's decline during the late-1990s has only strengthened this tendency. As long as the steel industry stays on its knees, the possibility of new social movements among American steelworkers will remain remote.

Jonathan Rees

BIBLIOGRAPHY

Brody, David. *Steelworkers in America: The Nonunion Era.* Cambridge, MA: Harvard University Press, 1960.

Fitch, John. *The Steel Workers.* Pittsburgh: University of Pittsburgh Press, 1989.

Hoerr, John P. *And the Wolf Finally Came.* Pittsburgh: University of Pittsburgh Press, 1988.

Krause, Paul. *The Battle for Homestead 1880–1892: Politics, Culture and Steel.* Pittsburgh: University of Pittsburgh Press, 1992.

Tiffany, Paul. *The Decline of American Steel.* New York: Oxford University Press, 1988.

GARMENT WORKERS MOVEMENT

In the 1970s, the International Ladies' Garment Workers' Union (ILGWU) pioneered the path of re-integrating labor with other social movements to bring about a more equitable society for all working people. Under new radical leadership, the ILGWU recognized that organizing women and the documented and undocumented immigrant workforce was a priority. This stance represented a marked detour from the majority view of organized labor, which argued that it was not possible to organize the undocumented. The new ILGWU leadership contended that labor–management accords represented a dead end for union building and instead, the rank-and-file had to be involved in building their own union. Through this involvement, workers would gain political understanding of the ongoing class struggle between labor and management and develop bold campaigns and labor–community coalitions. This new approach marked a radical departure from the past conservative ILGWU.

BACKGROUND

Since its inception in 1900, the ILGWU had a history replete with internal political strife. On the one side were the more moderate to conservative groups, who sought industry stability and accords with management to promote the union. The opposition represented Communists, Socialists, and other radicals, who argued that the best way to build the union was through rank-and-file involvement in militant actions, such as strikes and labor–community coalitions. The moderate to conservative group held leadership well into the twentieth century. David Dubinsky, an Eastern European Jewish immigrant, who represented labor–management cooperation, was president from 1932 to his retirement in 1966. The union was organized by craft in that there were separate locals for each craft, but it also was industrial in that all branches of the industry were organized. For the ma-

jority of its history, with the exception of a brief affiliation with the more democratic and radical Congress of Industrial Organization (CIO) in 1937, the union was affiliated with the more conservative American Federation of Labor (AFL) since 1940.

Throughout its history, the ILGWU was challenged by an industry that was mainly decentralized and based on piecework. In addition, the industry was replete with small shops or sweatshops, owned by contractors who were able to offer low job bids by continually cutting labor costs. Coined in the late nineteenth century, "sweatshop" referred to a workplace where relatively unskilled workers, usually immigrants, labored or sweated for meager pay in unhealthy and unsafe conditions for many hours. Throughout the years, the industry practiced many unfair labor practices such as minimum wage and overtime violations, homework, and child labor.

In the late 1970s, faced with a declining industry, the reappearance of sweatshops, and a shrinking workforce due to the domestic effects of globalization, the ILGWU, under more radical leadership, pioneered creative and aggressive organizing campaigns, which targeted immigrant workers, including the undocumented. They were one of the first unions to recognize that the inclusion of undocumented workers was essential for the success of organizing campaigns. During this time, many organizers received their training within the ILGWU and went on to develop bold campaigns in other unions which involved undocumented workers, such as the Hotel Employees and Restaurant Employees Union and the Service Employees International Union.

In 1995, the ILGWU merged with the Textile Workers Union and the Amalgamated Clothing and Textile Workers Union to form the 300,000-member Union of Needletrades, Industrial and Textile Employees (UNITE) in an effort to strengthen its declining union. UNITE emerged as one of the most

ROSE (RACHEL) SCHNEIDERMAN
(1884–1972)

Born in Savin, Poland, on April 6, 1882, Rachel Schneiderman immigrated to the United States in 1890. She later changed her name to Rose. She went to work in her early teens sewing caps, and in 1903, she helped organize a New York City local of the Jewish Socialist United Cloth Hat and Cap Makers' Union, taking the lead in getting women elected to the union. In 1904, she was elected to the union's executive board, the highest position yet held by a woman in any American labor organization. The following year she joined the Women's Trade Union League (WTUL), the national organization that led the fight to improve women's working conditions. She remained among the WTUL's most active leaders for forty-five years, serving as president from 1926 to 1950. She was also a national organizer for the International Ladies' Garment Workers' Union (ILGWU).

Schneiderman took a major role in several of the landmark events of the American labor struggle. In 1909, she called for the strike of women shirtwaistmakers. That same year, she took a role in organizing the garment workers, and she denounced all those who had contributed to the disastrous Triangle Shirtwaist Company fire in 1911. By the late 1910s, the WTUL was her major focus. As president of both the New York and national WTUL, she concentrated her efforts on lobbying for minimum wage and eight-hour-day legislation. In addition to her work with the WTUL, she worked for women's right to vote, serving as a key organizer for the National American Woman Suffrage Association.

In 1921, she helped organize the Bryn Mawr Summer School for Women Workers. In 1922, Eleanor Roosevelt joined the WTUL, and the two women began a lifelong friendship. Schneiderman tutored Roosevelt on the issues confronting women workers, the challenges facing the trade union movement, and the problems inherent in labor–management relations. The connection paid off later when President Franklin D. Roosevelt appointed Schneiderman to the Labor Advisory Board of the National Recovery Administration in 1933, on which she served for two years, the only woman to do so. She then served as secretary of the New York State Department of Labor from 1937 to 1943. She lectured widely before diverse audiences and served on various boards. When she died on August 11, 1972, she was one of the most respected spokespersons and activists for improving the conditions of laboring people.

James G. Lewis

innovative and progressive unions in the nation. UNITE built labor–community coalitions, spearheaded efforts to establish and enforce federal guidelines against sweatshops, exposed slave labor conditions among Thai undocumented workers in Southern California, worked for amnesty for undocumented workers, publicized the past and present conditions in the garment industry in cooperation with a Smithsonian Institute traveling exhibit, and aggressively organized garment workers throughout the United States.

THE INDUSTRY AND THE UNION

The International Ladies' Garment Workers' Union (ILGWU) was founded on June 3, 1900, by eleven male delegates representing 2,000 workers from four unions, although immigrant women were the predominant workforce. The first industrywide strike in 1909–1910, in New York City, was led by these immigrant women workers. Shirtwaist workers fought for better conditions and higher pay in the "Uprising of the 20,000," as it was called.

In the garment industry, a hierarchy existed with men at the top of the pay scale working as cutters and pressers and women at the bottom as helpers, finishers, and sewing machine operators. Pay scales were based on piecework, and the more skilled positions paid a higher rate. The industry consisted of large manufacturing concerns in which the entire manufacturing process took place and smaller shops were run by contractors, who bid on parts of the manufacturing process. Contractors fiercely competed for jobs by keeping labor costs low, in order to win bids for work. Because of the small capital investment required, a contractor could be a former worker, who operated out of a storefront or even his own home. These shops were often mobile, and some employed family members and friends, making organizing difficult. In the late twentieth century, the union recognized the potential alliance between contractors and workers against the large manufacturers and sought to neutralize them or win their support.

In the early twentieth century, Eastern European Jewish and Italian immigrants made up the workforce, whereas by the later twentieth century, Asian and Latino immigrants constituted the main workforce. In the latter era, the entrenched leaders had little awareness of the demographic changes that had occurred within the workforce, did not speak the workers' languages, and were not receptive to their needs. They maintained their mistaken views

Rose Schneiderman, longtime leader of the Women's Trade Union League, delivers an address at a rally in Madison Square Park in New York City, circa 1913. *(Brown Brothers)*

that neither women nor immigrants could be organized.

Conditions in the garment industry were miserable. New York City was the number one garment manufacturing site in the United States. Most factory laws required 250 cubic feet of air for each worker but did not say where it had to be located. In new loft buildings, the ceilings were quite high, so owners could crowd more workers into a given space. It was sweltering hot in summer and freezing in winter. Windows were nailed shut and doors were locked under the pretense of forestalling theft. Bathrooms were filthy or nonexistent. Safety conditions were deplorable, especially the constant threat of fire. Workers labored fifty-six to fifty-nine hours a week and were charged for needles, thread, use of electricity, the stools they sat on, and the water they drank; they were fined for mistakes, as well as for talking or singing.

THE UPRISING OF 20,000

In 1909, New York City shirtwaist workers led by Clara Lemlich, a young Jewish immigrant, began to challenge these terrible conditions by organizing ILGWU Local 25, the shirtwaist local. At that time, shirtwaists were practically the uniform for working women, and hundreds of large and small shops competed by driving labor costs as low as possible. Many unions, believing women to be nonorganizable, were reluctant to recruit them, despite the militant history of women workers, such as the Lowell women textile workers in the early to mid-nineteenth century. As conditions worsened, the Local, numbering 100 workers, pushed the International leaders to sanction a strike and began walking out of the shops. Within days, 20,000 workers were out, and more joined, until the numbers swelled to 30,000, which represented 75 percent of the workforce. Although the women strik-

With signs and flags, this picture captures the spirit, diversity, and patriotism of immigrant workers employed in New York City's garment industry in the early 1900s. *(Brown Brothers)*

ers were brutally beaten by police and thugs and jailed repeatedly, they held firm to their cause. The strikers actually received more support and publicity from affluent women of the Women's Trade Union League than they did from their own International and the AFL.

By February 1910, the strike was settled with the majority of workers being rehired, hours reduced to fifty-two with a two-hour limit on night work, and wages increased 15 percent. But the settlement also included the Protocols of Peace, which were pacts to settle conflicts without strikes and supposed to serve as a model of labor–management cooperation. The

Protocols were in sharp contrast to a more radical trade union philosophy, which viewed strikes as the workers' most effective weapon. The controversial no-strike provision later fueled disputes in the union.

A total of 345 firms signed contracts with the union, membership grew to 60,000, and Local 25's membership rose to 10,000. The significance of the 1909–1910 strike was that it was the first industry-wide strike and was led by immigrant women. Although the strike clearly disputed the male leadership's position that women and immigrants could not be organized or maintain a fierce strike, male

PAULINE NEWMAN (c. 1890–1986)

Pauline Newman was born in Lithuania around 1890 and came to the United States in 1901. Soon after her arrival in New York City, she went to work to help support her family working in a hairbrush factory and hand-rolling cigarettes. As a young teenager, she became employed at the Triangle Shirtwaist Factory trimming extra threads off of shirts. Working seven days a week, often for fourteen hours a day, she made a dollar and a half a week. She was no longer employed there by the time of the tragic fire in 1911.

Newman took to radical politics early and spent most of her career with the International Ladies' Garment Workers' Union (ILGWU), an organization dominated by Eastern European Jewish men. She balanced this loyalty with participation in the emerging arena of women-centered politics led by the Women's Trade Union League (WTUL). This coalition of wage-earning and middle-class women fought for the eight-hour day, decent wages, women's suffrage, and protective workplace laws. The tragic death of nearly 150 women in the 1911 Triangle Shirtwaist Factory fire galvanized the ILGWU, which pushed harder for improved working conditions. New York's state legislature imposed tougher municipal building codes and more stringent factory inspections.

A leader in the ILGWU, Newman became the first full-time woman organizer. She had her initiation into the labor movement as a speaker in the 1909 Shirtwaist Makers Strike and went on to become an organizer in the Northeast and Midwest, playing a role in numerous major strikes. She founded the ILGWU's Health Center and was director of health education from 1918 to 1980. Newman's other positions over the years included adviser to the United States Department of Labor in the 1930s and 1940s, the Board of Directors for the Bryn Mawr Summer School for Women Workers, and the WTUL. She died in Manhattan on April 8, 1986.

James G. Lewis

leaders still refused to relinquish their mistaken beliefs.

THE TRIANGLE SHIRTWAIST COMPANY FIRE

Although the Triangle Shirtwaist Company workers had been among the most militant and courageous leaders of the strike, the company was not one of the 345 firms that recognized the union. The Triangle Shirtwaist Company was located on the top three floors of a ten-year-old building, acclaimed to be fireproof. One of the key demands in the 1909–1910 garment strike had been for adequate fire protection, including fire escapes and sprinkler systems. The exterior was brick, but the interior was flammable wood. There were inadequate fire escapes and no sprinkler system. All doors opened inward, and all but one door to the staircases were kept locked, based on the employer's premise that this would prevent employee theft. Oil-soaked rags littered the floors; barrels of oil were lined up against the walls; piles of cloth, rags, and tissue were everywhere; and lint was heavy in the air.

On March 25, 1911, as 500 workers were preparing to leave at 4:30 P.M., a fire broke out on the eighth floor, and within minutes the "fireproof" building was engulfed in flames. Many were crushed trying to escape, and others jumped to their death 100 feet below. A total of 146 workers perished, all but 21 of whom were women. The owners were eventually acquitted of manslaughter charges, which incensed workers and their allies, who demanded an investigation. Based on the findings, fifty-six state labor laws were passed relating to safety and child labor. This hard-fought-for legislation served both as an example for other states to follow suit and as a model for the 1930s New Deal legislation.

POLITICAL DISPUTES WITHIN THE UNION

In the following decades, the union leadership continued to play a conservative role by making industry stability a priority over workers' needs and involvement. The labor–management accord continued to characterize the union activities and philosophy into the late 1960s and early 1970s. The hierarchical structure of the industry was replicated within the union, as women were not groomed for union leadership, which remained steadfastly male. The New York headquarters continued to have bitter political disputes involving Communists and Socialists who opposed this approach. Political disputes in Los Angeles were similar to those in New York and other parts of the country, but in Los Angeles popular leftists won leadership of a number of locals.

ILGWU IN LOS ANGELES

In Los Angeles, the industry followed similar patterns to those in New York City. After a militant strike in

Aftermath of the Triangle Shirtwaist Company fire of March 25, 1911, in which 146 workers died, many of them young women who, unable to escape, plunged to their deaths to the streets below. One of the worst industrial accidents in American history, the tragedy led to the passage of stringent fire safety laws. *(Brown Brothers)*

1919, ILGWU Local 52 made its presence felt within the burgeoning Los Angeles garment industry. By 1924, Los Angeles was the United States' fourth leading garment manufacturing center. One of the few women in ILGWU leadership, Vice President Molly Friedman, criticized the union for not actively recruiting the 3,000 mainly Jewish and Latina women workers. Friedman's organizing plan did not take effect until 1933 when Rose Pesotta, an ILGWU organizer, was allowed to undertake a major campaign in Los Angeles. Her 1933 successes enabled Pesotta to convince the International leadership to back an even more impressive organizing effort in 1941 against the formidable Mode of Day Company.

THE COLD WAR ERA

The Cold War era led to a fierce red-baiting campaign in many areas of U.S. society, including the trade union movement. Many union leaders were intent on ousting leftists and militants from key positions. The ILGWU was no exception. All officers within the trade unions were to sign a non-Communist disclaimer affidavit as part of the 1947 Taft-Hartley Law. Those who refused were to be removed from office in order for the union to receive certification from the National Labor Relations Board. The ILGWU leadership began a campaign to ensure that all officers sign the affidavit or resign. By 1950, the leadership had successfully removed all radical threats to its position throughout the union, including those in Los Angeles.

GLOBALIZATION OF GARMENT PRODUCTION

The 1960s to the 1980s were marked by increasing globalization as companies moved offshore to escape unionization, higher wages, and better benefits. By the late 1980s and early 1990s, owing to political instability in many of these countries, the garment industry began to bring the Third World home by providing jobs for undocumented workers and recreating the sweatshops of the nineteenth and early twentieth centuries. The most shocking and extreme situation occurred in 1995 in El Monte, California, when seventy-two Thai garment workers were discovered locked up in virtual slavery. These workers, defended by the Asian Pacific Legal Center and the union, later won millions of dollars in back wages. Large retailers such as Bloomingdale's, Nordstrom, Neiman-Marcus, and Disney were found to have sold clothes made by these workers.

By the early 1990s, 4,500 of Los Angeles's 5,000 garment shops were sweatshops; 2,000 of New York's 6,000 garment shops were sweatshops; and scores of others existed throughout the United States. These companies, contractors for the giant retailers and manufacturers, such as Guess, flagrantly violated labor laws involving minimum wage, overtime, and industrial homework, cheating workers out of hundreds of thousands of dollars. During the Clinton administration, Secretary of Labor Robert Reich found that violations of minimum wage and overtime laws were pervasive throughout the garment industry.

Since sweatshops were difficult to organize, and many garment industries had moved offshore, ILGWU membership declined from 457,517 to 125,000 by 1995. In 1995, the ILGWU joined with two other garment workers unions to form the Union of Needletrades Industrial and Textile Employees (UNITE). The new union, considerably strengthened with 300,000 members and with a newly elected militant and progressive leadership, went on to become a leader in innovative and bold organizing efforts. UNITE spearheaded many campaigns to enlist federal legislation and enforcement against sweatshop and garment industry labor law violations.

In 1996, 128 of the nation's largest retailers and manufacturers signed an agreement to comply with existing labor laws and to permit federal monitoring of domestic and offshore factories. Investigations revealed that some of the biggest names in entertainment and fashion were involved in contracting out their products to domestic sweatshops employing undocumented workers, including children. In addition, these same personalities were indirectly involved in offshore sweatshop production. Some embarrassedly joined public efforts to eradicate global sweatshop labor, but others were recalcitrant in their refusal to acknowledge their culpability in endorsing such products. UNITE, working with young socially aware entertainers, such as Rage Against the Machine, publicized the injustices in the garment industry. The union set up a special Sweatshop Watch unit to publicize the conditions in the garment industry in order to help pass state and federal legislation that would force retailers and manufacturers to comply with existing labor laws and to outlaw sweatshops.

COMMON THREADS

Reminiscent of the Women's Trade Union League, Common Threads was developed by professional women to publicize both sweatshop abuse and the relationship between garment workers and consumers. Working with UNITE, Common Threads developed successful campaigns against giants such as Guess, which led to a federal investigation and efforts to promote stricter guidelines regarding garment employment. Based on a grant from the California Council for the Humanities and UNITE, Common Threads installed nine storefront depictions of the history of the garment industry and union and offered tours and lectures of key moments in the union's history. The exhibit remained in place for one year, despite the strong opposition of the fashion and apparel industries.

THE SMITHSONIAN INSTITUTION SWEATSHOP EXHIBIT

In 1997, the Smithsonian Institution, in conjunction with a grant from UNITE and the National Retail Federation, documented the history of American sweatshops from 1820 to 1997. The exhibit was scheduled to travel throughout the United States, but the powerful retailers' and manufacturers' associations lobbied so hard against it that museums refused to allow it to be installed. One exception was the Museum of Tolerance in Los Angeles, which, despite threats of funding loss, courageously provided a home for the traveling exhibit.

TEAMX

In a unique move to illustrate how sweat-free conditions can produce quality garments, teamX Inc., a Los Angeles-based employee-owned manufacturer was created in 2001. teamX is fully represented by UNITE and is modeled upon the highly successful Mondragon Industrial Cooperative in the Basque Region of Spain. teamX's labor–management and manufacturing system is in the forefront of the garment industry. Their line of clothing, SweatX, is geared to the college market. Students and professors have organized campaigns at their campuses to ensure that their student stores purchase solely union-made garments, such as SweatX.

CONCLUSION

From its inception until the 1970s, the ILGWU was controlled by a leadership that promoted industry stability and labor–management accord. However, a more radical faction consistently argued against this philosophy and for rank-and-file involvement to increase workers' understanding of class struggle. In the 1980s, faced with decreasing membership and the reappearance of sweatshops, a more radical ILGWU leadership pioneered creative and bold organizing campaigns, which set an example for the entire labor movement. One of the key elements in their philosophy was the necessity to organize documented and undocumented immigrant workers.

In 1995, the ILGWU merged with two other unions to form the 300,000-member UNITE, emerging as one of the most progressive unions in the United States. UNITE built labor–community coalitions, spearheaded efforts to outlaw sweatshops, sponsored a worker-owned garment collective, fought for immigrant amnesty, and continued to creatively organize workers throughout the United States. Through its efforts, UNITE linked labor with other social movements for positive social change, bringing more equity within the United States.

Myrna Cherkoss Donahoe

BIBLIOGRAPHY

Danish, Max D. *The World of David Dubinsky.* Cleveland: World, 1957.

Laslett, John, and Mary Tyler. *The ILGWU in Los Angeles, 1907–1988.* Inglewood, CA: Ten Star, 1989.

Levine, Louis. *The Women's Garment Workers: A History of the International Ladies' Garment Workers' Union.* New York: B.W. Huebsch, 1924.

Louie, Miriam Ching Yoon. *Sweatshop Warriors: Immigrant Women Workers Take on the Global Factory.* Boston: South End, 2002.

Milkman, Ruth, and Kent Wong, eds. *Voices from the Front Lines: Organizing Immigrant Workers in Los Angeles.* Translated by Luis Escala Rabadan. Los Angeles: Center for Labor Research and Education, UCLA, 2000.

Pesotta, Rose. *Bread upon the Waters.* New York: Dodd, Mead, 1944.

Ross, Andrew, ed. *No Sweat: Fashion, Free Trade, and the Rights of Garment Workers.* New York and London: Verso, 1997.

Stein, Leon. *The Triangle Fire.* Philadelphia: J.B. Lippincott, 1962.

Tax, Meredith. *The Rising of the Women: Feminist Solidarity and Class Conflict, 1880–1917.* New York: Monthly Review, 1980.

The 1920s were dark days for the American labor movement. The decade began as the strike wave of 1919 was brutally suppressed and many local unions were effectively shattered. The Palmer Raids of the following year further stigmatized organized labor with the taint of radicalism and anarchism. Throughout the decade, seemingly every major institution of American life—the police, the courts, the federal government—allied to keep the "Open Shop" free from unionization. During the decade, union membership fell almost a third, from just over 5 million members in 1920 to 3.4 million in 1929. Whereas 19.4 percent of nonagricultural workers were union members at the start of the decade, just 10.2 percent were unionized in 1929. The number of strikes plummeted from 3,630 in 1919 to just 921 in 1929. Those contemporary observers who paid much attention to organized labor deemed it largely irrelevant. As President Calvin Coolidge observed in a January 1924 speech before the American Society of Newspaper Editors, "The chief business of America is business."

The pro-business, staunch individualist outlook was shared by all three Republican presidents during the decade and by many workers as well. Indeed, given the material advances during the decade, there was ample reason for optimism in the American working class. Between 1923 and 1928, average yearly wages increased 9.1 percent, from $1,285 to $1,405. The total annual amount paid in wages and salaries climbed from $36.4 billion in 1922 to $57.4 billion in 1929. To be sure, the increase paled in comparison to the climb in dividends, which more than doubled in the same period, from $3 billion to $6.3 billion. Although real wages inched up just 2 percent during the decade, more American workers were participating in the consumer economy thanks to the rapid spread of the installment plan. Although car and home ownership were still beyond the reach of many workers, radios, refrigerators, and other appliances became more commonplace in workers' homes in the 1920s. "Working men don't need unions nowadays," one Muncie, Indiana, businessman told Robert and Helen Merrell Lynd in their classic study of 1920s America, *Middletown: A Study in Modern American Culture*, adding, "We are much more in danger of coddling the working men than abusing them. Working people are just as well off now as they can possibly be except for things which are in the nature of industry and cannot be helped."

TRENDS IN MANUFACTURING JOBS AND EMPLOYMENT

The economic expansion of the 1920s owed much to the advances in productivity that transformed the American workplace in the first part of the century. As it had since the antebellum era, industrialization after the turn of the century emphasized machine production, technological advances, and unskilled labor in manufacturing goods; however, manufacturing work after 1900 was increasingly directed toward the making of durable goods for the consumer market. The most obvious symbol of the new consumer age in manufacturing was also its dynamic sector: the automobile industry. Nothing demonstrated the changing nature of manufacturing jobs in the twentieth century better than the assembly-line production at Henry Ford's Highland Park plant, opened in the Detroit suburb in 1909 to produce the Model T.

CONSUMERISM

Ford's factory put into practice the scientific management principles of Frederick Winslow Taylor, the most influential industrial engineer of the early twentieth century. Taylor preached simplification, routinization, and deskilling in the workplace. The use of standardized and interchangeable parts further increased worker productivity, as did the introduction of the assembly line. For workers, the assembly line represented not just technological innovation, but dehumanization as well: the exhausting pace of work led to a 380-percent turnover at Highland Park by 1913. To counter the problem, Ford announced a Five Dollar Day—actually, a base rate of $2.34 with additional incentive pay—to keep workers at the helm. Thousands stormed Ford's employment office in the wake of the announcement, and other automobile manufacturers were forced to follow suit. The establishment of high wage rates in the industry allowed autoworkers to begin participating in the mass consumer economy of the 1920s. Yet the wages of the auto industry did not become the norm across the economy. One survey showed that 47 percent of Ford workers owned cars in the 1920s, while just 26 percent of workers in San Francisco and 3 percent of unskilled Chicago laborers could make a similar claim.

UNEMPLOYMENT

As a result of these trends, productivity in the 1920s increased 72 percent in the manufacturing sector, 41 percent in mining, and 33 percent among the nation's railroad lines. Despite these impressive statistics, in the eyes of many employers, workers remained as interchangeable as the parts they installed on the assembly line. Since no federal agency collected unemployment figures until legislation directed the Bureau of Labor Statistics to do so in July 1930, estimates of jobless workers varied widely. Some social scientists calculated that unemployment never dipped below 10 percent, even during the economic expansion of 1923 to early 1929. Even optimistic observers admitted that the jobless rate stayed well above 5 percent during the decade, even during the boom years. More accurate studies were conducted by local observers and give a more revealing snapshot of the era. A Wharton School survey in April 1929 found that 10.4 percent of Philadelphia's workers were out of a job. But a simple measure of joblessness in itself could be misleading. A 1929 survey conducted in Buffalo, New York, showed that the city had a jobless rate of 10 percent, with another 6.5 percent of respondents working only part-time. Most telling of all, the Lynds' study of Muncie, Illinois, revealed that only 38 percent of wage earners in working-class families had steady work during a nine-month survey period in 1924.

LABOR IN THE WAKE OF THE GREAT WAR

In contrast to the erratic nature of the 1920s economy, American workers had enjoyed boom times during World War I. The turbulence in Europe interrupted immigration and led to a labor shortage. With orders for war materiel pouring in, employers had little choice but to raise wages. Workers also took the incentive to join labor unions during the war; for many unskilled workers, it was their first experience with organized labor, which had traditionally been confined to the ranks of craft unions. Between 1914 and 1918, membership in the American Federation of Labor (AFL) expanded from 2 million to 3.2 million.

END OF THE PROGRESSIVE ERA

This massive wave of organizing took place with substantial support from the federal government, which marked a significant policy shift from preceding generations. President William Howard Taft—later a notoriously antilabor Supreme Court chief justice—approved the creation of the Department of Labor during the lame-duck days of his administration in March 1913. Under President Woodrow Wilson, the Department expanded its scope to include a special mediation commission to craft wartime labor policies. The committee recommended that workers have the right to bargain collectively through independent labor unions; that the government set up a grievance board to mediate disputes between management and labor; and that the eight-hour day become standardized, with overtime pay beyond eight hours.

In April 1918, the War Labor Board (WLB)—with five representatives from labor's ranks, five from the employer's ranks, and two government officials—was established to implement these policies. By the end of World War I in November 1918, the WLB had mediated 1,100 labor disputes. Under the WLB, the federal government had reached into industrial affairs on an unprecedented scale. In mandating that employers pay overtime and recognize independent labor unions under collective bargaining agreements, the WLB was the pinnacle of Progressive Era labor reforms.

Events at war's end demonstrated just how fragile these gains were; indeed, the labor movement would have to wait another generation for the federal government to become permanently enmeshed in labor relations. Most employers had fought against the WLB's agenda from the start and commenced a new round of attacks on the agency after the Armistice. Among their charges were complaints that the WLB's presence in industrial relations had fostered unnecessary agitation among labor's ranks. Employers had enjoyed the federal government's support in labor disputes almost without exception up to the war, and they demanded a return to the pre-Progressive Era status quo. After lobbying by the National Manufac-

During the strike wave of 1919, Philadelphia police club demonstrators. Labor conflicts often provoked state-sponsored violence in the late nineteenth and early twentieth centuries. *(Brown Brothers)*

turers Association, the National Metal Trades Association, and other employers' groups, the WLB was disbanded by the end of 1918. Contrary to the business lobbyists' claims, the disappearance of the WLB did everything but bring calm to industrial relations. By the end of 1919, some 4.1 million workers took part in 3,630 strikes.

THE 1919 STRIKE WAVE

One of the largest strikes took place in Seattle, where shipyard workers walked off the job in January 1919. Within two weeks, about 25,000 other Seattle workers pledged their support in a general strike. From February 6 to 11, 1919, a General Strike Committee operated community kitchens, safety patrols, and other basic services, essentially running the city on the strikers' terms. Outraged local business leaders demanded state and federal intervention, by military force if necessary. Fortunately, federal mediators finally ended the strike without violence, although the initial demands of the shipyard workers were never resolved.

The peaceful end to the Seattle General Strike was an exception in one of the most violent years in American history. Typical of the unrest was the strike at the Willys-Overland automobile operations in Toledo, Ohio. Confronting a postwar slump, the city's largest

employer announced wage cuts early in 1919 that threatened to take away much of the wage gains made during the war. On May 5, 1919, more than half of the workforce walked out of the company's main plant, and the strike quickly spread to some of the city's other major factories. Willys-Overland management immediately got an injunction to limit picketing around the plant, and the business community banded together through the Merchants and Manufacturers Association. Typical of the Association's propaganda was a full-page advertisement in the May 9 edition of the *Toledo Blade* that declared, "We believe the great majority of these men and women, who have been forced out of employment are not in sympathy with the radical arbitrary demands of their self-appointed leaders . . . The vast majority of Toledoans are loyal, fair, and square. They will not stand for injustices, violence, disloyalty, or Bolshevism." In support of the injunction, the mayor deputized dozens of U.S. Army troops awaiting demobilization as deputy-soldiers to patrol the streets. After a deputy-soldier started an argument with local residents on June 4, a squadron of troops stormed into one neighborhood to put down an incipient riot. As the crowd fled, two were shot dead and nineteen others were injured by the soldiers. The strike dissipated in the wake of the violence, and unions for production workers at the Willys-Overland plant were obliterated for another seventeen years.

An equally dramatic conclusion followed the Boston Police Strike, which commenced on September 9, 1919. After the police commissioner, mayor, and governor refused to recognize a police officers' union and fired some of its leaders, three-fourths of the department declared a strike. After rioting broke out, Governor Calvin Coolidge sent the state militia in to quell the violence and crush the strike. Five citizens were killed by the militia and twenty others were critically wounded. Coolidge was unrelenting in his hostility toward the union and ultimately barred any of the strikers from being rehired. For his participation in putting down the strike, Coolidge was selected as the vice-presidential nominee by the Republican Party in 1920; he advanced to the presidency in 1923 upon the death of President Warren G. Harding. Elected to the presidency in his own right in 1924, Coolidge maintained his hostile stance toward labor throughout his term in office, which ended in March 1929.

THE RED SCARE AND PALMER RAIDS

Coolidge, like the other Republican presidents who served during the decade, was a staunch individualist who believed that the government had little place in labor relations aside from intervening to break strikes in the name of public safety and economic progress. The height of the government's direct efforts to break up left-wing labor organizations came with the Red Scare and Palmer Raids of 1919–1920. Ostensibly, the action was designed to root radicals and Anarchists out of American society; yet the effects on the labor movement were devastating.

After terrorists sent a series of bombs to government officials and business leaders during April–June 1919, Attorney General A. Mitchell Palmer ordered a general roundup of suspected Communists and Anarchists. The Palmer Raids, which took about 6,000 suspects into custody, began in November 1919 and lasted until March 1920. Spurred on by the Red Scare, vigilante groups conducted a campaign against some labor unions, including the Industrial Workers of the World (IWW). Along with such direct violence, twenty states passed criminal syndicalist laws that hounded the IWW out of existence. Typically, the laws made it a crime to advocate labor reform through illegal or violent acts, which the IWW had done. Having reached its peak of membership and influence in 1917, by 1924 the IWW had ceased to function as a force in the labor movement. The postwar Red Scare itself petered out in 1920 after the attorney general—perhaps hoping to raise his profile for a presidential run—predicted massive unrest on May Day.

When the day passed without incident, fears of a radical threat to American society quickly dissipated. Although the embarrassment effectively ended Palmer's political career, his actions had accomplished much of what employers had sought in the immediate postwar era. Labor unions were branded as radical and un-American; many labor officials had been jailed or deported; and many industrial unions had been wiped out of existence.

THE AFL IN THE 1920S

By 1920, the number of workers in unions had fallen back to its pre-World War I level. As before the war, most of them were concentrated among skilled craft unions in the American Federation of Labor (AFL). Yet the AFL was a weak advocate for the labor movement during the decade. On a national level, the AFL was debilitated not only by the hostile labor climate in general but by jurisdictional disputes among its member unions as well. A lack of creative, visionary leadership also hampered the organization's efforts. Longtime AFL president Samuel Gompers, who died in 1924, governed the body with his "pure and simple" vision of unionism. In Gompers's view, the AFL was best served by staying out of partisan politics, keeping the government out of labor relations, and focusing on the organization of skilled workers.

William R. Green, who succeeded Gompers in 1924, shared this conservative approach. Green valued consensus and conciliation over direct conflict, which put the AFL at a disadvantage as employers broke one local union after another in the 1920s. He was also unable to calm the factional storms that broke out whenever one AFL member union tried to poach members from another AFL union. Like Gompers, Green concentrated on keeping skilled craft workers as the base of the AFL, a tactic that eventually led to the formation of the rival Congress of Industrial Organizations for unskilled workers in 1935.

The constituent unions of the AFL varied widely in the political and economic power they exerted. The most powerful AFL union, the United Brotherhood of Carpenters, had a steady membership throughout the decade, with 322,000 members in 1929. Its president, William L. Hutcheson, stamped out rival organizing attempts from other AFL unions early on in the decade. Despite his potential for serving as a model for other union leaders, Hutcheson embodied the conser-

WILLIAM GREEN (1873–1952)

An important twentieth-century labor leader, William Green served as a major official in the United Mine Workers of America (UMWA) and as president of the American Federation of Labor (AFL). The son of a Welsh immigrant miner, Green was born in Coshocton, Ohio. He completed eight years of education and developed a lifelong, unshakeable commitment to evangelical Christianity. At the age of seventeen, Green began a twenty-one year stint as a miner. He married Jenny Mobley and raised six children. By 1891, he was an active member of the UMWA and served in a variety of local union offices.

The foundations of his union career were based on Christian ideals combined with an unyielding commitment to the efficacy of union-management cooperation. Eventually, his union activities took him out of the mines to leadership roles in the UMWA's national organization. He also served two terms as an Ohio state senator from 1910 to 1914. In both capacities, he was outspoken about his conviction to build partnerships with industrial capital that would benefit both sides.

In 1912, Green was elected national secretary-treasurer of the UMWA and then became a member of the AFL's executive council. During these years, he worked closely with UMWA president John L. Lewis. With the death of long-time AFL president Samuel Gompers in 1924, Green emerged as a compromise candidate and was elected president that year.

As AFL president, Green understood the conservative nature of the organization. Though personally committed to industrial unionism and social action, Green followed the lead of conservative craft unionists. He never developed a role as a social justice crusader. Instead, he used the presidency as a forum to push his beliefs that labor and management needed to form a close working relationship that would result in great benefits for all. He combined this strategy with a deep-seated belief in free enterprise, unconditional patriotism, and a rabid hatred of all forms of radicalism, especially communism.

When New Deal legislation provided the catalyst for major organizing drives in the 1930s, Green failed to exercise the necessary leadership. Still believing that employers would welcome unions, he hesitated to initiate industrial union drives to organize the mass production industries. This failure led to a major split between Green and Lewis and between industrial union advocates and AFL leadership. In 1937, several of these leaders separated from the AFL to form the Congress of Industrial Organizations.

Green did use supportive New Deal legislation and the protection of the World War II years to expand AFL membership. At the end of the war, with AFL membership at ten million, Green cultivated a true partnership with government and business but was devastated by consistent employer resistance and the Taft-Hartley Act (1947). By this time, AFL leaders gradually began to reassign Green's duties to future president George Meany. Green continued in office until his death in 1952.

R. David Myers

vative outlook that characterized the AFL's history. Having witnessed the destruction of ideological-minded union leaders countless times, Hutcheson embodied the pure and simple unionism of the Gompers era. At least Hutcheson could claim to have a degree of influence with the White House; he supported each of the Republican administrations and in turn was said to have turned down several offers to become the secretary of labor.

The most dynamic leadership in the AFL came from the president of the United Mine Workers of America (UMW), John L. Lewis. Although he had worked as a miner intermittently since his teenage years, Lewis's rise through the UMW's ranks began in 1910, when the thirty-year-old was elected president of a Panama, Illinois, local. He began serving as an AFL lobbyist in Springfield the following year and became an AFL vice-president in 1917. In 1920, when he assumed the presidency of the UMW, its membership base was already eroding from its wartime high of about 750,000 workers. As oil and gas challenged coal as sources of power and coal prices dropped, coal operators took advantage of the antilabor climate to attack the UMW in a seemingly endless series of confrontations.

Major strikes in 1922, 1923, and 1925–1926 set the tone for concession bargaining after 1928, when Lewis could no longer insist on a $7.50 a day wage in all the UMW's contracts. In some UMW districts, the daily wage rate dropped to $5.00—still better than the $1.50 nonunion coal operators received at the Pittsburgh Coal Company, which had violently mashed its UMW local in 1925—but the loss took away one-third of miners' wages nonetheless. By 1927, the UMW had fewer than 200,000 members.

TABLE 1. Labor Union Membership, 1920–1934

	Total Union Members	AFL-Affiliated Members
1920	5,034,000	4,079,000
1921	4,722,000	3,907,000
1922	3,950,000	3,196,000
1923	3,629,000	2,926,000
1924	3,549,000	2,866,000
1925	3,566,000	2,877,000
1926	3,592,000	2,804,000
1927	3,600,000	2,813,000
1928	3,567,000	2,896,000
1929	3,625,000	2,934,000
1930	3,632,000	2,961,000
1931	3,526,000	2,890,000
1932	3,226,000	2,532,000
1933	3,857,000	2,127,000
1934	3,728,000	3,045,000

Source: U.S. Bureau of the Census, *Historical Statistics of the United States: Colonial Times to 1970* (Washington, DC, 1975).

THE EMERGENCE OF THE AMERICAN PLAN

The election of Warren G. Harding to the White House in 1920 under the banner of a "Return to Normalcy" began twelve years of uninterrupted Republican Party rule of the White House. It also marked the end of the Progressive Era in American life; indeed, the private sector was much more active than the government in shaping the outlines of labor activity during the decade. Having reestablished the "Open Shop"—that is, a workplace rid of labor unions—employers were intent on keeping the status quo in the 1920s. Although many employers had openly participated in the orgy of violence in 1919, most of their efforts throughout the decade took a more subtle approach. By 1921, these efforts to use scientific management, personnel reforms, and welfare measures had taken shape under the rubric of "The American Plan," a term first publicized by the National Association of Manufacturers and the National Chamber of Commerce in 1921.

SCIENTIFIC MANAGEMENT AND PERSONNEL MANAGEMENT

One aspect of the American Plan encouraged scientific and personnel management innovations to control the workplace and increase productivity. Whereas Henry Ford had concentrated largely on the principles of Taylorism in his operations, the dominant management philosophy in the 1920s articulated the need to study human relationships in the workplace, not just

technological and mechanical improvements. The most significant example of this new outlook took place with a series of experiments conducted at Western Electric's (WE) Hawthorne Works from 1924 to 1933. Located in the western Chicago suburb of Cicero, Illinois, the Hawthorne plant made telephones and other electrical devices for WE. With a workforce that numbered up to 30,000 employees, the Hawthorne Works was the Chicago area's largest employer.

In the most widely publicized experiment, a study conducted by George Elton Mayo beginning in April 1928, a research group set up thirteen trials with five women from the assembly-line. Altering the workroom's illumination, the rest periods granted to workers, and the length of the working day and week, the researchers came to a surprising conclusion: there was no specific correlation between the changes made in the workplace and the level of worker productivity, which increased a total of 46 percent, even when working conditions were made measurably worse. Searching for a reason to explain this phenomenon, the researchers concluded that increased participation by workers in managerial decisions was more important than incentive pay schemes or physical conditions in improving output. WE implemented this conclusion by conducting over 10,300 interviews with its employees to discuss their opinions about their work environment in the hope of spurring company-wide productivity increases.

COMPANY UNIONS AND WELFARE CAPITALISM

Many employers cited these conclusions to demonstrate the importance of keeping the Open Shop. If a close relationship between employer and employee was the key to increased productivity and worker's satisfaction, then labor unions represented a threat to both these goals. Along these lines, many employers set up company unions to encourage workers to talk about efficiency, plant safety, and grievances with management. Company unions, sometimes called employee representation plans, were always controlled by management; the typical worker could vote for a representative to the union but otherwise had no say in its conduct. By 1928, over 1.5 million employees were enrolled in 399 company unions, and most of them worked for large-scale corporations such as Procter & Gamble and International Harvester.

An equally important part of the American Plan took the form of welfare capitalism, a term that encompassed a wide range of employer-sponsored benefits programs to win worker loyalty. At the Hawthorne Works, WE offered on-site medical care, a stock-ownership plan, after-hours educational courses, and sick benefits and vacation time that depended on the employee's length of service. WE also sponsored company sports teams and other social events for its employees and, like other employers, occasionally supported community institutions such as the YMCA or local churches through fund drives. Nationwide, a small but growing number of corporations sponsored a significant level of welfare capitalist programs in the 1920s; the programs were more common among large employers with secure market positions and less pressure to cut wages and costs.

Although the Hawthorne Works was invoked as the preeminent example of corporate America's beneficial influence on working-class life in the 1920s, welfare capitalist measures could take a more overtly paternalistic and anti-union form. The most notorious examples came from the textile towns of the North Carolina Piedmont region, where manufacturers had relocated from the late nineteenth century to avoid unionized workforces in New England. Everywhere in the Southern textile towns—from the company-owned housing to the company-controlled school to the company-run general store—workers were reminded of their employers' power. Employers claimed to keep the cost of living down by offering workers housing at half price, but workers were thrown out of their housing if they were suspected of supporting unions—or if they lost their jobs for any reason at all

The company-endowed and -operated schools also represented a bad bargain for workers. Poorly equipped and staffed, the typical mill school offered only eight grades, and children were routinely pulled from class to work during times of labor shortages. Company-run stores, where some workers, paid in company scrip, were forced to shop, also offered little real value for the mill hands. Although company stores typically offered credit to mill workers, the snare of debt trapped workers even further in poverty. If the company store was the only place to shop in town, workers were sure to pay a higher price for what they bought. Resentment against all of these factors contributed to a series of textile strikes in the Piedmont region in 1929 and 1930; all of them were crushed, typically with outright violence. With a wage rate of twenty-seven cents an hour for common labor in 1928—in contrast to the forty-nine cents that laborers in the Mid-Atlantic region earned—workers in the textile region remained among the most economically deprived in the country.

THE GREAT MIGRATION

While the labor movement faltered and the business community pressed its advantage in the 1920s, demographic trends proved equally important to the future of working-class life in America. The steady flow of European immigration was stopped by World War I, and restrictive immigration laws enacted in the 1920s kept the flow down to extremely low levels. Given the labor shortage induced by the war, a massive wave of internal migration of African Americans from the rural South took place to keep America's Northern industries running. Low cotton prices and the destruction of cotton crops by boll weevil attacks had already displaced thousands of agricultural workers during the war, and the repressive legal and social structure of the South served as an additional inducement to leave the region. From 1915 to 1920 at least 400,000 African Americans left for the North, and as many as one million joined them in the following decade in a movement known as the Great Migration. Chicago's African-American population jumped from 110,00 to 234,000 in the 1920s, and Detroit's increased from 6,000 on the eve of World War I to 120,000 in 1930.

The higher wages and less pervasive legal and social discrimination made the North "The Promised Land" to many of the migrants; yet restrictive covenants in housing and hiring practices that kept them from gaining higher wage jobs continued to make life a struggle for working-class African Americans. And although the direct violence of the Ku Klux Klan was not nearly as prevalent in the North as in the South, race riots took the lives of forty-nine victims in East St. Louis in 1917 and thirty-eight in Chicago in 1919. In East St. Louis, the riots were spurred by antagonism over the use of African-American workers as strikebreakers, a common tactic among anti-union Northern employers. Given the history of discrimination against African-American workers, racial tension proved to be a major stumbling block in the building of industrial unions in the 1930s.

ONSET OF THE GREAT DEPRESSION

Between the stock market crash in October 1929 and the end of Herbert Hoover's term as president in March 1933, the American economy seemed to be in freefall. Unemployment—never accurately measured in the previous decade but estimated by some officials to be between 3.2 and 5 percent in 1929—climbed to

25 percent in 1932. In some cities, the rate hit unimaginable heights: one-third of New Yorkers were without a job, as were half of Detroit's workers, 40 percent of Chicagoans, and 80 percent of Toledoans. U.S. Steel, one of the nation's largest corporations, had a workforce of zero full-time workers in 1933, in contrast to its workforce of about 225,000 workers in 1929.

The welfare capitalist measures of the 1920s mostly fell by the wayside after 1929, although some employers started food and clothing banks for their laid-off employees. Still others inaugurated part-time work schedules to spread wages around, or allowed employees to grow vegetables on unoccupied company land parcels. Public relief efforts were somewhat better organized but equally ineffective after the first two years of the Depression. As *Fortune* reported in a September 1932 expose under the scathing title "No-One Has Starved," local relief agencies had already buckled under the economic collapse: "Food only, in most cases, is provided and little enough of that. Rents are seldom paid. Shoes and clothing are given in rare instances only. Money for doctors and dentists is not to be had."

President Hoover appointed federal commissions to study the problem but stood by his claim that voluntary relief efforts would carry the nation through the crisis. Hoover's integrity took a final blow in a conflict with the Bonus Expeditionary Army on July 28, 1932. About 20,000 Bonus Marchers had come to the capital to demand the immediate payment of a bonus promised to veterans of World War I set to be paid in 1945. Hoover, seeing a radical insurrection unfolding, ordered troops to oust the protesters, who had encamped in various federal buildings and landed in the Anacostia section of Washington, D.C. Two veterans were killed in the ensuing conflict, and one infant later died of his injuries. Images of the burning Bonus Army camps revolted many Americans, who saw Hoover as a callous tyrant. His reputation never recovered from the incident.

In the end, Hoover's only substantial relief efforts came through the Reconstruction Finance Corporation (RFC), which made money available to states to support work-relief programs in 1932. Criticized as a "millionaires' dole," the RFC was a minimal response to the unfolding economic tragedy. In one last bid for working-class support as he started his reelection bid, Hoover even claimed credit for passage of the Norris-LaGuardia Anti-Injunction Act of 1932, legislation that he had long opposed. In addition to outlawing "yellow dog" contracts forbidding union membership in the workforce, the act severely limited the use of federal injunctions to break up strikes. It also freed union leaders from liability for damaging acts carried out by union members, unless such acts had been advocated by union leadership.

The Norris-LaGuardia Act was the only significant piece of legislation to favor the labor movement under the twelve years of Republican rule, and few were fooled by Hoover's last-minute capitulation to the Act's passage. In November 1932, Hoover lost his reelection bid when he retained less than 40 percent of the popular vote. In his place, New York governor Franklin Delano Roosevelt ended twelve years of Republican rule as he took over the White House.

THE PIVOTAL YEAR 1934

Throughout the 1920s, successive Republican administrations had scaled back or eliminated Progressive Era reforms that had improved working conditions while conservative federal courts issued injunctions to break strikes. As a result of Roosevelt's New Deal programs, the federal government reversed both of these trends by taking itself into labor relations on an unprecedented scale. For the labor movement, the most important act of Roosevelt's first year in office was the National Industrial Recovery Act (NIRA), which he signed into law on June 16, 1933.

The NIRA established a code of fair competition supervised by the National Recovery Administration (NRA) and temporarily suspended antitrust rules, which allowed businesses to plan production on an industrywide basis. In exchange for this favor, the NRA mandated a minimum wage, to be set by industry, and a forty-hour maximum work week. From the start, the NRA's work was roundly criticized. As they had during World War I, most business leaders resented the government's involvement in the private sector. Other critics argued that the NRA's reach did not go far enough in fundamentally restructuring the economy. Still others were simply baffled by the complex bureaucracy that the creation of the NRA entailed.

Nothing symbolized the controversy and confusion over the NIRA better than its Section 7(a). The section declared "That employees shall have the right to organize and bargain collectively through representatives of their own choosing, and be free from interference" by their employers in such efforts. The section also prohibited employers from forcing their workers to join company-controlled unions or from firing them for joining independent labor unions. Yet the NIRA did not specify penalties against employers for failing to follow Section 7(a); nor did it set up an administration to oversee the implementation of the article. Thus, while Section 7(a) seemed to place the weight of the government behind unionization, it did little to clarify how workers could actually organize labor unions. In the wake of the NIRA's passage, a new wave of labor unrest swept the country as business and labor tested the real impact of Section 7(a) in the work place.

THE AUTO-LITE STRIKE

The strike at the Auto-Lite factory in Toledo, Ohio, was one of the first to test the actual meaning of Section 7(a). A small group of workers at the auto parts plant had struck for union recognition in late February 1934, an action that made little headway with the company's staunchly anti-union management. On April 13, 1934, the majority of the plant's workers walked off the job again, with union recognition at the top of their list of demands. The strike quickly turned into a mass movement in the city, as four other major plants were also shut down by strikes. With thousands of strikers and their supporters gathering at the Auto-Lite plant throughout May 1934, the company armed its guards with machine guns and tear gas in preparation for an assault, even as it refused to bargain with the union.

After someone in the factory threw a steel bracket at striker Alma Hahn on May 23, 1934, a riot erupted among the 10,000 protesters. Four days of unrest, including the shooting deaths of one striker and one strike supporter, were finally put down by about 1,350 National Guardsmen; about two hundred others were injured. When Governor George White refused the company's request to forcibly reopen the plant, Auto-Lite's management finally agreed to recognize the union. With a five-cent increase in wages and a minimum wage set at thirty-five cents, the plant reopened on June 5, 1934, with AFL Local 18384 as the recognized bargaining agent for the factory's workers. The following year, after the establishment of the Congress of Industrial Organizations, Local 18384 became Local 12 of the United Auto Workers union.

THE TEAMSTERS' STRIKE

Workers in Minneapolis also tested the limits of the NIRA in 1934. After Teamsters organizer Ray Dunne led a successful strike by coal truck drivers in early February 1934, Local 574 signed up between 2,000 and 3,000 members and demanded union recognition, a wage hike, and overtime pay from employers. The conflict quickly went beyond the collective bar-

gaining table, however, as the anti-union Citizens' Alliance (CA) jumped into the fray. Declaring the Teamsters' action a bid to radicalize the city's working classes, the CA began arming its members for a violent confrontation. A series of battles between strikers and the CA at the city's public market on May 21–22 left two CA members dead. Under pressure from Governor Floyd Olson, who was sympathetic to the strikers, the employers' group signed an agreement to abide by Section 7(a) on May 25. The truce was short-lived as the CA broke its agreement just weeks later. On July 16, 1934, the Teamsters went out on strike again.

The second strike turned into a more protracted affair, lasting thirty-six days. Crowds of up to 100,000 union supporters poured into Minneapolis, and another violent confrontation on July 20 left two strikers dead and fifty injured. The governor declared martial law on July 26. After intense efforts by Roosevelt's representatives, the CA finally was brought into an agreement with the Teamsters, which gained undisputed recognition as a bargaining agent and a minimum wage for its members. Within two years of the strike, Local 574 represented members at 500 Minneapolis-area companies, and the Citizens' Alliance was effectively broken as a power in the city.

THE MARITIME WORKERS' STRIKE

The biggest of the three urban strike waves culminated in a general strike in San Francisco from July 16–19, 1934. On May 9, 1934, International Longshoremen's Association workers along the entire Pacific Coast (with the exception of Los Angeles) went on strike under the leadership of Harry Bridges. As in the other strikes, higher wages, reduced hours, and more equitable hiring practices were among the reforms demanded by strikers, along with their chief goal, union recognition in collective bargaining. The Industrial Association of San Francisco (IASF), a coalition of anti-union employers, took the lead in battling the maritime workers' strike. In conjunction with the local police, the IASF disrupted a July 5 strike protest by shooting into the crowd; two strikers were killed and dozens more were shot on that "Bloody Thursday," as the day became known. Over the next few days, a grassroots call for a general strike began brewing among San Francisco's workers. On July 16, with the reluctant support of most of the city's labor leadership, at least 130,000 workers essentially shut down the city.

The strike was called off three days later after

Tanks prepare to roll in to break the general strike in San Francisco in 1934. Some 130,000 strikers—including trolley drivers, construction workers, teamsters, and bartenders—had brought the city to a virtual standstill for four days. *(© Underwood Photo Archives, Inc.)*

pressure from the Roosevelt administration, and the maritime workers later achieved most of their demands in a federal arbitration ruling. Not only had the union won recognition as a bargaining agent, it also gained joint control with employers over the hiring process, higher wages, and an overtime provision. By the end of 1934, 1,856 strikes involving 1,470,000 workers had taken place.

Together with a renewed series of textile strikes in the Carolinas, the major urban strikes of 1934 demonstrated the problems in administering the vague clause of Section 7(a) of the NIRA. The NIRA itself was soon deemed irrelevant, however, when it was declared unconstitutional by the U.S. Supreme Court

in 1935. In response, the Roosevelt administration fought to pass the National Labor Relations Act (often called the Wagner Act), which the president signed into law on July 5, 1935. Unlike the NIRA, the Wagner Act not only guaranteed the right of workers to bargain collectively, but specified how that right would be enforced. It also created the National Labor Relations Board to issue injunctions over unfair labor practices, to oversee union elections, and to hear grievances between labor and management. The most significant piece of legislation to govern labor relations in the twentieth century, the Wagner Act opened up a new era in the history of the American labor movement.

TABLE 2. Work Stoppages and Workers Involved, 1920–1934

	Work Stoppages	Workers Involved
1920	3,411	*
1921	2,385	
1922	1,112	
1923	1,553	
1924	1,249	
1925	1,301	
1926	1,035	
1927	707	330,000
1928	604	314,000
1929	921	289,000
1930	637	183,000
1931	810	342,000
1932	841	324,000
1933	1,695	1,170,000
1934	1,856	1,470,000

*U.S. Bureau of the Census does not provide data for "Workers Involved," 1920–1926.
Source: U.S. Bureau of the Census, *Historical Statistics of the United States: Colonial Times to 1970* (Washington, DC, 1975).

SUMMARY

Coming as it did between the Progressive Era and the New Deal, it is tempting to dismiss the period from 1920 to 1934 as a mere interruption in the growth of the American labor movement's economic, social, and political power in the first half of the twentieth century. At the time, however, the powerful alliance of business and government seemed permanent. The conservative—and at times, reactionary—coalition of antilabor interests found expression in the politics of "normalcy," the rhetoric of unswerving patriotism, and the implementation of the American Plan. The impact of these forces meant that the era passed without significant labor reform, regulation, or legislation. They also ensured that wage gains for workers lagged far behind what was necessary to generate a sustainable consumer economy. A mass production, mass consumption economy as envisioned by Henry Ford and others during the Progressive Era would take another generation to achieve.

The labor movement itself—torn apart by ideological dissension, power struggles, and an almost universally lethargic leadership—in large part failed to rise to the challenges presented by what was admittedly one of the most antilabor periods in American history. Ideologically minded unions such as the IWW were no match for the might of the government's Palmer Raids and Red Scare. At the other end of the spectrum, the AFL's inability to reach out to unskilled workers in favor of a narrow vision of craft unionism was increasingly out of step with the modern industrial landscape. The best that can be said for the labor movement's generally conservative leadership is that in endorsing material goals over more visionary strategies, workers were particularly disillusioned when their consumerist dreams vanished with the Great Depression. The devastation was so complete that the majority of the working class turned their loyalties to their unions and Roosevelt's administration with a decisiveness that made the weaknesses of the prior decade's labor movement all the more telling.

Timothy G. Borden

BIBLIOGRAPHY

Bernstein, Irving. *The Lean Years: A History of the American Worker, 1920–1933*. Boston: Houghton Mifflin, 1966.

———. *Turbulent Years: A History of the American Worker, 1933–1941*. Boston: Houghton Mifflin, 1971.

Borden, Timothy. " 'The Salvation of the Poles': Working-Class Ethnicity and Americanization Efforts During the Interwar Period in Toledo, Ohio." *Polish American Studies* 56 (Autumn 1999): 19–44.

Brandes, Stuart. *American Welfare Capitalism, 1880–1940*. Chicago: University of Chicago Press, 1976.

Brody, David. *Workers in Industrial America: Essays on the Twentieth-Century Struggle*. 2d. ed. New York: Oxford University Press, 1993.

Chandler, Alfred D., Jr. *Scale and Scope: The Dynamics of Industrial Capitalism*. Cambridge, MA: Harvard University Press, 1990.

Cohen, Lizabeth. *Making a New Deal: Industrial Workers in Chicago, 1919–1939*. Cambridge, UK: Cambridge University Press, 1990.

Denning, Michael. *The Cultural Front: The Laboring of American Culture in the Twentieth Century*. London: Verso, 1996.

Edsforth, Ronald. *Class Conflict and Cultural Consensus: The Making of a Mass Consumer Society in Flint, Michigan*. New Brunswick, NJ: Rutgers University Press, 1987.

Faue, Elizabeth. *Community of Suffering and Struggle: Women, Men, and the Labor Movement in Minneapolis, 1915–1945*. Chapel Hill: University of North Carolina Press, 1991.

Freeland, Robert. *The Struggle for Control of the Modern Corporation: Organizational Change at General Motors, 1924–1970*. New York: Cambridge University Press, 2000.

Gillespie, Richard. *Manufacturing Knowledge: A History of the Hawthorne Experiments*. Cambridge, UK: Cambridge University Press, 1991.

Hall, Jacquelyn Dowd, et al. *Like a Family: The Making of a Southern Cotton Mill World*. New York: W.W. Norton, 1987.

Hooker, Clarence. *Life in the Shadows of the Crystal Palace, 1910–1927*. Bowling Green, OH: Bowling Green State University Popular Press, 1997.

Korth, Philip A., and Margaret R. Beegle, eds. *I Remember Like Today: The Auto-Lite Strike of 1934.* East Lansing: Michigan State University Press, 1988.

Lemann, Nicholas. *The Promised Land: The Great Black Migration and How It Changed America.* New York: Alfred A. Knopf, 1991.

Lynd, Robert S., and Helen Merrell Lynd. *Middletown: A Study in Modern American Culture.* 1929. Reprint, New York: Harcourt Brace Jovanovich, 1957.

Nelson, Daniel. *Farm and Factory: Workers in the Midwest 1880–1990.* Bloomington: Indiana University Press, 1995.

Nelson, Daniel. *Shifting Fortunes: The Rise and Decline of American Labor, From the 1820s to the Present.* Chicago: Ivan R. Dee, 1997.

"No One Has Starved," *Fortune Magazine,* September 1832.

Rachleff, Peter. "The Dynamics of 'Americanization': The Croatian Fraternal Union Between the Wars, 1920s–1930s." In *Labor Histories: Class, Politics, and the Working-Class Experience,* ed. Eric Arensen, Julie Green, and Bruce Laurie, 340–362. Urbana: University of Illinois Press, 1998.

Salvatore, Nick. *Eugene V. Debs: Citizen and Socialist.* Urbana: University of Illinois Press, 1992.

Schatz, Ronald W. *The Electrical Workers: A History of Labor at General Electric and Westinghouse, 1923–1960.* Urbana: University of Illinois Press, 1983.

U.S. Bureau of the Census. *Historical Statistics of the United States: Colonial Times to 1970.* Washington, DC, 1975.

Zieger, Robert. *John L. Lewis: Labor Leader.* Boston: Twayne, 1988.

COMMUNIST MOVEMENT

The Communist Party of the United States has had a variety of names and a complex history. It had deep roots in, and a significant impact upon, the multicultural U.S. working class and the American labor movement, as well as the intellectual and cultural life of the United States. Animated by a revolutionary interpretation of the Socialist theories of Karl Marx, and by the example of the Russian Revolution of 1917 led by Vladimir Ilich Lenin, it was part of a powerful international movement that arose in 1919 under the banner of the Communist International.

As part of that international movement, American Communism came under the domination of the Russian Communist Party, which had succeeded in establishing a revolutionary regime in what had once been the Russian empire, ultimately renamed the Union of Soviet Socialist Republics (USSR) or Soviet Union. As this regime became increasingly bureaucratic and authoritarian, there were problematical consequences throughout the world Communist movement, including the movement in the United States. One result was a three-way split in the late 1920s, with an overwhelming majority remaining in the organization that became increasingly subordinate to the ruthless dictator of the USSR, Josef Stalin.

Consequently, the Communist mainstream became marked by a combination of revolutionary idealism and the extremely negative qualities associated with the Stalinist dictatorship. This problematical reality weakened both the Communist Party and the American Left; nonetheless, a number of American Communists made substantial contributions to struggles for social change.

SOURCES

The rise of Communism in the United States cannot be understood without examining its sources and origins in a number of American realities. From the end of the American Civil War (1861–1865) through the 1890s, the capitalist economic and social order of the United States experienced a tumultuous transition of industrialization, corporatization, and expansion that had a powerful impact on various segments of the population. The country became the world's leading manufacturer, and dramatic increases in economic productivity brought phenomenal increases in the wealth of the nation.

The benefits and expenses of this development were unevenly distributed. Although tremendous opportunities opened up for enterprising financiers and industrialists, many smaller businesses were destroyed, and small farmers throughout the country found their farms and livelihoods placed in jeopardy by the dynamics of the new structures of power and market forces unleashed in this "Gilded Age" transition.

The country's working-class majority felt multiple impacts. Many skilled trades were increasingly replaced with occupations requiring unskilled (and cheaper) labor—more easily dominated and more intensively exploited by employers. Efforts to organize unions for improvements of wages and working conditions were routinely attacked and broken by employers (with the often violent assistance of both private "police" and governmental authorities). Massive waves of immigration also undermined gains that workers were able to win—flooding the labor market with impoverished and often desperate laborers from a variety of different cultures, often suffering ethnic and racial discrimination, and pitted against each other by employers seeking to control their workforce more effectively.

The most intense discrimination was usually reserved for African Americans who had been betrayed by a post-Reconstruction compromise that denied them equal citizenship rights and generally kept them on the lowest rungs of the socioeconomic ladder. Institutional racism was enforced by state and local governments throughout the South, buttressed by lynchings and Ku Klux Klan terrorism; in the North, systematic discrimination in defense of white privilege was widespread. Women of all races were also subjected to second-class citizenship—denied the right to vote, undermined by multiple varieties of legal and economic discrimination, and subjected to various forms of sexual harassment and double standards.

There were yet other negative developments—notably, the pervasive corruption of politicians by wealthy interests, multiple business abuses, the systematic cheating of consumers by unscrupulous manufacturers, and the despoliation of urban areas, rural areas, and nature itself for the purpose of maximizing profits for the greedy few. Periodically, the "boom-and-bust" business cycle would generate devastating depressions, throwing millions of people out of work and plunging them into poverty. Many charged that the immense concentration of wealth into a few hands was changing the American republic from a democracy into a plutocracy (rule by the rich instead of rule by the people). And there were growing concerns that U.S. foreign policy was evolving in the direction of imperialism—economic expansionism beyond the borders of the United States in search of business profits—that would embroil the country in oppressive and exploitative relations with weaker peoples and draw the United States into dubious wars.

Intellectuals and artists were among the first to give powerful expression to such concerns. But these developments generated an array of dissident currents and protest movements, the most dramatic being the Populist movement of the late 1880s and the 1890s as well as a number of feminist and antiracist efforts. Especially important was the growth of a substantial labor-radical subculture reflected in a succession of organizations—the National Labor Union, the Knights of Labor, the Eight Hour Leagues, the Workingmen's Party of the United States, the American Federation of Labor (AFL), the Socialist Labor Party, the International Working Peoples Association—as well as a series of often violent strikes and labor conflicts, such as the rail strike and labor upsurge of 1877, the 1886 eight-hour demonstrations culminating in the Haymarket "riot," the Homestead strike of 1892, and the Pullman strike of 1894.

BEGINNINGS

The Progressive Era of the early twentieth century saw the culmination of such protests and struggles in a nationwide political shift that caused some elements in both the Democratic and Republican parties to tilt in a radical direction toward challenging the power of big business. It also resulted in the political mainstream, which, under such presidents as Theodore Roosevelt and Woodrow Wilson, began to flow in a direction that favored an increase in government regulation of the economy and fostered reforms designed to eliminate corruption and abuses, as well as to help the disadvantaged, in order to dampen radical sentiments. Within this context, a variety of movements and organizations dedicated to far-reaching social reforms were established. Among these were the National Association for the Advancement of Colored People (NAACP), struggling for equal rights for blacks, and a new wave of feminism, focused on winning the right to vote for women but also struggling for greater educational and occupational opportunities as well as for access to birth control.

By 1901, many of the remnants and continuations of the labor-radical tradition combined with other elements (former Populists, Christian Socialists, radicalized feminists, leftward-moving intellectuals, battle-scarred trade unionists, and others) to form the Socialist Party of America. Its peak was reached in 1912, with 118,000 members throughout the country and with 323 publications (in English and other languages) with a total circulation of more than 2 million. The weekly newspaper *Appeal to Reason,* published in Girard, Kansas, had the largest circulation—more than 761,000. In 1912, Socialist leader Eugene V. Debs (who had led the 1894 Pullman strike) polled 6 percent of the presidential vote, and Socialists held 1,200 elected offices in 340 cities, including seventy-nine mayors in twenty-four states. Socialist congressmen were elected from New York City and Milwaukee, Wisconsin, and as late as 1918 Socialists elected thirty-two state legislators and were making a positive showing in several municipal elections. Socialists led and strongly influenced about one-third of the unions in the AFL, and many Socialists also played a central part in establishing the more militant Industrial Workers of the World (IWW), which assumed a vital role in organizing inclusive, multiethnic, multiracial struggles among unskilled industrial workers.

Sharp differences emerged between more reformist Socialist Party currents led by Representative Victor Berger (Socialist-WI) and labor lawyer Morris Hillquit on the one hand, and more revolutionary-minded figures such as Debs and IWW leader "Big Bill" Haywood. The moderate elements dominated the party apparatus and sought to minimize left-wing influence. In the face of the patriotic hysteria and fierce government repression unleashed by the United States' entry into World War I in 1917, the bulk of the Socialist Party held to its antiwar position. And when, in the same year, the Bolshevik revolution proclaimed the world's first "workers' state" in Russia (dramatically described in eyewitness reports in the Socialist press by radical journalist John Reed, whose classic account *Ten Days That Shook the World* would soon be published), the Socialist Party as a whole greeted it with enthusiasm.

But the Socialist left wing felt that the antiwar position was being soft-pedaled by the moderates and that U.S. Socialists should apply the Bolshevik model of organization and revolutionary strategy to American conditions. When it became clear in 1919 that the left wing was winning over a party majority, the moderates engineered massive expulsions, eliminating the bulk of the left wing and over half the membership. In addition to the bulk of the Socialist Party's left wing, many IWW activists and AFL militants were drawn to the example of the Russian Revolution. Among others who were attracted were some black Socialists who, led by Cyril Briggs and Richard B. Moore, organized in a significant group called the African Blood Brotherhood.

Under such circumstances, a newly formed Communist Party might have been expected to emerge with 80,000 members and substantial influence. But fierce government repression and no less fierce factional disputes (which resulted in two Communist parties being formed) guaranteed that this would not happen. The Communist Party of America (CPA) probably had fewer than 25,000 members, and the Communist Labor Party (CLP) may have had about 15,000.

The CPA, dominated by the foreign-language federations (especially the federation made up of Russian immigrants headed by Nicholas Hourwich and the Jewish federation led by Alexander Bittelman) that had been expelled by the Socialist Party, claimed to be more attuned to the Bolshevik model. As such, it attracted the talented young Italian-American intellectual Louis Fraina, the stalwart Ohio Socialist organizer Charles Ruthenberg, the dynamic former student Socialist leader Jay Lovestone and his classmate William Weinstone, millionaire Rose Pastor Stokes, the studious teacher Bertram D. Wolfe, and Juliet Stuart Poyntz, who had been education director of the International Ladies' Garment Workers' Union.

The Communist Labor Party, which claimed a greater connection with U.S. realities and the American labor movement, included the flamboyant "all-American" radical John Reed, the volatile Irish-American workers' leader James Larkin, Ben Gitlow (one of ten New York Socialist state legislators elected but refused their seats in the super-patriotic atmosphere of the times), the seasoned IWW organizer James P. Cannon, the experienced AFL Socialist militant William F. Dunne, and veteran Socialist Party organizer Ella Reeve Bloor.

Although most of these leaders remained in the Communist movement for years to come, many rank-and-file Communists found it difficult to endure the government repression, disillusionment over the failure of the hoped-for revolutionary upsurge to materialize in the United States, and the debilitating disunity. Both organizations ended up with fewer than 10,000 members combined, but continued to denounce each other and seek exclusive recognition as the "real" U.S. Communist Party from the newly formed Communist International. Instead, the leaders of the Communist International insisted on unity, which was finally achieved in 1921, although there was still a factional fight over whether the organization should be predominantly "underground" in the way that the Russian Bolsheviks had been. (The Russian leadership of the Communist International concluded that, given the relatively free conditions existing in the United States, maintaining such an underground existence made no sense.) The unified organization was able to establish a more stable existence, reversing the membership decline, and to begin attracting significant recruits, such as the famous leader of the 1919 steel strike, William Z. Foster.

The unified party took the name Workers Party of America. In 1925, the organization's name changed to the Workers (Communist) Party of America and, by 1930, to the Communist Party of the United States of America.

THE COMMUNIST INTERNATIONAL

The Communist International (also known as the Comintern and the Third International) was of decisive importance to the origins and subsequent development of American Communism. When established under the leadership of the Russian Communists, it was projected to be a world party of Socialist revolution in which all national sections and individuals would enjoy a comradely equality. Not surprisingly, however, it was the Russians who were naturally seen as the leaders inasmuch as they had made a successful revolution and were the hosts and financiers of the Comintern.

"In the first days of the October revolution—that

is the Bolshevik revolution—the Russians were leaders through prestige, through achievement, through the fact that they conquered one-sixth of the world for socialism," recalled Jay Lovestone, some years later. "We had an attitude of almost religious veneration toward them . . . But I must say in fairness to the Russian leaders at that time they did not advocate this, they did not nurture this." In fact, according to Lovestone "they tended to treat us as equals, with equal respect: respecting our opinions, and we appreciated that. They were big men, and because they were big men they did not act in little or small ways, but nevertheless the Russian influence was decisive."

According to James P. Cannon, he and his comrades "learned to do away forever with the idea that a revolutionary socialist movement, aiming at power, can be led by people who practice socialism as an avocation. . . . Lenin, Trotsky, Zinoviev, Radek, Bukharin—these were our teachers. We began to be educated in an entirely different spirit from the old lackadaisical Socialist Party—in the spirit of revolutionists who take ideas and programs very seriously." Bertram Wolfe concurred, noting that before 1925 it was *not* the case that "all important decisions for the American Communist party were being made in Moscow"—rather, communications from Lenin, Zinoviev, and other Comintern leaders "were intended only as helpful suggestions, often exciting ones, and as successful examples to imitate after adapting them to American conditions, but not as categorical commands."

Lovestone recalled that by 1924, when Comintern leader Gregory Zinoviev was allied with Josef Stalin against Leon Trotsky, there developed "sharp, unprincipled factionalism—I would say suicidal factionalism—in the Russian party, [and] the Comintern policies began to be involved in and determined by factional struggles inside the Russian party. . . . First there was the beginning of slavishness and mechanical transference, and what I called the Byzantine court at Moscow—kowtowing before the potentates, but it was not yet worked up into a system. . . . Then that culminated in the triumph of Stalin in Russia and thereafter the triumph of Stalin in the Communist International."

"Everything had been settled behind the scenes," Cannon observed about a typical situation in the Comintern of the mid-1920s. "The word had been passed and all the secondary leaders and functionaries in the Comintern were falling into line." When radical intellectual Max Eastman complained to Foster of a highhanded action of Comintern leadership, Foster responded: "Max, a lot of things happen here that I don't like. But we can't do anything about it. They've got the prestige. No revolutionary movement anywhere, as things stand now, can prosper without their backing."

THE POLITICAL ACCOMPLISHMENTS OF THE 1920S

Although the American Communists benefited from the revolutionary prestige of the early Soviet Republic, and from various forms of Comintern assistance, their own initiative and creative energy were decisive in making the Workers Party a significant force in the 1920s.

Under William Z. Foster's leadership, an influential network of leaders and activists was created in the AFL through the Trade Union Educational League (TUEL). In its monthly periodical *The Labor Herald,* and in its many pamphlets and public meetings, it sharply criticized corruption, exclusionary practices, and conservatism in existing unions. It also put forward a program that urged craft unions to amalgamate to form industrial unions; to establish a shop delegate system to ensure rank-and-file control of unions; to create a labor party; to enact reforms such as unemployment insurance; and to support the Soviet Republic in Russia and the eventual creation of a workers' republic in the United States. Progressive union leaders and activists rallied to many of these demands, and through sustained TUEL efforts a number of unions were influenced by the TUEL program, as were central labor councils in Chicago, Minneapolis, and other cities.

Trade union activists who had gotten experience through the TUEL (and through its early 1930s successor, the Trade Union Unity League) went on in the later 1930s and 1940s to play prominent, dynamic roles in building a powerful labor movement through the organizing drives that were part of the rising Congress of Industrial Organizations.

The American Communist Party was also involved in defending civil liberties, particularly those of workers, through the International Labor Defense (ILD). The ILD had been conceived of during discussions between "Big Bill" Haywood, Rose Karsner, and James P. Cannon (Cannon would become its national secretary when it was set up in 1925). The ILD provided aid to hundreds of "class-war prisoners," regardless of political affiliation, who had been imprisoned or otherwise persecuted during the fierce government repression during World War I, during the postwar "Red Scare," as well as in subsequent strikes, labor struggles, and other situations. It publicized the cases (through the *Labor Defender,* meetings, picket lines, and other means), raised money, and often secured legal assistance. During the 1920s, its most famous cases were those of the Italian Anarchists Nicola Sacco and Bartolomeo Vanzetti, as well as those of militant Socialists and trade unionists Tom Mooney and Warren K. Billings.

In the following decade, the ILD would become best known for its defense of Angelo Herndon, a black Communist arrested and imprisoned for making a radical speech in Georgia, and "the Scottsboro boys," nine young black men accused and convicted of raping two white women in Alabama (although the trial was blatantly unfair and one of the women later recanted). Such cases became important symbols of antiracist struggle.

Especially through the insistence of the Communist International, the American Communist Party began to give more consistent and careful attention to the problem of racism and the plight of African Americans than had ever been the case among U.S. leftwing organizations. A small but important core of black workers and intellectuals came to see, in the words of Harry Haywood, "the elimination of racism and the achievement of complete equality for Blacks as an inevitable byproduct of socialist revolution in the United States." In 1925, the American Negro Labor Congress was organized, headed by the flamboyant Lovett Fort-Whiteman (who later went to live in the USSR and perished in Stalin's purges), which published *The Negro Liberator.* A cadre of 200 black Communists developed, which was able to assume a major role during the struggles of the 1930s among the unemployed and unionizing industrial workers, against racism in the United States, and against fascism abroad.

The Communist slogan "black and white, unite and fight" was to be symbolized in the 1932 presidential election when black party leader James W. Ford was selected as the vice-presidential running mate of William Z. Foster. Several thousand blacks joined the Communist Party during that decade and began to wield a dramatically widening influence within the black community. As a result, Communists played a sometimes pivotal role in the antiracist struggle. Black lawyers such as Benjamin J. Davis (who later served as a Communist on New York City's city council) and William Patterson (who later headed up the ILD and later the Civil Rights Congress), such writers as Langston Hughes and Richard Wright,

singer and actor Paul Robeson, and the great African-American scholar W.E.B. Du Bois were among those drawn to the Party's ranks or periphery.

The Communists coordinated an impressive array of immigrant fraternal, cultural, and social organizations, and sought to help protect the rights of immigrants through the broad-based National Council for the Protection of the Foreign Born, which was established in 1926 and formed a coalition of organizations representing 700,000 members. It should be noted that a majority of U.S. workers in many areas in this period were first- and second-generation immigrants—the fraternal organizations were vitally important for affirming and preserving one's culture and protecting one's rights from a pervasive anti-immigrant bigotry. In the 1930s, this was broadened into a multiculturalism that was counterposed to the rising tide of fascism. The 1930s also saw the organization of the influential International Workers Order, organized by ethnic units (Italian, Jewish, Hungarian, Serbo-Croatian, Slovak, Ukrainian, Greek, Polish, and so on), which provided insurance and other benefits, sponsored various cultural and political activities, and had 150,000 members.

Women made up less than 20 percent of Communist membership throughout the 1920s (it was to rise by more than 10 percent in the 1930s). Nonetheless, Communism took a formal position in favor of equal rights for women, and several women were prominent in leadership positions (Ella Reeve Bloor, Rose Pastor Stokes, Juliet Stuart Poyntz, Rose Wortis, Sylvia Bleecker, Rose Karsner, among others). Attention was given to "the woman question" through articles, pamphlets, and books; through International Women's Day events on March 8 of every year; and through classes and discussions. Often this attention was accompanied by a rejection of "bourgeois feminism" and an emphasis on the special problems of working-class women, for example, through the United Council of Working-Class Women, headed by Kate Gitlow (mother of party leader Ben Gitlow), and the publication of the periodical *Working Woman.* As has often been pointed out, the Communist Party's views on "the woman question" could be quite narrow, although sometimes in Communist circles there was a linkage of gender-class-race issues that was remarkably ahead of its time. By the 1930s, women in and around the Communist Party were able to engage in discussions and activities (discussions around the 1936 Women's Charter asserting the rights of women to full equality in all spheres of social activity, activities to provide full rights and representation for

Members of the Washington Communist Party meet on March 6, 1930, to plan a demonstration in front of the White House. The Communist Party led the fight for integration, black empowerment, and workers' rights in the 1930s. (© Underwood Photo Archives, Inc.)

women in the workplace and labor movement) that helped create new perceptions of womanhood and set the stage for the later feminist resurgence.

The Young Workers League, later renamed the Young Communist League, was organized in 1922 for activists in their teens and twenties, with Martin Abern as national secretary and Max Shachtman as editor of the monthly *Young Worker*. By 1925, it had an estimated membership of 4,000. The Young Pioneers of America was established for children between the ages of seven and fourteen, with a magazine first called *Young Comrade* and then *Young Pioneer*.

Other Communist-sponsored organizations included the United Farmers Educational League, the Friends of Soviet Russia, the All-American Anti-Imperialist League, and many more—some of which evolved into larger and more influential organizations in the 1930s.

Through innumerable books and pamphlets published by International Publishers and Workers Library Publishers, through the *Daily Worker* (launched in 1924), through a variety of English- and foreign-language periodicals (twenty-seven journals in nineteen languages, with a total circulation of 177,000), through classes (including an impressive curriculum organized under the directorship of Bertram D. Wolfe for the Workers School in New York City), through rallies and Communist electoral campaigns, and through hard work in a variety of organizations and movements, the Communists sought to spread Marxist ideas and deepen socialist consciousness. The cultural and intellectual life of the Communists contributed to the ability of some members to contribute to the larger cultural and intellectual life of the United States during the 1920s and even more during the 1930s and 1940s—in scholarship, literature, music, graphic arts, theater, film, and more.

Although Party membership fluctuated between 7,000 and 12,000 throughout the 1920s, many thousands more were drawn to its activities and influenced by its efforts, and American Communists were positioned to play a significant role in coming decades. But the factional conflicts of the 1920s, and the final outcome of those conflicts, also did much to undermine the Communists' ability to realize the potential of their movement.

THE FACTIONAL WARS OF THE 1920s

In addition to a deep idealism, a profound opposition to oppression and exploitation, and an uncompromising commitment to the creation of a society of "the free and equal," the leadership of the Communist Party was marked by a variety of personalities, egos, ambitions, and "careerist" aspirations. In addition, serious differences arose as to how best to build the Communist Party and to advance the struggles of the workers and the oppressed. A major difference emerged around the issue of how to best impact the larger political life of the United States. As the Democratic and Republican parties shifted rightward and as "mainstream" politics pulled in a more conservative direction in the 1920s, a variety of oppositional currents in the working class, among farmers, and among intellectuals and "middle-class" reformers gave intense consideration to the creation of a third party.

By 1923, a Hungarian Communist and Comintern representative who went by the name of John Pepper (his actual name was Joseph Pogany) had insinuated himself into the leadership of the U.S. Communists, gathering around himself the party's general secretary Charles Ruthenberg, Jay Lovestone, Ben Gitlow, and others. Under Pepper's influence, they pushed the party into a set of disastrous adventures in the third-party movement. Progressive trade unionist John Fitzpatrick, head of the Chicago Federation of Labor and a powerful ally of William Z. Foster's TUEL, initiated

a conference to begin the development of a new radical farmer-labor party. Pepper's efforts culminated in the Communists packing the conference with representatives of their own "front" groups and pushing through—over Fitzpatrick's angry objections—the premature creation of a supposed farmer-labor party based on their own fantasies.

Fitzpatrick and other trade union progressives in the AFL immediately broke with the Communists and facilitated the destruction of TUEL influence in the AFL. A genuine farmer-labor effort—the Conference for Progressive Political Action (a broad-based coalition of unions, reformers, and Socialists)—excluded the Communists and ran Senator Robert M. La Follette (R-WI) for president in 1924 on the new Progressive ticket, which would receive 4 million votes. But by this time the Communists had been frozen out of the third-party movement, and differences among the Comintern leadership caused them to scuttle any efforts to reverse that process. The Communist Party ended up running its own candidates, Foster and Gitlow, in the presidential race, in a pale campaign that netted a paltry 33,000 votes.

Additional "clever" maneuvers of the Pepper–Ruthenberg–Lovestone leadership generated the rise of a strong oppositional current—an alliance of two caucuses led by William Z. Foster and James P. Cannon. The Foster–Cannon opposition, rejecting schemes that would cause the Communists to overreach themselves, insisted on building solid united-front efforts, with special attention to building a base within the Progressive wing of the AFL. The ability of the Foster–Cannon caucuses to secure a majority only intensified the factional conflict, for which Lovestone proved to be especially talented.

The Comintern pulled Pepper out of the United States and initially seemed to favor a semiharmonious balance between the factions. At one point, Cannon, Bittelman (breaking temporarily from the Foster caucus), and Weinstone (breaking temporarily from the Lovestone caucus) sought to cut across the factionalism to help create a more unified, "Bolshevized" Communist Party, but the factionalized situation continued. A remarkable intervention of the Comintern then tipped the scales in 1925—in effect dictating that the Ruthenberg–Lovestone faction should be the leadership of the Party. As it turned out, this represented a decisive move on the part of the Stalin faction inside the Russian Communist Party to bring various sections of the Comintern under its control. A special concern was exhibited to minimize the influence of potential left oppositionists who might be drawn into support for Stalin's chief rival, Trotsky. When Ruthenberg died in early 1927, Lovestone moved quickly to assume full leadership and to intensify an uncompromising struggle against anyone who might challenge that leadership.

COMMUNIST FRAGMENTATION

An anti-Trotsky campaign was being orchestrated throughout the Comintern, and under Lovestone's leadership—ably supported by Wolfe, Gitlow, and others—this campaign was advanced among the American Communists. Ludwig Lore, a prominent German-American Communist, had been expelled in 1925 at Lovestone's initiative, in part for defending Trotsky. "I know everyone of our boys is solid with Stalin," Lovestone asserted proudly when Trotsky and Zinoviev established a united opposition to challenge the crystallization of the bureaucratic dictatorship in the USSR in 1926. But the Party was shaken in 1928 when James P. Cannon and some of his closest associates (Max Shachtman, Martin Abern, Rose Karsner, and others) were brought up on charges and expelled for Trotskyism. Disgusted and disheartened by the factionalism and what he viewed as unprincipled maneuvering that seemed to characterize so much of the internal life of American Communism and the Comintern as such, Cannon had in fact been won over to Trotsky's critique of Stalinism. He and about 100 expellees promptly organized the Communist League of America in 1929, basing themselves forthrightly on Trotsky's revolutionary perspectives.

But 1929 also saw a dramatic "leftist" zigzag in Stalin's policies inside the USSR and its Communist Party, as well as within the Comintern. Over the objections of his moderate-Communist ally Nikolai Bukharin (with whom Lovestone and his associates had nourished a close relationship), Stalin had pushed through a brutal forced collectivization of the land and a rapid industrialization policy in the USSR. Stalin's decision brought extreme hardship and even death to millions of peasants and workers and was accompanied by an intensification of extreme dictatorial measures. Also over the objection of various elements in the Comintern (including Lovestone and his supporters), Stalin began imposing an ultra-left turn on Communist Parties throughout the world, calling on them to reject alliances with all others on the left, to split the trade union movement in order to establish Communist-led unions, and to prepare for an expected new wave of revolutions.

Backed by a majority of the American Communist Party, Lovestone organized a large delegation to go to Moscow to argue in the Comintern that the Stalin line would be a sectarian and ultra-left disaster if applied to U.S. conditions. In consultation with trusted aides in the United States (Jack Stachel and Robert Minor), Lovestone also took measures to keep American Party resources in "safe hands" in the event of a break with the Stalin leadership. Consummate factional infighter though he was, Lovestone was no match for Stalin's political machine. Brutally crushing them in Moscow as "right opportunists" and "American exceptionalists" who were "disloyal" to the Communist International, Stalin mocked: "No one will follow you but your wives and sweethearts." Stachel, Minor, and others of the Lovestoneite majority back in the United States were given the choice: break with Lovestone or break with the Comintern and the USSR. Along with a substantial portion of the delegation to Moscow, the great majority of Communists in the United States (including Stachel and Minor) repudiated Lovestone.

When Lovestone, Wolfe, Gitlow and other unrepentant co-thinkers finally were allowed to leave the USSR, they were able to establish a new organization in 1930 called the Communist Party (Majority Group). This was so far from the truth that the 200 Lovestoneites soon adopted the new name Communist Party Opposition.

William Z. Foster was not considered to be sufficiently trustworthy to represent the Stalinist line in the U.S. Communist leadership. As a result, the Comintern elevated a secondary figure from the Foster caucus, who had recently spent time in Moscow, Earl Browder, to serve as general secretary of the Communist Party of the USA. This appointment was made just as the Great Depression was devastating millions of workers and raising questions about whether the capitalist system was about to collapse. A majority of American Communists, losing patience for continued factional disputes, let alone critiques of the USSR and the Comintern, felt it was time to close ranks behind the leadership of Comrade Stalin, in the face of intensifying economic hardship, the rising tide of fascism, and the shadows of war.

As Peggy Dennis later commented, "in our political naivete . . . we younger comrades did not particularly connect our own internal struggle with that which had raged in the Comintern and the Soviet Communist Party," nor did many U.S. Communists comprehend that the Comintern's interventions into the affairs of the American Communist party were "part of Stalin's consolidation of his leadership within the Soviet party and the international movement, less than five years after Lenin's death." She added, "we

Mounted police club Communist demonstrators in Union Square in New York City on "Red Thursday," March 6, 1930. Hundreds of thousands of Communists worldwide rallied in Chicago, Detroit, San Francisco, London, Paris, and Berlin to protest unemployment and capitalism. *(Brown Brothers)*

eloquently echoed Stalin's published denunciations of Bukharinism and Trotskyism without even objecting to the fact that we were not allowed to read what Bukharin or Trotsky had said or written."

In the period of ferment and radicalization in the 1930s that was generated by the Great Depression and the threat of fascism, it was not just party members but also radicalizing non-Communists considering various points of view who were drawn to the arguments of the Communist Party's leadership. Listening to a debate between Stalinist V.J. Jerome and Lovestoneite Bertram D. Wolfe, George Blake Charney later recalled: "I was in no position to judge the respective merits of their arguments on Marxism. Both were learned men. In the end I was drawn to the position of the [Stalinist] party because it was positive and forward-looking, whereas Wolfe was carping and neg-

ative and offered so little hope at a time when we needed so much."

MIXED LEGACIES

Despite the drastic curtailment of internal democracy in the Communist Party and the Comintern, matched by the intensification of the brutal authoritarianism of the Stalin regime in the USSR, American Communists of the 1930s threw themselves into a variety of activities to defend the interests of the working class and the oppressed. The injustices that had drawn them to Communism had by no means vanished—and some of them had gotten worse. Organizational efforts and struggles were launched among the ranks of the unemployed—hunger marches, the building of Unemployed Councils, and the Workers Alliance. There were also union struggles—especially when the Con-

One of the most prominent leaders of the Communist Party of the United States from the 1920s to the 1950s, William Z. Foster ran for president in 1924, 1928, and 1932. He is shown here testifying before Congress on November 8, 1945. *(Bettman/Corbis)*

gress of Industrial Organizations (CIO) began organizing millions of mass production workers—in which Communist Party members and sympathizers often provided leadership. Communists played a pioneering and often dramatic role in struggles against racism and in some cases in struggles for women's rights. Struggles were ongoing against fascism, imperialism, and militarism. In the process, Communists made innumerable contributions to culture and consciousness that impacted millions of people throughout the country.

By the late 1930s, nearly 100,000 people were associated with the Communist Party. At the same time, in line with Earl Browder's slogan that "Communism is 20th Century Americanism," the Communists sought to avoid doing anything to alienate pro-capitalist liberals in the New Deal wing of Franklin D. Roosevelt's Democratic Party. This was part of the

People's Front orientation, designed by the Stalin leadership of the Comintern to create a broad, multi-class global coalition to block the spread of fascism (especially the variety represented by the Hitler regime that took power in Germany). In the words of Earl Browder, "Roosevelt's programmatic utterances of 1937, when combined with the legislative program of the CIO (his main labor support), provides a People's Front program of an advanced type," adding that "we can completely agree with such non-socialist democrats upon the united defense of democracy under capitalism." Years later, Browder boasted that the Communist Party thereby "rapidly moved out of its extreme leftist sectarianism of 1930 toward the broadest united front tactics of reformism for strictly limited immediate aims. It relegated its revolutionary socialist goals to the ritual of chapel and Sundays on the pattern long followed by the Christian Church. On weekdays it became the most single-minded practical reformist party that America ever produced."

The Trotskyists never attracted more than 2,000 members, sometimes existing in several organizations or even as independent individuals. Despite an often undeserved reputation for sectarianism, they were able to play an honorable role in the labor movement, especially through the impressive leadership they provided in the 1934 Minneapolis general strike. Pockets of working-class militants in various unions and industrial centers, as well as in unemployed and community struggles, continued to do what they could to advance class consciousness and the class struggle, and to keep alive revolutionary Socialist ideas. Trotskyist and Trotskyist-influenced intellectuals, writers, and artists made contributions to American culture, such as: James Burnham, Max Eastman, James T. Farrell, Sidney Hook, Irving Howe, Dwight Macdonald, Mary McCarthy, Philip Rahv, James Rorty, Meyer Schapiro, Edmund Wilson, and others (although some abandoned their left-wing commitments). One of the greatest legacies of the Trotskyists was their consistent anti-Stalinism in which they not only denounced Stalin's crimes, but also insisted that these were alien to Marxism, to the Russian Revolution of 1917, and to the goals and commitments of the early Communist movement. In later years, some also played a significant part in antiracist, antiwar, feminist, and other struggles.

The Lovestoneites have left a more complex legacy. Hoping that the Comintern would recognize them as having been right, they persisted in defending many of Stalin's policies—until by 1937 they recoiled with horror as the bloody purges of the 1930s made it clear that there was no way back for them. One of their greatest contributions was the magnificent left-wing mural history of the United States painted by the great Mexican revolutionary muralist Diego Rivera at their New Workers School. They also made significant contributions in certain union struggles, including (along with Socialists and "mainstream" Communists) during the sit-down strikes of automobile workers. However, their role in unsavory union factional fights finally destroyed their credibility in the United Auto Workers. On the other hand, a prominent Lovestoneite, the popular Charles ("Sasha") Zimmerman, rose in the leadership of the International Ladies' Garment Workers' Union (ILGWU), and Lovestone became a close associate of ILGWU chieftain David Dubinsky (and eventually a significant figure in the AFL, after Dubinsky assured other AFL leaders that "the son of a bitch converted" to their own anti-Communist outlook). This was after their organization dissolved in 1941, and Lovestone went on to help develop and implement Cold War foreign policy in collaboration with the State Department and Central Intelligence Agency. Bertram Wolfe became an anti-Communist authority on the USSR and State Department employee. Another Lovestoneite, Will Herberg, became a prominent Jewish theologian and conservative intellectual. Ben Gitlow moved even further to the right as an associate of the John Birch Society.

Much of this reaction was related to revulsion over the fact that the Russian Revolution, in which so many idealistic hopes were invested, gave way to the murderous dictatorship of the Stalin regime. This reality (and the defense or denial of the reality) is one of the most negative legacies of American Communism's mainstream. A related problematic legacy was the tendency for Communists in various social struggles to tailor their efforts to harmonize with the dictates of the Stalin regime, sometimes to the detriment of those struggles. In addition, some were drawn into spy networks to assist the "homeland of socialism"— through the Comintern underground apparatus, the Soviet secret service, Soviet military espionage—in its battle against the capitalist enemy. These made up only a very small minority of Communists, and in some cases their stories did not end well. There was, for example, Juliet Stuart Poyntz, who took on trusted "underground" assignments, became disillusioned with Stalinism, and suddenly disappeared (perhaps kidnapped and murdered) in the 1930s. There were Whittaker Chambers and "Red spy queen" Elizabeth Bentley, who were idealistically drawn into "secret work" and then repelled by aspects of what they were doing, causing them to turn on their comrades and become professional witnesses against Communism. Such reactions fed into the anti-Communist hysteria of the Cold War era beginning in the late 1940s and caused many to view American Communism as simply a treasonous conspiracy.

The fact remains that the legacy of American Communism cannot simply be reduced to this negative set of events. Too many were heroically involved in the struggle for the economic betterment of the working class, for racial equality and human rights and against poverty, imperialism and militarism, and fascism. Too many people had made such involvements fundamental commitments of their lives for us to be able to exclude such idealistic impulses from the Communist legacy. People were drawn to this movement because they sought a world in which our economic resources would be democratically controlled and utilized to provide dignity, freedom, and equality for all people. Although many reject this vision as an impossible dream, it endures.

From the 1950s through the 1960s and beyond, many children of Communists (nicknamed "red diaper babies")—while often rejecting the Communist Party—went on to play important roles in struggles for political, economic, and social change. "Most red diaper babies struggle with the need to adapt the socialist values of childhood to capitalist adult reality, to walk a fine line between individual fulfillment and social responsibility," note Judy Kaplan and Linn Shapiro in their anthology *Red Diapers*. Many without such family backgrounds have also looked to retrieve what might be positive from the mixed legacies of U.S. Communism as they struggle to make the world a better place.

Paul Le Blanc

BIBLIOGRAPHY

Aaron, Daniel. *Writers on the Left: Episodes in American Literary Communism.* New York: Harcourt, Brace and World, 1961.

Alexander, Robert J. *International Trotskyism, 1929–1985, a Documented Analysis of the Movement.* Durham, NC: Duke University Press, 1991.

———. *The Right Opposition: The Lovestoneites and the International Communist Opposition of the 1930s.* Westport, CT: Greenwood Press, 1981.

Barrett, James R. *William Z. Foster and the Tragedy of American Radicalism.* Urbana: University of Illinois Press, 1999.

Bart, Philip, Theodore Bassett, William W. Weinstein, and Arthur Zipser, eds. *Highlights of a Fighting History: Sixty Years of the Communist Party, USA.* New York: International, 1979.

Breitman, George, Paul LeBlanc, and Alan Wald. *Trotskyism in the United States: Historical Essays and Reconsiderations.* Amherst, NY: Humanity Books, 1996.

Browder, Earl. "The American Communist Party in the Thirties." In *As We Saw the Thirties: Essays on Social and Political Movements of a Decade,* ed. Rita James Simon. Urbana: University of Illinois Press, 1967.

———. *The People's Front.* New York: International, 1938.

Brown, Michael E., Randy Martin, Frank Rosengarten, and George Snedeker, eds. *New Studies in the Politics and Culture of U.S. Communism.* New York: Monthly Review, 1993.

Buhle, Mari, Paul Dan Buhle, and Dan Georgakas, eds. *Encyclopedia of the American Left.* New York: Oxford University Press, 1998.

Cannon, James P. *The First Ten Years of American Communism, Report of a Participant.* New York: Lyle Stuart, 1962.

———. *The History of American Trotskyism.* New York: Pathfinder Press, 1972.

Charney, George Blake. *A Long Journey.* Chicago: Quadrangle Books, 1968.

Denning, Michael. *The Cultural Front: The Laboring of American Culture in the Twentieth Century.* London: Verso, 1998.

Dennis, Peggy. *The Autobiography of an American Communist.* Westport, CT: Lawrence Hill, 1977.

Draper, Theodore. *American Communism and Soviet Russia.* New York: Viking, 1960.

———. *The Roots of American Communism.* New York: Viking, 1957.

Eastman, Max. *Love and Revolution, My Journey Through an Epoch.* New York: Random House, 1964.

Foner, Philip S., ed. *The Bolshevik Revolution: Its Impact on American Radicals, Liberals, and Labor.* New York: International, 1967.

Foster, William Z. *History of the Communist Party of the United States.* New York: International, 1952.

Freeman, Joseph. *American Testament, A Testament of Rebels and Romantics.* New York: Farrar and Rinehart, 1936.

Fried, Albert. *Communism: A Short History in Documents.* New York: Columbia University Press, 1997.

Gitlow, Ben. *I Confess: The Truth about American Communism.* New York: E.P. Dutton, 1940.

Haynes, John E. *Red Scare or Red Menace? American Communism and Anticommunism in the Cold War Era.* Chicago: Ivan R. Dee, 1996.

Haywood, Harry. *Black Bolshevik: Autobiography of an Afro-American Communist.* Chicago: Liberator, 1978.

Healey, Dorothy, and Maurice Isserman. *Dorothy Healey Remembers.* New York: Oxford University Press, 1990.

Hicks, Granville. *John Reed, The Making of a Revolutionary.* New York: Macmillan, 1936.

Kaplan, Judy, and Linn Shapiro. *Red Diapers: Growing Up in the Communist Left.* Urbana: University of Illinois Press, 1998.

Klehr, Harvey. *The Heyday of American Communism: The Depression Decade.* New York: Basic Books, 1984.

Klehr, Harvey, and John Earl Haynes. *The American Communist Movement: Storming Heaven Itself.* New York: Twayne, 1992.

Lovestone, Jay. "Testimony of Jay Lovestone, Secretary, Independent Labor League of America." In *Investigation of Un-American Propaganda Activities in the United States: Hearings Before a Special Committee on Un-American Activities* (Dies Committee), House of Representatives, 75th–76th Congress. Washington, DC: Government Printing Office, 1939–1940.

Morgan, Ted. *A Covert Life: Jay Lovestone, Communist, Anti-Communist, and Spymaster.* New York: Random House, 1999.

Nelson, Steve, James Barrett, and Rob Ruck. *Steve Nelson, An American Radical.* Pittsburgh: University of Pittsburgh Press, 1981.

Ottonelli, Fraser. *The Communist Party of the United States from the Depression to World War II.* New Brunswick, NJ: Rutgers University Press, 1991.

Palmer, Bryan. *James P. Cannon, Volume I (1890–1929).* Unpublished manuscript.

Reed, John. *Ten Days That Shook the World.* New York: International, 1926.

Ryan, James G. *Earl Browder: The Failure of American Communism.* Tuscaloosa: University of Alabama Press, 1997.

Solomon, Mark. *The Cry Was Unity: Communists and African Americans, 1917–1936.* Jackson: University of Mississippi Press, 1998.

Theoharis, Athan. *Chasing Spies: How the FBI Failed in Counterintelligence but Promoted the Politics of McCarthyism in the Cold War Years.* Chicago: Ivan R. Dee, 2002.

Weinstein, Allen, and Alexander Vassiliev. *The Haunted Wood: Soviet Espionage in America—The Stalin Era.* New York: Random House, 1999.

Wolfe, Bertram D. *A Life in Two Centuries.* New York: Stein and Day, 1977.

SACCO AND VANZETTI

On April 15, 1920, in Braintree, Massachusetts, a paymaster and his guard were carrying a factory payroll of $15,776. Two gunmen suddenly fired on them, grabbed the cash, and fled in a nearby automobile. Three weeks later, two friends, Nicola Sacco and Bartolomeo Vanzetti, were arrested for the crime. Thus, the stage was set for the most notorious political trial in the twentieth century.

Their arrest coincided with the "Red-Scare" of 1919–1920, a period in U.S. history immediately following World War I, during which many people feared those labeled as "Reds," "Anarchists," and "foreign-born radical agitators." Neither Sacco nor Vanzetti had a criminal record, but they were recognized by the authorities for their involvement in strikes and antiwar demonstrations and for their close association with the Italian Anarchist Luigi Galleani. Both were committed Anarchist activists. Many liberals and most radicals feel the two men were tried for their political beliefs and not because they committed the robbery.

TRIAL BEGINNINGS

In addition to the Braintree robbery, Vanzetti was charged with a holdup that had occurred on December 24, 1919, in Bridgewater, Massachusetts. Vanzetti was found guilty of this crime. Vanzetti's witnesses were primarily Italian immigrants who spoke little English, and he did not take the stand in his own defense. For this criminal offense, a crime in which no one was hurt, Vanzetti received a sentence much harsher than usual—ten to fifteen years. This signaled to the two men and their supporters a hostile bias on the part of the authorities that was political in nature and pointed to the need for a new defense strategy in the Braintree trial.

On the advice of the Anarchist militant and editor Carlo Tresca, new legal counsel was brought in—Fred H. Moore, the well-known Socialist lawyer from the West. He had collaborated in many labor and Industrial Workers of the World trials and was especially noted for his important role in the celebrated Joseph Ettor-Arturo Giovannitti case, which came out of the 1912 Lawrence, Massachusetts, textile strike. Moore decided it was no longer possible to defend Sacco and Vanzetti solely against the criminal charges of murder and robbery. Instead he would have them frankly acknowledge their anarchism in court, try to establish that their arrest and prosecution stemmed from their radical activities, and dispute the prosecution's insistence that only hard, nonpolitical evidence had implicated the two men in common crimes. Moore would try to expose the prosecution's hidden motive: its desire to aid the federal and military authorities in suppressing the Italian Anarchist movement to which Sacco and Vanzetti belonged.

ANARCHIST ROOTS

By trade, Sacco was a shoe worker and Vanzetti was a fish peddler. Both men were supporters of Galleani's journal *Cronaca Sovversiva*, the principal Italian Anarchist newspaper in the United States, which advocated "propaganda by the deed" (direct action in violent form) and revolutionary violence, including the use of dynamite and assassination. Such activities, they believed, were responses to the overwhelming violence of the state. During World War I, the paper was shut down for its radical views, and its editors, including Galleani, were deported to Italy in 1919 at the war's end.

Like most Anarchists, the followers of Galleani were against the war. In an article entitled "Matricolati!" (Registrants) published in *Cronaca Sovversiva*, Galleani advised his followers to avoid the draft and go underground. Heeding his call, Sacco and Vanzetti left for Mexico. Unable to find work, the two sneaked back across the border in September 1917. After working at a series of labor and construction jobs, Vanzetti bought a fish cart, knives, and supplies from a friend returning to Italy and became a fish peddler. Sacco continued to earn his living as a shoe worker. He worked in factories and was on good terms with his employers. Sacco was also devoted to his wife Rosina and his son Dante. The family also included a daughter, Alba, who passed away in 1906 when she was barely a month old. Vanzetti never married or had children.

The first Italian Anarchist group formed in 1885 in New York City. One of the precipitating factors in the development of Italian anarchism was the Haymarket Affair of 1886–1887, which began when Chicago police fired into a crowd of striking workers at the McCormick Reaper Works, killing and wounding several men. In response, Anarchist and Socialist labor leaders organized a meeting near Chicago's Haymarket Square, and a riot broke out between police and workingmen, ultimately killing more than half a dozen police officers. By the 1890s, there were Italian Anarchist groups in Boston, Philadelphia, Pittsburgh, Cleveland, Detroit, Chicago, and San Francisco.

As historian Paul Avrich notes in *Anarchist Portraits* (1988), "another important stimulus was the arrival from Italy of a series of distinguished anarchist writers and speakers." Some like Galleani and Tresca made the United States their home. Galleani arrived in the United States in October 1901 at the age of forty. Settling in Paterson, New Jersey, he assumed the editorship of *La Questione Sociale*, the leading Anarchist periodical in the United States. On June 6, 1903, he launched *Cronaca Sovversiva* in Barre, Vermont, among the Italian stone and marble cutters.

Sacco and Vanzetti, like many Italian Anarchists, revered Galleani as a "patriarch of the movement." They considered themselves Anarchist-Communists and were dedicated to social revolution, rejecting the state and private property. Galleani's brand of anarchism appealed to a broad section of the Italian working class, including garment and construction workers, stonecutters, shoe workers, barbers, tailors, and machinists.

Unlike the followers of Tresca who adopted anarcho-syndicalism, Sacco and Vanzetti avoided the unions owing to their suspicion of hierarchical organizations. However, they were participants in strikes, Sacco in Hopedale in 1913 and Vanzetti at Plymouth in 1916. This was the character of the movement to which Sacco and Vanzetti adhered. They subscribed to *Cronaca Sovversiva*, attended political lectures, frequented the concerts and picnics, and acted in Anarchist plays. They took part in demonstrations and agitated during strikes.

DEFENDING SACCO AND VANZETTI

From 1920 to 1927, the plight of Sacco and Vanzetti was the primary concern of the Italian Anarchists. They formed the Sacco-Vanzetti Defense Committee in order to raise funds and lecture in defense of their comrades. Other Anarchist ethnic groups—Jewish, German, Russian, and so on—rallied behind the cause. But the Anarchists were not alone. Moore's defense of the two men soon became so openly and energetically political that its scope quickly transcended its local roots. He organized public meetings, solicited the support of labor unions, contacted international organizations, initiated new investigations, and distributed tens of thousands of defense pamphlets throughout the United States and the world. Much to the chagrin of some Anarchist comrades, Moore would even enlist the aid of the Italian government in the defense of Sacco and Vanzetti. The Communist International urged all Communists, Socialists, Anarchists, and trade unions to organize efforts to rescue Sacco and Vanzetti. Moore's aggressive strategy transformed a little-known case into a cause celebre.

Leftists and liberals accepted Moore's assertion that Sacco and Vanzetti were being tried for their political beliefs. Moore urged that the prosecution was not using strictly nonpolitical evidence and that their case was based on facts that had no bearing on the murders. However, Moore's attempt to convince the jury that the goal of the prosecution was suppressing the Italian Anarchist movement fell on deaf ears. Following a six-week bitter trial, Sacco and Vanzetti were found guilty of robbery and murder on July 14, 1921.

But the guilty verdict was hardly the last page in their legal battle. It would drag on until 1927 during which time there were many motions, appeals, and petitions for a new trial on various court levels. The motions contained evidence of perjury and comments by Judge Webster Thayer referring to the two men as "those anarchist bastards."

After the failure of Moore's strategy, Sacco and Vanzetti hired a respected Boston lawyer, William Thompson. Thompson abandoned Moore's political approach and engaged strictly in jurisprudence. Nonetheless, the political dimensions of the case continued to be voiced by Anarchists, Socialists, liberals, and trade unionists.

Demonstrations took place in the major cities of

Despite a paucity of evidence, anarchists Bartolomeo Vanzetti (center) and Nicola Sacco (right) were convicted of murder in 1921. Many charged that they were really tried for their extreme political beliefs, and liberals and radicals worldwide mobilized in their defense. They were executed in 1927. *(Brown Brothers)*

the United States and in France, Italy, Switzerland, Belgium, Spain, Portugal, and Scandinavia. Thousands of French police troops were needed to prevent a mob from besieging the American embassy in Paris. Scientist Albert Einstein, English novelist H.G. Wells, English labor leader Thomas Mann, and even the Vatican were strong Sacco and Vanzetti supporters who protested their conviction.

Ultimately, all the efforts were to no avail. Sacco and Vanzetti were executed on August 23, 1927, a date that became a watershed in twentieth-century American history. Serious doubts still surround the verdict. Indeed, no other convicted murderers have received

a celebrated place in the *Dictionary of American Biography*. Furthermore, the Sacco-Vanzetti case was inspiration for a few movies, several poems, six plays, and nine novels. As historian Robert D'Attilio notes, "It became the last of a long train of events that had driven any sense of utopian vision out of American life."

Evan Daniel

BIBLIOGRAPHY

Avrich, Paul. *Anarchist Portraits*. Princeton, NJ: Princeton University Press, 1988.

———. *Sacco and Vanzetti: The Anarchist Background*. Princeton, NJ: Princeton University Press, 1991.

D'Attilio, Robert, and Jane Manthorn. *Sacco and Vanzetti: Developments and Reconsiderations, 1979*. Boston: Boston Public Library, 1979.

Ehrmann, Herbert B. *The Case That Will Not Die*. Boston: Beacon, 1969.

Glassgold, Peter, ed. *Anarchy!: An Anthology of Emma Goldman's Mother Earth*. New York: Counterpoint, 2001.

Pernicone, Nunzio. *Italian Anarchism*. Princeton, NJ: Princeton University Press, 1993.

Vanzetti, Bartolomeo. *The Story of a Proletarian Life*. Translated by Eugene Lyons. Boston: Sacco and Vanzetti Defense Committee, 1923.

Unemployment Movement

Following the collapse of the economy after the stock market crash of 1929, Americans confronted the specter of steadily increasing unemployment that robbed them of their jobs and led many to abandon the voluntaristic assumptions of laissez-faire economics. As the ranks of the jobless swelled with the advent of widespread unemployment, large numbers of displaced workers turned to left-led voluntary associations and political organizations for leadership in the struggle to meet the most basic of human needs. The result was the development of mass organizations that displayed the characteristic features of social movements, including evidence of spontaneity, grassroots pressure, and democratic control. As unemployed activism escalated, various political organizations embraced the cause of the jobless and worked to advance partisan programs through engagement in the unemployed movement.

Communist Party Councils

The first group to offer meaningful assistance to the unemployed was the Communist Party (CP), which had long championed the cause of the dispossessed in the American underclass. Always aggressive in their search for adherents, party organizers actively recruited on the breadlines, at the plant gates, and in relief offices in an effort to broaden their support base among the jobless. One of the earliest mass actions occurred on March 6, 1930, when in a coordinated nationwide demonstration hundreds of thousands filled the streets of the major cities and demanded government action to meet the needs of dislocated workers and their families. Even CP activists were stunned by the size and intensity of the International Unemployment Day demonstrations. Success fueled the party's determination to mount a mass movement by creating a national organization to promote the interests of the unemployed.

The result was the establishment in summer

What Was Planned
A poster appeal to the hunger marchers.

This gripping image conveys both the depth of the Depression and the determination of the unemployed to gain relief. *(Brown Brothers)*

1930 of the Unemployed Councils of the United States, a body intended to advance the agenda of the jobless and link them with employed workers in the struggle to improve the lives and status of impoverished workers and their families. In Detroit, New York, and Chicago, militant organizations carried out jobless demonstrations, eviction protests, and welfare office mediation on behalf of relief re-

Unemployed veterans of World War I descended on Washington, D.C., in the spring of 1932 to demand that Congress authorize immediate cash payments, or "bonuses," as compensation for their military service. With no place to stay, some of the bonus marchers camped out in front of the Capitol Building on July 13. Two weeks later, federal troops forcibly evicted some 2,000 veterans, killing two. *(Brown Brothers)*

cils worked to raise public and political consciousness of their program through a series of highly publicized national events, such as the national hunger marches of 1931, 1932, and 1933, the Bonus March of 1932, and selected efforts to establish the unity of employed and unemployed workers in strike situations. Led by the tireless Communist organizer Herbert Benjamin, the Councils worked to advance a national agenda that featured a demand for unemployment insurance, greater federal relief allocations, and public employment programs. Before 1934, the Unemployed Councils were at the forefront of the national unemployed movement, in part due to their persistence in local organizing and commitment to short-term goals. Their revolutionary rhetoric drew a tepid response, but their success in addressing human needs drew the support and gratitude of the jobless and dispossessed.

THE LEAGUE FOR INDUSTRIAL DEMOCRACY

So successful were the Communists in the early Depression years that other radical groups determined to enter the field. Struggling to break the hold of the Socialist old guard, Socialist Party (SP) militants moved to compete with the Councils for the loyalty and allegiance of the unemployed. These efforts began with the establishment of the Wisconsin Workers Committee and the Chicago Workers Committee on Unemployment. Active as early as 1932, the Illinois group expressed the spirit of a younger element in the SP that grew out of the League for Industrial Democracy (LID) and dedicated itself to organizing the unorganized rather than engaging in doctrinal debates. The LID Socialists, with the support of the party's national executive committee, moved to contest CP domination of the unemployed movement by employing some of the same techniques used by their adversaries. By emphasizing grassroots organizing at the local level, the Workers Committee competed with the Councils and by 1934 had become successful advocates for the jobless and established a firm foothold in such places as Chicago, Milwaukee, and New York. While the Unemployed Councils were declining in influence, the Socialist expression of the unemployed movement demonstrated remarkable growth that culminated in the organization of the SP-sponsored Workers Alliance of America at the national level in 1935. The Alliance, under the aggressive leadership of New Yorker David Lasser, soon came to dominate the evolving mass movement.

cipients. Although the Councils were loosely coordinated by the Communist Party's designated leaders, one of the greatest strengths of these organizations lay in the substantial independent initiative exercised by the local Councils and their leaders. This decentralization enabled local organizations to move quickly and decisively in response to emergency situations such as evictions or denials of public assistance. Although there is little evidence of mass conversion to Communist Party ideology, it is clear that the jobless knew that at the local level it was the Councils and their leaders who provided the most reliable support when they were confronted by personal crises. Consequently, party organizers enjoyed a level of respect and acceptance rarely achieved in post-Depression years.

Between 1929 and 1933, the Unemployed Coun-

MUSTEITES AND THE NATIONAL UNEMPLOYED LEAGUE

Still another entry into the field of unemployed organizing was the National Unemployed League, which grew rapidly in Pennsylvania, West Virginia, and Ohio. Led by the radical A. J. Muste and his followers, many of them associated with the Brookwood Labor College. This organization included Socialists, Communists, and Trotskyites, and often members of the Conference for Progressive Labor Action, which aspired to create an independent worker movement on the left capable of competing with the American Federation of Labor. Combining forces with the Seattle-based self-help cooperative known as the Unemployed Citizens League, the Musteites and their allies came to be called the National Unemployed Leagues. The organization was strongest in the coal-mining and steel-producing areas of the East and Midwest. Formally established in 1933 at a national conference in Columbus, Ohio, the League experienced disagreements between the advocates of self-help cooperative programs and radicals determined to engage in labor actions and high-profile demonstrations. Perhaps the most important success for the Musteites occurred in the Toledo Auto-Lite strike of 1934, when the Lucas County Unemployed Leagues joined hands with striking workers in a dramatic illustration of unity between employed and jobless workers, thus realizing the early dream of the Unemployed Councils.

By 1935, the Workers Alliance of America had grown into a major national organization with a membership of 400,000 jobless workers in eighteen states. Truly national in scope, the Alliance had eclipsed the Unemployed Councils and enhanced the prestige of the Socialist Party among the nation's unemployed. In early 1936, the stage was set for the next major development in the unfolding unemployed movement. By this time, the Communist Party had entered the Popular Front period, during which it endorsed cooperation with the non-Communist left, including Socialists and New Deal Democrats. The change in approach facilitated a new openness to the idea of a unified unemployed movement, which ended in the merger of the Councils, Leagues, and the Workers Alliance in 1936. Although the majority of the Alliance's restructured national executive board was non-Communist and Lasser retained his position as president, Benjamin assumed the important position of national executive secretary.

These changes coincided with the launching of the New Deal's ambitious program for the unemployed under the Emergency Relief Appropriation Act of 1935, which created the Works Progress Administration (WPA). The new federal work relief program was a direct stimulus to increased militancy and organizational activity among Workers Alliance participants. The burgeoning federal work relief program provided the Alliance with a fertile field for organizational growth, as the concentration of workers on the projects facilitated recruitment. With this expansion, the unemployed movement entered a new phase characterized by an emphasis on lobbying at the national level for favorable legislation and high-profile intervention on behalf of the jobless. The practical consequence was that from 1936 on, the Workers Alliance came to function more as a legitimate labor union for its unemployed members and less as an advocate for relief recipients and their families. Lasser and Benjamin interacted easily with Roosevelt administration officials, who came to regard them as representatives of workers on government projects.

As a result of this gradual integration into the New Deal structure, the unemployed movement was eventually coopted by the forces of liberalism, though radicals like Benjamin continued to exercise strong influence on its policies and direction. Similarly, many of the Alliance's most gifted organizers were drawn into the Congress of Industrial Organizations' (CIO) struggle to organize the unorganized in the mass industries such as steel, auto, and rubber. Led by the United Automobile Workers (UAW), some CIO unions moved to incorporate unemployed organizing into the fabric of the international unions. Their goal was to maintain Depression-era membership and educate the jobless as a bulwark against their use as strikebreaking pawns in the labor-management struggle. As a result of such strategies, the unemployed movement functioned as a training ground for union organizers who became the shock troops of the industrial union movement of the late 1930s and early 1940s.

As the economy revived with the advent of World War II, some leaders of the unemployed movement reinvented themselves as advocates for the "unemployables" of the labor force: women, youth, and the handicapped. From Michigan, for example, the UAW Welfare Department exerted political pressure in Washington in hopes of converting WPA into an agency that might meet the needs of these traditionally ignored elements in the workforce. Simultaneously, the smaller and politically isolated Workers Alliance devoted its energies more and more to the chronically unemployed and long-term relief recipients. The Alliance's shrinking membership base and the cumulative impact of Red-baiting attacks doomed the organization to obscurity in an era marked by an expanding economy.

By 1939, economic recovery and renewed employment opportunity had begun to undermine the unemployed movement as a vibrant social force. The movement was also damaged by sharpened allegations of Communist infiltration as both the House Committee on Un-American Activities and the Committee on Appropriations took aim at the Workers Alliance. Charges of Communist influence, cooptation by New Deal liberalism, the reality of economic revival, engagement in the mainstream union movement, shrinkage of WPA employment, and the onset of war all combined to fatally weaken a movement that had played a key role in sheltering the jobless and the hard core "unemployables" in capitalism's darkest hour.

CONCLUSION

Although the movement faded with the economic upturn, it had contributed in significant ways to the advancement of Depression victims' interests. Advocacy efforts for welfare recipients and public works employees had filled an important gap in the social safety net by shielding workers from economic disaster. Eviction reversals, benefit increases, counseling, and assistance in establishing entitlement were among the concrete services the movement provided for the discards of Depression America. Pressure group activity and lobbying also aided in the enactment of unemployment compensation legislation and complemented liberal efforts to expand WPA programs and other public employment opportunities in the troubled 1930s. Moreover, one of the key achievements of the unemployed movement was certainly its role as a school for unionism, in which the jobless were reminded of the common interests shared by employed and unemployed workers as part of the working class.

When the unemployed refused to cross picket lines and took their organizing experiences into the nation's factories upon reemployment, they often became dedicated union activists who brought industrial unionism to a receptive workforce. Under radical leadership, the unemployed movement had demonstrated how collective action could meet the needs of individuals who committed themselves to participation in a wider social community of human interest. In the process, grassroots unemployed organizers served the most immediate interests of the jobless by creating a web of organizations and activists that constituted an influential mass movement rooted in unprecedented, if transitory, class solidarity

James J. Lorence

BIBLIOGRAPHY

Folsom, Franklin. *Impatient Armies of the Poor: The Story of Collective Action of the Unemployed, 1808–1942.* Niwot: University Press of Colorado, 1991.

Klehr, Harvey. *Heyday of American Communism.* New York: Basic Books, 1984.

Leab, Daniel J. " 'United We Eat': The Creation and Organization of the Unemployed Councils in 1930." *Labor History* 8 (Fall 1967): 300–315.

Lorence, James J. *Organizing the Unemployed: Community and Union Activists in the Industrial Heartland.* Albany: State University of New York Press, 1996.

Piven, Frances Fox, and Richard A. Cloward. *Poor People's Movements: Why They Succeed, How They Fail.* New York: Pantheon, 1977.

Rosenzweig, Roy. "Organizing the Unemployed: The Early Years of the Great Depression, 1929–1933." *Radical America* 10 (July–August 1976): 37–61.

———. "Radicals and the Jobless: The Musteites and the Unemployed Leagues, 1932–1936." *Labor History* 16 (Winter 1975): 52–77.

———. " 'Socialism in Our Time': The Socialist Party and the Unemployed, 1932–1936." *Labor History* 20 (Fall 1979): 485–509.

UNEMPLOYED COUNCILS

The unemployed movements of the 1930s were a powerful response to an economic disaster that helped to give hope and sustenance to unemployed people and their families throughout much of the United States. It was at one and the same time a national movement and a highly localized movement. In addition to providing immediate assistance to many thousands of people, it helped to create significant pressure on local, state, and national governments to provide relief, including substantial social legislation, for those afflicted by unemployment and poverty. It also helped to give significant numbers of people political experience and organizational training that would be utilized in other struggles—most dramatically, the organizing drives and strikes of mass production workers during the 1930s and 1940s spearheaded by the Congress of Industrial Organizations (CIO). It was an important instance in which left-wing organizations in the United States played a vital role and achieved mass influence.

THE GREAT DEPRESSION

The stock market crash in October 1929 signaled the beginning of the Great Depression that afflicted the United States and the world economy for a decade. A salient feature of the economic downturn, of course, was massive unemployment. The number of those who were jobless rose from 492,000 at the time of the crash to 4,065,000 three months later in January 1930. By September of 1930, the number passed 5 million, and in November, 6 million. In January 1931, it was up to 8 million, and by October, it was more than 9 million. It soared to over 12 million by 1933, and before the year was over there were more than 15 million unemployed.

Joblessness led to an inability of millions of workers and their families to secure income for food, clothing, shelter, as well as fuel and other necessities. For many, the consequences were hunger, utility shutoffs, and foreclosures on homes with unpaid mortgages or apartments with unpaid rents. Individual people and individual families dealt with these problems as best they could—seeking help from other family members, relying on charity, asking for food and odd jobs wherever they might be found, and in some cases building little shacks for shelter outside of city limits (in some instances these mushroomed into shantytowns called "Hoovervilles" in bitter tribute to President Herbert Hoover, with his false promise that "prosperity is just around the corner").

THE EARLY UNEMPLOYED MOVEMENT

The unemployed movement was a response to these circumstances—and to a realization by many people that these were common problems that could be adequately solved only through collective action. Much of this movement took the form of collective self-help—people working together to secure food, clothing, shelter, and fuel through a variety of methods: raids on grocery stores, negotiations with farmers to gather crops that would otherwise be wasted, digging and operating illegal "bootleg" coal mines, and setting up increasingly complex bartering systems (selling labor for food, selling food for clothes, selling clothes for food, selling food for haircuts, etc.).

The most effective expressions of the movement were organized by left-wing organizations. The first to take dramatic action was the Communist Party, affiliated with the Communist International, which was able to point out that the Union of Soviet Socialist Republics, under Josef Stalin, was the only country not suffering from this capitalist economic collapse. The Communist Party organized a network of Unemployed Councils that came together as the Unemployed Council of the USA in 1930 and was reorganized in 1934 as the national Unemployed Council.

Some of the most innovative efforts were carried

Americans thrown out of work by the Great Depression, such as these in Philadelphia, organized Unemployed Councils throughout the country.
(© Underwood Photo Archives, Inc.)

out by an offshoot of Brookwood Labor College, the Conference for Progressive Labor Action (CPLA), led by A.J. Muste (hence sometimes referred to as "the Musteites"). The CPLA later became the American Workers Party and then merged with dissident Communists influenced by the ideas of Russian revolutionary Leon Trotsky (known as Trotskyists) into the Workers Party of the United States. The Communist Party organized the Unemployed Councils of the United States of America. The Musteites organized what were generally called Unemployed Leagues, culminating in the formation of the National Unemployed Leagues in 1933.

The more moderate Socialist Party—particularly as radical young activists entered its ranks under the impact of the Depression—soon played a prominent role in a number of areas. Socialist-led formations had various names (the Chicago Workers Committee, the People's Unemployed League of Baltimore, the Unemployed Workers League, etc.) but finally merged with each other (and with the Association of the Unemployed, led by dissident Communists associated with Jay Lovestone) to form the Workers' Alliance of America in 1935.

Historians have sometimes been inclined to dismiss such organizational divisions in the unemployed movement as reflecting sectarian "turf battles" between competing left-wing groups. While this sort of thing was not absent, there were more substantial reasons for the divisions.

In the early 1930s, the Communist Party was guided by the view of Stalin and others that the revolutionary period initiated by the Russian Revolution of 1917 had in the 1920s given way to a second period of capitalist stabilization and prosperity. Now, the Communists maintained, the Depression signaled *a third period* in which capitalism would be overthrown under the leadership of Communist Parties throughout the world. This third-period Communism was often characterized by a recklessly "revolutionary" attitude and a refusal to work in coalition with other left-wing organizations—qualities that affected much Communist work in the unemployed movement.

While the Unemployed Councils developed a reputation for being militantly confrontational, for example, in bodily blocking evictions, the Socialist Party often involved itself in efforts to work with local relief authorities to secure financial assistance for threatened families. The Unemployed Leagues effectively blended both approaches and also often sought to root their efforts in local self-help efforts and to generate revolutionary consciousness among participants. They did so not with appeals to the Russian Revolution, but with references to American revolutionary traditions (such as the frequent use of the "Don't Tread on Me" flag of 1776).

DRAMATIC ACTION

Various components of the unemployed movement engaged in a number of dramatic actions. The Unemployed Councils organized massive protests on March 6, 1930, turning out perhaps half a million nationwide, in about twenty cities: 100,000 each in New York City and Detroit, about 50,000 each in Chicago and Boston, 30,000 in Philadelphia, 25,000 in Cleveland, 20,000 apiece in Pittsburgh and Youngstown, and so on. In many cases, the police attacked the demonstrations, arresting more than 200 and injuring at least 200 more ("Communists have no Constitutional rights," insisted the police commissioner of Los Angeles)—though a number of city governments also pledged aid to the unemployed.

Hunger marches were organized in dozens of cities in the following year. In 1931 and again in 1932, the Unemployed Councils organized hunger marches in Washington, D.C.—the first consisting of less than 1,700 delegates from various cities, and the second with 3,000 delegates, who were attacked by the police.

National marches on the nation's capital were also staged by less radical ideologues. Father James R. Cox, a Catholic priest from Pittsburgh, led a 1932 hunger march of 12,000. Later that year, 22,000 unemployed veterans from World War I converged on Washington, setting up a shantytown and calling on the government for early payment of a $1,000 bonus that had been promised to each of them by law. The law stipulated that the bonus would be paid in 1945, but the veterans argued that they needed it now. Eventually, President Herbert Hoover had troops forcibly disperse the veterans and burn down their shanties. "The Bonus march in the summer of 1932 was one of the most instructive things that ever happened in this country," commented novelist John Dos Passos. "Both its failures and its successes cast light on the realities of popular government under the great monopolies." (In the radical high-tide of 1936—overriding the veto of President Franklin Roosevelt—Congress would pass the Patman Bill, which finally gave the veterans their bonus.)

Perhaps more important for the lives of those suffering from the Depression were the activities taking place in the neighborhoods. Richard Boyer and Herbert Morais have offered a composite anecdote that gives a sense of a more localized dramatic action, of friends and neighbors who came to the aid of unemployed Peter Grossup and his wife, when they were being evicted from their house, after missing mortgage payments, by five deputies from the sheriff's department:

> A tall Negro, apparently in charge, stood next to Mr. Flaherty [his neighbor]. . . . Mr. Flaherty pulled at him again and said, "We're from the Unemployed Council. We want to help."
>
> "Well, my God," shrieked Mr. Grossup, "if you want [to] help, do something then!"
>
> The tall Negro looked briefly at the five deputies on the porch and then at his thirty unemployed.
>
> "Move it back," he said.
>
> In an instant before Mr. Grossup's very eyes all of his prized possessions, his easy chair, even the big refrigerator, the bed posts, the pictures, everything was streaming back into his home. The neighbors began grabbing pots and pans and mattresses and stumbling a little and laughing wildly and calling out in excited tones, clumping up onto the porch and into the house. There was a little scuffle once on the porch with the deputies but more and more neighbors were helping and they just pressed in.
>
> Mr. Grossup never knew how it all happened. It was a happy blur. He had his home again. He had strength. He had friends. . . .

Such activities had effects on a number of levels. "Social workers everywhere told me that without street demonstrations and hunger marches of the Unemployed Councils no relief whatever would have been provided in some communities," according to one reporter, "while in others even less help than that which had been extended would have been forthcoming." One of the leaders of the Unemployed Leagues, A.J. Muste, later described such struggles as "providing an outlet to the unemployed who were no longer passively submitting to their lot, actually ameliorating their condition somewhat, and contributing to the channeling of dissent which, among other things, led to the election of Roosevelt in 1932."

Thousands of protesters—mobilized by Unemployed Councils, Unemployed Leagues, and the Workers' Alliance—converged on state capitols at various times, putting pressure on the legislators. One of the most dramatic protests was a 1936 sit-in at the New Jersey State Legislature, staged by the Workers' Alliance, with unemployed workers occupying the seats normally filled by politicians. They made humorous speeches, "passed" legislation to aid the unemployed, and attracted considerable media attention. The Workers' Alliance issued a pamphlet describing the event by a young militant named George Breitman, who expressed the views of many who were radicalized in this period:

> The interests of the ruling, the boss class, are opposite to those of the exploited, the ruling class; therefore the workers can expect nothing but betrayal from the representatives of the ruling class, their politicians, and must be prepared to fight them for everything they want.

One of the most dramatic developments involved the militant Toledo Auto-Lite Strike in 1934, in which the Lucus County Unemployed League mobilized masses of unemployed workers to join in actively supporting the embattled workers, helping them to win their strike. But people demonstrated loyalty to the radical organizations of the unemployed because of the practical efforts described by Ernest Rice McKinney, a black leader of the Unemployed Leagues:

> We actually got them placed on relief, we actually kept them on relief, we fought the relief organization on behalf of the unemployed very concretely. We got food orders for them, we got houses for them to live in, we got clothing for them. We put their furniture back in the house when it was set out on the street.

We actually turned their gas on when it had been turned off. We wired their houses for electricity when the current had been cut off. We did very concrete things.

UNITY AND DECLINE

By 1936, the various left-wing currents seemed to be converging sufficiently to facilitate the unification of the major components of the unemployed movement. After Musteites merged with Trotskyists in 1935, and then the combined organization began to gravitate toward the radicalized Socialist Party in 1936, the Unemployed Leagues decided to merge into the Workers' Alliance. As the Communist Party shifted away from its earlier "third-period" ultra-leftism toward favoring united-front efforts with other leftwing and even liberal currents, the Unemployed Councils also merged into the Workers' Alliance, with Socialist David Lasser and Communist Herbert Benjamin sharing the leadership of the unified movement.

The reasons for unification were also related to larger developments. At the beginning of the Depression, people responded in very personalized ways, and as individual responses were transformed into collective action, the targets were initially local relief agencies, landlords, and city governments—then state governments. The business and laissez-faire orientation of the national government under Herbert Hoover made it an ideal target for angry protests, but not a likely source of assistance. By the second year of Franklin D. Roosevelt's "New Deal" in 1934, however, national pressure on the policies of the federal government would have greater impact.

Roosevelt initiated a number of important programs that helped the unemployed. A Public Workers Administration (PWA) received billions of dollars in the course of the Depression. The Civilian Conservation Corps (CCC) was established in 1933, and over a nine-year period it employed a total of 2.5 million young men (though only 300,000 to 500,000 at any one time)—living in rural camps, planting millions of trees, fighting hundreds of forest fires, building 42,000 dams, creating hundreds of parks and public camp sites and thousands of miles of hiking trails, laying 45,000 miles of telephone lines. Even more ambitious was the Works Progress Administration (WPA), established in 1935 and employing as many as 2 million men and women at any one time (though drastically fewer before it went out of existence in the early 1940s. In addition to manual workers (building roads, bridges, schools, swimming pools, parks and post offices), the WPA employed clerical workers, teachers, writers, artists, musicians, and others. Of course, there were other forms of government assistance as well; by 1938, a total of 6,641,000 households (representing 20,581,000 individuals, about 20 percent of the population) were receiving some form of public assistance from local, state, and federal agencies, but of these about one-third were on WPA.

In addition to pushing for such programs as these (and for even greater funding to help expand them), the Workers' Alliance, as had the various earlier groups, fought hard for other legislation, including Social Security and unemployment insurance. More than this, the Workers' Alliance organized WPA and CCC workers, functioning as a union of federal employees, struggling for and even going on strike for improved working conditions, for back pay, and for increased pay when hours were increased. By 1938, it claimed a membership of 800,000.

A weakness of the Workers' Alliance, over time, was its increasingly close relationship with, and even growing dependency on, the Roosevelt administration. This relationship may have been understandable given some of the New Deal policies, and it was also related to the pro-Roosevelt shift in Communist Party perspectives, as its united-front orientation evolved into what the Communist International hailed as the People's Front. This emphasized that—in the face of Hitler's aggressive policies toward the USSR and other countries—the choice was not between capitalism and socialism but instead "between bourgeois democracy and fascism," and that Roosevelt's programs (major social reforms in the United States and friendly relations with the USSR) represented, as Communist leader Earl Browder put it, "a People's Front program of an advanced type."

When Roosevelt began to slash New Deal programs in the late 1930s, shifting toward preparations for World War II, the Workers' Alliance was not in a position to provide an effective challenge. Moreover, when the Communist Party defended the September 1939 Hitler-Stalin Non-Aggression Pact (which shocked many on the left), there was an eruption of sharp Socialist-Communist conflict within the Workers' Alliance, culminating in the angry resignation of Lasser and other Socialists.

The unemployed movement had been significantly weakened by other factors as well. There were built-in stabilities. Unemployment is a difficult and demoralizing situation, often making it difficult to sustain ongoing political activity. The most energetic and highly motivated individuals in the unemployed movement will generally seek to end their unemployment if possible through obtaining good jobs in the private sector—and once they do that, they normally leave the unemployed movement. The decisive factor, of course, was that the Depression came to an end with U.S. preparations for World War II, and the evaporation of unemployment naturally brought the evaporation of the unemployed movement.

Nonetheless, the unemployed movements of the 1930s had an enduring impact in more than one way. Hundreds of thousands of people throughout the country benefited from direct contact with these movements, and millions benefited from their successful campaigns for relief to the unemployed. Countless numbers of people crossed racial, ethnic, and religious barriers to join in a common struggle that benefited all—and this had a powerful impact on the consciousness of many. The political education and experience gained by participants was also felt in innumerable ways—particularly among mass production workers who returned to work and helped build powerful industrial unions of the CIO, but also among those who would struggle for civil rights and a variety of social reforms in future years.

Paul Le Blanc

BIBLIOGRAPHY

Bernstein, Irving. *The Lean Years: A History of the American Worker 1920–1933.* Boston: Houghton Mifflin, 1966.

Boyer, Richard O., and Herbert M. Morais. *Labor's Untold Story.* New York: Cameron, 1955.

Breitman, George. *The Trenton Siege by the Army of Unoccupation.* 1936. Reprint, New York: Fourth Internationalist Tendency, 1986.

Feeley, Dianne. In Unity There Is Strength: The Struggle of the Unemployed Throughout the 1930s. Pittsburgh, unpublished manuscript, September 28, 1983.

Folsom, Franklin. *Impatient Armies of the Poor: The Story of Collective Action of the Unemployed, 1808–1942.* Niwot: University Press of Colorado, 1991.

Hacker, Louis M., and Benjamin B. Kendrick. *The United States Since 1865.* 3d ed. New York: F.S. Crofts, 1946.

Muste, A.J. "My Experience in the Labor and Radical Struggles of the Thirties." In *As We Saw the Thirties: Essays on Social and Political Movements of a Decade,* ed. Rita James Simon. Urbana: University of Illinois Press, 1967.

Preis, Art. *Labor's Giant Step: Twenty Years of the CIO.* New York: Pathfinder, 1972.

Rosenzweig, Roy. "Unemployed Movements of the 1930s." In *Encyclopedia of the American Left,* ed. Mari Jo Buhle, Paul Buhle, and Dan Georgakas. New York: Oxford University Press, 1998.

STRIKES OF 1934

The strikes of 1934—particularly those in Toledo, Minneapolis, and San Francisco—were a turning point in the revitalization of the U.S. labor movement, opening the way to the dramatic upsurge through which millions of industrial workers, and others as well, joined the ranks of organized labor. Through tireless organizing efforts and militant strikes, these workers went on to bring dramatic improvements to the quality of life of the U.S. working class and to change the face of the American political scene.

The early years of the Great Depression found the organized labor movement at a low point after a decade of decline during the 1920s. Through business assaults (supported by the government), union membership declined from 5 million in 1920 to 3.5 million in 1923, with the membership of the American Federation of Labor (AFL) remaining steady at just under 3 million throughout the decade. Labor journalist Edward Levinson commented that "from 1923 to 1933 was the Federation's period of sterility." AFL leaders tended to emphasize their respectability, their opposition to all forms of "radicalism," and their desire to contribute to the "efficiency" of the business economy. More than this, they tended to dismiss the possibility of organizing the majority of unskilled and semi-skilled mass production workers, favoring craft unions of skilled workers. Critics denounced the AFL as the "American Separation of Labor" because, ignoring the mass of unorganized workers, it focused on the separate jurisdictions and the various jurisdictional disputes of the craft unions. Nor did they put forward any vision for dealing with the Great Depression, which began in 1929, that was significantly different from that of the conservative Republican president, Herbert Hoover.

The massive unemployment dramatically contributed to the further erosion of AFL membership, which sagged to 2 million. Employers launched an assault on the wages and working conditions of those workers still "lucky enough to have jobs"—and the only significant labor battles of the early Depression years were those engaged in by unemployed workers, led by the political radicals who were despised by the AFL chieftains.

Elements in the labor movement—ranging from dissidents associated with Brookwood Labor College to John L. Lewis, the relatively conservative (but shrewd) autocrat of the United Mine Workers of America—had been pressing for the AFL to shift to a more inclusive, active, and bold orientation required to match the changing times. The explosions of 1934 would provide them with irrefutable arguments.

MILITANT UPSURGE

In Minneapolis, Vincent Raymond Dunne and other dissident Communist followers of Leon Trotsky (who were opposed to Josef Stalin's dictatorship, which had taken over in the decade following the 1917 Russian Revolution) led thousands of Teamsters and others to victory through a militant general strike that used bold new tactics. In San Francisco, mainstream Communists allied with Harry Bridges led West Coast longshoremen to a partial victory after a hard-fought general strike. In Ohio, Toledo Auto-Lite workers, led by A.J. Muste and his Socialist followers in the American Workers Party, won a similar victory.

The Toledo Auto-Lite Strike began on February 23 and stretched to June 4. The Minneapolis Teamsters strikes came in three phases: a strike of coal-yard workers, February 7–9, which established Local 574 of the International Brotherhood of Teamsters, which went on to wage citywide strikes from May 15 to May 25 and July 16 to August 22. The San Francisco longshoremen's strike erupted on May 9 and was settled on July 31. There was a labor upsurge throughout the country during the year, with gains being made by mine workers, garment workers, clothing workers, and others.

Most dramatic was a national textile workers strike lasting from September 1 to September 22 under the leadership of the United Textile Workers; this strike was especially notable for mobilizing thousands of hard-pressed workers throughout the South who displayed remarkable determination and courage. But with minimal strike funds and illusions that the administration of Franklin D. Roosevelt would support them, they could not withstand the brutal and violent repression (sixteen workers were killed and many others were wounded) orchestrated by powerful mill owners and their political friends. Unlike so many of the other battles of 1934, the national textile strike went down to bitter defeat (15,000 workers were fired and blacklisted), setting back the cause of southern labor for many years to come.

Yet the balance of power in the labor struggles of 1934 tilted decisively in labor's favor. The strikes that proved to be decisive were those of Toledo, Minneapolis, and San Francisco.

COMMON PATTERNS

As outlined by A.J. Muste, the three struggles shared several key elements.

> The methods employed in the Auto-Lite strike—calm defiance of injunctions, cooperation between unemployed organizations and unions, dramatization of the strike issue to bring the masses out to observe and participate in picketing, the threat of a local general strike by the city central body, persistent effort by groups of advanced workers with a revolutionary outlook but a realistic union policy—brought the Auto-Lite strike to an end with a partial victory for the union. Before a year passed, these methods had led to the complete unionization of the Auto-Lite plant and of the entire auto parts industry in Toledo. In other cities and industries these same methods, in many cases applied by workers consciously following the Toledo example, brought complete or partial victory in a great series of struggles which made the year 1934 one of the most notable in the history of the American working class.

Of special importance were the left-wing groups that helped to provide, influence, and back up the capable people with fiercely radical ideas who led the struggles. "The dynamic intervention of a revolutionary workers organization, the American Workers Party, seemed to have been required before that outcome could be achieved," noted Muste's comrade, strike leader Louis Budenz. "The officials in the [AFL-sponsored] Federal Automobile Workers Union would have lost the strike if left to their own resources."

"Our policy was to organize and build strong unions so workers could have something to say about their own lives and assist in changing the present order into a socialist society," V.R. Dunne matter-of-factly explained when he spoke of his efforts in leading workers of his hometown to victory. "Probably four or five hundred workers in Minneapolis knew 'Ray' personally," journalist Charles Walker later commented. "They formed their own opinions—that he was honest, intelligent, and selfless, and a damn good organizer for the truck drivers' union to have. They had always known him to be a Red; that was no news."

In addition to the basic methods Muste described from the Toledo experience, innovations in the Minneapolis strikes included: the use of "flying squadrons" (roving pickets utilizing automobiles and directed via radio from a central command point); the establishment of a strike headquarters that would include a commissary to help feed strikers and their families, and a hospital; the development of a women's auxiliary to facilitate involvement in the strike of wives, sisters, mothers, and sweethearts (among others) in the multiple activities and tasks connected with the struggle; the production of a fairly professional daily strike newspaper to tell the strikers' side of the story, *The Organizer,* which was full of information and humor.

On the West Coast, Harry Bridges, leader of the radicalized International Longshore and Warehouseman's Union that emerged from the San Francisco strike, did not hesitate in expressing the opinion that "the capitalistic form of society . . . means the exploitation of a lot of people for a profit and a complete disregard of their interests for that profit, [and] I haven't much use for that." Relying on a substantial core of left-wing activists (with the Communist Party in particular committing its newspaper, legal and other professional assistance, and its substantial cadres to the struggle), Bridges was able to mobilize a powerful force capable of doing battle with the immense power deployed by West Coast business interests.

As in Toledo and Minneapolis, there was a need for mass picketing, and the willingness to engage in pitched battles with company thugs and the forces of "law and order" that were defending the rights of employers to break unions resulted in casualties on both sides. In all three cases, the National Guard was brought in, and martial law was declared. In San Francisco, the deaths of two strikers occasioned a call for a massive funeral march—"a stupendous and reverent procession that astounded the city," wrote the *San Francisco Chronicle,* as thousands of union members marched to honor the martyrs and their cause. And as with the other two key strikes, the entire labor movement was drawn into the struggle, largely through rank-and-file pressure, through a general strike that brought the city to a standstill.

In Toledo, Minneapolis, and San Francisco, the strikes ended with compromise settlements and partial victories. But in each case, this decisively shifted the balance of power and provided the essential foothold through which more gains were rapidly achieved. Each city soon attained the status of strong "union town."

PAVING THE WAY

The 1934 strikes not only inspired workers in many other areas to go and do likewise, but it convinced certain key AFL figures—John L. Lewis of the United Mine Workers, Sidney Hillman of the Amalgamated Clothing Workers, David Dubinsky of the International Ladies' Garment Workers' Union, and others—that it was time to form a Committee for Industrial Organization (CIO, which later formed a separate Congress of Industrial Organizations). This soon resulted in a decisive break with the more conservative leadership of the AFL.

Under the CIO banner, a number of powerful new industrial unions came into existence, representing auto workers, steelworkers, electrical workers, rubber workers, longshore and maritime workers, transit workers, and many more. These unions were built, in large measure, by following the example and utilizing the techniques associated with the 1934 victories. The AFL leadership responded by shifting away from its outright opposition to industrial unionism. By 1937, the CIO had 1.5 million members, and the AFL had grown to 2.5 million. Both federations would continue to grow through the 1940s.

This not only brought immediate and tangible gains to the workers who won union recognition and consequent improvements in working conditions and living standards, but it also created an organized force that pushed many politicians (including President Roosevelt) to adopt pro-labor policies. As a result, the balance of power in U.S. politics would be changed for many years to come.

Paul Le Blanc

BIBLIOGRAPHY

Bernstein, Irving. *The Turbulent Years: A History of the American Worker 1933–1941.* Boston: Houghton Mifflin, 1969.

Dobbs, Farrell. *Teamster Bureaucracy.* New York: Pathfinder Press, 1977.

———. *Teamster Rebellion.* New York: Pathfinder, 1972.

Korth, Philip A. *The Minneapolis Teamsters Strike of 1934.* East Lansing: Michigan State University Press, 1995.

Korth, Philip A., and Margaret Beegle. *I Remember Like Today: The Auto-Lite Strike of 1934.* East Lansing: Michigan State University Press, 1988.

Le Blanc, Paul. *A Short History of the U.S. Working Class.* Amherst, NY: Humanity Books, 1999.

Levinson, Edward. *Labor on the March.* New York: Harper & Row, 1938.

Muste, A.J. "The Automobile Industry and Organized Labor." *New Frontiers,* September 1936: 5–47.

Nelson, Bruce. "San Francisco General Strike." In *Encyclopedia of the American Left,* ed. Mari Jo Buhle, Paul Buhle, and Dan Georgakas, 718–720. New York: Oxford University Press, 1998.

———. *Workers on the Waterfront: Seamen, Longshoremen, and Unionism in the 1930s.* Urbana: University of Illinois Press, 1988.

Preis, Art. *Labor's Giant Step: Twenty Years of the CIO.* New York: Merit, 1964.

Quinn, Mike. *The Big Strike.* New York: International, 1979.

Riehle, David. "Minneapolis Teamsters Strike." In *Encyclopedia of the American Left,* ed. Mari Jo Buhle, Paul Buhle, and Dan Georgakas, 499–501. New York: Oxford University Press, 1998.

Walker, Charles Rumford. *American City: A Rank-and-File History.* New York: Farrar and Rinehart, 1937.

BROOKWOOD LABOR COLLEGE

Brookwood Labor College, one of the outstanding educational institutions in the United States, played an essential part in the training of labor activists—intellectually and organizationally—who revitalized the labor movement through the creation of the Congress of Industrial Organizations (CIO) in the 1930s. Established in Katonah, New York, in 1921, it was animated by the tension between an institutionalized union movement functioning as part of a capitalist economy and the vision of democratic and militant workers' struggles that would create a future free from oppression and exploitation. The tension intensified and culminated in fissures among the school's founders and faculty, and finally in Brookwood's closing in 1937.

WORKERS' EDUCATION AND BROOKWOOD'S BEGINNINGS

In the wake of the radicalization that issued from the disillusionment over World War I and the hopes generated by the Russian Revolution, many left-wing trade unionists and radical educators in the United States—in part influenced by workers' education efforts in England—moved to establish "labor colleges" across the United States. In 1921, a Workers Education Bureau was created to help coordinate such efforts, and its first president was James Maurer, who explained that "the underlying purpose of workers' education is the desire for a better social order . . . and the ultimate liberation of the working masses." He urged that it not be utilized to help students rise out of the working class, but rather that it help them to "serve the labor movement in particular and society in general."

Some workers' education efforts took the form of evening classes sponsored by unions and central labor councils, whereas others involved summer schools, such as the Bryn Mawr Summer School for Women or the Wisconsin School for Workers (affiliated with the University of Wisconsin). A third form consisted of residential labor schools, of which Brookwood Labor College was the most prominent.

At the end of World War I, well-to-do pacifists William and Helen Fincke, deeply influenced by Walter Rauschenbusch's Christian Socialist Social Gospel perspectives and by John Dewey's approach to progressive education, had sought to establish a school for working-class children in Westchester County, on a beautiful wooded estate about forty miles from New York City. Concluding (in consultation with their close friends Toscan and Josephine Bennett) that the effort should be shifted in the direction of workers' education, the Finckes called a conference of left-wing labor activists to discuss such a project.

Among those who gathered at Katonah were John Brophy, president of District 2 of the United Mine Workers of America; Jay Brown, president of the International Timber Workers Union; Fannia Cohn, education director of the International Ladies' Garment Workers' Union; John Fitzpatrick, president of the Illinois Federation of Labor; Charles Kutz, head of Pennsylvania Railroad employees in the International Association of Machinists; Abraham Lefkowitz, vice president of the American Federation of Teachers; James Maurer, president of the Pennsylvania Federation of Labor; A.J. (Abraham Johannas) Muste, president of the Amalgamated Textile Workers of America; Joseph Schlossberg, secretary-treasurer of the Amalgamated Clothing Workers of America; and Rose Schneiderman, president of the Women's Trade Union League. They agreed on four basic points that would be the basis for the establishment of Brookwood Labor College:

1. A new social order was needed and was coming—in fact, it was already on the way.
2. Education would not only hasten its coming, but

would also reduce to a minimum and perhaps entirely eliminate the need to resort to violent methods.

3. The workers themselves would usher in the new social order.
4. There was an immediate need for a workers' college with a broad curriculum, located amid healthy country surroundings, where the students could completely apply themselves to the task at hand.

A Socialist perspective lay at the core of Brookwood's philosophy, but it was intimately intertwined with a commitment to practical trade union organizing within the framework of the American Federation of Labor (AFL). "Socialist ideas were not offered as a substitute for trade unionism, but rather as a supplement, a means of strengthening the union," as John Brophy explained. He and the others formed a board of directors for the Brookwood Labor College, and they selected A.J. Muste to be the day-to-day director of the college. A tall, lean thirty-six-year-old who had been an effective leader of the 1919 Lawrence Textile Strike, Muste had before that event been a scholarly pastor, associated with the pacifist Fellowship of Reconciliation, animated by the Social Gospel and by an enthusiasm for the socialism of Eugene V. Debs.

Although day-to-day activities at Brookwood would be determined by the faculty in consultation with the students, policy was set by the ten-person board of directors. The board would be made up of labor representatives, with a nonvoting Educational Advisory Committee, and with representatives of the faculty having four votes and of the students having two votes.

Fifteen students enrolled in 1921, and eventually the yearly number of students would average fifty. This was the beginning of a venture that would eventually educate close to 500 organizers and activists who would later help transform the American political scene.

A.J. MUSTE'S FACULTY AND STUDENTS

With a few significant exceptions, the workers enrolled at Brookwood Labor College were young labor radicals, who were either open to or already influenced by various currents of left-wing thought. One early Brookwood student, Len De Caux, later described Brookwood's director in this way:

A.J. Muste was the man who ran Brookwood, resident labor college, of the Twenties. We could not then have

Revolutionary and pacifist A.J. Muste directed Brookwood Labor College, a school devoted to working-class organization and militancy in the 1920s and 1930s. (Karen Eberhardt/Walter P. Reuther Library, Wayne State University)

imagined his later career as militant activist in radical and pacifist causes—in his eighties he matched the youth as man of action against the Vietnam war. To us young Brookwooders, A.J. was essentially the moderate. We respected his counsels of caution, practicality, a relative labor conformism. But our favorite crack was that he always looked for the center with his "On the one hand . . . But on the other hand. . . ." I would have expected him to progress ever rightward, a typical social-democrat. Youthful impatients, we didn't suspect that fires like our own might burn beneath the diplomatic calm of this lean and eager man.

Muste's own evaluation of the faculty, staff, and students at Brookwood is also revealing. "Above all, the men and women . . . with whom I worked closely for a decade or more at Brookwood, in the general

A.J. MUSTE (1885–1967)

Abraham Johannes Muste was born on January 8, 1885, in Zierikzee, the Netherlands. A pacifist who became a Marx-Leninist revolutionary and then a pacifist again, Muste served as a minister in three different Christian denominations. Known to the public as A.J. Muste, he was sometimes called "America's Gandhi" because he was a leading influence on twentieth-century social movements in the United States.

Muste came to the United States at age six and was raised by a Republican family in the strict Calvinist traditions of the Dutch Reformed Church. In 1909, he was ordained a minister in that church and married Anna Huizenga, with whom he raised three children. He was class valedictorian at Hope College and received a degree from Union Theological Seminary, graduating magna cum laude.

In 1914, increasingly uncomfortable with the Reformed Church, he became pastor of a Congregational Church. When war broke out in Europe, Muste, inspired by the Society of Friends (Quakers), became a pacifist. Three years later his antiwar stance cost him his church, whereupon he took a church post with the Quakers in Providence in 1918. He then started working with the fledgling American Civil Liberties Union in Boston. In 1919, as executive secretary of the Amalgamated Textile Workers (1919–1921), when the textile industry strikers appealed for help from the religious community, he suddenly found himself thrust into the center of the great labor strikes in Lawrence, Massachusetts. From 1921 to 1933, Muste served as director of the Brookwood Labor College in Katonah, New York. Its curriculum, which consisted of the theory and practice of labor militancy, supported his efforts to train labor activists.

For several years during the 1920s, Muste served as chairman of the Fellowship of Reconciliation but steadily drifted toward revolutionary politics, and in 1929 he helped form the Conference for Progressive Labor Action (CPLA), seeking to reform the American Federation of Labor from within. When the Great Depression hit, the CPLA became openly revolutionary

and was instrumental in forming the American Workers Party in 1933, in which Muste played the leading role. He abandoned his Christian pacifism and became an avowed Marxist-Leninist. He was a key figure in organizing the sit-down strikes of the 1930s and merged his own political group with another to form the Trotskyist Workers Party of America.

In 1936, Muste traveled to Norway to meet with Leon Trotsky. It is not clear what took place, but Muste returned that same year as a Christian pacifist. Although he did remain active in the labor movement, in 1940 he became executive secretary of the religious pacifist organization Fellowship of Reconciliation (FOR), a post he held until 1953. The organization adopted radical methods of civil disobedience under Muste's leadership and inspired the organization of the Congress on Racial Equality, the first of the militant civil rights groups.

At age sixty-eight, Muste "retired" and wrote several books. In retirement he became the leader of the Committee for Nonviolent Action, an organization that actively protested nuclear power and arms proliferation. Muste was close to the emerging liberation movements in Africa, and he helped organize the World Peace Brigade, which worked closely with Kenneth Kaunda of Zambia and Julius Nyerere of Tanzania. In the United States, Muste served as close friend and mentor to Martin Luther King Jr. and his wife, Coretta Scott King.

Muste also became a pivotal figure in organizing opposition to end the Vietnam War. In 1966, he led a group of pacifists to Saigon, where, after trying to demonstrate for peace, they were arrested and deported. Later that same year, he flew with a small team of religious leaders to Hanoi where they met with Ho Chi Minh. Less than a month later, on February 11, 1967, Muste died suddenly in New York City. At his death, messages of condolence came from sources as diverse as Ho Chi Minh and Robert Kennedy. A brilliant thinker, he produced no single body of theoretical work but did leave behind a remarkable legacy of fighting for peace and social justice.

James G. Lewis

field of workers' education, and in various phases of labor organization and strike activity, were people of integrity," Muste later recalled. "They had their shortcomings, in a few cases distressing or irritating ones, but they were solid and clean, incapable of playing cheap politics, though by no means political babes or bunglers."

Muste himself taught courses in the history of Western civilization and the United States. Specializing in U.S. and international labor history was David J. Saposs, who had been a student and associate of John R. Commons and had co-authored with Commons, Selig Perlman, and others the classic *History of Labor in the United States*. His minor classic *Left-Wing*

Unionism: A Study of Radical Policies and Tactics (1926) (whose arguments against radical "dual unionism" coincided with those of William Z. Foster) was published by the Communist Party's International Publishers in 1926—though Saposs was not a member of the Communist Party (Brookwood students remembered him as being more moderate than Muste) and was destined to become a member of the National Labor Relations Board. Mark Starr—who taught economics and labor journalism—had been involved in the National Council of Labor Colleges of England; he would later become education director of the International Ladies' Garment Workers' Union and co-author a standard popular text, *Labor in America* (1944), for use in high schools and labor education classes in the late 1940s and 1950s. He met his future wife, Helen Norton (a rail worker's daughter and college graduate from Kansas), on the Brookwood faculty, where she trained students in labor journalism and helped them produce the *Brookwood Review.*

One of the most popular and most radical of the teachers was Arthur W. Calhoun. Calhoun had an undergraduate degree from the University of Pittsburgh and a Ph.D. from the University of Wisconsin, and teaching experience at Clark University; he was also the author of a pioneering three-volume *Social History of the American Family from Colonial Times to the Present* (1917–1919) and taught sociology, economics, and even courses in Marxism, while his wife Mildred taught courses in English. (Calhoun was replaced in 1929 by an instructor from the Seattle Labor College, John C. Kennedy.) Another popular Brookwood stalwart was Josephine Colby, a high school teacher with a degree from the University of California; she was an instructor in English (also teaching English as a second language to many of the immigrant workers who came to Brookwood), literature, and public speaking, and directed many of the plays put on by the Brookwood Labor Players. Tom Tippett, who developed as an energetic labor educator during his years as a radical mine workers' organizer, served as director of Brookwood's extension program, organizing classes for central labor councils, state labor federations, and local unions. According to one student, he was "a stimulating and colorful teacher who correlates theory with practical activity"; he also became involved in union-organizing efforts in the South, which he described in the classic *When Southern Labor Stirs* (1931).

Workers from mostly urban and largely industrial environments were not brought into a well-organized and beautiful campus in a rural setting for the pur-pose of duplicating normal "higher education," which Brookwood supporter Jean Flexner described as catering to "the inexperienced, impressionable dilettante, who drifts with open and colorless mind through a kaleidoscope of courses to emerge without deep convictions or definite objectives." Seasoned labor radical Clint Golden—Brookwood's field secretary, who raised money, secured union support, and scouted for students—explained that workers needed "expert knowledge as a weapon in their struggle for justice," emphasizing: "By developing and controlling our own institutions of learning, for the men and women of our movement, we will educate the workers into the service of their fellow workers rather than away from the labor movement, as is so often the case when the ambitious unionist enters the average university." And yet, according to Cara Cook (the librarian who also oversaw much of the administrative work and tutored as well), a distinctive characteristic of Brookwood was that "we were always singing." One of the songs gave a humorous sense of faculty and staff:

> There's A.J. Muste, a teacher, He used to be a preacher . . .
> And Polly Colby makes them speak, With phrases smooth and manner neat . . .
> Dave Saposs tells them stories, About past union glories . . .
> And Helen Norton makes them write, For labor papers day and night . . .
> Tom Tippett teaches classes, In the field to union masses . . .
> While J.C. Kennedy does his stuff, and Makes them learn their Marx enough . . .
> Mark Starr does British labor, With considerable British flavor . . .
> And Cara Cook does this and that, and runs the Secretariat . . .

Singing, socializing, putting on plays, playing baseball, communing with nature—all were essential elements of the Brookwood experience. So was physical labor, with all students and faculty expected to help with the work that was necessary to prepare meals, wash dishes, do the laundry, clean the various facilities of the institution, maintain the grounds, repair and expand the school's buildings, and so on. "The importance and dignity of hand work and head work are both fully appreciated," Brookwood's founding committee affirmed.

Another aspect of the Brookwood curriculum was

fieldwork. This involved practical experience assisting unions (sometimes in strike situations or assisting in the efforts of union reformers) or engaging in other campaigns—such as participating in the struggles to save the lives of the famous Italian Anarchists sitting on Death Row, Nicola Sacco and Bartolomeo Vanzetti, or participating in antiwar activities. Faculty as well as students were expected to do such fieldwork.

Students could attend Brookwood for either one or two years. The first year offered more basic courses, and the second (for those returning) offered more advanced training. In addition to courses designed to give a background in history, sociology, economics, and other academic areas, there were courses designed to teach practical skills for labor activists: Trade Union Organization, Structure, Government and Administration of Trade Unions, Labor Journalism, Labor Legislation and Administration, The Strategy of the Labor Movement, Public Speaking, Labor Dramatics, and Training in Speaking and Writing. A typical first-year student might, for one term, study economics two mornings a week, English three mornings a week, and in the afternoons have drama twice a week and sociology three times a week. A typical second-year student might have morning courses in public speaking and drama twice a week, journalism twice a week, and labor issues twice a week; with the afternoons involving intensive labor history and social psychology courses.

The evenings might involve social or cultural activities—or educational discussions with guest speakers: novelist Sinclair Lewis, labor historian Norman Ware, A. Philip Randolph of the Brotherhood of Sleeping Car Porters, Norman Thomas of the Socialist Party, Father John A. Ryan of the Catholic Social Welfare Council, Communist Party educator Bertram Wolfe, philosopher John Dewey, economist Scott Nearing, Fenner Brockway from the British Labor Party, J. Olson of the Norwegian Labor Party, Socialist educator and journalist Oscar Ameringer, Roger Baldwin of the American Civil Liberties Union, John Keracher of the Proletarian Party, historian Harry Elmer Barnes, and many others.

Diversity was a hallmark of Brookwood's student body, which ranged in age from teens to people in their fifties (though a majority were between twenty-one and thirty years old). About one-third of the student body was female (much higher than the percentage of women in the labor movement of that time). A survey of forty-two students in 1927 reveals that about 52 percent were native-born and 48 percent foreign-born, with the great majority (thirty-three students) coming from families of industrial workers, and half had completed no more than eight years of school (some significantly less). Although the largest number of students came from the industrial Northeast, many came from the South and Midwest, and some from the far West as well as from other countries. There was also significant ethnic diversity, including African-American workers and activists. Ideological diversity was also represented in different religious backgrounds and different political orientations. A mixture of Socialists from various organizations (and from no organization at all) mixed with Anarchists and "pure and simple" trade unionists, as well as workers who didn't identify themselves with such labels.

GOMPERS AND LENIN

Debate and discussion were encouraged at Brookwood, and all were urged to see themselves as part of the effort to revitalize the labor movement. Dominant currents within the AFL increasingly saw this approach as a threat; as the 1920s unfolded, they were increasingly inclined to become even more conservative than the ex-Socialist, "pure and simple" AFL president Samuel Gompers had been. They certainly did not want to be "revitalized." Ultimately, this tension deepened and finally tore Brookwood apart.

Along with Gompers and many others in the labor and Socialist movements, most of Brookwood's faculty, staff, and students threw themselves into the 1924 third-party presidential campaign of Progressive Robert M. La Follette. La Follette netted an impressive 4 million votes, but the AFL leadership reared back from what it considered a terrible failure. In contrast, Brookwood spokesmen continued to advocate the creation of an independent labor party. They also were increasingly inclined to criticize the exclusive craft-union focus on skilled workers favored by the dominant forces in the AFL, calling for new industrial unions that would organize unskilled mass production workers. Moreover, they were tolerant or even actively sympathetic toward various forms of labor radicalism that challenged the AFL's top leadership.

The list of guest speakers, as we have seen, included a large percentage of left-wing figures, some of whom were members of or close to the Communist Party, which was anathema to the AFL leadership. For that matter, several of the faculty members—Calhoun, Saposs, Colby, and Tippett—were identified (falsely) by some AFL conservatives as being Communist Party members.

The school staged memorials to commemorate the

deaths not only of AFL founder Samuel Gompers, but also of Russian Communist leader Vladimir Ilich Lenin and U.S. Socialist leader Eugene V. Debs. May Day celebrations featured portraits of all three, along with such others as Rosa Luxemburg and Leon Trotsky. (Muste later commented: "The composition of the student body being what it was, some of them were as irked at having Gompers' picture on the wall as others were by Lenin's, but it was in accord with the catholicity we observed in these matters that both were there and the entire student body took part in the meeting.") Then too, some songs sung at Brookwood may have proved offensive to labor conservatives. One of these songs was written by student Edith Berkowitz and contained, in part, the following words: "They've refused to heed our suffering, But they'll hear our marching feet! We have the workers' Red Flag unfurled. We come to take back our world."

After several years of fruitless efforts to force Brookwood to submit to their more conservative labor orientation, in 1928 the AFL leadership—relying on informants placed within the student body—released a sensational public denunciation of Brookwood Labor College as Communistic and called on its affiliates to sever relations. Many of them refused to do so when Brookwood denied the charges, and many prestigious pro-labor liberals and radicals rallied to the college's defense. And yet the situation created terrible tensions—which were complicated by the Communist Party's attacks on Brookwood in the same year.

Among the Communists attending the college at that time were Sylvia Bleeker and her companion Morris Lewit, who—in the factional disputes within the Communist Party at that time—were aligned with William Z. Foster against the organization's general secretary Jay Lovestone. Factional infighter that he was, Lovestone made a point of having the Party press attack Brookwood in 1928 as "class-collaborationist," serving as "a cloak for the reactionary labor fakirs." He publicly berated the "Fosterites" at the college for co-signing the Brookwood statement allegedly "denouncing the communist movement and kowtowing to the American Federation of Labor bureaucracy." This began an irreversible development of Communist Party hostility to Brookwood that continued well after Lovestone lost his factional fight. (Under the influence of Soviet dictator Josef Stalin, U.S. Communists from 1929 through 1934 would attack all Socialist groups and labor organizations not controlled by the Communist Party.)

Adding to the tangle was the fact that Brookwood faculty member Arthur Calhoun publicly disassociated himself from the college's defensive statement. While insisting that he was not a member of the Communist Party, he argued that the college should openly break from reactionary AFL leadership and politically align itself with the revolutionary orientation that the Communists represented. In response, Muste and the majority of the faculty (including those who had been red-baited by the AFL leaders) urged the board of directors not to renew Calhoun's contract. This created new dissensions among Brookwood's remaining supporters.

And then the Great Depression came. This, combined with the attacks from the AFL, caused Muste and some of the others associated with Brookwood to assume a more radical trajectory. Since 1924, the Socialist magazine *Labor Age*—edited by labor activist Louis F. Budenz—had become increasingly associated with Brookwood, and by 1929 Muste was working with Budenz and others in the milieu of the magazine and college to establish the Conference for Progressive Labor Action (CPLA). A number of Brookwood graduates and supporters became involved in the new venture—which began with a call for (1) organizing the unorganized workers into unions, (2) working to transform the craft unions of the AFL into more inclusive industrial unions, (3) breaking down all exclusion from union membership for racial, political, economic, social, or religious reasons, (4) launching government programs providing unemployment benefits and other forms of social insurance, (5) creating a labor party based on the trade unions, (6) persuading the U.S. government to recognize the Soviet Union; and (7) encouraging anti-imperialist and antimilitarist policies by the U.S. labor movement, which would lead to "a closer union of all workers of the world."

With the coming of the Depression, however, a majority of activists in the CPLA became more intensely involved than ever in the struggles of the unemployed (building militant Unemployed Leagues), as well as in desperate strike actions. Through the early 1930s, a powerful dynamic of radicalization drew Muste and a number of CPLA members to the conclusion that—in competition with what they saw as the "sectarian" Communist Party and the hopelessly compromising Socialist Party—the CPLA should evolve into a revolutionary vanguard party that operated according to the principles of democratic centralism. This would mean that its members would be "workers and fighters in the revolutionary movement"—with "the policies which they carry out in a disciplined manner . . . worked out by these members themselves on the basis of the most democratic discussion." Muste urged that "Brookwood be transformed into a training base" for "CPLA fighters" and that it focus less on general education and more on "action and direct involvement in the labor struggle."

A majority of Brookwood's faculty (including Colby, Norton, Saposs, and Starr) and the board of directors decisively rejected this version of the CPLA in 1933. The break was painful. Muste and his supporters left the college to pursue their radical course. Brookwood continued for almost four more years under the capable and energetic leadership of Tucker P. Smith, who was recruited not from the labor movement but from the pacifist Fellowship of Reconciliation. Among the new faculty was Roy Reuther, who with his brothers Walter and Victor (both of whom also visited Brookwood) would play a key part in the creation of the United Auto Workers. Those remaining sought to adhere to Brookwood's original goals, yet the college's spirit was altered and its base significantly eroded by what had taken place. Lack of funds forced it to close its doors in 1937.

LEGACIES

Brookwood Labor College was a vital moment in the history of the American labor movement; though itself unable to endure, it left an enduring legacy. Its faculty formed Workers Education Local 189 of the American Federation of Teachers, which expanded beyond Brookwood during the 1930s to embrace labor educators in many locations. Internal differences led to a shift in affiliation to the Communication Workers of America, but Local 189 has continued into the twenty-first century as a gathering place for labor educators and as the symbolic high point in workers' education.

Many Brookwood veterans played an essential role in the battles, strikes, and organizing efforts that created the Congress of Industrial Organizations. Although the Socialist future that had animated them never came into being, many of them went on to assume important posts in the CIO (and after 1955 in the AFL-CIO) and its various union affiliates, as well as in the fields of education, politics, and government. While many of these former radicals became very much a part of the trade union "establishment," younger labor radicals seeking to revitalize the labor movement have often looked to the Brookwood experience for inspiration and useful lessons.

Muste and those who followed him away from Brookwood with the CPLA went on, during the early years of the Depression, to militant actions of the Unemployed Leagues and "class struggle" activities. One of the most dramatic of these activities was the Toledo Auto-Lite Strike of 1934. The CPLA evolved into the American Workers Party at the end of 1933, and then it merged with the Communist League of America (followers of Leon Trotsky) at the beginning of 1935. Some of Muste's comrades stayed with the Trotskyists for many years, others ended up in other groups, and some dropped out of left-wing politics altogether. Muste himself soon returned to his radical pacifist and Christian roots in the Fellowship of Reconciliation, where he played a leadership role in antiwar and antiracist struggles for many years afterward.

The Brookwood experience impacted on other radicals who had a major impact on the civil rights movement of the 1950s and 1960s. Myles Horton visited and studied Brookwood as a partial model for the Highlander Folk School, which he and other radical educators established in Tennessee during the 1930s and which shifted from training labor activists to training civil rights activists in the 1950s. One Highlander associate who was centrally involved in establishing both the Southern Christian Leadership Conference (SCLC) of Martin Luther King Jr. and the Student Non-Violent Coordinating Committee (SNCC) was Ella Baker—who was also a graduate of Brookwood Labor College.

Paul Le Blanc

BIBLIOGRAPHY

Allen, Devere. *Adventurous Americans.* New York: Farrar and Rinehart, 1932.

Altenbaugh, Richard J. *Education for Struggle: The American Labor Colleges of the 1920s and 1930s.* Philadelphia: Temple University Press, 1990.

Bernstein, Irving. *The Lean Years: A History of the American Worker 1920–1933.* Boston: Houghton Mifflin, 1966.

Bloom, John. "Workers Education." In *Encyclopedia of the American Left,* ed. Mari Jo Buhle, Paul Buhle, and Dan Georgakas. New York: Oxford University Press, 1998.

Brameld, Theodore. *Workers Education in the United States.* New York: Harper and Brothers, 1941.

Brooks, Thomas R. *Clint: A Biography of a Labor Intellectual, Clinton S. Golden.* New York: Atheneum, 1978.

Calhoun, Arthur Wallace. *A Social History of the American Family from Colonial Times to the Present.* Cleveland, OH: The Arthur H. Clark Company, 1917–1919.

Commons, John R., et al. *History of Labour in the United States.* New York: Macmillan, 1921–1935.

Conference for Progressive Labor Action. *CPLA Program-Policies.* New York: Futuro, n.d.

De Caux, Len. *Labor Radical: From the Wobblies to CIO, A Personal History.* Boston: Beacon, 1970.

Faulkner, Harold U., and Mark Starr. *Labor in America.* New York: Harper & Row, 1949.

Foner, Philip S. *History of the Labor Movement in the United States.* Vol. 9. New York: International, 1991.

Hentoff, Nat. *Peace Agitator: The Story of A.J. Muste.* New York: Macmillan, 1963.

Howlett, Charles F. *Brookwood Labor College and the Struggle for Peace and Social Justice in America.* Lewiston, NY: Edwin Mellen, 1993.

Le Blanc, Paul, and Michael Steven Smith. "Morris Lewit: Pioneer Leader of American Trotskyism (1903–1998)." In *Revolutionary Labor Socialist: The Life, Ideas, and Comrades of Frank Lovell,* ed. Paul Le Blanc and Thomas Barrett. Union City, NJ: Smyrna, 2000.

Lovell, Frank. "Sylvia Bleeker (1901–1988): Union Organizer, Socialist Agitator and Lifelong Trotskyist." In *Revolutionary Labor Socialist: The Life, Ideas, and Comrades of Frank Lovell,* ed. Paul Le Blanc and Thomas Barrett, 295–301. Union City, NJ: Smyrna, 2000.

Lovestone, Jay. *Pages From Party History.* New York: Workers Library, 1928.

Muste, A.J. "My Experience in Labor and Radical Struggles." In *As We Saw the Thirties: Essays on Social and Political Movements of a Decade,* ed. Rita James Simon, 125–150. Urbana: University of Illinois Press, 1967.

———. "Sketches for an Autobiography." In *The Essays of A.J. Muste,* ed. Nat Hentoff, 1–174. New York: Simon and Schuster, 1970.

Robinson, Joanne Ooiman. *Abraham Went Out: A Biography of A.J. Muste.* Philadelphia: Temple University Press, 1981.

Saposs, David J. *Left-Wing Unionism: A Study of Radical Policies and Tactics.* New York: International Publishers, 1926.

Tippett, Tom. *When Southern Labor Stirs.* New York: Jonathan Cape and Harrison Smith, 1931.

LABOR MOVEMENT 1935–1947

The birth of the Congress of Industrial Organizations (CIO) represented a watershed in American labor history. At the center of labor activism during two crucial decades, the CIO not only exercised a key role in the establishment and expansion of collective bargaining in the nation's core industries, but it also provided a political voice for the nation's working class. During the era of the New Deal and World War II, the CIO pioneered and supported political initiatives that involved economic policy and social welfare. In the process, the CIO aided in the forging of the New Deal Democratic coalition, which dominated American politics for nearly forty years.

Besides involving itself in domestic affairs, the CIO and its ideologically diverse leadership engaged in debate surrounding the politics of anti-Communism both at home and abroad, especially in the early years of the Cold War. Overall, CIO leaders acted as critical supporters of the government's anti-Communist foreign policies, while at the same time, they molded their practices of modern political action initiatives in the domestic political arena, especially in the area of civil rights, of which they were pioneers. Extensive debate surrounding the political dimension of the industrial union crusade and the competing visions on how to advance organized labor characterized the CIO in the years following World War II. The diverging political currents among CIO leaders, which included but were not limited to communism, the role of government in regulating organized labor, and a cautious approach in the organizing of African Americans in the South, were greatly responsible for its failure to organize workers in Operation Dixie. All of those issues, and especially growing government intrusion into the internal affairs of the CIO as reflected in the 1947 Taft-Hartley Act, weighed heavily in its decision to merge with the American Federation of Labor (AFL) in 1955.

THE FORMATIVE YEARS

Begun in November 1935, as an attempt to encourage the growth of industrial unionism within the American Federation of Labor (AFL), John L. Lewis, of the United Mine Workers of America (UMW) and other unions, created the Committee for Industrial Organization. Benefiting from the financial resources provided by the UMW, the CIO had a high degree of activism that contrasted sharply with the AFL's craft unions' organizational inertia. Specifically, the AFL had failed to seize opportunities for industrial unionism afforded by national legislation aimed at economic recovery during the early years of the Great Depression and the New Deal.

Signed into law on June 16, 1933, the National Industrial Recovery Act (NIRA) created the National Recovery Administration (NRA), which was responsible for restructuring the entire nonagricultural economy. For workers, the relevance of the legislation involved the creation of codes in each industry that regulated work hours and established minimum wages. Of particular importance to organized labor were Sections 7a and 7b, which proclaimed the right of workers to establish unions of their own choosing, free from employer domination.

For the remainder of 1933 and through 1935, industrial workers responded enthusiastically to this legislation, which was reflected in a remarkable surge in union membership and activism. Between 1933 and 1935, AFL membership grew by 30 percent as the UMW and garment workers' unions rebuilt their organizations, which had fallen victim to the successful anti-union employer offensive that had dominated the 1920s. These AFL industrial union outposts were joined by workers forming new unions in mass production industries, such as the steel and auto, rubber, textiles and electrical goods, all of which sought AFL affiliation. By 1935, AFL membership had reached 3

DAVID DUBINSKY (1892–1982)

The president from 1932 to 1966 of the International Ladies' Garment Workers' Union (ILGWU), Dubinsky was born in Brest-Litovsk, Poland, on February 22, 1892. He was a baker in his father's shop in Lodz (then in Russian Poland) and joined the baker's union at age fourteen. The General Jewish Workers' Union, or *Bund*, was a highly political organization of Jews from Poland and other parts of the Russian empire. The union looked to socialism as the best solution for preserving and promoting Jewish culture and bringing relief to the workers of the world, a belief that Dubinsky carried with him the rest of his life. A year after joining, he became the secretary for the local union. He was arrested a year later and banished in 1908 to a Siberian prison. He escaped and reached the United States in 1911, where he became a cloak cutter and joined the ILGWU.

At the time he joined, and for the remainder of his time in the union, Dubinsky led the fight within the union against the Communists and helped make unions a bulwark of democracy. Before and during World War II, the fight spread to the American Labor Party, a Socialist political party in New York State that Dubinsky helped to found in 1936. Like the Garment Workers' Union, it was also largely comprised of East European Jewish refugees who were divided into pro- and anti-Communist factions. When the Communists seized control of the party, Dubinsky and his fellow Socialists left the party in 1944 to form the Liberty Party, which soon overtook his old party in membership numbers.

Dubinsky rose rapidly through the ranks of the Garment Workers' Union and became president in 1932, serving for thirty-four years. Under his guidance, he transformed the union from a struggling financial entity on the verge of collapse to one with assets in the hundreds of millions of dollars. The union took on issues such as the provision of health insurance, severance pay, retirement benefits, and a thirty-five-hour work week. He also worked to abolish the sweatshops that were ubiquitous in the industry. He led the expansion of membership of the ILGWU during the Great Depression, when union membership jumped in numbers because of federal support for them.

Although a vice president of the American Federation of Labor (AFL), Dubinsky led (1935–1936) his union in joining with the Committee (later Congress) of Industrial Organizations (CIO), which organized unions by industry. When the AFL, which organized unions by trade, suspended the CIO unions in 1936, Dubinsky resigned from the AFL. However, he opposed the establishment of the CIO on a permanent independent basis, and in 1938 he also broke with it, thus making the ILGWU independent.

In 1940, the ILGWU reaffiliated with the AFL. Dubinsky then launched a campaign to rid the AFL of mob ties, but struggled against a reluctant and frightened leadership. In 1945, he again became a vice president and member of the executive council of the AFL. After a change of leadership in both organizations in 1952, he saw his opportunity and worked for a merger of the two, which took place 1955. He again pressed for cutting mob ties. His lengthy efforts to oust corrupt union leaders who had mob connections culminated in the anti-racket codes adopted by the AFL-CIO in 1957. He retired from the presidency in 1966 and served as director of the union's Retirees Service Department. He was awarded the Presidential Medal of Freedom in 1969, the nation's highest civilian honor. He died on September 17, 1982.

James G. Lewis

---

million. Although Lewis and the UMW provided seasoned organizers and financed much of the new activity, he and his UMW staff received help from a variety of veteran and emerging trade union leaders who understood that tapping into the mass activism was not enough. A revitalized and assertive American labor movement required disciplined leadership.

Leaders like Sidney Hillman, head of the Amalgamated Clothing Workers of America (ACWA), and David Dubinsky of the International Ladies' Garment Workers' Union (ILGWU) were nominal Socialists and were critical of the AFL and its leaders. Yet they were also ardent supporters of the New Deal and President Franklin D. Roosevelt. At the same time, they adhered to the AFL principles and tradition of placing collective bargaining at the top of the union agenda and the notion that effective unionism necessitated centralized and authoritative leadership guided by an unflagging belief in the American free-enterprise system.

Lewis's most reliable allies, however, and those most responsible for overseeing the union organizing drives in mass production industries during the latter part of 1930s, were two UMW stalwarts and former adversaries, John Brophy and Adolph Germer. Brophy, defeated by Lewis for the presidency of the UMW in 1926, was a capable organizer with ties to radical political groups. As a veteran activist known for his independence and integrity, he filled the position as director of the CIO's daily operations. Immediately, Brophy appointed Germer, another former UMW activist, as the organization's first field representative. Circulating throughout the heartland in 1935 and 1936 in an attempt to align the CIO with the increasing militancy of workers in that region, Germer emerged as a full-time adviser to rubber workers, who during those years tenaciously struggled to establish industrial unionism in Akron, Ohio.

STRIKES, POLITICS, AND ORGANIZATIONAL INDEPENDENCE

The rubber workers of Akron not only battled the likes of the Goodyear, Goodrich, General, and Firestone Tire companies, but they also had fought among themselves, because those enterprises had established company unions that had obtained a significant degree of credibility over the years. In July 1935, however, Congress enacted the National Labor Relations Act (NLRA) after the Supreme Court had ruled the NIRA unconstitutional. A key provision of the NLRA was prohibition of overt company support for labor organizations. This element of the law, along with other sections that declared a number of management practices toward worker organization illegal, provided space for rubber workers to organize.

The AFL had denied the United Rubber Workers' Union a full charter under the auspices of the NRA and instead advocated reliance on the federal government and cooperation with employers to bring collective bargaining. This strategy had failed to produce improvements in wages and working conditions, or to address the problem of employer disciplining of union activists. After Goodyear fired 137 tire builders in February 1936, workers walked out and eventually formed an eleven-mile picket line around the huge factory complex. A month later the strikers emerged victorious. But even after strikers earned recognition from the company, Germer complained to Brophy that the URW was dominated too much by irresponsible militancy.

The thrust of CIO organizing then moved to the steel industry where slightly more than a half million workers encountered employment instability, arbitrary and capricious promotion and discipline policies, along with confusing pay schedules and job assignments. The NRA had provided the impulse for thousands of steelworkers to join the AFL-affiliated Amalgamated Association (AA) with the hope that it

would remedy their problems. In addition, the AFL had been advocating an expanded organizing drive among the workers in America's quintessential heavy industry. Like their rubber industry counterparts, the steel magnates had established company unions to blunt workers' efforts to form independent organizations and representation. As in the case of the rubber workers, AFL inertia had left eager-for-organization steelworkers disillusioned. On June 12, 1936, Lewis announced the formation of the Steelworkers Organizing Committee (SWOC). Lewis staffed the SWOC board with UMW hands, Philip Murray and David J. McDonald, while infusing the organizing drive among steelworkers with $500,000 from the miners' union treasury. SWOC published a newspaper, established a research department, and hired full-time legal counsel. But the organizing drive lacked the enthusiasm characteristic of the rubber workers' struggle, and the campaign developed slowly as a result.

This lack of vitality combined with the fact that the upcoming 1936 presidential election detracted CIO attention away from organizing. A consensus had developed among the CIO hierarchy that Franklin Roosevelt's reelection was crucial to the success not only of its current organizing initiatives, but also to the very survival of the CIO itself. In May 1936, the CIO established an ad-hoc committee to support Roosevelt and other progressive candidates. Throughout the fall campaign Lewis frequently visited industrial America, met with Roosevelt personally on a number of occasions, and addressed the nation on the radio calling for support of the president. For his part, Murray shifted resources and organizers from SWOC to the political campaign. Roosevelt's November landslide ensured that the NLRA would not be repealed. It also cleared the way for more organizing as union leaders and workers were confident that the president, after overwhelmingly receiving the labor vote, would surely support the expansion of collective bargaining.

Following the election, the CIO succeeded in bringing industrial unionism to most key sectors of the economy. Besides finally making breakthroughs in the steel and automotive industries, CIO collective bargaining entered the workplace in transportation, the appliance industry, meatpacking, and on the docks in the nation's ports. Some of those victories, however, proved ephemeral. Although the SWOC signed an agreement with U.S. Steel, companies employing over 150,000 workers known as Little Steel fiercely resisted, and the struggle culminated in the police murder of ten Chicago strikers on Memorial

John L. Lewis, president of the United Mine Workers, leads a meeting of mineworkers participating in a mock trial of American Federation of Labor President William Green. He is being tried for unfriendly acts against the union for their participation in the Committee for Industrial Organization.
(© Underwood Photo Archives, Inc.)

Day, 1937. The rubber barons in Akron still resisted the URW and CIO, and organizing drives among textile workers in the South had stalled. Although Henry Ford's company carried out a reign of terror inside his huge Detroit and Dearborn plants, the United Automobile Workers (UAW) signed agreements with Chrysler and General Motors (GM). The bargaining agreements materialized as a result of the 1937 sit-down strike in Flint, Michigan.

Representing the apex of mass production industry with its featured assembly line, the auto companies had become masters of high-performance workplace innovations. Constant restructuring and redefining skills combined with the latest in union-busting tactics to forestall unionization in the industry for more than two decades. But as the Depression dragged on, autoworkers grew more vocal and employed bold tactics in their protest against worsening conditions. First, the NRA, and later the NLRA, helped to galvanize union sentiment as autoworkers marched and went on strike. In late 1936, autoworkers everywhere were demanding union recognition by using a new tactic, the sit-down strike.

On December 30, 1936, workers sat down in two GM Fisher Body plants in Flint. Shutting down the machines, the Flint autoworkers ejected foremen and company guards and stopped GM production of all Chevrolet, Buick, and Pontiac models. With broad

Spectators outside the Fisher Body Plant on January 17, 1937, watch as sit-down strikers refuse to evacuate the auto plant. The sit-down strikers played a crucial role in the organization of the United Auto Workers union. *(Brown Brothers)*

support from the community, the strikers and their wives fought off police attempts to storm the plants and crush the rebellion. Meanwhile, acting as the CIO's chief spokesperson, John L. Lewis skillfully negotiated through elected public officials in the state of Michigan and at the level of the federal government to bring GM to the bargaining table. The result was a February 11, 1937, agreement that ended the six-week struggle and obliged GM to recognize the UAW as the exclusive bargaining representative. The Flint sit-down strike was a monumental leap forward in the establishment of industrial unionism in the automotive industry, and, at the same time, it lent credibility to the CIO course of militancy, which sharply contrasted with the more cautious approach of the AFL.

Success in the organization of auto industry workers not only swelled CIO membership, but also enhanced organized labor's political influence and clout. In 1938, over the objections of many pro-business politicians in the North and Southern conservatives, Congress passed the Fair Labor Standards Act, which established the minimum wage as well as the regulation of hours and the requirement of overtime pay. The legislation, along with the Social Security Act passed in 1935, was viewed by many as proof that the CIO had emerged as a key player in helping the advance of New Deal reform initiatives. This factor, combined with successful organizing campaigns in a variety of industrial sectors, resulted in the CIO's formal break with the AFL in 1938, when it adopted its permanent name, the Congress of Industrial Organizations.

THE CIO, LABOR, AND WORLD WAR II

Almost immediately following the break with the AFL, serious infighting developed among the organization's central figures. From the CIO's beginning, differences existed, but they largely had been submerged and subordinated to the idea of building up the ranks of organization. But as the economy continued to worsen in 1939 and CIO membership remained stagnant, troubles mounted. Serious disagreements that emerged over the CIO's relationship to the federal government as the nation drifted toward war divided the leadership. These problems mounted on top of the ILGWU departure in 1938 and an intense factionalism within the UAW that almost resulted in an organizational implosion. In 1940, Lewis and Sidney Hillman engaged in open conflict over Roosevelt's seeking an unprecedented third term as well as his foreign policy, which Lewis claimed was moving the nation toward war. As a result, Lewis departed from the CIO and turned the reins of leadership over to steelworkers' head Philip Murray.

Lewis's leaving the CIO paralleled the outbreak of World War II, which began on September 1, 1939. The war in Europe also was responsible for sharpening the conflict and the growing rift between Lewis and Hillman. Although Lewis was now outside the CIO, he was still recognized as America's principal labor leader, and his publicly expressed views on war mobilization and organized labor's relationship with the federal government reached a broad audience. Although Hillman closely identified with the administration's foreign policy, Lewis was an ardent isolationist. Hillman, especially after May 1940, when Germany invaded France, sought to tie organized labor to government plans for war preparation, which involved implementation of a program for dramatically increasing industrial production. Consistent with his philosophy that government-labor cooperation was optimal for advancing the CIO, Hillman accepted Roosevelt's offer to be appointed as labor's representative to coordinate the rising military production. Lewis, meanwhile, constantly expressed antiwar views and criticized Hillman for allowing the government to award contracts to industrial firms that violated federal labor laws with impunity.

In 1940, Lewis supported Roosevelt's opponent, utilities executive, Wendell Willkie. After Pearl Harbor, more of the U.S. economy became enmeshed in war production, and the Roosevelt administration received a no-strike pledge from CIO leaders. The agreement was possible because in January 1942, Roosevelt abolished the National Defense Mediation Board (NDMB) and replaced it with the National War Labor Board (NWLB). Created in March 1941, the NDMB was a tripartite body charged with trying to settle union disputes with companies holding defense contracts by issuing nonbinding recommendations. Although it had worked for Lewis and the UMW during a nationwide strike of mines owned by the steel firms, the CIO and the government desired a mechanism that would be more decisive and therefore better serve to stabilize industrial relations and production during wartime.

Unlike the NDMB, the NWLB had power to issue "directive orders" without Roosevelt's approval. NWLB jurisdiction extended to any labor-management dispute that might interrupt work and thereby contribute to the effective prosecution of the war. In effect, virtually the entire U.S. economy became subject to the NWLB. And with Roosevelt linking labor peace directly to national security, the NWLB and the courts, as highlighted in the *Little Steel* case, required workers to maintain union membership during the life of the union contract. Despite these legal advances for organized labor, Lewis, not willing to surrender the right to strike and rely exclusively on the judgment of the NWLB, severed UMW ties with the CIO in 1942. Although the ranks of the CIO grew by some 40 percent and membership approached 5 million, the AFL emerged from World War II larger than the CIO. Despite the CIO no-strike pledge, many rank-and-file acted independent of the leadership and ignored the policy, striking war-related industries frequently. Consequently, the AFL succeeded in portraying itself as more responsible and better able to stabilize production. Accordingly, many employers opted for recognizing AFL unions rather than run the risk of experiencing disruptive work actions by angry CIO rank-and-file members.

Strikes also fueled antilabor sentiment, which resulted in the Republicans gaining seats in both the House of Representatives and the Senate in 1942. In June 1943, Congress passed the Smith-Connally Act, which, among other things, authorized government seizure of war and military production operations threatened by labor disputes, and banned strikes in federally operated plants. Smith-Connally also limited union political activity. The CIO responded by creating a Political Action Committee (PAC), which resulted in bringing closer ties between the labor organization, Roosevelt, and the Democratic Party. Be-

JOHN L. LEWIS (1880–1969)

Born in Cleveland, Iowa, on February 12, 1880, Lewis was the son of a Welsh immigrant coal miner. Between 1898 and 1907, Lewis tried coal mining, farming, construction, and business before entering the labor movement. Working as a miner after 1906, he rose through the union ranks, and by 1909 he had become a national organizer for the American Federation of Labor (AFL) and then president of the United Mine Workers of America (UMW) in 1920, a post he held until 1960. Lewis fought vigorously to build up the declining union in a sick industry, won the loyalty of the miners, and thus consolidated his own power. He did so by courting management. He was welcomed by business-people and even served as chair of the Republican Party's National Labor Committee.

In the midst of the Great Depression in the 1930s, he joined the Democratic Party in 1932 hoping that the national government would help stabilize industrial relations in the coal industry. He worked closely with Franklin Delano Roosevelt after his election in 1932 and had welcomed the New Deal. Frustrated with the AFL's failure to organize mass production workers, he split with the AFL. Taking several of the largest unions with him, Lewis founded a new organization, the Committee (later Congress) of Industrial Organizations (CIO) in 1935, and became its first president. By 1937, the CIO had taken control of the nation's two largest mass production companies, General Motors and U.S. Steel, and Lewis was at the peak of his power. When Lewis felt President Roosevelt took labor for granted, he supported Republican candidate Wendell Willkie for the presidency in 1940 in hopes that a Republican candidate elected with labor votes might support the union in general and Lewis specifically. He staked his CIO presidency on Willkie's victory. When Roosevelt won, Lewis resigned from the CIO but remained head of the UMW.

Increasing antagonism between Lewis and Philip Murray, the new head of the CIO, led to a break, and in 1942 the UMW withdrew from the CIO. Lewis maintained power despite the separation. During World War II, Lewis faced a hostile War Labor Board and unfavorable public sentiment because of the many strikes of the coal miners in the "no-strike" period. Although they did win the demands of the miners, these strikes alienated public support and may have helped to pave the way for later anti-strike legislation. Between 1945 and 1950, he led four national coal strikes. The UMW again joined the AFL but split off a year later in 1947, once more in a dispute over means of combating the restrictive Taft-Hartley Act. Lewis's failure to obey a federal court order to end a protracted coal strike led to a heavy fine for criminal contempt of court in 1948.

After 1950, Lewis ended his more aggressive tactics and followed a policy of accommodation with the declining coal industry. He steadily improved the material conditions of union members, and won esteem as an apostle of "cooperative capitalism" because his cooperation stabilized the industry. Despite the improvements for his workers, they suffered in the long run when they became victims of technological change. He voluntarily resigned as president of the UMW in 1960 and served as chairman of the UMW's Welfare and Retirement Fund after his retirement. He died on June 11, 1969.

James G. Lewis

cause Smith-Connally declared direct union financial contributions in general elections illegal, PAC activity focused on nonpartisan voter registration and education campaigns. The political activity combined with the no-strike pledge played an instrumental role in gradually guiding the CIO to rely more on political and institutional structures rather than on mass mobilization and work actions as the principal means to better the lot of American workers.

THE 1945–1946 STRIKES: CIO LEADERSHIP AND STRATEGY

As the war ended, however, a temporary shift away from this trend was necessitated by the fact that, during World War II, basic wage rates had eroded. Although stable employment, job upgrading. and ample opportunity to work overtime hours during the war years enabled workers to earn income, inflation continued to eat away at their standard of living. After the end of the war, orders for factory goods disappeared. Unemployment among the civilian workforce increased 25 percent. Although the CIO urged government to stimulate economic growth and provide security through housing and welfare programs, increases in wages remained at the core of the postwar CIO bargaining agenda. The CIO joined prominent economists in arguing that mass purchasing power was necessary to generate and sustain economic growth and essential in avoiding a return to the conditions of the 1930s. The CIO and some economists asserted that American business could afford to give substantial wage increases without raising prices. But business chafed at union demands for wage increases. And the most strike-riddled episode of American history followed.

In the last few months of 1945, America lost over 28 million man-days to strikes. In November, 180,000 UAW members struck GM. By January 1946, 500,000 steelworkers, 200,000 electrical workers, and 150,000 CIO packinghouse workers had joined them on the picket lines. In February, the nation lost almost 20 million man-days to strikes. In the end, the strikes won substantial wage hikes for workers in those industries, increases that ranged between 15 and 20 percent. As a result, the CIO increased the number of workers it represented and were covered by contract to over 1.7 million. Although relatively successful, in the end, the strikes revealed sharp, divergent views among the CIO leadership over the future direction of the organization, especially in terms of how to build and define collective bargaining structures in a modern, industrial economy.

Whereas steelworkers' chief Philip Murray advanced the notion of business-labor cooperation with the government providing general oversight, Walter Reuther, the emerging leader of the UAW adopted a more confrontational approach. He emphasized capitalizing on worker militancy and mobilizing public opinion to hold American business accountable not only to labor, but to the average American citizen as well. Reuther argued that, when giant firms such as GM claim they cannot afford to give workers wage increases, they should be required to open their books to public scrutiny. The UAW leader claimed his position was consistent with the fact that the collective bargaining process itself was widely publicized, and that wages and other terms and conditions of employment for mass production workers were known to the general public.

But Reuther's strategy for organized labor backfired when President Harry Truman reacted to mounting political pressure. In December 1945, Truman called upon Congress to enact some form of antistrike legislation. At the core of Truman's request was a proposal for preventing strikes in industries affecting the public interest. It involved cooling-off periods during which presidential fact-finding boards would gather and examine evidence and issue nonbinding recommendations. Although Congress did not act on Truman's proposal, it planted the seed for future

antistrike legislation, which would result in weakening organized labor overall.

Other factors emanating from the strike wave of 1945–1946 also forecasted hard times for the CIO and organized labor. Overall coordination of the strike movement by the CIO was nonexistent. In its place, for example, unions such as the United Electrical Workers (UE) and the UAW, which both represented 30,000 workers at GM's Frigidaire Division, competed against one another by pursuing strategies and making tactical decisions based exclusively on their own interest. Also not boding well for building a stronger CIO was the emerging issue of Communism. This factor, along with others, including a failure by the CIO leadership to reach consensus on linking membership to broader social purposes, such as civil rights, greatly impacted organizing in the immediate postwar years, especially as it related to Operation Dixie.

OPERATION DIXIE

Although the CIO suffered from internal divisions, the results of 1945–1946 ushered in optimism surrounding the building of membership, especially in the South. World War II had produced significant gains for the CIO in the region, as its membership in Dixie reached 225,000. At war's end, CIO unions were administering 42,000 collective bargaining contracts with Southern-based textile firms. Oil workers had doubled their prewar membership in Louisiana and Texas, pulp and paper workers had unionized in Virginia, and the URW had established strong locals in Memphis and Gadsden, Alabama. Accordingly, in early 1946, CIO leadership permanently established the Southern Organizing Committee (SOC).

From its inception, important aspects of Operation Dixie were well planned and funded. SOC deployed teams of organizers, which formed functioning unions that were integrated into the various CIO affiliates. The USWA (United Steelworkers of America), UAW, and UE all provided hundreds and thousands of dollars for the campaign, and organizers collected a one-dollar initiation fee from new recruits. SOC leaders and organizers hoped to recruit military veterans, who were exempt from the initiation fee, and native Southerners. The strategy reflected the desire by CIO leaders not to have the organizers labeled as radicals or Northern carpetbaggers. Despite careful planning on various levels, the leadership failed to design an overall strategy that would provide direction, framework, and purpose.

Initially, CIO and SOC leadership had hoped to rekindle the militancy of the 1930s. Soon, however,

Operation Dixie evolved into a campaign that was not about a militant crusade, but one that resembled more of a business proposition. Conservatives dominated Southern congressional delegations, and their ranks received a boost with the election of more Northern Republicans to Congress in 1938 and 1942. In addition, no effort was made to build upon the already existing CIO Communist-led, biracial unions in logging, tobacco, food processing, and woodworking. Lurking in the background throughout the duration of Operation Dixie were the politics of anti-Communism. Ultimately, this combined with the insistence that the campaign not mix organizing with politics, thereby rejecting the notion that Operation Dixie would link itself with any crusade for civil rights. The organizing drive focused almost exclusively on the white worker-dominated textile industry and largely ignored lumbering, pulp and paper, tobacco, and other industries where great numbers of African Americans were employed. SOC leaders also actively discouraged African Americans from applying for organizing positions.

This strategic drift complemented employer tactics designed to stymie organizing and reinforce the traditional paternalism that for so long had characterized the Southern employment relations system. SOC leaders relied heavily on the unfair labor practices provisions of the National Labor Relations Act. Even during the 1930s, textile employers had been successful in delaying legal proceedings under the provisions, and during Operation Dixie they refined these practices. Propaganda launched by public officials and local journalists also aided textile employers in the fight against the CIO. Besides playing themes that traditionally had resonated with Southern whites, such as that industrial unionism would bring social and economic equality to African Americans, they also asserted that a CIO victory would destabilize the South's institutions and destroy regional economic progress. The result was a failure by the SOC to establish strong, local unions, identified in the beginning by CIO leadership as key to a successful campaign.

Meanwhile, a string of National Labor Relations Board (NLRB) election defeats in the textile mills added woes to a campaign that already was under serious financial stress. By the end of 1946, it was clear to CIO leadership that Operation Dixie had failed. Refusing to link the growth of industrial unionism in the South to the African-Americans' struggle for civil rights, CIO leaders played into the hands of the Southern economic elite, who already had a wealth of experience in deploying the issue of racial equality to divide Southern workers.

Within the context of the politics of anti-Communism, which loomed increasingly important in the internal affairs of the CIO, the fact that unions with a heavy concentration of African Americans were Communist-led served to undermine the possibility of success for Operation Dixie. Operation Dixie's failure helped to reinforce the anti-Communism fixation inside the CIO, and as the general public embraced the Cold War political framework, industrial unionism was increasingly challenged.

TAFT-HARTLEY WEAKENS THE CIO

On the heels of Operation Dixie, the CIO focus shifted dramatically toward politics. However, despite increased PAC activity in support of pro-labor candidates, the Republicans scored huge victories in the 1946 congressional and state races. For the first time since 1932, Republicans had control over both the House and the Senate. The public mood had turned decidedly antilabor. The 80th Congress reflected the hostility toward organized labor by escalating efforts to radically alter the NLRA. The result was the enactment of the Taft-Hartley Act, passed over President Truman's veto on June 23, 1947. The major thrust of the legislation aimed at curbing the power of unions and strengthening the hand of employers in resisting unionization.

The legislation incorporated a list of unfair union practices and expanded presidential power in forcing unions to delay strike action. Both the NLRB and employers could seek injunctions against unions, and it allowed employers the right to actively dissuade employees from joining unions. A section of the law allowed states to adopt so-called right-to-work laws, thereby undermining union security and organizing activity. Workers in right-to-work states who benefited from union contracts could now refuse to join unions and not pay union dues. It prohibited union contributions to candidates in primary and general elections, which severely restricted union political activity. Probably more damaging for CIO internal affairs and organizational health was a provision requiring that all union officers and those seeking remedy from the NLRB sign and file affidavits with the Labor Department stipulating they were not Communists.

Although CIO leaders, including President Philip Murray, who spoke out in opposition to what he called the law's "loyalty oath," initially opposed the

GEORGE MEANY (1894–1980)

George Meany, the long-term (1955–1979) president of the AFL-CIO (American Federation of Labor-Congress of Industrial Organizations), spent almost his entire working life as an official in the union movement in one capacity or another. Born the son of a plumber on August 16, 1894, Meany dropped out of high school at sixteen, passed the apprenticeship test for the plumbers union on his second try, and worked briefly in the trade. Despite these humble beginnings, he became the leader of the AFL-CIO, a remarkable accomplishment for a man who proudly proclaimed that he had never walked a picket line or led a strike.

In 1917, Meany joined Plumbers Local 463 in New York. Typical of AFL unions of that day, the organization's chief mission was not recruiting members or organizing new locals, but controlling the supply of plumbers in order to set wages. AFL unions in general represented only skilled craftsmen and excluded recent immigrants, people of color, and women—policies that persisted throughout Meany's tenure and beyond. Meany was elected business agent of Local 463 in 1922 and secretary of the New York City Building Trades Council a year later. In 1934, he was elected president of the New York State Federation of Labor, a position he retained over five elections. He was politically astute and influential with the state legislature, shepherding the passage of seventy-two pro-labor bills.

During the 1930s and 1940s, Meany's influence with the Democratic Party grew. As part of the Franklin D. Roosevelt coalition of liberals, labor, ethnic minorities, and Southern Democrats, Meany delivered the votes of its unionized skilled trades workers. In the 1930s, the AFL was challenged by the CIO, a new federation that emerged to unionize industrial workers, a constituency previously ignored by organized labor.

In 1939, Meany rose to the position of secretary-treasurer of the AFL, a position he held until the death of AFL president William Green in 1952. He was then elected president of the AFL by its executive council. His major accomplishment occurred in 1955 when he helped engineer the merger of the AFL and CIO. Subsequently, he was elected unanimously, essentially appointed by the executive board he controlled. Meany was a chief proponent of "business unionism"—the concept that unions should work in concert with business, eschewing strikes and radicalism, working for better wages and benefits, and defending only its members, within the capitalist system. A rabid anti-Communist, Meany practiced an essential conservatism

that led him to grow increasingly out of touch with the needs and aspirations of the rank-and-file. Although he saw himself as a foreign policy expert, his staunch opposition to cooperation with Communist China and the Soviet Union and his support of the Vietnam War put him far to the right of most of his constituents and the Democratic Party by 1972.

Meany's statements on international affairs throughout the era resound with warnings against "appeasement" at nearly every turn, demonstrating how even pre-World War II events deeply influenced the thinking of Americans. The blend of historical events which included World War I, the Bolshevik Revolution in Russia, and subsequent events in the Soviet Union, the interwar years, World War II, and especially the Cold War dramatically influenced the way Americans, and especially influential leaders like George Meany, came to view the world around them. Meany sincerely believed that a monolithic international Communism was out to conquer the world and that it was the AFL-CIO's duty to involve itself in international affairs to help counter this threat. He was able to convince the majority of leaders within the AFL-CIO that this was so. Meany did not answer directly to the rank-and-file, having been, in essence, appointed as president for life by his executive board. In turn, he controlled the board that kept him in power. He supported American policy in Vietnam during the Johnson and Nixon administrations, disregarding the growing opposition within his own organization and among the American workers he represented.

Meany's tenure saw the number of unionized American workers rise to over 30 percent. It also witnessed the decline, by 1971, to 22 percent. By the end of his career in 1979, he was clearly an anachronism and was even partially responsible for the decline of the union movement in the United States. In his early years, he espoused organizing the unorganized, but by 1971 he declared organizing useless and unnecessary. In 1972, Meany declared the AFL-CIO's neutrality in the presidential election between Republican Richard Nixon and Democrat George McGovern, contributing to Nixon's landslide victory. Though initially supportive of Nixon and especially his policies on Vietnam, he later turned on Nixon after the Watergate scandal, demanding his resignation or impeachment. In 1979, Meany declined to seek reelection to the presidency of the AFL-CIO, and he died the following year at age eighty-five.

Frank Koscielski

signing of non-Communist affidavits, foreign policy issues and domestic loyalty soon trumped CIO unity on the issue. As public debate concerning the containment of Communism abroad and the threat of subversion at home intensified, tensions between pro-Soviet and anti-Communist elements in the CIO sharpened. When Walter Reuther became UAW president, he convinced the UAW executive board to sign the affidavits. Other CIO unions followed, and on July 29, 1949, Murray reluctantly signed an affidavit, leaving the Communist-dominated UE, Mine, Mill, and Smelter Workers, Farm Equipment Workers, and Food, Tobacco, and Allied Workers' unions the only holdouts.

Walter Reuther then began to aggressively employ the affidavit against the nonsigning unions and attempted to raid their membership, especially the UE and the Mine, Mill, and Smelter Workers. The UE, at least initially, successfully fought off the raids, due to its leadership and resources. Soon, however, rival factions within the UE emerged, and James Carey challenged its leadership. After the UE completely broke with the CIO in mid-1949, President Murray chartered an electrical workers' union, the International Union of Electrical Workers (IUE), to compete against the UE. During raiding activity, the IUE received critical support from the Roman Catholic Church and the Federal Bureau of Investigation, as well as from Carey's testimony before the House Committee on Un-American Activities, popularly known as the House Un-American Activities Committee (HUAC), which conducted investigations into Communist subversion of American institutions, including Hollywood and the Screen Actors' Guild. Although unions like the UE survived, they emerged from the raiding wars battered. This process alone contributed heavily to the overall weakening of the CIO. The AFL, meanwhile, absorbed affiliates and members while charting steady, organizational growth during the period. By the early 1950s, this factor, along with others, led CIO leaders into serious discussion concerning the possibility of merging with their rival.

THE REALPOLITIK OF MERGER

Besides the problems associated with the politics of anti-Communism, CIO postwar leadership faced the challenge of the changing dynamics of the American workforce. CIO leaders proved unprepared to deal with the growth of the service, white-collar, and other nonindustrial sectors. With manufacturing saturated, AFL unions successfully outmaneuvered the CIO in organizing workers in the goods-handling, white-collar, and public sectors. As the AFL expanded, it also began drawing former CIO affiliates into its ranks, especially among packinghouse, textile, food, and chemical workers. In addition, the growth of skilled jobs in the metal trades, particularly in small shops, made tool-and-die makers and millwrights look to the traditionally craft-oriented AFL for affiliation. By 1950, the AFL legitimately claimed double the membership of the CIO. The only consolation for the CIO was the success it enjoyed enlisting the Communications Workers of America (CWA), which included a large number of telephone operators, the overwhelming majority of whom were female.

Although CIO attacks on the AFL's racial policies were still credible, by 1950 the AFL counted more black members than the CIO. This occurred despite the CIO establishing itself as a significant force in the national civil rights legislative initiative. The CIO wrote an *amicus brief* for the Supreme Court in *Brown v. Board of Education*. Strong rhetoric and civil rights statements from CIO leaders like Walter Reuther did not correspond to how the federation's affiliates treated African Americans in the workplace. The UAW, for example, did nothing to break the monopoly white workers enjoyed in the skilled trades. In contrast, AFL leaders like George Meany, although part of the racially exclusive building trades, had at least established good relations with black unionists, such as A. Philip Randolph, head of the AFL-affiliated Brotherhood of Sleeping Car Porters. In addition, Meany and the AFL supported the contours of the CIO's liberal, legislative agenda, including civil rights and an expansion of New Deal-type social reforms.

Other factors also contributed to the drift toward merger. In the area of foreign policy, CIO leaders, while supporting the government's anti-Communist crusade, and in particular the Central Intelligence Agency (CIA) overthrow of Jacobo Arbenz Guzman in Guatemala in 1954, never penetrated the inner circle of established, international AFL operatives, relegating the once rebel federation to a marginal role. Like their AFL counterparts, however, CIO leaders saw Communist influence fostered by the Soviet Union behind every movement of economic nationalism and independence in the Third World during the Cold War years, a factor that would end up damaging the labor movement in future years.

Most importantly, the CIO had long abandoned the militant and confrontational approach toward employers, and by the early 1950s it had embraced the long-standing AFL philosophy of order and discipline in the workplace. CIO leaders enthusiastically backed employer prerogatives to boost productivity and economic growth. The CIO exchanged the notion of spontaneous protest for higher wages and benefits and shop floor peace. Over the years, the CIO had gradually adopted this position, playing a critical role in the establishment of the modern system of collective bargaining and industrial relations. In 1953 and 1954, the AFL and the CIO signed important no raiding agreements, which served as precursors to their eventual merger in December 1955. In the end, the unification represented a general consolidation of organized labor's public activity, rather than an agreement concerning organizing, particularly as it existed in the legislative and political arenas, which long before 1955 had arrived to dominate the agenda of both federations.

CONCLUSION

The emergence of the CIO during the height of the Great Depression provided hope for hundreds of thousands of American workers during one of the nation's most turbulent periods of history. The CIO rekindled the labor activism of the early twentieth century that had been submerged by an aggressive employer counteroffensive during the 1920s. When the United States entered World War II, CIO leadership successfully channeled that labor activism into fostering productivity, which exercised a significant role in the defeat of the Axis powers. That process contributed heavily to the growth of collective bargaining and the establishment of a formal industrial relations system. The CIO also immersed itself in politics, and in so doing, it gave the nation's working class its first coherent and effective voice by creating a modern political action vehicle, which has endured to the present day. Its political action arm, especially after World War II, was key in the struggle for civil rights. In the years immediately before the merger with the AFL, the CIO political program incorporated a legislative agenda that provided one of the cornerstones of American liberalism.

Through the channeling of labor activism into institutional structures such as collective bargaining, and along with it the acceptance of government regulation, the CIO did limit the exercise of workers' power. This also resulted from CIO insistence that it participate as a player within a Democratic Party coalition, rather than exercise political independence, such as the brand exhibited by John L. Lewis in his opposition to Franklin Roosevelt in 1940. In addition, CIO acceptance of Cold War policy in the Third World and its congruence with the AFL on what constituted labor internationalism eventually contributed to the erosion of union membership at home. American corporations gradually began to locate production in countries where anti-Communist regimes guaranteed a more pliable and docile workforce.

In the final analysis, however, the CIO dramatically improved working conditions for vast numbers of laborers toiling in American industry. Through collective bargaining it helped to establish higher standards of living and, in the process, elevated the social status of ordinary working people. Autoworkers, steelworkers, rubber workers, electrical workers, and other factory hands earned decent incomes and achieved personal dignity. As a result, their offspring attended college and many moved upward in American society. For those reasons alone, the CIO has to be considered as one of the most important social movements in American history.

Norman Caulfield

BIBLIOGRAPHY

Bernstein, Irving. *The Turbulent Years: A History of the American Worker, 1933–1941.* Boston: Houghton Mifflin, 1971.

Brody, David. *Workers in America: Essays on the 20th Century Struggle.* New York and London: Oxford University Press, 1980.

Cohen, Lizabeth. *Making a New Deal: Industrial Workers in Chicago: 1919–1939.* New York: Cambridge University Press, 1990.

Dubofsky, Melvyn. *The State and Labor in Modern America.* Chapel Hill: University of North Carolina Press, 1994.

Dubofsky, Melvyn, and Warren Van Tyne. *John L. Lewis.* Urbana and Chicago: University of Illinois Press, 1986.

Fine, Sidney. *Sit Down: The General Motors Strike of 1936–1937.* Ann Arbor: University of Michigan Press, 1963.

Fraser, Steven. *Labor Will Rule: Sidney Hillman and the Rise of American Labor.* New York: Free Press, 1991.

Galenson, Walter. *The CIO Challenge to the AFL: A History of the American Labor Movement, 1935–1941.* Cambridge, MA: Harvard University Press, 1960.

Griffith, Barbara. *The Crisis of American Labor: Operation Dixie and the Defeat of the CIO.* Philadelphia: Temple University Press, 1988.

Lichtenstein, Nelson. *Walter Reuther: The Most Dangerous Man in Detroit.* Urbana and Chicago: University of Illinois Press, 1997.

McKenney, Ruth. *Industrial Valley.* Ithaca, NY: ILR, 1992.

Morris, James O. *Conflict Within the AFL: A Study of Craft Versus Industrial Unionism, 1901–1938.* Ithaca, NY: Cornell University Press, 1958.

Nelson, Daniel. *American Rubber Workers and Organized Labor, 1900–1941.* Princeton, NJ: Princeton University Press, 1988.

Pfeffer, Paula. *A. Philip Randolph. Pioneer of the Civil Rights Movement.* Baton Rouge: Louisiana State University Press, 1990.

Preis, Art. *Labor's Giant Step: Twenty Years of the CIO.* New York: Pathfinder, 1972.

Radosh, Ronald. *American Labor and U.S. Foreign Policy.* New York: Alfred A. Knopf, 1969.

Richter, Irving. *Labor's Struggles, 1945–1950.* New York and Cambridge: Cambridge University Press, 1992.

Taft, Philip. *The A.F.L.: From the Death of Gompers to the Merger.* New York: Harper & Row, 1959.

Terkel, Studs. *Hard Times: An Oral History of the Great Depression.* New York: Pantheon, 1970.

Vorse, Mary Heaton. *Labor's New Millions.* New York: Ayer, 1938.

Zieger, Robert H. *The CIO: 1935–1955.* Chapel Hill: University of North Carolina Press, 1995.

LABOR LAW

Social movements, including the labor movement, affect the development of law. Labor law focuses on *collective* action, addressing issues between organized capital and organized labor. An important distinction needs to be made between labor law and another closely related body of law, employment law. The latter focuses on *individual* workers' rights and issues such as workers' and unemployment compensation, health and safety, wages and hours, discrimination, pensions, and Social Security regulations. Labor law, on the other hand, applies to workers who belong to a union and or are seeking union representation. Strikes create the impression that the battle for labor reform takes place on the picket lines or in the streets; however, most labor struggles are ultimately decided in the halls of the legislature and then, finally, in the courts. Legal cases focused on labor have a long history, but most present laws regulating labor-management relations are rooted in the National Labor Relations Act (NLRA) passed in the 1930s.

Most major legal decisions regarding labor took place after the Civil War. Still, significant cases dealing with strikes and picketing went before the courts before the industrial revolution reached America. As trade and manufacturing advanced in Colonial America, the first labor organizations began to form in occupations such as shoemakers, printers, tailors, and carpenters. The first documented strike in the United States occurred in Philadelphia in 1768 when printers sought a minimum wage of $6 per week. When strikes occurred, employers argued that labor organizations were illegal conspiracies. A conspiracy, according to English "common law," is the collusion of two or more persons to harm the public good. The conspiracy charge was the basis for legal opinions regarding labor in America both before and after the revolution. In addition to limiting workers' ability to fight against low wages and poor conditions, the common-law doctrine helped legalize forced labor systems such as indentured servitude and slavery.

At least twenty-one conspiracy trials were held in the United States between 1805 and 1842. Judges of the period were generally conservative, and they made decisions based on middle-class principles. So, not surprisingly, organized workers only won six cases as judges continued to use common-law conspiracy doctrines as their guiding principles. Because they were attempting to raise wages and reduce hours through "combinations," strikes by workers amounted to conspiracies. Labor organizations were forced to disband and pay heavy fines. The first union to be convicted of engaging in a criminal conspiracy was Philadelphia's Journeymen Cordwainers in the 1806 legal decision, *Commonwealth v. Pullis*. Despite setbacks, workers continued to campaign against the conspiracy doctrine, arguing that it was developed by British judges and had no place in the United States. The efforts proved worthwhile. One of labor's early legal victories came in 1842 in *Commonwealth v. Hunt* in which Chief Justice Lemuel Shaw of Massachusetts held that unions did not amount to conspiracies, even if the union's actions meant lower profits for an employer or a reduction in trade. Gradually, the courts abandoned criminal conspiracy doctrine to prevent unionization, and charges against striking workers based on this area of law slowed in the 1850s and 1860s.

The postbellum period witnessed the development of large labor organizations such as the Knights of Labor and the American Federation of Labor, and the strike emerged as the most significant form of social protest in the United States. A dramatic increase in the number of strikes and large-scale industrial struggles—such as the Haymarket Affair of 1886, the Homestead Lockout of 1892, and the Pullman Boycott of 1894—brought national attention to the problems of labor. The first nationwide strike took place in 1877 when railroad workers struck in the middle of a severe economic depression. There was court action in response to the strikes in the late nineteenth and early twentieth centuries; however, the legal intervention took the form of the injunction rather than conspiracy charges. An injunction is a court order by a judge demanding that certain parties stop performing certain actions which threaten other people's property. The labor injunction was a powerful tool for employers to break strikes, pickets, or boycotts. Injunctions enabled management to circumvent pro-labor juries because the decision to grant an injunction rested solely with a judge—who was often very friendly with capital. When there was picketing or organizing, or even when unions planned to pay strike benefits or operate soup kitchens, employers rushed into both state and federal courts seeking injunctions, claiming that union action caused property loss. An injunction could usually be granted quickly, and any union that defied the order and continued to strike was held in contempt of court. Union officers and members could be punished immediately or thrown in jail.

Labor injunctions were first issued in the 1880s. A key example of the effectiveness of the injunction for capital occurred during the Pullman Strike of 1894. The strike against the Pullman Palace Car Company officially began on Friday, May 11, 1894, although factory workers had been unhappy about wages and rents in the company town for years. The walkout took on a new dimension weeks later when the American Railway Union (ARU), led by Eugene Debs, officially intervened in the strike and refused to handle Pullman cars. When the boycott went into effect, it proved enormously successful. A key moment in the strike came when the courts issued a "blanket injunction" that outlawed any activity that could be deemed as support for the striking workers. Injunctions were also issued against Debs and other union officers. Because the strike continued, the labor leader was charged with contempt of court and conspiracy. Despite the efforts of his attorney, Clarence Darrow, he was sentence to six months in jail. The case is striking because of the involvement of the U.S. Supreme Court. In the case *In re Debs,* the Supreme Court upheld the use of the blanket injunction, as well as the conviction of Debs and other union leaders. With support from the courts, the use of injunctions in labor disputes on both the state and federal level increased from 1890 to 1930. In the late 1890s and early 1900s, some state and federal anti-injunction bills appeared. However, the Supreme Court again struck a blow against labor by declaring these laws unconstitutional.

Labor did gain some strength in national politics during the Wilson administration (1913–1921). For example, the Department of Labor, which was originally formed as a branch of the Department of the Interior in 1884, was elevated to cabinet status in 1913 with a mission to "foster, promote, and develop the welfare of wage earners." Labor made gains in the courts as well. In the past, employers had used government regulations such as the Interstate Commerce Act of 1887 and the Sherman Antitrust Act of 1890 as an antistrike tool. The acts were intended to discourage monopolies and trusts, but some courts also deemed the normal activities of trade unions as "restraint of trade" under the antitrust legislation. For example, when a strike by New Orleans longshoremen began, the United States attorney won an antistrike decree by claiming that the unions were blocking interstate and foreign commerce. Finally, in 1914, Congress enacted the Clayton Act which provided some protection for organized labor by declaring that antitrust laws did not apply to unions since "the labor of a human being is not a commodity or article of commerce." In 1926, another step forward for labor occurred with passage of the Railway Labor Act, which required employers to bargain collectively with unionized workers employed with interstate railroads. Unions also learned to use the injunction to its benefit in the opening decades of the twentieth century. A small number of pro-labor injunctions were issued to forbid lockouts or blacklisting. Injunctions were also issued on labor's behalf to keep employers from breaking collective agreements. Advances were also made in the courts regarding picketing. In the nineteenth century, state courts took the position that all picketing—a major weapon of the worker—was illegal. By 1930, however, state courts allowed peaceful employee picketing.

When the United States' economy collapsed in 1929, conditions resulted which encouraged organization by both the unemployed and employed. Workers demonstrated, picketed, and formed unions. Faced with an increase in radicalization among the masses, the 1930s witnessed great gains for unions and the right to organize and strike. The first hint of change came with passage of the Davis-Bacon Act in 1931, which required that construction contracts entered into by the federal government specify a minimum wage to be paid to persons employed under those contracts. The closing year of the Hoover administration in 1932 was marked by passage of the Norris-LaGuardia Act. The legislation became known as the Anti-Injunction Act because a key provision, Section

4, barred federal courts from issuing injunctions against labor unions and individuals. The act also made the "yellow-dog contract" (which forced workers to promise not to join a union or discontinue union membership) unenforceable in federal court. In general, if there was a labor dispute, the injunction had been removed from the employer's arsenal. They could still obtain injunctions from state courts; however, several state legislatures followed the federal lead and passed their own anti-injunction bills. The initial impact of the Norris-LaGuardia Act was weakened by court challenges but the Act was finally declared constitutional in 1937.

Following the inauguration of President Franklin Delano Roosevelt in March of 1933, Congress passed the National Industrial Recovery Act. Under the legislation, a friend of labor, Senator Robert F. Wagner of New York, insisted on the inclusion of Section 7(a), which provided that "employees shall have the right to organize and bargain collectively through representatives of their own choosing, and shall be free from the interference, restraint or coercion of employers of labor." Section 7(a) also stated that "no employee and no one seeking employment shall be required as a condition of employment to join any company union or to refrain from joining, organizing, or assisting a labor organization of his own choosing." The inclusion of Section 7(a) in the NIRA represented a substantial shift of economic power to unions. Union membership began to grow, moving from approximately three-and-a-half million in 1935 to over ten million in 1941.

Labor's excitement over 7(a) was dimmed in 1935 when the Supreme Court declared the NIRA unconstitutional. Workers, however, continued to organize and pressured lawmakers to devise a substitute for the labor sections of the NIRA. The result was passage of a bill sponsored by Senator Wagner, the National Labor Relations Act in July 1935, also known as the Wagner Act. The legislation represents one of labor's strongest victories, making illegal a host of management activities that had been previously used against labor. A sampling of unfair labor practices established by the Wagner Act includes:

- threatening workers with job loss for union activity.
- using industrial espionage.
- privately interrogating workers about union membership.
- hiring strikebreakers to engage in violence or create fear in workers.

- using the "Mohawk Valley Formula" (organizing citizens' committees, spreading false rumors, etc.) to break a strike.

Under the Wagner Act, the National Labor Relations Board (NLRB) was established as an independent agency to investigate complaints by unions or employees about possible violations of the NLRA. One weakness of the Wagner Act, according to its critics, is that court orders are needed to enforce NLRB rulings—a time-consuming process. It has also been argued that the Wagner Act has resulted in more union bureaucracy and defuses worker militancy and direct action. Nonetheless, the Wagner Act was clearly a step forward for the working class. Another significant triumph for labor on the legal front in the 1930s was passage of the Byrnes Act of 1936, also known as the Anti-Strikebreaker Law, which made it a felony to transport individuals across state lines as a threat against nonviolent picketing or as a measure against organizing or bargaining.

Labor gains in the 1930s were modified following World War II when a period of antilabor sentiment ensued. The Taft-Hartley Labor Act of 1947 was passed over the veto of President Harry Truman—who felt the measure was antilabor. Taft-Hartley retained most of the basic guarantees of workers' rights in the Wagner Act, particularly provisions dealing with collective bargaining. However, it contained a variety of restrictions and amendments and nullified parts of the Anti-Injunction Act of 1932. Significant provisions of Taft-Hartley include:

- outlawing of the closed shop by which an employer can hire only union members.
- banning the union shop in which all workers must join the union within some time period but need not be members when hired.
- outlawing sympathy strikes and secondary boycotts.
- making excessive or discriminatory initiation fees or dues an unfair labor practice.
- prohibiting strikes against the government.

One of the most controversial sections in Taft-Hartley was Section 9(g), which compelled all union officers to sign sworn statements that they were not members of the Communist Party. As a result of this section, radicals and leftists were driven from unions and some unions were destroyed. Section 9(g) was ultimately amended under the Labor-Management Reporting and Disclosure Act of 1959 (also known as the Landrum-Griffin Act), but Communists were still restricted from holding union office. The amended version of Section 9(g) was ultimately declared unconstitutional by the Supreme Court.

The Landrum-Griffin Act of 1959 was the result of Senate committee hearings into charges of labor management corruption, including the use of violence by labor leadership and the misuse of funds. The act prevented former Communist Party members from holding union office for a period of five years after resigning membership. A similar provision was included for convicts. It also sought to guarantee union members freedom of speech and freedom of assembly, and it called for the use of a secret ballot for the election of union officers as well as tighter regulation of union funds.

The 1960s and 1970s witnessed a variety of gains for workers in the area of employment law. The Work Hours Act of 1962 provided regulations for overtime. Discrimination was curbed in the Civil Rights Act of 1964 and the Age Discrimination in Employment Act of 1967. Workplace safety rules and inspections were tightened under the Occupational Safety and Health Act of 1970, which created the Occupational Safety and Health Administration (OSHA). Efforts to protect pension plans were launched in 1974 with the Employee Retirement Income Security Act of 1974. In the 1980s, under the Reagan and Bush administrations, attempts were made to reduce labor regulations in an effort to make America's industries more competitive.

Few major labor laws were passed in this timeframe; however, in 1990, the U.S. Supreme Court delivered a ruling making it harder for companies to replace union workers with nonunion workers.

Mark A. Noon

BIBLIOGRAPHY

Anglim, Christopher. *Labor, Employment, and the Law: A Dictionary.* Santa Barbara, CA: ABC-CLIO, 1997.

Forbath, William. *Law and the Shaping of the American Labor Movement.* Cambridge, MA: Harvard University Press, 1991.

Novkov, Julie. *Constituting Workers, Protecting Women: Gender, Law, and Labor in the Progressive Era and New Deal Years.* Ann Arbor: University of Michigan Press, 2001.

Orren, Karen. *Belated Feudalism: Labor, the Law, and Liberal Development in the United States.* New York: Cambridge University Press, 1991.

Taylor, Benjamin, and Fred Witney. *U.S. Labor Relations Law: Historical Development.* Englewood Cliffs, NJ: Prentice Hall, 1992.

Tomlins, Christopher. *Law, Labor, and Ideology in the Early American Republic.* New York: Cambridge University Press, 1993.

———. *The State and the Unions: Labor Relations, Law, and the Organized Labor Movement in America, 1880–1960.* New York: Cambridge University Press, 1985.

Tomlins, Christopher, and Andrew King, eds. *Labor Law in America: Historical and Critical Essays.* Baltimore, MD: Johns Hopkins University Press, 1992.

Woodiwiss, Anthony. *Rights v. Conspiracy: A Sociological Essay on the History of Labour Law in the United States.* New York: Berg, 1990.

CANNERY WORKERS MOVEMENT

In his 1939 study, *Factories in the Fields: The Story of Migratory Farm Labor in California,* Carey McWilliams posed the question of why it had been so difficult to organize agricultural-related workers. He contended that until organizers understood that agricultural-related work, which included farm workers and cannery workers, was essentially the same as other factory work, they could not make headway. He argued that the myth of the small farmer remained for many years, but agribusiness was the reality. A number of radical organizations understood this myth, and pioneered organizing efforts among farm workers and cannery workers. They had to overcome a conservative trade union movement that held onto the myth. These organizers had to meet the challenges emanating from the immigrant diversity in the workforce and the power of the growers and food processors. Finally, the organization of agricultural-related workers was inherently connected to United States policy on Mexican immigration, which was a revolving door policy.

HISTORY

The struggle to organize cannery workers was always closely linked to that of organizing agricultural workers. Organization was especially difficult because many of the workers were Mexican nationals, who were deported when growing season was over or when the United States economy was in a downward cycle. Both areas employed many women; in fact, the canneries consisted of a primarily Latina workforce. Conditions were abysmal, with low wages, seasonal work, unventilated rooms, and no toilet facilities. Workers often lived in makeshift tents with no running water. With the exception of agricultural unions, most mainstream labor organizations did not admit immigrants into their organizations.

CANNERY AND AGRICULTURAL WORKERS INDUSTRIAL UNION

Under the auspices of the Communist Party, one of the earliest attempts resulted in the Cannery and Agricultural Workers Industrial Union (CAWIU), which was formed during the throes of the Great Depression. Although workers were competing for fewer jobs, CAWIU led many Southwestern agricultural-related workers strikes throughout the 1930s. A major strike occurred in 1938 against the Southern Pecan Shelling Company in San Antonio, Texas. Southern Pecan was one of the few pecan companies not mechanized because it was more cost-effective to pay low wages to their predominantly Mexican workforce than to maintain machines. When the company tried to cut the already low wages, thousands of workers struck and won a favorable settlement. Since the majority of the workers were women, CAWIU recognized that it was essential for women to play a major role in leading and coordinating agricultural strikes. Important leaders were Manuela Solis Sager, Emma Tenayucca, and Luisa Moreno. All three remained committed to integrating Mexican workers into the organized labor movement and working for social change.

By the late 1930s, the union had led dozens of major strikes. CAWIU's successes were met by the wrath of the growers, who utilized police, national guards, and the legal system against them. CAWIU leaders faced prosecution under California's criminal syndicalism law. The resultant legal battles depleted their meager resources. Although the union was destroyed, its impact was extensive and laid the groundwork for future organizing among agricultural-related workers. Wage gains won by CAWIU's successful strikes amounted to millions of dollars, and workers gained important experience and political knowledge based on these unionization drives.

Cannery workers hurl stones and other objects at guards and strike-breakers during a labor conflict in Stockton, California, in 1937.
(© Underwood Photo Archives, Inc.)

LA CONFEDERACIÓN DE UNIONES DE CAMPESINOS Y OBREROS MEXICANOS

As CAWIU was being crushed, Mexican workers were forming a new independent union, La Confederación de Uniones de Campesinos y Obreros Mexicanos (CUCOM), under the leadership of radicals. The organization grew rapidly, going on to launch successful strikes and win increased wages from the growers. Again, the growers, with all forces of the state at their disposal, sought to destroy the Confederation. To strengthen their position, CUCOM linked themselves to the U.S. labor movement and also joined with labor leaders from the Filipino and Japanese communities to form the Federation of Agricultural Workers Union of America (FAWUA) in 1936. FAWUA's strike efforts met with fierce resistance from the growers, and their efforts to affiliate with the American Federation of Labor (AFL) never came to fruition, due to the resistance of the conservative AFL. In 1938, based on the lessons learned from CAWIU, CUCOM, and FAWUA, radical

trade unionists organized the United Cannery, Agricultural, Packing, and Allied Workers of America (UCAPAWA), which affiliated with the newly organized and more militant Congress of Industrial Organizations (CIO). Through its successful campaigns, UCAPAWA went on to become the seventh largest CIO union.

LUISA MORENO

From its inception, UCAPAWA was dedicated to trade union democracy and believed in promoting the leadership of immigrant workers and women workers at all levels. Luisa Moreno, a Guatemalan immigrant with a long history of involvement in labor organizing, was among the founders of the union and served as vice president for many years. Moreno had extensive trade union experience before helping to build UCAPAWA. She had organized cotton workers in Texas, beet workers in Colorado, and 60,000 cannery workers in California. Moreno was one of the main leaders of the Southern Pecan Strike in Texas. Moreno, as other UCAPAWA leaders, clearly understood the relationship between unionism, civil rights, and social change. She consistently argued for the recruitment of immigrants and women and their inclusion as leaders. She helped found the *El Congreso de los Pueblos de Habla Español* (the Congress of Spanish Speaking Peoples) in 1938. The Congress was nationwide and included workers, educators, politicians, students, and artists. Its purpose was to promote understanding between Anglo-Americans and Mexicans, to improve the economic, social, and cultural life of Mexican people, to actively unionize, and to fight all forms of discrimination. Moreno traveled all over the United States promoting the Congress and arguing for the rights of Spanish-speaking peoples. She explained how Mexican workers were constantly being brought to the United States by large growers' associations as a cheap workforce and then sent back, making organizing difficult.

FOOD, TOBACCO, AGRICULTURAL AND ALLIED WORKERS OF AMERICA (FTA)

Since UCPAWA had made significant gains among tobacco workers, its name was changed in 1944 to the Food, Tobacco, Agricultural and Allied Workers of America (FTA). The plans of the union continued to be the building of strong cannery units, which would serve as a basis for organizing farm workers. FTA served as a model of social unionism as they actively recruited women and immigrants and consciously groomed them for leadership. Women recruiting women proved to be pivotal to the union's organizing success.

In 1945, backed by the CIO, FTA took on the challenge of organizing cannery workers in central California. This task was made more formidable as they found themselves competing with the AFL-sanctioned International Brotherhood of Teamsters (IBT), who had a condescending attitude toward cannery workers. Utilizing their democratic approach, FTA sought to reach the diverse workforce, which included Chinese, African-American, Italian, Portuguese, and Mexican workers. Multilingual literature was distributed, and multilingual meetings were held. Although FTA overwhelmingly won NLRB certification elections, the IBT retaliated by boycotting canneries under FTA contract. The IBT also won over the California Processors and Growers Association (CPG), who preferred their labor/management accord approach over the more radical FTA. The NLRB elections were challenged, and the IBT began to sign "sweetheart" or illegal contracts.

Because of the fierce anti-Communist, anti-Progressive movement of the Cold War years, especially in the McCarthy era, the IBT and the AFL repeatedly attacked the FTA as subversive. As a result of the 1947 Taft-Hartley Act, which eroded many of labor's gains won through the 1935 National Labor Relations Act, FTA, along with other left-led democratic unions, was expelled from the CIO in 1950, weakening the labor federation considerably. IBT became firmly entrenched among the cannery workers in California.

By 1990, a democratic faction won control of the IBT and attempted to transform the union. IBT still held sway over cannery workers, but during the 1990s, before the union could be democratized, thousands of California cannery and other agricultural-related workers found themselves displaced as plants located offshore. Although regions such as Watsonville, San Pedro, and San Diego enjoyed flourishing food processing industries for almost fifty years, by the twenty-first century, most were gone.

CONCLUSION

The organizing of cannery workers was intertwined with the organizing of farm workers. These workers were predominantly women and documented and undocumented immigrants. Organizing immigrants was difficult since they were vulnerable and always subject to deportation. During the Depression, many Mexicans, including U.S. citizens, were deported or "repatriated" to Mexico. Despite intimidation, harassment, and the severe economic conditions of the Depression, Mexican workers, especially women, were at the forefront of the trade union movement. Women and Mexican workers coordinated organizing campaigns and formed democratic unions in the cannery and agriculture-related industries. Fierce red-baiting campaigns on the part of the government, business, the church, and conservative unions all joined to destroy these unions in the 1940s and 1950s. At the end of the twentieth century, in the search for cheaper labor, the canning and agriculture-related industries moved offshore, leaving thousands of workers jobless.

Myrna Cherkoss Donahoe

BIBLIOGRAPHY

Acuna, Rodolfo. *Occupied America: A History of Chicanos.* New York: Harper & Row, 1981.

Gonzalez, Gilbert. *Labor and Community: Mexican Citrus Worker Villages in a Southern California County, 1900–1950.* Urbana: University of Illinois Press, 1994.

McWilliams, Carey. *Factories in the Field: The Story of Migratory Farm Labor in California.* 1939. Reprint, Santa Barbara, CA: Peregrine, 1971.

Ruiz, Vicki L. *Cannery Women/Cannery Lives: Mexican Women, Unionization, and the California Food Processing Industry, 1930–1950.* Albuquerque: University of New Mexico Press, 1987.

Labor Movement   1948–1981

Between the end of World War II and the first Reagan administration, the American labor movement completed a trajectory of growth that began in the 1930s, survived a period of stagnation, and initiated a decline that would continue throughout the end of the century.

After a revival of militancy in the immediate aftermath of World War II, labor retreated from the social agenda it had advanced during the New Deal and accepted the more limited role of bargaining agent for its members. At the labor movements' apogee in the mid-1950s, unions comprised one-third of nonfarm workers. Organized labor was remarkably successful in procuring high wages, pension benefits, and health insurance against the background of Cold War politics and the resurgence of conservatism. These hard-won gains indirectly benefited the whole working class as some nonunion firms followed similar wage patterns.

Looking from the perspective of a steady decline of the labor movement in the past two decades, historians have located the seeds of its downfall in the postwar period. They argue that the labor movement developed into a mainstream institution, which supported corporate capitalism and the Korean and Vietnam wars and abandoned its reformist goals. Critics have also observed that material gains were often achieved only in exchange for increased input on the job—an alienating experience for the average worker on the line.

Labor, during the period under examination, also contended with internal opponents among social groups that criticized its bias toward male and white members. Organized labor accommodated to these pressures in a variety of ways, according to the political inclinations of its various affiliates. However, following the social transformations of the 1960s, discontent also grew among white workers, spurring a series of rank-and-file movements that challenged the industrial order of corporate capitalism.

This agitation diminished in the mid-1970s when the economic crisis and the restructuring of mass production started eroding labor's negotiating leverage and jeopardized millions of jobs. In the 1980s, the Reagan administration put forward a neoliberal agenda that included a direct attack on the prerogatives of organized labor. The managerial offensive that ensued accelerated the decline of the labor movement and eroded its influence in American society.

LABOR IN THE WAKE OF WORLD WAR II

The end of World War II opened a period of confrontation between labor and capital that resulted in the refashioning of the system of industrial relations initiated during the New Deal. After VJ Day, industrial unions—mostly gathered under the umbrella of the Congress of Industrial Organizations (CIO)—lifted the No Strike Pledge they had underwritten to sustain the wartime production effort. Fear of a renewed depression among workers, which seemed confirmed by cutbacks in production and plant closures, led to a wave of strikes of a magnitude second only to the one of 1919–1920. Thousands of strikes occurred among automobile, steel, electrical, and coal workers, but also in the shipbuilding, telephone, railway, lumber, meatpacking, and other industries. Industrial workers comprised over two-thirds of the strikers.

The CIO, under the leadership of Philip Murray, saw in the reconversion an opportunity to broaden the role of labor and the scope of its influence in government decision making. However, inside the organization different personalities disagreed on the best way to achieve this goal. Although Murray favored a smooth transition through negotiation with corporations and government, others—and prominent among them was Walter Reuther, head of the United Automobile Workers (UAW)-General Motors (GM) department—preferred a showdown, thereby exploiting workers' willingness to strike. Eventually, this second

WALTER P. REUTHER (1907–1970)

More than any other individual, Walter Reuther defined the structure, mission, and outlook of the United Automobile Workers (UAW). Although he was neither the labor union's founder nor its first president, his influence spans the decades from the years of the Great Depression into the twenty-first century.

Reuther was born on September 1, 1907, to a German immigrant couple in Wheeling, West Virginia, the second of five children. They were strong unionists and staunch Socialists who believed that a Socialist commonwealth would eventually replace the predatory capitalist system extant in the United States in the early twentieth century.

In 1927, Walter moved to Detroit to work in the burgeoning automobile business. After a brief stint at Briggs Manufacturing, a supplier of auto bodies, Reuther landed a job at Ford Motor Company and remained there for five years. Victor, Walter's brother, joined him in Detroit in 1930, and they began working together in the election campaign for Socialist candidate Norman Thomas. Although Reuther eventually abandoned the Socialist cause per se, the ideals of economic and social equality remained.

After Walter was laid off, the brothers embarked on a three-year tour of Europe that eventually led them to work in the Soviet Union's Gorki auto plant for eighteen months. Upon their return in 1935, the two brothers worked at organizing industrial workers for the newly formed Congress of Industrial Organizations (CIO), which organized all workers in a certain industry regardless of skill level or craft affiliation, unlike the long-established American Federation of Labor (AFL). Reuther's skill at organizing and a new weapon, the sitdown strike, brought success to the newly formed UAW. Walter Reuther was elected president of newly chartered Local 174 in Detroit. Organizing successes at General Motors (Flint, Michigan) and Chrysler (Detroit and Hamtramck, Michigan) in 1937 and at Ford in 1941 cemented the UAW as a fixture in the American auto industry. In 1937, Reuther and other organizers were severely beaten by a Ford goon squad in the famous Battle of the Overpass at the company's Rouge River Plant in Dearborn, Michigan. He survived an assassination attempt in 1948 that left him severely wounded.

During the war years, 1941–1945, most unions, including the UAW, agreed to the "No Strike Pledge," which demonstrated union loyalty to the nation while giving up workers' ultimate weapon against employers. Despite the pledge, thousands of unauthorized wildcat strikes took place in the auto plants. The plants had been converted to war production, partially as a result of Reuther's "500 planes a day" plan.

In 1948, Reuther negotiated the "Treaty of Detroit" with General Motors, which gave autoworkers quarterly cost-of-living adjustments and a 2 percent annual improvement factor. An even more generous five-year contract in 1950 expanded healthcare benefits and established a monthly pension plan. The UAW grew in numbers and political clout, especially in the Democratic Party, reaching a peak of 1.5 million members in 1965. In exchange for monetary and benefits packages, however, the UAW gave up control over issues of production, corporate investment, and the nature of the workplace.

In 1955, Reuther helped negotiate the merger of the AFL and CIO. But in 1968, because of personal and organizational differences with AFL-CIO President George Meany, Reuther led the UAW out of the AFL-CIO. Chief among these differences was Meany's conservative views on civil rights and foreign policy, especially the Vietnam War. Reuther had supported U.S. President Lyndon Johnson because of the War on Poverty and Johnson's progressive actions on civil rights and rebuilding the inner cities until late 1967 and early 1968. Reuther's muted opposition to the war alienated both Johnson and Meany, who supported American efforts in Vietnam to the bitter end in 1973.

Reuther was a strong supporter of the civil rights movement and marched alongside Martin Luther King Jr. in Detroit and Washington in 1963.

Walter Reuther died with his wife, May, on May 9, 1970, in a plane crash. They were on their way to view Reuther's final project, an extensive UAW training facility at Black Lake in northern Michigan. Although he can be criticized for his failures, he should be praised for his vision and his attempts to create a just society in which working people could participate in the American Dream.

Frank Koscielski

line proved more popular among rank-and-file workers, who had contended with inflation, wage freezes, and speedups during the war period.

The longest confrontation, and a crucial one for the fate of American labor, was the 1946 General Motors strike led by Walter Reuther himself. The GM strike lasted 113 days and shut all the company's plants. Most were concentrated in Detroit, Flint, Toledo, and Cleveland. The UAW demanded a 30 percent wage increase without a rise in the cost of cars. Reuther claimed that, due to rising wartime productivity and "cost plus" government contracts, GM had the ability to pay, and provocatively asked the company to open its books to a panel of government experts to demonstrate the contrary. Reuther embraced Keynesian economics and argued that only a redistribution of income could forestall another depression by sustaining consumers' spending.

If wage hikes were passed on to consumers, they would undermine sustained growth. He called upon the government to maintain price controls and working-class living standards. President Harry Truman, however, was not going to assume such a role. By not giving full support to the UAW, the president encouraged GM to resist the kind of social ambitions that the labor movement had nurtured during the war. GM manager Wilson, on behalf of the entire business community, upheld the principle that unions should not intrude in management matters such as prices, profits, or organization of work. The GM strike therefore concerned essentially what sphere labor would occupy in the postwar period. Eventually, the UAW's position was also undermined by the settlement of the United Steel Workers and United Electrical Workers—the latter striking against the same employer—who settled with a pay rise of 18.5 cents an hour. Reuther, left with little space for maneuvering, had no alternative but to accept these conditions.

Although the postwar strikes delivered only limited gains in wages, they did show the extent of workers' power and solidarity, even in the face of internal failure to coordinate CIO strategy. The fact that violent clashes with police occurred only in sporadic cases suggested that organized labor enjoyed a greater legitimacy among the general public than before the war. However, subsequent events also showed the fragility of industrial unionism power.

Successes among Southern unions during the war and the desire to revive the organizing spirit of the 1930s led the CIO to announce in 1945 an ambitious drive to unionize the low-wage South—unofficially dubbed "Operation Dixie." With less resoluteness, the craft union–based American Federation of Labor (AFL) also launched its own organizing drive. But wartime success proved ephemeral, and both organizing campaigns faced an entrenched anti-union sentiment not only among employers but among workers too. For the CIO in particular, the failure was upsetting since it had initially committed considerable, though insufficient, resources, together with its credibility. The campaign suffered from dubious strategic choices, which included the privileging of textile industries, the eschewing of the racial question, and the exclusion of left-wing organizers. Operation Dixie dragged on until 1953 when it was discontinued in the face of CIO affiliations dropping out of the drive among the discomfort of the in-field organizers. The AFL had already stopped its drive in 1947.

TAFT-HARTLEY AND THE PURGE OF COMMUNISTS

One circumstance that hindered Operation Dixie was the growing conservative climate in national politics. The onset of the Cold War and the strike wave after VJ Day contributed to create a backlash against labor that gave Republicans the majority in the elections of 1946. For Republicans the repeated strikes exposed the inadequacies of the existing labor legislation, which gave a "monopolistic" power to unions. Employers, too, waited for a chance to reform the Wagner Act. These sentiments resulted in passage of the Taft-Hartley Act. The first major political attack on the New Deal political order, the act marked the transition to the postwar era in labor law. The act sought to restrict unions' influence at a political level and interunion solidarity by banning sympathy strikes, supportive boycotts, and campaign contributions. It complicated the procedure for the union shop and, most important, for the future of organized labor, allowed states to bypass federal law and ban the closed shop. This provision in particular nullified Operation Dixie. Finally, the new law required all union officeholders to sign affidavits affirming that they were not members of the Communist Party. Any union whose officers refused to sign affidavits would lose the protection provided by the Wagner Act and access to the National Labor Relations Board (NLRB) mechanism.

The Taft-Hartley Act reinforced the effect of contracts stipulated at industry level in seriously delimiting the union's space for maneuvering both at the national level and on the shop floor. The clause that allowed the U.S. president to seek an injunction end-

No law was more universally despised by organized labor than the 1947 Taft-Hartley Act, which banned sympathy strikes and the closed shop and curtailed union influence nationwide. In this 1953 cartoon, labor leaders John L. Lewis, Walter Reuther, and George Meany ride a horse with an axe head, galloping toward the Taft-Hartley Act in hopes of chopping it down and repealing it. *(Library of Congress)*

ing strikes that "imperil the national health," though never seriously implemented, lowered public support for unions by portraying them as selfish economic actors that were harmful to the nation. The act, by redefining the term *employee* in a way that excluded foremen, impaired the efforts of this category to build up a union in the form of the Foremen Association of America. As historian Nelson Lichtenstein has demonstrated, the foremen's efforts to build a union drove them increasingly into a collaboration with the CIO, thereby depriving management of the fundamental instrument to regiment rank-and-file. Manufacturers' victory in keeping foremen strictly on management's side represented an insurmountable limit for the expansion of unions' rights to other categories. The cumulative effect of the provisions in the new labor legislation was to discourage unions from pursuing a

strategy of structural reform of the American political economy.

The Taft-Hartley Act and the announcement of the Truman Doctrine of worldwide containment of the Soviet Union opened a period of internal struggle within the CIO that resulted in the purge of Communist-led unions and Communist officers. Although Communists were only a minority within the CIO, they played a major role in the 1930s in building the organization. They occupied key posts in the United Electrical, Radio and Machine Workers (UE), the Food, Tobacco, and Allied Workers (FTA), and the International Longshoremen's and Warehousemen's Union (ILWU). Other unions, such as the UAW and the United Packinghouse Workers of America (UPWA), counted staunch Communist locals in their ranks. During the Cold War, the presence of Communists became a central issue. On the one hand, the CIO became increasingly enmeshed in supporting the Truman administration and its foreign and defense policy. On the other hand, genuine anti-Communists like former UE president James Carey and UAW president Walter Reuther used the issue to win factional struggles on their own turf.

In 1947, CIO affiliates followed a divided course in reference to international politics, for instance, in reference to the Marshall Plan. However, during the 1948 presidential election a split became inevitable as pro-Soviet unions and leaders supported third-party candidate Henry Wallace, while AFL-CIO leaders endorsed Truman. The provision of the Taft-Hartley Act that decertified from the NLRB unions whose officers did not sign the anti-Communist affidavit played into the hands of Reuther and the like because it made "Communist" unions more vulnerable in relations with employers and to takeover by other unions. During 1948 and 1949, for instance, the UAW raided UE and Farm Equipment (FE) locals. In the same period, the CIO expelled many affiliates with Communist leadership or orientation, thereby losing hundreds of thousands of members and some of the finest organizers. The AFL, on the other hand, had no record of Communist infiltration, and it had enthusiastically adopted the anti-Communist affidavits. In the Cold War period, in collaboration with the State Department and the Central Intelligence Agency (CIA), the AFL played an important part in undermining Communist unions in Europe and in creating the International Confederation of Free Trade Unions. In the process, labor became part of the liberal establishment by consolidating its alliance with the Democratic Party, especially through the activity of CIO's Political

Action Committee and AFL's League for Political Action. The Communist purge therefore defined the character of labor for the next twenty-five years and opened a period that is often called the Corporate Consensus, in which organized labor participated in the American government's program of military spending and Communist containment abroad, reaping the benefits of the economic boom at home.

COLLECTIVE BARGAINING AND THE POSTWAR LIBERAL CONSENSUS

The Korean War can be considered the beginning of a period of maximum fortune for organized labor. In these years the two characters that defined postwar labor ascended to a presidential position in their respective organizations: George Meany in the AFL and Walter Reuther in the CIO. During the Korean War, labor renewed its commitment to the Democratic foreign agenda, but contrary to its stance in World War II it did not consent to a no-strike pledge. Therefore, during the Korean conflict the system of industrial relations developed into its mature form, according to the lines already designated by the 1946 UAW-GM contract.

In that instance, the automobile manufacturer had expressed the employer's concern to limit the scope of collective bargaining to matters deemed not critical to management efficiency. The control of the production process on the shop-floor level was the most important sphere from the managerial point of view, for it invested its prerogative to determine the production output and its cost. The existence of collective bargaining rested on the shared assumption between unions and manufacturers that it would have to be enacted at the expense of shop-floor bargaining. In fact, by specifying workers' rights on the shop floor through a contract, unions and manufacturers also severely limited them. This system, which historians have called workplace contractualism, regulated workers' discontent with a grievance procedure articulated in several steps. At every stage, union and management negotiated to solve the problem according to the contract. Often the way a grievance would be solved depended on a *quid pro quo* between the two sides, and not on conformity to an abstract rule. For instance, management could revoke a disciplinary action toward a worker if the union, in exchange, pardoned an increase in the work pace. If the grievance could not be solved at the lower level of the hierarchy, it would go higher up, until, eventually, it would be submitted to arbitration by a neutral third party with a binding decision.

There is little discussion that the grievance procedure, as it was implemented, aimed at neutralizing potential disruptive conflict on the shop floor. It buttressed management control of the workforce and production process because it left unions with only one legitimate instrument to counter an adverse managerial decision: to file a grievance. This system was also in itself ineffectual in attacking inequalities in the workplace inasmuch as union officials and managers could, in practice, simply ignore a grievance. Finally, the sheer volume of grievances granted that only a small proportion would be submitted to every step of the procedure.

Collective bargaining pursued economic efficiency and orderly industrial relations by rendering most types of job actions illegal during the life of the contract. It transformed shop stewards into guardians of the rank and file insofar as they had to restrain actions that violated the contract. Collective bargaining also affected the internal organization of unions, as only full-time officials could administrate the complex body of contract rules. Officials at the local level were responsible for the application of the contract for the central organizations. A UAW bylaw required three conditions for a strike: that the conflict could not be solved through the grievance procedure; that the strike be voted by a majority of the local members; and that the strike be approved by the International Executive Board. Collective bargaining therefore reinforced the decisional power of the hierarchies at the expense of the rank and file, although always within a system formally committed to internal democracy.

By 1950, unions such as the UAW had completed their trajectory from a catalyst of mass movement to pillars of the social order based on the "Corporate Consensus." The CIO had joined the AFL in definitely abandoning more radical aims in order to co-manage a capitalistic economy base on the assumption of a constant growth of the auto industry and a national prosperity underpinned by the Cold War "military-industrial complex." The CIO slogan "What's Good for America Is Good for the CIO" is telling in this respect. The 1950 UAW-GM contract has been traditionally regarded as the most significant example of this trend. The contract included a $125-a-month pension and a cost of living allowance (COLA) linked to inflation. Most remarkably, the contract ran for the unprecedented length of five years.

The press hailed the agreement as the "Treaty of Detroit," and it was compared to as sweeping an innovation as Ford's five-dollar day. Reuther boasted that the contract was "the most significant development in labor relations since the mass production industries were organized." The UAW proved that organized labor was able to provide a high standard of living for the working class, without impairing manufacturers' growth. Indeed, as in previous UAW-GM contracts, the "Treaty of Detroit" was a trendsetter not only in the auto industry, but also in the entire manufacturing sector. COLA soon spread to all major union contracts and, as inflation increased, to Social Security pensions and even some nonunion contracts. However, the contract also marked the end of the union's effort to intervene in the management of the industry—the four-year-old request to "open the books" seemed four decades away—and testified to the end of the liberal hope for an expansion of the welfare state by accepting a company-centered welfare.

Operating in a high-technology and high-profit sector, the UAW broke ground in achieving the material betterment of its workers, but in all the manufacturing sectors, unions successfully expanded health insurance, pension plans, unemployment benefits, and, in particular, wages, which for the average workers rose, in real terms, 31 percent between 1950 and 1965. Outside the CIO, the United Mine Workers, led by the legendary John L. Lewis, negotiated in 1947 a forward-looking medical fund to protect miners from the frequent work-related injuries and diseases. In the 1950s, only a few radical observers contradicted the common wisdom that the American worker had entered the middle class. Suburban residential patterns and the constant growth of consumers suggested that the American worker was integrated into the system. On the other hand, the upsurge of white-collar employment, which in 1956 surpassed blue-collar employment, pointed to a future disappearance of the traditional working class.

Organized labor's successes in collective bargaining concealed its inability to put forward a social welfare agenda at the national level. Labor turned toward firm-based benefits because plans for a public healthcare program had plummeted by 1949. By doing so, labor created in the manufacturing sector a privileged working class disinterested in advancing the social legislation liberals sought for lower-income groups in the segmented U.S. labor market. There was an "Other America," in the words of writer Michael Harrington, that did not reap the benefits of the expanding U.S. economy as union workers did. Furthermore, the failure to shift welfare items from the collective bargaining agenda to national politics impeded further gains in wages and working conditions.

Efforts to repeal the brakes imposed by the Taft-Hartley Act were also unsuccessful, and actually labor stood on the defensive during the 1950s against further Republican attacks on union rights. Finally, within the private sector, even the most powerful unions like the UAW and the United Steelworkers of America (USWA) failed to curb employers' resistance to a guaranteed annual wage and a shorter work week.

THE 1950s: LABOR IN THE AFFLUENT SOCIETY

The 1950s were therefore at the same time years of achievement and years of stagnation for the labor movement. While in absolute terms, the number of unionized workers increased, its proportion in the total workforce actually shrank. In 1954, for instance, union membership stood at about 17 million and represented 34.7 percent of nonagricultural workers. By 1968, although the first figure had risen to almost 19 million, it represented only 27.8 percent of the labor force. Also responsible for this development were the managerial strategies of development and restructuring in key unionized sectors, such as automobile, steel, and meatpacking. Manufacturers consented to the unions' presence only grudgingly and, even if they accepted the unions as bargaining partners, they endeavored to find ways to undermine their clout. At the industry level, this meant mainly experimenting with technology that would reduce the need for human labor while augmenting production. In the late 1940s, the specialized press dubbed this phenomenon "Automation"—a term that soon appeared in virtually every discussion on the future of American manufacturing.

When Ford introduced automation in 1947, it meant the operation of automatic transfer machines that would move material between different lines without the employment of workers. However, automatic devices gradually spread in many industries, substituting for workers in a number of occupations. Mechanization threatened both skilled and unskilled workers but exacted a greater toll among the unskilled as it often concerned labor-intensive operations. Automation changed the American industrial landscape in many ways that affected the labor movement. Since it required an initial large investment for its introduction, automation favored the tendency of American capitalism toward further concentration, as smaller manufacturers who could not afford the technology lagged behind in productivity and were eventually driven out of the market. Unions in the industrial sector therefore confronted increasingly powerful corporations.

Automation caused the quick obsolescence of plants. The new transfer lines worked best on a large horizontal surface area. Manufacturers always preferred to build new plants on cheap land outside large urban centers rather than to renew the old multistory plants. Furthermore, they used this opportunity to increasingly relocate their operations to areas with low levels of unionization, leaving the old industrial heartland deindustrialized, with terrible social and economic consequences. These developments therefore eroded unions' power precisely in those segments of the labor market in which they were supposed to be strong. In the long run, more than any other strategic or organizational mistake, it would be the restructuring of the industrial economy that would weaken unions' leverage in the political arena.

By the mid-1950s, labor had become an established component of the American polity. Organized labor claimed 18 million members, and of these, 9 million belonged to the AFL, 6 million to the CIO, and the rest to independent unions such as the UMW and the railway brotherhoods (these figures, however, were probably inflated). However, labor would have to overcome its many divisions if it was to countervail in the long term the powerful anti-union forces. Efforts to mend the separation between the different components of the house of labor were in vain during the late 1930s and the 1940s, but in the 1950s the original antagonism between the AFL and the CIO had diminished as the difference between craft and industrial unionism faded in the bureaucratization of the postwar labor movement.

The ascendancy in 1952 of the first Republican president since 1933 prompted the two organizations to look for a greater unity. Truly, Reuther and Meany were two different men: Reuther was committed to pursue a social democratic agenda, whereas Meany was a bread-and-butter unionist who proudly declared that he had never led a strike. However, both fitted C. Wright Mills's characterization of "managers of discontent" insofar as they were instrumental in channeling working-class insurgency into mainstream institutions.

Two obstacles that had precluded the merger in the past—the respective charges of Communist influence in the CIO and the negative record of racketeering in some AFL affiliates—became less conspicuous.

As we have seen, by 1950 the CIO had purged its Communist affiliation and was a leading supporter of anti-Soviet politics. In 1953, the AFL moved to attack illegal practices in the International Longshoremen's Association (ILA), especially in its power base on the New York docks (whose underworld was depicted by Elia Kazan in the controversial 1954 film *On the Waterfront*). Failing to meet the requests of the federation regarding the transparent system of paying and the employment of officers with clean police records, the ILA was finally expelled from the AFL later that year.

The AFL and the CIO eventually merged in 1955 after having settled (though not in a definitive way) the thorny matter of AFL raiding on CIO locals and (rarely) vice versa. Since the AFL was the larger of the two, the presidency was assigned to Meany. On the other hand, Reuther contented himself with being a vice president in charge of the Industrial Union Department where he thought he would be in control of the resources necessary to launch a new organizing drive. In fact, he saw in the merger the opportunity to revitalize the campaign to organize the unorganized, which had stalled since the end of Operation Dixie. Reuther thought that the merged federation could amass $15 million and organize up to 4 million workers in a few years.

In the end, the merger did not open the road for such a development, and organized labor did not move forward, but instead continued to stall. The AFL-CIO never initiated the kind of momentum that Reuther envisioned. Meany persevered in the customary AFL skepticism of central organizing. He thought this was best left to single unions or to workers themselves: they would have joined unions if they wanted to. Frustrated by the many obstacles he encountered in the AFL-CIO, Reuther in 1967 temporarily brought the UAW into an alliance with the Teamsters, charging that the federation lacked "the necessary vitality, vision, and imagination, as well as social invention to make it equal to the challenging problems of a changing world."

This coalition was short-lived because the two organizations represented two different types of unionism: the UAW was one of the most forward-looking, democratic, and reformist unions; the Teamsters, though equal, or bigger, in size, had not severed their ties with organized crime that had caused their expulsion from the AFL-CIO in 1957. The Teamsters adopted dubious practices in their organizing raids and were politically on the other end of the spectrum, being close to the Republicans.

THE MERGER OF THE AFL AND CIO

After nearly twenty years of union rivalry between the American Federation of Labor and the Congress of Industrial Organizations, organized labor in the United States reunified under the umbrella of one federation with the creation of the AFL-CIO in February 1955. The following is the preamble to the new federation's constitution.

PREAMBLE

The establishment of this Federation through the merger of the American Federation of Labor and the Congress of Industrial Organizations is an expression of the hopes and aspirations of the working people of America.

We seek fulfillment of these hopes and aspirations through democratic processes within the framework of our constitutional government and consistent with our institutions and traditions.

At the collective bargaining table, in the community, in the exercise of the rights and responsibilities of citizenship, we shall responsibly serve the interests of all the American people.

We pledge ourselves to the more effective organization of working men and women; to the securing to them of full recognition and enjoyment of the rights to which they are justly entitled; to the achievement of ever higher standards of living and working conditions; to the attainment of security for all the people sufficient to enable workers and their families to live in dignity; to the enjoyment of the leisure which their skills make possible; and to the strengthening and extension of our way of life and our democratic society.

We shall combat resolutely the forces which seek to undermine the democratic institutions of our nation and to enslave the human soul. We shall strive always to win full respect for the dignity of the human individual whom our unions serve.

With Divine guidance, grateful for the fine traditions of our past, confident of meeting the challenge of the future, we proclaim this Constitution.

Source: AFL-CIO, Washington, DC.

LABOR AND THE RACIAL QUESTION

One basic issue that had retarded the AFL-CIO merger was their different commitment to racial equality. The AFL had a negative record on civil rights. Although the federation included about 600,000 black workers and one black-led union—the Brotherhood of Sleeping Car Porters—many affiliates continued to blatantly discriminate against African Americans. All AFL skilled craft unions de facto excluded blacks from their ranks, and so did the building trades unions, musicians, papermakers, and others. Apart from generic statements denouncing racism, the federation never disciplined these cases, nor did it allow an extended debate about the issue. The approach of the AFL to racial matters had not changed much since its formative years in the nineteenth century when blacks were not part of the industrial working class.

On the other hand, African Americans had played an important part in building the CIO in the 1930s. By 1945, over 300,000 black workers were members of CIO affiliates. They were particularly numerous in auto manufacturing and meatpacking, so that the UAW and the UPWA became outspoken supporters of civil rights as well as steel and longshoring workers. Postwar industrial contracts helped narrow the gap between white and black workers' income. In 1950, the average African-American income was 60 percent that of whites, compared to 41 percent in 1939. CIO leaders frequently asserted the need to end racial discrimination, though often in the Cold War context of avoiding negative Soviet propaganda.

Upon closer inspection, however, the positive reputation of CIO unions for civil rights was only relative to the situation in the AFL. Although the UPWA systematically fought prejudicial practices and discriminatory contracts, other CIO unions were vocal supporters of civil rights but did not always consistently live up to their own words. The UAW, for instance, staunchly endorsed civil rights legislation, it generously donated to the NAACP, and it created at its internal core a Fair Practices Committee to consider cases of discrimination within the automobile industry. However, its internal hierarchies remained exclusively white. In 1962, the first African American was elected to its executive, but blacks remained grossly underrepresented among the top officers. Similarly, the UAW never challenged its skilled trades practices of racial exclusivity, thereby contributing to keep blacks in the most unpleasant jobs.

Given these precedents, a merger between the two federations sounded ominous to civil rights activists in the labor movement because it also suggested that the CIO would renounce its timid commitment to the black cause. The AFL-CIO convention in 1955 did ratify an article in the constitution that committed the organization to "encourage all workers, without regard to race, creed, color, national origin, or ancestry, to share equally in the full benefits of union organization." However, in the following years, proposals to implement this clause were frustrated by the fact that white delegates from conservative unions dominated the convention. President Meany personally opposed expelling unions that practiced discrimination. To the insistence of A. Philip Randolph, the combative president of the Brotherhood of Sleeping Car Porters, demanding to expand the power of the civil rights committee, he famously replied "Who in hell appointed you as the guardian of the Negroes members [sic] in America?"

Moving into the 1960s, the AFL-CIO continued to refuse to throw its weight to achieve full racial equality in its ranks. Liberal unions such the UAW worked closely with the civil rights leaders. The civil rights leaders acknowledged the UAW's contribution when they called Reuther to share the podium in the 1963 March on Washington where Martin Luther King Jr. delivered his poignant "I Have a Dream" speech.

Meanwhile, the UAW's internal contradictions were exposed in Detroit by the activists of the Trade Union Leadership Council (TULC), who demanded a stronger black presence in the leadership and in the skilled trades. Other liberal unions also came under attack. In 1962, NAACP labor secretary Herbert Hill denounced the International Ladies' Garment Workers' Union for discouraging African-American and Puerto Rican members from running for office. Revelations of discrimination within industrial unions proved even more disturbing than the surveys that showed racial exclusivity among AFL craft unions; the AFL craft unions, after all, had never publicly advanced racial justice. This discrepancy between public statements and private truths increasingly drove a wedge between labor and the black movement.

WOMEN IN THE LABOR MOVEMENT

As in the case of African Americans, the labor movement's record in regard to women is mixed. From the outset, trade unions had been male-dominated and male-oriented organizations, and women made inroads into equality only slowly, facing a number of obstacles. The lack of manpower for defense industries during World War II led to increased employment of women, helped question some of the boundaries that defined the gendered division of work in manufacturing, and exposed the arbitrariness of these divisions.

Women adjusted to jobs as welders and assemblers, jobs traditionally reserved for men. As their per-

centage among the workforce increased many times over, women also entered union politics. In unions such as the UAW and UE, during World War II women represented up to 40 percent of the membership. Their defense production experience prepared women to resist the massive layoffs after the Japanese surrender in 1945. While for men workers layoffs lasted only from the time of reconversion to civilian activities, women workers were often discriminated against and not hired again. In many cases, men with no history of employment were preferred to women with three years of seniority. Employers now asserted that women were not suited for certain jobs.

Although the labor movement acknowledged the problem of sexual discrimination at work, union leadership tended to marginalize women's problems in favor of the demands of the male majority. Verbal commitments to sex equality did not translate into equal access to a position of power in the union hierarchy or in an agenda centered on equal access to jobs for women. As a result of this kind of patriarchal resistance among both managers and laborites, the percentage of women in the industrial workforce shrank to 10 percent by the 1950s.

Thus, women's battle for equality in the workplace had to start inside the unions, with local leadership often proving harder to overcome than national officers. In the UAW, where Walter Reuther sincerely believed in the opportunities for democracy offered by the labor movement, local leaders often ignored recommendations and directives to bargain equal access to jobs or disregarded female workers' grievance against unfair managerial practices. Women's insistence on defending their rights made an impact on the UAW policy. In 1955, the international leadership granted them continuing funding for the Women's Bureau, an independent department from which women could advance their collective bargaining objectives.

In the UE, the largest union expelled from the CIO in the Communist purge, the internal Fair Practices Committee equally fought against sexism and racism, and the union often succeeded in eliminating discriminatory clauses in the contracts. However, few other unions could boast the same commitment to the advancement of women. The ILGWU, a union composed in the majority of women, had a leadership almost exclusively male, and the AFL craft unions did not bother to organize women. Finally, no woman sat on the AFL-CIO executive board.

A breakthrough in the position of women in the labor movement occurred only in the 1970s. The rise of the feminist movement with its emphasis on gender equality revitalized women's effort inside the unions and gave them greater political leverage. Meanwhile, the unionization of the service sector increased the percentage of women inside the labor movement. In 1974, hundreds of female delegates from all over the country founded the Coalition of Labor Union Women (CLUW) in Chicago. CLUW demanded affirmative action in the workplace to end sexual discrimination, pledged to organize women in the labor movement, and encouraged women's empowerment in the workplace and in the union. Although influenced by the feminist resurgence of the decade, CLUW was fully within the tradition of pressure groups in the labor movement and was successful in exerting influence in the AFL-CIO toward women's concerns and in promoting women to leadership inside their unions.

THE 1960s: LABOR AND ITS DISCONTENTS

Although discontent grew within its ranks, in the 1960s labor enjoyed a return to grace in Washington. Both John F. Kennedy and Lyndon Johnson shared labor's belief in a Keynesian economy, and under their presidencies the decade became a moment of liberal ascendancy. Kennedy chose as his secretary of labor Arthur Goldberg, a CIO man. Goldberg was later elected to the U.S. Supreme Court, thus giving labor an influence at the highest political level. Kennedy's assassination opened the way to his successor's program of civil rights, social legislation, and government spending—exactly the type of welfare state labor leaders like Reuther had demanded for a decade. Johnson routinely consulted with union leaders and enlisted their support for both the Great Society and the Vietnam War.

The Labor-Liberal alliance was, however, destined to collapse under the thrust of a radicalized civil rights movement and the mounting protest against the war. Johnson's War on Poverty could not redress ingrained economic inequalities without infringing the corporate power that had created them, and this was clearly outside the scope of his administration. Poverty programs instead targeted specific aggrieved groups—which came to be identified with poor African Americans—with insufficient funds to ameliorate their condition, but with sufficient publicity to irritate more privileged sections of the working class. White and ethnic voters, so far the bulwark of liberalism, shifted to the right when they began to believe

that the expansion of the welfare state had occurred at their expense but not for their benefit. Urban riots and turbulence in the universities contributed to create the feeling that America was "coming apart" and that a shift toward traditional values was needed.

The escalation of the Vietnam War, together with the growth of Black Power and the counterculture, set the emerging New Left apart from organized labor. Young workers in the factories did not recall the CIO militant organizing days or its postwar battles for social reforms. They regarded unions in a different way: bureaucratic organization disciplining the workforce on the account of the employers; mainstream institutions that supported the war and sanctioned American capitalism.

Not surprisingly, in the wake of the urban riots of the late 1960s, black workers were the first to clash with their unions and to create dissent groups in the workplace. In Detroit, a city where the rapid deindustrialization hit mainly the large black population, black workers at Chrysler organized into revolutionary movements, which coalesced in 1969 under the League of Revolutionary Black Workers. Blending Marxism-Leninism and Black Nationalism, the League demanded better working conditions and more black supervisors and union officers. Its methods—wildcats (unauthorized strikes) and "illegal" picket lines—and its aggressive rhetoric challenged the status quo of labor relations developed throughout the postwar period. Unions—the UAW in this case—moved against these groups with all their strength as they undermined labor's principal negotiating resource: the capacity to govern the shop floor.

American unions were potentially losing the support of a whole generation of workers. The late 1960s and the early 1970s were characterized by a wave of wildcats that challenged both management and the union. Rank-and-file agitation demonstrated that the *labor movement* did not always coincide with the *union movement*. On the contrary, in many cases what triggered the wildcats were not only unbearable working conditions or low pay, but also the bankruptcy of the grievance procedure and of the contractual system of shop-floor representation that did not address workers' problems at the point of production.

Toward the end of the 1960s, when the productivity push coincided with a slowdown of the economy and a number of union concessions on wages and benefits, rank-and-file rebellion spread outside the revolutionary groups of Black Nationalist and young hippies. In some cases, the rank and file built organizations at the industry level to challenge union leadership. The most successful of these endeavors was the Miners for Democracy (MFD). Born in 1969 after the assassination of the opposition candidate for the UMW presidency, Joseph "Jock" Yablonski, MFD toppled the corrupt (and murderous) Tony Boyle in 1972 and proceeded to dismantle the centralized and authoritarian structure of the union. In the Teamsters, the Teamsters for a Democratic Union and the Teamsters United Rank and File sought to achieve the same result but with no success. In the UAW, a union with a more sophisticated and democratic leadership, the United National Caucus—after the defeat of the League of Revolutionary Black Workers—was one of the opposition groups behind the series of walkouts that shut Chrysler plants in Detroit in the summer of 1973. The UAW rationalized the accelerated succession of wildcats in that city as the product of pernicious external influence from Black Nationalist or Communist groups.

At the origin of the protests, there were instead the hazardous safety conditions in the aging Detroit plants and the continuous speedup of the lines necessary to produce the same output of the automated plants of Chrysler competitors. The wildcat summer of 1973 famously ended in Detroit with a clash between the UAW "flying squadron" and the militant rank and file on the picket lines, in which UAW officers carrying baseball bats broke the strike of their fellow workers. As historian Nelson Lichtenstein wrote in *Labor's War at Home* (1987), this episode "symbolized to many the distance traveled by even the most progressive unions of the old CIO."

UNIONS IN THE PUBLIC SECTOR

Although unionism had lost its vitality in key industrial sectors, the labor movement did ascend in one important domain: the public sector. Public employees had largely remained unorganized during the 1950s. They were excluded from the coverage of the labor laws, and many of them enjoyed a white-collar status that arguably made them less prone to be organized. Two factors favored the growth of unionism in this sector. First, the surge in public unionism reflected the change in the character of public work. In many cases, government workers were as hard-pressed and burdened as factory workers and not paid as copiously. Second, with President Kennedy's endorsement in 1962 of federal employees' right to organize and bargain collectively, public employees found in state and federal governments a more benevolent opponent than workers in the private sector. By the early 1970s, unions like the American Fed-

eration of State, County, and Municipal Employees (AFSCME), the American Federation of Teachers, and other unions of public employees had organized over 4 million workers.

At its height, in 1975, 50 percent of public workers were unionized. With the degradation of the status of public employment, minorities, women, and African Americans had been recruited; therefore, the growth of public unionism also has to be seen in relation to the social movements that saw protagonists in these categories.

Two examples of public employees' militancy are illustrative here. The postal workers' strike of 1970 was one instance of how workers generally reputed to be passive and loyal turned militant in the face of deteriorating wages and job conditions. The strike spread from New York to other cities in the country, even with the threat of severe penalties for its participants inasmuch as they had taken the oath to stay on the job. President Richard Nixon declared a national emergency and called in the National Guard to deliver New York mail. However, the soldiers lacked the necessary knowledge and often sympathized with the strikers, so that Nixon was forced to enter into a compromise with the strikers, delivering substantial improvements in wages and bargaining rights.

The American Federation of Teachers is another example of a public employee union that became more militant during the 1960s. By the late 1970s, it represented the majority of public school teachers. Often under scrutiny during McCarthyism, through strikes and hard-won collective bargaining, teachers achieved better workplace conditions, pay rises, and guarantees against unfair dismissal.

THE 1970S: HARD TIMES FOR ORGANIZED LABOR

The rank-and-file movement exposed the many weaknesses of the postwar model of industrial unionism: the bloated bureaucracy; the centralized organization; the parochial political vision; the connivance with employers. Rank-and-file militancy collapsed during the 1974–1975 recession, the worst since the Great Depression, revealing a labor movement ill-equipped to respond to the declining U.S. economy of the 1970s.

In 1974–1975, the U.S. gross national product shrank by nearly 2 percent, and industrial production fell nearly 10 percent. Unemployment rose to its highest level in the postwar era, 8.5 percent, with even higher rates in manufacturing. A rising inflation drove real wages down. The crisis accelerated the restructuring of the American economy. In the 1970s, the United States faced global competition from the European and Japanese economies, whose productivity rates during the 1950s and 1960s had grown faster. Competition spurred at home the further use of labor-saving technology (like numerically controlled machines), managerial requests of higher productivity from workers, and a reorganization of the productive structures through mergers, buyouts, divestment, and downsizing.

U.S. corporations in fact increased their investments abroad and moved their production to right-to-work states and to selected developing countries like Mexico, Taiwan, and Hong Kong. The latter trend has been conspicuously increasing in the last thirty years with corporations taking advantage of the perfect union-free environment offered by the free-trade zones around the globe. The first *maquiladoras*—plants in Mexican free-trade zones near the American border—were licensed in 1969 for 72 U.S. plants; five years later the number had become 655, prompting the Mexican government to open new *maquiladoras* farther south from the border. By reorganizing production on an interregional and international scale, manufacturers were able to shake the very foundation of labor's power.

A growing number of manufacturers found an even cheaper way to do business by stopping producing altogether and instead outsourcing production to subcontractors abroad. In these cases, the core of the companies was no longer constituted by the now nonexistent factories, but by swelling headquarters and marketing departments, the only corporate presence to be located on American soil.

The deindustrialization wave of the 1970s exerted a heavy toll on jobs (some have calculated 3.2 million manufacturing jobs lost per year) and destroyed working-class communities. Basic industries such as automobile, steel, and tires have been the hardest hit by this retrenchment. One of the most famous plant closings was the shutdown of the Youngstown Sheet and Tube Company in Ohio during the 1970s, once a large and profitable steelmaking firm. In Youngstown, the New Orleans–based Lykes Corporation that had purchased the firm used the cash produced by steel to finance operations in more profitable sectors: chemical firms, shopping malls, and real estate. Lykes's strategy of planning divestment at Youngstown reflected the growing trend toward achieving profits through financial wizardry and eventually led to the failure of the Sheet and Tube Company.

In Youngstown, considerations of capital mobility and short-term profit presented a formerly thriving community with the social costs of thousands of unemployed. For many of these victims of deindustrialization, the domestic side of "globalization" meant long periods of unemployment, the loss of health insurance and pension benefits, and decrease of self-esteem. For the communities, it meant reduced tax revenues and less money available for social spending, leading to rapid urban decay and the rise of crime.

With its clout in the workforce substantially undermined, labor could not oppose the threats of layoffs and plant closings. Nonetheless, together with the strategic choice to shift production abroad, in the 1970s business started to squeeze labor costs at home. The loss of American economic supremacy and the waning of the liberal coalition prompted manufacturers to extract more concessions from unions and to reverse previous arrangements about wages packages and working conditions. Workers were often asked to sacrifice hard-won gains to cover for management deficiencies. When Chrysler teetered on the brink of bankruptcy in 1979, the UAW agreed to grant $650 million in concessions, thereby breaking the custom of uniform contract in the industry and setting a dangerous precedent of retreat. By the end of the decade, wage cuts, unheard of during the 1950s and 1960s in unionized firms, became increasingly frequent as workers accepted a reduction in their standard of living in the vain hope of salvaging their plants.

These developments accelerated the shift in the labor market from industrial, manufacturing jobs to service employment, thereby cutting the strength of the labor movement at its base. With the loss of well-paid manufacturing jobs and the growth of downtown jobs needed to manage, market, and counsel the restructured economy, American society began polarizing between an upper tier of the labor market inhabited by professionals and a lower tier of underpaid workers: cashiers, janitors, waiters, chambermaids, retail salespersons. An overwhelming proportion of these workers were (and are) low-paid, part-time, and temporary and therefore difficult to organize for a new generation of unionists.

CONCLUSION: THE REAGAN ERA

After a decade of steady decline in the level of unionization, the election of Ronald Reagan to the presidency signaled the business community that the administration would curb the remnant of labor's influence in the nation. The early manifestation of this policy was Reagan's handling of the Professional Air

Traffic Controller Organization (PATCO) strike. The grievances of the air traffic controllers had accumulated under Carter but exploded during the first year of the Republican administration (they had supported Reagan during the presidential election). PATCO went on strike in August 1981 demanding a pay rise and a shorter work week.

Forty-eight hours after the beginning of the strike, Reagan fired the 11,350 air traffic controllers who had not returned to work and drafted the military to keep Americans flying. For the first time since the 1920s, the government directly attacked organized labor and unabashedly discredited unions in the public opinion. However, Reagan's election was itself related to the rise of neoliberal conservatives, and the restructuring of the economy had occurred in the previous decade.

The defeat of the air traffic controllers' strike opened the door, in the 1980s, to a wave of concession bargaining. In 1982, in a reversal of the "Treaty of Detroit," the UAW and GM signed a new contract that included $2.5 billion in union givebacks. Once again their relationship symbolized the changing character of labor relations. In fact, contrary to Chrysler a few years earlier, GM was a still profitable firm, turning hundreds of millions of dollars of profits, but it could now extract these concessions simply by threatening plant closings and outsourcing.

By the end of the Reagan and Bush administrations, union membership in the core industries had collapsed. The UAW lost 500,000 members, and the USW an equal or superior number. But union membership was also to decline among industries free from foreign competition: construction, food processing, and transportation. As a proportion of the entire workforce, organized labor reached the all-time low of 16 percent in 1991.

From its radical origins in the 1930s, labor moved to become a mainstream institution in the 1950s. However, by the 1980s, this development gradually eroded its bargaining power and finally left it without a political strategy in the face of the economic recession and the loss of influence in Washington. In the following decades, an era that has often been labeled "postindustrial," labor had to come to grips with a society that considered it a marginal institution and often held it in low esteem. Whether labor will recover its lost vitality in the future will eventually depend on its capacity to return to collective action and to reintroduce workers' rights into the national political agenda.

Nicola Pizzolato

BIBLIOGRAPHY

Asher, Robert, and Charles Stephenson, eds. *Labor Divided: Race and Ethnicity in United States Labor Struggles, 1835–1960*. Albany: State University of New York Press, 1990.

Bluestone, Barry, and Bennett Harrison. *The Deindustrialization of America: Plant Closings, Community Abandonment, and the Dismantling of Basic Industry*. New York: Basic Books, 1987.

Boyle, Kevin. *Organized Labor and American Politics, 1894–1994: The Labor-Liberal Alliance*. Albany: State University of New York Press, 1998.

Bright James R. *Automation and Management*. Boston: Harvard University Press, 1958.

Davis, Mike. *Prisoners of the American Dream*. London: Verso, 1986.

Foner, Philip S. *Women and the American Labor Movement: From the First Trade Unions to the Present*. London: Collier Macmillan, 1982.

Gabin, Nancy F. *Feminism in the Labor Movement: Women and the United Auto Workers, 1935–1975*. Ithaca, NY, and London: Cornell University Press, 1990.

Goldfield, Michael. *The Decline of Organized Labor in the United States*. Chicago: University of Chicago Press, 1987.

Halpern, Rick. *Down on the Killing Floor*. Urbana and Chicago: University of Illinois Press, 1997.

Harrison, Bennett. *The Great U-turn: Corporate Restructuring and the Polarizing of America*. New York: Basic Books, 1988.

Laslett, John H.M., ed. *The United Mine Workers of America: A Model of Industrial Solidarity?* University Park: Pennsylvania State University, 1996.

Lichtenstein, Nelson. *Labor's War at Home: The CIO in World War II*. Cambridge and New York: Cambridge University Press, 1987.

———. *The Most Dangerous Man in Detroit*. New York: Basic Books, 1995.

———. *State of the Union. A Century of American Labor*. Princeton, NJ: Princeton University Press, 2002.

Lichtenstein, Nelson, and Stephen Meyer, eds. *On the Line: Essays in the History of Auto Work*. Urbana and Chicago: University of Illinois Press, 1989.

Lipsitz, George. *A Rainbow at Midnight. Class and Culture in Cold War America*. New York: Praeger, 1981.

Milkman, Ruth. *Farewell to the Factory*. Berkeley: University of California Press, 1997.

Milkman, Ruth, ed. *Women, Work, and Protest : A Century of US Women's Labor History*. Boston and London: Routledge & Kegan Paul, 1985.

Mills, C. Wright. *The Power Elite*. New York: Oxford University Press, 1957.

Moody, Kim. *An Injury to All*. London and New York: Verso, 1988.

Stein, Judith. *Running Steel, Running America*. Chapel Hill: University of North Carolina Press, 1998.

Thompson, Heather Ann. *Whose Detroit? Politics, Labor, and Race in a Modern American City*. Ithaca, NY, and London: Cornell University Press, 2002.

Tomlins, Christopher. *The State and the Unions: Labor Relations, Law, and the Organized Labor Movement in America, 1880–1960*. New York: Cambridge University Press, 1985.

Zieger, Robert H. *American Workers, American Unions*. Baltimore and London: Johns Hopkins University Press, 1994.

———. *The CIO. 1935–1955*. Chapel Hill: University of North Carolina Press, 1995.

PUBLIC WORKERS MOVEMENT

The rise of the public workers movement in the United States is often understood as a product of the social movements of the 1960s. Through that decade, successful organizing campaigns of public sector unions often highlighted a tendency to merge workplace issues with larger community concerns, forging a social movement unionism that transformed labor relations in the United States. Central to the development of this community–labor coalition were the broader demographic shifts in the U.S. workplace, especially expansions in government services, health care, and education, and the increasing numbers of women, African Americans, Latinos, and other groups that had often been overlooked by traditional industrial unionism. Although the growth of public worker unions in the 1960s marked the most powerful moment in the history of these organizations, the origins of this movement have deep roots in U.S. history, with connections to multiple issues such as civil service reform, civil rights, and progressivism.

NINETEENTH-CENTURY PUBLIC WORKER MOVEMENTS

The earliest movements of public workers in the United States can be traced to the presidency of Andrew Jackson, when hundreds of civilian naval shipyard workers on the eastern seaboard petitioned the federal government for a ten-hour day. Pointing to existing standards in private industry, workers on government contracts lobbied Congress and other federal officials to administer the change in policy, while presenting their cause to the public and organizing isolated strike activity. Through these actions, in 1836, naval shipyard workers succeeded in pressuring federal officials to establish the principle of prevailing wages between government and private shipyards. Four years later, President Martin Van Buren extended this policy, signing an executive order making ten

hours the standard in all federal offices. Over the next thirty years, government employees were successful in maintaining these parallel standards in wages, hours, and working conditions. Despite these gains, this early period of government workplace activism did not see the development of permanent workplace institutions, with the causes of government employees represented through the lobbying of national labor federations such as the National Trades Union, the National Labor Union, and regional labor councils.

Government employees were bound in a political environment where job security was linked to the fortunes of political parties and specific political patrons, thus curbing the formation of permanent independent associations. Enactment of the Civil Service Act of 1883 transformed the federal workplace, limiting the power of politics and giving employees a permanent stake in their positions and allowing for permanent workplace organizations. Initial organizing drives came from the federal government's largest service department, the post office. By 1886, numerous branches representing letter carriers were chartered with the Knights of Labor in New York, Brooklyn, Chicago, Buffalo, Omaha, and other cities.

Through their collective efforts, these postal organizations petitioned successfully for changes in hours and wages, leading to the formation of the first national post office union, the National Association of Letter Carriers, in 1890. Other organizations for railroad postal workers and clerks also formed during this time, including the Chicago Post Office Clerks Union No. 8703, the first local made up exclusively of government employees chartered by the American Federation of Labor. By 1900, public worker organizations around the country were expanding to include white-collar federal clerical workers, local schoolteachers, and a wide range of local benevolent societies for police and firefighters.

GOVERNMENT LABOR UNIONS

This rise of government employee labor unions was met with resistance from departmental officers across the federal service. In 1902, President Theodore Roosevelt issued an executive order forbidding federal employees from joining trade associations, an edict that came to be known as the gag rule. For the next decade, this order shaped federal labor relations, curtailing the collective agency of government workers while trickling down to shape anti-union policies in state and local governments. Through these years, federal workers pressed for the overturn of the gag rule through aggressive lobbying efforts and occasional workplace unrest. In 1912, following extensive pressure from the American Federation of Labor, the Lloyd-La Follette Act was passed, overturning the gag rule and assuring the right of federal employees to organize in their own interests. Yet even with this legal precedent, many within the ranks of organized labor understood that the organizational potential of government employees was still far from secure. In 1920, AFL president Samuel Gompers was still cautious about government labor relations, arguing against a platform in support of the nationalization of railroads as a potential threat to the security of railroad union members.

The peculiar relationship of government employees within the ranks of organized labor centered on the question of the legal right of public workers to strike. Standard arguments claimed that, as public servants, government employees did not have the right to strike because their actions would have profound effects by stopping important government functions and threatening the public well-being. This issue came to the fore in 1919 when members of the Boston Police Department, in protest of low wages and excessive work hours, voted to seek AFL recognition. When their demands were not met, 1,200 police officers walked off the job, an act that resulted in several nights of looting and the destruction of millions of dollars of property. In response, Massachusetts governor Calvin Coolidge called out the state National Guard to restore order, issuing the famous declaration that "there is no right to strike against the public safety by anybody, anywhere, anytime." Coolidge's decisive action brought him national prominence, lifting him into the Republican vice-presidential nomination the following year, while the policemen's strike and their union were destroyed.

Following the defeat of the Boston police strike, public employee unions across the United States went into decline. However, organizational activities among public workers, at federal, state, and local levels, rapidly increased in the following decade. Although public workers were excluded from the protections of the National Labor Relations Act guaranteeing U.S. workers the right to organize, membership in public worker unions increased dramatically after 1932.

Expansions in federal, state, and local government operations, as a result of New Deal–era initiatives, introduced thousands of young, pro-union workers into government agencies, increasing membership in federal unions such as the American Federation of Government Employees and the National Association of Letter Carriers, as well as promoting rapid growth in the membership of teachers, fire, and police unions. Developments were made in municipal services, with nearly 30,000 workers in New York City's transportation system organized by the Transit Workers Union by 1938, a drive that spread to cities across the United States by the 1940s.

PUBLIC SECTOR UNION ORGANIZING

Perhaps the most important development in public sector organizing in the New Deal period came from the rise of local and state organizations into national bodies. The most significant municipal employee union to emerge during this time was the American Federation of State, County and Municipal Employees (AFSCME). Formed in Wisconsin in 1932 following a political upheaval that threatened the state civil service system, AFSCME gained an AFL charter in 1936 and began an aggressive national organizing campaign. Reflecting the divisions in the national labor movement, AFSCME split in 1937, with the similar-sounding State, County and Municipal Workers of America (SCMWA) forming as its CIO rival. Despite this schism, both organizations embraced similar visions based on government reform programs rooted in the Progressive Era that stressed the expansion of the merit system based on a well-regulated civil service. Both organizations succeeded in organizing a broad range of workers, extending from clerical and technical staff to sanitation workers, police officers, zookeepers, and street repair crews. By 1946, AFSCME claimed a membership of 78,164 to the SCMWA's 70,000.

Historians have noted that the primary difference between the rival state, county, and municipal unions stemmed from political divisions. Led by New York City social worker Abram Flaxer, SCMWA's political program was left-leaning, compared to AFSCME's more liberal politics. In 1947, SCMWA merged with

Students and teachers picket City Hall in New York City on September 16, 1968. A divisive teachers' strike closed the city's public schools for weeks.
(AP Wide World Photos)

the CIO's organization of federal workers, the American Federation of Government Employees (AFGE), to form the 100,000-member United Public Workers of America. Openly critical of the United States' Cold War policy, the left-leaning UPW drew considerable attention from the federal government and suffered losses in membership through the late 1940s. In 1950, the CIO expelled the union, on the basis that they were in sympathy with the Communist Party, leaving AFSCME as the primary national union representing state and municipal employees.

Despite the expansions in public worker unions through the 1930s and 1940s, these organizations were still perceived as peculiar within the ranks of organized labor. Lacking the legal rights of industrial

workers, public workers were limited in their dealings with the government employer. Also, with political conditions varying from region to region, public sector unions developed as very decentralized organizations, limiting their presence as strong national bodies. Nonetheless, public sector unions made significant advancements in the 1950s. By far the most important development in public worker organization during this period was the rise of hospital unions. Although numerous hospital unions had existed with varying degrees of success in Hawaii, Michigan, Philadelphia, and San Francisco, hospital workers were still rarely represented by unions. This changed in 1957 when workers at New York City's Montefiore Hospital organized and attained formal recognition the following year, initiating a national union drive over the coming decade. The establishment of Hospital Workers Union 1199 highlighted a new moment in union organizing in the United States, reaching out to a new working class made up of a majority of women, African-American, Latino, and other groups traditionally overlooked by unionization drives. These successful campaigns would provide the groundwork for the new spirit of public sector unions in the 1960s.

Public worker unions grew by amazing proportions after 1960. Encouraged in part by John F. Kennedy's signing of Executive Order 10988 in 1962, which further strengthened the rights of federal employees, government workers gained new confidence in organizing. Successful unionization drives by teachers, sanitation workers, clerical staffs, hospital workers, and other public workers assumed central importance in the labor conflicts of the era. By 1967, public sector unions accounted for 1.5 million members, up from 900,000 in 1955.

Throughout the period, public workers asserted their rights in new, militant ways. New York City teachers conducted major strikes in 1960 and 1962 in defiance of state law, gaining bargaining rights and wage increases with the United Federation of Teachers. In 1964, Jerry Wurf, leader of New York's District Council 37, took over as AFSCME international president, pledging the union to a policy that embraced direct action tactics, strikes, and formal collective bargaining. Strikes by hospital workers, trash collectors, street repair crews, firefighters, and the epic strike of 200,000 postal workers in 1970 revealed the unique ability of public workers to impact the functions of everyday life, marking a significant shift in labor relations.

AFRICAN AMERICANS IN THE PUBLIC SECTOR UNION MOVEMENT

Observers of the new militancy of public workers in the 1960s pointed to the prominent roles played by African-American workers, as both leaders and rank-and-file activists, and their blending of workplace and community struggles. One of the most dramatic examples of the labor–community coalition building by public workers during this period was the 1968 Memphis sanitation strike. Striking for better wages and safety conditions, black sanitation workers identified their struggle with the broader fight for civil rights across the city and the nation, and gained the support of the city's African-American churches and commu-

nity organizations. Their strike took on national proportions when civil rights leader Martin Luther King Jr. joined the strikers, embracing their cause as part of the national Poor People's Campaign that he was initiating. While in Memphis, King was assassinated on April 4, 1968, marking a turning point in the national black freedom struggle.

Following King's death and growing national pressure, the sanitation workers won the strike, establishing a new era of workplace relations and community power in Memphis. Using a rhetoric that transcended the workplace and addressed community issues, such as access to health care, police behavior, racial relations, and the position of women, public workers crafted a new organizational approach that transformed labor relations in the United States.

WOMEN IN THE MOVEMENT

The rise of public sector unions in the 1960s and 1970s was in part the result of continuing shifts in the demographics of workplaces across the United States. Increasingly, women made up a larger proportion of the unionized workforce, gaining more power in nationally prominent public sector unions, influencing the policies and programs adopted by their organizations. By 1978, 49 percent of the American Federation of Government Employees were women, with women also making up 60 percent of the American Federation of Teachers (AFT) and the National Education Association (NEA). Through their presence as leaders and rank-and-file activists, women asserted new roles within their unions. In the 1970s, the national Coalition of Labor Union Women (CLUW) was formed with support from women in public sector unions, providing an institutional base that has continued to shape official union policies at both the local and national levels. Maxine Jenkins (AFSCME Local 101), Sandra Feldman (AFT), and Mary Moultrie (Hospital Workers Union 1199) have been central national leaders who shaped the successes of their national unions. Since this time, public sector unions have taken the lead in placing women's health issues, job training, and pay equity as central tenets of public sector unionism.

The growing power of public employee unions through the 1960s and 1970s led to unprecedented political power and influence at all levels of government. Both the NEA and AFT have been influential in shaping national education policy within Democratic administrations, leading to repeated attacks against these groups as "special interests" in presidential campaigns through the 1980s and 1990s. Increasingly, public sector unions came under attack for their power in effecting local and national policies. The most aggressive act against public workers came in 1981 when President Ronald Reagan summarily fired all members of the striking air traffic controllers in the Professional Air Traffic Controllers Organization (PATCO), an act that has come to be seen as the opening volley in a period of vigorous anti-union campaigns in both public and private sectors. The political realignment that followed into the 1990s has placed the job security and expansion of government workers and their unions at the center of political debates. Since the 1980s, public workers unions have organized against managerial initiatives that stress increased privatization, a primary concern of all public employee unions.

PRESENT AND FUTURE PROSPECTS

At the start of the twenty-first century, public workers and their unions no longer remain peculiar members of the labor movement but have become part of the mainstream, influencing the policies of the AFL-CIO at the highest levels. Public sector union membership, totaling more than 3 million members, far exceeds membership in industrial and manufacturing industries. In 1995, a coalition led by public sector unions succeeded in electing Service Employees International Union leader John Sweeney to the presidency of the AFL-CIO. Sweeney's platform, committed to giving a "New Voice" to labor in the United States, embraces the community spirit and militant tactics that have marked the public workers movement since the 1960s. Seeking to build coalitions with community organizations and academics, and dedicated to the empowerment of women and the organization of non-English speakers through aggressive organizing campaigns, the policies of the AFL-CIO will likely continue to be shaped by the legacy of the public workers movement for many years to come.

Francis Ryan

BIBLIOGRAPHY

Brenner, Aaron. "Striking Against the State: The Postal Wildcat of 1970." *Labor's Heritage* 7 (Spring 1996): 4–27.

Dark, Taylor E. "Debating Decline: The 1995 Race for the AFL-CIO Presidency." *Labor History* 40:3 (1999): 323–343.

Estes, Steve. "I AM A MAN! Race, Masculinity, and the 1968 Memphis Sanitation Strike." *Labor History* (May 2000): 153–170.

Fink, Leon, and Brian Greenberg. *Upheaval in the Quiet Zone: A History of Hospital Workers' Union Local 1199.* Urbana and Chicago: University of Illinois Press, 1989.

Flaxer, Abram. "State, County and Municipal Workers of America." *Public Management* 19 (October 1937): 262–264.

Freeman, Joshua B. *Working-Class New York: Life and Labor Since World War II.* New York: New Press, 2000.

———. *In Transit: The Transportation Workers Union in New York City, 1933–1966.* Philadelphia: Temple University, 2001.

Goulden, Joseph C. *Jerry Wurf: Labor's Last Angry Man.* New York: Atheneum, 1982.

Hamilton, Randy. "The New Militancy of Public Employees." *Public Affairs Report* 8:4 (August 1967).

International Association of Chiefs of Police. *Police Unions and Other Police Organizations.* Bulletin on Police Problems No. 4, Washington, DC, 1944.

Johnston, Paul. *Success While Others Fail: Social Movement Unionism and the Public Workplace.* Ithaca, NY: Cornell University Press/ Institute for Labor Relations, 1994.

Marx, Herbert. *Collective Bargaining for Public Employees.* New York: H.W. Wilson, 1969.

Ozanne, Robert W. *The Labor Movement in Wisconsin: A History.* Madison: State Historical Society of Wisconsin, 1984.

Riccucci, Norman M. *Women, Minorities and Unions in the Public Sector.* Westport, CT: Greenwood Press, 1990.

Shaffer, Robert. "Where Are the Organized Public Employees? The Absence of Public Employee Unionism from U.S. History Textbooks, and Why It Matters." *Labor History* 43:3 (2002).

Slater, Joseph. "Public Workers: Labor and the Boston Police Strike of 1919." *Labor History* 38 (1989): 7–27.

Spero, Sterling D. *Government as Employer.* New York: Remsen, 1948.

Spero, Sterling D., and John Cappozzola. *The Urban Community and Its Unionized Bureaucracies.* New York: Dunellen, 1973.

Zander, Arnold. "The American Federation of State, County and Municipal Employees." *Public Management* 19 (October 1937): 259–261.

LABOR MOVEMENT AND THE VIETNAM WAR

The Vietnam War divided the American people in ways not seen since the Civil War. Indeed, in the words of historian George Herring, it was "America's Longest War" and it is the only war that the United States has ever lost. American involvement in Vietnam can be traced from the end of World War II in 1945 to 1975 and beyond, with the actual "hot war" dating from the Gulf of Tonkin Resolution in 1964 to the total withdrawal of American troops in 1973. It was a war that cost over 58,000 American lives and countless casualties. Adding to the controversy of America's involvement is the fact that war was never actually declared by Congress. It was part of the ongoing war on Communism known as the Cold War. The Vietnam War created bitter divisions in American society that have yet to heal. Nowhere were these rifts more evident than in the American labor movement where the American Federation of Labor-Congress of Industrial Organizations (AFL-CIO) came into conflict with some of its affiliates, the largest being the United Auto Workers, and with the leadership and rank and file of many union locals across the nation.

ORGANIZED LABOR'S SUPPORT FOR THE WAR

The actions of AFL-CIO president George Meany and his International Executive Board created, in the American mind, the impression of a labor movement solidly supportive of U.S. actions in Vietnam. The reality, however, is that workers and their unions were no more supportive of American actions in Vietnam than the general population. Some survey research concluded that support for the war tended to increase with an individual's educational attainments. Thus, those with a high school diploma or less actually tended to be more dovish on the war. Labor's response to the war was much more complicated and nuanced than many have contended; working people held multiple, diverse, and often divergent views on the war, and these views changed over time.

In 1965, following the commencement of "Rolling Thunder" (the U.S. bombing campaign on North Vietnam), the AFL-CIO Executive Board pledged its "unstinting support" of the Johnson administration's actions. Throughout the ensuing years, the federation's official announcements grew more strident as the public's support for the war dwindled, particularly after the 1968 Tet Offensive. By 1969, the majority of the country, including its working people, had concluded that the war was a mistake. After the election in 1968 of Republican Richard Nixon, Meany and the AFL-CIO continued its support for administration actions in Vietnam. When Nixon chose to expand the war and invade Cambodia in 1970, a wave of disbelief and revulsion spread across the country. Yet Meany congratulated the president, lauding him for his "courage and conviction," while reiterating the federation's support.

Nixon's actions in Cambodia led directly to a resurgence of what had been a relatively quiescent antiwar movement. One demonstration, at Kent State University in Ohio, culminated in the deaths of four students at the hands of National Guardsmen. In New York, as demonstrators prepared to march in reaction both to Nixon's escalation of the war and to Kent State, they were set upon and beaten by a group of construction workers, the so-called hardhats. A few days later, about 100,000 hardhats marched in Manhattan in support of the Nixon administration. But these events have largely been misinterpreted. They were not, for the most part, a manifestation of prowar sentiment. On the contrary, they were the actions of a group of overwrought individuals who saw antiwar protesters as people of privilege who could afford to demonstrate rather than work and who were able to avoid military service because of their class status. In addition, most of the construction workers were paid their day's wages by their employers, contingent on their participation in the march. By 1970, most Americans believed that the country's most pressing problem was not the war but protest and national unrest.

Although many believed that Nixon had broken his 1968 campaign promise to end the war in short order, Meany and the AFL-CIO felt that Nixon was trying to achieve "peace with honor." They could not countenance the idea that their powerful nation could actually lose a war to the international Communist movement. Thus, as young men, many of them workers, died in the jungles of Vietnam, the federation continued its support until direct U.S. involvement finally ended in 1973.

Meany and the AFL-CIO leadership did represent the sympathies of some in the rank and file, at least in the early years of the war. As time went on, however, and the war fell out of favor with the American people, it did so with workers as well. Meany refused to recognize or reflect the changing sympathies of those he was supposed to represent. In 1974, after the end of direct American involvement, he finally admitted that he had been mistaken in his support for both the Johnson and Nixon administrations on the war.

THE UAW OPPOSES ESCALATION OF THE WAR

Meany and the AFL-CIO were not representative of all union workers or even all national union leadership. The actions of the United Automobile Workers, represented by Walter Reuther and his International Executive Board (IEB), followed a decidedly different path. In 1965, Reuther and the IEB reacted to President Johnson's escalation of the war with some ambivalence. The UAW's IEB did not immediately embrace the Johnson administration's actions. Secretary-Treasurer Emil Mazey was only the first to express his reservations. Reuther himself urged a more moderate resolution on the war than the AFL-CIO's. He decried further escalation, insisting on negotiations and suggesting that the United Nations step in, but he later revised his resolution to express more support for the administration.

What followed over the years to 1968 was a tug of war within the UAW international that echoed events in the nation more than within the AFL-CIO. The UAW IEB was much more ready to buck its leader. Reuther's own brother, Victor, declared early opposition, as did others on the IEB. Family and friends, and those in the rank and file who were not ready to go along with Johnson on the war, had a profound influence on Reuther. But his struggles were not as difficult as those of some workers, whose children were being sent off to fight.

Reuther chose to support Johnson, almost until 1968, in order to achieve the civil rights revolution and the Great Society. The UAW and the Democratic Party were linked through mutual self-interest. In the end, however, the war split the Democratic coalition and ultimately cost the Democrats the election. Reuther realized that the war served the interests of neither the nation nor his rank and file, but he was reluctant to join forces with an antiwar movement that seemed to be anti-American and pro-Communist. The UAW did support the 1969 Moratorium, a national protest against the war. When Nixon invaded Cambodia in early 1970, Reuther reacted publicly and vocally in horror and disgust. His death in a plane crash shortly thereafter did not affect the UAW International's opposition to the war.

Under the leadership of Leonard Woodcock, the UAW continued its opposition to the Nixon administration's conduct of the war. It promoted a 1970 Detroit referendum against the war, supported George McGovern against Nixon in the 1972 election, and helped organize Labor for Peace.

THE WORKING CLASS AND THE WAR

At the local union level, opposition to the war appeared early, though rarely garnering a large and vocal contingent. Individual unions charted their own courses on nonunion issues, not always adhering to the positions taken by the international organizations. During the early days of the war, opposition tended to be subdued where it existed and varied among different trades. But it was at the local level that people paid the price for America's Vietnam misadventure and so were more apt to react adversely to the war.

Left-leaning unions such as Dearborn, Michigan's, UAW Local 600 (at that time the nation's largest local union), the United Electrical Workers (UE), and the International Longshoremen's and Warehousemen's Union (ILWU) were among the earliest to protest the war. In 1967, the Labor Leadership Assembly for Peace, which had been formed in 1966 as the Trade Union division of SANE (the Committee for a Sane Nuclear Policy), drew 523 labor leaders from around the country to Chicago. Both Emil Mazey and Victor Reuther spoke at the assembly. This group considered the war to be immoral, in direct contradiction to George Meany and the AFL-CIO.

Another development that made dissent more palatable to the rank and file was the formation of the Vietnam Veterans Against the War (VVAW) in 1967.

The VVAW operated from the bottom up, for as close to 50 percent of the VVAW was drawn from working-class families, while only 30 percent came from professional or managerial families. According to the VVAW, "We believe that true support for our buddies still in Viet-nam [sic] is to demand that they be brought home . . . before anyone else dies in a war the American people did not vote for and do not want."

It must be noted that the Vietnam conflict was truly, as historian Christian Appy notes, a working-class war. Unlike college students, who held draft deferments throughout most of the Vietnam period, working people were subject to the draft, which often plunged young people directly from the workplace into jungle battlefields. Thus, it was difficult for parents and co-workers to be against the war and still support their "boys" in Vietnam.

Workers did not generally participate in mass antiwar protests. Many working people hated the war and were aware that they were paying its price in dollars and blood. But they also hated the antiwar movement they had come to know primarily through the media. As the movement became more mainstream, especially after 1970, more workers did raise their voices in protest. Thus, the idea of unequivocal labor support for the war and the concept of the average worker as antiwar crusader are incorrect. Though support for America's actions in the Vietnam War was strong among some of the elites of the international unions, local unions and the rank and file were more likely to oppose the war while supporting those who fought it.

Frank Koscielski

BIBLIOGRAPHY

Appy, Christian G. *Working Class War: American Combat Soldiers and Vietnam.* Chapel Hill: University of North Carolina Press, 1993.

Herring, George C. *America's Longest War: The United States and Vietnam, 1950–1975.* Philadelphia: Temple University Press, 1986.

Koscielski, Frank. *Divided Loyalties: American Unions and the Vietnam War.* New York: Garland, 1999.

Foner, Philip Sheldon. *U.S. Labor and the Vietnam War.* New York: International, 1989.

BLACK LUNG MOVEMENT

Three medical doctors, a United States congressman, and thousands of West Virginia coal miners were part of the most successful agitational movement in the soft-coal industry in the second half of the twentieth century. The three physicians were Dr. I.E. Buff, a cardiologist of Charleston, West Virginia; Dr. Donald L. Rasmussen, a pulmonary specialist of Beckley, West Virginia; and Dr. Hawey Wells, a pathologist of Johnstown, Pennsylvania. The United States congressman was Ken Hechler, a Democrat from Huntington, West Virginia. The movement, known as the Black Lung Movement, was a campaign on the part of miners in the states of West Virginia, Kentucky, Pennsylvania, and Ohio, and their allies, to gain workers' compensation laws that would provide benefits for miners disabled with the disease.

Beginning early in 1968, the Black Lung Movement grew until, at its peak in the spring of 1969, over 40,000 miners were actively involved in the struggle. With the passage of workers' compensation legislation in West Virginia in March 1969, the movement shifted the focus of its efforts to Washington, D.C., where the Federal Coal Mine Health and Safety Act of 1969 was passed by Congress and signed into law by President Richard Nixon in December of that year. In little more than eighteen months, coal miners created the most significant and successful agitational effort the bituminous coal industry had ever seen.

RECOGNITION OF BLACK LUNG

Coal workers pneumoconiosis, or "black lung," is the result of inhaling microscopic particles of coal dust during the process of mining coal. Over time, and after considerable exposure to this dust, the lungs cease to be able to transfer oxygen to the blood supply. As the lungs' ability to transfer air fails, the heart becomes enlarged, and massive heart failure produces death. In intermediate steps, the miner is often short of breath and unable to function effectively.

Black lung became an issue in coal mining after World War II as mines made greater use of mechanical equipment that created greater amounts of dust. By the early 1960s, the disease was recognized in Europe as a significant health problem and had received some attention in America.

The early efforts of Dr. I.E. Buff, in 1968, to direct attention to the problem of black lung were largely unsuccessful. The government of West Virginia, the United Mine Workers of America (UMW), and the medical profession all failed to take any action to deal with the disease and its effects. The federal government, under President Lyndon Johnson, had proposed a comprehensive coal mine health and safety act late in 1968, but that proposed legislation did not include references to black lung. All of this changed dramatically in November of that year when a major explosion shook Consol Number 9, a large mine that lay between the communities of Farmington and Mannington, West Virginia.

The explosion trapped some seventy-eight miners underground. After nine days of futile rescue attempts, the mine was sealed. The tragedy of Consol Number 9 received worldwide media attention. Families across America, sitting down to their Thanksgiving dinners, could watch newscasts of the unending vigil of the miners' families waiting for news. Coal mine safety became an overnight issue of importance. Buff took advantage of that attention to attend a series of meetings held throughout West Virginia and eastern Kentucky, trumpeting his message of the dangers of black lung. His two colleagues, Donald Rasmussen and Hawey Wells, joined him in this effort. They styled themselves the Physicians for Miners Health and Safety Committee and held audiences spellbound as they discussed the problems of coal workers pneumoconiosis.

Philip Trupp, in his *Washingtonian* article, described how Buff would bark out phrases like "Black Lung is what's killing all of you. But the company says you're sick in the head, shiftless, or stupid. The company says you've got compensationitis. You're dying, and the killing will go on..." Rasmussen, a redhead with a beard, gave his miner audiences an accurate picture of the nature of the disease itself. Brit Hume, in *Death and the Mines* (1971), described the third member of this "traveling medicine show," Dr. Wells, as a pathologist, who would give speeches "laced with rabble-rousing rhetoric and calls for political action." Wells used a particularly flamboyant device. He would take dried sections from diseased lungs and crumple them to dust, exhorting his audience to action.

RISE OF THE BLACK LUNG MOVEMENT

Considerable attention was brought to the miners' cause at the first Charleston, West Virginia, mass meeting held in late January 1969. Over 3,000 miners from around the state participated in the ninety-minute meeting that included speeches by the three doctors, Congressman Hechler, other state politicians, and a number of miners. Ben Franklin, writing in the *New York Times*, called the miners "strangers to protest," yet they "demonstrated here today that they could be organized to make unexpectedly militant demands upon their union and their government."

Miners who attended this and other meetings held throughout West Virginia in January of 1969 became disgusted with the inaction of the UMW and formed their own lobbying organization, the Black Lung Association. The BLA hired a former member of the West Virginia State Senate, Paul Kaufman, to serve as its chief lobbyist. Attention then moved to the West Virginia legislature, where a number of bills dealing with black lung were introduced, some by the UMW and others by the Black Lung Association.

Throughout the early days of the legislative session, coal miners were in attendance, wearing armbands and buttons with the numbers "78/4" referring to recent deaths in mines. On several occasions, they brought a large coffin to the rotunda of the capitol building and held mock funerals for their comrades. The major legislative event was a lengthy joint hearing before the Judiciary Committees of the West Virginia Senate and House of Delegates on February 11, 1969. The hearing brought out the various positions of the proponents and opponents. The major point made by the proponents was that black lung was a distinct and identifiable disease, and not silicosis, and that the disease was not easily diagnosed, particularly not by X rays. The opponents argued that the concept of presumption—assuming that a miner who had spent significant years in mines had the disease as a matter of course—was a dangerous legal concept. They further argued that X-ray evidence was a vital part of diagnosis. Left out of the medical testimony was the earlier claim of the West Virginia medical profession that the ailment was the result of the excessive smoking done by miners when they were off work.

As the West Virginia legislature entered the final weeks of its two-month session, the lobbying efforts of the miners intensified. Many of the lobbyists were disabled miners or widows of coal miners, some of whom belonged to the Association of Disabled Miners and Widows. Many of them had never been to Charleston or the state capitol before. Although the professional lobbyists scoffed at this "grassroots" effort, their presence had an effect.

RANK-AND-FILE WORKERS, THE UNION, AND THE INDUSTRY COUNTEROFFENSIVE

There were two essential facts in favor of the coal industry when it came to responding to the Black Lung Movement. The first was the strong tie between the operators and the UMW. If they were both in agreement on a bill, it was highly likely to gain passage into law. The second was the historic and traditional influence of the coal operators with the leadership of the West Virginia legislature. The central attack on the legislation proposed in West Virginia focused on the burden that additional compensation benefits would place on the coal industry. Provisions in federal bills that required coal mines to maintain certain levels of dust in order to reduce the prevalence of the disease aroused concern in the industry.

One of the primary conflicts of the Black Lung Movement was between the leadership of the UMW and the rank-and-file members of the union. The UMW had often proclaimed its interest in fighting for new health and safety legislation but evaded any real action by claiming that current laws were satisfactory. The UMW leadership was caught in a bind: they had strongly proclaimed their intention to fight for compensation laws, yet they didn't want to press for laws that would alienate the coal operators and disturb their long alliance. But the leaders were faced with a growing discontent and activism on the part of their rank-and-file members in a year that was to see the election of top union offices. The union's first response was to discredit both the doctors and Congressman Hechler by asserting that they were just agitators, out to incite trouble. The most significant

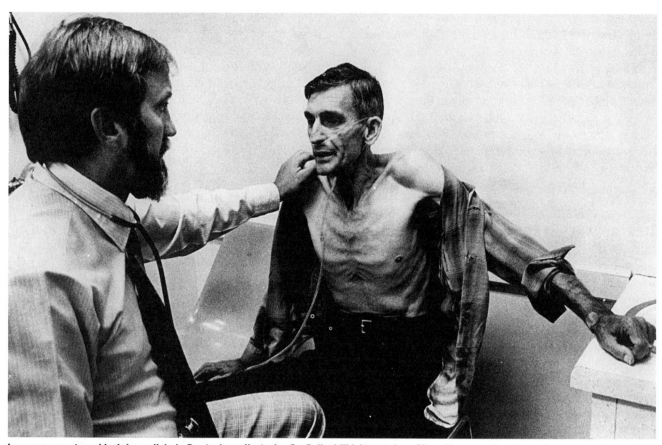

In a government-run black lung clinic in Prestonburg, Kentucky, Dr. Ballard Wright examines Oliver Moore, a miner in need of an operation in 1983. The Black Lung Movement persuaded the federal government to enact health and safety measures on behalf of miners. *(AP Wide World Photos)*

union effort to suppress the movement came after the January Charleston rally when several UMW districts ordered their members to support UMW bills and not the one introduced by the Black Lung Association. The implication of this demand was clear: any UMW member who supported or joined an organization that was deemed a "dual organization" was subject to suspension or expulsion from the UMW, losing medical benefits. This threat, though a serious one, had little effect on the movement.

The climax of the struggle came near the end of the session of the West Virginia legislature. By agreement of the legislative leadership, the House of Delegates was given initial responsibility for developing black lung legislation. When the House had passed a bill, the Senate would act. Miners had been promised that a bill would be reported to the floor of the House a week after the February 11 hearing.

When the House Judiciary Committee seemed stalled, and no bill appeared, the miners escalated the struggle. On Tuesday morning of February 18, some 282 men at the East Gulf Mine of the Winding Gulf Coal Co. refused to enter the mine. The miners indicated that they felt that they had to support Dr. Buff and the struggle for legislation. By the following morning, the strike had spread to nine mines in both Raleigh and Wyoming counties. By Thursday, reports had over 4,000 miners idled; by Friday the estimated number was 7,000 throughout the southern West Virginia coal fields. The wildcat strike took leaders of the Black Lung Association by surprise, and the miners were urged to return to work, as a strike was not seen as a solution to getting good legislation. Dr. Buff and his colleagues, however, saw the strike as a spontaneous response from the miners and urged them to continue. Once again national media attention was focused on coal miners, this time in Charleston and in the halls of the West Virginia capitol. By Wednesday, February 26, it was reported that some 30,000 miners had closed the mines in the southern part of the state, and that more than 50 percent of the northern ones were shut as well. The UMW response was to take out full-page advertisements urging their members to return to work, as the strike was not lawful under their contract.

It was too late. The afternoon of that same day the second giant rally was held in Charleston. Many of the same speakers were heard again—Drs. Buff, Rasmussen, and Wells, and Congressman Hechler. Miners from many parts of the state spoke, expressing solidarity with their brothers. At the end of the meeting, the 2,000 assembled miners poured from the Civic Center and began their march to the capitol, a mile and a half away. They marched down Kanawha Boulevard, a wide, divided four-lane road that runs along the Kanawha River almost the length of the city of Charleston, which lies in the narrow river valley.

As they approached the capitol, they were some fifty abreast, and they turned and marched up the flight of stairs to the central doors of the gold-domed capitol building. Inside, on the third floor, overlooking the stairs, were the members of the House Judiciary Committee in session. They looked out on a sight that none of them had ever seen before—hundreds of coal miners marching up the steps and into the building.

The coal industry tried to bring an end to the strike and sought a court injunction, which was denied. The UMW held meetings at union locals urging members to return to work. That effort failed. By Monday, March 8, the striking miners numbered over 40,000 and had closed down the coal industry in West Virginia, then the nation's largest coal-producing state. When the walkout first began, a UMW official was reported in *The New Republic* to have said: "Don't worry about it. The boys just got a little excited. They'll be back to work tomorrow or the next day." The striking miners stayed out for over three weeks, not returning until after Governor Arch Moore signed into law the black lung bill on Tuesday, March 11. Passage of federal legislation that included support for a federal compensation program followed later in the year, with President Nixon signing the Federal Coal Mine Health and Safety Act of 1969 into law on December 30.

The Black Lung Movement, born in 1968, nurtured by an evangelistic West Virginia physician, rallied by a maverick congressman, joined and supported by over 40,000 striking coal miners, had achieved its goal. America's disabled coal miners—slowly dying from an almost unpronounceable disease—at last had hopes of living out their lives with a measure of dignity.

William N. Denman

BIBLIOGRAPHY

"The Boys Who Got Excited." *The New Republic,* March 22, 1969, p. 7.

Denman, William N. "The Black Lung Movement: A Study of Contemporary Agitation." Ph.D. diss., Ohio University, 1974.

Franklin, Ben A. "Miners Organize to Reduce Risks." *New York Times,* January 27, 1969, p. 30.

Hume, Brit. *Death and the Mines: Rebellion and Murder in the United Mine Workers.* New York: Grossman, 1971.

Trupp, Philip. "Dr. Buff Versus the Black Lung." *The Washingtonian,* April 1969.

Labor Movement

The labor movement in the United States faced enormous challenges in the 1980s and 1990s. A conservative political shift, an employer offensive against unions, and economic restructuring devastated the ranks of American trade unions. Between 1983 and 2001, the percentage of workers in the United States who belonged to unions declined from 20.1 percent to 13.5 percent. The decline of unions had a negative effect on the lives of the American working class. As unions shrank, workers became poorer and faced greater insecurity. In the 1970s and 1980s, workers' income dropped 13 percent, and between 1978 and 1999 average employer compensation for workers decreased by 8.6 percent.

During the same time workers' productivity increased. The labor movement responded in various ways to the crisis that it faced in the last two decades of the twentieth century. In the 1980s, rank-and-file unionists challenged the cautious leadership of the country's largest labor federation, the American Federation of Labor-Congress of Industrial Organizations (AFL-CIO) and organized militant campaigns against plant closings and concessions. In the 1990s, a new group of leaders came to power in the AFL-CIO who energized an increasingly militant working class. Despite continued decline in membership, the labor movement sought to return to its roots as a social movement. It committed more resources to organizing, made broader alliances with religious, civil rights, and other community groups, and gradually embraced more militant tactics to improve the lives of all workers.

Employer Offensive and Conservative Backlash

In the 1980s, the labor movement had to confront declining influence in American society. Between 1980 and 1986, trade union membership dropped from 24 million to approximately 17 million. The percentage of unionized workers also declined, from 27 percent in the early 1970s to just 18 percent by 1986. The country's largest and most powerful industrial unions lost hundreds of thousands of members. The United Auto Workers (UAW) lost close to 500,000 members between 1979 and 1985. Its total membership shrank from 1,499,000 in 1979 to just over 1 million. In the same period, United Steelworkers of America's membership declined from 964,000 to 572,000. Other major unions like the United Rubber Workers, the International Association of Machinists, and the International Union of Electrical Workers lost tens of thousands of dues-paying members in the early 1980s.

A variety of economic and political forces led to the decline of organized labor. Deindustrialization had a significant impact on the fate of American unions. In the 1980s, the United States lost millions of jobs in the heavily unionized manufacturing sector of the economy. Between 1980 and 1985, the country lost 2.3 million manufacturing jobs. Automation and a severe economic recession in the early 1980s that led to plant closings and layoffs fueled deindustrialization. But the loss of manufacturing jobs resulted largely from corporations' decision to relocate their production facilities to low-wage regions in the Third World. Manufacturers that remained in the United States often relocated their plants to the lower wage and less unionized South. Plant relocations to the Southern states contributed to the decline of manufacturing jobs in the Midwest and Northeast.

Many of the workers "dislocated" by deindustrialization were unemployed for long periods of time or did not find new jobs. Unemployment remained high through the late 1980s, particularly for African-American and Latino workers. The laid-off workers who found employment primarily entered the service sector, where most of the country's job growth occurred. These new service jobs were largely nonunion, part-time, and low-wage. On average, factory workers who had been laid off between 1979 and 1983 and found jobs by 1984 saw their earnings drop by 16 percent.

Unions had to confront an increasingly hostile political climate in the 1980s. In 1981, the newly elected president, Ronald Reagan, began to undermine the power of the labor movement. In August 1981, Reagan sanctioned an aggressive stance against labor when he fired and permanently replaced the striking members of the Professional Air Traffic Controllers Organization (PATCO). Reagan weakened federal agencies set up to protect workers' rights, like the Occupational Safety and Health Administration and the National Labor Relations Board (NLRB). The NLRB became increasingly pro-business and less responsive to union grievances under the tenure of the Reagan-appointed chair of the NLRB, Donald Dotson. The NLRB gave employers the right to exclude plant closings as a collective bargaining issue and more power to fire union members. The percentage of pro-business rulings that the Dotson NLRB issued increased significantly compared to earlier boards, favoring unions in only 55 percent of its unfair labor practices cases and 25 percent in cases involving union-organizing drives.

The conservative political shift bolstered a broad employer offensive to keep unions out of their workplaces. Employers hired labor consultants and attorneys, known as union-busters, to lead campaigns to decertify unions and defeat organizing drives. By the early 1990s, union busting had become a billion-dollar industry employing thousands of consultants. Employers and their consultants used a variety of tactics, often in violation of labor law, to create union-free workplaces. To eliminate existing unions, employers, who are banned from initiating a decertification drive, persuaded pro-company workers to file for decertification or during strikes hired replacement workers who would vote out the union. To defeat organizing drives, employers, ignoring labor law, used threats and intimidation.

During the 1980s, employers often threatened to cut jobs in response to a pro-union vote, fired thousands of union organizers, and spread many more negative rumors about key union activists to undermine their credibility. The pro-business stance, slowness, and low fines of the NLRB emboldened anti-union employers who acted illegally to keep unions out. Employers adopted tactics that less blatantly violated labor law, such as holding captive-audience meetings where employees had to listen to speeches opposing the union and watch anti-union films or slide shows.

Unions faced an increasingly difficult bargaining climate during the 1980s. Employers successfully forced unions to make numerous concessions during negotiations. Since World War II, unions had regularly negotiated three- to five-year contracts that provided their members with wage increases and improvements in their benefits. Often, these contracts were negotiated on an industrywide basis. In the 1970s, employers in various industries such as meatpacking and rubber had forced unions to take cuts in wages and benefits. But concessionary bargaining gained momentum in 1979, when politicians and bankers demanded concessions from the UAW in exchange for massive bailout loans to a financially troubled Chrysler.

The UAW acquiesced and between 1979 and 1981 took wage and benefit cuts worth over $1 billion. To prevent a competitive advantage for Chrysler, soon the other big two automakers, Ford and General Motors (GM), demanded concessions. Concessionary bargaining gripped industry and continued even after the recession of the early 1980s ended and among profitable firms. Union workers in steel, meatpacking, transportation, communications, and many other industries faced wage cuts, reduced benefits, and loss of control over work rules.

THE LABOR MOVEMENT RESPONDS TO THE CRISIS

The labor movement was divided over how to respond to the employer offensive and the conservative political shift. The leadership of labor's umbrella organization, the AFL-CIO, responded cautiously. The AFL-CIO executive board during the 1980s, led by Lane Kirkland, was hostile to grassroots challenges to employers and sought to empower labor through established channels. The AFL-CIO spent much of its energy in the decade building support for the Democratic Party, largely through large financial contributions and electoral mobilizations. The Democratic Party, however, had become increasingly pro-business and offered less to workers in return for their political support.

Business unionists also advocated top-down control of union affairs and a nonadversarial approach with employers. They pressured their members to accept concessions and supported a growing number of labor–management cooperation schemes. In 1980, for example, UAW president Doug Fraser accepted a seat on Chrysler's Board of Directors in exchange for accepting wage and benefit cuts. The team concept that emphasized cooperation between unions and management became increasingly popular. Unionists joined programs such as Quality of Work Life (QWL) where they exchanged ideas with supervisors about how to improve conditions in the plants. Many workers complained that instead of empowering workers, management used employees' ideas to streamline production and eliminate jobs. The AFL-CIO's leadership also offered very little response to declining union membership, committing only a small percentage of its resources to new organizing.

A segment of organized labor advocated militant challenges to attacks on unions. In some unions, rank-and-file dissidents organized reform movements against the business union agenda. One of the most successful reform movements in organized labor emerged among members of the International Brotherhood of Teamsters. In the late 1970s, rank-and-file Teamsters, primarily Socialists affiliated with the International Socialists, organized the Teamsters for a Democratic Union (TDU). In the late 1970s and early 1980s, TDU organized to make the highly centralized and notoriously corrupt Teamsters more democratic and willing to challenge employers. The TDU defeated a 1983 contract proposal that included major concessions to the freight industry, supported other striking workers fighting concessions, won internal reforms like the right to directly elect national officers, and took control of the executive board in the 1991 elections.

The UAW's shift toward concessionary bargaining triggered a reform movement called New Directions among unionized autoworkers. In the face of opposition from the UAW's ruling Administrative Caucus, New Directions candidates won important union offices, and through work slowdowns and strikes challenged concessions like faster production lines.

Union workers led dramatic strikes during the 1980s to defeat concessions. In 1985, members of P-9 of the United Food and Commercial Workers union, in opposition to their international leaders, went on strike against wage cuts, deteriorating safety conditions, and other concession demands by the Hormel meatpacking company at its Austin, Minnesota, plant. A broad community campaign emerged involving numerous labor, civic, religious, and political organizations that lent their support to the striking meatpackers. Strikers and their supporters organized rallies, parades, pickets, blockades at the plant gates,

sit-ins at Hormel headquarters, and many other nonviolent direct action tactics to pressure the profitable company to provide decent wages and working conditions.

The Austin workers also hired the pro-union Corporate Campaign Inc., led by Ray Rogers, to launch a "corporate campaign" that involved a media campaign and mobilizing pressure on First Bank System, which financially backed Hormel. Corporate campaigns, developed initially by Rogers in the late 1970s, became a widely used tactic by striking workers in the 1980s. The strike ended in 1986 when the UFCW's international leaders, who had ordered an end to the strike, with the backing of the courts placed P-9 in a trusteeship and agreed to Hormel's concessions. Court injunctions against P-9 actions, arrests of union leaders, and National Guard troops that protected replacement workers had also weakened the strike.

Hormel workers in Austin were not the only unionists to strike against concessions in the 1980s. Although the number of strikes declined in the 1980s from 187 in 1980 to 54 in 1985, workers in steel, communication, paper mills, food processing, transportation, and other industries led important work stoppages to reverse declining wages and working conditions. Most faced the same fate as P-9 in Austin. In 1983, the United Steelworkers and twelve other unions representing workers at Phelps Dodge's copper mines in Arizona and Texas led a year-long strike when the company sought to withdraw from an industry pattern agreement and concessions.

Strikebreakers and a successful company-backed decertification campaign broke the Phelps Dodge strike. Three years later, 22,000 steelworkers struck USX Corporation but were defeated after agreeing to a contract that cut wages, holidays, vacations, and other benefits. An eleven-month strike by 1,700 members of the United Mine Workers in 1989 at the Pittston Coal Company proved more successful. Unlike P-9, Pittston workers had the support of their international, led by the reform-minded Richard Trumka. Through community coalitions, a corporate campaign, and civil disobedience, including blocking coal trucks and occupying a mine, Pittston workers successfully fought the company's demand for concession and its attempt to withdraw from the industrywide contract pattern.

Plant closings did not go unchallenged by America's unionists during the 1980s. Most business unionists rarely opposed plant shutdowns, accepting them as a corporate prerogative. They also tended to share employers' commonly used argument that foreign competition (particularly from Japan) in industries such as steel, automobiles, and electronics led to plant closings. Labor leaders joined with big business in Buy American campaigns and lobbying for higher tariffs on foreign imports.

The focus on foreign competition often tapped into the racial prejudices of white workers and led many Americans to scapegoat Asians and Asian Americans for their plight. In at least one case in June 1982, a twenty-seven-year-old Chinese-American man named Vincent Chin was killed by two white autoworkers in Detroit during a dispute at a bar. Prior to murdering Chin with a baseball bat, auto plant foreman Ronald Ebens and his accomplice, laid-off autoworker Michael Nitz, misidentified Chin as Japanese, calling him a "Jap" and telling him that he had cost them their jobs. Ebens and Nitz escaped jail time and were sentenced to probation. But the Chin murder and the light sentences Ebens and Nitz received helped trigger the contemporary Asian-American equal rights movement.

Some workers offered more complex explanations for the plant closings and presented militant challenges. A number of unionists charged that plant closings were more likely the result of corporate mismanagement and greed than of foreign competition or, as many employers maintained, of high union wages and government regulation. In numerous cases, plant-closing activists found that companies had refused to modernize profitable plants, "milked" profits from one plant to pay for other investments, set artificially high prices, and sought to move plants to achieve greater flexibility and profits in nonunion environments. Workers and community activists in western Pennsylvania and eastern Ohio organized to prevent the shutdown of steel factories in Youngstown, Ohio. In the late 1970s through the 1980s, activists organized the Ecumenical Coalition of the Mahoning Valley in Youngstown and the TriState Conference on Steel in Pittsburgh to prevent shutdowns. Activists held pickets and demonstrations, occupied U.S. Steel headquarters, and filed lawsuits to prevent plant closings. They also advocated worker or worker-community ownership schemes through community and government financing.

Organized labor also sought to respond to declining union membership. Unionists, however, were divided about how to increase their numbers. Some unionists emphasized militant organizing campaigns among workers in nonunion workplaces, including the growing number of workers employed in the service sector. The Service Employees International

Union (SEIU) launched campaigns to organize healthcare workers employed by nursing homes. In the mid-1980s, SEIU organized Justice for Janitors, which led successful campaigns to organize mostly African-American, Latino, and immigrant custodial workers who cleaned office buildings in America's major cities.

But most AFL-CIO unions advocated a more cautious approach, accelerating the trend toward union mergers. Larger unions often absorbed smaller unions that represented workers from different industries, like the Insurance Workers with the United Food and Commercial Workers or the Amalgamated Meat Cutters and the Retail Clerks International Union, which merged in 1979. As many as 2,100 unions merged between 1979 and 1984, consolidating labor's shift away from craft or industrial jurisdictions toward general unionism. Some unionists argued that mergers strengthened unions, particularly the smaller, less powerful locals that might otherwise not survive. Critics charged that smaller unions lost influence in mergers and that mergers led to less internal democracy as unions expanded their bureaucracy to deal with a more diversified membership.

LEAN PRODUCTION AND NEW CHALLENGES TO THE LABOR MOVEMENT

In the 1990s, the AFL-CIO adopted an increasingly militant stance that led many observers to pronounce a resurgence of organized labor. The militant shift was connected partly to the victory of the New Voice slate over Thomas Donahue's slate in the 1995 AFL-CIO elections. New Voice was led by its presidential candidate, SEIU head John Sweeney, candidate for secretary-treasurer, UMWA president Richard Trumka, and vice presidential candidate, Linda Chavez-Thompson, vice president of the American Federation of State, County, and Municipal Employees (AFSCME).

New Voice insurgents charged that, under the leadership of Lane Kirkland, the labor movement had become too bureaucratic, cautious, and willing to compromise with management. In an effort to thwart New Voice, Kirkland, who had been AFL-CIO president since 1979, stepped down in 1995 in favor of the secretary-treasurer, Thomas Donahue. The New Voice platform called for a greater emphasis on new organizing and labor solidarity and increased political activism and alliances with progressive organizations and social movements. It also advocated stronger ties with the growing number of women and people

SUMMARY OF THE GREENGROCER CODE OF CONDUCT   2000

The Greengrocer Code of Conduct was New York State Attorney General Eliot Spitzer's effort to enforce national wage and hour laws ignored by a growing number of employers in recent years. In 2000, workers in delis and groceries in New York typically paid new immigrants well below minimum wage, with no overtime, for seventy-two hours a week.

1. Min. Wage & Overtime

   • Pay all employees at least minimum wage, now $5.15 per hour.
   • Pay all employees "overtime"—1½ an employee's regular hourly rate for all hours worked past forty per week.

2. Timely Pay

   • Pay employees in a timely manner.

3. Records & Pay Stubs

   • Keep all payroll & time records required by state and federal law.
   • Give each employee a weekly pay stub of hours and wages (gross & net).

4. Rest

   • Give each employee one full unpaid day of rest per week.
   • Give each employee at least ½ hour uninterrupted for meal break and others as required by law.

5. Rights Poster

   • Post this Code on a wall in an easy-to-see location.
   • Post a notice on a wall about basic wage and hour rights.
   • The Code and notice will be in at least English, Spanish, and Korean.

6. Days off

   • For employees who have worked at the store for at least one year: provide 2 paid sick days and one workweek of paid vacation days per year.
   • For employees who have worked at the store for at least two years: provide 3 paid sick days and one workweek of paid vacation days per year.

7. Seminars

   • Attend at least one labor law seminar by Attorney General's Office.

8. Not Retaliate

   • The Code employer will not discharge or retaliate against any employee for making a complaint to the employer, the government, or the Monitor about violations of the Labor Law or this Code.

9. Organizing

   • The Code employer recognizes employees have legal right to organize and to join labor unions of their own choosing, and that the law prohibits retaliation against employees for organizing or joining a labor union.

10. Monitoring

   • The Code employer agrees to submit to unannounced monitoring of compliance with the Code at least two to three times per year.
   • When monitoring occurs, the Code employer will show all payroll and time records, and make employees available for private, confidential interviews.

11. Consumers

   • A Code of Conduct Seal will be displayed in the store window as long as the Code Employer is in good standing.
   • A list of Code members in good standing is available at the New York State Attorney General's website: www.oag.state.ny.us.
   • Code members no longer in good standing must post a notice stating as such, and will also be listed on the website.

12. Hotline

   • Call 1-800-729-1180 with complaints of violations.

Source: Office of New York State Attorney General Eliot Spitzer. Labor and Employment Rights. Available at www.oag.state.ny.us/workplace/final_ggcode_english _short.pdf.

During the election for president of the AFL-CIO, candidates John J. Sweeney (left) and Thomas Donahue (right) shake hands after a debate in 1995. Sweeney won the election. *(AP Wide World Photos)*

of color in the workforce and in unions. Between 1986 and 1995, the number of white men in unions declined from 55.8 percent to 49.7 percent. In the 1980s and 1990s, the percentage of black, Latino, and Asian Americans in the American workforce increased at a dramatically faster pace than the overall labor force. To connect with these workers, New Voice backed Linda Chavez-Thompson, the first woman of color AFL-CIO executive officer, and after their victory reserved spots for people of color on the AFL-CIO's executive board.

The progressive vision of the AFL-CIO's new leadership benefited from a change in political leadership in Washington, DC. After twelve years of Republican control of the White House, Democrats Bill Clinton and Al Gore were elected president and vice president. Both men symbolically supported labor by appearing with AFL-CIO leaders and publicly defending workers' right to organize unions. The Clinton ad-

ministration supported some aspects of labor's political agenda. Clinton pushed for an increase in the minimum wage and signed the Family and Medical Leave Act of 1993, which gave workers the right to take twelve weeks of unpaid leave after the birth of a child or to take care of a seriously ill relative. He also signed an International Labor Organization treaty against certain kinds of child labor. He strengthened unions by issuing an executive order that prevented firms with federal contracts worth over $100,000 from permanently replacing striking workers. Clinton also vetoed the Team Act, which would have allowed employers to form company unions in nonunion workplaces.

The labor movement and the workers it represented, however, continued to face enormous challenges in the 1990s. Clinton and Gore, political centrists, proved inconsistent allies, often supporting pro-business initiatives at the expense of organized labor and working people. Clinton signed the North American Free Trade Agreement (NAFTA), which opened up markets among Canada, the United States, and Mexico. Although NAFTA advocates argued that the agreement would create jobs in the United States, the effects have been the reverse, and it has undermined union strength. Between the implementation of NAFTA in 1994 and 2002, hundreds of thousands of high-paying manufacturing jobs, many in unionized plants, disappeared as companies shifted their operations to Mexico in search of cheap labor.

American employers increasingly used NAFTA as a tool to undermine union organizing drives, by threatening to relocate their plants if workers decided to unionize. Clinton supported other free-trade initiatives like the General Agreement on Tariffs and Trade (GATT) and the World Trade Organization (WTO), which was formed in 1995 to enforce global trade rules, including GATT. The WTO limited the rights of member nations to pass laws that might create barriers to trade and limit the ability of a company to maximize its profits. For example, nations belonging to the WTO can sue other WTO member nations to overturn laws designed to protect labor, environmental, and human rights.

Corporations continued to pursue policies in the 1990s to eliminate unions from their workplaces and to cut labor costs. American firms continued a forty-year trend toward moving their production facilities overseas, favoring Eastern Europe and Southeast Asia, for their low wages and lax environmental and labor regulations. By 2002, many American firms that relocated to Mexico in the 1990s had closed their Mexican plants and shifted once again to Asia in search of even cheaper wages. Companies also developed "lean production" or "Just-in-Time" methods as a way to maximize profits and, in the case of manufacturers, to reduce inventories. Businesses "outsourced" work to nonunion subcontractors.

The Big Three auto manufacturers, GM, Ford, and Chrysler, relied on auto parts firms to supply them with noncore parts that would arrive at their factories as they were needed in the production process. Other employers, like universities and public schools, privatized their custodial services, and the federal government hired a growing number of private nonunion–subcontractors.

A growing number of firms turned toward "downsizing" and part-time temporary labor as a way to boost profits. In January 1994, 108,946 workers lost their jobs as a result of corporate downsizing. General Motors laid off close to 70,000 workers, Sears fired 50,000, and IBM cut 38,500 employees from its payroll. Corporations also began to hire more temporary workers, who often received lower wages and lacked benefits like healthcare, unemployment, sickness, disability, or pensions. Although the number of part-time workers is debated, some estimate that between 16 and 18 percent of the entire workforce is contingent. Part-time employment agencies like Manpower became Fortune 500 companies and by 1996 became the second-largest employer in the United States. In 1997, temporary employment agencies placed 2.5 million workers in jobs.

By 2000, capital flight and lean production had increased the gap between the rich and the poor. In the 1990s, the economy grew rapidly and corporate profits soared, while workers earned less, produced more, and worked longer hours. In 1980, on average, CEOs earned 42 times the pay of workers in blue-collar jobs, which increased to 85 times in 1990 and by 2000 531 times. CEOs of major corporations continued to receive high pay, an average of $20 million in 2000, even as corporate profits fell and as a corporate crime wave unfolded at the turn of the millennium. In 2001 and 2002, investigations into corporate abuses revealed that a number of CEOs attained enormous wealth by selling their stock options just prior to public knowledge of poor earnings for their companies. Investigators also showed that, throughout the 1990s, many corporations led by highly paid CEOs had posted artificially high profits by manipulated their accounting, often illegally and in collaboration with accounting and investment firms and banks.

NEW VOICES AND MILITANCY IN THE LABOR MOVEMENT

Organizing

The labor movement responded to these challenges more vigorously than it had in decades. The AFL-CIO committed more resources to organizing new workers. The labor body advocated a more expansive approach to organizing, relying less on professional union staff and more on rank-and-file workers and coalitions with community and student groups. The AFL-CIO expanded its Organizing Institute to train people who wanted to become full-time union organizers. In 1996, it established Union Summer to build support for union drives. During Union Summer, students, workers, and community activists participated in a four-week internship helping to organize picket lines, distributing literature, and demonstrating on be-

MODEL LIVING WAGE ACT

Privatization and the growth of low-wage jobs have prompted a growing number of labor organizations to encourage municipalities to sponsor "living wage acts" to mandate that employers pay workers more fairly. The following is an excerpt of a model living wage act by the Center for Policy Alternatives.

SECTION 1. SHORT TITLE

This Act shall be called the "[STATE] Living Wage Act."

SECTION 2. FINDINGS AND PURPOSE

(A) Findings—The legislature finds that:

1. The state of [STATE] awards contracts that result in the employment of thousands of individuals. Many of these individuals, employed indirectly by the state, receive sub-poverty level wages.
2. The creation or promotion of jobs that pay sub-poverty level wages is shortsighted economic and social policy. Such jobs do not lead to a self-sufficient workforce or support sustainable community development. Instead, they increase the need for government services, such as public assistance for food, housing, health care, and child care.
3. The state is not an innocent bystander in the payment of sub-poverty level wages. It is necessary and appropriate for the state to require that contractors working on state business pay at least a living wage.

(B) Purpose—Recognizing that the state is a major contractor for services, this law is enacted to increase the wages of service employees who indirectly work for the state in order to improve public health and welfare, promote the economic strength of our society, and take pressure off state social service programs.

SECTION 3. LIVING WAGE

(A) Definitions—In this section:

1. "Secretary" means the Secretary of the Department of [LABOR], or the Secretary's designee(s).
2. "State" means the state or a principal unit of state government.
3. "State contractor" means a for-profit or not-for-profit entity that has a state contract.
4. "State contract" means: a. A contract for services with the state valued at $100,000 or more; or
    b. A subcontract valued at $25,000 or more for providing part or all of the services covered by another entity's contract for services with the state valued at $100,000 or more.

5. "Basic health insurance benefits" means an insurance plan where an employer pays 100 percent of the premium for individual coverage or 80 percent of the premium for family coverage if the health insurance:
    a. Covers at least 80 percent of the costs of office visits, emergency care, surgery, and prescriptions; and
    b. Has an annual deductible of no more than $1,000.

(B) Payment of Living Wage

1. Any state contract for services must require state contractors to pay an hourly wage rate that is at least the living wage.
2. During the duration of a state contract, a state contractor shall pay to each employee who is working on the state contract an hourly wage rate that is at least the living wage.
3. If a state contract is subject to prevailing wage requirements under [appropriate citation], the state contractor shall pay the living wage or the prevailing wage, whichever is higher.

(C) Calculation of Living Wage

1. The initial living wage shall be $10 per hour without basic health insurance benefits or $8.50 per hour with basic health insurance benefits. . . .

(D) Waivers and Exemptions

1. A not-for-profit entity that is subject to this section may apply to the state agency that is responsible for the state contract for a waiver of the living wage requirement, based on economic hardship. . . .

(E) Enforcement

1. No state contractor shall discharge, demote, harass or otherwise take adverse actions against any individual because such individual seeks to enforce this section, or testifies, assists, or participates in any manner in an investigation, hearing, or other proceeding to enforce this section.
2. No state contractor shall split or subdivide a contract, pay an employee through a third party, or treat an employee as a subcontractor or independent contractor to avoid payment of a living wage. . . .

Source: "Living Wage Act." Center for Policy Alternatives. Available at www.stateaction.org/issues/workcompensation/livingwage/legislation.cfm.

half of unionizing workers. Between 1996 and 2001, Union Summer had over 2,300 interns. The AFL-CIO more successfully built unions among the growing number of low-wage immigrant workers in the United States.

The SEIU continued to build on the successes of Justice for Janitors. In Los Angeles, in alliance with religious and community groups, Justice for Janitors waged militant campaigns that increased the percentage of unionized custodians in the city from 10 percent to 90 percent between 1987 and 1995. In 1999, in one of the largest union victories in fifty years, 74,000 mostly Latina and African-American women home-healthcare workers gained the representation of SEIU.

A significant movement to unionize graduate students employed as teachers and researchers at American universities gained momentum during the 1990s. Teaching assistants at the University of Wisconsin formed the first graduate student union in 1966, the Teaching Assistants' Association, followed shortly by graduate students at the University of Michigan who formed the Graduate Employee Organization. In the 1990s, public attention turned toward a growing number of successful organizing drives among graduate employees at America's major public and private universities, including the University of Iowa, the University of California, New York University, Temple University, and Wayne State University. Graduate unions affiliated with various international unions, including the UAW, the United Electrical Workers (UE), the American Federation of Teachers (AFT), the Communication Workers of America, and the National Education Association. By 2002, twenty-seven graduate employee unions existed representing 20 percent of the graduate employee workforce, and many graduate employees at other universities were leading union campaigns.

Graduate employees argued that by the 1990s universities functioned increasingly like corporations. They cut costs by turning toward cheap labor, in this case graduate students and part-time adjuncts. At some universities, graduate students taught as much as 40 percent of the undergraduate courses with little compensation. Graduate employee unions demanded and won contracts with higher pay, health benefits, and grievance procedures.

Despite the energy and dynamism of the new organizing, union membership continued to decline due to job loss, the growth of nonunion service sector jobs, and continued corporate attacks on union rights. Between 1990 and 2001, the percentage of union workers dropped from just over 15 percent to 13.5 percent, or 16.3 million workers. Government workers, particularly teachers, firefighters, and police, remained the most highly unionized segment of the workforce at 37.4 percent. By 2001, however, the labor movement represented just 9 percent of private nonagricultural workers. As in the 1980s, much of the union growth that occurred during the 1990s was a result of mergers. Two of the larger mergers occurred in 1995 when the International Ladies' Garment Workers' Union joined with the Amalgamated Clothing and Textile Workers to form the Union of Needletrades, Industrial, and Textile Employees (UNITE), and the United Rubber Workers affiliated with the United Steel Workers. Some continued to argue that mergers increased the union's bargaining power, and efficiency critics claimed that mergers lacked strategic focus. Critics argued that instead of merging with writers and university employees, the UAW and UMWA should focus on organizing the numerous nonunion workers in their industries.

Strikes

Workers continued to lead militant and successful strikes to improve their conditions in the 1990s. Although the number of strikes of at least 1,000 workers dropped to a ten-year low in 1995, strike activity increased in the following years. In 1996, the number of strikes rose to 37 from 31 in 1995 and involved 273,000 workers compared to 192,000 the previous year. In 1997 and 1998, these figures jumped to 339,000 and 387,000 workers on strike, respectively.

The strikes of the 1990s focused less on wages and benefits and more on fighting a growing corporate trend toward "lean production," a trend that involved downsizing, outsourcing production to nonunion subcontractors, and increasing workloads. Between 1990 and 1998, UAW local unions led twenty-two strikes against General Motors, in large part to protect jobs and prevent outsourcing.

In 1998, two strikes by the UAW at two key GM parts plants in Flint, Michigan, the Flint Metal Center and Delphi parts plants, virtually shut down GM and forced the company to retreat from its plans to outsource jobs. The strikes cost GM over $1 billion in profits, forced the company to close twenty-seven of its twenty-nine assembly plants, and idled close to 200,000 workers. The success of the strike was partly the result of corporations' shift to Just-in-Time production, which reduced its parts inventory and dispersed its production facilities, which allowed workers at strategically located plants to disrupt the entire chain of production.

The year before the Flint autoworkers struck, the Teamsters led a dramatic and successful strike against United Parcel Service (UPS). UPS, like many corporations in the 1980s and 1990s, had shifted toward part-time temporary labor and had moved toward outsourcing. Close to 60 percent of its diverse workforce of women, men, blacks, and Latinos worked part-time, and the company planned to subcontract the work of its full-time drivers. The starting part-time pay of $8 per hour had not increased since 1982, and many part-time employees worked over the thirty-five hour maximum for part-time work but were denied full-time pay and benefits.

The work was fast, with sorters handling around 1,200 packages an hour. In August, 180,000 UPS workers struck for higher wages and sought to force the company to turn 10,000 of its part-time jobs into full-time jobs. The strike was widely supported by Americans who responded to the Teamsters' demand for decent jobs. After fifteen days, UPS settled, promising to create more full-time jobs and to increase full-time pay by 15 percent and part-time pay by 37 percent.

Not all unionists struck or organized traditional unions to improve their conditions. A number of Latina and Asian immigrant women who labored long hours in sweatshops around the country built innovative labor organizations to challenge exploitation. In 2001, thousands of mostly immigrant women worked in 22,000 garment shops in the United States. Subcontractors often manufactured the clothes for retailers like K-Mart, Wal-Mart, Dayton Hudson, and Nordstrom.

Sweatshop workers sometimes earned less than $2 per hour, worked more than 100 hours per week, and suffered injuries from hours of back-bending labor on sewing machines. The women's immigrant status made them especially vulnerable to abuses. In New York, the community-based Chinese Workers and Staff Association (CWSA), formed in 1979, became an important vehicle for Chinese women to improve their conditions. The CWSA provided a welcome alternative to traditional unions that sometimes either ignored or misunderstood immigrant workers or treated them disrespectfully. The CWSA offered language, citizenship, and women's empowerment classes and in the 1990s led a growing number of campaigns against sweatshop abuses. In the early 1990s, the CWSA started a back-wage campaign to reclaim unpaid wages and in 1996 led a campaign against workplace injuries. Other community-based labor groups emerged around the country to advocate

for immigrant workers such as the Korean Immigrant Workers Advocates, the Asian Immigrant Women Advocates, La Mujer Obrera, and Fuerza Unida.

Politics

The labor movement increased its level of political activism. In 1996, the AFL-CIO launched a high publicity campaign spending $35 million to reelect Clinton and Gore and elect pro-labor candidates. At the same time, the labor movement proved more willing to challenge their Democratic allies. In 1995, labor lobbied to defeat the Clinton-backed NAFTA and in 1997 helped build a broad-based campaign to defeat a fast-track trade proposal to give the president broader authority to negotiate trade agreements. Fast track did not require the president to include any labor or environmental protections in the trade agreements. In 1999, the AFL-CIO and several affiliated unions joined a wide coalition of religious, student, environmental, gay and lesbian, animal rights, and human rights groups to protest the World Trade Organization at its meeting in Seattle at the end of November. The labor movement was particularly concerned about the WTO's effect on labor rights abroad and its role in facilitating capital flight from the United States.

AFL-CIO leaders Linda Chavez-Thompson and John Sweeney addressed protesters in Seattle and led a march of 50,000 trade unionists. Other trade unionists, in the face of police batons and pepper spray, joined in nonviolent sit-downs that prevented WTO representatives from entering their meetings. The "Battle of Seattle," as it became known, revealed a growing dissatisfaction with unregulated globalization and the willingness of diverse social movements to make alliances. Labor's concern with the effects of globalization led unions in the United States to strengthen their ties with progressive activists and unions in other countries who were leading campaigns to improve workers' lives.

CONCLUSION

The last two decades of the twentieth century were some of the most difficult years in U.S. history for the labor movement. Union membership declined dramatically, strike activity slowed, and union members accepted reductions in their wages and benefits. The conservative political environment, free-trade policies, and the loss of manufacturing jobs and growth of nonunion service jobs made it increasingly difficult to build the labor movement. Workers earned less and worked harder as corporate profits soared. Unionists also had to confront increased diversity in their ranks as women, immigrants, and people of color began to make up a majority of organized labor. But the labor movement survived and met these challenges creatively. Rank-and-file reform movements, strikes against concessions, campaigns against plant closings, grassroots organizing methods, political mobilizations, and community and labor alliances provided important alternatives to economic exploitation and offered hope for an equal and just society.

David M. Lewis-Colman

BIBLIOGRAPHY

Blau, Joe. *Illusions of Prosperity: America's Working Families in an Age of Economic Insecurity*. New York: Oxford University Press, 1999.

Bluestone, Barry, and Bennett Harrison. *The Deindustrialization of America: Plant Closings, Community Abandonment, and the Dismantling of Basic Industry*. New York: Basic Books, 1982.

Kelley, Robin D.G. *Yo' Mama's Disfunktional: Fighting the Culture Wars in Urban America*. Boston: Beacon, 1997.

Levitt, Martin Jay. *Confessions of a Union Buster*. New York: Crown, 1993.

Louie, Miriam Ching Yoon. *Sweatshop Warriors: Immigrant Women Workers Take on the Global Factory*. Cambridge, MA: South End, 2001.

Lynd, Staughton. *The Fight Against Shutdowns: Youngstown's Steel Mill Closings*. San Pedro, CA: Singlejack, 1982.

Masters, Marick. *Unions at the Crossroads: Strategic Membership, Financial, and Political Perspectives*. Westport, CT: Quorum, 1997.

Moody, Kim. *An Injury to All: The Decline of American Unionism*. New York: Verso, 1988.

———. *Workers in a Lean World: Unions in the International Economy*. New York: Verso, 1997.

Rachleff, Peter. *Hard-Pressed in the Heartland: The Hormel Strike and the Future of the Labor Movement*. Boston: South End, 1993.

Rothstein, Lawrence. *Plant Closings: Power, Politics, and Workers*. Dover, MA: Auburn, 1986.

Sweeney, John. *America Needs a Raise: Fighting for Economic Security and Social Justice*. Boston: Houghton Mifflin, 1996.

Tillman, Ray M., and Michael S. Cummings, eds. *The Transformation of U.S. Unions: Voices, Visions, and Strategies from the Grassroots*. Boulder, CO: Lynne Rienner, 1999.

PATCO AND REPLACEMENT WORKERS

On August 3, 1981, over 12,000 air traffic controllers left their jobs with the U.S. Federal Aviation Administration (FAA), staging a walkout in defiance of a law that prohibits federal workers from undertaking strikes. President Ronald Reagan warned the disgruntled members of the Professional Air Traffic Controllers Organization (PATCO) that he would permanently replace them if they did not return to work within forty-eight hours. When roughly 11,300 controllers remained on strike, Reagan authorized their permanent replacement on August 5, 1981, banning them from reemployment with the FAA. PATCO, the controllers' union, was subsequently decertified and broken. As the most significant union-busting event of the post–World War II era, the PATCO debacle represented a turning point in U.S. labor history. It marked the end of a half-century during which employers rarely attempted to break an established union during a strike.

THE USE OF REPLACEMENT WORKERS IN STRIKES PRIOR TO 1981

Prior to the advent of the New Deal in the 1930s, U.S. employers regularly exercised their common-law right to permanently replace workers on strike. Blacklists were common during this era, and employers enforced them through private employment bureaus and labor spies. But the passage of the National Labor Relations Act, also known as the Wagner Act, in 1935 altered this situation, granting workers the right to organize and bargain collectively, spelling out unfair labor practices that employers were forbidden to undertake. By the end of World War II, employer efforts to break unions on strike by operating with replacements were increasingly rare events.

The use of permanent replacements to break strikes became rare even though the law continued to recognize private employers' rights to use this tactic. In the midst of labor's resurgence in 1938, the U.S. Supreme Court issued a decision in the case of *NLRB v. Mackay Radio and Telegraph* that clarified these rights for employers. In its opinion in the case, the Court held that the Wagner Act allowed management to permanently replace strikers in economic strikes in cases where the conditions of employment rather than unfair labor practices were at issue, as long as employers could prove that legitimate and substantial business interests were served by this strategy.

For many years after World War II, employers generally did not attempt to make use of their *Mackay* rights. Employers' reluctance (or inability) to exercise those rights was one of the hallmarks of what some call the era of "labor–management accord" following World War II. On those occasions when employers did use replacement workers, union members usually reclaimed their jobs after strikes were settled (sometimes working side by side with replacement workers) and a union contract usually still obtained. In the 1960s, the courts issued a series of decisions that regulated the treatment of replacement workers and returning strikers, protecting the rights of union members from management discrimination in favor of replacement workers in the aftermath of a strike settlement. Operating under such decisions, employers who did make use of replacement workers usually did so to gain bargaining leverage against a union in a negotiation that assumed that the union itself would survive.

By the 1970s, however, labor–management relations deteriorated, and a variety of developments gave employers both the opportunity and the incentive to consider aggressive tactics to break union power. The weakening of the labor movement's allies on the national political stage; the growth of global trade; the comparative high costs of union labor in the United States; the refinement of management tactics of union avoidance; and the possibilities of dramatically increased profits in nonunion environments—these were among the factors that both prodded and enticed private sector employers into an increasingly hostile stance toward unions. Yet while private employers grew increasingly anti-union by the 1970s, they did not embrace the tactic of permanent replacement of strikers until the 1980s. Had not the federal government led the way, private sector employers may not have used striker replacement as a tactic as early and as effectively as they subsequently did.

THE PATCO STRIKE

The 1981 PATCO strike was a turning point long in the making. PATCO formed in 1968, six years after President John F. Kennedy issued Executive Order 10988, which allowed federal employees to organize and bargain collectively. Since its formation, PATCO had emerged as one of the most aggressive government employee unions in the United States. PATCO initiated slowdowns in 1968 and 1969 that snarled air traffic around the United States to dramatize the poor working conditions that characterized the nation's air traffic facilities. In an effort to secure its organization, PATCO staged a massive sick-out in March 1970 that curtailed air travel across the nation. Despite the FAA's vow that it would terminate the thousands of 1970 "strikers," no such threat was carried out, and PATCO won official recognition as the bargaining unit of air traffic controllers. Over the course of the 1970s, PATCO initiated several more slowdowns to advance its agenda. These were usually successful, though the FAA grew increasingly determined to battle PATCO as the decade wore on. By the late 1970s, the FAA's increasing intransigence led to a growing sentiment among PATCO members that the union would never get a satisfactory contract that addressed pressing issues of workplace stress and underpay until it could effectively shut down the nation's airports by a walkout. If that walkout was successful, PATCO activists reasoned, its illegality would be inconsequential. Just as the government rehired controllers following the 1970 sickout, the government would be forced to rehire controllers after a successful national strike.

Beginning in 1978, PATCO leaders began planning for that strike. PATCO created a network of local union activists to coordinate the walkout. Dubbed "Choirboys," the activists generally did not come from the ranks of elected union officers. Their identity was not publicized so that they could coordinate a walkout even if the government arrested elected union officials for striking in defiance of legal injunctions. Over time, the Choirboys became a powerful faction within the union, pushing for a strike in 1981 behind the slogan "Be One in '81." The Choirboys' influence helped shake up PATCO's national leadership in January 1980. At that time, PATCO's executive board delivered a no-confidence vote to the union's president, John Leyden, who had held the union's presidency since 1970. Union militants saw Leyden as too moderate to lead a major illegal strike against the government. Leyden promptly resigned and was succeeded by the union's vice president, Robert Poli, who had been in charge of formulating the 1981 strike plan. Under Poli's leadership, the strike preparations gathered momentum.

That momentum only temporarily subsided when PATCO endorsed Ronald Reagan's successful campaign for the presidency in 1980. Reagan sought this endorsement by promising PATCO that if elected he would work to address controllers' grievances. When PATCO's contract expired in March 1981, however, the union found the Reagan administration to be a tough negotiating partner. After months of contentious bargaining, a near strike in June 1981, and the failure of PATCO's membership to ratify a tentative contract offer in July 1981, PATCO finally voted to strike on August 3, 1981.

The FAA had been planning for this strike for many months. The agency immediately implemented a contingency plan under the direction of FAA administrator J. Lynn Helms, a former aviation industry executive who prided himself on his ability to deal forcefully with unions. Helms's plan saw airlines cancel thousands of flights, supervisors step in to take on controllers' duties, and the Defense Department assign hundreds of military controllers to the jobs of strikers. Meanwhile, the full force of the government came down on the PATCO strikers even as replacement workers were hastily trained. Around the country, U.S. attorneys sought injunctions and costly fines against PATCO officers, and several strike leaders were arrested for contempt of court for refusing to obey injunctions. Most important, President Reagan strode into the Rose Garden hours after the strike began to warn controllers that if they didn't return to work they would be permanently replaced. Although less than 10 percent of the strikers heeded Reagan's warning, the president followed through on his threat.

Public opinion polls showed that most Americans initially backed Reagan's response to the strike. Attempting to sway public opinion in a more favorable direction, the American Federation of Labor-Congress of Industrial Organizations (AFL-CIO) immediately expressed support for PATCO. Yet national union leaders were privately outraged that PATCO never consulted with other aviation industry unions or the AFL-CIO prior to calling its walkout. In the end, the

AFL-CIO rejected calls for sympathy strikes or mass pickets to close down airports. Instead, the AFL-CIO confined its support for PATCO to fundraising for strikers' families, issuing public statements in favor of a negotiated solution to the strike, and making Reagan's intransigence a major theme of the September 19, 1981, Solidarity Day demonstration, which drew hundreds of thousands of unionists to Washington, D.C. Grassroots support for PATCO among union activists around the country was strong, as many activists saw Reagan's stand against PATCO as signaling the onset of an aggressive new anti-union drive in the United States. Yet grassroots support for PATCO was unable to force the Reagan administration to back down, and PATCO was successfully broken.

STRIKER REPLACEMENT AND THE DIMINISHING EFFECTIVENESS OF STRIKES SINCE 1981

It is doubtful that any private sector employer could have engaged in such a costly effort to replace union strikers. By some estimates, it took years for the nation's air traffic system to recover from the firing of PATCO strikers and cost taxpayers billions of dollars, although it is difficult to assess the strike's ultimate cost. Significantly, the permanent replacement of thousands of striking air traffic controllers, whose technical skills had led many to assume that they were irreplaceable, shocked trade unionists and galvanized many private sector employers. In the years immediately following the PATCO strike, a number of highly visible private sector employers followed Reagan's lead. Hormel, International Paper, Greyhound, and Phelps Dodge were among the corporations that employed permanent replacement strategies during strikes in the decade following the PATCO walkout. Although strikers' ability to regain their jobs in these strikes was limited, the Supreme Court strengthened the hands of replacement workers in 1983 by finding that they could not be legally dismissed in favor of returning strikers if their employer had recruited them with the promise of retaining them.

Employers' willingness to permanently replace strikers in the aftermath of PATCO dramatically eroded the effectiveness—and hence the incidence—of strikes in the United States. Between 1947 and 1980, the Bureau of Labor Statistics reported at least 180 strikes each year involving more than 1,000 workers each in the United States. Since 1982, the number of such strikes has never once reached even half that level. Rather, figures showed a sharp decline from the

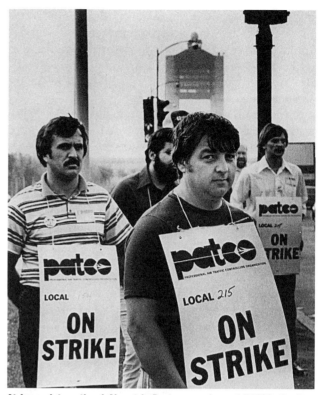

At Logan International Airport in Boston, members of PATCO, the Professional Air Traffic Controllers Organization, picket on August 3, 1981, the day 12,000 union members went on strike. President Reagan hired replacement workers—or "scabs," as strikers called them—and broke the strike, dealing a major blow to the American labor movement. *(AP Wide World Photos)*

235 strikes involving a total of one million workers in 1979 to a record low of 17 walkouts, involving only 73,000 workers, two decades later in 1999. Between 1947 and 1980, the United States averaged 300 major strikes annually. In the years between 1981 and 2000, the annual average was 47 major strikes.

In the 1990s, several unsuccessful efforts were made to prohibit employers from permanently replacing strikers. H.R. 5, passed by the U.S. House of Representatives in 1991, would have eliminated the permanent replacement tactic, but labor could not muster the sixty votes required to bring the bill to a vote in the Senate. In 1993, a similar bill failed to survive a Senate filibuster. Since the Republican takeover of the House of Representatives in 1994, there has been little prospect of altering the law on this issue. When President Bill Clinton signed an executive order in 1995 prohibiting the federal government from doing business with firms that permanently replaced strikers, court decisions effectively gutted the order and left the *Mackay* doctrine intact. Meanwhile, courts made clear that the votes of replacement workers could be counted in efforts to decertify unions after strikes. The failure to alter such legal doctrines greatly diminished workers' practical right to strike in the United States.

The result was that in the years after 1981 credible strike threats by U.S. unions became increasingly rare. Significantly, the effective use of the strike weapon failed to improve even during the economic boom of the mid-1990s, even though unions have traditionally used strikes more effectively during periods of economic growth. Although the outcome of the PATCO strike alone was not responsible for organized labor's diminished power, the precedent that the 1981 strike set for the permanent replacement of striking workers was undeniable. Ultimately, no single event better symbolized the declining fortunes of U.S. trade unionism as the twentieth century drew to an end.

Joseph A. McCartin

BIBLIOGRAPHY

Babson, Steve. *The Unfinished Struggle: Turning Points in American Labor, 1877–Present*. Lanham, MD: Rowman & Littlefield, 1999.

Crampton, P., and J. Tracy. "The Use of Replacement Workers in Union Contract Negotiations: The U.S. Experience, 1980–1989." *Journal of Labor Economics* 4 (1998): 257–276.

Getman, Julius. *The Betrayal of Local 14: Paperworkers, Politics, and Permanent Replacements*. Ithaca, NY: Cornell University Press, 1998.

Nordlund, Willis J. *Silent Skies: The Air Traffic Controllers' Strike*. Westport, CT: Praeger, 1998.

Northrup, Herbert R., and Amie D. Thornton. *The Federal Government as Employer: The Federal Labor Relations Authority and the PATCO Challenge*. Philadelphia: Industrial Research Unit, Wharton School, University of Pennsylvania, 1988.

Shostak, Arthur B. *The Air Controllers' Controversy: Lessons from the PATCO Strike*. New York: Human Sciences, 1986.

Singh, Parbudyal, and Harish C. Jain. "Strike Replacements in the United States, Canada, and Mexico: A Review of the Law and Empirical Research." *Industrial Relations* 40:1 (January 2001): 22–53.

UNITED PARCEL SERVICE STRIKE

During the summer of 1997, the Teamsters waged a fifteen-day strike against the Atlanta-based United Parcel Service (UPS), garnering overwhelming public support and winning wage increases along with a promise of 2,000 new full-time jobs. This was ultimately a promise on which the company did not deliver, and UPS workers continue to struggle for secure full-time positions. However, the 1997 UPS strike was the largest ever waged by the Teamsters against a single employer. It brought public attention to the problem of job casualization—the increasing reliance on low-paying, part-time workers who are given neither benefits nor job security.

At a time when the weakened labor movement struggled to deal with a new, increasingly casualized service economy, the Teamsters waged a very public struggle that attempted both to highlight the labor demands of this new workforce and to redeem the Teamsters themselves from the internal political corruption for which they had become so famous.

At the time of the strike, UPS was America's third-largest private employer, with more than 300,000 workers, two-thirds of whom were Teamsters members. The company delivered about 12 million packages each day, carrying 80 percent of the country's ground delivery. The Teamsters walkout brought UPS trucks across the country to a standstill, ultimately costing the company more than $750,000. It also allowed UPS's main competitor, Federal Express, to double its ground delivery business at the expense of a long-time UPS monopoly on ground transport of goods.

UPS strikers had the support of the public from the early days of the strike; at times the public favored the strikers two to one over the company. The conflict was highly visible, both in the press and on front porches and doorways across the country. The Teamsters' clear victory in the arena of public opinion

served as a catalyst for effective organizing campaigns across the country, from corrections officers on the West Coast to fast-food employees in the Midwest and Canada. Part-time workers nationwide benefited from new public awareness of their position in the workforce and the extent to which they were exploited by large corporations.

A SHOW OF LABOR STRENGTH AT A TIME OF LABOR WEAKNESS

The years leading up to the UPS strike were difficult for the labor movement. Depressed wages, increased hours, and poor access to affordable housing and health insurance had plagued American workers since the 1970s. Weakened unions, bad contracts, and what labor historian Robert H. Zeiger called "general antagonism toward unions" set the backdrop for the UPS struggle. In 1981, the Reagan administration stifled a strike of 13,000 air traffic controllers, ushering in an era of labor defeats both on the picket line and in law and public policy. One legislative blow after another hindered workers' attempts at halting casualization, improving wages and benefits, and strengthening both contracts and membership rolls.

Between 1978 and 1991, the Teamsters union—like its counterparts in the building, auto, and steel trades—saw membership losses of more than a half-million members. This loss has been credited to a combination of the loss of manufacturing jobs, generational distrust of unionism, and the labor movement's inability to organize the growing ranks of service and clerical employees. Whereas public sector unions experienced measurable growth, private sector unions suffered dramatic losses. At the same time, a trend toward the permanent replacement of striking workers raised the stakes for work stoppages. The 1981 air traffic controllers' strike ended with permanent replacements. Greyhound Bus Company permanently replaced its striking drivers in the spring of

1990, and in 1992, management at the Caterpillar Tractor factory in Peoria, Illinois, permanently replaced 13,000 strikers.

In the 1980s and 1990s, union-busting law firms flourished as corporations took advantage of a management-friendly National Labor Relations Board (NLRB), often dragging labor grievances through the courts for up to and exceeding three years. Although there were laws to protect the rights of workers, employers could break them without much fear of reprisal. The proceedings required to hold management accountable for such violations were too costly and time-consuming for most weakened unions to endure. The adverse conditions for labor during the years leading up to the Teamsters strike at UPS underscore the intensity of the union's fight and the magnitude of its accomplishment.

ISSUES

The 1997 UPS strike involved three major contract issues: the hiring of part-time workers and its resultant two-tiered wage structure, job safety, and control of worker pensions. The Teamsters' pension plan, often the subject of highly publicized tales of Teamsters corruption (culminating in a 1989 lawsuit that led to outside supervision of the funds), required UPS to pay into a pension fund that supported both Teamsters members in UPS jobs and those who drove for other employers. UPS wanted to terminate its involvement with the Teamsters plan and support its workers independently, which they claimed would increase pension payment to workers by more than 50 percent. UPS asserted that the part-time issue, for which the Teamsters enjoyed such overwhelming public support, was simply a smokescreen for the pension concern. Management charged that the Teamsters drivers were essentially striking to maintain corrupt financial practices by protecting their right to retain control of worker pensions.

Although the Teamsters' reputation for corruption and shady financial dealings was no secret, those who drove for UPS faced serious wage and job security issues that were anything but a smokescreen. By the time of the strike in August 1997, nearly 60 percent of UPS employees were part-time workers earning an hourly wage of approximately $9. By contrast, full-time workers doing the same jobs made approximately $20 per hour. Between 1993 and 1997, UPS filled 40,000 to 45,000 new union jobs, and more than 80 percent of these were of the part-time variety. These part-time employees, most of whom received

Fighting "to save the American dream," thousands of United Parcel Service workers—including these members of the Teamsters in Chicago—went out on strike in August 1997. The strike proved largely successful, as workers won wage increases and promises of new jobs. *(AP Wide World Photos)*

no benefits, often put in full-time hours at their second-tier salaries.

FIGHTING FOR JOB SAFETY AND SECURITY: COUNTERING MANAGEMENT'S CONTRACT CAMPAIGN

In the years leading up to the strike, drivers continued their ongoing fight for job safety. In the winter of 1994, in an attempt to increase productivity, UPS management raised the package weight limit from 70 pounds to 150 pounds without consulting the union and without increasing safety standards or precautionary measures. Full-time and part-time employees joined forces to mobilize for a February 1994 safety walkout in protest of the new weight limits. A few months later, the Teamsters' International launched what would turn out to be a three-week strike against a number of major trucking companies in response to the proliferation of $9-per-hour part-time positions. Although this Teamsters attack on corporate exploitation of part-time drivers predates the 1997 UPS strike that garnered so much public attention, it wasn't until the familiar workers in their brown uniforms moved from trucks and front porches to picket lines that the general public, by a two-to-one margin, expressed support for the Teamsters.

Following the 1995 three-week strike, UPS intensified its "Team Concept" campaign, an initiative taken by many large corporations in the early 1990s to undercut worker organizing and assert company control over worker concerns. For UPS, this meant preventing coalitions between part- and full-time workers. The goal was for employees to feel as though they had a voice in the decision-making process through participation in "work teams" organized by management to consider workplace issues; the upshot was the undermining of workers' right to collective bargaining. The Teamsters responded with its own campaign that included a widely circulated video, "Actions Speak Louder Than Words," in which they pressed issues of job safety, wages, benefits, and increased reliance on part-time labor.

Over the next few years, as contract deadlines approached and negotiations commenced, stalled, and started again, part-time workers across America grew increasingly frustrated. Movements like Jobs for Justice, women worker rights groups, and Occupational Safety and Health coalitions gained steam as UPS workers across the country prepared to walk off the job, giving up salaries of up to $50,000 per year for strike pay of about $55 per week.

UPS management launched a number of contract campaigns in the months—and even years—leading up to the August 1997 strike, most of which served only to fuel rank-and-file organizing. Although the company was making more than $1 billion a year in profits, it expanded subcontracting, granted lower wage increases, and continued to hire part-time workers. Management's required "pre-work communication meetings" attempted to undercut union organizing, but the 206 Teamsters locals with UPS employees countered with strong member-to-member networks. The international union immediately assigned nineteen field staff to boost organizing efforts and take on UPS's expensive and extensive contract campaign. By contrast, the union's campaign, based on networking and worker and community unity, spent nothing on advertising or promotion.

FROM NEGOTIATION TABLE TO PICKET LINE TO HEADLINE

The Teamsters' strategy centered around uniting part-time and full-time workers to support more full-time positions and better contracts for all. Their video, "Make UPS Deliver," emphasized the common interest of all UPS workers. As the first round of contract negotiations approached, the union organized workplace rallies in seven cities. Before the next round of negotiations, the number of rallies doubled. Tens of thousands of workers participated in job security rallies, blowing high-pitched whistles outside of UPS office buildings. Efforts to unite part- and full-time workers proved fruitful, and six weeks before contract expiration, 100,000 Teamsters signed a petition for the creation of more full-time positions.

On Thursday, July 31, 1997, UPS contracts expired. For the next few days, heated and intense negotiations ensued at which UPS offered one "final offer" after another. Each offer was followed by a union counterproposal reflecting the union's three principal demands: more full-time positions, control of the pension program, and greater attention to job safety. When UPS management refused to concede, Teamsters officials walked out on negotiations at 10 P.M. on Sunday, August 3, marking the official start of the strike.

The following morning the story broke with reports that 2,000 UPS pilots would honor the Teamsters' picket line. UPS announced that, while operating at 30 percent capacity, they were prioritizing the delivery of medical supplies, which would be delivered by nonunion drivers and management. President Bill Clinton expressed concern for the scale of the walkout and voiced vague sentiments of support for the hundreds of thousands of employees, stating he would not intervene in the dispute.

Despite public support for UPS management on the sparsely publicized pension issue, Americans saw their UPS men and women as a part of their community. This was partly the result of the company's own emphasis on customer service. The courteous, conscientious service that UPS demanded of its employees made its delivery men and women friends and neighbors to their customers. That summer, *Time* magazine listed UPS workers among "Elvis impersonators and telecom execs" as the top "winning" American occupations. "Americans don't like strikes," the author proclaimed, "but they love their delivery guys." Only ten days into the strike, a Gallup poll showed 55 percent of the public supported the strikers, while only 27 percent supported the company.

ORGANIZING DOOR-TO-DOOR AND COAST-TO-COAST

The strikers' public support did not come without considerable effort. Local unions held family days to bring community members into rallies. Strikers went door-to-door in local communities to explain the strike issues. Rank-and-file workers—familiar faces in the cities and towns to which they delivered—served as central and highly visible media spokespeople. The Teamsters personally carried surveys and fliers to UPS members around the country. Just as their UPS delivery drivers brought door-to-door service to UPS customers, Teamsters organizers launched a community-based campaign relying on close personal networks and face-to-face communication.

Support from workers of all kinds throughout the country brought more media attention to the strike. In Manhattan, 2,000 telephone workers marched in support of the striking UPS workers. High-profile political leaders, including Jesse Jackson, also joined the picket line. The strike became an international effort as UPS workers in Europe wore stickers, passed out leaflets, and blew whistles outside company headquarters. German employees wore white socks, drawing attention to their usually dark ankles to demonstrate their support for the American UPS strikers. With Congress on vacation and the summer news characteristically slow, the UPS strike was a national front-page story.

THE TEAMSTER IMAGE: INTERNAL UNION POLITICS AND THE UPS STRIKE

Increased media attention forced the Teamsters to prioritize their public image at a time when a strong, united body of leadership was most vital. Internal reform initiatives such as UPSurge and Teamsters for a Democratic Union (TDU) dated back to the 1970s and worked to democratize the leadership while improving the image of a union that was historically fraught with allegations of corruption. This reputation for scandal predated both the "disappearance" of Teamsters boss Jimmy Hoffa Sr. and the 1957 expulsion of the Teamsters from the American Federation of Labor-Congress of Industrial Organizations (AFL-CIO) for its alleged unsavory dealings with the mob. Since the 1970s, these reform movements within the union have variously divided, weakened, united, and strengthened the Teamsters, but one thing remained constant for UPS drivers: management's continued attempts to casualize the workforce and depress wages. The TDU's reform efforts culminated in 1991 with the first direct election of the Teamsters' international leadership. Newly elected Teamsters president Ron Carey was a twelve-year veteran driver who rode to victory on an anti-corruption platform.

Often, union politics compromised both the strength of contracts and the loyalty of workers to their union leadership. In 1982, the "old guard" Teamsters higher-ups approved an $8 per hour wage freeze for part-time workers. This settlement laid the groundwork for the two-tier wage structure that the company cultivated throughout the years by dividing part- and full-time employees. This division further weakened the internally strained and increasingly member-poor union, sapping worker loyalty to a leadership often seen as unresponsive to worker needs and overly responsive to company recommendations. Even reform leader Carey's anti-corruption platform would eventually prove ironic following the post-strike reversal of his 1996 reelection in light of charges of campaign finance improprieties.

Political unrest and allegations of corruption within the Teamsters only exacerbated the tensions in the rank and file's relationship with its union. In 1989, following charges of corrupt financial practices, the courts ordered independent supervision of the Teamsters' pension program. It was this same pension system that would become one of the major contract issues during the 1997 strike.

THE OUTCOME

In retrospect, UPS seems an unlikely corporation to battle successful union mobilization. A close eighty-two-year relationship between the Teamsters and UPS management, and a low 4 percent job turnover rate, suggest that a walkout would have been unlikely. UPS drivers were among the highest paid in the country. But UPS's reputation as a "good employer" enabled it to mask its exploitative hiring practices and wage structure, and it was this two-tiered wage system that set the company up for attack. By fostering such a divided workplace, UPS made the inequalities more visible, illuminating for both its workers and the general public its own attempts to transform its payroll into a fully casualized workforce.

The effective community and network-based organizing carried out by new Teamsters leadership and rank-and-file members gave UPS what one magazine writer called a "public relations thrashing," and the contract that was settled on August 18, 1997, brought an increase in hourly salaries of $3.10 for full-time employees and $4.10 for part-timers. UPS also promised thousands of new full-time positions to reverse the casualization trend. Despite worker gains and company embarrassment, the limitations of the 1997 UPS strike illuminate two of the challenges facing labor: internal union politics and the uncooperative nature of American law and legislation when it comes to labor relations. Just as the outcome of the strike ultimately proved to be a disappointment when UPS failed to deliver on many of its promises for new full-time positions, the progress toward Teamsters union democratization was ultimately mired in charges of inappropriate financial practices during Carey's re-election campaign.

REPERCUSSIONS: CORPORATE RECOVERY AND THE RETURN OF THE OLD-GUARD LEADERSHIP

Shortly after the strike, Carey's 1996 reelection was overturned in response to financial corruption charges levied against some of his campaign staff (although not against Carey himself). UPS stalled on its contract promises, while the reinstated old-guard union leadership, led by James Hoffa Jr., instituted a nonaggressive course of action, following normal grievance procedures to address the company's inaction.

UPS struggled to recover from the financial damage caused by the strike, emphasizing more profitable services like next-day air, cutting back ground service, and laying off more than 100,000 workers, many of whom were full-time employees. Ground service suffered substantially because Federal Express had picked up much of UPS's lost business. UPS attempted to bounce back through a new computerized management system by which drivers were expected to make up to twenty deliveries in an hour based on computerized productivity calculations. This "Taylorization" of the delivery process severely compromised the customer service that had made UPS so successful.

The company's public image and business reputation also felt the effects of cutbacks in truck cleaning and maintenance. UPS stonewalled on its promises to create more full-time positions, claiming it could not do so until it had more ground business, while at the same time cutting back on ground delivery services. A year after the end of the strike, many UPS employees were still filing grievances about management harassment and retaliation, despite company claims that morale remained high.

THE FIGHT CONTINUES

The tensions that surfaced five years later, as the 1997 contract neared expiration, showed that the struggle for more full-time positions, improved wages, and stronger contracts had not ended. In May 2002, Teamsters nationwide voted by a 93 percent margin to approve another strike. The rocky relationship between UPS and the union was only further disrupted by what the Teamsters saw as newly elected Republican president George W. Bush's close alliance with UPS management. Indeed, the company's top executives donated more than $300,000 to the campaign to elect a leader whose record, unsurprisingly, was not union-friendly. Between the 1997 strike and the year 2001, UPS increased its revenue by 36 percent while increasing the starting wage of part-time workers by only 50 cents per hour.

With a contract expiration date of July 31, 2002, UPS and the Teamsters hoped to avoid a work stoppage by beginning contract negotiations in January of that year rather than waiting until June as they had in 1997. The climate for negotiation was different this time in a number of ways. The shipping giant that had once controlled nearly 80 percent of the ground delivery market now could claim only 55 percent. Furthermore, its share faced new threats from the U.S. Postal Service, which planned to release a new "delivery confirmation tracking service" that summer to compete with private shipping companies.

Sixteen days before the contract was set to expire, Teamsters officials conditionally (upon ratification of its membership) approved a much stronger contract than they had won with a strike five years earlier. In what was, at the time, the largest private sector contract negotiation of 2002, Teamsters won a 22 percent pay increase over six years and a guarantee of 10,000 new full-time positions. This amounted to a $5 hourly increase for full-time workers and a $6 increase for part-time workers over the course of the six-year contract. The new contract also offered improvements in health insurance and benefits for retirees and part-time workers, as well as limits on excessive overtime. This 2002 settlement narrowly averted a repeat of the protracted 1997 conflict. The gains won in 2002 would have been impossible without the massive organizing efforts of those who struck five years earlier.

Mandi Isaacs

BIBLIOGRAPHY

Cancelada, Gregory. "UPS Workers Hope Strike Can Be Averted as Contract Negotiations Continue." *Business News,* June 7, 2002.

Durr, Barbara. "Teamster Strike Threat Puts Dent in UPS." *The Financial Times,* July 13, 2002, p. 8.

Jardine, Jeff. "UPS, Union Hope to Settle Contract, Avoid Repeat of Costly 1997 Strike." *Tribune Business News,* June 5, 2002.

PBS. "Return to Sender." Transcript of feature on UPS strike and Elizabeth Farnsworth interview with Ron Carey and UPS negotiator David Murray, August 4, 1997. http://www.pbs.org/newshour/bb/business/july-dec97/ups_8-4a.html.

"The Perils of Ron Carey: The Teamsters' Boss Calls a Strike Against UPS, But If He Doesn't Win, More Than Trucks Are Going to Roll." *Time,* August 18, 1997.

Rachleff, Peter. *Hard Pressed in the Heartland: The Hormel Strike and the Future of the Labor Movement.* Boston: South End, 1993.

"Win One, Lose One: Ron Carey's Election as Teamster President Is Voided, Taking the Shine off Labor's Victory at UPS." *Time,* September 1, 1997.

Witt, Matt, and Rand Wilson. "The Teamsters' UPS Strike of 1997: Building a New Labor Movement." *Labor Studies Journal* 24 (Spring 1999): 58.

Zeiger, Robert H. *American Workers, American Unions.* 2d ed. Baltimore, MD: Johns Hopkins University Press, 1994.

HOTEL AND RESTAURANT WORKERS MOVEMENT

The Hotel Employees and Restaurant Employees Union (HERE) emerged in the latter part of the twentieth century as one of the most progressive unions in the United States. This change from a relatively conservative history was based on the election of young militant leaders, like Maria Elena Durazo, president of Local 11 in Los Angeles. The new philosophy of the union was based on the importance of rank-and-file involvement; the necessity to include documented and undocumented immigrant workers in the union movement; the need to build strong labor–community coalitions; and organizing as a priority to provide a quality life for working people.

By the mid- to late twentieth century, the hospitality industry had changed as a result of mergers and takeovers, resulting in firms that did not honor previous contracts and the influx of immigrant workers, many undocumented. Although the industry was growing, the union was faced with a declining membership. The conservative leadership did not see organizing as a priority and were resistant to the idea of organizing immigrant and women workers. The union leadership was not responsive to the needs of its members, many of whom were Spanish speaking. The union leadership operated on the mistaken idea that labor-management accords would build the union. By the 1980s, young organizers came to the fore and began a struggle to wrest control from the entrenched leadership. Since they were closely tied to the rank and file and attuned to their needs, they eventually won control and changed the nature of the union by making organizing a priority, especially the inclusion of immigrant workers. HERE collaborated closely with unions holding a similar philosophy. It built strong labor–community coalitions, fought for amnesty for immigrant workers, launched bold and creative organizing campaigns, and set an example for all working people. In the modern era, the union represented more than 300,000 members in over 120 local unions in the United States and Canada.

UNION HISTORY AND ORGANIZING DRIVES

HERE began in 1891 as an American Federation of Labor (AFL) union for bartenders, porters, cooks, maids, waiters, and waitresses. The union grew from 10,000 in 1901 to 300,000 in 1945. As was true of all AFL unions, for many years the international union was organized along craft lines, with locals representing waiters, bartenders, cooks, and waitresses. In 1973, international president Edward T. Hanley sought to merge all locals to represent members by industrial affiliation rather than craft.

A Las Vegas, Nevada, strike in 1984 proved a major landmark for the international union. The casino owners made a concerted effort to destroy the union, but the union waged a successful strike. After sixty-seven days, in one of the longest, most violent and bitter strikes in Las Vegas history, a number of hotels, including the MGM Grand, the Tropicana, and the Sands, settled. Then, in 1991, members of the Culinary Workers Union Local 226 and Bartenders Union Local 165, both HERE affiliates, struck the Frontier Hotel and Gambling Hall in Las Vegas. This strike lasted six years. Not one of the 550 striking workers crossed the picket line. Although the Frontier was bought by Bellagio Resort Hotel and Casino in 1998, the new owners accepted the union contract. Creating an organizing environment for other casino workers, HERE's membership grew to 20,000 in Las Vegas. By the twenty-first century, Las Vegas was one of the most unionized cities in the nation.

The experiences of Los Angeles's Local 11 serves as an example for the history of the union in the mid- to late twentieth century. Local 11's president, Maria Elena Durazo, provided leadership that revitalized the Los Angeles labor movement. Coming to HERE in 1983 from a long involvement in labor–community

After a six-year-long strike, picket signs fill a garbage can at the Frontier Hotel and Casino in Las Vegas on October 28, 1997. The strike by the Culinary Workers Union and Bartenders Union forced owners to sell the property, spelling the end of the walkout. *(AP Wide World Photos)*

organizing in the International Ladies' Garment Workers' Union (ILGWU), Durazo was shocked by the racism in Local 11. Despite the fact that the majority of members were Latino immigrants, the white male union leaders refused to translate the meetings into Spanish and were not attuned to members' needs.

HERE workers saw wages and benefits deteriorate as the hospitality industry was taken over by multinationals, who engineered decertifications of the union. A radical change was needed that would take into account the changing face of the workforce and industry. Backed by Latino groups, community, religious, and academic groups, and sympathetic unions, Durazo undertook a campaign to win the presidency and control of Local 11 in 1987. The campaign was ugly. Ultimately, the international intervened and

placed the local under its trusteeship for two years but with Durazo as a staff director. Working with the international strengthened her support in the local. Two years later, in 1989, Durazo was elected president with little opposition and began to put her plans into practice.

Under her leadership, Local 11 set an example for all working people by utilizing a variety of street and media tactics to publicize its cause. Backed by the international, the local undertook extensive research and community outreach both to maintain its membership and to organize the nonunion workers in the industry. The local recognized the necessity to organize the immigrant workforce, including the undocumented. Members staged sit-ins in hotel lobbies, committed civil disobedience in busy intersections, and engaged in many visible, lively demonstrations and rallies. The public demonstrations won much support for the workers' cause.

The union produced a controversial video, *City on the Edge,* showing the social inequities and class stratification of Los Angeles. The video portrayed how low-wage jobs were contributing to the overall decay of Los Angeles's infrastructure and why the tourist industry had a responsibility to reverse this trend. Ironically, the video was released at the exact time of the civil unrest, which took place throughout Los Angeles in 1992. Responding to the publicity, the Hotel Employers Council agreed to settle health and pension benefits, which covered 5,000 Local 11 workers.

Organizing nonunion workers was a much more difficult challenge. But Local 11 argued that the city of Los Angeles could not recover or be rebuilt from the 1992 civil unrest, unless workers received a living wage. Coming from an immigrant farmworker family, Durazo understood well that it was vital to include immigrant labor as part of the organized labor movement. Most unions prior to the 1980s were resistant to this idea, but the International Ladies' Garment Workers' Union (ILGWU) was openly organizing immigrant labor and working with community groups to teach immigrant workers their rights. Durazo, who received her initial union organizing experience in the ILGWU, applied this training to HERE and won major contracts for Hyatt Hotel workers, some airport hotel workers, and downtown hotel workers. Local 11 firmly believed in making house visits to workers, building labor–community bridges, and generally getting workers involved in their own battle for unionization.

HERE Local 2 represented 13,000 workers in the San Francisco Bay Area by the twenty-first century. Similarly to other areas, more than half the members were women and over 70 percent people of color, mainly immigrants from all over the world. Until the 1970s, the leaders were older white males. In the mid-1980s, women of color ran for office, and one won the presidency. The union staff consisted of members of every race, nationality, sex, age, and every workplace department. The local argued that immigrant issues and women issues were concerns for all workers. Similarly to other areas, Local 2 worked closely with community groups, especially immigrant worker groups, to educate their members about their rights.

CONCLUSION

By the twenty-first century, HERE consisted of immigrant workers taking the lead in revitalizing the labor movement. HERE collaborated closely with the ILGWU, now UNITE, as sister unions to coordinate efforts; the two unions made plans to merge in 2004. HERE recognized the need to make organizing a priority, to build on the untapped reservoir of immigrant workers, and to ensure that workers were involved in the building of their union. HERE not only organized immigrant workers, but also set examples in their strategy and tactics for all organizing campaigns to fight for a quality life for all working people.

Myrna Cherkoss Donahoe

BIBLIOGRAPHY

City on the Edge. HERE Research Department, Los Angeles, CA, 1992, videocassette.

Milkman, Ruth, and Kent Wong, eds. *Voices from the Front Lines: Organizing Immigrant Workers in Los Angeles.* Translated by Luis Escala Rabadan. Los Angeles: Center for Labor Research and Education, UCLA, 2000.

One Day Longer: The Story of the Frontier Strike. HERE Research Department, 1999, videocassette.

Siegel, Lou. "Local 11 Takes on L.A." *Labor Research Review* 12:1 (Spring/Summer 1993): 21–23.

WILDCAT STRIKES

A "wildcat" action is a strike waged by workers without the instruction or endorsement of union leadership. A possible origin for the term is the word "wildcatter," used to describe nineteenth-century oil drillers who went out on their own, without company knowledge, to dig for oil. The exact definition leaves room for interpretation; the term also sometimes applies to any strike that is illegal, goes against a union contract, or is aimed at eliciting responses from a union rather than an employer.

During wartime, "no-strike pledges" made work stoppages illegal in many industries. Strikes waged by auto workers, machinists, or other necessary wartime labor during that era were called "outlaw strikes" in that they defied both the law and the official union position. Very little academic attention has been devoted to the examination of wildcat strikes. Although much has been written on the story of individual wildcat actions, less has been studied about the plant and workplace conditions, worker grievances, and the national labor climate that generally instigated and fostered such "outlaw" strikes.

Workers often organize wildcats on short notice to protest an official union decision not to strike, or in response to disciplinary actions taken against a fellow worker or group of workers. Wildcats illuminate the limitations and challenges of unionism—particularly in the presence of racism and corruption—and under the pressures of capitalism. As a strike against the concessions of official union leadership or a strike in the absence of official union endorsement, the wildcat marks the point at which a labor union fails to serve its membership.

The line between official and unofficial (wildcat) strikes is often blurred by both the dynamic nature of labor unrest and the complex power relationship between union leaders, management, and workers. Sometimes a formal union-sanctioned strike will spin out of the union officials' control, perhaps as a result of union concessions or the failure of union leadership to recognize the demands of the rank-and-file. In such cases, an official strike could become a wildcat when workers ignore union officials' orders to end the strike and return to work. Another form of ambiguity comes from a phenomenon called the "pseudo-wildcat" in which the union leadership maintains concealed influence in orchestrating a strike that masquerades as an act of defiance against the union. Union officials may also be quick to assert that all strikes—even those planned and led by union officials—are "spontaneous" or "unsanctioned" in order to absolve themselves of responsibility in the eyes of management.

MOTIVATIONS

Historically, wildcat strikes are seldom motivated strictly by wage demands, but rather by rank-and-file discontent with official union negotiations or settlements. Another common motivation is the disciplinary repercussions of work actions. Some labor historians blame poor economic times for upsurges in wildcat strikes, arguing that when the economy is bad, unions are forced to accept wage cuts and other concessions that anger union members and eat away at rank-and-file support for union leadership.

During World War II, labor unions agreed to a "no-strike pledge" in support of the war effort, effectively making any strike a wildcat. Nonetheless, workers waged unofficial strikes throughout the war to protest frustrating bureaucratic delays caused by the newly established War Labor Board (WLB, now the National Labor Relations Association—NLRA), which oversaw all labor grievances and disputes. Under WLB procedures, even the gains that unions had already won through negotiations, such as back pay, could take more than six weeks to reach the pockets of frustrated workers. In such cases, a wildcat strike often came before the rulings made their way through the bureaucratic WLB process. Many workers staged wildcats in protest of WLB rulings. Neither the Board nor the courts tended to be favorable to workers, the courts often ordering strikers to "go to work or go to jail," as in the case of a 1969 miner's strike in West Virginia, which sought to call company attention to high rates of black lung disease.

One frequent cause of wildcat strikes is union and company reaction to other wildcats; for this reason, they tend to reproduce themselves. For example, a drill press operator might walk off the job in protest of dangerous and destructive speedups, and subsequently be disciplined by the company in the form of a dismissal or a dock in pay. In response, a wildcat strike might ensue, and the company might respond by firing those who led that unsanctioned walkout. If the union does not demonstrate its loyalty to workers by responding with criticism of the company's actions, workers might stage another wildcat strike in protest of their union officials' failure to act. At each step, the number of workers involved tends to increase dramatically.

WILDCAT TRENDS AND THE CHANGING WORKPLACE

A company's productivity is ultimately beneficial to the worker, so union leaders must work with both management and rank-and-file to achieve it. However, in that negotiation process unions risk losing the support of workers when concessions such as wage cuts, loss of benefits, speedups, and mandatory overtime become "necessary," either for union-management politics or for company survival. Often employees perceive such concessions as indicative of union leadership loyalty to management rather than to the worker. The result is often worker discontent, loss of faith in the union leadership, and, ultimately, unsanctioned job actions ranging from slowdowns and small acts of sabotage to massive wildcat strikes.

Until the late 1950s, wildcat strikes were even more common than official, union-sanctioned strikes in many industries. Before that time, workers in any given plant did very different kinds of work under one roof and one body of management. It was difficult for the particular grievance of one worker to get the support and backing of a union that was responsible to a very large and diverse group of employees. As a result, most work stoppages during this period were orchestrated on a small scale and were organized by occupation without the consent of the union leadership.

By 1959, changes in the organization of industry and the workplace created a work environment in which similar kinds of workers did similar kinds of work under one roof. One union represented these occupationally organized workers, making it easier to get union support for strikes. Consequently, more union-sanctioned strikes occurred, while the number of wildcat strikes decreased. However, unsanctioned strikes continued to flare up when workers became frustrated or impatient with either their union leadership or the bureaucracies that delayed strike authorization.

Labor historians are often skeptical about government statistics on strikes—and on wildcat strikes in particular—because they rarely reflect the frequency or severity of job actions. Sources like newspaper coverage fail to register less obvious or publicly visible acts of worker resistance waged in the absence of union consent, such as slowdowns, group "sick days," sabotage, unofficial and clandestine "parties" on company time in company facilities, and worker redistribution of labor. Many wildcat strikes, according to one historical account, are "nothing but group absenteeism." In both government records and media representations, such collective and complicated acts of resistance often fail to register.

HISTORICAL PERSPECTIVE

Although wildcat strikes have always had a consistent presence in the labor movement, three particular periods in U.S. history have seen a high occurrence of unofficial strikes. In 1919, a wave of wartime wildcats struck the railroads and coal mines. During World War II, a second intense wave of defense–industry wildcats responded to "no-strike" pledges, mandatory overtime, speedups, and increased bureaucratization of labor grievance procedures. Finally, in the 1960s and 1970s, an increasingly diverse and divided workforce waged wildcats against employers and a union leadership that seemed increasingly alienated from its rank-and-file and increasingly allied with management. Wildcat strikes returned to the coal mines in 1969. Cargo, correspondence, and packages across the country sat idle that same year while both U.S. postal workers and the Teamsters waged wildcats.

Wildcats of World War I: Railroads and Coal Mines

An 1894 strike by the American Railway Union (ARU) demonstrated the extent to which railroad employees could control the fate of American commerce. The

Pullman strike, named after the Pullman Palace Car Company and the Illinois company town it controlled, ended only with the full force of the U.S. Army. In the years that followed, government intervention in the railroad industry intensified. By 1920, the rails remained under government control, and the right to strike remained suspended.

Between 1914 and 1920, consumer prices rose 100 percent in the United States, while railroad worker wages increased by only 50 percent. Without the right to strike, this caused highly combustible discontent among railroad employees. When a Chicago Yardsmen Association leader was demoted in April of 1920, 700 switchmen on his line—already angry about their lack of power and diminished economic viability—needed little more incentive to walk off the job. Within a few days, every Chicago rail line had become involved in the wildcat strike that ultimately brought 9,000 switchmen to picket lines across the country.

Within a few more days, the strike had spread to engineers, firemen, and conductors from coast to coast. So had the union's anti-wildcat drive. Railway union leaders claimed that the strike violated union rules and contracts; in fact, there actually was no contract that spring because the railroads had just recently been released from government control. Nonetheless, union leaders and railroad management accused strikers of being "Bolsheviks" and threatened them with termination. Tens of thousands did lose their jobs and were replaced by strikebreakers brought in by the union leadership.

To mount this offense against their employers, their government, and their own union leadership, striking workers formed what labor historian Jeremy Brecher calls temporary "outlaw" organizations, such as the United Railway Workers of America. Throughout the month of April, newspaper headlines reported raids and arrests at these "outlaw" meetings throughout the country. Ultimately, it was the arrest of more than twenty strike leaders for violation of the Lever and Sherman Acts that put an end to the strike. Weakened wildcat leadership could not sustain the struggle in the face of the newly established Railroad Labor Board, appointed by President Woodrow Wilson in response to the work stoppage. The board asserted the authority of the official union leadership and refused to acknowledge the demands of "outlaw" groups, but it did negotiate a wage increase for all railroad employees that summer.

Meanwhile, wildcats in the coal mines demonstrated how organized worker actions opposing their own union leadership can extend beyond mobilizing a work stoppage or walkout to creating an alternative union platform. During the week of July 4, 1919, as many outlaw railroad strikers returned to the job, workers throughout the country struck to protest the imprisonment of Socialist Party leader and railroad union organizer Tom Mooney on implications in a 1916 bombing at a rally in San Francisco.

Like workers in other industries and regions, coal miners in the Belleville subdistrict of Illinois had their pay docked for taking part in that strike, which was itself illegal. Miners at Nigger Hollow Mine No. 2 called a "spontaneous mass meeting" after protesting fruitlessly to management about their loss of pay. They drew up a petition asking the union chairman to call an official union meeting on the topic. When that petition was ignored, the miners selected their own chairman and held their own meeting, at which they voted that the collection of fines was illegal. They also voted for a work stoppage and sent word to the miners at a nearby mine to join in their strike. That same night, at a joint meeting of the strikers from both mines, a union official showed up and demanded that the miners return to work. The official was promptly booed and ejected from the meeting, and soon word had spread throughout the region.

Effectively, these wildcat strikers had rejected their official union leadership and had reformed their goals, grievances, and strategies with leaders from among their own ranks. Contradicting the common perception of wildcats as unplanned, disorganized, and caustic, these miners drafted statements in which they called their union leaders "apologists" and criticized the "futility" of reforms such as wage increases and shorter working days. The Bellville miners sent delegates to other mines in the region to increase their numbers. Not only did they petition the union for a state convention, but they also planned their *own*, which was, in effect, a wildcat convention.

Meanwhile, the UMW hired strikebreakers to suppress (and often harass) their own members. With the union dues paid by the striking miners, union leaders hired some of their own men as "deputy sheriffs," who then arrested wildcat strikers. Ultimately, the union spent $27,000 to repress their own membership. Their strikebreaking efforts only further alienated rank-and-file workers and brought more miners to the picket line. President Wilson criticized the strike and sent federal troops into the mines. On November 8, more than four months after the start of the strike, federal courts ordered the workers to return to the mines. While acting UMW president John L. Lewis declared, "We are Americans, we cannot fight our government," the strikers proved him wrong and ignored the court order.

For another month—as the weather grew cold and the demand for coal became more urgent—the miners continued their strike, and coal rations grew increasingly severe. Schools closed for lack of heat. The railroads scaled back, and factories fell quiet. Federal troops drove scabs past the picket lines into Montana coal mines. In North Dakota, the governor declared martial law. What began as clandestine meetings of a few workers in an Illinois mine had, in a matter of months, left the entire nation out in the cold. After President Wilson proposed a 14 percent wage increase and an arbitration commission, many went back to work, but not for long. With miners dissatisfied with results, the summer of 1920 was also fraught with coal-mine wildcats.

Wildcats of World War II

Throughout World War II, consistent government and industry efforts to silence labor and increase production in the name of the war effort led to frequent labor unrest. In March of 1941, President Franklin D. Roosevelt created the National Defense Mediation Board to keep labor disputes from interfering with war production, and across the country, union leaders signed "no strike pledges." Nonetheless, by April of that year, wildcat strikes began to flare up in defense-related workplaces across the country.

War demands sped up production, forcing workers to put in more hours at a faster work pace. In September 1942, in response to a war economy, Congress froze wages with passage of the Stabilization Act. Union recruitment grew increasingly difficult as workers began to see the unions—stripped of the right to strike and weak in numbers—as powerless against management. In response to this problem, the passage of "maintenance of membership" provisions automatically signed up new employees and prohibited the termination of union membership during the duration of a contract. Unions relied on this provision to protect their numbers, and it was common for management to threaten its revocation to strong-arm union officials into making concessions. This forced unions into closer alliances with management in order to protect the provision, which contributed to a growing sense of abandonment among rank-and-file workers.

Expanding bureaucracies made this a frustrating time for both union leadership and rank-and-file members. Throughout the war, augmenting this rank-and-file distrust of union leadership was the sense that management and union leadership often used the existence of the War Labor Board to avoid dealing with grievances. Claims sent to the government agency were subjected to great delays and considerable dilution. All labor grievances had to go through the War Labor Board, and they often took years to process. The result was many unsanctioned work stoppages in protest of both specific grievances and the slow, unresponsive manner by which they were processed. These wildcats, often called "quickies" because of the speed with which they were organized and executed, reflected increasing worker frustration with wartime labor bureaucracies and unresponsive unions. For many skilled workers putting in seventy to eighty hours a week, these strikes were also much-needed breaks in the grueling work routine. Sympathy strikes—those in which workers in one plant or department walk out in support of other striking workers—were very common during the war.

During the World War II era, wildcat strikes became part of the initiation into the work culture for a new generation of industrial workers. Contrary to the perception that the high number of World War II-era wildcats was a result of a young, unruly workforce, long-time employees encouraged many new workers to defy the unreasonably high production rates that wartime industry demanded. These "old timers," as one labor study called them, would lead new, younger workers in organizing defiance of both management and the union.

Although the 1940s were frustrating for many workers, they were also—for those who were skilled, white, and male—a period of unprecedented labor strength. A wartime labor shortage gave workers leverage, often allowing them to demand higher wages and to pick and choose among jobs and plants. This was not the case for African-American workers, who continued to face job discrimination and unequal wages when working alongside white laborers in the same job. The wartime era also brought with it a new awareness of discriminatory practices and job inequalities as a result of this more diverse workforce.

Workplace diversity brought racial unrest, and many of the era's most severe wildcats—like those of a generation later—were racially motivated. During World War II, 80 percent of black workers were not unionized, either because they were excluded by racist union members and leadership or because, perceiving unions to be part of a white America fraught with racial hostility, they doubted a union would fairly represent their interests. Black workers often waged wildcats in response to wartime hate strikes in which white workers walked off the job to protest having to work alongside black workers. Black workers also often staged wildcats to protest union or management acts of racism.

In 1944, nearly 5,000 recorded "quickies" nationwide baffled management and union leadership and resulted in massive losses of man-hours. Each of these five-to-six-day wildcat strikes played its part in forcing improvements in industrial working conditions. Government reactions to wildcat strikes provide much fodder for the image of labor conflict as armed, militaristic, and disorderly. Uniformed military officers were a common sight at war production plants during the wildcat year of 1944, but not for the purpose of controlling unruly strikers. The military presence was often to ensure that employees returned to work and stayed on the job. Soldiers also served as armed escorts for strikebreakers and sometimes even took the place of striking workers so that production could continue.

In determining the effectiveness of wartime wildcats, it is important to note that during the wildcat year of 1944, "labor efficiency" was down by anywhere from 20 to 50 percent, depending on the industry and workplace in question. If labor's aim in mounting a strike is to withhold valuable services from management, then this drop in efficiency indicates a labor victory.

Auto Workers, Teamsters, and Postal Workers in the 1960s and 1970s

If 1944 was the year known for wartime wildcat strikes, then Detroit was the place. As the heart of the auto industry and a wartime destination for large numbers of black migrants from the south, it became the center of the United Auto Workers (UAW) labor conflicts—from hate strikes to wildcats—each of which took on complex and intense racial and class dimensions. This was also true a generation later, in 1973, which one historian of Detroit's labor history called "Wildcat Summer."

For Detroit workers, the second half of the 1960s brought a steady decline in the real income of industrial workers. At the dawn of the 1970s, the U.S. Department of Housing and Urban Development reported that only half of these workers could afford a "decent home." For auto workers in Detroit, a growing number of whom were African American, the UAW's tendency to ally itself with management left employees struggling for a voice in the plant to win improvements in working and living conditions. As

production sped up, management at the General Motors plant forced workers to put in overtime by depressing wages. Speedups led to unsafe working conditions, and accidents became more frequent and more severe.

In order to get the attention and support of its own union, Detroit's black workforce waged one wildcat strike after another, in forms ranging from highly publicized work stoppages to more subtle and covert forms of resistance like sabotage, group sick days, and slowdowns. This wave of wildcats in Detroit grew both into and out of a revolutionary social movement based at the Dodge plant known as the Dodge Revolutionary Union Movement (DRUM); this movement organized outside the plants, advocating mass political education through its publications and demonstrations. As historians Dan Georgakas and Marvin Surkin point out in *Detroit, I Do Mind Dying: A Study in Urban Revolution* (1998), the media's emphasis on the role of this revolutionary movement ultimately distracted from working conditions and striker demands.

Wildcat strikers of the 1960s and 1970s, whether they were postal workers in New York, coal miners in West Virginia, auto workers in Detroit, or Teamsters in Illinois, were often portrayed negatively in the media. The mass-produced image of disorderly renegades resorting to warlike tactics is best exemplified by coverage of the 1970 Teamsters' wildcat. During that conflict, Ohio's governor called in more than 4,000 national guardsmen and ordered another 13,000 to remain on "standby" while "open warfare" took place on Ohio highways. The 145th Infantry, which had gained notoriety in the last few years by its responses to urban riots, descended upon West Akron. Meanwhile, police officers staked out known Teamster bars waiting for the rebels to emerge.

The Teamster wildcat began following the settlement of a national contract that offered drivers a raise of $1.10 over a period of thirty-nine months. Outraged, drivers in sixteen cities halted their vehicles and launched mobile wildcat pickets. Companies tried to reroute drivers, but their attempts to avoid the pickets only resulted in widespread violence and the loss of a half-million jobs. Eventually, the teamsters' resilience won them a two-thirds raise and elimination of the unsatisfactory contract.

Postal workers demonstrated that same resolve in their own 1970 strike, which became the first nationwide strike of government employees and ultimately forced President Richard Nixon to declare a national emergency. After 200,000 postal workers in fifteen states walked off the job, the president sent 25,000 troops to post offices across the country, proclaiming, "the mails must go through!" On St. Patrick's Day of 1970, 25,000 postal workers honored a picket line in New York City, even though striking was a felony offense for government employees, carrying a penalty of a year and a day in prison, along with a $1,000 fine.

Such fines would have been particularly difficult for New York City postal employees to pay, according to a 1968 government study showing that many of the city's postal employees were forced onto public assistance to make ends meet. The study uncovered mass discontent among U.S. Postal Service employees in New York, citing poor working conditions, high cost of living, and limited job mobility. "Sick-outs" among postal workers had been fairly common since 1967, but it was ultimately their 1970 wildcat that brought the country's circulatory system to a halt. Soldiers sent in as scabs to push the mail through expressed solidarity with the strikers by deliberately creating even more chaos behind post office walls. Ultimately, the postal workers won wage increases of 6 percent for all government employees, along with an additional 8 percent for themselves.

Examining labor history by emphasizing only official strikes, or by discounting those actions taken by workers against or without the consent of their labor unions, ignores not only a large part of the story, but also a large portion of the actors. Many workers who constitute the "labor" in American labor history were neither recognized nor supported by official unions. Inclusion of wildcat strikes accounts for the hardest-fought labor battles and holds union leadership accountable for its acts of exclusion and omission. Wildcat strikes mark the visible eruptions of the labor fringe, at which the demands of rank-and-file workers oppose the politics (and often the economic realities) of official union negotiations and settlements.

Mandi Isaacs

BIBLIOGRAPHY

Brecher, Jeremy. *Strike!* San Francisco: Straight Arrow Books, 1972.

Georgakas, Dan, and Marvin Surkin. *Detroit: I Do Mind Dying: A Study in Urban Revolution.* Boston: South End, 1998.

Glaberman, Martin. *Wartime Strikes: The Struggle Against the No-Strike Pledge in the UAW during World War II.* Detroit: Bewick, 1980.

Gouldner, Alvin W. *Wildcat Strike: A Study in Worker-Management Relationships.* New York: Harper, 1954.

Honey, Michael K. *Southern Labor and Black Civil Rights: Organizing Memphis Workers.* Chicago: University of Illinois, 1993.

Scott, Jerome F., and George C. Homans. "Reflections on the Wildcat Strikes" *American Sociological Review* 12:3 (June 1947): 278–287.

Zetka, James R., Jr. "Union Homogenization and the Organizational Foundations of Plantwide Militancy in the US Automobile Industry, 1959–1979." *Social Forces* 73:3 (March 1995): 789–810.

ORGANIZED LABOR, CONSUMPTION, AND BOYCOTTS

The relationship between consumption and social and political change has a long history in the United States. Indeed, consumer actions like boycotts date back to the years before the nation was born, to the colonial era. Before the first glimmers of a revolution were at hand, colonial craftsmen persuaded elite and ordinary colonists alike to boycott imported British goods in favor of domestically produced goods. The nonimportation movement, as it was called then, signified the beginning of a long tradition of consumer actions in the United States. Nearly a century later, the labor organizations that developed in the decades after the Civil War sought to revive that history with boycott and label movements of their own.

The connections between consumption and the labor movement have focused on the ability of unions to influence consumers' shopping habits and thus favor union-made goods. Labor activists sought to harness the economic power behind consumption and transform it into a source of political and negotiating strength. Whether through union labels or boycotts of nonunion goods, union leaders hoped that they could convince consumers to choose union-produced goods over nonunion-produced goods and thus gain additional influence and power at the negotiating table. However, the process of convincing consumers to consider labor conditions and issues of solidarity over price was often a difficult one. The most popular consumer actions of the late twentieth century relied on sophisticated advertising appeals to get the message out. But, even then, consumers tended to be fickle and focused on the bottom line; thus, the connection between consumption and the labor movement proved difficult to maintain over long periods of time. Nevertheless, the moments in history in which labor unions did succeed in influencing consumer choice yielded benefits that were profound for organized labor.

THE LABOR MOVEMENT AND CONSUMPTION CAMPAIGNS

The earliest link between consumption and the labor movement dates back to 1875, when members of the Cigar Makers' Association of the Pacific Coast in San Francisco began to consider ways of persuading consumers to choose their cigars over nonunion-made cigars. The union devised a conspicuous white label that would be placed on each box of cigars to help consumers identify the source of manufacture. The label read, "CIGAR MAKERS' ASSOC'N. The cigars contained in this box are made by WHITE MEN." The label's specific and intentional identification of white men as the producers was an important part of the design. For in addition to seeking to increase their power by increasing consumption of union-produced cigars, this first union label also functioned as a tool of racial exclusion.

Chinese and Chinese-American cigar makers posed a threat to white men's control of the cigar industry in San Francisco, and thus the union devised a label to act not only as a tool of solidarity, but also as a way to discredit Chinese laborers. Rather than attempt to include Chinese and Chinese-American workers in their union, white cigar makers used the white label to signify not only a union-made product, but also the racial origins of the product. Cigar makers in other cities soon adopted the label technique for themselves. Four years after the pioneering efforts of the Cigar Makers' Association of the Pacific Coast, cigar workers in St. Louis reported that local manufacturers were "unable to sell cigars without [our] union label." In 1881, the national organization of cigar workers, the Cigar Makers' International Union of America, issued its first union label, bringing the technique to a national audience.

Other trade unions soon followed the cigar workers' lead and developed their own union label campaigns. A few decades later, near the turn of the twentieth century, can makers similarly sought to undercut a group of workers through the use of a union label. This time the excluded workers were women, whom male unionists viewed as a threat because of their apparent willingness to work for lower wages and their perceived weak union loyalty. In addition to the availability of cheaper female laborers, male can makers worried that increasing levels of mechanization in the can-making industry would undermine their hard-won union wages. So, male can makers created a stamp that was placed on the bottom of each can, assuring consumers of the "hand-made" quality and sanitary conditions of each can's production.

GENDER AND THE UNION LABEL

At the same time, the stamp was intended to persuade consumers to pay more for goods in the preferred cans and thus increase the marketability of goods in cans made by men unionists as opposed to those produced by women workers. In addition, the organized can makers wanted consumers to associate good quality with masculine production. In these very early union label campaigns, ethnicity, race, and gender were central issues of union solidarity.

Gender posed an interesting conundrum for the labor movement at the turn of the twentieth century, in terms of both organizing and consumer activism. Women were specifically excluded from the union label strategy in much the same way that they were often excluded from trade unions. Despite the fact that working-class women were typically responsible for determining a great percentage of their family's consumption, one study of the efficacy of the union label strategy in 1910 complained that in order for the label strategy to be successful, the labeled goods needed to be purchased by men consumers.

Women consumers lacked a sense of solidarity and industrial experience and were thus unable to maintain consistent support for union labels, or so the argument went. The reasoning behind working-class women's wavering support for union labels actually had more to do with the reality of small budgets and higher-priced union goods. It was the working-class woman's responsibility to stretch her meager dollars to the maximum, which often meant choosing lower-priced nonunion goods over labeled union goods. The consumer actions favored by trade unionist husbands and leaders often conflicted with women's need to stretch their husband's (and often, their own) working-class wages to meet their family's needs.

Still, not all union label activists dismissed women. As the label technique grew more sophisticated in the early twentieth century, some union leaders eventually turned to women and demanded their support for union labels. They had finally come to understand that women of all economic classes, as the arbiters of household consumption, wielded a substantial amount of power in the marketplace. Seeking to harness that power, many unions and even the American Federation of Labor (AFL) decided to target their union label campaigns at women. In 1909, the AFL established its own Union Label and Service Trades Department. Eventually, organized labor came to realize that the success or failure of the union label strategy depended, in large part, upon the support of women.

Middle-class women reformers in the Progressive Era took the union label technique and made it their own. In 1898, a group of reform-minded activists, most of them women, joined together to harness the power behind consumption as a force for improving working conditions and created the National Consumers League (NCL). The early NCL used the standard techniques established by trade unions to advocate for their goals. For instance, like the cigar makers, the NCL devised a white label to designate goods produced in favorable circumstances. In addition, they developed a "white list" that identified department stores with good working conditions. From the very beginning, women played a central role in supporting such label efforts by labor unions and coalitions of activists working outside the realm of organized labor. The NCL was not, strictly speaking, a division of organized labor; however it was part of a larger movement that sought to improve working conditions, eliminate sweatshops, and create minimum standards in industry. In that way, trade unions and the NCL were working toward the same goals.

As the ready-to-wear apparel industry and its accompanying sweatshops flourished at the turn of the century, organized labor found new uses for the union label strategy. By 1900, the two primary apparel workers' unions, the International Ladies' Garment Workers' Union (ILGWU) and the United Garment Workers (UGW) had developed their own distinctive labels to be sewn into garments produced by union workers. The initial label campaigns of the ILGWU and UGW suffered, however, from spotty regulation. Labels were sometimes granted to substandard shops, even sweatshops and nonunion shops, thus undercutting the efficacy of the strategy.

The onset of World War I in 1914 had the effect of increasing the number of Americans on union rolls as women, African Americans, and even unskilled workers found temporary positions in industries that had previously spurned them. But immediately after the war's conclusion, the Red Scare swept the nation. Labor unions scrambled to purge radicals from their rolls, and, in the process, the movement became more conservative and less demanding of American business and industry. It was in this environment that organized labor greeted the Great Depression. Some leaders of the AFL supported an extension of the union label strategy to a "Buy American" movement, arguing that consumption of American goods, in addition to union goods, would increase the availability of jobs in the nation. During the Great Depression, the AFL's Union Label Department expanded its endorsement of union goods to include goods made in America by Americans, enveloping its appeals in a patriotic veneer. Union goods were, by definition, American goods, and what was good for organized labor was good for the millions of unemployed Americans. In addition, the AFL could earn some political advantages by appearing as if it was working to solve the Great Depression.

In 1941, America's entry into yet another global conflict once again swelled the membership rosters of labor unions in the United States. Because of the mobilization effort for World War II, both the trade-oriented, conservative AFL and the more progressive Congress of Industrial Organizations (CIO) fared well during the war. The number of unionized workers grew from 10.5 million at the start of the war to 14.7 million by the end of the conflict. After the war, unions turned once again to their label campaigns. By this time, there was a general consensus about the importance of women consumers to the success or failure of label campaigns. This was particularly true in the apparel industry. Apparel was one of the most frequently purchased of union-labeled goods, and the men's clothing workers union, the Amalgamated Clothing Workers of America (ACWA), wasted no time in reviving its label campaign. This time, however, the union directed its appeal to trade unionists as well as to the general public through radio promotions and advertisements in both trade and popular journals. In the 1950s, cities and towns across the nation, even in the notoriously anti-union South, sponsored union label weeks that often included essay contests and raffles of union-made products. Many of the postwar union labels, especially those initiated by the apparel unions, were directed at women consumers. Union label advocates recognized that women purchased not only their own clothing, but also the clothes for their husbands and children.

The post–World War II union label campaigns also employed sophisticated advertising techniques. The ILGWU, for instance, hired a well-known advertising firm to lead its label campaign in 1958. Mary Rockefeller, then the First Lady of New York State, kicked off the campaign by sewing the first ILGWU label onto a garment. A few years later, Eleanor Roosevelt stitched the one billionth label into another union-made garment. Photographs of these two promotional events appeared in union advertisements in women's journals. With the help of such prominent women and sophisticated advertising that targeted women consumers, the union label appeared to have staying power.

"BUY AMERICAN" CAMPAIGNS

The flood of cheaper, imported goods that began in the 1960s with the Kennedy Round of the General Agreement on Tariffs and Trade's (GATT's) massive tariff reductions posed an enormous threat not only to domestic industries like apparel and auto manufacturing, but also to their respective unions. The threat was real and substantial. From the early 1960s to 1976, the percentage of imported apparel in the United States grew from a mere 2.5 percent to over 30 percent. In the 1970s, the ILGWU sought to bring its label campaign to the forefront of the battle against imports. The national offices of the ILGWU worked steadily, often with participation of its sister union, the Amalgamated Clothing and Textile Workers Union (ACTWU; created by a merger of the ACWA and the Textile Workers Union of America in 1976) to enforce label standards and to make the connection between union-made and American-made apparel. Then, in 1975, organized labor's use of the label as a weapon against imports reached its high point. In November of that year, the ILGWU's famous "Look for the Union Label" television commercial first hit the airwaves, bringing the pro-union "Buy American" message into living rooms across the nation. The commercial's catchy jingle, "Look for the union label, when you are buying a coat, dress, or blouse," soon caught on. Within a few months of its initial broadcast, most Americans were familiar with the tune and its pro-union, "Buy American" message. The song's lyrics linked the pro-union agenda with the "Buy American" campaign, claiming that the ILGWU's label was good for America. The AFL championed the commercial's success and its message, calling it the "cry of the modern trade union movement."

The appeal of this particular label campaign extended beyond that of earlier versions. This time, the union's strategy envisioned women as workers, unionists, and consumers. The mostly female signers in the "Look for the Union Label" commercial were an ethnically and racially diverse group. African-American, Latina, and Asian women all had a prominent place in the commercial, thus broadening its appeal. The success of the commercial is difficult to measure, but without doubt it did succeed in getting the message out. Versions of the commercial appeared on television shows like *Jeopardy* and *The Merv Griffin Show*. The very popular *Saturday Night Live* program even poked fun at the commercial in one of its more memorable skits. It was clear that the commercial succeeded in making consumers aware of the union label. However, it did little in the long run to stem the ever-increasing flood of imported apparel.

CONSUMER BOYCOTTS

Where the union label campaigns sought to gain influence by urging consumers to spend money on particular goods, boycotts functioned in exactly the opposite way. Boycotts demanded that consumers withhold their money. By not purchasing certain specified products, unions hoped to compel employers to negotiate more fairly over issues such as union recognition, wages, and working conditions. Both boycotts and union labels were strategies designed by organized labor to increase the power and influence of labor unions in America. However, union-sponsored boycotts suffered under much stricter governmental supervision and legislative restrictions than label campaigns.

In the four decades before World War II, the right of organized labor to initiate boycotts was the focus of several court decisions and federal legislation. One of the most famous early boycotts initiated by organized labor in this time period was the subject of the famous 1908 U.S. Supreme Court decision *Loewe v. Lawlor*, or the Danbury Hatters case, as it was more commonly known. After Dietrich Loewe, the company owner, refused to recognize the United Hatters, the union organized a boycott of all scab-manufactured hats. The United Hatters' organizers and rank-and-file unionists attacked any establishment across the nation that sold hats made by Loewe's scab workers. The AFL supported and popularized the boycott when they added Loewe hats to their "Don't Patronize List."

The boycott ran into trouble when the American Anti-Boycott Association (AABA) joined forces with Loewe and filed suit against the hatters. The AABA amassed a powerful lobby of attorneys who argued that boycotts across state lines constituted a violation of the Sherman Anti-Trust Act because, just as certain combinations of employers were illegal because they constituted collusion, so were combinations of workers. The courts agreed and ordered the hatters to pay three times the actual damages sustained by Loewe. Subsequent federal court decisions extended the boycott limitations provided in the Danbury Hatters case, and eventually, virtually all boycotts of retail establishments were prohibited by the federal courts and their broad interpretation of the Sherman Anti-Trust Act. The courts claimed that unions and other combinations of workers had no right to boycott retail establishments because they were secondary to the complaint itself. That is, the stores that sold scab-made products were not, in fact, the subject of the workers' or unions' complaints and therefore should not have to suffer the consequences of a union-organized boycott.

In the 1930s, boycotts enjoyed a reprieve from the limitations that federal courts imposed in previous decades. With the passage of the Norris-LaGuardia Act in 1932, Congress expressly gave unions permission to use the secondary boycott strategy. Three years later, passage of the Wagner Act reinforced a wide range of freedom with respect to secondary boycotts. But the reprieve was to be short-lived, and few unions were willing to venture into the legal quagmire, fearing lawsuits and devastating monetary fines such as the one suffered by the United Hatters as a result of the Danbury Hatters case. The passage of the 1947 Taft-Hartley amendments to the National Labor Relations Act once again banned secondary boycotts in most industries. As a result of the long history of legal restrictions of boycotts, organized labor has used this type of consumer action cautiously and infrequently.

THE UNITED FARM WORKERS

Of the unions that attempted to use the boycott strategy, the United Farm Workers (UFW) was one of the most successful. Under the charismatic leadership of Cesar Chavez in the 1960s and 1970s, the UFW launched and executed several boycotts. The UFW first adopted the boycott strategy in 1965 and targeted wine grapes produced by a large and well-known agricultural corporation. A few years later, the union broadened the target to include all table grapes. Then, in the 1970s, lettuce was added to the list of boycotted agricultural products. The UFW successfully avoided court injunctions by extending their appeals beyond unionists to include the general public. In this way, the boycott was not specifically a union action and therefore not subject to the wide variety of legal re-

Carrying a "Don't Eat Grapes" sign, United Farm Workers leader Cesar Chavez joins a march in Pittsburgh in 1969 urging consumers to boycott grapes.
(AP Wide World Photos)

strictions. Chavez publicized the plight of the largely Latino farm workers in California. He passionately campaigned for union recognition, better wages, and improved working conditions. Television interviews further illustrated the terrible plight of Latino farm workers. Chavez fought against long hours, terrible pay, anti-union intimidation, and unsafe and unsanitary working conditions. He urged the consuming public, especially housewives, to boycott wine grapes, table grapes, and lettuce until improvements were achieved. The UFW went beyond targeting fellow trade unionists and included religious organizations, student groups, and nonaffiliated consumer organizations in their boycott appeals. Nevertheless, other branches of organized labor threw their support be-

hind the UFW's efforts. For instance, in 1974 a local branch of the Coalition of Labor Union Women organized a picket line in front of a Newark, New Jersey, grocery store in support of a UFW boycott. The national media also paid close attention to the UFW's boycotts. The *New York Times* and the *Wall Street Journal* both chronicled the ongoing struggle in many editions of their newspapers over the years. Eventually, the UFW's boycotts faded from national attention, and by 1978, the union transferred several boycott administrators back to California for union elections and contract negotiations. The transfer of resources signified a measure of success for the UFW, for the union did succeed in gaining several election victories. But the availability of undocumented workers willing to work for low, nonunion wages and the passage of several laws in Congress allowing companies to hire temporary immigrant workers limited the achievements of the UFW boycotts.

The ACWA also employed the boycott strategy in the 1970s. In March of 1972, twenty-six workers walked off their jobs at the Farah Manufacturing Company in El Paso, Texas. The mostly Latina group of workers initiated the walkout to protest their low wages, lack of job security, and oppressive work environment. Within a month, that strike led the ACWA to begin an impressive national boycott of all Farah's products. The boycott was one of the most successful in the history of the American labor movement as evidenced by its widespread popularity and the attention of the national media. Many observers point to the boycott as the critical factor in the union and workers' victory over Farah. Once again, the ACWA used advertisements that targeted women consumers and included pictures that portrayed the overwhelmingly female strike force in militant and strong stances.

The union solicited support from a wide range of sources. The Catholic Church provided important institutional support for the boycott, allowing union meetings to take place on church property and publicizing the boycott through its own communication network. Politicians, academics, and celebrities joined the Citizens Committee for Justice for Farah Workers and allowed their signatures of support for the boycott to be published in newspapers with national readerships. Although the National Labor Relations Board issued an injunction against union picketing of stores that sold Farah garments, in effect saying that such action constituted a secondary boycott, the boycott continued. Although there is controversy over the lasting effects of the strike and boycott, one thing is certain: the boycott dealt a serious blow to the financial health of the Farah Manufacturing Company and figured prominently in the company's decision to sign a union contract with its workers in 1974.

Exact figures vary, but according to the company's own financial report, Farah suffered an $8.3 million loss for the fiscal year of 1972 alone. As successful as the ACWA's boycott strategy may first appear, the long-term results were quite different. For although the boycott did result in a union contract and numerous NLRB decisions in the workers' and union's favor, the end result was that most of the Farah plants in the United States closed by the 1980s.

The Latina workers who had struggled so hard to achieve union recognition and better working conditions ultimately lost their jobs.

CONCLUSION

Although the labor movement's many attempts to control consumption have yielded a record of both success and failure, the lingering desire to instill a moral dimension in consumers' marketplace choices lingers on the horizon even today. The AFL-CIO continues to publish a list of union products and retailers and to support a widespread "Buy Union" and boycott campaign. Most recently, an antisweatshop movement has captured the attention of a small but vocal minority of college students and has brought new attention to the labor movement. Boycotts and union labels are, in effect, different sides of the same coin. Although one strategy urges consumers to withhold their money, the other encourages them to spend it. Either way, it is a contest over the very significant power of consumption.

Michelle Haberland

BIBLIOGRAPHY

Coyle, Laurie, Gail Hershatter, and Emily Honig. "Women at Farah: An Unfinished Story." In *A Needle, a Bobbin, a Strike: Women Needleworkers in America*, ed. Joan M. Jensen and Sue Davidson, pp. 227–277. Philadelphia: Temple University Press, 1984.

Dereshinsky, Ralph M., Alan D. Berkowitz, and Philip A. Miscimarra. *The NLRB and Secondary Boycotts*. Rev. ed. Labor Relations and Public Policy Series, no. 4. Philadelphia: Trustees of the University of Pennsylvania, 1985.

Ernst, Daniel R. "The Danbury Hatters' Case." In *Labor Law in America: Historical and Critical Essays*, ed. Christopher L. Tomlins and Andrew J. King, pp. 180–200. Baltimore, MD: Johns Hopkins University Press, 1992.

Ferris, Susan, and Ricardo Sandoval. *The Fight in the Fields: Cesar Chavez and the Farmworkers Movement*. New York: Harcourt Brace, 1997.

Forbath, William E. *Law and the Shaping of the American Labor Movement*. Cambridge, MA: Harvard University Press, 1991.

Frank, Dana. *Buy American: The Untold Story of Economic Nationalism*. Boston, MA: Beacon, 1999.

———. *Purchasing Power: Consumer Organizing, Gender, and the Seattle Labor Movement, 1919–1929*. New York: Cambridge University Press, 1994.

Glickman, Lawrence B., ed. *Consumer Society in American History: A Reader*. Ithaca, NY: Cornell University Press, 1999.

———. *A Living Wage: American Workers and the Making of Consumer Society*. Ithaca, NY: Cornell University Press, 1997.

Honig, Emily. "Women at Farah Revisited: Political Mobilization and Its Aftermath Among Chicana Workers in El Paso, Texas, 1972–1992." *Feminist Studies* 22:2 (Summer 1996): 425–452.

Jacobs, Meg. "Democracy's Third Estate: New Deal Politics and the Construction of a 'Consuming Public.'" *International Labor and Working-Class History* 55 (Spring 1999): 27–51.

Jenkins, Craig J. *The Politics of Insurgency: The Farm Worker Movement in the 1960s.* New York: Columbia University Press, 1985.

Majka, Linda C., and Theo J. Majka. *Farm Workers, Agribusiness, and the State.* Philadelphia: Temple University Press, 1982.

McCreesh, Carolyn Daniel. *Women in the Campaign to Organize Garment Workers, 1880–1917.* New York: Garland, 1985.

Rose, Margaret. "From the Fields to the Picket Line: Huelga Women and the Boycott, 1965–1975." *Labor History* 31:3 (Summer 1990): 271–293.

Sklar, Kathryn Kish. "The Consumers' White Label Campaign of the National Consumers' League, 1898–1918." In *Getting and Spending: European and American Consumer Societies in the Twentieth Century,* ed. Susan Strasser, Charles McGovern, and Matthias Judt, pp. 17–36. Cambridge, UK: Cambridge University Press, German Historical Institute, 1998.

Spedden, Ernest R. *The Trade Union Label.* Baltimore, MD: Johns Hopkins University Press, 1910.

Tyler, Gus. *Look for the Union Label: A History of the International Ladies' Garment Workers' Union.* Armonk, NY: M.E. Sharpe, 1995.

LABOR CULTURE

The American labor movement has been strengthened considerably by its multifaceted culture. Strike novels, industrial songs, union banners, picket-line chants, workplace narratives, union-sponsored films, labor plays, and working-class poetry are just a few of the art forms that have been used to promote union causes. Some labor art may not have attracted a wide audience; however, images of labor, workers, and unions in the arts continue to play an important role in the struggle for social change.

The earliest cultural images of the American worker offer an emphasis on the individual worker rather than the collective, organized laborer. In the early nineteenth century, depictions of work were often tied to the American work ethic and reflect rural, small-town society dominated by self-employed craftsmen, shopkeepers, professionals, or farmers. Positive images of the worker prevailed as the working class was celebrated as the builders of the nation in poems such as Walt Whitman's "A Song for Occupations" (1855) and Henry Wadsworth Longfellow's "The Village Blacksmith" (1841). Songs were also a popular genre for relating the exploits of heroic workers like Paul Bunyan, the Minnesota logger, Casey Jones, the engineer, and the steel-driving man, John Henry. The song remained a popular form as labor organizations grew in the postbellum period, frequently appearing in political or labor journals that were seeking to rally workers. Reese E. Lewis's "March of the Rolling-Mill Men" was published in the *National Labor Tribune* in 1875:

> Rouse, ye noble sons of Labor,
> And protect your country's honor
> Who with bone and brain and fibre
> Make the nation's wealth.
> Lusty lads, with souls of fire
> Gallant sons of noble sire,

> Lend your voice and raise your banner
> Battle for the right.

The use of music to promote the cause of labor would continue as activist songwriters put pen to paper to address issues of working conditions, fair wages, and employment security. A popular song of the 1870s was Felix O'Hare's "The Shoofly." The tune was written in response to the closing of a Pennsylvania coal mine and is just one of many union songs and legends compiled by George Korson. The genre probably reached its height in the early twentieth century with the Industrial Workers of the World (IWW). Described as the "singingest union" America ever had, the IWW would hand with every union card a copy of a book, *IWW Songs: To Fan the Flames of Discontent* (also known as the *Little Red Songbook*). The tunes in the *Songbook* were often parodies of well-known hymns and popular songs, and the music would ring out at union meetings, on the picket lines, and in jails. Some of the most popular selections, like "The Preacher and the Slave," "Casey Jones, the Union Scab," and "Pie in the Sky," were written by the nation's first well-known labor troubadour—Joe Hill (1879–1915). In the same year that Hill was executed in Utah on questionable murder charges, another IWW poet and artist, Ralph H. Chaplin (1887–1961), penned what has been considered labor's national anthem. "Solidarity Forever," which is sung to the melody of "The Battle Hymn of the Republic," can still be heard in union halls today:

> When the Union's inspiration through the workers'
>   blood shall run,
> There can be no power greater anywhere beneath
>   the sun.
> Yet what force on earth is weaker than the feeble
>   strength of one?
> But the union makes us strong.

Solidarity forever! Solidarity forever!
Solidarity forever! For the union makes us strong.

When the Great Depression prompted labor militancy, musicians like Woody Guthrie, Huddie Ledbetter (Leadbelly), and Aunt Molly Jackson were ready to continue the tradition established by Hill and Chaplin and give voice to the struggles of workers and the unemployed. Aunt Molly Jackson, while expressing the benefits of union representation, also injected a feminist perspective into the struggle in such songs as "I Am a Union Woman":

I am a union woman,
Just as brave as I can be,
I do not like the bosses,
And the bosses don't like me.
Join the CIO, come join the CIO.

Between 1941 and 1942, CIO organizing campaigns were also supported by the Almanac Singers, a group founded by Pete Seeger. Following World War II, People's Songs emerged—an informal group of folk musicians who worked to establish a library of protest songs, many of which could be used by trade unions. Songs that were traditionally utilized by unions played an important role in the protests of the 1960s. "We Shall Not Be Moved," an adapted spiritual that could be heard at civil rights protests and freedom marches in the turbulent decade, was first used in the 1920s by striking African-American textile workers in North Carolina. Similarly, "We Shall Overcome" was originally a Baptist hymn titled "I'll Be All Right" and was developed as a protest song by unionized tobacco workers in the 1940s. Labor has also been addressed by rock and roll artists who have used the guitar to explore their working-class backgrounds.

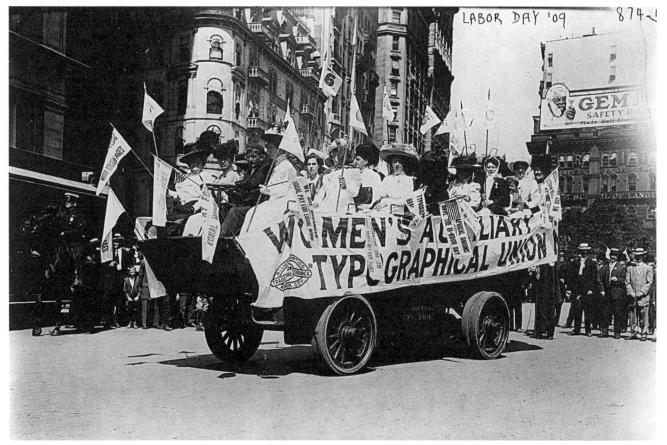

Members of the Women's Auxiliary Typographical Union proudly display their banners—along with the union label—in New York City on Labor Day, 1909. Since the early 1880s, workers have paraded in Labor Day celebrations to promote unity, build solidarity in the labor movement, and raise public awareness of their contributions to society. *(Library of Congress)*

WOODROW WILSON "WOODY" GUTHRIE (1912–1967)

Woody Guthrie was born on July 14, 1912, in Okemah, Oklahoma. He was the second-born son to Charles and Nora Guthrie. His father was a cowboy, land speculator, and local politician who constantly made and lost money and the family home in the oil booms. His Kansas-born mother profoundly influenced Woody by teaching him songs that he would later adapt. Guthrie learned harmonica as a boy and guitar as an adolescent. The death of his sister in a fire followed by the financial and physical ruin of the family and the institutionalization of his mother around 1923 devastated the young boy's family and home. These incidents helped give Guthrie a uniquely wry and rambling outlook on life. From the age of thirteen, he was an itinerant musician and laborer, and by age twenty-one he wound up in Texas, where he married and started a family.

Unable to find work, Guthrie took to the road during the Great Depression, singing for his meals, and wrote hundreds of songs that praised migrant workers, pacifists, and underdogs of all kinds. He headed west with other migrant workers to California in 1937, where Guthrie experienced the intense hatred and antagonism of resident Californians who were opposed to the influx of outsiders. His identification with outsider status would become a major part of his political and social positioning, one that gradually worked its way into his songwriting. It is especially evident in his Dust Bowl ballads such as "I Ain't Got No Home," "Goin' Down the Road Feelin' Bad," "Talking Dust Bowl Blues," "Tom Joad," and "Hard Travelin'."

Guthrie was always deeply involved in union and left-wing politics, and he wrote many of his over 1,000 published songs on themes of social injustice, poverty, and politics. In 1939, he moved cross-country to New York City, where he befriended such artists as Huddie Ledbetter, Pete Seeger, and Ramblin' Jack Elliott. Together they took up such social causes as union organizing, antifascism, and strengthening the Communist Party, all of which they supported through their political songs of protest. In 1940, folklorist Alan Lomax recorded Guthrie in a series of conversations and songs for the Library of Congress. Also during the 1940s, he recorded extensively for Moses Asch, founder of Folkways Records. The recordings from this period, which have been reissued under the Smithsonian Folkways label, have remained influential for young folk music singers/songwriters everywhere. He published his first novel, *Bound for Glory*, in 1943. A semiautobiographical account of his Dust Bowl years, *Bound for Glory*, generally received critical acclaim. His second marriage to Marjorie Mazia in 1946 produced four children, including son Arlo, who later followed his father into the music business as a singer-songwriter.

Guthrie's best-known songs are "So Long, It's Been Good to Know You" and "This Land Is Your Land," which is actually a Socialist anthem. He helped to form the Almanac Singers in the late 1940s, a group that advocated public power at workers' rallies. Some members of the group would later re-form as the Weavers, the most commercially successful and influential folk music group of the late 1940s and early 1950s. Guthrie's solo and group work exerted a strong influence on younger performers, notably Bob Dylan. In 1952, he was hospitalized with Huntington's chorea, and after fifteen years of suffering, Guthrie died on October 3, 1967. By that time a new generation, including Joan Baez and Dylan, had learned his songs and adopted his causes.

James G. Lewis

Key examples include Bruce Springsteen, who brings union imagery into such songs as "Youngstown" from the album *The Ghost of Tom Joad* (1995). Billy Joel hit the charts in the 1980s when he tackled the deindustrialization of America in the song "Allentown."

In comparison with labor songs, fiction was a less successful genre for promoting the cause of labor. Prior to the Civil War, prose writers did not totally ignore the factory system and working-class life. For example, the textile mills of Lowell, Massachusetts, are addressed in an early strike novel, Day Kellogg Lee's *Merrimack: or Life at the Loom*, and a hint of protest can be found in some of the selections in the *Lowell Offering* written by the young women who labored in the mills. In Elizabeth Turner's "Factory Girl's Reverie," published in the *Offering* in 1845, a sad sense of pastoral longing is offered by a young woman in a noisy factory:

> When the bell calls I must go: and must I always stay here, and spend my days within these pent-up walls, and this ceaseless din my only music?
>
> O that I were a *child* again, and could wander in my little flower garden, and cull its choicest blossoms,

and while away the hours in that bower, with cousin Rachel. But alas! that dear cousin has long since ceased to pluck the flowers, and they now bloom over her grave.

The novel, however, was not yet the venue for working-class themes since the form often dealt with matters of property and inheritance. Even as industrialization increased in the aftermath of the Civil War, full-scale industrial narratives failed to appear in great numbers. Rebecca Harding Davis set the American precedent for the subject in 1861 when her novella *Life in the Iron Mills* appeared in the *Atlantic Monthly*. Forty years would pass before the appearance of what many consider the next landmark novel of industrialization appeared—Upton Sinclair's *The Jungle* (1906). Within these perimeters, most novels that address factory life handle working-class themes in a subliterary, cursory fashion, reflecting the fact that professional novelists of the time often came out of the upper echelons of society and wrote with middle-class readers in mind.

Gradually, however, more authors would offer treatments of the conditions of the American working-class—Elizabeth Stuart Phelps, Edward Bellamy, Stephen Crane, Theodore Dreiser, Jack London, and Mary Wilkins Freeman. These novelists drew on the major labor struggles of the Gilded Age and Progressive Era to provide insight into the industrial scene and union activity. Works like Theresa Serber Malkiel's *The Diary of a Shirtwaist Striker* (1910), which richly documents the New York Shirtwaist Makers' Strike of 1909–1910, and Ernest Poole's *The Harbor* (1915), a highly successful novel that draws on the Chicago Stockyard Strike of 1904 and the Paterson Silk Strike of 1913 also offered insight into the gains made by the Socialist Party and the IWW during this period.

The Great Depression brought renewed interest in working-class issues and problems, and editors and publishers looked for works dealing with labor struggles. The period witnessed the rise of the worker-writer and the proletarian novel. Novels such as Mary Heaton Vorse's *Strike!* (1930), Grace Lumpkin's *To Make My Bread* (1932), Jack Conroy's *The Disinherited* (1933), John Steinbeck's *In Dubious Battle* (1936), and William Attaway's *Blood on the Forge* (1941) are just a few examples of the successful integration of labor themes into fiction.

In the genre of popular film, organized labor has not fared well. A majority of silent films were highly antilabor, often linking union members and strike leaders as agitators. Films like *Gus—the Anarchist*, *The Dynamiters*, *Murderous Anarchists*, and *Lazy Bill and the Strikers* depicted the strike as a worthless form of protest that only results in death, destruction, and lost jobs. Such films were often supported by employers' associations in their fight against unionization. In 1910, the American Federation of Labor (AFL) addressed the image of unions in films at their convention and passed a resolution encouraging members to protest at theatres where such movies were shown.

The labor union also pressed for the production of "moving pictures depicting the real life and ideology of the working class." Such films would be few in the subsequent decades as Hollywood filmmakers often failed to follow the lead of the proletarian novelist of the 1930s. The film version of John Steinbeck's *The Grapes of Wrath* (1940), for example, offers insight into the struggle of workers but minimizes the political message of the novel. Other noteworthy films provide a hint of the possibility of social progress through organized labor but also show the darker side of corrupt unionism. In *On the Waterfront* (1954), Terry Malloy (played by Marlon Brando) takes a stand against a corrupt, violent, dictatorial labor union; however, he continues to believe in the organization of workers—as long as it is not built on intimidation and fear.

Another film released the same year as *On the Waterfront* is considered one of the finest radical films ever made—*Salt of the Earth*. Director Herbert Biberman, writer Michael Wilson, and producer Paul Jarrico (who were all on Hollywood's blacklist) were inspired by a strike by mostly Mexican-American zinc miners at Silver City, New Mexico, and made the film with the cooperation of the International Union of Mine, Mill, and Smelter Workers. The Mine-Mill trade unionists in the film are portrayed as victims of police who are controlled by the company. An important theme of the film is also sexual repression as the strikers' wives play a pivotal role in the ultimate union victory. The filmmakers overcame a host of obstacles to complete the project—including intimidation from vigilante groups that opposed the production. The director used actual strikers for leading and supporting roles in the movie. Anti-Communists worked hard to suppress the film, and those who did opt to see the movie at the few sites it was shown were greeted by protesters and Federal Bureau of Investigation (FBI) agents. The film, of course, was a financial failure; however, it began to be shown in the late 1960s as interest in radical feature filmmaking intensified, and it now plays an important part in filmmaking classes as well as studies of the blacklist period.

In the decades that followed the production of

Salt of the Earth, pro-labor films would be rare. Director Martin Ritt addressed labor struggles from a working-class perspective in *The Molly Maguires* (1970) and *Norma Rae* (1979). Similarly, writer-director John Sayles tells the story of union organizing in West Virginia coal country in *Matewan* (1987). Sylvester Stallone played a teamster organizer in *F.I.S.T* (1978). *Hoffa* (1992), with Jack Nicholson in the title role, offers a less than positive portrait of union activity.

Labor issues have been more successfully addressed in the genre of documentary filmmaking. Union Films was formed following World War II and produced a series of films in cooperation with the CIO and United Electrical, Radio, and Machine Workers of America. In 1964, the Amalgamated Clothing Workers marked its fiftieth anniversary by producing a film, *The Inheritance*, a history of labor beginning in 1900. The 1970s can be considered a high point in labor documentaries. Barbara Kopple's *Harlan County USA*, dealing with a strike by Kentucky mine workers, captured an Academy Award in 1977. In addition, films like *Union Maids* (1977), *Eugene Debs and the American Movement* (1977), and *The Wobblies* (1979) captured labor's past through extensive use of archival photographs and film.

Theatre has also played a significant role in labor culture. A prime example occurred during the Paterson Silk Strike of 1913 when over 1,000 workers dramatized the labor struggle in the "Pageant of the Paterson Strike" at Madison Square Garden. The pageant successfully gave expression to the struggles of the strikers, but it failed to generate much-needed strike funds. Beginning in the 1920s, workers' education leaders and labor colleges recognized theatre's ability to instruct and inspire. Labor unions like the International Ladies' Garment Workers' Union and Local 65 of the United Wholesale and Warehouse Employees produced their own shows to "entertain" both workers and the public. Labor issues were also the focus of political theatre in the 1960s through 1980s: In Detroit, for example, Unstable Coffeehouse Productions produced *Sitdown '37* for an audience of United Auto Workers to mark the twenty-fifth anniversary of the sit-down strike that unionized General Motors. Emmanuel J. Fried, a former labor organizer with experience with Group Theatre in New York, turned to writing labor plays in the 1960s, including *The Dodo Bird* and *Drop Hammer*. Alternative theatres in most major U.S. cities performed these plays. More recently, two plays by John Schneider, *The Line*, dealing with a strike by Milwaukee area meatpackers, and *Out of the Darkness*, focused on a 1898 woodcutters strike in Oshkosh, were performed by Theatre X in Milwaukee.

Photography has also played a key role in raising awareness of American working conditions. Sweatshop and child labor conditions in New York were captured in the work by Jacob Riis, *How the Other Half Lives: Studies Among the Tenements of New York* (1890). Another example of a photographer who worked to capture working-class people was Lewis Hine, who produced inspiring pictures of workers in Pittsburgh as well as at the construction of the Empire State Building in New York. The 1930s were a particularly strong period for documentary photographs, with many photographers working on projects sponsored by federal agencies such as the Farm Security Administration. Excellent photographs of workers were also produced by members of the radical Film and Photo League, which completed a host of documentary projects during the Great Depression. A noted photographer of anthracite coal miners is George Harvan of Pennsylvania whose pictures have been widely displayed.

A number of organizations, including labor unions and historical societies, have recognized the ability of computer websites to preserve and promote the culture and history of the American labor movement. A large number of sites addressing labor arts is now available online, giving viewers the opportunity to tour labor art exhibitions. Collections include a wide range of buttons, badges, ribbons, cartoon art, murals, photography, songbooks, and sheet music. Some websites examine specific episodes in labor history such as the Haymarket Affair and the Triangle Shirtwaist Factory Fire. Web pages also include audio files of labor songs. Some sites also offer information on labor theatre groups, plays, labor festivals, and public arts projects.

Mark A. Noon

BIBLIOGRAPHY

Blake, Fay. *The Strike in the American Novel*. Metuchen, NJ: Scarecrow, 1972.

Bromell, Nicholas. *By the Sweat of the Brow: Literature and Labor in Antebellum America*. Chicago: University of Chicago Press, 1993.

Denning, Michael. *The Cultural Front: The Laboring of American Culture in the Twentieth Century*. New York: Verso, 1990.

Dietrich, Julia. *The Old Left in History and Literature*. New York: Twayne, 1996.

Enstad, Nan. *Ladies of Labor, Girls of Adventure: Working Women, Popular Culture, and Labor Politics at the Turn of the Twentieth Century.* New York: Columbia University Press, 1999.

Foner, Philip. *American Labor Songs of the Nineteenth Century.* Urbana: University of Illinois Press, 1975.

Gutman, Herbert. *Work, Culture, and Society in Industrializing America: Essays in American Working-Class and Social History.* New York: Knopf, 1976.

Harris, Jonathan. *Federal Art and National Culture: The Politics of Identity in New Deal America.* New York: Cambridge University Press, 1995.

Hyman, Colette. *Staging Strikes: Workers' Theatre and the American Labor Movement.* Philadelphia: Temple University Press, 1997.

Reuss, Richard. *American Folk Music and Left-Wing Politics.* Lanham, MD: Scarecrow, 2000.

Rideout, Walter. *The Radical Novel in the United States, 1900–1954.* Cambridge, MA: Harvard University Press, 1965.

Rosenzweig, Roy. *Eight Hours for What We Will: Workers & Leisure in an Industrial City.* New York: Cambridge University Press, 1983.

Ross, Steven. *Working-Class Hollywood: Silent Film and the Shaping of Class in America.* Princeton, NJ: Princeton University Press, 1999.

Sloan, David. "The Image of Labor in American Literature and the Arts: The Conflict Between Nineteenth-Century Individualism and Twentieth-Collective Action." *Essays in Arts and Sciences* 12: 2 (1983): 49–69.

Stead, Peter. *Film and the Working Class: The Feature Film in British and American Society.* New York: Routledge, 1989.

Trachtenberg, Alan. *The Incorporation of America: Culture and Society in the Gilded Age.* New York: Hill and Wang, 1982.

Walsh, Francis. "The Films We Never Saw: American Movies View Organized Labor." *Labor History* 27:4 (1986): 564–580.

Zaniello, Tom. *Working Stiffs, Union Maids, Reds and Riffraff: An Organized Guide to Films about Labor.* Ithaca, NY: Cornell University Press, 1996.

5

NATIVE AMERICAN MOVEMENT

INTRODUCTION

Most people have come to accept the theory that there were contacts with the so-called New World before 1492. There is evidence of contact with peoples from the South Pacific, North Pacific, Africa, the Mediterranean, as well as other European countries. Recently, some have speculated that China had been a source of exchange. And many are familiar with Leif Eriksson, the Norse explorer who sailed west from Greenland and visited parts of Newfoundland and Nova Scotia. Yet many still choose to date the North American experience from 1492 as if there was nothing—or no one—in this region before the explorer Christopher Columbus came and "discovered" this landmass and claimed it for the Spanish crown.

When Columbus came upon these shores, the first thing he did was rename the islands that he encountered, even when he knew the name given to that place by those who lived there. Of course, in that process of naming was the process of taking possession of the islands—and the native peoples—who lived on them.

While taking possession of the islands and the peoples of the Caribbean, Columbus wrote about the indigenous peoples whom he had encountered: they had no religion, they could not speak, and they were naked (and without shame). He stated that, because of their ignorance of steel weapons, with a hundred men he could conquer them all. It was not long before the Spaniards were doing just that: raping, kidnapping, and pillaging the indigenous communities they encountered.

The Europeans who arrived in North America acted as they did because they had the might to do so, possessing the military technology they needed to impose their will. Moreover, the Europeans believed they had a mandate from God to alter the cultures that they encountered. Thus, armed with steel weapons, the Bible, and an unswerving sense of self-righteousness, the early colonizing Europeans set in place a monumental apparatus of social engineering.

At the very beginning of this massive undertaking, which occurred in the time immediately following Columbus's discovery, the debate in Europe was over whether or not the beings that were encountered in the Americas were actually humans. If they were human beings, then Christian charity demanded that they be treated with respect; conversely, if they were something other than human beings worthy of God's charity, they could be forced under the yolk of European dominance—for the Bible gave man "dominion" over the beasts of the earth. This belief led to a debate in Europe over whether or not the indigenous peoples of the Americas were "naturally inferior" and therefore "naturally" fit for slavery and exploitation by their Spanish "superiors."

One side of the debate argued that the native peoples of the Americas should be treated with respect and Christian charity; the opposing view was that they were fair game for extermination if they refused the "civilizing" influence of the Spanish. Both sides defended the right of the Spanish to convert the peoples of the Western Hemisphere to Christianity and lead them to a more "civilized" life. Unfortunately, the end result of this social debate had little practical effect on colonial depredations. Indeed, in what is today Central America and Mexico, anywhere from 90 to 95 percent of the native population was lost either through disease, maltreatment, suicide, or outright genocide in the century following first contact.

But one should not assume that the native peoples of the Western Hemisphere were defenseless in the face of these depredations. For example, because the Caribbean islanders were in no position to match Columbus militarily, their immediate resistance consisted of what can only be called a rather sophisticated wild goose chase whereby one community would simply tell the Spanish that they were misinformed—the gold they sought was really not on this island, but if they left and went to some other distant island they were sure to find lots of gold *there*. By reading Columbus's journal of his first trip, you can readily see that this "resistance" was very effective, with Columbus racing from one island to another in search of gold that turned out to be more illusory than real.

Resistance to the Spanish followed them to the mainland as well, as the Aztecs fought a six-month war against Cortez and his native allies. Here the resistance was broken, not so much by the force of arms as by the incredible destruction wrought on the residents of Tenochtitlan, the Aztec capital, by a smallpox epidemic that ravaged the city. In what is now the United States, the Spanish northward advance suffered a serious blow in 1680 when the Pueblo, under their leader Popé, led a resistance that drove the Spanish from their territory. In large part, the Pueblo "revolt" was a response to the Spanish imposition of Christian ritual throughout their "Empire" in the Western Hemisphere.

Of course, many native peoples were reluctant to give up their way of life and the religions of their culture, and realized that the underlying message most often was either to convert or be killed. Thus, the Europeans' religious proselytizing throughout the Western Hemisphere became the biggest experiment in social engineering that the world has ever seen.

Although much of this discussion is focused on the Spanish, other colonizing powers behaved similarly, with one notable North American exception: the French. Early on, the French adopted a more benign attitude toward the native peoples they interacted with, treating them more as equals than as slaves. As a result, the French often intermarried with the indigenous population and adapted themselves to a more thoroughly indigenous lifestyle. In fact, the French/Native American mixing gave rise to an entirely new and unique cultural group called the Métis, whom the Canadian constitution recognizes as "Aboriginal people." Although the French came to dominate this cultural grouping, many Métis arose out of other (non-French) European/Native American mixtures.

After the defeat of the French in 1760, the British sought to impose many restrictions on the native peoples of North America. This led many to resist the new British overlords. One of the most notable and successful of these efforts to reverse the imposition of British cultural values was "Pontiac's Rebellion" in 1763. With the aid of many warriors, Pontiac enlisted the support of Neolin, a Delaware prophet, who called for a return to traditional ways as far removed from the influence of Europeans as was possible. For example, Pontiac and Neolin allowed for the continued use of European firearms in order to reverse the advances of the British.

Following the same principle as Neolin, we see the prophets Tenskwatawa (brother of Tecumseh), Handsome Lake, Wovoka, Smohalla, and many others, all preaching for a return to more traditional ways. These leaders all saw the revitalization of traditional life as a way to preserve their culture and heritage and represented one of the most resilient forms of social resistance to European efforts to "civilize" the native peoples wherever they were encountered. The one constant (as mentioned earlier) that Native Americans resisted was the demand by Europeans that they give up their "pagan" religions and adopt some form of Christianity, all in the name of "civilization." Often, this religious proselytizing came with the additional demands for monogamous marriage, private land ownership, and a settled way of life based on farming (which, of course, meant an abandonment of the hunt).

Indigenous "social movements" should all be examined through a lens of resistance; Native Americans were never passive actors whenever Europeans attempted to impose imperial hegemony over them. Native peoples all over the world have vigorously resisted those who would impose Western culture upon them, while defending their way of life with that same vigor. As the essays in this section unfold, we will see just how deep-seated the resistance to this European compulsion to assimilate the indigenous peoples of the world has been. Quite possibly, this culture clash—the attempts by the Europeans to "civilize" all they meet and the resistance to these attempts—will prove to be *the* dominant "social movement" that has occurred since the late 1400s.

Phil Bellfy

NATIVE AMERICAN MOVEMENT
COLONIAL ERA—1800S

After the first English settlers landed at Jamestown in the seventeenth century, they and other colonists who followed were preoccupied with "civilizing" the indigenous population. In the century that followed, the English, following the example set by the Spanish, assumed the responsibility of reform by imposing Christianity and Western values in an attempt to create a race of "red Christian farmers." After the Revolutionary War, some reformers argued that citizenship in the new nation was an additional requirement for civilization. During the course of these various reform movements, resistance by the native peoples varied. Some Native Americans adopted European lifeways, others rejected them outright, and still others synthesized parts of those lifeways into their own cultures. As a consequence, the lifeways of native peoples in the United States have been severely altered since European contact.

When English colonists referred to efforts to "civilize" natives, they usually meant Christianizing them as well, for most Europeans believed that Christianity was a prerequisite for civilization. Consequently, most of the colonies relied on missionaries to spread the Gospel to the native peoples and bring them into the fold of European society. In the beginning, these missionaries were Puritans (now called Congregationalists), Presbyterians, and Anglicans, though Quakers and Moravians sent out their own missionaries to natives in the eighteenth century. In 1631, John Eliot, a Puritan minister called the Apostle to the Indians, began to found "praying towns" for Native Americans in Massachusetts, arguing that newly converted natives should live separately in godly communities to keep them from falling under the influence of their pagan brothers and sisters. The outbreak of King Philip's War in 1675 effectively ended Eliot's efforts. In 1754, Eleazar Wheelock, an itinerant New England preacher, founded the Moor's Charity School, a coeducational institution that emphasized manual labor

as an integral part of native students' instruction and conversion.

For the most part, Eliot, Wheelock, and other missionaries did not believe that native peoples had any religion at all. It is not surprising, then, that some groups chose to ignore the missionaries entirely. As colonization continued, it became harder for natives to stay free from contact with whites, whether through trade, displacement, or war, and native groups began adopting some of the material and intellectual aspects of the white lifestyle, although they still generally resisted religious conversion. Elite members of Native American communities, along with some "mixed-bloods" who were the children of native and white parents, had more contact with colonists and were most receptive to missionaries' conversion efforts.

Using similar religious themes, many of the prophetic movements associated with native wars during the late eighteenth and early nineteenth centuries were actually movements to reform native cultures from within, although these reforms were designed to undo the missionaries' efforts. Pontiac, an Ottawa Indian chief who allied with the French to drive out British colonists squatting on lands belonging to the Ottawa tribe in 1763, acted in accordance with the religious practice preached by the Delaware prophet Neolin. Neolin argued that native peoples were losing their lands and succumbing to alcoholism and disease because they had forsaken the ancient ways given them by the Great Spirit. Only through reforming their lives could Native Americans regain what they had lost. Although most of what Neolin preached grew out of indigenous spiritual traditions, he included the Christian notions of heaven, hell, and a punishing deity in an apparent attempt to appeal to those already under the influence of Christian ideology.

Immediately after the Revolution, the newly

Unita Bailey keeps a lookout over Ute territory in the Wasatch Mountains, 1873. *(Western History Collections, University of Oklahoma)*

formed U.S. government signed a series of treaties with native groups who ceded vast amounts of land to the government in order to feed the land-hunger of colonists. Because many of those treaties had been negotiated with Native Americans who had no authority to do so, some native groups went to war to reclaim their lands. Ironically, some of the leaders of these groups were the same mixed-bloods and elites who were educated by missionaries. For example, Alexander McGillivray, a mixed-blood Creek political leader educated in Charleston, South Carolina, encouraged his people to keep fighting after the Revolution when Georgia expanded onto Creek lands.

In order to end this series of costly frontier wars, Henry Knox, secretary of war under George Washington, suggested that the government return to the British colonial practice of purchasing rather than conquering Native Americans' lands. This tenet was made firm in the Northwest Ordinance of 1787, and it, along with the policy of providing for the "civilization" of native groups in treaties, formed the basis of the U.S. government's Indian policy for many

years. For example, in exchange for land cessions, the 1790 treaty with the Creek gave the tribe the animals and tools it needed to become settled agriculturalists. This treaty was also the first to state that a native group was under the "protection" of the government, essentially making Native Americans wards of the state.

This wardship policy expanded under the presidency of Thomas Jefferson. Jefferson and his officials believed that with changes in their environment and proper education, Native Americans could assimilate with whites, become productive citizens, and be convinced to give up tribal lands that, as republican farmers, they no longer needed. Thus, the Jeffersonian presidency saw attempts to reform Native Americans through legislation. The end result of these reforms would not just be civilized native peoples but more land for white settlers. The legislative reforms therefore proved very difficult to force upon the native peoples since the government still assumed that whites should advance at their expense.

These reforms also led to a new round of missionary activity among native peoples. Congregationalists, Presbyterians, Methodists, and Baptists all ministered to various native groups, establishing schools and preaching their own versions of Christianity. Native Americans, as was their reaction previously, did not always respond favorably. Not surprisingly, indigenous revitalization movements emerged in some of the tribes of the Old Northwest under tremendous pressure by settlers. One of the most notable movements was that of the Seneca prophet Handsome Lake, who preached a message of purification and resistance to white influence similar to that of Neolin. His movement also selectively accommodated some white influences, encouraging the adoption of white methods of farming, for example, so that the Seneca could survive in an increasingly white-dominated area.

Other groups, especially those in the Southeast, seemed to at least outwardly accept the "civilization" program imposed by the dominant society. By concentrating their efforts among the elite and mixed-blood members of these groups, missionaries were able to "convert" a significant number of the Cherokee, Choctaw, Chickasaw, Creek, and Seminole to the Christian cause. In fact, they were so successful that these Southeast tribes became known as the "Five Civilized Tribes." In an odd twist of irony, the Cherokee, who were considered the most acculturated of these groups, took the ideology of civilization to its next logical step and adopted their own national constitution in 1827. The document and its assertion that the Cherokee alone had sovereignty over their lands alarmed the Georgia state government, which then extended its own legislative authority over the Cherokee in an attempt to keep the tribe's land open to white settlement.

Consequently, the Cherokee action stood in stark contrast to Georgia law and the federal policy of encouraging land cession to facilitate white expansion. The result of this clash was the passage of the Indian Removal Act, signed into law in 1830 by President Andrew Jackson. The Act provided for the removal of the Five Civilized Tribes from their land in the Southeast to Indian Territory, which encompassed parts of the present states of Arkansas and Kansas and all of Oklahoma.

The debate over the provisions of the Removal Act pitted reformer against reformer and native against native. Many abolitionists, including Lydia Maria Child and Wendell Phillips, spoke out strongly against removal. Congregationalist missionaries Samuel A. Worcester and Elizur Butler went to prison for their efforts to show solidarity with their indigenous constituents. In Native American communities, those who still followed traditional ways staunchly opposed giving up their ancestral lands, while many of the mixed-blood converts came to understand the danger inherent in armed resistance and became advocates of removal. Consequently, removal had proponents and opponents in white and in Native American communities.

The main humanitarian argument espoused by pro-removal reformers was that it would take native peoples away from the influence of "bad" whites who had a tendency to get natives drunk in order to rob them blind. Missionary Isaac McCoy thought of removal as a chance to establish an ideal native Christian community in the West. Some mixed-blood natives, such as Cherokees John Ridge and Elias Boudinot, favored removal because of increasing harassment from local residents and state governments in the Southeast. The removal arguments won the day, and in 1836 the Cherokee were the first to undertake the forced march west along the Trail of Tears. Other tribes east of the Mississippi, from south to north, were also removed.

After removal, the government, still believing that eventually Native Americans would assimilate into the mainstream, continued to funnel aid money through missionary organizations. This government aid was essential to the Native Americans' own survival; consequently, many native tribes reluctantly allowed missionaries to establish religious and educational institutions in their territories. At the same time, they often openly resisted the proselytizing reforms that were an integral part of missionary efforts.

As white settlement spread across the continent in the period between removal and the Civil War, government officials became more interested in finding a permanent solution to the perennial "Indian problem." By the 1850s, commissioners of Indian Affairs such as Luke Lea and George Manypenny were advocating fixed homes for native peoples in the Far West along the lines of a reservation system. The reservation system was presented as a way to protect natives from the ever-present problem of squatters and "bad" whites.

In the two and a half centuries following the arrival of English colonists, the ultimate goal of reformers remained the same: the "civilization" of the indigenous peoples through Christianity and education. After the Revolution, reformers added citizenship in the form of republican land ownership as the third requirement for civilization. The civilization project, however, was always subordinate to white settlers' desire for land. The degree to which native peoples adopted white ways also depended on both the press of white settlement and the ability of the natives to fight it off. Adoption of civilization, however, did not mean that native peoples would likewise subordinate their interests to those of whites. In this way, white reformers' efforts were always doomed to failure.

Rebecca McNulty

BIBLIOGRAPHY

Cave, Alfred A. "The Delaware Prophet Neolin: A Reappraisal." *Ethnohistory* 46:2 (Spring 1999): 256–290.

Prucha, Francis Paul. *The Great Father: The United States Government and the American Indians.* Abridged ed. Lincoln: University of Nebraska Press, 1986.

Ronda, James P. " 'We Are Well as We Are': An Indian Critique of Seventeenth-Century Christian Missions." *William and Mary Quarterly* 34:1 (January 1977): 66–82.

Szasz, Margaret Connell. *Indian Education in the American Colonies, 1607–1783.* Albuquerque: University of New Mexico Press, 1988.

Wallace, Anthony F.C. *The Death and Rebirth of the Seneca.* New York: Alfred Knopf, 1970.

———. *The Long Bitter Trail: Andrew Jackson and the Indians.* New York: Hill and Wang, 1993.

NATIVE AMERICAN MOVEMENT
WORLD WAR I TO THE INDIAN NEW DEAL

After 1890, with the "settling" of the American frontier, the last of the Native American resisters were sent to prison and the remaining natives were confined to reservations. No longer able to hunt freely and without access to riverbeds, Native Americans witnessed the disintegration of the economic basis of tribal life and became increasingly dependent on the federal government for their subsistence. In the 1880s, reformers were convinced that to solve the "Indian problem," Native Americans must assimilate into the greater society as individual property owners, farmers, laborers, and, above all, English-speaking Christians. Communal lands were broken up, children were sent away to Indian boarding schools, and traditional gender roles were severely threatened. From the Progressive Era to the New Deal era in the mid-1930s, reformers and policymakers continued their efforts to "civilize" Native Americans. During President Franklin D. Roosevelt's administration, federal Indian policy took a drastic turn. Allotment ended, and the segregated boarding schools were closed as revitalization of Indian rights and lands began under the "Indian New Deal."

AMERICANIZATION AND ALLOTMENT

Reformers and policymakers from several fronts attacked tribal life. Native cultures were suppressed through legislation and policy forbidding religious ceremonies, dancing, and group feasting. "Americanization" efforts were applied uniformly to all native peoples, with complete disregard for differences in lifestyles and living environments. "Friends of the Indian" advocated dismantling the reservations as the best way to push Native Americans into the modern world where they would learn habits of thrift and industry. In 1887, Congress passed the General Allotment Act, sponsored by Senator Henry Dawes (R-MA), to abolish reservations and allot land to individual American Indians as private property. This new policy terminated communal ownership of land, pushed the native peoples into mainstream society, with the underlying assumption that they wanted and had the capacity to be farmers.

Reservations were surveyed, and tribal rolls were prepared prior to allotment. Those who refused to come in and be listed on the rolls did not receive allotments. Supposedly, listed tribal members were allowed to select their own allotments (160 acres to heads of families, 80 acres to unmarried adults and orphans), but often reservation agents made the selections for them. "Surplus" lands were then sold to anxious settlers and investors, creating a "checkerboard" effect on reservations. Allottees who proved themselves to be "civilized" farmers were to be granted citizenship at the end of a twenty-five-year period, during which time the federal government held title to the land.

Protections provided these native allottees were steadily eroded. In 1902, Congress allowed heirs to sell inherited land without approval from the secretary of interior. In 1906, the Burke Act declared that those American Indians whom the secretary of interior deemed "competent" to manage their own affairs could be granted land patents in fee simple without waiting out the twenty-five-year trust period to sell their allotments. Nationwide competency commissions were especially devastating, easily subject to fraud and manipulation.

On the White Earth reservation in Minnesota, powerful lumber interests bought up timber-rich allotments for a fraction of their value. Senator Moses A. Clapp (R-MN) attached a rider to the annual Indian appropriations bill, which automatically deemed "competent" any "mixed-blood" adult. According to Melissa Meyer in *The White Earth Tragedy: Ethnicity and Dispossession at a Minnesota Anishinaabe Reservation, 1889–1920* (1994), the Clapp rider "brought grief" to White Earth. Speculators hired witnesses to "subscribe to affidavits that the Indian in question had white blood in his veins and in many cases the white blood ran through the branches of the family for many generations to some remote Canadian Frenchman." At White Earth and other allotted reservations, as resources and lands dwindled, social and political conflicts arose. Until allotment officially ended in 1934, over 90 million acres—two-thirds of the Native Americans' land base—were lost.

ASSIMILATION THROUGH EDUCATION

In addition to breaking up the communal land base through allotment, reformers and policymakers also attacked the family unit by putting children in Indian boarding schools. It was believed that by "civilizing" the children while turning adults into Christian farmers and housewives, the goal of assimilation would be met within a generation. The following excerpt from an *Atlantic Monthly* article entitled, "How Shall the American Savage Be Civilized?" aptly describes society's attitude. "The kind of education they are in need of is one that will habituate them to the customs and advantages of a civilized life . . . and at the same time cause them to look with repugnance on their native state."

First attributed to Captain Richard Henry Pratt, founder of the Carlisle Indian School in Carlisle, Pennsylvania, the phrase, "kill the Indian and save the man," came to represent the philosophy behind the assimilationist movement. Between 1879 and 1902, the federal government opened twenty-five boarding schools for Native American children. Pratt's model of education differed from the existing modes of educating native children in reservation day schools and reservation boarding schools. Children were forbidden to speak their native languages and were immersed into the daily routines of academics combined with training in husbandry and domestic skills. With shortly cropped hair, boys were dressed in military-style uniforms, while girls were forced to wear tight, Victorian-style dresses.

Many students quickly excelled in other areas of the early boarding school curricula such as athletic competitions and debate. The Carlisle bands frequently toured the country. Select students regularly accompanied Pratt to Washington, D.C., where their academic and handcraft achievements were showcased. Although many children were very homesick as well as physically ill from the change in diet and climate, their new common language created the base for the first modern Pan-Indian movement that arose in the second decade of the twentieth century. "Re-turned students" were usually anomalies on their reservations, often serving as interpreters. Many did take up farming, but the majority worked for the Indian Bureau and became teachers and clerks. The plan for complete assimilation within a generation proved to be a failure.

"RED PROGRESSIVES" AND CITIZENSHIP

The circle of college-educated Native Americans in the early twentieth century was small. Several first-generation Indian boarding school students and other educated natives became part of the first modern Pan-Indian movement. In 1911, the Society of American Indians (SAI) was founded. Executive board members were all Native Americans, including Arthur C. Parker (Seneca anthropologist), physicians Charles Eastman (Santee Sioux) and Carlos Montezuma (Yavapai Apache), Angel DeCora (Winnebago), and Arapaho minister, Sherman Coolidge, to name a few. Many of the members' paths crossed through Carlisle at some point in their lives either as students, teachers, or staff members. While leadership was restricted to Native Americans, the bulk of the associate membership was made up of noteworthy reformers, such as Richard Henry Pratt and Fayette McKenzie. McKenzie, professor of sociology at Ohio State University, was instrumental in bringing the group together, providing the initial forums for their meetings.

SAI members were proponents of tribal values as well as advocates of complete assimilation. Their common cause was social progress and a better image for Native Americans across the country. The SAI published the *American Indian Magazine*, a quarterly journal that featured editorials, reports of Indian policy, literature, historical essays, and self-publicity. The SAI represented the first instances of an intellectual, activist movement. Native intellectuals came together for a specific project, to promote their race.

In 1916, the SAI declared "American Indian Day" to be a national holiday. The handbook published for the national event included guidelines for the "second Friday in May for schools, Saturday for field day, and Sunday for Religious Exercises." American Indian Day was endorsed by the Commissioner of Education, governors, historical societies, and patriotic societies.

The Society of American Indians campaigned vigorously for citizenship for Native Americans. They supported the United States in World War I, encouraging enlistment of native men in the armed forces and Red Cross activities for native women. Eventually, disagreements within the leadership over peyote usage on reservations and the degree of involvement of the Indian Bureau caused factionalism that split the group apart in the early 1920s.

NATIVE AMERICANS IN WORLD WAR I

At a time when few Native Americans held citizenship status, the majority of natives supported the war effort as Americans. Native American men began enlisting in the army a full year before the United States officially entered the war on April 6, 1917. The federal government initiated a nationwide draft registration for Native American males in June 1917. Protests arose on a number of reservations, especially where American Indians were not "citizen Indians," such as the Navajo in Arizona and the Goshutes in Utah. The draft proved unnecessary however, for over 12,000 Native American men enlisted in the U.S. armed forces during the Great War, with 1,000 of them serving in the U.S. Navy. These figures represented approximately 25 percent of the adult male Native American population.

Reformer and expedition photographer Joseph Dixon along with Secretary of the Interior Franklin Lane were proponents of all-native units within the army. They prompted several congressional bills calling for the creation of special American Indian regiments. The Society of American Indians, the Indian Rights Association, and the Commissioner of Indian Affairs, Cato Sells, took stands against segregating native soldiers. Despite the policy of integrating native American men within white regiments, the army inadvertently established a few all-native units.

Although Native American soldiers filled a variety of positions within the army, the majority of men served in infantry combat units in Europe. Their legendary reputation as natural "fighters," combined with popular stereotypes of "instinctive" soldiers, caused hundreds of native soldiers to be assigned as scouts, messengers, and snipers on the front lines. As the war progressed, U.S. military officials began using Native American soldiers to transmit telephone messages in their native languages in attempts to confuse German code breakers. This set an important precedent for the now-famous Navajo "code-talkers" of World War II. Many Native American soldiers won medals for meritorious service and received commendations from their commanders. Native soldiers and those at home hoped the United States would bestow full citizenship upon them as reward for their loyalty. Congress, however, approved application for citizenship only to returning veterans.

Citizenship for Native Americans proved to be a double-edged sword. The U.S. Supreme Court ruled in *United States v. Nice* (1916) that American Indian citizenship was not incompatible with continued federal guardianship. Thus, according to Thomas Britten in *American Indians in World War I: At Home and at War* (1997), "the government could maintain many of its regulations over Indian life." This is exactly what happened with the "competency commissions" set up by Commissioner of Indian Affairs Cato Sells in 1917. Land titles, with patents in fee simple, were issued whether or not native allottees applied for them. Native Americans, unskilled in land transactions and business deals, soon lost their lands and their monies. To Sells and like-minded reformers, this meant reduced appropriations by the government and more independence for native peoples. So while Native Americans were participating wholeheartedly in the war effort, both as soldiers and as home-front supporters, the administration was taking care of its "Indian problem."

WAR EFFORTS ON THE HOME FRONT

Native Americans at home also made significant contributions to the war effort. Native women were among the most important participants in Red Cross activities and fundraising events. Women knitted socks and mufflers, sewed hospital garments, and packaged comfort kits to support American soldiers. Native American women readily embraced these activities as an extension of traditional female roles supporting their warriors in battle. An estimated 10,000 home-front natives joined the Red Cross during World War I. Native American ranchers donated cattle and sheep, while Native American farmers participated in the "Great Plowup," a national campaign to grow more food for the war effort and put more land into agricultural production.

The national media gave much attention to the Native Americans' purchase of Liberty Bonds and war stamps. Numerous articles appeared in *American Indian Magazine*, the quarterly journal of the Society of American Indians, and Indian School publications entitled "Indians Work for Victory Loans" and "Indians Are Aiding Uncle Sam Win War." Cherokee Chief White Elk sold $1.8 million in Liberty Bonds in one week of speaking engagements, as reported in the *New York Times* article, "How Indian Chief Helped Uncle Sam" (January 26, 1919). Secretary Lane took advantage of Native Americans' participation in the war and their purchase of Liberty Bonds. Tribal funds, held in trust by the government, as well as soldiers' paychecks (signed by reservation agents), were being used to buy Liberty Bonds. When the time came to redeem the funds, in what Thomas Britten calls "classic Indian bureau paternalism," Secretary Lane frequently denied requests because he feared natives would "make poor use of the money" or because "they did not really need [it]." Thus, while Native Americans were "competent" enough to die for their country, sacrifice life savings, and labor for the war effort they were still treated as wards of the federal government.

REFORM EFFORTS IN THE 1920S

In 1921, Secretary of Interior Albert Fall issued a series of potentially damaging and malevolent proposals. The former senator from New Mexico was well-known as being hostile to Native American rights. The 1922 Bursom Bill, in short, proposed to buy out the federal responsibilities of Pueblo Indians in New Mexico using the tribes' own monies. This and other ruthless proposals affecting Apache allotment, as well as oil and gas leasing, caused heightened concern for Native American affairs, not only within well-established reform groups such as the Indian Rights Association (IRA), but also within a national civic umbrella organization, the General Federation of Women's Clubs (GFWC). These groups worked together in the field on the national level, involved with land issues in New Mexico in 1922 and the Oklahoma Indian guardianship scandals in 1924.

The GFWC sponsored research agents in the early 1920s, who in turn, founded Native American reform organizations of their own. Former social worker John Collier, a GFWC research agent in New Mexico, founded the American Indian Defense Association (AIDA) in 1923. The AIDA was a reform group of non-natives, with several "Red Progressives" on its advisory board. One of these was former SAI member Gertrude Bonnin, who was instrumental in the formation of the GFWC's National Indian Welfare Committee in 1921 and also served as GFWC research agent in Oklahoma in 1923–1924. The AIDA and the IRA also participated in the investigation concerning the Five Civilized Tribes and Osage Indians in Oklahoma. The subsequent report was titled *Oklahoma's Poor Rich Indians: An Orgy of Graft and Exploitation of the Five Civilized Tribes—Legalized Robbery* (1924). Because Bonnin was a native woman, she was able to elicit the stories of not only fraud victims, but also those who feared for their lives—stories that would not be shared with white, male investigators. Bonnin wrote, "[t]he smothered cries of the Indian for rescue from legalized plunder came in a chorus from

all parts of eastern Oklahoma." The report, which included exposure of the circumstances surrounding the murder by poison of a young Choctaw girl, Ledcie Stechi, among other atrocities, prompted a full Senate investigation.

Bonnin, along with her husband Captain Raymond T. Bonnin, went on to form the National Council of American Indians (NCAI) in 1926. The council, with its exclusively Native American membership, disbanded in 1938 shortly after Gertrude's death in 1938. The NCAI's mission was to ensure that the reservations be kept up to date on legislative matters concerning native affairs. Whenever the standing Senate and House Committees on Indian affairs were in session, Gertrude was present, listening for her native brethren. She transcribed, typed, and mimeographed periodic newsletters, which she financed with stipends from speaking engagements. These newsletters were always signed, "yours for the Indian cause."

Reform in the 1920s continued with the inauguration of the first national advisory board on Indian affairs in 1923 and the passage of the Indian Citizenship Act in 1924, which allowed American Indians who were not yet citizens to vote in national elections. The Committee of One Hundred, formed by Commissioner of Indian Affairs Hubert Work in 1923, was a select group of prominent citizens, including celebrities, activists, ministers, and anthropologists. Former SAI members, Henry Roe Cloud, Thomas Sloan, Charles Eastman, and Arthur C. Parker, were among the Native American members. Reformers still firmly believed that individual property ownership and Christian-based lifestyles and education were the answer to the "Indian problem." In the 1920s, however, reform efforts began to concentrate on the actual conditions under which native peoples lived and sought some major effort by the federal government to improve the situation. Several reports were written during the 1920s that focused on health, education, and substandard quality of daily life. The most famous report was *The Problem of Indian Administration* (1928), undertaken and published by the Brookings Institution. Commonly known as the Meriam Report, the information contained in over 500 pages finally woke people up to the deplorable living conditions of Native Americans.

Another native-led organization, the Indian Defense League of America (IDLA), had very specific goals, working to ensure border-crossing rights. Former U.S. Army veteran of the Spanish-American War, Clinton Rickard, Tuscarora chief and activist, was opposed to the Citizenship Act because it excluded Canadian Indians, who had been traveling back and forth across the Canadian-U.S. border all their lives. He founded the Indian Defense League of America (IDLA) in 1926. Rickard and the League lobbied long and hard for border-crossing rights, often traveling to Washington, D.C., to testify before committees at his own expense. Rickard demanded that the Jay Treaty of 1794 and the 1812 Treaty of Ghent, both of which guaranteed border-crossing rights for Canadian and American Indians, be upheld. These rights were achieved on April 2, 1928, when President Calvin Coolidge signed House Resolution 11351 into law. Although considered a "traditional" Native American, Rickard chose to work within the existing federal system on this and other issues affecting Six Nations Indians.

THE INDIAN NEW DEAL

Until 1934, native tribes were rarely consulted on the legislation introduced for their supposed benefit. Commissioner of Indian Affairs John Collier, appointed by President Roosevelt in 1933, was the first Indian commissioner who seemed to listen to Native Americans. The Indian Reorganization Act (IRA), also known as the Wheeler-Howard Act, is one of the most important of any piece of legislation enacted in the twentieth century. Largely the brainchild of Commissioner Collier, the IRA provided, for those 181 tribes that adopted it, an end to the devastating allotment policy and an opportunity to interact within the federal system as native entities. A complete new way of thinking, resulting in legislation that became known as the "Indian New Deal," is reflected in John Collier's own words. In *Indians of the Americas: The Long Hope* (1947), he wrote, "This task of the guardian government, to make free the people who are its dependencies, demands not only sincerity of disinterested purpose but also deep knowledge of what those peoples are, and of the material environment within which they [live]."

Few can deny the positives of cultural regeneration for Native Americans and native land reform. On the other hand, the adoption of constitutionally based governments, which was a provision of the IRA, fractionalized many tribes. Seventy-eight tribes rejected the switch from consensus rule to majority rule. Historian Colin Calloway, in *First Peoples: A Documentary Survey of American Indian History* (1999), wrote, "Indian traditionalists felt strongly against the imposition of rigid and alien political and economic systems on [their] communities." In some regards, the "Indian New Deal" was not new, but merely another pater-

nalistic attempt by non-natives to do what they regarded as the "right thing" for Native Americans. John Collier's twelve-year tenure as commissioner of Indian affairs did chart a new direction in federal Indian policy, but its blueprint for reform, which mandated one policy for all native peoples, offered little recognition of the tremendous diversity within Indian America.

CONCLUSION

As the survival and practice of native traditions and ceremonies attest, attempts at "cultural genocide" and religious oppression were, at best, only partially successful. Although tribal life was disrupted for a few decades during the allotment and boarding school eras, the resilience of native cultures and spirit is evident in today's world. As reform efforts shifted from the focus of "civilization" and assimilation during the Progressive Era to cultural renewal during the Indian New Deal, policymakers were still doing what they thought was best for Native Americans. It would be several more decades before self-determination was realized by the native peoples and the federal government began to reassess the ward to guardian relationship.

Susan Dominguez

BIBLIOGRAPHY

Adams, David Wallace. *Education for Extinction: American Indians and the Boarding School Experience, 1875–1928*. Lawrence: University of Kansas Press, 1995.

Bonnin, Gertrude, Charles H. Fabens, and Matthew K. Sniffen. *Oklahoma's Poor Rich Indians: An Orgy of Graft and Exploitation of the Five Civilized Tribes—Legalized Robbery*. Philadelphia: Office of the Indian Rights Association, 1924.

Britten, Thomas. *American Indians in World War I: At Home and at War*. Albuquerque: University of New Mexico Press, 1997.

Brookings Institution, Institute for Government Research. *The Problem of Indian Administration*. Report of a Survey Made at the Request of Honorable Hubert Work, Secretary of the Interior, and Submitted to Him, February 21, 1928. Baltimore, MD: The Johns Hopkins Press, 1928.

Calloway, Colin G. *First Peoples: A Documentary Survey of American Indian History*. Boston: Bedford/St. Martin's, 1999.

Collier, John. *Indians of the Americas: The Long Hope*. New York: Mentor Books, 1947.

Deloria, Vine, Jr., and Clifford M. Lytle. *American Indians, American Justice*. Austin: University of Texas Press, 1983.

———. *The Nations Within: The Past and Future of American Indian Sovereignty*. Austin: University of Texas Press, 1984.

Hertzberg, Hazel W. *The Search for an Indian Identity*. Syracuse, NY: Syracuse University Press, 1971.

"How Indian Chief Helped Uncle Sam." *The New York Times*, January 26, 1919.

Hoxie, Frederick E. *A Final Promise: The Campaign to Assimilate the Indians, 1880–1920.* Lincoln: University of Nebraska Press, 1984.

Meyer, Melissa L. *The White Earth Tragedy: Ethnicity and Dispossession at a Minnesota Anishinaabe Reservation, 1889–1920.* Lincoln: University of Nebraska Press, 1994.

Nabakov, Peter, ed. *Native American Testimony: A Chronicle of Indian-White Relations from Prophecy to the Present, 1492–2000.* New York: Penguin Books, 1991.

Nielsen, Nancy J. *American Indian Lives: Reformers and Activists.* New York: Facts on File, 1997.

Nies, Judith. *Native American History: A Chronology of a Culture's Vast Achievements and Their Links to World Events.* New York: Ballantine Books, 1996.

Society of American Indians. *American Indian Day: A New Sort of American Day.* Washington, DC: SAI, 1916.

Wison, George. "How Shall the American Indian Be Civilized?" *Atlantic Monthly*, November 1882, 604.

RISE AND REPRESSION OF THE AMERICAN INDIAN MOVEMENT

In both communities, African-American and American Indian, the civil rights effort produced powerful youth components. Among blacks, the Student Nonviolent Coordinating Committee (SNCC) was most prominent. For Native Americans, it was the National Indian Youth Council (NIYC), a group arising from the so-called Chicago Conference organized at the University of Chicago by Cherokee anthropologist Robert K. Thomas during the summer of 1961. Whereas SNCC harnessed its energies to desegregation campaigns and voter registration drives in the Deep South, NIYC devoted itself to the struggles of the Muckleshoot, Puyallup, Nisqually, and other peoples indigenous to the Pacific Northwest to (re)assert their treaty-guaranteed fishing rights.

In June of 1965, Stokely Carmichael, at the time head of SNCC, announced that the organization was shifting its emphasis from a traditional civil rights agenda to the pursuit of "Black Power." At about the same time, he indicated that SNCC, which had suffered severe repression in the course of its activities in the southern states, was abandoning its philosophical commitment to the ideals of nonviolence. Instead, he advocated the principle of "armed self-defense" practiced by the Louisiana-based Deacons for Defense and Justice and by National Association for the Advancement of Colored People (NAACP) leader Robert Williams in Monroe, South Carolina, during the early years of the decade. Never one to engage in idle chatter, Carmichael immediately set about applying his ideas in Lowndes County, Alabama, reputedly one of the most violently racist locales in the entire South. Within months, he'd succeeded in organizing an area previously believed impossible to approach.

Carmichael's Lowndes County Freedom Organization, as he called it, employed the picture of a black panther as its logo. During the spring of 1966, the image was adopted by a pair of Merritt College students, Huey P. Newton and Bobby Seale, while found-

ing what was originally called the Black Panther Party for Self-Defense in Oakland, California. Built around a ten-point program aimed at securing self-sufficiency and self-determination for North America's "black colony," and the idea that anyone is entitled to meet force with force in defending these rights, the party shortly emerged as the most dynamic black radical organization in the United States, its membership swelling from about a dozen at the outset to more than 5,000 arranged in some forty local chapters just two years later (another 125,000 African Americans indicated "active support" to Gallup pollsters in late 1968). By 1969, Federal Bureau of Investigation (FBI) Director J. Edgar Hoover was describing the Panthers as the most serious of all threats to the stability of America's white supremacist status quo.

The spectacular growth of the Black Panther Party—the "for Self-Defense" phrase was deleted from its name in 1967—heralded a shift in the locus of Black Power politics from the rural South to the urban North, as well as a decisive turn away from Afroamerica's traditional embrace of pacifism as a viable political strategy. At a popular level, this was eloquently symbolized in a series of inner-city revolts marking the "long hot summers" of 1965–1968. In more self-consciously political circles, the same trend was signified by the temporary absorption of SNCC by the Panthers in 1968, and the replacement of the word "Nonviolent" with the word "National" in SNCC's name by H. Rap Brown, Carmichael's successor as the organization's chair, a year later. At another level still, the public resonance achieved by the Panthers signaled a transition from the ideology of Black Power to one demanding the outright liberation of Afroamerica. The latter is most evident in the names of several other African-American organizations making their appearance in the late 1960s and early 1970s: the Revolutionary Action Movement (RAM), for example, as well as the Republic of New Afrika (RNA) and the Black Liberation Army (BLA).

Corollaries to Stokely Carmichael's Black Power pronouncement in 1965 were being made by Cherokee anthropologist Robert K. Thomas and NIYC head Clyde Warrior, among others, throughout the period. It was not until 1969, however, that National Congress of American Indians (NCAI) director Vine Deloria Jr.'s bestselling "Indian Manifesto," *Custer Died for Your Sins,* put the concept of "Red Power" on the popular radar screen. Fortuitously, the book's release coincided with the seizure of an abandoned federal prison on Alcatraz Island, in San Francisco Bay, by a group calling itself Indians of All Tribes (IAT). Although native people had been pursuing an increasingly confrontational style of politics for some years (e.g., in connection with the fishing rights struggle in Washington State, and with regard to treaty rights in upstate New York), it was the protracted takeover of Alcatraz initiated at decade's end that finally captured substantial public attention.

The momentum was sustained into 1970 by the continued occupation of Alcatraz as well as the release of Deloria's *We Talk, You Listen: New Tribes, New Turf* and Dee Brown's wildly successful "Indian History of the American West," *Bury My Heart at Wounded Knee.* Brown's tract neatly reversed the time-honored polarity of Indians as bad guys/whites as heroes. Hollywood also weighed in with a pair of "revisionist westerns"—Arthur Penn's *Little Big Man* and Ralph Nelson's *Soldier Blue,* which, though intended as analogies to U.S. comportment in the Vietnam War, did much to confirm the accuracy of Brown's historical interpretations in the public mind. Then, in September, a group calling itself the American Indian Movement (AIM) occupied the ground atop George Washington's head at the Mount Rushmore National Monument in South Dakota's Black Hills.

THE AMERICAN INDIAN MOVEMENT

AIM was founded in Minneapolis during the fall of 1968 by a group of Anishinabe, including Dennis Banks, Mary Jane Wilson, George Mitchell, and Pat Ballanger. Modeled after the Black Panther Party—the Panthers sported black berets, whereas AIM wore red—the new organization gained credibility in its home community in precisely the same manner as the Newton/Seale group had: mounting street patrols to "police the police," who had long and savagely abused the nonwhite residents of America's teeming urban ghettos. Later, AIM would also emulate aspects of the Panthers' broader program, including the es-

In a rally in Rapid City, South Dakota, a demonstrator raises his fist in support of maintaining the territorial integrity of the Black Hills. *(AP Wide World Photos)*

tablishment of alternative schools, a multimedia news service, legal and health clinics, food give-aways, a housing initiative, and job placement services. Like the Panthers, AIM would eventually, and with limited success, field candidates in local, state, and national elections.

During the occupation of Alcatraz, however, AIM was mostly looking to follow the Panthers' example by extending its reach beyond the Minneapolis/St.

DENNIS BANKS (1932–)

Dennis Banks was born on April 12, 1932, in Leech Lake, Minnesota, as a member of the Anishinabe tribe. Educated in Bureau of Indian Affairs boarding schools, he cofounded, with George Mitchell, the American Indian Movement (AIM) in 1968. Its original purpose was to help Indians in urban ghettos who had been displaced by government programs that effectively forced them from the reservations. Its goals eventually encompassed the entire spectrum of Indian demands—economic independence, revitalization of traditional culture, protection of legal rights, and, most especially, autonomy over tribal areas and the restoration of lands that they believed had been illegally seized.

The movement was involved in the occupation of Alcatraz Island in 1969, as Banks attempted to force the federal government to honor all of the treaties that had been made and subsequently broken with the many American Indian tribes. AIM held Alcatraz for nineteen months. In the early 1970s, Banks became increasingly confrontational after years of frustrations that yielded little action. His 1972 Trail of Broken Treaties March on Washington, and the subsequent occupation of the Bureau of Indian Affairs building for six days, was a precursor to the events that would rock the nation less than a year later.

Under Banks's leadership in 1973, AIM took up arms in resistance. On the Pine Ridge Indian Reservation in South Dakota, AIM took control of Wounded Knee for seventy-one days. The occupation provided an outlet for AIM to publicize its goals of tribal sovereignty and self-determination. Later on that year, after a settlement had been reached, Banks again appeared in Custer, South Dakota, as American Indians held a protest after a jury acquitted a white man convicted of murdering an Indian.

After the protest, Banks was arrested, along with 300 of his fellow protesters. While he was found innocent of charges at Wounded Knee, his involvement at Custer landed him a jail sentence. Refusing to serve time, Banks fled to the underground until then-California governor Jerry Brown granted him asylum the following year. He returned to South Dakota in 1984 to serve eighteen months in prison for his roles in American Indian protests. He was appointed the first American Indian chancellor at Deganawidah-Quetzalcoatl University in 1980, a two-year college in California dedicated to providing alternative ideas and methods of education to Native American people. He has organized several cross-country runs originating from the campus designed to raise awareness of Native American issues. In the 1990s, he remained active in Native American politics but remained out of the national spotlight. During the first half of 1994, Banks organized a five-month Walk for Justice across the United States on behalf of imprisoned native activist Leonard Peltier. He also appeared in a handful of movies in the 1990s, including *The Last of the Mohicans* in 1992.

James G. Lewis

Paul area. Dennis Banks was therefore openly recruiting from the moment he first visited the island in December 1969. His major coup in this respect was his success in bringing into the fold IAT's oratorically gifted spokesperson, a young Santee named John Trudell (now an acclaimed poet) who went on to fulfill the same function for AIM from 1970 to 1979. Also signed up was Russell Means, a reservation-born but urban-raised Oglala Lakota imbued with what many saw as a strong ability to garner the attention of the media. It was Means who conceived of and led the Mount Rushmore occupation during the fall of 1970, as well as a sequel carried out the following June. It was Means, too, who organized AIM's seizure of the *Mayflower* replica anchored at Plymouth, Massachusetts, on Thanksgiving Day, 1971; the ship itself was briefly used as a podium from which a list of Indian grievances was delivered, while Plymouth Rock was painted red.

Simultaneously, other AIM members were busily engineering a series of confrontations and Alcatraz-style occupations designed to attain more concrete goals. The 1971 takeover of unused military facilities at Fort Lawton, near Seattle, for instance, ultimately resulted in the construction, on the site, of an American Indian cultural center. Confrontations in Oklahoma and Minnesota precipitated Indian control over schools in both states. Another confrontation in Denver led to improved healthcare for native people in that city. Under these circumstances, AIM chapters began to sprout up all over North America; by late 1972, the unofficial count was forty-three in the United States and another half-dozen in Canada; a year after that, AIM could boast solid alliances with the Crusade for Justice, a Denver-based radical Chicano organization headed by Rodolfo "Corky" Gonzales, the Los Angeles–based Brown Berets and Chicano Moratorium, Jesse Jackson's Operation Push in Chi-

Cofounder of the American Indian Movement, Dennis Banks pursued increasingly confrontational tactics in the 1970s in support of tribal sovereignty and self-determination. *(AP Wide World Photos)*

cago, the Puerto Rican Young Lords Party in New York, and the remnants of the Black Panther Party in Oakland.

This promising "Rainbow Coalition"—the term was coined by Fred Hampton, a Panther leader assassinated by the Chicago police in 1969—also included a hefty Euroamerican constituency, both through the involvement of organizations like Venceremos and Vietnam Veterans Against the War (VVAW), and through Cherokee activist Jimmie Durham's organization of a continentwide galaxy of mostly white Native American Support Committees (NASCs). A genuine international dimension was also added by a relationship with the All-African People's Revolutionary Party (A-APRP), headed by Stokely Carmichael, who by this point was a citizen of Guinea and was known as Kwame Turé.

For all its other successes, however, it was in the small town of Gordon, Nebraska, just south of the Pine Ridge Reservation in western South Dakota, that AIM truly consolidated its reputation among native people as an organization that could get things done.

There, one Saturday night in January 1972, a pair of local toughs, Melvin and Leslie Hare, tortured and murdered a middle-aged Oglala named Raymond Yellow Thunder. When local authorities refused to act—as was routine in those days—the victim's family appealed to AIM for help. Russell Means thereupon assembled a caravan of more than a thousand Indians to go to Gordon. At a rally in the town square, he announced that AIM had come to "put Gordon on the map," and, he concluded, "if these two guys aren't charged with murder within 72 hours, we're coming back to take this place *off* the map." In short order, the Hare brothers became the first whites in the history of Nebraska to be prosecuted, convicted, and imprisoned for killing an Indian.

AIM's unprecedented victory in the Yellow Thunder case attracted hundreds of new members, as well as the respect of traditionalists everywhere. The traditionalists in particular had begun to view the movement as a modern warriors' society, dedicated to defending the people's interests regardless of personal risk. For the younger people who flocked to AIM's banner, the movement's aggressively confrontational style of politics, which released Indians from a lifelong sense of disempowerment, was often reason enough to join. Soon, deliberately ostentatious displays of "Indianness"—braids, ribbon shirts, chokers, and the like—had joined bumper-stickers reading "Indian and Proud" as standard fashion statements wherever native people gathered. The "shame of being born into oppression" had definitely been cast off in Indian country.

Among those who had openly embraced AIM by 1972 was Leonard Crow Dog, a staunch Brûlé Lakota traditionalist from the Rosebud Reservation, adjoining Pine Ridge. In reciprocation, the movement anointed him its spiritual leader, with many members participating in his annual Sun Dance, conducted in early August. During an informal meeting convened after completion of the ceremonies that year, it was agreed that AIM had arrived at a point where it might "carry the struggle forward into a new phase." The best way of accomplishing this, it was decided, would be to organize delegations from as many peoples as possible to converge on Washington, D.C., on the eve of the U.S. presidential election, upcoming in November.

The strategy underlying what immediately became known as the "Trail of Broken Treaties" was to use the timing of the event to force Richard M. Nixon—the presidential incumbent, all but certain to win reelection—to publicly acknowledge a range of defects in the country's relations with American In-

On July 30, 1973, members of the American Indian Movement (AIM) gather in a show of solidarity at the Tulsa International Airport, en route to a convention at White Oak, Oklahoma. The emergence of AIM in the 1970s signaled a growing militancy among American Indians. *(AP Wide World Photos)*

dians. From there, it was reasoned that Nixon would have little alternative but to promise correction of the government's long-standing pattern of violating treaties with Indians, usurping their governments, and expropriating their lands and resources. As a result of this treatment, native people had been left by far the most impoverished of any population group reflected in the U.S. census. (Annual per capita income on Pine Ridge was barely $1,200 in 1972, for instance, while unemployment hovered at about 90 percent and male life expectancy averaged only 44.6 years.) "Trail" participants would thus be ideally positioned to submit a twenty-point program through which Nixon could accomplish the desired result during his second term.

Arrangements were made with federal authorities for the planned demonstrations to be conducted in an orderly manner, but officials reneged at the last moment. Permission was even refused for ceremonies to be held at the grave of the hero Ira Hays at Arlington National Cemetery. A Pima, Hays was one of the Marines who had raised the flag on Iwo Jima during World War II. When promised food and housing support also failed to materialize, several hundred infuriated protesters stormed the Bureau of Indian Affairs (BIA) headquarters in the government sector of the Capitol, renaming it the "Native American Embassy," conducting regular press conferences on its steps, and refusing to leave until Nixon personally agreed to a point-by-point response to the twenty-point program they'd come to present.

Faced with the nightly spectacle of Russell Means appearing as a "noble savage" on the 6 o'clock news, the president not only consented but provided more than $66,000 of his own campaign funds to buy airplane tickets so that those in the BIA building could leave in a hurry. The occupiers then withdrew, taking with them a huge quantity of the Indian Bureau's most confidential paperwork in the process. Over the next several months, the files were copied, the originals returned to the BIA, and duplicates distributed to the various peoples whose assets and affairs they concerned. In some cases, analysis of these papers took years, but among the many revelations they contained, they uncovered the existence of an involuntary sterilization program secretly administered by the BIA's Indian Health Service (IHS). It has been estimated that about 40 percent of all native women of childbearing age were subjected to such treatment between 1970 and 1975. This disclosure caused the IHS to be relocated from the BIA to the Department of Health, Education and Welfare (now the Department of Health and Human Services) in 1976.

The papers also revealed all manner of duplicitous leasing practices and the like with respect to the minerals and other assets "managed in trust" by the BIA under an authority deriving from the "plenary power" over Indians asserted by the United States in 1903. On average, Indians were receiving through BIA-negotiated leases only about 10 percent of the royalties they would have received had they been allowed to sell their resources on the open market. Armed for the first time with the details of how they had been officially defrauded, many of the victimized peoples were eventually able to force changes in the way their lands and other resources were being administered. AIM's forced disclosures also revealed irregularities with regard to the disposition of rents, mineral royalties, and other revenues impounded by the BIA under pre-1972 interpretations of its trust authority and thereafter "lost." At present, an estimated $40 billion or more may have been involved in this "prima facie pattern of official theft."

The Nixon administration, of course, was nonetheless outraged by what had been done, comparing it to Daniel Ellsberg's leaking of the top-secret "Pentagon Papers" to the New York Times in 1971. As a result, a smear campaign was launched to discredit the movement and, by extension, whatever information it might seek to convey. Sensational stories quickly surfaced in the press claiming, falsely, that

AIM "vandals" had done more physical damage to the Capitol than anyone since the British had sacked the city during the War of 1812. Figureheads from the federally funded National Tribal Chairman's Association were also flown in to denounce Banks, Means and other AIM leaders as irresponsible and independent revolutionaries with no constituency among Indians. Meanwhile, the FBI was instructed to target AIM and to politically neutralize the organization.

WOUNDED KNEE

For their part, most AIM members returned home triumphant, or tried to do so. On Pine Ridge, Russell Means, despite the fact that he was enrolled and owned land there, found himself barred from the reservation by thugs working for the recently installed tribal president, Dick Wilson. Apparently intent upon establishing a "feudal barony" on Pine Ridge and willing to sign away a large and mineral-rich tract of reservation land in exchange for being allowed to do so, Wilson had been provided with federal funds to create a paramilitary entity calling itself first the Tribal Rangers and later the Guardians of the Oglala Nation (GOONs). Heavily overlapping with the local BIA police, the GOONs were employed in an effort to terrorize Wilson's opponents, mostly local AIM supporters, into submission. In response, the opposition organized itself as the Oglala Sioux Civil Rights Organization (OSCRO), headed by Pedro Bissonette, and set about impeaching him.

It was against this backdrop that Dennis Banks issued a call in January 1973 for AIM members to come to Rapid City to undertake a major civil rights campaign in western South Dakota. Barely had they begun to arrive in significant numbers when the news broke that a young Oglala named John Wesley Bad Heart Bull had been stabbed to death in the tiny adjacent town of Buffalo Gap. When, as in the Yellow Thunder case a year earlier, local authorities made no effort to bring appropriate charges against the killer, a non-Indian named Darold Schmidtz, the victim's mother requested assistance from the movement. However, when the resulting AIM contingent arrived in Custer, the county seat where charges against Schmidtz would have to be filed, things were much different than they had been in Gordon the year before.

For starters, an anonymous caller had caused the Rapid City Journal to print an announcement that morning, February 6, that the demonstration had been canceled because of bad weather. Hence, only about 200 Indians turned out to participate. They were met by a combined force of local, county, and state police tactical units, overseen by FBI observers. In the ensuing mêlée, the Custer County Courthouse and the local chamber of commerce building were set ablaze. Most of the Indians, including Means, Banks, and Bad Heart Bull's mother, Sarah, were arrested on charges of riot and arson. The trials would last for years, resulting in convictions of virtually everyone accused. Sarah Bad Heart Bull was sentenced to serve a year in jail, while her son's killer never spent a day behind bars.

AIM had barely managed to bail the last of its members out of jail when word came that the impeachment effort against Wilson on nearby Pine Ridge had been thwarted. Although OSCRO had managed to obtain more signatures calling for his removal from office than had voted for Wilson in the first place, the BIA had placed him in charge of his own impeachment proceedings. A sixty-man Special Operations Group (SOG) of U.S. marshals—essentially a large SWAT unit—had been posted to the reservation to back him up. A day before the impeachment hearing was scheduled to occur, Wilson had instructed his BIA police *cum* GOON units to arrest all tribal council members likely to vote against him and hold them in jail until the proceeding was over. Afterward, he held a press conference at which he proclaimed a reservation-wide ban on political meetings of any sort "until further notice."

Stymied in their efforts to resolve their grievances by conventional due process remedies, the elders comprising the traditional Oglala leadership called upon AIM to intervene. Hence, on February 26, it was decided to convene a press conference the following morning at a symbolic site—the mass grave containing the remains of some 350 Lakotas massacred by the U.S. Army at Wounded Knee Creek in 1890—to expose what was happening on Pine Ridge. That evening, an advance party of about 150 AIM members entered the tiny reservation hamlet to prepare for the event, while a smaller group began to notify the media. At dawn, however, those inside Wounded Knee realized that, overnight, Wilson's GOONs had set up roadblocks on every road by which the press could enter the hamlet, simultaneously sealing the AIM people in. Shortly thereafter, SOG personnel began setting up reinforcing positions. Then, FBI men began to arrive. By the end of the day on February 27, a pair of "consultants"—special warfare experts, actually—had been dispatched to the scene by General Alexander Haig, Richard Nixon's military affairs adviser.

Thus began the seventy-one-day Siege of Wounded Knee, 1973. Initially unprepared for either an armed confrontation or a protracted occupation under South Dakota's severe winter conditions, the surrounded AIM contingent quickly equipped itself with weapons and ammunition from a local trading post and began to jerry-rig defensive emplacements—"bunkers," as they were called—at key points around the "Wounded Knee Perimeter." The expertise provided by several combat veterans among the besieged AIM members was shortly augmented by that of a seven-member, all-white countersniper team sent in as a gesture of solidarity by VVAW. (They stayed for the duration and were naturalized as Oglala citizens by traditional Lakota headman Frank Fools Crow.) A system was also worked out for area supporters to keep those inside Wounded Knee supplied, using the cover of darkness to backpack food and clothing, as well as additional arms and ammunition, through the federal siege lines.

The federal forces also geared up very rapidly. By March 7, nearly 300 marshals and over a hundred FBI agents had been deployed on Pine Ridge. Also on hand were about 250 BIA police officers, most of them SWAT team members imported from other reservations. Wilson's GOONs added another 150 or more, with non-Indian vigilante groups contributing an approximately equal number. State and local police departments in a five-state area surrounding South Dakota were placed on continuous alert to intercept persons suspected of heading for Wounded Knee. (Some 1,200 persons were arrested over a two-month period.) General Haig's on-site consultants, Colonels Volney Warner and Jack Potter, arranged for the provision of equipment ranging from armored personnel carriers (APCs) to M-79 grenade launchers out of restricted military inventories. An elite "rapid deployment force" was pre-positioned at Fort Carson, Colorado, in case an airborne assault of the hamlet was deemed necessary, while planes from Strategic Air Command's Ellsworth Air Force Base, just outside Rapid City, conducted continuous aerial reconnaissance.

Altogether, during the course of the siege, a half-million rounds of military ammunition were fired into the Wounded Knee perimeter, killing two Indians (an Apache, Frank Clearwater, and an Oglala, Buddy Lamont), and wounding numerous others. More flares were used to illuminate the perimeter at night than were expended by all U.S. forces in Vietnam during any year of the war. When this failed to staunch the flow of supplies, authorities resorted to burning off the grass for a half-mile in all directions. Wilson's

In efforts to reach a truce during the bloody siege at Wounded Knee, South Dakota, in 1973, a leader of the American Indian Movement hands a peace pipe to Kent Frizzell (right), assistant United States attorney general. To the left of Frizzell are Wallace Black Elk (kneeling), Russell Means, Dennis Banks (wearing a headband), and Carter Camp (wearing a vest). They are meeting in a teepee. *(AP Wide World Photos)*

GOONs are believed to have murdered as many as thirteen people captured while attempting to slip into the siege zone. In the end, however, even these draconian measures proved fruitless, and the confrontation ended only when federal officials agreed to conduct a full-scale investigation of the Wilson regime and to meet with traditional Oglala leaders concerning U.S. violations of the 1868 Fort Laramie Treaty, which legally defined U.S./Lakota relations.

To be sure, the authorities promptly sandbagged the ceasefire agreement, but AIM's purpose in going to Wounded Knee had been accomplished. By the time the siege ended on May 7, 1973, the situation on Pine Ridge—and conditions in Indian country more generally—had riveted international attention for more than two months. In barely a year, AIM would translate this media attention into establishment of its "diplomatic arm," the International Indian Treaty Council (IITC), directed by NASC's Jimmie Durham

and charged with putting the question of indigenous rights before the United Nations. By 1977, IITC would be the world's first Native organization to have attained formal consultative status with the United Nations. In addition, Durham had been instrumental in organizing the so-called Indian Summer in Geneva, a conference that led, in 1982, to establishment of the United Nations Working Group on Indigenous Populations (a subdivision of the UN Economic and Social Council, ECOSOC). The working group itself was charged with providing a regular forum in which violations of native rights could be reported and with drafting a Universal Declaration of Rights of Indigenous Peoples for adoption by the General Assembly. The latter was completed in 1998 and is currently in the process of presubmission review.

In May of 1973, however, all of this lay long in the future. AIM's immediate task was to survive the 185 indictments of its members following in the wake of Wounded Knee. On this front, Russell Means alone had been charged with thirty-seven felonies and three misdemeanors, and was facing a potential combined sentence of "triple life, plus 199 years," as he put it. Banks and others were in little better shape. The bail set in most instances was extravagant, especially considering that many of the accused were among the poorest people in the country: the amount set to obtain Pedro Bissonette's release was $152,000, for example; that for Means, $150,000; a $35,000 bond was required even to free the medicine man, Leonard Crow Dog. Scores of people languished in jail for weeks, sometimes months, before the funds could be raised to get them out.

THE AIM TRIALS

The first to go to trial were Means and Banks, beginning in February 1974; they were charged with everything from criminal conspiracy and kidnapping to car theft and assaulting federal officers. For this one case, the prosecutors pulled out all the stops in an effort to win convictions; they even used the testimony of an "eyewitness" who had actually been in California when the event in South Dakota had occurred. After an eight-and-a-half month proceeding, however, the judge dismissed all charges with prejudice, observing that "the waters of justice have been polluted" by the introduction of the false witness and other extreme government misconduct. Worse than that, shortly thereafter, it was learned that the FBI had maintained an infiltrator in the defense team throughout the trial.

By the end of 1974, the government had prosecuted forty Wounded Knee cases, obtaining only five minor convictions. Late in the fall, the Wounded Knee Legal Defense/Offense Committee (WKLDOC; pronounced "Wickle-Doc"), an AIM legal defense apparatus created by attorneys Ken Tilson and Beverly Axelrod during the siege, mounted a challenge to the assertion of U.S. jurisdiction over the remainder of the accused as a violation of the 1868 Treaty. In January 1975, Judge Warren Urbom handed down a decision stating to the effect that, while this challenge would once have been true, the United States had so long and so regularly violated the treaty that its legal force had been eroded. On this novel basis, the way was cleared for the trials to continue. At that point, the Justice Department, apparently embarrassed by adverse publicity concerning the meager 7 percent conviction rate it was achieving in return for the expenditure of millions in taxpayer dollars, seems to have decided that the charade had for the most part

served its intended purpose. Fifty pending cases were thereupon dismissed.

The remaining twenty "leadership trials" dragged on for another year, however, with the major government "victory" coming in June 1975, when Crow Dog, Oklahoma AIM leader Carter Camp, and Stan Holder, a Wichita combat vet who had served as head of security at Wounded Knee, were convicted of interfering with a group of marshals who had attempted to enter the AIM perimeter on March 11, 1973, disguised as "postal inspectors." All told, after more than sixty trials involving nearly three times that many defendants and literally hundreds of charges put to juries, federal prosecutors could boast of only fifteen guilty verdicts, and none of them for substantial offenses, setting an all-time record low. As it turned out, officials did not seriously expect to obtain better results. Instead, they had pursued a neutralization strategy perfected by the FBI in a 1967 campaign against RAM, making arrests on every possible pretext until the targeted activists were hopelessly mired in judicial proceedings, their organization bankrupted by the demands of bail and legal defense.

Nor did the government's legal offensive end when the Wounded Knee trials had run their course; it simply became more selective. Russell Means, for instance, was confronted with one charge after another for several years and was even tried for murder in 1976, despite the fact that his alleged victim, an Oglala named Martin Montileaux, repeatedly stated before dying that Means had *not* been among his assailants. Although every case ended with his acquittal, the sheer tediousness of it all eventually exhausted Means' patience. His and other AIM members' refusal to rise upon entry of the judge presiding over Sarah Bad Heart Bull's 1974 trial on charges stemming from the Custer Courthouse confrontation led to an all-out courtroom brawl and to Means' only felony conviction a year later. Found guilty of violating a riot clause in an ancient and never-before-used South Dakota antisyndicalism statute, he was sentenced to four years imprisonment (since the law was repealed while Means was in prison, he will forever be the only person thus convicted).

Dennis Banks was convicted of the Custer charges in July 1975 and, facing a fifteen-year sentence, skipped bail, becoming a fugitive. A year later, California governor Jerry Brown, a Democrat, granted him sanctuary in that state, citing a statement by South Dakota attorney general William Janklow that "the way to deal with AIM leaders is to put a bullet between their eyes" as evidence that Banks's life would be in danger were he to return to Janklow's jurisdiction. (Janklow had also campaigned for his position on a pledge to "put the AIM leaders either in jail or under it.") In 1982, upon the election of Brown's republican successor, George Deukmejian, Banks again went underground, surfacing a few weeks later under another sanctuary arrangement on the Onondaga Reservation in upstate New York. It was not until September 1984, when satisfactory assurances of his safety were made by Janklow (who had been elected governor in the interim), did Banks finally surrender. Sentenced to two concurrent three-year sentences; he served thirteen months.

Meanwhile, in November 1975, during his first stint as a fugitive, Banks, along with his wife, Kamook, and AIM members Kenny Loud Hawk and Russell Redner, were charged with federal explosives and firearms violations. The case was dismissed in 1976 for lack of evidence but was reinstated by the Ninth Circuit Court in March 1980. In 1983, the case was again dismissed, this time on grounds that the government had violated the defendants' right to a speedy trial. But in January 1986, the U.S. Supreme Court again reinstated the charges. In July 1986, the case was again thrown out by an angry district court judge, Andrew Redden, because of "additional due process violations" by federal prosecutors. The Justice Department was seeking reinstatement yet again, when, in late 1988, a weary Dennis Banks accepted a bargain wherein he entered a pro forma guilty plea in exchange for a suspended sentence and the dropping of charges against his codefendants.

Still another exceptionally sordid case concerned Los Angeles AIM members Paul "Skyhorse" Durant and Richard "Mohawk" Billings, accused in 1974 of the ugly torture/murder of a cab driver named George Aird. Although the police arrested the likely culprits within hours of the slaying, and the district attorney's office was preparing charges against them, the FBI apparently convinced them to immunize the accused as state's witnesses and to charge Skyhorse and Mohawk instead. Pretrial maneuvering dragged on interminably, amidst a barrage of anti-AIM publicity and with the defendants denied bail the whole time. When the trial finally began in June 1977—it would last an astonishing eleven months—it soon became obvious that such evidence as existed was either meaningless or crudely fabricated. After one of the state's star witnesses admitted under cross examination that it was he rather than Skyhorse or Mohawk who'd stabbed Aird to death, their acquittal was an all but foregone conclusion. By then, however, they

had spent nearly four years of their lives in lock-up, and AIM's reputation in California was irreparably damaged by a raft of news stories comparing AIM to the Manson Family.

WKLDOC attorney William Kunstler concurred, observing that "the purpose of the trials [was] to break the spirit of the American Indian Movement by tying up its leaders and supporters in court and forcing [it] to spend huge amounts of money, time and talent to keep [its] people out of jail, instead of building an organization that can work effectively for the Indian people." The approach, noted Charles Garry, attorney for the Black Panther Party, was identical to that the FBI had adopted in its drive to destroy the political effectiveness of Garry's clients during 1969–1971. The truth of such views was readily borne out during the 1990s, with the release after decades behind bars of one-time high-priority Panthers. In each case, it was conclusively demonstrated that the government had falsified evidence against the victims in precisely the same manner it had done in the Banks/Means, Skyhorse/Mohawk, and other AIM trials.

THE REIGN OF TERROR

During the siege, Dick Wilson had openly announced that "AIM will die at Wounded Knee." That venue, despite an official ban placed on media personnel going within fifteen miles of the perimeter, proved entirely too public for the commission of outright mass murder, however. Wilson was therefore deeply, and again quite openly, frustrated with the outcome. So, too, in its much quieter way, was the FBI, a matter clearly expressed in a 1973 internal document entitled "Paramilitary Operations in Indian Country." These sentiments were communicated by manifestations of hostility by both the GOONs and on-site FBI personnel toward the U.S. Marshals Service, which was nominally in charge of the siege and which both Wilson and FBI special operations expert Richard G. Held felt was entirely too "soft" in its handling of the situation.

When the siege ended, however, the marshals were withdrawn, leaving the FBI in charge of law enforcement on Pine Ridge. Even before the marshals departed, the GOONs—whom, after several confrontations, Chief U.S. Marshal Wayne Colburn had come to view as a "menace" and ordered his men to disarm—had begun to turn up with brand-new, fully automatic, army-issue M-16 rifles, state-of-the-art military communications gear, and the like. Years later, Duane Brewer, a prominent GOON leader, would acknowledge that the FBI had been secretly passing along weapons, munitions, and equipment faster than the marshals could impound it. Once the marshals left, there was nothing at all to disrupt the flow of lethal paraphernalia. The FBI claims it provided such items only to the BIA police, but, as was common knowledge, about two-thirds of the reservation police force doubled as GOONs. The arrangement was quite similar to that prevailing between the FBI and local police *cum* Ku Klux Klan members in the Deep South during the early 1960s.

The result was that during the three years spanning the months March 1973–March 1976, at least sixty-nine AIM members and supporters were murdered on or near Pine Ridge. Calculated against the overall reservation population base of 10,000, the murder rate on Pine Ridge, using *only* documented political deaths, was 170 per 100,000. That is more than *eight times* the 20.2 per 100,000 rate evident in Detroit, the reputed "murder capital of the United States," during the same period.

The grisly particulars attending the Pine Ridge slaughter are often instructive. Among the first fatalities was OSCRO leader Pedro Bissonette, who was shot point-blank in the chest with a 12-gauge shotgun and then left on the road to bleed to death after being stopped at a police roadblock on the night of October 17, 1973. In the predawn hours of March 27, 1975, Bissonette's apolitical sister-in-law, Jeanette, was also—and, at the time, inexplicably—shot to death; according to Brewer, she had been mistaken for Ellen Moves Camp, a prominent Pine Ridge activist. On September 10, 1975, AIM supporter Jim Little was severely beaten by four men; he died during the hour it took for an ambulance to arrive from the BIA hospital, located only two miles away. On January 30, 1976, anti-Wilson attorney Byron DeSersa was shot and left to bleed to death in a ditch. Although numerous witnesses identified the assailants—all known GOONs—FBI personnel on the scene made no arrests, other than that of one of the *witnesses,* an elderly Cheyenne named Guy Dull Knife, who, the agents said, had become "abusive" when they failed to act.

Although the death toll rose at a rate described as "awesome" even by South Dakota's notoriously anti-AIM attorney general, William Janklow, another 340-odd AIM members and supporters on Pine Ridge suffered serious physical assaults and/or attempts on their lives. On the night of March 3, 1975, the home of seventy-year-old Matthew King, an assistant to Chief Fools Crow (and an uncle of Russell Means), was riddled with gunfire by "party or parties unknown." Two nights later, the same culprits burned Fools Crow's own house to the ground. The home of

anti-Wilson tribal council member Severt Young Bear was shot up so frequently that he "lost track" of the number of incidents. On June 8, Russell Means himself was shot in the back, the bullet penetrating a kidney, by a BIA police officer who claimed the action was justified because Means was engaged in "rowdy behavior." On November 17, BIA police officer Jesse Stone opened fire on the house of AIM supporter Chester Stone with an M-16, wounding Stone, his wife, and two small children (one of whom, three-year-old Johnny Mousseau, was permanently crippled as a result).

From the outset, AIM and its supporters sought to resolve the conflict by resorting to due process remedies, beginning with OSCRO's effort to impeach Dick Wilson. This was followed by AIM's demand for a criminal investigation of the Wilson regime, advanced as a condition for ending the Wounded Knee standoff. (In 1975, the Government Accounting Office finally completed an audit in which it was concluded that the Wilsonites could not account for more than $300,000 in federal highway funds, but no charges were ever filed.) Then, in the fall of 1974, Russell Means faced off with Wilson in an electoral bid to unseat him. Means outpolled his opponent by a margin of 677 votes to 511 in the primary, but ostensibly lost the runoff by a 200-vote margin. The Denver office of the Justice Department's Civil Rights Division investigated Means's charge that the results were rigged and found evidence of massive fraud—Potato Creek, a district "swept" by Wilson, had forty registered voters but eighty-three ballots cast. Altogether, 154 such "problems" were catalogued, but the results were allowed to stand.

Since many or most of the crimes against AIM and its supporters were committed by the BIA police, no redress could be expected from that quarter. As for the FBI, which exercised preeminent jurisdiction on Pine Ridge during the critical period, George O'Clock, special agent in charge of the Bureau's Rapid City Resident Agency, explained to the press that he was too "short of manpower" to investigate homicides, attempted homicides, assaults, and other acts of political terrorism against AIM. On the other hand, O'Clock—who had at his disposal the greatest ratio of agents to citizens in the history of the FBI—had sufficient manpower available to amass more than 316,000 separate investigative file classifications on the victims. In June 1975, he had even assigned not one but two of his men to track down a seventeen-year-old AIM member named Jimmy Eagle, accused of stealing a pair of used cowboy boots. Given such priorities, it is unsurprising that the FBI has been "unable" to achieve a satisfactory resolution of *any* of the scores of cases at issue. Many remain "pending" to this day.

In early July 1975, Denver Civil Rights Division investigators William Muldrow and Shirley Hill Witt returned to Pine Ridge for purposes of assessing the reasons for the "ubiquitous climate of violence" there. It was their mutual determination that the Wilson regime, with the complicity of federal authorities, including the FBI, had visited a veritable "reign of terror" upon reservation residents for more than two years. Among other things, they recommended that a planned congressional inquiry concerning the FBI's operations on Pine Ridge, "indefinitely postponed" a few weeks earlier, be immediately resumed. It never has been resumed. In 1987, however, Duane Brewer, still confident that his service as a GOON leader would immunize him and his "boys" from prosecution, confirmed much of what Muldrow, Hill Witt, and AIM itself had suspected. For all practical intents and purposes, the GOONs had functioned as a death squad, coordinated by the FBI in much the same fashion in which the Central Intelligence Agency (CIA) has controlled such entities in Latin America and elsewhere.

Such an arrangement is entirely consistent with the procedures outlined in "Cable Splicer" and "Garden Plot," a pair of "domestic counterinsurgency scenarios" developed by Louis O. Giuffrida, director of the California Civil Disorder Management School, at the behest of then-governor Ronald Reagan in 1970. It is a matter of record that both Giuffrida and British counterinsurgency expert Frank Kitson had briefed Pentagon and FBI officials on the nature of such "low-intensity warfare" strategies as early as 1971 and that one of Giuffrida's ranking staff members, Colonel Vic Jackson, was on-site at Wounded Knee in 1973. It is also telling that, in internal memoranda dating from the crucial period, the FBI referred to AIM members not as "radicals" or "militants"—the traditional vernacular employed by its political neutralization specialists—but rather as "insurgents."

Therefore, it appeared that the FBI was, in a sense, field-testing Giuffrida's scenarios against AIM in the years following Wounded Knee, and that what transpired on Pine Ridge, far from being an example of "law enforcement gone awry," was actually an exercise in outright counterinsurgency warfare conducted by domestic police agencies. To the extent that this is so, the FBI's campaign to neutralize AIM represents a dramatic escalation rather than an abandonment of the already highly illegal counterintelligence operations—known as "COINTELPROs"—that were revealed in the 1975 Senate Select Committee *Report on Intelligence Activities and the Rights of Americans* as having been conducted by the FBI in its drive to "disrupt, destabilize and destroy" the Black Panther Party.

In any event, when Ronald Reagan became president in 1981, one of his first significant acts was to create the Federal Emergency Management Agency (FEMA). A primary task of FEMA is to coordinate the operations of local, state, and federal (including military) forces, along with those of selected "private citizen organizations" in times of "civil disorder." This is exactly the script laid out in Garden Plot and Cable Splicer, and is very much the thrust of what was done on Pine Ridge. Accordingly, Reagan's choice as founding director of FEMA was Louis O. Giuffrida. In turn, Giuffrida concocted ever more refined versions of his original scenarios, "war-gaming" them in exercises dubbed "Rex-84," "Rex-85," and so on. The basis on which the 1973–1976 reign of terror on Pine Ridge was imposed has, as a consequence, been formally adopted as national policy, applicable to all dissident groups, and, at least in principle, to the citizenry as a whole.

FIREFIGHT AT OGLALA

The problem with the FBI's counterinsurgency initiative on Pine Ridge is that it didn't work. By the spring of 1975, having absorbed at that point some fifty fatal casualties, hundreds wounded or seriously injured, and the great bulk of the Wounded Knee trials, the resistance on Pine Ridge remained very much unbroken. Indeed, given that AIM's security component had begun to organize itself in armed defensive clusters at various places around the reservation, there was every indication that a resurgence was in the offing. Since this was beyond the capacity of the GOONs' roving hit teams to deal with—according to Brewer, they had already begun to back away, considering attacks upon the AIM strong points to be "suicidal"—a pretext was needed that would allow the FBI itself to (re)enter the reservation with sufficient force to wrap things up, once and for all.

The incident designed to serve this purpose materialized during the late morning of June 26, 1975, when two agents, Ron Williams and Jack Coler, approached an encampment established by the Northwest AIM Group, one of the movement's more proficient security teams, on the property of Harry and Cecelia Jumping Bull, elderly traditionalists who lived a few miles south of the reservation town of

Oglala. Although the FBI men were ostensibly there to serve the earlier-mentioned arrest warrant on Jimmy Eagle (a document that in reality did not yet exist), they made no attempt to do so. Instead, stopping their cars in an open field a short distance from the treeline in which the AIM camp was located, they opened fire. In short order, receiving heavy return fire, they were radioing frantically for backup. Soon thereafter, both were dead.

Given the remote location in which the altercation occurred, the help they had requested had nonetheless begun to arrive almost immediately. The FBI would later claim that some 150 BIA SWAT personnel prepositioned in the immediate area were "coincidentally" there because of an unrelated training exercise. This does not explain, however, why the bureau itself had an equivalent force of its own SWAT men already assembled at its Quantico, Virginia, facility, apparently awaiting the signal that the fighting had begun. (They, along with SWAT teams assigned to the Minneapolis, Chicago, Denver, and other FBI field offices, were on-site at the Jumping Bulls' before the firing stopped, late the same afternoon.) Nor does it explain why William Janklow just "happened" to be waiting by his phone in Pierre, the South Dakota state capital, a plane ready at the airport to whisk him halfway across the state to Hot Springs, in time to round up a group of local vigilantes and drive seventy-five miles to the scene while the firefight was still raging.

Although the FBI's planning is murky, it appears that Coler and Williams were sent to instigate a gun battle that would trigger first an overwhelming assault on the Northwest AIM position by BIA SWAT teams and then an avalanche of FBI SWAT personnel to mop up similar "compounds" elsewhere on the reservation. It was anticipated that there would be no more than eight AIM security men in the encampment when the two agents approached, however. In the event, there were more than thirty, and it was this miscalculation that cost them their lives. The BIA men, unnerved by the unexpected volume of gunfire coming from the AIM group, took up blocking positions around the Jumping Bull property rather than mounting an attack. As FBI units arrived, they did the same. Not only were Coler and Williams abandoned to their fate thereby, but—with the exception of an AIM member from Couer d'Alene, Idaho, named Joe Stuntz Killsright, killed by a sniper at long range—all the "insurgents" involved managed to escape.

Seeking to put the best face on a tremendously embarrassing situation, the FBI immediately barred the press from coming near the scene and, in the morning, convened a press conference. At that point, Tom Coll, a "public information specialist" flown in overnight from Washington, "explained" what had happened. The agents had been "lured" into an "ambush" by "AIM guerrillas" who had fired on them with "automatic weapons" from a "sophisticated bunker complex." Each man, Coll continued, had been "riddled by as many as thirty bullets fired at point-blank range," then "stripped," and, in one account, "scalped." Coll even provided reporters with the last words of one of the agents, supposedly uttered a moment before he was "viciously executed." How Coll could possibly have known this, unless he or some other agent had been close enough to hear, was an obvious question, left unasked by the assembled media representatives.

None of this was true, as the FBI was well aware. The bureau had, after all, *sent* the slain agents to the Jumping Bulls', so there was no question of their having been "lured." The FBI also knew that both men had suffered only three—not "thirty"—wounds and that neither had been stripped or scalped. It had also controlled the crime scene for more than eighteen hours before the press conference was held, so it knew there were no "bunkers." It would be more than a week before this admission came, however. In the meantime, headlines across the country were depicting AIM as "a gang of mad dog killers" (lurid stories concerning the Skyhorse/Mohawk case were running simultaneously). Misled in this manner, the public raised no objection as the FBI went swarming onto Pine Ridge 400 strong, decked out in army-issue combat fatigues, armed with military M-16s, and equipped with APCs and Huey helicopters. For the next two months, these forces conducted Vietnam-style "sweeping" operations across Pine Ridge, kicking in doors, and mounting what it referred to as "air assaults" on the properties of known AIM members on both Pine Ridge and Rosebud. Before it was over, several people were dead, and even a few of the GOONs were protesting that things had gone too far.

With attention thus distracted, federal officials seized the opportunity to have Dick Wilson fulfill his end of the bargain that had propelled him into office in the first place. In early July, he traveled to Washington where he signed a preliminary document transferring title to the northwestern one-eighth of Pine Ridge—an area known as the Sheep Mountain Gunnery Range—to the Interior Department's National Park Service, ostensibly so that it could be incorporated into the Badlands National Monument. Unbeknownst to the combatants slugging it out on the reservation, and most likely to Wilson himself, the department had been aware for some time that the parcel contained a rich deposit of uranium intermixed with molybdenum. The public law by which Congress formalized U.S. possession during the spring of 1976 was later amended to allow the Oglalas to recover the surface area involved, but *not* the subsurface mineral rights.

This accomplished, and with AIM finally pounded into something resembling total disarray, FBI special operations chief Richard G. Held, who had been sent to Pine Ridge to oversee the bureau's blitzkrieg, quietly informed his superiors that his mission was complete. In September, he returned to Chicago, where he had earlier been assigned as the special agent in charge of handling the FBI's role in the 1969 assassinations of Illinois Black Panther leaders Fred Hampton and Mark Clark. So exemplary was his service considered in both the Pine Ridge and Hampton/Clark connections that, although he had already reached retirement age, his term of service was extended so that he could be promoted to the position of FBI associate director. Others involved in the reservation offensive—among them Held's son, Richard W., who had excelled in the Los Angeles field office's COINTELPROs against the Panthers a few years previously—were also proportionally rewarded.

RESMURS AND THE CASE OF LEONARD PELTIER

By the fall of 1975, the FBI had undoubtedly come to view its Pine Ridge operation as an overall success, but a few loose ends remained to be tied up. One of these concerned the fact that the loss of Coler and Williams represented the first time two FBI men had been killed in a single confrontation since the bureau's "gangbuster days" of the mid-1930s. Public image and agent morale alike dictated that *somebody* would have to pay. It also seemed advisable to undertake follow-up measures designed to ensure that AIM would be unable to once again reconstitute itself in the wake of the battering it had received. The means to both ends resided in an "investigation" captioned RESMURS ("REServation MURderS"; the acronym applied *only* to the deaths of Coler and Williams, *not* to the scores of unsolved Indian homicides with which the bureau was then—and is still—backlogged).

Although the bureau was aware from the first that a number of local Oglalas had participated in the firefight, it elected to target Bob Robideau, Dino Butler, and Leonard Peltier, men perceived as forming the backbone of Northwest AIM. There is no indication that the FBI actually believed the three were any more responsible for what had happened than anyone else. Rather, since they were all "outsiders," focusing on them was simply a convenient way of dividing AIM and its supporters among themselves. In effect, defending the accused would require local Oglalas to potentially incriminate one or more of their own; their failure to do so, however, would sever the bonds of trust underlying AIM's effectiveness on Pine Ridge. Accordingly, charges initially brought against Jimmy Eagle as a "fourth defendant"—a matter of appearance, since Coler and Williams were supposedly pursuing him when the firefight occurred—were unceremoniously dropped so that "the full prosecutorial weight of the federal government" could be brought to bear against the preferred defendants.

Dino Butler was captured during an air assault on Crow Dog's Sun Dance in early August 1975, and Bob Robideau a short while later, after he was temporarily blinded by the explosion of his car on the Kansas Turnpike, near Wichita. Peltier had meanwhile escaped to Canada, where he found refuge in Small Boy's Camp, a traditional Cree community in the mountains of west-central Alberta. Arrested by the Royal Canadian Mounted Police in February 1976, he petitioned for a grant of political asylum. This petition was denied, and he was extradited to the United States in June the same year, mainly on the basis of a fraudulent "eyewitness affidavit" prepared by the FBI and introduced in Canadian court. This official submission of false evidence, a flagrant violation of the U.S./Canadian extradition treaty, was later revealed and led to a formal protest and demand that Peltier be returned to Canada's jurisdiction. So serious was the treaty fraud considered that, in 1986, the Canadian parliament also entertained the possibility of canceling its extradition agreement with the United States altogether.

It was originally planned that Butler, Robideau, and Peltier would be tried together, on the premise that they had acted in concert and as part of a mutual conspiracy to murder FBI agents. Since Peltier was still fighting extradition during the spring of 1976, prosecutors proceeded against Butler and Robideau in Cedar Rapids, Iowa, on June 7. At trial, the government's credibility was once again undermined by its reliance on transparently false witnesses. Contentions that AIM was a "terrorist" organization were countered by calling FBI director Clarence Kelley to the stand; questioned by defense attorney William Kunstler, Kelley was forced to concede that the

American Indian Movement activist Leonard Peltier stands in prison in 1986. Although he was convicted of the 1975 murder of two FBI agents, many believe he was innocent. *(AP Wide World Photos)*

bureau possessed "not one scintilla" of evidence to support such allegations. To cap things off, the plausibility of Butler's and Robideau's claim that they'd acted in self-defense received substantial reinforcement when they called William Muldrow to describe the FBI-instigated reign of terror he and Shirley Witt had discovered on Pine Ridge.

On July 16, an all-white jury returned verdicts of not guilty on all counts, noting that the defendants had "done only what any reasonable person would do, under the circumstances" created by the FBI itself. It was clear—since Bob Robideau had testified that he'd personally shot both agents—that the jury believed no murders had occurred. This placed the Justice Department in a serious quandary. The outcome of a high-level meeting to discuss their options, however, resulted in a stint of judge-shopping in which officials secured the services of Paul Benson, a North Dakota district jurist who was willing to restrict to the scope of evidentiary consideration solely "to the

events of June 26, 1975," and thus rule the entire Cedar Rapids trial record inadmissible. Prosecutors then proceeded against Peltier with the argument that he had acted as a "lone gunman," a premise they could not have believed, assuming they were in the least sincere about the truth of the case they had presented against Butler and Robideau.

During Peltier's trial, which began on March 21, 1977, defense attorneys, unable to cross-examine effectively because of the judge's evidentiary rulings, were forced to listen as FBI men gave substantially different accounts of events from those they had sworn were true in Cedar Rapids. The capstone came with the testimony of an agent name Fred Coward, who had not even been mentioned during the Butler/Robideau trial. He claimed to have seen Peltier through a rifle scope on the fatal day, carrying an AR-15 rifle in close proximity to the dead agents' bodies. This evidence was crucial because FBI ballistics expert Evan Hodge also claimed, on the basis of a mysterious shell casing allegedly found in the trunk of Coler's car, that the final rounds hitting Coler and Williams had been fired from an AR-15. Moreover, Hodge claimed, his overall examination of crime scene evidence indicated that AIM members had used only one such weapon during the firefight. *Ipso facto,* whichever AIM member could be linked to an AR-15, as Coward did with Peltier, would appear to the jury to be the killer. Hodge also testified that a toolmarks comparison matched the key shell casing to an AR-15 recovered from Robideau's burned-out car along the Kansas Turnpike (thus "proving" that the Northwest AIM Group had been in possession of the "murder weapon").

With this groundwork laid, prosecutor Lynn Crooks used his closing argument to depict in graphic detail exactly how Peltier was supposed to have cold-bloodedly "executed" both agents, even borrowing from Tom Coll's long-discredited fabrications to recount how one of the agents had begged his killer not to pull the trigger. On April 18, 1977, after only six hours of deliberation, the jury found Peltier guilty of double-homicide, and, on June 1, Benson sentenced him to serve back-to-back life sentences. Although this was his first conviction, he was taken directly to the federal "supermax" prison at Marion, Illinois, a draconian facility ostensibly reserved for "incorrigibles" who had already proven unmanageable in regular penal settings.

WKLDOC attorneys quickly submitted an appeal based on Benson's handling of the trial. It was considered by a three-judge panel of the Eighth Circuit Court, chaired by Chief Judge William Webster. Toward the end of 1978, the panel delivered a finding that, although the record revealed more than thirty reversible errors, any one of which would have been sufficient to send a normal case back to trial, Peltier's conviction would be allowed to stand. The opinion had been written by Webster, who by the time it was read had already left the court to take up a new position as director of the FBI. The Eighth Circuit declined to conduct an *en banc* hearing to reconsider Webster's plainly conflicted decision, and the U.S. Supreme Court refused to review it as well.

While all this was going on, WKLDOC had also filed a suit under the Freedom of Information Act (FOIA) to obtain all FBI documents relating to the RESMURS investigation. This resulted in the release, in 1981, of some 12,000 pages of often heavily redacted material that had not been disclosed to the defense before or during Peltier's trial. (The FBI stated that it was withholding an additional 6,000 pages on

"national security" grounds, but, in 2002, it was forced to admit that it had "overlooked" a further 42,000 pages when the original release was made.) Among the documents was an October 12, 1975, teletype flatly contradicting Evan Hodge's trial testimony. A comparison of the firing-pin markings made by the "Wichita AR-15" and those on the all-important mystery shell casing had actually produced negative results. Peltier's attorneys were therefore able to file a second appeal, resulting in hearings on the FBI's ballistics evidence in 1984. Interrogated by William Kunstler, Hodge unraveled on the stand, being caught in the process of committing perjury and having to admit that AIM members had used not one but *several* AR-15s during the Oglala firefight.

In oral arguments before another panel of the Eighth Circuit Court on October 15, 1985, Lynn Crooks did his best to salvage the situation, arguing—in diametrical opposition to his own closing statement to the jury—that, although he had "no idea who actually shot the agents," it didn't really matter, since Peltier had "actually" been convicted, not of murder, but of "aiding and abetting whoever committed the murders." When a judge asked who Peltier might have aided and abetted, since his codefendants had been acquitted, Crooks replied that perhaps he had aided and abetted himself. It took the three judges eleven months to craft a finding in which they both rejected Crooks's new theory and declared the circumstantial case presented against Peltier at trial to have been false and misleading while *still* allowing his conviction to stand. Once again, the U.S. Supreme Court refused to review the matter.

Since then, although Peltier has been moved to the "normal" federal maximum security prison at Leavenworth, Kansas, he has been routinely denied parole. (He is still serving the first of his life sentences.) The government has ignored petitions for a retrial signed by more than 14 million people internationally, requests by several foreign governments to the same effect, a finding by Amnesty International that Peltier is a "prisoner of conscience" (i.e., a wrongfully incarcerated political prisoner), and much else. In January 2001, faced with significant public protests by FBI agents—the first such demonstrations in the history of the bureau—President Bill Clinton failed to sign a long-promised commutation of his sentence. Peltier therefore continues to serve his time, a symbol of the federal government's arbitrary ability to repress the legitimate aspirations to liberation of indigenous people.

AFTERMATH

By the time of Peltier's conviction and initial appeal, the movement was in serious decline. Its reputation even among activists suffered badly as the result of rumors, quite possibly true, that in February 1976 AIM members had murdered one of their own, a Mik'maq named Anna Mae Pictou Aquash, in the mistaken belief that she was an FBI informant. (Aquash had been "bad-jacketed," a standard COINTELPRO technique—employed with devastating effectiveness against the Black Panther Party—by which legitimate activists are made to appear to be police infiltrators.) In 1979, shortly after his entire family—his wife, Tina, their three children, and his mother-in-law, Leah-Hicks-Manning—were murdered on the Duck Valley Reservation in Nevada, John Trudell resigned his position as the only remaining "national" AIM officer and announced that all comparable positions had been abolished. No one disputed his statement, for there had been no general membership meeting since 1975.

There were occasional flurries of activity, as when, in 1978, Dennis Banks utilized his California sanctuary as a base from which to organize The Longest Walk, a march from San Francisco to Washington, D.C., designed to protest pending legislation introduced by reactionary Congressman Lloyd Meeds and others to repeal all treaties with American Indians. The walk undoubtedly figured in the bills' subsequent defeat, but a larger reason was probably the fact that U.S. claims to the legitimacy of its territorial title are based largely on those very same treaties. Thereafter, although he has coordinated a virtually endless series of walks and runs meant to draw attention to native issues, Banks, too, announced his "retirement" from AIM.

In 1979, Jimmie Durham, along with IITC's associate director, Paul Chaat Smith, resigned their positions as well, citing the development of the organization's overly cozy relations with certain governments and an encroaching sense of "professionalism" on the part of several of the organization's trustees as their reason. During the mid-1980s, Durham's and Smith's observations were amply borne out when the IITC incorporated itself and appointed a handpicked board to replace the council of traditional elders at whose behest it had been founded and who had overseen its functioning. The new board immediately propelled the Treaty Council into alignment with Nicaragua's Sandinista government, in opposition to the self-determining rights of the country's in-digenous peoples. This maneuver splintered what was left of AIM and fractured the unity previously displayed by native delegations to the UN. Founding trustee Russell Means, who protested IITC's abandonment of principle, was thereupon "expelled." Although IITC continued to claim representation of "98 indigenous nations throughout the Western Hemisphere," most of these had distanced themselves by 1986. The Treaty Council itself continues to exist but without a discernible base of grassroots support. It has thus become essentially an appendage of the very statist entities it was created to oppose.

In 1981, having by then completed the parole stemming from his criminal syndicalism conviction, Means spearheaded the seizing of an 880-acre tract in the Black Hills National Forest, near Rapid City. Dubbed "Yellow Thunder Camp," after Raymond Yellow Thunder, the site was continuously occupied until 1985, during which period the FBI and U.S. Marshals Service were legally enjoined from intervening as AIM battled the National Park Forest Service in court for the right to stay. AIM actually won a landmark decision at the district level: Judge Robert O'Brien entered a ruling that the Lakotas, and thence other Indians, were entitled to view entire geographic areas as sacred sites, and therefore to enjoy use and in certain instances occupancy of them. But the victory was soon nullified by the U.S. Supreme Court's adverse decision in the so-called G-O Road case (*Lyng v. Northwest Indian Cemetery Protective Association* [1988]).

Probably the last major hurrah of the American Indian Movement came during the early 1990s, when Means, along with Colorado AIM leader Glenn Morris, organized a coalition of twenty-five local organizations in Denver to conduct a sustained series of demonstrations protesting the annual Columbus Day parades held in that city. The outcome was a last-second cancellation of the event in 1992, the year a particularly extravagant "celebration of genocide" was planned in honor of the five hundredth anniversary of Columbus's "discovery of America." A particular highlight occurred during the summer of 1992, when a jury considering charges that Means, Morris, and two other Colorado AIM leaders had violated the First Amendment rights of Columbus Day organizers in 1991 by blocking their parade route, not only acquitted the four but stated their belief that the city of Denver had violated international law by issuing a permit for the event.

AIM's Denver victory stimulated signs of life in chapters located elsewhere in the United States. These flashes of even modest resurgence produced indica-

At a gathering in Pueblo, Colorado, on Columbus Day, 1998, Russell Means leads a protest against the hanging of a wreath on a statue of Christopher Columbus. *(AP Wide World Photos)*

Power politics—those of AIM in particular—transformed the circumstances of native North America in ways that may well prove irreversible. If nothing else, the "shock troops of Indian sovereignty," as a grassroots Lakota named Birgil Kills Straight once called them, moved "like a hurricane" through Indian country long enough to instill a sense of pride among people in whom it had been long and terribly diminished, forced Indian issues into the public consciousness for the first time in generations, and proved that gains could be made by going—and sometimes *only* by going—toe-to-toe with the oppressor. That such understandings have not been lost is reflected in the armed confrontations with authorities undertaken by the Mohawk Warriors Society at Oka, near Montreal, and elsewhere during the 1990s. Where this will lead during the new century remains to be seen, but the future surely seems brighter than it did a half-century ago, given the success of militant struggles for Native American rights.

Ward Churchill

BIBLIOGRAPHY

American Friends Service Committee. *Uncommon Controversy: The Fishing Rights of the Muckleshoot, Puyallup and Nisqually Indians.* Seattle: University of Washington Press, 1970.

Anderson, Robert, et al. *Voices from Wounded Knee, 1973.* Rooseveltown, NY: Akwesasne Notes, 1974.

Brown, Dee. *Bury My Heart at Wounded Knee: An Indian History of the American West.* New York: Holt, Rinehart and Winston, 1970.

Burnett, Robert, with John Koster. *The Road to Wounded Knee.* New York: Bantam Books, 1974.

Carson, Clayborne. *In Struggle: SNCC and the Black Awakening of the 1960s.* Cambridge, MA: Harvard University Press, 1981.

Churchill, Ward. "Death Squads in the United States: Confessions of a Government Terrorist." In *From a Native Son: Selected Essays in Indigenism, 1985–1995,* 231–270. Boston: South End, 1996.

Churchill, Ward, and Jim Vander Wall. *Agents of Repression: The FBI's Secret Wars Against the Black Panther Party and the American Indian Movement.* Classical ed. Cambridge, MA: South End, 2002.

———. *The COINTELPRO Papers: Documents from the FBI's Secret Wars Against Dissent in the United States.* Classical ed. Cambridge, MA: South End, 2002.

Cleaver, Kathleen, and George Katsiaficas, eds. *Liberation, Imagination, and the Black Panther Party: A New Look at the Panthers and Their Legacy.* New York: Routledge, 2001.

Deloria, Vine, Jr. *Behind the Trail of Broken Treaties: An Indian Declaration of Independence.* New York: Delta Books, 1974.

———. *Custer Died for Your Sins: An Indian Manifesto.* New York: Macmillan, 1969.

———. *We Talk, You Listen: New Tribes, New Turf.* New York: Macmillan, 1970.

tions that the FBI was still at work making sure the genie stayed in its bottle, however. In a bizarre twist, a barrage of notices were shortly issued by an entity calling itself the National American Indian Movement, claiming that the Colorado chapter was fraudulent, that its leadership was composed of "white men masquerading as Indians" and "probable police agents," and that the entire group had therefore been "summarily expelled" from AIM. As it turned out, "National AIM" was actually a Minnesota-chartered/Minneapolis-based nonprofit corporation, with no "membership" as such, subsisting on hefty infusions of federal funds. Nonetheless, the confusion it generated before its true nature was revealed was sufficient to negate any potential for a genuine revitalization of the movement.

Despite their demise after the mid-1970s, Red

Dillingham, Brint. "Indian Women and IHS Sterilization Practices." *American Indian Journal* 3:1 (January 1977).

Johansen, Bruce, and Roberto Maestas. *Wasi'chu: The Continuing Indian Wars.* New York: Monthly Review, 1979.

Johnson, Troy R. *The Occupation of Alcatraz Island: Indian Self-Determination and the Rise of Indian Activism.* Urbana: University of Illinois Press, 1996.

Johnson, Troy, Joane Nagel, and Duane Champaign, eds. *American Indian Activism: Alcatraz to the Longest Walk.* Urbana: University of Illinois Press, 1997.

Jones, Charles E., ed. *The Black Panther Party [Reconsidered].* Baltimore, MD: Black Classics, 1998.

Matthiessen, Peter. *In the Spirit of Crazy Horse: The Story of Leonard Peltier.* 2d ed. New York: Viking, 1991.

Means, Russell, with Marvin J. Wolf. *Where White Men Fear to Tread: The Autobiography of Russell Means.* New York: St. Martin's, 1995.

Sayer, John William. *Ghost Dancing the Law: The Wounded Knee Trials.* Cambridge, MA: Harvard University Press, 1997.

Smith, Paul Chaat, and Robert Allen Warrior. *Like a Hurricane: The American Indian Movement from Alcatraz to Wounded Knee.* New York: New Press, 1996.

Weyler, Rex. *Blood of the Land: The U.S. Government and Corpcrate War Against the American Indian Movement.* 2d ed. Philadelphia: New Society, 1992.

Treaty Rights and Indian Activism from Alcatraz to NAGPRA

American Indian lands are, in some sense, *not* truly Indian lands. Reservations, established by treaty (or, after 1871, by executive order), are held "in trust" for the tribe by the federal government. The federal government has maintained quasi-colonial oversight of tribes and their territories, administered by the Bureau of Indian Affairs (BIA) in the paternalist tradition of the guardian-ward relationship. Established in 1824, the BIA has the dubious distinction of being the oldest and most deeply entrenched federal agency. By the 1960s, many BIA employees were Native Americans hired to facilitate federal administration of tribal lands and lives. Tribal governments, meanwhile, especially Indian Reorganization Act (IRA) governments, were "puppets": elected and organized according to federal guidelines. Dependent upon federal appropriations and approval, they were seriously disconnected from their constituent communities. With the BIA and tribal government determining policy and process, the majority of reservation residents were left without power or voice. Fueled by military experience, urban residence, and education, intertribal associations developed to fill the political void. Emerging demands for "Treaty Rights" and "Red Power" evolved into a social movement for self-determination that continues to be pressed, with uneven success, to this day.

Native American treaty rights, always lurking in the background of federal-native relations, paradoxically gained the spotlight during Termination. Serving the goal of getting the federal government "out of the Indian business," the Indian Claims Commission, established in 1946, sought to settle old grievances and allow the government to move on to new concerns. Terminating old grievances was often associated with terminating tribes themselves and thus tribal treaty rights. Everyone "knew" that tribes were disappearing, and with their disappearance, the future of treaties was also clear: they would become vacuous, null, and void. The Indian Claims Commission was established in part to hasten, or at least facilitate, that process, compensating treaty violations with cash payments. By its very focus on treaties as the source and substance of claims, however, the commission catalyzed treaty rights activism. It is not surprising, then, that the occupation of Alcatraz, which initiated a new era of Native American activism, asserted their "treaty rights" to the island.

Treaty rights, as special rights of legally distinct groups of American citizens, defy civil rights as the equal rights of individual American citizens. In 1968, the Indian Civil Rights Act (ICRA) made all too clear the tension between tribal rights and civil rights; ICRA provided protections to individual tribal members and simultaneously extended federal controls on tribal governmental process. The same year saw the founding of the American Indian Movement (AIM) in Minneapolis to advance native civil rights there (especially in regard to poor housing, high unemployment, and police brutality). Energized by the broader civil rights movement, Native American activists elsewhere publicized the contemporary relevance of treaty rights and the contemporary reality of native peoples and "Indian issues" in their occupation of the decommissioned federal penitentiary on Alcatraz Island and at many other sites across the country.

Alcatraz

Actually, there were two occupations of Alcatraz: both claimed the island based on the 1868 Fort Laramie Treaty with the Sioux Nation. In 1964, five Lakota men occupied Alcatraz for four hours, claiming it for all Native Americans but on the basis of the 1868 treaty with their tribe. Five years later, eighty-nine Indians of All Tribes, only some of whom were Lakota, claimed their right to occupy the land based on the same 1868 Sioux treaty. The treaty, they asserted, gave Native Americans the right to unused or decommis-

Demanding that the federal government return possession of Alcatraz Island to Native Americans, members of the Indians of All Tribes Inc. stand in solidarity on November 25, 1969. The seizure of the island in San Francisco Bay five days earlier marked the rise of modern Native American militancy. *(AP Wide World Photos)*

sioned federal land anywhere in Indian Country. A devastating fire at the San Francisco Indian Center had left the local native peoples without a gathering place: Alcatraz was reclaimed in part to provide a new, intertribal space in the Bay Area.

The occupation of Alcatraz included and introduced hundreds of Native Americans from around the country, catalyzing a new activism later described as "Red Power." The occupation itself lasted nineteen months, until June 1970, when the remaining fifteen protesters were removed by federal marshals. Failure to gain the land, however, was offset by success in winning media attention and public support. Vine Deloria has said that "Alcatraz was the master stroke of Indian activism," simultaneously galvanizing native identity and action and demonstrating the continuing, contemporary reality of native peoples and Native American issues in America. Wilma Mankiller, later highly acclaimed principal chief of the Oklahoma Cherokee, said of her Alcatraz experience:

I'd never heard anyone actually tell the world that we needed somebody to pay attention to our treaty rights, that our people had given up an entire continent, and many lives, in return for basic services like health care and education, but nobody was honoring these agreements. For the first time, people were saying things I felt but hadn't known how to articulate. It was very liberating.

Wilma Mankiller's experience typified that of many other "warriors without weapons," who resisted by their silence, often melting into the formal educational pot. Eventually, this silence grew into civil disobedience and political demonstration under the leadership of urban intertribal organizations and individuals. Tribal issues and treaty rights were what distinguished Native American issues and were of paramount concern to activist groups, including AIM and its gender-based offshoot, Women of All Red Nations (WARN). In the United States, tribes were "domestic dependent nations," compromised in their sovereignty and vulnerable—especially after the U.S Supreme Court's *Lone Wolf v. Hitchcock* (1903) decision—in their treaty rights. Well aware of this conundrum, the members of the International Indian Treaty Council pursued self-determination and treaty rights in the international arena. Their work led to the convocation of the first United Nations meeting of Indigenous Peoples in Geneva (1977), the United Nations Working Group on Indigenous Populations (1982), and eventually, to the Declaration of Rights of Indigenous Peoples (1992), which established a new standing for native nations in international law.

Since the 1961 American Indian Chicago Conference (AICC), intertribal "Indian" identity, arbitrarily imposed by federal policy and legislation, had become a proactive political and social reality. The NIYC (National Indian Youth Council), formed at the AICC, ensured the future of such intertribal activism. NIYC members cut their political teeth on treaty rights activism in Washington and Oregon. "Fish-ins," although named and organized following the civil rights "sit-ins" in the South, focused on the special rights of Native Americans as tribal citizens, not the equal rights of all people as American citizens. Many of those involved in the fish-ins were not members of the tribes whose treaty rights to fish at the "usual and accustomed stations" had been violated: they demonstrated on behalf of the specific rights of certain native peoples, but also on behalf of treaty and tribal rights in general. Fish-ins were followed by legal action in regard to reserved fishing rights, notably in what is generally known as the Boldt decision (*U.S. v. Washington*, 1974), upholding a century-old treaty guaranteeing off-reservation fishing rights to tribes in the Northwest. The Boldt decision was seen throughout the country as a substantial victory for treaty activists and provided hope that the legal institutions of the United States would provide a forum for redress for native peoples.

A small group of attorneys, including John Echohawk and others associated with the University of New Mexico law school, began to pursue tribal and treaty rights in the courts as others advanced Red Power by political action. The Native American Rights Fund, now located in Boulder, Colorado, was established for this purpose in 1970, the same year the occupation of Alcatraz ended and 48,000 acres including Blue Lake, taken illegally from the people of Taos, were returned to the Pueblo. While the differing modes of action—political and legal—were not coordinated, they served the same goal and were, in general, mutually supportive.

Alcatraz had convinced young Native Americans of the possibility and the potential of political protest. It contributed directly to the AIM-organized cross-country "Trail of Broken Treaties" caravan from the West Coast to Washington, D.C., in 1972. The Twenty Points position paper, drawn up by Minneapolis AIM, put treaty rights first. The document called for the repeal of 1871 legislation ending federal treaty making with American Indian nations; sought the establishment of a treaty commission to sign new treaties and a presidential commission to recommend corrective action for federal violations of existing treaties; called for Senate review of the many signed but unratified treaties; and noted that a federal injunction on actions that threatened treaty rights was to be available during lengthy court determinations. Finally, and importantly, the *Indian* interpretation of treaties was to be declared binding unless successfully challenged in court. Unfortunately, serious consideration of the Twenty Points was lost in the organizational and spatial melee of the BIA takeover with which it unexpectedly ended. Perhaps it is not surprising, then, that, mere months later, violence became part of AIM action at Wounded Knee.

AMERICAN INDIAN MOVEMENT

AIM organized and energized the 1973 siege of Wounded Knee as it had the Trail of Broken Treaties only months before. Its involvement on Pine Ridge had begun the year before with a protest march in reaction to the murder of Raymond Yellow Thunder

in nearby Gordon, Nebraska. That earlier action was lauded by the majority of Pine Ridge residents, whereas the Wounded Knee action addressed and inflamed intratribal and intergenerational tensions. An AIM-encouraged effort to impeach Chairman Richard Wilson as a puppet leader had solidified tribal political factions, which ultimately expressed their differences in a violent and armed conflict with repercussions well beyond the reservation borders. The seventy-one-day conflict resulted in the death of two Native Americans, federal causalities, and injuries of unknown numbers of people on both sides, and it also ended in lawsuits and prison terms. When the siege ended on May 9, 1973, political tensions persisted. The now familiar Treaty of 1868 was again invoked; again in a questionable manner, by Russell Means, reiterating the central role of treaties in Native American social movements:

> The FBI must have known from the first day, when we presented our demands . . . that Wounded Knee was about our treaty rights—about the [1868] Fort Laramie Document that affirmed Oglala sovereignty. We were risking our lives not only for the right to select our own officials, but also to choose our own system of government.

AIM occupation and activism on reservations continued, and continued to point out differences in political perspective between generations as well as between urban and reservation native peoples. On the newly restored Menominee reservation, the Menominee Warrior Society adopted AIM tactics in its takeover of the Alexian Brothers novitiate building, in an effort to dramatize self-determination. Much of the focus of activism, AIM or otherwise, seems to have been about self-determination. The number and voice of native peoples residing in cities were important aspects of this focus. During the 1970s, the number of Native Americans in cities was approaching, if it had not already equaled, the number on reservations. (Census counts of the urban native population are notoriously low, whereas reservation counts tend to be more accurate.) The urban experience, including formal education, the impact of 1960s-style radical thinking and activism, and the construction of difference in urban identity politics encouraged a rethinking of Native American cultures and histories and a renewed commitment to self-determination.

Improbably, President Richard Nixon agreed. Nixon's policy of "self-determination without termination" meant that the federal government would be held to its treaty agreements with Native American tribes, and tribes would take a more active role in their own governance and development. In addition, to prepare Native American children for a self-determined future, tribes were to be afforded the primary role in education. The 1975 Indian Self-Determination and Education Assistance Act was the legislative expression of this new federal policy. It directed the secretary of the Interior to contract directly with tribal organizations to plan, direct, and execute tribal programs, including those currently administered by the BIA. That 1975 act has been amended, improved, and expanded over the years, but it continues today as the fundamental legislative assertion of tribal right to determine and administer services owed as a result of treaties.

In 1975, "education" referred primarily to pre-college education in survival schools that followed the AIM model in the Heat of the Earth school in Minneapolis. The future of self-determination, however, depended upon succeeding generations of tribal leaders being able to hold their own in government-to-government negotiations and being educated in tribal and Native American histories and issues. Tribally controlled community colleges developed to fill the postsecondary void in reservation education, taking as their mission education for self-determination and self-determined education. A new type of "warrior" had arisen. The "warriors without weapons" gave way to groups like AIM and the Menominee Warrior Society; the new warrior was the "briefcase warrior," whose weapons were education and the law.

The Tribally Controlled Community College Assistance Act, providing federal education funds for tribal colleges, was passed in 1978, still under the Nixon administration. The same year saw the American Indian Religious Freedom Act, the Indian Child Welfare Act, the land claims settlement for the Passamaquoddy in Maine, and the *Santa Clara v. Martinez* and the *Oliphant v. Suquamish* U.S. Supreme Court decisions, which interfered with tribal self-determination and sovereignty. It was a legally schizophrenic year, reflecting the fundamental contradictions between the reality of treaty rights, federal Native American law, and "domestic dependent nation" status, and the inevitable tensions arising out of these often conflicting realities.

Most important in the American Indian Religious Freedom Act were the *whereas*-es, which recognized the limitations on religious rights. The act itself carried scant remedy and compelled little change, but it

certainly and clearly acknowledged the (sometimes incidental) abuse of the native peoples' religious freedom by federal departments and agencies. First Amendment nonestablishment protections defeated essentially every sacred lands case that came before the Court, making it clear that Native Americans were to have their religious freedom, but not the sacred lands upon which that depended, even though the control of those lands had been taken from them in violation of treaty agreements. A ski resort in the West, camping and motorcycles in the Black Hills, recreational boating on Lake Powell, logging in California, were all considered "compelling state interests" that trumped Native American claims to sacred lands. The differences in native and Court interpretations were highlighted in the *G-O Road* case (*Lyng v. Northwest Indian Cemetery Protection Association,* 1988) where the Yurok high-country stood between finished segments of a major logging road and was considered unimportant in terms of Yurok religious freedom since, it was claimed, so very few people ever went there.

The Indian Child Welfare Act (ICWA), however, had a large and lasting impact. ICWA affirmed tribal control of tribal domestic issues, especially in regard to the removal and placement of neglected and abused children. More than any other act, ICWA caused non–Native American court systems to recognize and respect tribal courts. Indeed, it led to the establishment of courts in many tribes that had not yet developed them. In these ways, ICWA provided a strong legislative statement of Native American sovereignty and self-determination. Native families were supported in both titles of the act: extended family members were given priority in the placement of children removed from their parents, and family supportive services were mandated.

In the Court, *Martinez* seemed to underscore tribal self-determination by supporting the tribal right to determine its own membership through sovereign immunity as rendered in the decision. *Oliphant v. Suquamish* decidedly interfered with tribal sovereignty and self-determination, denying tribal criminal jurisdiction over nonmembers. The Court seemed in some sense at odds with the Congress: that was not new. But at odds with itself, again, the inherent tensions in federal Native American law were revealed. The legal struggle continued and continues: when the Court is understood as conservative and ill-disposed to Native American rights concerns, attention is focused on congressional lobbying efforts. Such is the situation at the time of this writing. Briefcase warriors must be politically savvy as well as legally knowledgeable to defend and assure tribal sovereignty and self-determination.

The conjunction of legal action and political demonstration addressing both land rights and religious freedom can be seen in the struggle over the Black Hills. In 1979, the U.S. Court of Claims ruled that the 1877 federal seizure of the Black Hills was unconstitutional, and entered a judgment in favor of the Lakota for $105 million. The decision was affirmed by the U.S. Supreme Court in 1980. The tribe, however, would not accept compensation and sued for the return of the Black Hills as well as $11 billion in damages. The case was dismissed on the grounds of the sovereign immunity of the United States. Members of AIM then established the "Yellow Thunder Camp" (named after Raymond Yellow Thunder, whose murder first introduced AIM to the Pine Ridge reservation) to gain public support and reiterate the Lakota claim. To this day, the Lakota have continued to refuse financial compensation for the taking and to press for the return of their lands.

Although the Nixon administration supported significant advances in Native American self-determination, the appropriations to support that self-determination were lacking. Native American social movements in the decade of the 1980s focused on reservation economic development. Reservation communities invariably came in at the bottom of all the poverty and social parameters measured by the census and other instruments. Self-determination, it was argued, cost money: without funds, sovereignty was a ruse. But a few voices called for a new perspective on the relationship between sovereignty and economy: the relationship was inevitable, but the order was reversed. Sovereignty preceded economic development instead of following it: sovereignty was the foundation upon which tribal economic development could and must proceed.

Gaming is certainly the best-known and most lucrative example of this logic. Tribal gaming depends on the special legal and political status of recognized tribes and the exemption of reservations from state regulations, including state gaming regulation. Tribal business became the new locus of tribal self-determination. Certainly, however, it is not the only such endeavor. As Rennard Strickland summarized: "A shift from the courtroom to the boardroom" had begun. With improved funding for the PL 638 Indian Self-Determination and Assistance Act contracts,

more and more were negotiated, expanding tribal autonomy. Tribes continue to decrease their reliance on the BIA and other federal agencies and to increase their own direct control of tribal services and governance.

Reservation economic development commonly implies environmental deterioration. In the 1970s and 1980s, coal development on the Northern Cheyenne reservation in southeastern Montana provided a potential source of revenue to one of the poorest of the nation's tribes. Yet, a vocal and active group of tribal members derailed major coal development, seeking to sustain both natural resources and the environmental quality of the reservation for the generations to follow. Tribal members were between a rock and a hard place. Members of that small but successful group became the butt of physical and verbal attacks on the reservation for many years thereafter: they had effectively denied badly needed income to reservation families. Environmental issues rose to the fore throughout Indian Country in the 1980s as another expression of land, treaty rights, and religious freedom. Environmental concerns were addressed in both legal action and political demonstration. The relationship between tribe and national environmental groups was complex and problematic: the banning of eagle feathers, listed as one of the *whereas*-es in AIRFA (American Indian Religious Freedom Act), certainly anticipated this. Tribal air and water rights included rights to air and water quality, however, and such rights protected non–Native American as well as native peoples, as was clear in the Ladysmith mining case. In the region of the Ladysmith mine, the Great Lakes Indian Fish and Wildlife Commission (GLIFWC) consulted on behalf of constituent tribes on issues of the environment and treaty rights management. That the GLIFWC helped to organize treaty rights demonstrations makes clear the coincidence of legal, political, scientific, and social action work typical of the time. Most tribes today have enacted environmental and conservation ordinances that guide executive action.

As might be expected, anti–Native American backlash organizations and attitudes began to develop: among them, ERFE (Equal Rights for Everyone), STA (Stop Treaty Abuse), and PARR (Protecting American Rights and Resources) attracted a considerable following based on what were considered to be "sacred" American principles. Such groups were notable, especially in the Midwest, where the legacy of Fred and Mike Tribble's action to claim off-reservation inland spearfishing rights reserved to Great Lakes

Ojibwe set off widespread anti-spearfishing demonstrations and a chain of legal decisions. The popularity of "Treaty Beer," a fund-raising scheme for anti-treaty groups, attests to both the marketing ability of these groups and the continuing lack of understanding of Native American status and issues in the general population.

An unintended but nonetheless significant consequence of native activism was the "hardening" of ethnic categories and the identity markers by which they are claimed and ascribed. As tribal and Native American rights became front-page news, as the newly recognized and racially diverse Pequot Tribe established the largest and most lucrative gaming enterprise in the country, as Wilma Mankiller made the cover of *Time* magazine, and as *Dances with Wolves* (1990) played on romantic ideals, Native Americans began to focus on ownership of their own representations. Ownership and control of cultural resources became as important as ownership and control of land and natural resources. Museums were criticized as colonialist institutions, and museum collections came under scrutiny for holding sacred objects illegally obtained. The Smithsonian returned two war god statues to the Zuni, and the Heye Foundation repatriated sacred wampum belts to the Iroquois, both as the result of tribal legal and political initiative. Human remains held in museums became the focus of native activist interest in this period of time. The "civil rights of bones" and the human rights of native peoples were hotly debated, as local demonstrations, many of which included members of AIM, publicized Native American perspectives and claims. In Illinois, for example, the Dickson Mounds exhibit over a burial of unknown tribal affiliation was forced to change as a result of intertribal (including AIM) action.

The remarkable result of such actions and such claims was the Native American Graves Protection and Repatriation Act (NAGPRA) of 1990. Recognizing tribal ownership interest in human remains and associated funerary items and in sacred objects or objects of cultural patrimony, NAGPRA mandated the return of such remains or objects to recognized tribes that could clearly identify their affiliation with them. The legal reasoning behind NAGPRA holds that sacred items and items of cultural patrimony are owned by the community, not by individuals within it, and can only be alienated by the community: those held by gift or purchase from individuals, then, are illegally held. NAGPRA became the first federal act not only to acknowledge but also to incorporate Native American perspectives in a legal definition. Consul-

tation with tribal representatives in the identification of sacred objects and objects of cultural patrimony is mandated by the law, thus recognizing diversity in worldview and requiring the incorporation of tribal knowledge into mainstream legal process. The legislation envisions a consultative rather than an adversarial approach. Federal Native American policy as articulated in NAGPRA clearly shows the impact of more than two decades of political and legal action. NAGPRA process and pragmatics, however, remain problematic.

The success of NAGPRA has been stymied by lack of congressional funding. The cost of reviewing inventories, consulting with museums and universities, and the logistics of particular repatriations are frequently beyond the financial abilities of the tribes. As a result, human remains and sacred items languish in federally funded institutions across the United States, still waiting to be returned. Demonstrating the cultural affiliation of human remains and sacred items has also proved cumbersome and contentious. Some academics and museum personnel have preferred pursuing their own research agendas to working in a cooperative spirit with the tribes, as has been amply illustrated in the controversy surrounding The Ancient One/Kennewick Man. Sacred items and objects of cultural patrimony held in private collections in this and other countries are, moreover, not covered in the act, which addresses only institutions receiving federal funding.

Native American activism around treaty rights, land, and religious freedom took its initial energy from urban communities where diversity of tribe, class, education, and experience provided significant fuel. Action was focused, however, on tribes and reservations considered to be the locus of native identity and community. By the 1980s, the integration of an urban-reservation social system became clear to Native Americans, if not to the government, which continued to insert a wedge between reservation and urban communities. Indian Country expanded: gaming moved off reservations and into Duluth, Detroit, Milwaukee, and other cities. Tribes set up satellite offices in urban communities, and several included representation on the tribal council for off-reservation members. Treaties clearly never stipulated Native American identity nor recognized it as synonymous with reservation residence: the reservation-based wedge began to lose its grip.

Throughout the quarter of a century between Alcatraz and NAGPRA, and beyond, treaty rights, land, and religious freedom were frequently and significantly understood to intersect or even coincide. Modalities of social action have included silence, education, peaceful demonstration, civil disobedience, legal action, economic development, and environmental protection. While Native American social movements are clearly encouraged and influenced by issues and modes of activism in other ethnic communities, the political and legal status of Native Americans always and inevitably differentiates their issues from those of other "minorities." Native American activism, from Alcatraz to NAGPRA, whatever its specific focus or modality, has reiterated the spirit and the significance of treaties (constitutionally described as "the supreme law of the land"), advanced tribal self-determination, and established the continuing and contemporary insistence of the recognition of an American Indian presence in the greater American population.

Terry Straus and John Low

BIBLIOGRAPHY

Cornell, Steve, and Joseph Kalt. "What Can Tribes Do?" Harvard Project on Reservation Economic Development, 1992.

Deloria, Vine, Jr. *God Is Red*. New York: Putnam, 1973.

MacGregor, Gordon. *Warriors Without Weapons*. Chicago: University of Chicago Press, 1946.

Mankiller, Wilma. *American Indian Activism*. Champaign: University of Illinois Press, 1997.

Means, Russell. *Where White Men Fear to Tread: The Autobiography of Russell Means*. New York: St. Martin's, 1995.

Nagel, Joane. *American Indian Ethnic Renewal*. New York: Oxford University Press, 1996.

Nesper, Larry. *The Walleye Warrior*. Lincoln: University of Nebraska Press, 2001.

Prucha, Francis Paul. *American Indian Treaties: The History of a Political Anomaly*. Berkeley: University of California Press, 1994.

Straus, Anne Terry. "A Rock and a Hard Place." In *Anthropology Exchange* (Special Edition), 1978.

Strickland, Rennard. *Tonto's Revenge*. Albuquerque: University of New Mexico Press, 1997.

PAN-INDIANISM MOVEMENT

The term *Pan-Indianism* refers to the joining together of different American Indian peoples, tribes, or nations for a common purpose. Pan-Indian movements include political confederacies such as the Haudenosaunee, or League of the Iroquois; military alliances such as those led by Pontiac and Tecumseh; and civil rights organizations such as the Society of American Indians and the American Indian Movement (AIM). The term itself is redundant, since Indian already refers generically to the native peoples of the Americas, each of whom has his own specific community, language, and traditions. Pan-Indianism is frequently used today to describe gatherings or events sponsored by and attended by a variety of Native American peoples, particularly the powwow.

Powwows are social gatherings of native peoples from one or more tribes, centered around drumming, singing, dancing, and feasting. Traditional powwows are more community-focused, usually held on tribal powwow grounds or at urban native centers; while contest powwows feature competition drumming and dancing, and often attract more spectators from outside the community. Powwows grew out of traditional dances from many different parts of Indian Country, but external forces in the nineteenth and twentieth centuries, including intertribal contact, exhibition dancing, the world wars, hobbyist participation, and the standardization of competition, helped to shape the powwow as a modern Pan-Indian movement. At the same time, many powwows retain specific regional or tribal elements.

The Indian Removal Act of 1830 began the forced relocation of eastern tribes to Indian Territory, west of the Mississippi River. Under pressure from expanding American settlements, other tribes began moving westward. Shifting into new territories meant increasing contact with other native peoples. The pace of intertribal borrowing accelerated from subsistence techniques to spiritual movements. Dance complexes were exchanged, and by the late 1800s, the war dance,

grass dance, and drum dance had spread throughout the Plains and Great Lakes.

Indian boarding schools were another avenue for intertribal contact. The federal government established schools, removed Indian children from their families, and brought them together. Students from many different tribes were thrown together and began to interact. They were not allowed to speak tribal languages, and English became the *lingua franca* of the boarding schools, making intertribal communication easier. Taken from their homes and required to learn a new language and culture, students formed strong emotional ties with fellow students, which fostered an overall "Indian" ethnic identity.

By the late 1800s, native tribes had been brought into the reservation system. No longer a threat to expanding white settlement, they became objects of curiosity. White showmen and entrepreneurs recognized the potential entertainment value in exhibitions of native dancing and began recruiting Native Americans for participation in entertainments for white audiences. Gloria Young chronicled the rise of the Wild West shows in "Powwow Power: Perspectives on Historic and Contemporary Intertribalism" (1981). Wild Bill's Wild West Show, the Pawnee Bill Historic Wild West Exhibition and Indian Encampment, and Comanche Bill's Wild West Show toured the United States and Europe. Native Americans from many different tribes participated, sharing their dances and learning from each other.

World War I and II influenced the development of the Pan-Indian powwow in several ways. Native Americans who served in the military came in contact with native peoples from other areas, creating new intertribal contacts. Friendships begun in the military continued after the wars, with intertribal visiting and sharing. Dances and songs shared by soldiers became part of the developing powwow repertoire. Returning veterans from both wars were honored at celebrations

At a powwow in Peshawbestown, Michigan, on May 28, 2000, Chris Bussey, a member of the Grand Traverse Band of Ottawa and Chippewa Indians, performs a ceremonial dance. An ancient tradition of native peoples, powwows are intertribal gatherings that feature music, dance, storytelling, and contests. *(AP Wide World Photos)*

in their home communities. Traditional war songs and dances were revived to acknowledge the deeds of Native American soldiers in World War I. New songs and dances were borrowed or created and added to the existing traditions.

White interest in native culture also contributed to the expansion of the powwow. As William K. Powers has documented, beginning in about 1900, American Indian "hobbyists" emerged as a group of non-natives interested in Native American culture, particularly dancing and singing. The Boy Scouts, Girl Scouts, Indian Guides, Camp Fire Girls, and other youth groups focused on outdoor activities and native crafts and lore. Some adults continued this interest,

giving public presentations of native dancing and costumes, and sometimes participating in powwows. Hobbyists leaned toward Plains-style dress and dance, contributing to a Pan-Indian flavor at powwows.

Many scholars mark the beginning of the modern powwow in the 1950s, with the introduction of competition and standardized categories in which dancers compete. Categories for contests include men's traditional, grass and fancy dances; women's traditional, jingle and fancy shawl dances, and junior or children's categories. Prize money can be substantial, particularly at large powwows with several hundred contestants. Even in traditional powwows, these categories have become standardized. Rather than contests, there are demonstration dances in the various categories.

Despite these substantial Pan-Indian influences, differences in powwows exist at both the regional and tribal level. Two styles of powwows are recognized today, Northern and Southern, reflecting differences in histories of intertribal contact. In the Northern Plains, reservations are more isolated, and so intertribal exchange has been slower than in the South. In the Southern Plains, exchange has been more prevalent, particularly reflecting the influence of southeastern tribes removed to Oklahoma. Northern-style drums usually have four to six singers, who sing at a higher pitch than Southern singers. Southern drums have more singers, as many as ten or twelve. Northern-style traditional dancers more often wear buckskin and furs, while Southern-style traditional dancers tend to wear cloth shirts and dresses.

Today, many powwows emphasize tribal elements in language, dress, dance, and community recognition. As Anya Peterson Royce pointed out in *The Anthropology of Dance* (1977), as native peoples have worked to revive their cultures, they have incorporated their own traditions into the Pan-Indian powwow. The invocation at a powwow is almost always given in a tribal language, most often in the language of the host tribe. Individuals who speak their tribal languages are in demand for powwow blessings. Dancers seek to incorporate stylistic elements that mark their tribe into their powwow outfits, particularly in traditional dance styles. Iroquois men dancers incorporate their traditional headdresses, *gustoweh*, with specific numbers and placement of feathers to denote membership in one of the Six Nations of Iroquois. Seminole women dancers wear the distinctive patchwork dresses, with multiple layers. Ho-Chunk (Winnebago) women wear ribbonwork decorations on their cloth dresses, in a style known as Ho-Chunk Applique. The Ho-Chunk people have even created a new contest category just for this style of dress.

Powwows serve as an important gathering place for native peoples, a coming together of the community. Particularly in urban areas, powwows can be a way to bring a diversity of tribes together, as described by Joan Weibel-Orlando in *Indian Country, L.A.: Maintaining Ethnic Community in Complex Society* (1999). However, as examined in *Powwow: Native American Performance, Identity, and Meaning* (2003), edited by Luke Eric Lassiter, powwows can and do reinforce and revitalize specific tribal traditions, in addition to strengthening a sense of shared purpose and identity among Native American peoples.

Susan Applegate Krouse

BIBLIOGRAPHY

Lassiter, Luke Eric, ed. *Powwow: Native American Performance, Identity, and Meaning.* Lincoln: University of Nebraska Press, 2003.

Powers, William K. "The Indian Hobbyist Movement in North America." In *Handbook of North American Indians*, Vol. 4, *History of Indian-White Relations*, ed. Wilcomb E. Washburn. Washington, DC: Smithsonian Institution, 1988.

Royce, Anya Peterson. *The Anthropology of Dance.* Bloomington: Indiana University Press, 1977.

Thomas, Robert K. "Pan-Indianism." In *The American Indian Today*, ed. Stuart Levine and Nancy Oestreich Lurie. Deland, FL: Everett Edwards, 1971.

Weibel-Orlando, Joan. *Indian Country, L.A.: Maintaining Ethnic Community in Complex Society.* Rev. ed. Urbana: University of Illinois Press, 1999.

Young, Gloria A. Powwow Power: Perspectives on Historic and Contemporary Intertribalism. Ph.D. diss., Indiana University, 1981.

SOVEREIGNTY AND THE SELF-DETERMINATION MOVEMENT

As the twenty-first century unfolds, indigenous people will have to struggle against the same forces that wreaked havoc on uncounted numbers of their cultures, both in the Americas and throughout the world, during the last 500 years. Just as monocultural agriculture can be threatened by a single pathogen, a social monoculture often lacks the diversity and flexibility needed to survive in an uncertain and quickly changing world. So, given the unique worldview of each indigenous culture, Native Americans will be working to preserve each and every culture and each and every bit of knowledge that has been assembled within these cultures over thousands of years. The major thrust of their efforts to survive as intact cultures will be the assertion of their sovereignty and their inherent right to self-determination.

Of course, preserving cultures will be a futile effort if industrial societies render the planet as unlivable. Therefore, indigenous societies will focus much of their future efforts on educating the dominant society as to the necessity to maintain a livable planet for those generations yet unborn.

ENVIRONMENTALISM

The popular culture belief that indigenous people are natural conservationists is indeed based on their connection to the land, but indigenous people did not survive and thrive on this planet by conserving its resources. Instead, they figured out how to utilize and change the natural environment so that it would not only benefit those alive at the time, but also "improve" the existing resources in order to ensure their availability for future generations. So we see a tremendous movement today by indigenous people to continue to live in harmony with the planet as human beings have done for all but a brief period of our existence on this planet (that is, since the Industrial Revolution).

Such environmental philosophies are embodied in an indigenous worldview, which, in turn, is embodied in Native American languages. So, the next 500 years will see a movement to revitalize tribal languages, together with the cultures and worldviews that are embodied within those languages. This is a critical time in human history. Of the thousands upon thousands of world languages extant in 1492, many thousands have already been lost; and of the 6,000 to 7,000 remaining in the world today, it has been estimated that half of these will not survive into the next century. Only a few languages indigenous to North America are expected to be among those that survive, so the work of tribal people struggling to maintain the cultural workings of their language and worldview hovers on the edge of desperation. It is a huge challenge, made even more difficult by the ubiquitous nature of Western culture and its influence on individuals, cultures, and societies around the globe.

Although cultural survival is embodied within the Native American languages and worldview, the modern political world also demands that Native Americans fight to maintain what vestiges of sovereignty they have been fortunate enough to retain. In the United States, the fact that American Indian tribes signed treaties with the government is an implicit recognition of their sovereign status. Canada's constitution recognizes the "inherent rights" of Aboriginal people, although the definition and interpretation of those rights (and who is and who is not "Aboriginal" in both the American and Canadian context) are always subject to judicial review.

Of course, sovereignty is only as valid as it is accepted by other sovereign peoples, and the record all over the world has not been good for indigenous people. Although the United Nations has recently set up a forum for indigenous voices, not one of the United Nations 191 member-states is representative of any indigenous peoples—they are truly "stateless" and virtually without a voice in world affairs. With the world's political organization based quite simply on the nation-states that grew as a result of European water in the West, Native American tribes are struggling to regain rights to waters that were, decades ago, "allocated" to various farming and industrial interests in violation of treaties. This is not merely one parochial interest trumping another parochial interest, but rather a struggle to see which worldview will prevail—that of native people or the "water as a commodity" view of the dominant society.

As the tribes of the Western United States struggle to regain their rights to their own resources, Canada may provide some guidance on where Aboriginal people are going in their continuing struggle for self-determination. Canada's Constitution contains this clause: "The existing aboriginal and treaty rights of the aboriginal peoples of Canada are hereby recognized and affirmed" (Section 35[1]). This clause gives the Aboriginal people of Canada constitutional protection that their counterparts in the United States do not enjoy. Of course, just as in the case of a unilateral assertion of sovereignty, aboriginal rights are only those that can be fought for and won in the Canadian court system.

In a famous Canadian Supreme Court case, *Mitchell v. MNR* (2001), a chief of the Mohawk asserted an aboriginal right to bring some goods for personal use and trade with other First Nations people into Canada without having to pay duty. This right to bring goods across the border duty-free has been a long-standing concern for native people all along the U.S./Canadian border, and Chief Mitchell's case was just one more in a very long string of cases that all refer back to Jay's Treaty (1794) where the right of duty-free passage was expressly stated—"nor shall the Indians passing or repassing with their own proper goods and effects of whatever nature, pay for the same any impost or duty whatever" (Article III).

Although Chief Mitchell won in the lower courts when they agreed that he had a constitutional "aboriginal right" to bring a small quantity of personal goods into Canada from the United States, the Canadian Supreme Court ruled against him, stating that it is the sovereign right of nations to impose import duties and that, therefore, it would be an abrogation of Canadian sovereignty to allow anyone—including Aboriginal people—to abridge that right. So, for the immediate future, the struggle of Canada's Aboriginal people will be to test the limits of their constitutionally protected "aboriginal and treaty rights."

Another very important feature of the Canadian Aboriginal experience is the fact that Aboriginal people in British Columbia have no historical treaty relationship with the government, either with the

Nita Gonzales (seated, left) of Escuela Tlatelolco, Glenn Morris (seated, right) of the American Indian Movement, and members of the Transform Columbus Day Alliance gather on the steps of the Colorado State Capitol Building in Denver on October 5, 2001. The group, which represents more than eighty community-based organizations, opposes traditional celebrations of Columbus Day and seeks alternative ways to commemorate the first encounter between Europeans and Indians in 1492. *(AP Wide World Photos)*

colonization and domination of indigenous peoples, we can expect that this struggle will only intensify as our "global village" shrinks in size and as the world moves closer to a true monoculture—which will be "Western" and "modern" to be sure.

RIGHTS TO RESOURCES

The survival of a livable planet, sovereignty, and the struggle against cultural genocide are obviously global issues, but there are some more "local" issues that should be recognized as important for the survival of future generations. Water rights in the Western United States are one of those critical, local concerns, as indigenous tribal rights are often set aside in favor of individual "rights." In the case of

Crown or with provincial authorities. The first of these "modern" treaties was negotiated with the Nisga'a people and ratified on April 13, 2000. It gives the Nisga'a sovereignty over 2,000 square kilometers and a degree of self-government that will be the precedent for other First Nations peoples across Canada as they negotiate modern agreements with Canadian government officials. This, of course, not only is an agenda of those Aboriginal people in Canada, but will serve as a model for Native Americans in the United States as they assert their rights.

FEDERAL RECOGNITION AND CASINOS

Although there are over 550 federally recognized tribes in the United States, there are over 200 more that seek federal recognition. Federal recognition allows tribes to enter into a government-to-government relationship with the United States. The effort by tribes to gain federal recognition is a process that has been going on for many decades. Some tribes were denied recognition during the Depression when the government simply couldn't afford to recognize any more tribes, so their applications have been "pending" since the 1930s. For other tribes, the effort to gain federal recognition is a more recent phenomenon, fueled in some cases by the desire to obtain official recognition in order to open a casino. Casinos are often seen as the means whereby tribal people can achieve a degree of economic well-being that has been denied to them by centuries of exploitation and neglect by the dominant society. Of course, gaming is only one of the economic areas that tribal people are hoping to exploit in order to bring themselves out of the abject poverty that many have faced for a long time—and successful casino operations can only be mounted in areas that have a population large enough to support them, making gaming an option that is not available to many of the poorest, rural tribes.

Casinos and other economic enterprises are only one element of the huge puzzle that indigenous people are struggling to piece together in order to achieve even a minimal level of self-sufficiency. Obviously, the "wardship" status of native people severely restricts their ability to provide services that adequately meet the needs of their members. As can be seen by any discussion of the last 500-plus years of government "reform" efforts, these efforts have often not borne any fruit that is worthy of being emulated and repeated. So the dilemma facing many Aboriginal people both in the United States and in Canada has been to determine how to balance their absolute need for government assistance—often mandated by treaty—

with their strong desire to escape from the yoke of dependency, which is engendered by that very same life-support assistance.

ECONOMIC SURVIVAL

So while Aboriginal people on both sides of the U.S. and Canadian border face different governments and different dependency relationships to those governments, the one thing that all will agree upon is the need to escape the grinding poverty and hopelessness that large numbers of native people face. It's not because they live in resource-poor areas—although many do—but more because those resources are generally not being managed for the benefit of the tribe from whose land these resources are being extracted. Perhaps the most egregious example of the U.S. government failing in its responsibility to Native people can be seen in the unfolding scandal over the government mismanagement of tribal "trust funds." These trusts are established to manage the many billions of dollars the government collects on tribes' behalf (often in the form of lease revenue or royalties from resource extraction activities on tribal lands). The scandal that is now unfolding is pointing at the inability of the Bureau of Indian Affairs to account for over $2 billion in just a twenty-year period (from 1973 to 1992). No one can even estimate how many more billions have disappeared over the last 180 years (the Bureau of Indian Affairs was established in 1824).

But the economic sustenance provided for by even the admittedly mismanaged trust funds was often all that was available to many of the poorest of tribal people. And it is difficult to think about how to achieve economic self-sufficiency when you're not sure where your next meal will come from. So, the very strong movement toward economic self-sufficiency that is being promoted by many tribal leaders is often tempered by the reality that governments can—and often do—implement programs that will adversely affect the people that these same programs are ostensibly designed to help.

The road to self-sufficiency that many tribes will be traveling in these next 500 years will be found to be full of potholes with numerous detours along the way—many down blind alleys. But Native American people are still going to travel those back roads because their cultures demand that they look to providing for future generations. The dual goals of self-sufficiency and self-determination can be viewed as simply the two sides of the same coin. It seems that these are the challenges of native people everywhere. As the world moves closer and closer to a universal monoculture based on the "American" standards of *individual* "democratic" and economic rights, more local and "parochial" concerns seem to be moving to the fore.

For the long term, we may hope that people are discovering that a consumer-driven need for instant (and private) gratification doesn't make for a culture that sustains the very human need to be a *social* creature (especially when contrasted to the media-derived "need" to be an *economic* creature). In the next 500 years, people may discover what indigenous people have known all along: that we need each other to survive and that the "meaning of life" (if such a thing can be examined) can be explained as a need to live in harmony and balance with all of the elements of creation, not just those that can be bought and sold at a profit, and, of course, with each other. Perhaps it's not too late. Perhaps the way that worked so well for over 2 million years and was only abandoned in the last 200 will once again provide people with what they need. Perhaps all that is needed for the next 500 years is the example provided by indigenous people, who have survived this last 500 years with their cultures, if not unscathed, at least still alive. The struggle

then is to maintain (or, in some cases, regain) the cultural knowledge that Native Americans have developed over time and to maintain that worldview as embodied in their languages.

Phil Bellfy

BIBLIOGRAPHY

Bemis, Samuel Flagg. *Jay's Treaty; a Study in Commerce and Diplomacy.* New Haven, CT: Yale University Press, 1962.

Canada Supreme Court. *Mitchell v. M.N.R.* Ottawa: SCC 33. File No. 27066, 2001.

Churchill, Ward, ed. *Critical Issues in Native North America.* Copenhagen: IWGIA, 1989–1991.

Deloria, Vine, Jr., and Clifford M. Lytle. *American Indians, American Justice.* Austin: University of Texas Press, 1983.

Hawkes, David C. *Aboriginal Peoples and Constitutional Reform: What Have We Learned?* Kingston, Ontario: Institute of Intergovernmental Relations, Queen's University, 1989.

Mercredi, Ovide, and Mary Ellen Turpel. *In the Rapids: Navigating the Future of First Nations.* Toronto: Viking, 1993.

NARF. *Native American Rights Fund Annual Report.* Boulder, CO: NARF, 2002.

IDENTITY, MASCOTS, AND PLAYING INDIAN

At the 1754 Albany Congress held near the Mohawk Nation in Albany, New York, Benjamin Franklin stuck a feather in an Englishman's cap and called him an American by making direct, and allegorical, reference to the Iroquois Confederacy in the drafting of the Albany Plan of Union. When Franklin dipped his quill into the inkwell and wrote the words "Sachem and Grand Council" as a way of describing a union of thirteen English colonies, in this famous precursor to the Articles of Confederation and the U.S. Constitution, he symbolized a new national movement. At this early stage of revolutionary sentiment, Franklin's words marked the beginning of what would become an age-old association with the stereotypical image of the American Indian. Thereafter, the American Indian, converted to a standardized and usable image, became an emblem of American identity and the origin of the stereotypical Indian mascot and logo.

In 1773, nineteen years after the Albany Congress and on the eve of the American Revolution, the Sons of Liberty paid tribute to this earlier effort at union by dressing as Mohawk warriors and throwing English tea overboard into Boston harbor. On that glorious oak stage, for the world to see, the Boston Tea Party participants identified themselves as Mohawks as a symbol of their American background and patriotic protest. With this purposeful display, they directly associated themselves with Benjamin Franklin's Albany Plan of Union, the first intellectual discourse on federal representative self-rule and confederation. The Sons of Liberty first appeared in the 1760s as an organization created in opposition to "taxation without representation," the Stamp Act, the Quartering Act, and other oppressive legislation.

At the Boston Tea Party, men dressed as and played Indian for symbolic, and revolutionary, purposes; they had no desire to become "savages" themselves. The Boston Tea Party "Mohawks" planned no subterfuge to disguise their identities. They fully expected arrest and trial. In fact, they avoided the pitfalls of savage behavior, as they perceived it, by practicing peaceful civil disobedience and dramatic and symbolic protest. A broadside issued in Boston in 1774 and entitled "Tea Destroyed by Indians" emphasized this point: "Ye GLORIOUS SONS OF FREEDOM, brave and bold, / That has stood forth—fair LIBERTY to hold; / Though you were INDIANS, come from defiant shores, / Like MEN you acted— not like savage Moors." Even though war paint and war clubs do appear on the surface as implements of savagery, the Boston Tea Party "Mohawks" demonstrated to the world that they were not savage warriors but civilized men making a symbolic point. They did no harm to anyone, nor did they destroy property other than the hateful tea.

THE SONS OF LIBERTY AND ITS DESCENDANTS

The Sons of Liberty created the archetypal model of invented American Indian ritual, warrior look, custom, and caricature. With the image and symbol of their invented Indian, they made their European social antecedents decidedly "American." They did not reject their Western civilized origins. To convert socially accepted secret organizations of European origin, like the society of Free and Accepted Masons, to a uniquely American version, or to invent new ones with an American flavor, the image of the Indian served the American patriots well. Often, a weathervane, fashioned in the form of a Native American archer, identified a secret meeting place, usually a barn, where Sons of Liberty patriots would gather. Like the Freemasons, the Sons of Liberty adopted elaborate rituals, but instead of creating rituals echoing and paying homage to ancient Egypt, the Americans invented rituals echoing the culture, dress, and manners of the American Indian. They donned an Indian warrior guise, sang Indian songs, and smoked an Indian pipe of their own invention. Tar and feathering, tomahawks embedded in entranceways, and the menacing presence of Americans dressed as Indians at doorsteps signaled to their enemies their patriotic and serious intent. They acted in a controlled savage manner against their English opponents, but they still believed in their civilized and European origins. Because they communicated an American identity rather than a Mohawk one, the Sons of Liberty sought to portray a generic, standard image of an American Indian with very little relation to any existing tribe.

According to Sons of Liberty lore, the Delaware chief, Tammany, was their source of indigenous inspiration. Tammany, or Tamanend, was believed to be the Delaware "king" of the Lenni Lenape Confederacy, which was a precolonial power occupying the territory later known as Pennsylvania. His legendary life and history are purported to be an invention of the Sons of Liberty, though some aspects of his life are supposedly based on fact. R.G. Horton writes in his *History of Tammany Society, or, Columbian Order* (1865): "The Sons of Liberty were determined that America should not be behind other countries in the illustrious character of her productions, and hence they invented the legendary accounts of the distinguished chieftain." These legendary accounts told of a proud and brave leader of native people who was vigorous in mind and body. And though he "devoted himself to the acts of peace," he waged war on the "evil spirit" that would deny his people liberty and happiness. To colonial Americans, these notions of liberty through self-determination and defended with a warrior's strength were powerful and admirable concepts. The sanctity of these notions was embodied in the very person of Chief Tammany, the fierce warrior hero who would not submit to a loss of his liberty or of his rights. Because of these qualities, and the fact that he was a product of the American environment, he was "without question, one of the most distinguished red men who ever lived"; therefore, he was ideally suited to symbolically represent the revolutionary cause. "Liberty" was a word that became synonymous with the word "Tammany" and was thought to be a direct translation of the Delaware word and name of the great chief. According to R.G. Horton, "Their watchword was 'Tammany and Liberty.' " Not surprisingly, the Sons of Liberty were often called the Sons of Tammany.

Once the association with the American Indian was clearly established as symbol and mascot, the newly formed American government would also honor their war heroes with medals bearing this image, or logo. During the American Revolution, for example, Anthony Wayne, for his retaking of Stoney Point, and Daniel Morgan, for his heroism at the Bat-

tle of Cowpens, were each awarded a medal that displays an American Indian warrior with a quiver of arrows bestowing a wreath of *laurus nobilis* to a white gentleman dressed in a military uniform of the Revolutionary army. Clearly, the association is symbolic. The civilized gentleman honored by and associated with the noble savage is the meeting of the two halves of American identity. The minting and the granting of these peculiar medals show the importance of American Indians as emblems of independence and democracy. The most famous and enduring examples are the U.S. coins that depict the head of an American Indian warrior, a tradition carried on with the issuing of the Sacajawea dollar coin in 2000.

After the Revolution, the Tammany Society and the Society of Cincinnati would continue the prerevolutionary traditions of the Sons of Liberty; they were organizations that incorporated "classical" history as myth as well as "Indian democracy." They, too, would adapt features of American Indian warrior life into their organizations and rituals. In 1830, the Improved Order of Red Men was formed along similar lines. This order claims to be the oldest secret society of purely American origin. The Improved Order of Redmen did not admit "real Indians" as members. "Improved" meant that members had to be an American of *European* descent. American meant those males who could trace ancestors to the American colonial experience and to the American Revolution. Civilized Americans, in this sense, "improved" the natural condition of the positive qualities of the savage redman. They, like the Sons of Liberty, believed they were the true sons and inheritors of North America who would, in a predestined manner, replace the original inhabitants.

The most famous descendants of the Sons of Liberty were the Sons of St. Tammany; they were officially known as the Tammany Society or Columbian Order. They were organized in 1789 in favor of democratic ideas and principles as opposed to monarchical and aristocratic ones. As Marcus Jernegan notes in his study "The Tammany Societies of Rhode Island" (1887), they were strictly a political organization rather than a hobbyist or honor society. Their original purpose was to perpetuate and protect principles that "grew out of their belief in liberty, representative government, social and political equality." To symbolize this purpose, they adopted the banner of the spirited patriot soldiers and zealous Sons of Liberty. Jernegan adds: "It is usually maintained that certain troops from Pennsylvania under Washington's command first inscribed St. Tammany on their banners and dubbed him a saint." Tammany, the American Indian warrior, philosopher, statesman, and patron saint of America, served as the emblematic model for native warrior virtues.

GAMES AND RITUALS

After the American Revolution and once native populations were killed or otherwise displaced, "playing Indian" became a common game among children of all generations, past and present, to the point that it became a rite of passage of sorts. Young boys will often play with toy forts, toy Indian warriors, toy cowboys, and toy cavalry. These games provide a way for children to experience something about the hardships of settlement and survival in the North American continent, the invention of the United States, and Manifest Destiny. Often the play centers on the fighting of American Indians in heroic and romantic settings. Killing them in mock "cowboy 'n' Indian" fights, the role playing of "braves or chiefs," or even the practicing of native skills, like canoeing, archery, stalking, and scouting, can teach children something about the myth of the American frontier and its place in American history.

In Massachusetts, around 1853, William Wells Newell, a collector and analyzer of games played by American children, remembered how much native tribes occupied the imagination of young Americans. He recorded numerous American Indian games played by boys and girls alike. Such games of the early 1800s would be adapted and played by generations of American children in the years after. Games are rituals, and the games played by children are often unique and revealing of subliminal cultural beliefs and practices. Once real Indians were no longer a threat, American adults and children alike were free to imagine their own versions of fantasy warriors for play and for more utilitarian purposes as well.

In the early 1900s, Ernest Thompson Seton's handbook, *The Birch-bark Roll of the Woodcraft Indians*, and his other books, including *How to Play Indian* (1903), would carry on traditions of playing American Indian. Although Lord Baden-Powell of England wrote the first Boy Scout handbook, he has acknowledged that most of its organizational content was adopted from Seton's *Birch-bark Roll of the Woodcraft Indians*. Baden-Powell merely eliminated reference to Native Americans and adopted a more conventional military uniform for his boys. Nevertheless, in 1910, when the Boy Scouts of America (BSA) was formed in New York City, the American Indian was considered integral to America's scouting movement. Seton's *Boy Scouts of America: A Handbook of Woodcraft,*

Scouting, and Life Craft (1910) was written as the American version of the British Boy Scout handbook. American heritage and American ideals had to be made a part of the organization, handbook, and movement. American Indians are especially highlighted in the BSA's honor society, called The Order of the Arrow. Within a few years after 1910, the BSA had in itself become an American tradition. By 1926, according to the BSA handbook, the popularity of this movement had been confirmed, for over half the men attending college at that time had been Boy Scouts.

LOGOS AND MASCOTS

Paralleling the rise of the Boy Scout movement was the rise of the use of images of American Indians as commercial symbols that became very popular eye-catchers because they are subliminal reminders of American heritage and identity. As trademark designs, American Indian warriors mark the product as authentic, American, and original. From the late 1800s to today, Hiawatha Corn, Wampum Canned Goods, Bow-String Rubber, Cherokee Coal, American Copper and Cable, Calumet Baking Powder, American Baking Powder, Red Warrior Axes, Savage Arms, Red Cloud Chewing Tobacco, and Big Chief Sugar, to name a few, have successfully used images of American Indian warriors to sell and promote their products.

By the 1950s, names, war weapons, cognomens, and caricatures suggesting American Indian warriors or culture were appearing not only as logos for consumer products but as logos and mascots for sports teams. In the arena of sports, team names like Chippewas, Redskins, Indians, Chiefs, Braves, and Warriors reveal a connection to Americanism and the invented Indian of Revolutionary times. The display of the invented Indian as a logo or a mascot to a hungry spectator culture eager for these historical and contemporary distortions stands for, and symbolizes, the ultimate appropriation and conquest of the North American continent. The use of American Indians as logos and mascots shows the end development of an emblematic and readily consumable native warrior guise. Spectators and players recognize the symbolic qualities of the indigenous identity. The practice of the so-called tomahawk chop at Atlanta Braves baseball games is yet another example of this symbolic use.

With the seemingly endless visual, oral, and dramatic representations of the invented Indian in contemporary society, Americans find it difficult to sort through the pseudo-Indian fabrications and art fakery to find some sense of authenticity that is not steeped in romanticism and nostalgia. This is especially evi-

Carrying a poster of various sports team Indian mascots, Jan Saiz of Madison, Wisconsin, and Hugh Danforth of Oneida, Wisconsin, denounce the stereotyped images as racist and demeaning at a demonstration in Madison on March 22, 2002. The mascot in the center represents the Cleveland Indians, one of Major League Baseball's oldest teams. *(AP Wide World Photos)*

dent when you consider the lack of attention and interest in the historical place and role of contemporary Native Americans in modern society. As can be easily ascertained, Americans want to keep Indians in the past, dressed in war paint and moccasins. Examine some of the images found on the wrappers and packaging of products sold at your local grocer, like *Big Chief Sugar*, or examine closely some of the American Indian logos pasted to the helmets and caps of high school, college, and professional sports teams to confirm this point. Not many Native Americans are de-

picted in graduation caps and gowns, grasping their diplomas in eager anticipation of what the future holds for them. Although dressing up like an American Indian warrior, or accepting a team's logo that depicts one, may be symbolic of what it means to be an American, it is at the same time an ominous expression of prejudice and racism because its adherents do not realize that what they do is harmful to current-day Native American people. However, the majority of Americans believe the use of these images is harmless and, ironically, respectful.

Apart from the fact that the Sons of Liberty were predisposed to use deadly force, their behavior—the dressing up, the war paint, the cult of violence—had much in common with the modern-day sporting event, especially with the use of American Indian mascots and logos, and the "dressing up" of spectators. Contemporary Americans, however, are befuddled over questions concerning the "proper" or "improper" use of American icons such as an image or caricature of an American Indian. Unlike the Boston Tea Party Mohawks who knew the difference between the Mohawks they depicted and the real Mohawks they fought and killed on the frontier, fans and players in modern times do not understand the distinction between the "Indian" invented by the Founding Fathers and real-life, flesh-and-blood, natives who signed treaties with the United States. On the other hand, Colonial Americans, the Sons of Liberty in particular, understood the origin of the native people they honored and Benjamin Franklin realized that the use of American Indians as symbolic devices had historical significance. Over the course of 200 years of American history, this historical connection has diminished to a litany of unanswered questions and has dissolved into the vagaries of mass culture.

In other American art forms—literature, sculpture, paintings, and photography—and in forms of American popular culture—dime novels, Wild West shows, movies, and television—the image of the American Indian endures with ever-increasing popularity. In this new millennium, corporations, universities, and grade schools throughout the United States still adopt the visages of the invented Indian for use as trademarks, logotypes, and mascots. These images of Indians, which often symbolize corporate identity and school pride, affirm the importance of the invented Indian and of playing Indian in American history and culture. The image and likeness of the native warrior has certainly become an enduring feather stuck in Yankee Doodle's cap but has little to do with real Native Americans themselves.

Patrick LeBeau

BIBLIOGRAPHY

Burton, Bruce. "The Iroquois Had Democracy Before We Did." In *Indian Roots of American Democracy*, ed. Jose Barreiro. *Cultural Encounter I. Northeast Indian Quarterly*, IV, V (1988): 45.

Franks, Ray. *What's in a Nickname? Exploring the Jungle of College Athletic Mascots*. Amarillo, TX: Ray Franks Publishing Ranch, 1982.

Fryatt, Norma R. *Boston and the Tea Riots*. Princeton, NJ: Auerbach, 1972.

Hirschfelder, Arlene B. *American Indian Stereotypes in the World of Children*. Metuchen, NJ: Scarecrow, 1982.

Horton, R.G. *History of Tammany Society, or, Columbian Order*. New York: Tammany Society, 1865.

Jernegan, Marcus W. "The Tammany Societies of Rhode Island." *Papers from the Historical Seminary of Brown University* 8 (1887): 10–15.

Johansen, Bruce E. *Forgotten Founders: How the American Indian Helped Shape Democracy*. Harvard and Boston, MA: Harvard Common Press, 1987.

"Journal of the Proceedings of the Congress Held at Albany, in 1754." In *Collections of the Massachusetts Historical Society*, pp. 9–74. Boston: John H. Eastburn, 1836.

Newell, William Wells. *Games and Songs of American Children*. New York: Dover, 1963.

Preuss, Arthur. *A Dictionary of Secret and Other Societies*. London: B. Herder Book, 1924.

Rosenthal, Michael. *The Character Factory: Baden-Powell and the Origins of the Boy Scout Movement*. New York: Pantheon Books, 1984.

Seton, Ernest Thompson. *The Birch-bark Roll of the Woodcraft Indians*. New York: A.S. Barnes, n.d.

———. *How to Play Indian*. New York: Curtis, 1903.

———. *Boy Scouts of America: A Handbook of Woodcraft, Scouting, and Life Craft*. New York: Doubleday, 1910.

———. *Two Little Savages: Being the Adventures of Two Boys Who Lived as Indians and What They Learned*. New York: Grosset & Dunlap, 1911.

Stedman, Raymond William. *Shadows of the Indian: Stereotypes in American Culture*. Norman: University of Oklahoma Press, 1982.

Whalen, William J. *Handbook of Secret Organizations*. Milwaukee, WI: Bruce, 1966.

INDIGENOUS PEOPLE AND ENVIRONMENTALISM

The Indigenous environmental movement grew steadily throughout the last decades of the twentieth century and continues to grow in the twenty-first. Its growth correlates with the resurgent native religious systems that are built on earth-centered values: most aboriginal cultural groups have deeply rooted ecological traditions, even though they vary widely in the specifics of their religious beliefs. Traditional teachings generally refer to the interconnectedness and sacredness of all organisms within the web of life; the importance of respect for the Earth Mother; and the understanding that any damage done to flora, fauna, and the land itself affects all living things, including humankind, because all things are interconnected. Traditional native belief is built on a "theology of place" in which people do not separate themselves from the land: to that end, Gregory Cajete quotes an elder's explanation that "This is the place that made us." The religious connection to the earth, as well as a history of complicated and protracted land conflicts, may explain the focus of the most visible and publicized contemporary environmental movements. In recent decades, aboriginal activism has been predominantly focused on protecting traditional lands from development, stopping destructive land use, reclaiming lost land rights, and battling against widespread environmental racism. Environmental racism is broadly defined as economic and political policies that disproportionately expose discrete communities of color to dangerously poor environmental conditions, negatively affecting public health and safety. The Economic Justice movement arose as an answer to the devastating impact which systematic exposure to toxic waste, highly polluting mineral extraction, environmental degradation, and economic divestment were having on communities. (For more information on Environmental Justice, see Robert A. Bullard's *Dumping in Dixie: Race, Class and Environ-*

mental Quality [2000] and *Unequal Protection: Environmental Justice and Communities of Color* [1994.])

ENVIRONMENTAL ACTIVISM

It is useful to think of the history of native peoples since the arrival of Christopher Columbus as an ongoing struggle for the right to occupy and determine the use of land. The continuing conflict over natural resources results from very different views of what land is and what it is for. Euro-American environmental policy has been built on the ideas that the human is the child of God, land is a commodity, and natural resources are gifts from God for people to consume. Most indigenous cultures believe that they are part of the land and that they have an enduring religious/ecological obligation to protect it—and therefore protect themselves. As a result of this conflict, when there was a question over who would retain possession of any particular area, Euro-American economic needs (such as grazing lands and commercial fishing) nearly always outweighed aboriginal cultural heritage (roaming buffalo herds and summer subsistence fisheries). In most situations, the governmental body would reallocate natural resources as it desired, and the native community was relocated, decimated, or prevented from continuing their traditional practices. Native peoples continue to view environmental conflicts as attacks upon culture, religious rituals, and their entire cosmological system.

There are other ways in which indigenous activists are different from other parts of the environmental movement. In contrast to large-scale organizations such as No Nukes, the Nature Conservancy, and Greenpeace, contemporary native environmental activists have often been weakened by their relative isolation. They frequently come together as a grassroots response to specific, localized problems associated with toxic waste, fishing rights, resource extraction, and other instances of Environmental Racism. The difficulties that these organizations face are endemic to their problems. Many campaigns emerge in rural communities (such as reservations and reserves) with a specific problem, so they have less political clout and fewer sources of funding for their campaigns. They are often led by people with less organizational experience and less access to high-quality legal representation, and they have staffs that can't match the media savvy of the corporations and political bodies they challenge. Without financial resources, publicity, and wide-ranging expertise, they have had limited success in fighting their battles.

They have been aided, however, by communication channels such as the Internet, which helps to combat the divide-and-conquer strategy often used to weaken individual environmental initiatives. The Internet has enabled the maintenance of umbrella organizations such as the Indigenous Environmental Network (IEN), which coordinates international symposia and acts as an information clearinghouse for regional campaigns. Organizations such as the IEN have implemented Internet-based initiatives, significantly augmenting the small amount of mainstream broadcast media coverage with native-produced news stories across all forms of media.

SAVING THE LAND FROM DEVELOPERS AND POLLUTERS

The increasing numbers of activists have begun to overcome the historic limitations of the indigenous environmental movements, and today's many campaigns continue to focus on a broad range of primarily land-related issues. Among the best places to begin searching for examples of issues-based campaigns is two-time Green Party vice presidential candidate and Mississippi Band Anishnaabe Winona LaDuke's *All Our Relations: Native Struggles for Land and Life* (1999), which explains much of the root of land-use issues in native communities: "our lands are home to a wealth of resources. Two-thirds of the country's uranium; one-third of all western low-sulfur coal; and vast hydroelectric, oil, and natural gas resources are all situated on Native land." LaDuke provides primers and historical frameworks for understanding such issues as the impact of coal mining on the Northern Cheyenne. She tells how the Northern Cheyenne fought to void substantially underpriced mineral-rights contracts negotiated on their behalf by the U.S. Bureau of Indian Affairs. They have invoked federal clean air standards to protect their communities, and they have helped form an organization called the

At a demonstration at the University of Minnesota on May 20, 2002, environmentalist and former Green Party vice-presidential candidate Winona LaDuke denounces gene mapping of wild rice. LaDuke and many fellow Native Americans liken the dangers of using plants for genetic research to desecrating sacred land. *(AP Wide World Photos)*

Council of Energy Resource Tribes (CERT) to aid other tribes in their negotiations with corporations and the U.S. government.

LaDuke describes the Mother's Milk Project, which advocates for the rights of the Akwesasne Mohawk people, who have been exposed to PCB poisoning in the St. Lawrence River for decades. They continue to fight for reparations and cleanup by corporations such as General Motors, Reynolds Aluminum, and Domtar. Aside from the direct impact of PCBs on individuals, the Akwesasne Mohawk have had to systematically change their diets and forego their fishing culture, contributing to significant public health changes such as increased rates of diabetes, heart problems, and obesity. She also explains the impact of Everglades destruction on the Florida Seminole, low-level jet combat training on the Nitassinan Innu, and nuclear weapon testing and waste storage on the Western Shoshone.

The Western Shoshone have consistently opposed the establishment of a centralized nuclear waste dump within Yucca Mountain, a site that is sacred to them and has also been deemed scientifically unfit for this sort of storage. In the summer of 2002, President George W. Bush cited the $8 billion of research into the project as his main justification of its continuance. Native groups and other environmentalists pledged to continue to fight during the construction phase, which will take nearly a decade. Yucca Mountain is a particularly good example of the issues that face native peoples, especially reservations. Because of their comparative remoteness, control of large tracts of land, and long history of impoverishment, reservation lands are excellent candidates for hosting toxic dumps. When an economically destitute community is presented the opportunity to bring in millions of dollars in exchange for allowing waste sites on their lands, the overwhelming temptation is to gamble that there will be no seepage into ground water or containment leaks. Communities must choose between poverty today and the potential for illness in the future. Many are tempted to opt for the latter, hoping that they are not contributing to irreparably harming the land to which their people have historical, cultural, and religious ties.

For these same reasons, Inuit whaling and aboriginal fishing rights in the United States and Canada are continuous points of contention. As outgrowths of treaty land-rights issues, they seem to be places in which native peoples would split from the mainstream environmental movement. However, these conflicts are nearly as much about resource management and the prevention of devastating effects on commercial fishing as they are about maintaining traditional cultural practices. What often gets lost in the conversations is the fundamental difference between a permanent community engaging in subsistence-style fishing versus broad-based harvesting of a series of regions. The former helps to maintain populations, whereas the latter devastates them and moves on to the next. Among the newest issues is a growing conflict over the introduction of genetically modified wild rice to the rice fields of Minnesota. Because wild rice

is a staple that the Anishnaabeg consider one of the Creator's most significant gifts, and one that must be protected and maintained, there are significant religious implications if that crop is substantially altered or harmed.

This same conflict—with the same underlying politics of land ownership and stewardship—arises in Donald Grinde (Yamasee) and Bruce Johansen's *Ecocide of Native America: Environmental Destruction of Indian Lands and Peoples* (1995) which adds several more cases to LaDuke's. After discussing historical approaches to the last 400 years of indigenous ecological history, they focus largely on mining and farming in Navajo country, fishing rights, and uranium mining, and they provide another perspective on PCBs in Akwesasne. Ward Churchill's *Struggle for the Land: Native North American Resistance to Genocide, Ecocide, and Colonization in Contemporary North America* (1999) provides an in-depth analysis of the relationship between aboriginal sovereignty and land issues. He includes additional perspectives on some of the issues mentioned above, and he discusses hydroelectric dams in Quebec, the Alberta Lubicon Cree's claims of cultural genocide and land misappropriation, and land wars in Navajo country. Other sources, such as Jace Weaver's *Defending Mother Earth: Perspectives on Environmental Justice* (1996) and Jill Oakes et al.'s *Sacred Lands: Aboriginal World Views, Claims, and Conflicts* (1998), further explore aboriginal world-views and environmental justice.

When looking at the broad range of abuses that native peoples are combating, often the fear becomes pervasive that all the sacred lands are being destroyed and that no fights can be won. This is not the case: there have been some successes. Perhaps the most visible recent example was led by the Gwich'in Athabaskans, who have sought to stop exploratory oil drilling in the coastal plains of the Arctic National Wildlife Refuge in northeast Alaska. In preventing the development of oil fields, they have been able to maintain the calving grounds of the porcupine caribou and protect one of the largest tracts of pristine land in the United States. LaDuke also writes of the White Earth Land Recovery Project, in which the White Earth Ojibwe of Minnesota have reacquired a portion of their traditional lands, largely through purchase. She also describes the successes of the NativeSun project, which is introducing alternative, renewable energy sources to the Hopi and Navajo communities. NativeSun hopes to empower the Hopi and Navajo peoples by ending their reliance on the power grid and helping them to assume control of their own energy needs in a way that will be respectful to the earth and reduce pollution as much as possible.

Jefferson Faye Sina

BIBLIOGRAPHY

Bullard, Robert A. *Dumping in Dixie: Race, Class and Environmental Quality*. Boulder, CO: Westview, 2000.

———. *Unequal Protection: Environmental Justice and Communities of Color*. San Francisco: Sierra Club Books, 1994.

Cajete, Gregory. " 'Look to the Mountain': Reflections on Indigenous Ecology." In *A People's Ecology*, ed. Gregory Cajete, 3–20. Santa Fe, NM: Clear Light, 1999.

Churchill, Ward. *Struggle for the Land: Native North American Resistance to Genocide, Ecocide, and Colonization in Contemporary North America*. Rev. and Expanded Edition. Winnipeg: Arbeiter Wing, 1999.

Freeman, Milton M.R., et al. *Inuit, Whaling, and Sustainability*. Walnut Creek, CA: Altamira, 1998.

Grinde, Donald A., and Bruce E. Johansen. *Ecocide of Native America: Environmental Destruction of Indian Lands and Peoples*. Santa Fe, NM: Clear Light, 1995.

Kawagley, A. Oscar. *A Yupiaq Worldview: A Pathway to Ecology and Spirit*. Prospect Heights, IL: Waveland, 1995.

LaDuke, Winona. *All Our Relations: Native Struggles for Land and Life*. Cambridge: South End, 1999.

Oakes, Jill, Rick Riewe, Kathi Kinew, and Elaine Maloney, eds. *Sacred Lands: Aboriginal World Views, Claims, and Conflicts*. Calgary: University of Alberta, 1998.

Osawa, Sandra Johnson. *Lighting the Seventh Fire*. Seattle, WA: Upstream Productions, 1994, 48 min.

Vecsey, Christopher, and Robert W. Venables, eds. *American Indian Environments: Ecological Issues in Native American History*. Syracuse, NY: Syracuse University Press, 1980.

Weaver, Jace, ed. *Defending Mother Earth: Perspectives on Environmental Justice*. Maryknoll: Orbis Books, 1996.

Struggle for the West: U.S. Indian Policy from Sand Creek to Wounded Knee

U.S. Indian policy went through a number of changes from the time of the Civil War, but in almost all cases, despite the good intentions of many people, the policies were unsuccessful. American Indians were stripped of their land, their culture, and, in some cases, their very lives. In almost every case the desires of the native peoples were discounted, while the individuals struggling to help the natives thrust upon them their own personal views of what would be best.

When the Civil War broke out in 1861, many of the western tribes found the pressure that had been placed upon them was temporarily relieved, as soldiers were withdrawn to fight further east. The Five Civilized Tribes in Indian Territory found themselves caught up in the struggle between North and South as each side struggled to gain the loyalty of these strategically located tribes. The Confederacy, through the promise of more liberal treaties than the United States had ever offered, and the more active presence of agents, eventually won the support of the majority of the members of the Choctaw and Chickasaw tribes. The Cherokee, Creek, and Seminole were more deeply divided.

Inaction by the Lincoln administration and early Confederate victories on the battlefield bolstered support for the pro-Confederate factions of these tribes, and in October 1861 the Cherokee formally severed their relationship with the United States. Within a year, however, the tides of war had begun to change, and the Indian Territory became vulnerable to Union attacks. Many Native Americans who had supported neutrality or the North quickly abandoned their loyalty to the South and tried to rebuild their ties with the Union but met a cold reception.

Forced Concessions

When the war came to an end, the Union used the Five Civilized Tribes' defection to the South as justification to force new concessions from them. Each of the tribes was forced to sign a treaty that effectively cut its land holdings in half. The confiscated lands on the western half of Indian Territory would be used to create reservations for other Western tribes.

The Civil War also affected the Sioux on the Northern Plains. The Santee Sioux, who had agreed to settle on reservations prior to the Civil War, were especially affected. With the advent of war, keeping reservations properly supplied was a low priority. The lack of promised supplies combined with poor crops caused the Santee Sioux to become restless. As hunger increased on the reservation, the Sioux were forced into action. A group of natives broke into the reservation's storehouse to steal enough food to feed themselves and avoid starvation. The government and the Indian agents' continued neglect called for more extreme action. Many young warriors talked openly of attacking the whites in the area and driving them out. Abraham Lincoln's withdrawal of several units of soldiers to fight the Confederates further emboldened them. Only the dire warnings of Little Crow, one of their chiefs, kept them from taking immediate action.

The telling blow occurred in 1862 when a group of Sioux stole eggs from a party of settlers and, after a brief altercation, murdered five of them. When Little Crow was told of the event, he immediately called a council and, despite his feelings to the contrary, decided to lead a preemptive strike against the settlers of Minnesota before they could seek revenge for the murders. The Sioux rose up *en masse* and attempted to rid the Minnesota Valley of white settlers. Their key mistake came when, ignoring the advice of Little Crow, they refused to launch an immediate attack on Fort Ridgely, the only stronghold in the vicinity. As a result, when the Sioux finally turned their attention to the fort, the number of defenders had swelled considerably, having been augmented by refugee pioneers.

It was nearly a month before General Henry Hastings Sibley led a party of Minnesota volunteers and militia to defeat the Sioux in a battle at Wood Lake. The victory dispersed the natives and ended organized resistance. Many fled west to join their kinsmen on the plains, while others surrendered. A hastily held trial of almost 400 captured Native Americans led to the conviction of 303, who were sentenced to death. President Lincoln eventually overturned all but thirty-nine of the sentences. In the largest mass execution in U.S. history, thirty-eight were eventually hanged. Tensions between the settlers and the Minnesota Sioux eventually led to the complete expulsion of the native peoples from the state, and a new reservation was created for them in the Dakota Territory.

SAND CREEK MASSACRE

In the Central Plains, the Cheyenne and Arapaho found themselves under pressure when gold was discovered in their region. For several years, the natives attacked miners and settlers who invaded their lands, alarming local Coloradoans. A group of Cheyenne and Arapaho under the leadership of Black Kettle desired peace and agreed to relocate to the area of Sand Creek. Other natives, however, continued to harass settlers and miners, hoping to drive them from the area. In 1864, Colonel John Chivington led a force of cavalry and militia to suppress the hostiles but attacked Black Kettle's band of peaceful Native Americans instead. The result was the Sand Creek Massacre, where over 100 men, women, and children were killed and their bodies were horribly and sexually mutilated. Although the carnage was widespread, Black Kettle and others did manage to escape.

When word of the Sand Creek Massacre reached Washington, D.C., there was widespread condemnation of Chivington and his actions. Many congressmen began agitating for a new policy concerning Native Americans, but the demands were necessarily set aside because of the constraints of the Civil War. A new treaty was finally negotiated in 1865 with the Cheyenne and Arapaho, as well as with the Comanche and Kiowa on the Southern Plains, but amendments to the treaties by the Senate ensured that the nations would not get the land promised by the treaties.

MILITARISM AND REPRESSION

Still, with the Civil War concluded, pressure mounted to establish a new policy to deal with the Indians. In December 1866, when Captain William Fetterman and eighty soldiers were ambushed and killed by a party of Sioux led by Chief Red Cloud on the Bozeman Trail in Wyoming, the need for a new policy became more urgent. After an intense investigation into the causes of conflict and the reasons for the decline of the tribes, two opposing factions emerged. One group favored peace, while the other favored a military solution. The peace faction urged creating reservations for each of the various tribes and teaching them English, farming, and the other skills thought necessary to make them productive citizens. The force faction argued that nothing less than continuous military harassment of the Native Americans, until their spirit was broken and their numbers decimated, would subdue them.

The resulting policy, often referred to as the peace policy, was actually a combination of the two. Tribes would be given individual reservations to live on and would receive subsidies and gifts to encourage them to accept their new lives. Those Native Americans who refused to settle on the reservations were to be suppressed militarily. Some tribes, realizing the futility of resistance, reluctantly accepted reservations obtained through treaties.

In 1867, a government commission met at Medicine Lodge Creek in southwestern Kansas to negotiate with the Southern Plains Indian tribes. Five thousand Comanche, Kiowa, Kiowa Apache, Arapaho, and Cheyenne attended the discussions. The treaty that emerged created two reservations in the western half of Indian Territory. One reserve would be established for the Comanche, Kiowa, and Kiowa Apache, and other would be created for the Arapaho and Cheyenne. Through a combination of gifts, promises, and threats, the commission acquired the agreement of all five tribes.

Two prominent chiefs, Roman Nose of the Cheyenne, and Satanta of the Kiowa, however, refused to sign the treaty and took their followers out into the plains. The commission, feeling that it had accomplished the majority of its goal, headed north to treat with the Northern Plains Indians. At Fort Laramie, in 1868, the commission gradually negotiated and signed treaties with the Crow, Northern Cheyenne and Arapaho, and the Sioux. The treaty created the "Great Sioux Nation" and called for the expulsion of all U.S. military from the region. Even the recalcitrant Red Cloud, who had been holding out, eventually signed the treaty.

Many individual Native Americans refused to accept reservation life and continued to travel across the plains to hunt the buffalo and, at times, cause depredations. The army had the impossible task of policing the entire plains and hunting down these "nontreaty" natives and forcing them to submit. Corruption by government officials exacerbated the problem. Indian agents received huge sums of money to keep the native peoples well-provisioned and to pay them subsidies, but often used the funds to purchase inferior-quality supplies or spoiled food while pocketing the savings. Increasingly, natives fled the reservation to live the freer life on the plains where they could obtain their own supplies and fresh buffalo meat.

In late 1868, General Philip Sheridan launched an extensive winter campaign to subdue the natives on the Southern Plains and force them to stay on their assigned reservations. One detachment pursued warriors into the peaceful encampment of Black Kettle, the survivor of the Sand Creek Massacre, who had scrupulously obeyed the provisions of the Treaty of Medicine Lodge Creek. The soldiers attacked the village, killing over 100 warriors, including Black Kettle. By early 1869, Sheridan's campaign of total warfare had killed many hostiles and nonhostiles, but concluded with the confinement of the remaining members of the tribe on their reservations.

The death of Black Kettle and other peaceful Native Americans led Congress to create the Board of Indian Commissioners that same year. The board was led by Christian leaders, determined to win over the natives through missionary programs. Although the board members no doubt believed that they were serving the best interests of the tribes, they refused to take into consideration the Native American beliefs or customs and insisted that they convert and accept Christian ideals. Interdenominational rivalry and resistance from government officials bent on profiting from the natives' plight caused most of the board's recommendations to be rejected. The board did abolish the treaty system, however, as this idea fit well with Congress's plans. After 1871, Native Americans would no longer be considered members of a nation or tribe but wards of the federal government. Within a decade, the original members of the board had been replaced with individuals more malleable to the desires of Congress and government agencies.

EXPROPRIATION AND ANNIHILATION

Meanwhile, the army had realized that as long as the buffalo roamed the plains, the natives could not be forced to stay on the reservation. In fact, many treaties had granted the Native Americans permission to leave the reservation to hunt buffalo to supplement their food supply. Any time they felt abused or mistreated, or sometimes because they simply wanted to

return to their old lifestyles, groups would flee the reservations to live the free life on the plains, which supplied them with all the necessities of life.

Prior to the 1870s, buffalo had been hunted sporadically by hunters hired by railroad companies to supply cheap meat for workers, or by sportsmen for the thrill of the kill. But by 1871 eastern industries discovered a commercial use for buffalo hides, and professional hunters joined the action. Within a decade the buffalo herds were decimated to the point of near extinction. Indian hunting parties rarely if ever encountered buffalo on their off-reservation jaunts and now had little choice but to accept the dismal life on the reservation.

As the organized buffalo hunts began, and the Native Americans saw their way of life being obliterated, Indian raids flared up once again. In 1874, a large party of Kiowa, Comanche, and Cheyenne attacked a party of buffalo hunters at Adobe Walls in the Texas panhandle. Although the hunters held off the attackers, their eventual withdrawal after the fight encouraged more natives to join the uprising. Soon the Southern Plains in Texas, New Mexico, Kansas, and Colorado were swarming with native warriors intent on driving the buffalo hunters out. General Sheridan was once again called upon to subdue them in what would become known as the Red River War. Sheridan launched a multipronged invasion of the area and ruthlessly pursued the Native Americans through the winter of 1874–1875, burning camps, destroying supplies, and killing or capturing natives. One by one, the tribes surrendered. By the summer of 1875, the last holdouts, a band of Comanche, surrendered at Fort Sill.

Once the war ground to a halt, the government hoped to ensure there would be no further outbreaks by imprisoning a number of prominent chiefs. As further insurance, additional native leaders and prominent warriors were exiled to Florida, where they remained until finally released in 1878. By that time most of the southern tribes had realized the futility of resistance and reluctantly accepted reservation life.

AGGRESSION AND RESISTANCE ON THE NORTHERN PLAINS

On the Northern Plains relations had been relatively peaceful. The powerful Sioux nation was effectively divided into two groups. One group led by Chiefs Red Cloud and Spotted Tail lived on the Great Sioux Reservation in South Dakota. The other group roamed the unceded lands in the Powder River and Bighorn Mountains region. The nomadic, nonreservation na-

Chief Sitting Bull led Sioux warriors in a victory over General George Armstrong Custer at the Battle of Little Big Horn on June 26, 1876. *(Denver Public Library)*

and was annihilated. Custer's defeat caused a public outcry in the East and resulted in more troops being sent to subdue the Native Americans. The natives, having no supply lines, could not keep a large force in the field for any length of time and eventually had to break into smaller bands. One by one, the bands were hunted down and forced to surrender. Crazy Horse and more than 1,000 natives surrendered in the spring of 1877. Sitting Bull and his followers fled to Canada, refusing to submit, although he eventually returned and surrendered in 1881. With Sitting Bull's surrender, even the powerful Sioux tribe realized the futility of resistance and, without the buffalo, survival off the reservation was all but impossible.

Other western tribes soon capitulated as well. In 1877 the Nez Perce led the U.S. Army on a dramatic 1,700-mile chase in a largely unsuccessful effort to escape to Canada. The Bannock, Shoshone, and Paiute in the Northwest rose up briefly in 1878–1879, only to be crushed by the army and ushered back to their reservations. Likewise, the Ute in Colorado staged a brief rebellion in 1879. The last Native Americans to be subjected to the force of military campaigns were the Apache in the mountains of New Mexico and Arizona. There, a small band led by Geronimo, successfully defied the army's attempts to contain them on reservations until the Apache, too, surrendered in 1886. In order to prevent any further problems, the government shipped Geronimo and 500 Apache to Florida to be imprisoned.

EFFORTS AT INCORPORATION

With the conclusion of organized resistance, and the gradual reduction of the size of reservations, the government attempted to incorporate the natives into the American system. The goal was to eventually eliminate the need for reservations completely and convert the natives into "productive" citizens. The assimilation policy revolved around two basic tenets. First, tribal unity had to be destroyed to teach the Native Americans individuality. This would be accomplished by taking them away from tribally owned reservations and giving them individual allotments of land to live upon. Second, children would be educated in specially created Indian boarding schools. They would be taught American culture away from the influence of their parents and the tribal mentality.

The passage of allotment legislation was hindered by reformers who feared that Native Americans did not sufficiently grasp the concept of private property. Reservations were community property, and few Indians understood how land could be "owned." To as-

tives were led by Sitting Bull and Crazy Horse. Both groups lived virtually unmolested until gold was discovered in the Black Hills, an area held sacred by the Sioux and part of the Great Sioux Nation. The flood of prospectors into the area—led by General George Armstrong Custer in violation of the 1868 treaty—necessarily caused friction with the natives. As hostilities erupted, the government stepped in and ordered all the Sioux to congregate at the reservation, thereby reducing their contact with gold hunters and freeing the gold-rich lands. The order was followed by an announcement that all Indians not on the reservation by early 1876 would be considered hostile and would be hunted down and brought in by military force.

Many Sioux had no intention of returning to the reservation; they, along with some Cheyenne allies, rallied around Sitting Bull and Crazy Horse. When the deadline passed, troops were sent to round up the natives. On June 26, 1876, General Custer led his troops in an attack on a large party at Little Big Horn sign them allotments, argued many reformers, would simply result in them selling these parcels of land off to the first white person who offered them money, resulting in a population of destitute, homeless natives. The problem was nuanced with the passage of the Dawes Act in 1887. According to the act, Indians would be allotted 160-acre plots, which would be held in trust by the government for twenty-five years, thus preventing them from selling it off. Once the reservation lands had been allocated to individuals, the "surplus" lands would be sold to white settlers.

The Dawes Act was an unqualified failure. It resulted in the loss of approximately 70 percent of tribal lands. The Native Americans, most of whom saw farming as degrading "women's work," refused to become the farmers that reformers expected. Instead of making them more independent, the Dawes Act actually increased their reliance on the American government for sustenance and support.

Education of the native children resulted in similar disappointment. The concept of educating the native peoples was not a new idea. Almost every Indian policy had included provisions for education, but they had all failed to yield the desired results. The latest idea was to remove the native children from the influence of their parents and tribal culture and place them in Indian boarding schools miles away from their families. In these more remote schools, it was reasoned, the children could be immersed in American culture and would be more susceptible to conversion. The first boarding school, the Carlisle Indian Industrial School, was opened in 1879; additional schools soon followed. The schools were set up in military fashion, with students wearing uniforms and held to a strict regimen, and emphasized learning English as the first step toward "civilization" (those caught speaking a tribal language were often subject to severe discipline). They also taught subjects like reading, writing, and arithmetic, but focused more on pragmatic skills that they thought would help students successfully blend into American society. Therefore, female students learned domestic skills, while male students were introduced to farming and industrial pursuits.

The success of the boarding schools is arguable, although school attendance increased fourfold between 1877 and 1890 (attendance was compulsory). The schools did have some success in destroying the Native American identity of many students, but at the same time that success caused resentment toward the white American culture that had destroyed this identity. Many of the graduates also found themselves out-

casts when they returned home, seen almost as traitors by their families and friends.

MASSACRE AT WOUNDED KNEE

The final blow to the Native Americans came at Wounded Knee in 1890. In the 1880s, a Paiute mystic named Wovoka emerged as an "Indian messiah." Wovoka preached that the Indians should give up their warlike ways and that if they performed a ceremonial dance known as the Ghost Dance, God would reward them by returning the buffalo and allowing their people, both living and dead, to (re)inherit the earth. Wovoka's influence spread rapidly across the west as Native Americans who lived degraded lives on reservations grasped at the glimmer of hope offered by his teachings.

The Sioux sent a delegation to interview Wovoka and learn more of his teachings. The delegates returned to the Sioux reservation with a more militant version of the Ghost Dance, which spread quickly among the reservation's population. Sitting Bull became one of the religion's staunchest advocates. As the natives became more and more frenzied with their performance of the dance, Indian agents became alarmed and called upon the army to end the dance. The army decided that the most effective way to disrupt the performances would be to arrest the leaders, especially Sitting Bull. Realizing that soldiers would not be allowed to take Sitting Bull without violence, the army sent in Indian police to arrest him. Sitting Bull's followers realized the intent of the native police force and moved to protect their revered leader. In the scuffle that ensued, Sitting Bull was killed. In the hope of escaping the army, many native people, under the leadership of Big Foot, attempted to join Red Cloud on his reserve and fled the reservation. Custer's old unit, the since re-formed Seventh Cavalry, was sent to return these Native Americans to the reservation. The cavalry caught up with the natives at the small village of Wounded Knee and surrounded them on December 28, 1890. The next morning, as the army was disarming the natives, one of their guns discharged and the army opened fire. When the smoke cleared, over 200 Sioux men, women, and children lay dead. Apparently in retaliation for Custer's defeat, and in a repeat of the shameful acts at Sand Creek, the bodies were again horribly mutilated.

The Wounded Knee Massacre brought a final and decisive end to armed native conflict. There would be no more uprisings, but the issue of how to handle the Native American population still remained. Attempts to concentrate the native peoples on reservations had failed when both natives and whites violated the boundaries set up in treaties. Attempts to Americanize the natives through individual plots of land and educating them to the American way also ended in failure. Wounded Knee only re-emphasized the need for a new policy to deal with Native Americans and showed clearly the failure of previous policies to have the desired effect. A new wave of legislation would be introduced at the turn of the century, and several new policies would be attempted to bring the American Indian into the American melting pot, but most would have no more success than those of the previous 100 years.

Jeffrey D. Carlisle

BIBLIOGRAPHY

Andrist, Ralph K. *The Long Death: The Last Days of the Plains Indians.* New York: Macmillan, 1964.

Brown, Dee Alexander. *Bury My Heart at Wounded Knee: An Indian History of the American West.* New York: Holt, Rinehart and Winston, 1973.

Hoig, Stan. *Tribal Wars of the Southern Plains.* Norman: University of Oklahoma Press, 1993.

Prucha, Francis Paul. *The Great Father: The United States Government and the American Indians.* Abridged edition. Lincoln: University of Nebraska Press, 1986.

Utley, Robert Marshall. *Frontier Regulars: The United States Army and the Indian, 1866–1891.* New York: Macmillan, 1973.

Weeks, Philip. *Farewell, My Nation: The American Indian and the United States, 1820–1890.* Wheeling, IL: Harlan Davidson, 1990.

IDENTITY AND LITERATURE

The use of literature to explore identity issues is not unique to the indigenous culture of North America. Some of America's most renowned works, for example, J.D. Salinger's *Catcher in the Rye* (1951), deal with the subject superbly. Yet, long before Salinger, native people used literature to explore identity issues and to present themselves and their culture to the broader, dominant society. Early works by native authors were often autobiographical religious tracts like those of George Copway and Peter Jones, missionaries who used their English-language skills and indigenous identity to spread Christianity among native people. Others, like Simon Pokagon and Andrew Blackbird, used their literary skills to tell the stories of their lives and their tribes, often with the intent to bring to light the many problems faced by native people struggling against the encroachments of "civilization."

These early authors (and many, many others) faced the issue of indigenous identity directly by working in the genre of autobiography. Others, like D'Arcy McNickle in *The Surrounded* (1936), turned away from autobiography to tell the story of native people struggling to maintain their identity through a more fictional and tribal approach. Often, these early fictional accounts of native people on the cusp between traditional life and "civilization" met with wide success and brought a large measure of respectability to the emerging field of Native American literature.

The rise of the civil rights movement in this country, coupled with the emergence of "Red Power," led many authors to write stories that confronted the issue of Native American identity as less of a tribal issue—like *The Surrounded*, for instance—and created unique characters whose identity crisis could be confronted head-on through personal and probing literature. One of the most stunning of these works is *Winter in the Blood* (1974), by the Blackfeet/Gros Ventre author James Welch. In this dark novel, the main character is not even given a name; instead, he is a young man very troubled about his identity who spends much of the book searching for his roots and his place in modern society (when he's not drinking or off on some seemingly self-destructive adventure). Of course, by the end of the book, Welch has the protagonist finding his home—both physically and spiritually—back on the reservation of his birth.

Another dark and troubling story of the search for identity can be found in Oscar Zeta Acosta's *The Autobiography of a Brown Buffalo* (1972). Although Acosta returns to the autobiographical style utilized by earlier indigenous authors, his is not a story of "my life as an Indian." Instead, Acosta painfully explores American discrimination and alienation by delving deep into his Chicano roots, eventually finding himself broke and broken in Mexico, where he finally escapes from his tormented life to discover his place in North America as an indigenous person (hence the *Buffalo* reference in the title). In the end, he returns to his native California and embarks on a public life of activism for Chicano/Native American causes. Oscar Acosta, ironically true to the tumultuous, troubled life he led, disappeared around 1974 and is presumed dead.

Many other writers have focused on the cultural confusion that confronts many people of mixed blood and is manifested in identity crises typified by that of Oscar Zeta Acosta. In the Ojibway author Louise Erdrich's widely acclaimed novel, *Tracks* (1989), the character Pauline is tortured by her mixed-blood status; she is not truly comfortable or accepted in either the white or the native world. For the teenage Pauline, the ambiguity is too much to bear, and she rejects her identity as an American Indian, converts to Christianity, and eventually claims that Christ has declared her to be "pure white," like her grandfather. Contrasted to Pauline in the novel is an elder of Pauline's tribe, Nanapush, who is anything but confused about his heritage. Instead of doubt and rejection, Nanapush sees his mission in life as the teacher and exemplar of native identity not only for his fellow tribal members, but for those in the surrounding (and encroaching) white community. For Louise Erdrich (herself a mixed-blood), the novel *Tracks* is a masterful and imaginative exploration of what it means to be Native American in a world that demeans such traditional ways as superstition and seeks to impose a modernity upon a people who are—up to that point of culture conflict—comfortable knowing who they are.

Another brilliant exploration of native identity in modern fiction can be found in Laguna Pueblo author Leslie Marmon Silko's *Ceremony* (1977). Here the main character, Tayo, is another very confused and troubled mixed-blood who is rejected by both cultures. After failing to protect his full-blood cousin in World War II, and abandoning his uncle (who dies while he is gone) to go off and fight in the "whiteman's war," Tayo returns to his Southwestern reservation, which is in the midst of a drought. Suffering from post-traumatic stress syndrome and his personal guilt over the effects of the drought (he cursed the rain while in the South Pacific during the war), Tayo embarks upon a ceremonial process to restore his mental health, end the drought, and find his uncle's lost, half-breed cattle. Along this ceremonial path, he comes to accept that his "cure" lies in a warm embrace of his indigenous culture, always just outside of his reach owing to the fact that his rejection by the community was always a corollary to the pride and hope that was lavished on his full-blood cousin with whom he was raised as a brother. In the end, Tayo finds the mixed-blood cattle—who were returning to their southern, Mexican "roots"—and by doing so, completes the healing ceremony as it was laid out by a mixed-blood "medicine man." Aside from the obvious comparison between the lost cattle and Tayo's struggle for identity, Silko also uses the identity of Tayo's cousin/brother, Rocky, to explore the difficulties inherent in rejecting one's cultural heritage. Here she has Rocky as a full-blood who is hell-bent on rejecting his Native American heritage and making a "success" of himself in the dominant, non-native society. Yet he is senselessly killed fighting in "their" war, while his half-blood cousin/brother—in tune with his indigenous roots—survives. Profound ironies abound.

A distinctly different portrayal of a native protagonist is found in Pueblo/Yaqui writer Martin Cruz Smith's *Stallion Gate* (1986). In this novel of the building of the atomic bomb, Smith creates a "Super Indian" character named Joe Peña. Joe Peña, the driver for General Groves of the Manhattan Project, is as far from the unnamed James Welch character or Silko's Tayo as you can get—an accomplished jazz pianist, a combative and anti-authority GI, a champion boxer, a confidant (and adviser) to those building the atomic bomb, a spy-chaser, a womanizer, an important Indian dancer, an expert marksman, and general all-around Super Everyman. In this novel, Smith uses the accomplishments of Joe Peña to undermine and dispel the stereotypes of the lost, identity-less, and searching character so common in many of the books that explore Native American identity.

A great number of other important indigenous writers explore the theme of identity in their works—such as Charles Eastman (*Indian Boyhood*, 1902), Mourning Dove (Hum-ishu-ma) (*Cogewea, the Half-blood: A Depiction of the Great Montana Cattle Range*, 1981), Sarah Winnemucca (*Life Among the Piutes: Their Wrongs and Claims*, 1883), and the Pulitzer Prize–winning N. Scott Momaday, who won the prize for his novel *House Made of Dawn* (1968) in 1969. Native writers also produce and publish a tremendous amount of poetry based on the theme of identity—poets like E. Pauline Johnson, Joy Harjo, Paula Gunn Allen, Duane Niatum, and Gerald Vizenor have all used their poetic skills to explore what it means to be indigenous in a predominantly non-native world. It should also be noted that the world of "identity politics" is not restricted to the writings of novelists and poets. Contemporary North American playwrights like Drew Taylor, screenplay writers like Sherman Alexie, film directors like Chris Eyre, comedians like Charlie Hill, songwriters and musicians like Robbie Roberson, and rap-artists like Lightfoot all bring identity issues to their work and all serve the broader movement toward cultural survival and self-determination that is at the heart of what it means to be a Native American in today's world.

Phil Bellfy

BIBLIOGRAPHY

Acosta, Oscar Zeta. *The Autobiography of a Brown Buffalo*. San Francisco: Straight Arrow Books, 1972.

Eastman, Charles Alexander. *Indian Boyhood*. New York: McClure, Philips, 1902.

Erdrich, Louise. *Tracks*. New York: Harper & Row, 1989.

McNickle, D'Arcy. *The Surrounded*. New York: Dodd, Mead, 1936.

Momaday, N. Scott. *House Made of Dawn*. New York: Harper & Row, 1968.

Mourning Dove (Hum-ishu-ma). *Cogewea, the Half Blood: A Depiction of the Great Montana Cattle Range*. Given through Sho-pow-tan; with notes and biographical sketch by Lucullus Virgil McWhorter. Lincoln: University of Nebraska Press, 1981.

Ruoff, A. LaVonne Brown. *American Indian Literatures: An Introduction, Bibliographic Review, and Selected Bibliography*. New York: Modern Language Association of America, 1990.

Salinger, J.D. *The Catcher in the Rye*. Boston: Little, Brown, 1951.

Silko, Leslie. *Ceremony*. New York: Viking, 1977.

Smith, Martin Cruz. *Stallion Gate*. New York: Random House, 1986.

Vizenor, Gerald, ed. *Native American Literature: A Brief Introduction and Anthology*. New York: HarperCollins College, 1995.

Welch, James. *Winter in the Blood*. New York: Harper & Row, 1974.

Wiget, Andrew. *Native American Literature*. Boston: Twayne, 1985.

Winnemucca, Sarah. *Life Among the Piutes: Their Wrongs and Claims*. Edited by Mrs. Horace Mann. Boston: Cupples, Upham, 1883.

Witalec, Janet, ed. *Smoke Rising: The Native North American Literary Companion*. Detroit: Visible Ink, 1995.

GENERAL INDEX

BIOGRAPHICAL INDEX